the Unofficial Guide™ to Having a Baby

Ann Douglas
and
John R. Sussman, M.D.

Macmillan • USA

Macmillan General Reference
A Pearson Education Macmillan Company
1633 Broadway
New York, New York 10019-6785

ISBN: 0-02-862695-8

Manufactured in the United States of America

10 9 8 7 6 5 4 3 2 1

First edition

To Julie, Scott, Erik, and Ian, for the wonderful times we shared both before and after your births; and Laura, the baby I never got to take home.

—Ann Douglas

To my family, colleagues, and patients, I give my thanks for your support, encouragement, and patience. You have taught me invaluable lessons both about being a doctor and being a man.

—John Sussman

Acknowledgments

A book of this scope requires the behind-the-scenes efforts of a lot of people. In addition to our editors at Macmillan and our research assistants Janice Kent and Barb Payne, we would like to thank the following individuals who assisted us during the research of this book: Winston Campbell, M.D., Professor of Obstetrics/Gynecology and Director of Maternal-Fetal Medicine at the University of Connecticut Health Center; Miriam DiMaio, Senior Genetic Counselor, Department of Genetics, Yale University School of Medicine; Janet Estes, founder of the online Infant Loss Mailing List; Siobhan Furst, pediatric nurse, Hospital for Sick Children; Robert Greenstein, M.D., Ph.D., Professor in Pediatrics and Director of the Division of Human Genetics at the University of Connecticut Health Center; Sara Grimes, founder and co-administrator of the Subsequent Pregnancy After Loss online mailing list; Elizabeth Hawkins-Walsh, nursing professor, Catholic University of America; Susan Hays, Director of the Health Sciences Library at New Milford Hospital; Herman Hein, Professor of Obstetrics at the University of Iowa Hospitals and Clinics; Tracy Keleher, Producer, Canadian Parents Online; Michael Nettleton, co-administrator of the Sub-sequent Pregnancy After Loss online mailing list; Linda Omichinski, Registered Dietitian; John Rodis, M.D., Associate Professor of Obstetrics/Gynecology and Pediatrics and Director of Perinatal Genetics at the University of Connecticut Health Center; and Jennifer Zint, expert on surrogacy.

We would also like to thank the parents who shared the most intimate details of their lives with us while serving on our parent panel or by participating in individual interviews:

Nicole Alexander, Wilma Anderson, Laura Augustine, Jennie Baird, Heidi Barrett, John Beck, Krista Beck, Leila Belhadjali, Serene Blascovich, Melissa Bolton, Andrea Brenton, Susan Breuker, Michelle Brown, Laura Buren, Charlene Busselaar, Noel C. Kurtz, Sue Cain, Anne Cavicchi, Dawnette Chadwick, Catie Chi Olson, Nancy Clanton, Debbie Clanton-Churchwell, Dawn Clapperton, Melanie Clark, Holly Clawson, Helena Cright, Debby David, Molly Davies, Jennifer Dawson, Joanna Delavan, Bob Dony, Cherisa Duncan, Cindy Durrett, Erin Dwyer, Susan Erhardt, Jennifer Fariel, Amy Fessler, Janet Flach, Deirdre Friedrich, Robin Frojen-Andersson, Tanya Frojen-Andersson, Danielle Gardiner, Jim Gastle, Laura Gazley, Olivia Gerroll-Kelley, Angela Goldie, Stacy Graham, Victoria Grandy, Stephanie Griffin, Lou Guimond, Jennifer Hanskat, Lori Harasem-Mitchell, Heather Harms, Elaine Harper Nugent, Barbara Hennelly, Mary Hernandez-Froment, Sarah Hetherington, Steve Hiller, Marilyn Copley Hilton, Troy Hilton, Anne Hoover, Johnna Horn, Toni Howard, Marie Hughes, Vidya Iyer, Tracy Myers Janevic, Bridget Kelley, Aricka Krier, Grace Lacson, Therese Lafferty, Joanna Lasiter, Erika Lingo, Marcie Longstaff, Karen Lyall, Rhona Lyons, Allison Martin, Marie Martorella, Randa McBride, Jacqueline McKenzie, Heather McKinnon, Wendy McWilliams, Rhonda Melanson, Michele Minietta, Janna Skura Mintz, Cindy Mount, Lisa Mullen, Olivia Mundahl, Debbie

Myers, Christa Newbold, Ellen Newlands, Ashley Ocampo, Jennifer Ogle, Vicki Paradine, Jackie Patrick, Allison Peck, Sandra Pendak, Jane Pendergast, Carrie Petersen, Heather Petit, Tola Plusnick, Brenda Pressler, Suzi Prokell, Diana Quin-Conroy, Kathi Rawnsley, Charity Reed, Lisa Reed, Kseniya Reinoehl, Karen Rolfe, Amie Rossini, Marianne Salas, Debbie Saltrick, Kimberley Sando, Kim Schrader, Colleen Shortall, Nicola Shute, Collette Smith, Julie Snyder, Destiny Sparks-McAffrey, Andrea Stalnecker, Beth Starks, Terrie Tarnowski, Jane Tracogna, Thomas Viano, LeeAnn Volle, Linda Wacht, Lisa Wagley, Jodi Walker, Ruth Ann Wallace, Tina Walsh, Trina Walsh, Kama Warner, Meredith Webb Feinberg, Jessica Lauren Weiss, Lori Wells, Jennifer Welter, Lynne Whitman, Helen Williams, Margaret Williams, Leslie Wilson, Ginny Wood, Jeffrey Wooten, Christy Young, Susan Yusishen, Suzanne Zavesky, Beth Zerbest, and Melissa Ziegler.

Contents

The *Unofficial Guide* Reader's Bill of Rights

We Give You More Than the Official Line

Welcome to the *Unofficial Guide* series of Lifestyles titles—books that deliver critical, unbiased information that other books can't or won't reveal—*the inside scoop.* Our goal is to provide you with the *most accessible, useful* information and advice possible. The recommendations we offer in these pages are not influenced by the corporate line of any organization or industry; we give you the hard facts, whether those institutions like them or not. If something is ill-advised or will cause a loss of time and/or money, we'll give you ample warning. And if it is a worthwhile option, we'll let you know that, too.

Armed and Ready

Our hand-picked authors confidently and critically report on a wide range of topics that matter to smart readers like you. Our authors are passionate about their subjects, but have distanced themselves enough from them to help you be armed and protected, and help you make educated decisions as you go through your process. It is our intent that, from having read this book, you will avoid the pitfalls everyone else falls into and get it right the first time.

Don't be fooled by cheap imitations; this is the *genuine article Unofficial Guide* series from Macmillan Publishing. You may be familiar with our proven track record of the travel *Unofficial Guides*, which have more than three million copies in print. Each year thousands of travelers—new and old—are armed with a brand new, fully updated edition of the flagship *Unofficial Guide to Walt Disney World*, by Bob Sehlinger. It is our intention here to provide you with the same level of objective authority that Mr. Sehlinger does in his brainchild.

The Unofficial Panel of Experts

Every work in the Lifestyle *Unofficial Guides* is intensively inspected by a team of three top professionals in their fields. These experts review the manuscript for factual accuracy, comprehensiveness, and an insider's determination as to whether the manuscript fulfills the credo in this Reader's Bill of Rights. In other words, our Panel ensures that you are, in fact, getting "the inside scoop."

Our Pledge

The authors, the editorial staff, and the Unofficial Panel of Experts assembled for *Unofficial Guides* are determined to lay out the most valuable alternatives available for our readers. This dictum means that our writers must be explicit, prescriptive, and above all, direct. We strive to be thorough and complete, but our goal is not necessarily to have the "most" or "all" of the information on a topic; this is not, after all, an encyclopedia. Our objective is to help you narrow down your options to the best of what is available, unbiased by affiliation with any industry or organization.

In each *Unofficial Guide* we give you:

- Comprehensive coverage of necessary and vital information
- Authoritative, rigidly fact-checked data
- The most up-to-date insights into trends
- Savvy, sophisticated writing that's also readable
- Sensible, applicable facts and secrets that only an insider knows

Special Features

Every book in our series offers the following six special sidebars in the margins that were devised to help you get things done cheaply, efficiently, and smartly.

1. "Timesaver"—tips and shortcuts that save you time.
2. "Moneysaver"—tips and shortcuts that save you money.
3. "Watch Out!"—more serious cautions and warnings.
4. "Bright Idea"—general tips and shortcuts to help you find an easier or smarter way to do something.
5. "Quote"—statements from real people who are intended to be prescriptive and valuable to you.
6. "Unofficially..."—an insider's fact or anecdote.

We also recognize your need to have quick information at your fingertips, and have thus provided the following comprehensive sections at the back of the book:

1. **Glossary:** Definitions of complicated terminology and jargon.

2. **Resource Guide:** Lists of relevant agencies, associations, institutions, Web sites, etc.

3. **Recommended Reading List:** Suggested titles that can help you get more in-depth information on related topics.

4. **Important Documents:** "Official" pieces of information you need to refer to, such as government forms.

5. **Important Statistics:** Facts and numbers presented at-a-glance for easy reference.

6. **Index.**

Letters, Comments, and Questions from Readers

We strive to continually improve the Unofficial series, and input from our readers is a valuable way for us to do that. Many of those who have used the *Unofficial Guide* travel books write to the authors to ask questions, make comments, or share their own discoveries and lessons. For lifestyle *Unofficial Guides*, we would also appreciate all such correspondence, both positive and critical, and we will make best efforts to incorporate appropriate readers' feedback and comments in revised editions of this work.

How to write to us:

Unofficial Guides
Macmillan Lifestyle Guides
Macmillan Publishing
1633 Broadway
New York, NY 10019

Attention: Reader's Comments

The *Unofficial Guide* Panel of Experts

The *Unofficial* editorial team recognizes that you've purchased this book with the expectation of getting the most authoritative, carefully inspected information currently available. Toward that end, on each and every title in this series, we have selected a minimum of three "official" experts comprising the "Unofficial Panel" who painstakingly review the manuscripts to ensure: factual accuracy of all data; inclusion of the most up-to-date and relevant information; and that, from an insider's perspective, the authors have armed you with all the necessary facts you need—but the institutions don't want you to know.

For *The Unofficial Guide to Having a Baby,* we are proud to introduce the following panel of experts:

Barbara Hotelling, B.S.N, R.N., is an Independent Childbirth Educator in Rochester, MI. She is the owner and director of Birth & Parenting Educators, which provides childbirth education classes and professional labor support. She has held positions as a Perintatal Support Coach, Labor Support Coach, and Volunteer Support

Coach. She has written numerous articles about pregnancy, birth, and baby care for the *International Journal of Childbirth Education, Birth,* and other journals.

Richard Whatley, M.D., C.C.F.P., has practiced Family Medicine in Peterborough, Ontario, for 17 years. He graduated from the Family Medicine Program at Ottawa Civic Hospital in 1971. He is the father of four children.

Lisa Mandelbaum, R.D., is a nutrition specialist and coordinator of patient care and counseling at Peak Wellness in Greenwich, CT. Lisa provides nutritional counseling and leads related community outreach programs at local public and private schools. She also maintains a private practice in New York City, where she counsels children and adults on a variety of nutritional issues, including nutrition during pregnancy and lactation.

Introduction

Introduction

One of the most exciting and important decisions you'll ever be faced with is whether or not to have a child. Assuming you decide to take the plunge, you're in for a wild and exciting ride.

First there's the business of trying to get your body in the best possible condition to support a pregnancy: eating properly, staying active, and avoiding substances that could be harmful to your baby.

Then there are the joys and frustrations of trying to conceive: struggling to distinguish between the symptoms of early pregnancy and those of PMS; running to the bathroom every half hour on the day that your period is due in an effort to determine whether that month's Baby Olympics have paid off; and spending an obscene amount of money on home pregnancy tests in an effort to get the answer you want.

If you don't manage to conceive as quickly as you would like, you will have to find some way of coming to terms with the fact that this is one aspect of your life over which you have only a limited amount of control. As difficult as it may be for you to even consider the possibility, you could, like ten percent of American women, find yourself experiencing fertility problems. If you and your partner are unable to conceive naturally, you may decide to consider other avenues to becoming pregnant—assisted reproductive technologies, surrogacy, adoption, and so on—or you may decide to abandon your dream of having a child altogether.

Assuming that you do manage to conceive fairly quickly—and the odds of this happening are, by the way, decidedly in your favor—you will still have a lot of physical and emotional adjustments to make. Starting long before the pregnancy test comes back positive, your body will begin to undergo a remarkable metamorphosis that will allow it to grow a baby during the weeks and months ahead. And then there are the emotional changes of pregnancy. During the months that it takes to grow a baby, you'll likely experience the full gamut of emotions—euphoria, worry, joy, depression, and everything in between. It's the emotional changes of pregnancy that are, for most women, both the most difficult and the most wondrous aspect of being pregnant. One moment you may be feeling totally euphoric about the miracle that is taking place in your very own body, convinced that deciding to have a baby is the best thing you've ever done. The next moment you may be making yourself totally crazy, worrying about all the various ways that having a baby is going to change your life—and your partner's life—forever.

As if that weren't enough to contend with, then there's the whole business of giving birth—a process that is both miraculous and terrifying to most women. You need to trust that your body will know what to do when the big moment arrives, and then come to terms with any fears you may have about what may happen during the birth.

While first-time mothers tend to focus their attention on the moments leading up to the birth, experienced mothers know that the rollercoaster ride doesn't end when your baby arrives. If anything, it is just beginning. While you may initially view this new littler person in your life with more curiosity than love, the emotions of motherhood don't take long to set in. The feelings you experienced when you fell in love for the first time may seem almost insignificant as compared to the love that begins to blossom between you and your baby.

Made in America

The road to parenthood may not be the easiest of journeys, but it's certainly one of life's most rewarding. If you're thinking about having a baby in the near future, the news is good: the odds of having a healthy baby are decidedly in your favor. Consider the facts for yourself:

- Eighty-five percent of couples who are trying to conceive will be pregnant within one year. Even those couples who don't manage to conceive right away have a good chance of becoming parents through either fertility treatments, adoption, or surrogacy.

- While the rate of early miscarriage is high, 90% of women whose pregnancies are confirmed will carry their babies to term.

- According to the Centers for Disease Control and Prevention, only 2% to 3% of babies are born with any major congenital anomaly.

While there are no guarantees that everything will go perfectly during pregnancy, there is plenty of good news for women who are hoping to conceive and carry children. Consider the facts for yourself:

- New methods of treating infertility are making motherhood a possibility for women who might not otherwise have been able to become pregnant. (We discuss many of these options in Chapter Two.)

- New research into the causes of miscarriage and stillbirth has allowed women who might otherwise have lost their babies to carry those babies to term. (See Chapter Eleven for details.)

- American women are receiving better quality prenatal care than ever before. In fact, the Center for Health Statistics reports that of the 3,899,589 babies born in 1995, more than 80% were born to mothers who received prenatal care from the first trimester onward. Since earlier prenatal care means healthier babies, this is good news for all concerned.

While there's plenty of good news to report on the childbearing front, we'd be guilty of whitewashing the facts if we tried to pretend that everything is rosy. There are still a few rather significant blemishes on America's childbearing record: the country's infant mortality rate is higher than that of many other industrialized nations, and, despite all the advances in obstetrical care, just as many American women today give birth to low birthweight babies as did some twenty years ago.

It's difficult to imagine an area of American life in which the gap between the "haves" and the "have nots" is more pronounced than childbirth. According to Herman Hein, professor of obstetrics at the

University of Iowa Hospitals and Clinics, it's an underprivileged class of women—those who, for complex socioeconomic reasons, choose to opt out of proper prenatal care and who continue to smoke, drink, and take drugs during their pregnancies—who are responsible for the nation's poor infant mortality rate.

While Hein insists that America has the infant mortality rate that it deserves, given the fact that 25% to 30% of women continue to smoke during pregnancy, he is quick to note that the country's rate isn't quite as bad as it might seem at first glance. The problem is that methods of reporting infant deaths vary considerably from country to country. America's record—although not lily white—would certainly be a whole lot more respectable on a level playing field. In Japan, for example, the death of a Japanese baby who weighs one pound at birth but only lives for two or three days is not classified as an infant death, whereas the same death of an American baby would be treated as one. This, according to Hein, is one of the reasons why the American infant mortality rate in 1995 was 7.2 deaths per thousand while the Japanese rate was 4.4—or, to put it another way, why the Japanese had the best infant mortality stats in the world, while the U.S. ranked 25th.

Statistics also help to illustrate how the whole nature of giving birth in America is changing, both for better and for worse. Here are some facts you'll want to consider as you go about planning for your own delivery:

- The rate of cesarean section in America has been steadily declining since the late 1980s. Eighty percent of the babies born in 1995 were delivered vaginally, and 20% by cesarean section.

- Surgical interventions are now the norm in delivery rooms across the country. According to the National Center for Health Statistics, there were 1.4 million episiotomies, 618,697 inductions, and 752,000 artificial ruptures of membranes (AROM) performed in 1995.

- There's been a marked increase in the number of women giving birth to more than one baby. The number of women giving birth to twins, triplets, and other multiples soared to 26.1 per 1000 births in 1995—a statistic that reflects the growing use of fertility-enhancing drugs and procedures.

- The birth rate for women between the ages of 40 and 44 has increased by 74% since 1981.

- Prenatal care is becoming increasingly high tech. 2.4 million babies are monitored by ultrasound and 3.1 million via electronic fetal monitoring equipment each year.

As helpful as the numbers may be in understanding what your childbirth experience may be like, they don't tell you everything. You have to dig a little deeper to find out what it's really like to have a baby in America today. And that, in a nutshell, is what this book is all about.

The Mother of All Pregnancy Books

If you've spent much time in bookstores lately, you already know that most pregnancy books fall into one of two basic categories: those that manage to scare you to death by piling on details about every conceivable pregnancy-related problem and expect you to follow a prenatal diet and fitness regime that would have even boot camp recruits begging for mercy; and those that are so full of new age warm-and-fuzzies that you couldn't find a cold hard medical fact to save your life.

Then there's this book, the Mother of All Pregnancy Books—a book that is overflowing with facts, tips, and resources galore—to say nothing of pages. While most *Unofficial Guides* come in at approximately 400 pages, we knew we needed at least 800 pages to do this subject justice. Fortunately, the editors at the *Unofficial Guides* agreed with us and gave us carte blanche to write a pregnancy book that is packed with the very types of information that expectant parents both want and need.

At the heart of this book is something that most pregnancy books tend to neglect: first-hand accounts of what it's really like to have a baby. You'll hear real parents talk about the joys and frustrations of trying to conceive, the raging hormones of early pregnancy, the wonder of feeling your baby's first kick, the legendary discomforts of the third trimester, the experience of coping with a pregnancy that doesn't end when your due date rolls around, the challenge of trying to decide whether or not you're really in labor, and the wondrous experience of giving birth to a child and becoming a parent.

If some of this material sounds like the kind of information you might share with a friend over a cup of coffee, it's certainly for good reason. There were a lot of real live parents involved in the planning of this book.

We pulled together a panel of 150 new and expectant parents and asked them to share their pregnancy wisdom. As you will see as you get into the heart of the book, the parents on our panel were surprisingly frank about their experiences, baring their souls about such highly intimate aspects of their lives as the sexual positions they used while trying to conceive their babies, how they and their partners really felt about being pregnant, and what it was really like to give birth. Time and time again, they thanked us for giving them the opportunity to pass along the very types of pregnancy wisdom that they wished someone else had told them when they were embarking on their own journeys to parenthood.

The panel came up with practical tips on every pregnancy-related situation imaginable: keeping the fun in sex when you're trying to conceive, coping with morning sickness on the job, convincing your boss to agree to the best possible maternity leave package, choosing a caregiver and a place to give birth, weathering the physical and emotional highs and lows of pregnancy, and finding unbelievable bargains on health insurance, prenatal vitamins, maternity wear, baby gear, and much more.

The result of all their input is the book that you're holding in your hands—one that is unlike anything else you're likely to find on the bookstore shelf because it's drawn from the experiences of real parents like you.

The book is also far more comprehensive than most pregnancy books. Rather than spouting a few cliches about prenatal nutrition, uttering some reassuring words about pregnancy complaints, and insisting that you'll be "just fine" when it comes time to deliver, we delve into the nitty-gritty, boldly going where no other pregnancy book has gone—at least until now. You'll find facts drawn from the latest medical journals and statistical databases and lists of resources that you can use to follow up on points that we raise in the text. The text is also liberally sprinkled with the URLs of Internet sites that you owe it to yourself to visit and the subscription information for Internet mailing lists where you can compare notes with other parents and parents-to-be.

Like any complex issue, the facts about pregnancy are often more grey than black and white. In situations in which the data conflict or an issue is particularly controversial, we present you with the facts on both sides of the argument and allow you to make up your mind for yourself.

Since pregnancy can also be a fun time in your life, we've thrown in a bit of less serious stuff too—like information about all those Old Wives' Tales you've probably heard by now, interactive pregnancy calendars galore, and the URL of a Web site that shows you how to improvise a diaper if you find yourself unexpectedly caught short. (Now there's one site you'll want to bookmark!)

We've got plenty of other goodies in store for you, including the following:

- A frank discussion of the pros and cons of having a baby—everything from physical and emotional concerns to financial matters and the potential career fallout (i.e., the truth about the Mommy Track).

- The inside scoop on getting pregnant fast, and tips on coping with the emotional rollercoaster ride that you can find yourself on if you don't conceive as quickly as you'd like. We allow you to step inside the bedrooms of the members of our parents panel and find out what worked for them, and why. We give you valuable

information designed to help you find your way
through the infertility maze, providing you with
clear definitions of the fertility-related lingo
you'll need to understand, as well as practical
advice on choosing a fertility clinic.

- Detailed information on the symptoms of early
  pregnancy, advice on coping with your partner's
  reaction (good, bad, or ugly), and tips on breaking the news to your boss. This is where you'll
  get a crash course on what the Family Leave Act
  means to you and what rights you have as a pregnant employee.

- Tips on finding the caregiver and birth environment that's right for you as well as the inside
  scoop on where midwives, doulas, and other
  types of caregivers fit into the whole childbirth
  picture.

- The lowdown on choosing childbirth classes
  that are actually worth attending—and tips on
  which ones are to be avoided like the plague.

- The pros and cons of prenatal testing and the
  facts you need to consider when deciding
  whether or not you're prepared to hop on this
  particular medical merry-go-round. (Obviously,
  this is where we get into such heart-wrenching
  issues as deciding whether or not to terminate a
  pregnancy if the news that comes back is less
  than what you'd hoped for.)

- The facts you need to make healthy choices
  throughout your pregnancy, especially when it
  comes to nutrition, medication, sex, exercise,
  and staying on the job.

- A detailed examination of topics that other
  books tend to gloss over or ignore completely:

coping with a high-risk pregnancy; preparing for a multiple birth; becoming pregnant after years of infertility; being pregnant and single, pregnant and gay, and so on.

- A comprehensive chapter on pregnancy loss, written by someone who's actually lived through the heartbreak of both miscarriage and stillbirth. We give you the facts about miscarriage, stillbirth, and neonatal death—information that no pregnant woman can afford to ignore. This chapter is jam-packed with information that we hope you'll never have to use, like coping with the loss of your baby, making funeral arrangements, and coping with the physical and emotional challenges of a subsequent pregnancy.

- The scoop on maternity wear and baby gear: what you need, what you don't need, and where to find the bargains. We even tell you how to obtain the maximum allowable coverage from your HMO or insurance company and give you the inside track on some of the valuable freebies that may be yours for the asking.

- Comprehensive information on the physical and emotional changes you may experience during your pregnancy, including how your body is changing, how your baby is growing, what you need to be concerned about, and important issues that you might want to think about as your pregnancy progresses. We provide you with helpful tips on coping with such common pregnancy complaints as morning sickness, backaches, urinary tract infections, yeast infections, and more.

- The facts about important decisions you will need to make before, during, or after the birth: whether or not to be induced if you go overdue, the pros and cons of various types of pain relief during labor, and what you need to know about circumcision.

- A sneak preview of labor and delivery (i.e., what labor really feels like, how to distinguish between true and false labor, when to call your caregiver, why you may or may not want to invite others to the birth, and what to expect during both a vaginal and cesarean delivery).

- The truth about life after baby (i.e., what babies are really like, how to cope with a sick baby or a baby who has special needs, how to survive the postpartum period, and how to make breast-feeding or bottle-feeding work for both you and your baby).

- The latest news on contraception and some advice on spacing your family and preparing an older child for the birth of a new baby.

- A set of appendices that are packed with information designed to help you to make the best possible health-related choices for yourself and your baby. You'll find a detailed glossary of fertility, pregnancy, childbirth, and baby-related terms; a resource directory packed with leads on the hottest Internet sites and the names, addresses, and phone numbers of the pregnancy and parenting-related organizations that every American or Canadian parent needs to know about; leads on magazine and journal articles, books, and other materials you may wish to consult in order to round out your knowledge; a sample birth plan; a sample contract for hiring a doula; and valuable information on emergency childbirth procedures, including tips on what to do while you wait for the ambulance to arrive.

As you can see, we've packed a lot of useful information into *The Unofficial Guide to Having a Baby.* So toss this book in your handbag, put it on your night table, or stash it in your desk drawer at work so that we'll be there when you need us during the exciting months that lie ahead.

The Truth about Getting Pregnant

PART I

Preparing for Pregnancy

S carlett O'Hara said it best: "Death and taxes and childbirth. There's never any convenient time for any of them." If Margaret Mitchell had written her famous novel *Gone With the Wind* today rather than in an era when family planning was even less of an exact art than it is now, she might have noted that there's never an ideal time to conceive a child.

There is, after all, always a good reason to postpone a pregnancy: too much is happening at work, you don't have enough money in the bank, you want to lose the extra weight you've been carrying around since your freshman year at college, and so on.

The biological clock waits for no woman, however. If you postpone your family too long, you reduce your chances of being able to have your own biological child. In a recent article in *Business Week*, Dr. Zev Rosenwaks, director of the Center for Reproductive Medicine and Infertility at New York Hospital–Cornell Medical Center, made the point that women who decide to postpone childbearing

3

Unofficially...
They're not getting older, they're getting pregnant!
According to a recent article in *Town and Country* magazine, the number of births to women in their early 40s has increased by 50% since 1970. In 1992, 55,702 babies were born to women between the ages of 40 and 44, and 2,008 to women between the ages of 45 and 48.

until it's the "right time" need to be aware of the risks: "If you can try to become pregnant at a younger age, you should. You're likely to get pregnant more often and earlier. You're likely to have a healthier pregnancy because you're less likely to have a miscarriage and less likely to have a chromosomal abnormality. You're likely to have as many children as you want."

David Meldrum, a reproductive endocrinologist at the Center for Advanced Reproductive Care in Redondo Beach, California, echoed those thoughts in a recent interview with *The Atlanta Journal and Constitution:* "Women aren't told enough about the decline of fertility with age. Many don't realize that if they wait, motherhood may pass them by."

That said, the biological clock isn't the only factor that warrants consideration when you're contemplating a pregnancy. It's important to consider such additional factors as your physical and emotional readiness for parenthood, the career costs of having a baby, and your financial situation.

First things first

The time to start taking care of your body is before you get pregnant. Studies have shown that you increase your odds of having a healthy baby if you are in the best possible physical condition before you conceive.

Your answers to the questions in our Preconception Checklist should give you an idea of how physically ready your body is to support a pregnancy. These are also the types of questions your caregiver is likely to ask at your first appointment.

CHECKLIST: PRECONCEPTION
■ Do you skip meals regularly?

- Are you on any type of special diet that might prevent your body from getting the range of nutrients required to support a pregnancy?

- Do you smoke?

- Do you consume alcohol?

- Do you drink coffee?

- Are you using any prescription medications or using any other types of drugs?

- Are you taking any vitamins?

- Do you currently have or have you ever had any sexually transmitted diseases, such as genital herpes, gonorrhea, chlamydia, syphilis, venereal warts, or HIV/AIDS?

- Do you have any chronic health conditions, such as epilepsy, lupus, diabetes, high blood pressure, heart disease, PKU, or kidney disease?

- Have you been immunized against rubella (German measles)?

- Have you been screened for Hepatitis B?

- Have you had your flu shot? (Getting a flu shot is not de rigueur unless you have serious health problems, such as asthma, heart disease, and diabetes, which could place you at risk for flu-related complications.)

- Is your workplace free of hazards that could jeopardize the well-being of your baby?

- Are you more than 20% overweight or 15% underweight?

- Are you anemic?

- Have you ever had problems with your uterus, tubes, or cervix? Have these problems required surgery?

← Note!
Bring a copy of your answers to your preconception checkup so that you can discuss any areas of concern with your doctor or midwife.

- Did your mother take a drug called DES when she was pregnant with you?
- Have you had two or more abortions during or after the 14th week of pregnancy?
- Have you had three or more miscarriages?
- Have you had five or more pregnancies?
- Have you given birth within the previous 12 months?
- Have you ever given birth to a baby who was either less than $5^1/2$ pounds or more than 9 pounds at birth?
- Have you ever given birth to a stillborn baby?
- Have you ever given birth to a baby who died within the first month of life?
- Have you ever given birth to a baby with a birth defect?
- Have you given birth to a baby who required care in an intensive-care nursery?
- Have you experienced vaginal bleeding late in pregnancy?
- Do any of the following medical problems run in your family: high blood pressure, diabetes, hemophilia, birth defects, mental retardation, cystic fibrosis, Tay-Sachs disease, sickle-cell anemia, or thalassemia?

Now let's consider what a "yes" answer to any of these questions could mean in terms of your ability to conceive and carry a baby.

Do you skip meals regularly?

If you make a habit of skipping meals, your body could be missing out on some important nutrients, including folic acid and iron.

It's particularly important to ensure that your diet contains adequate quantities of folic acid. Studies have shown that women who consume at least 0.4 mg of folic acid each day reduce their chances of giving birth to a child with a neural tube defect (for example, anencephaly or spina bifida) by 50% to 70%.

To increase your intake of this important nutrient, you should consume foods that are naturally high in folic acid, such as oranges, orange juice, honeydew melon, avocados, dark green vegetables (broccoli, brussel sprouts, Romaine lettuce, spinach), asparagus, bean sprouts, corn, cauliflower, dried beans, nuts, seeds, bran cereals, whole-grain products, wheat germ, and fortified breakfast cereals. Talk to your doctor about taking a folic acid supplement as well.

Because neural tube defects can occur very early on in pregnancy, it's important to ensure that you have adequate levels of folic acid in your diet before you conceive. That's why most doctors recommend that you consume adequate amounts of folic acid throughout your childbearing years.

It's also important to ensure that your diet contains sufficient quantities of iron. During pregnancy, a woman's iron needs to double. The extra iron is required to create additional red blood cells that carry oxygen from your lungs to all parts of your body as well as your growing baby.

If you find that you are tired all the time, it could be because you're low on iron. Try boosting your iron intake by consuming iron-rich foods, such as whole-grain and enriched cereals, lean meats, dried peas and beans, dark green vegetables, and dried fruits. Because vitamin C helps your body absorb

Bright Idea
Your mother was right. Breakfast is the most important meal of the day. If you skip breakfast because you're not hungry first thing in the morning, stop eating after 6 p.m. If you skip breakfast because you're in too much of a rush in the morning, throw a banana, a cup of yogurt, and a couple of ice cubes into the blender and make a breakfast shake you can sip in the car on the way to work.

iron, consume these iron-rich foods with a glass of orange juice or other foods that are high in vitamin C, such as melons, strawberries, grapefruits, raspberries, kiwi, broccoli, tomatoes, sweet potatoes, and so on.

Are you on any type of special diet that might prevent your body from getting the range of nutrients required to support a pregnancy?

If you are a vegetarian or on a special diet to control diabetes or some other type of medical condition, be sure to consult with a nutritionist before you start trying to conceive. Your body may be lacking some important nutrients.

Do you smoke?

Unofficially...
A 1996 University of California Berkeley study showed that smoking 10 cigarettes a day reduces a woman's chances of conceiving by 50%. Source: BabyCenter's Preconception Page

Smoking during pregnancy increases your chances of having a low-birthweight baby and places your baby at increased risk of dying from Sudden Infant Death Syndrome (SIDS). The reason is simple: nicotine causes vasoconstriction (that is, a tightening of the blood vessels, including those leading to the placenta and the baby). To make matters worse, smoking also reduces the amount of vitamin C circulating throughout your body, thereby interfering with the absorption of iron and possibly leading to iron-deficiency anemia.

As a rule of thumb, you should stop smoking before you stop using birth control. This will allow your body to be nicotine-free by the time you conceive.

If you're finding it hard to kick the habit, you might want to try gradually cutting back on the number of cigarettes you smoke (that is, reduce your daily intake of cigarettes by one at the end of each week).

Do you consume alcohol?

Babies who are exposed to alcohol prenatally can be born with serious medical problems. Why take the chance? Stop consuming alcohol when you begin trying to conceive.

Do you drink coffee?

Coffee may be your early-morning beverage of choice right now, but it's best to give it up or switch to decaf once you start trying to conceive. Caffeine is thought to restrict the growth of a developing baby by constricting blood vessels and reducing blood flow to the uterus. What's more, a few studies have indicated that excessive consumption of caffeine (that is, more than three cups of drip coffee per day) may contribute to fertility problems. (The jury is still out on this, however.)

Are you using any prescription medications or any other types of drugs?

Both prescription and nonprescription drugs can affect a developing baby. Ask your doctor what drugs you should and should not be taking during pregnancy.

Are you taking any vitamins?

Large doses of vitamins can be harmful to your baby. This is one of those cases when too much of a good thing can be a bad thing. Your best bet is to stick with a vitamin that has been specially formulated for use during pregnancy.

Do you currently have or have you ever had any sexually transmitted diseases, such as genital herpes, gonorrhea, chlamydia, syphillis, venereal warts, or HIV/AIDS?

Your sexual past can come back to haunt you when you start trying to conceive. Here's why:

Watch Out!
Acne medications such as Acutane (isotretinoin) have been proven to cause birth defects. To increase your chances of having a healthy baby, you should stop taking the drug at least one month before you start trying to conceive.

Bright Idea
Ask your doctor to test you for chlamydia at your next pelvic exam. Five percent of American women are infected with the disease, which can cause infertility, ectopic pregnancy, and recurrent pelvic pain. You should be particularly vigilant about being tested if either you or your partner have had sex with someone else at any time.

- Unrecognized genital herpes can be harmful—even fatal—to your baby.

- Gonorrhea and chlamydia can scar your fallopian tubes and either make it difficult for you to conceive or increase your chances of having an ectopic (tubal) pregnancy.

- Syphillis, if uncured, can cause birth defects. *Note:* some types of genital warts can be a symptom of syphillis.

- If you are HIV positive or have full-blown AIDS, your pregnancy will have to be carefully managed to reduce the risk of infecting your baby.

Your doctor can provide you with information on ways of treating or controlling these diseases both prior to and during pregnancy. You'll find additional information on managing these diseases in Chapter 10.)

Do you have any chronic health conditions, such as epilepsy, lupus, diabetes, high blood pressure, heart disease, PKU (phenylketonuria), or kidney disease?

Women who suffer from serious medical conditions require special care during pregnancy. Here are some examples of the types of issues that women with these types of conditions must confront during pregnancy:

- Women with poorly controlled insulin-dependent diabetes are four to six times more likely to give birth to a baby with birth defects than nondiabetic women. That's why it's so important for diabetic women to ensure that their blood sugar is well controlled both prior to and during pregnancy.

- Women who are epileptic need to carefully consider the risks of taking antiseizure medications during pregnancy. Although some medications increase the chances of birth defects, seizures can themselves be harmful to the developing fetus.

■ Women with lupus—an autoimmune disorder in which the body attacks its own tissues—are at increased risk of experiencing miscarriage or preterm labor. As a rule of thumb, women who have been symptom free for six months prior to conceiving are likely to have a healthy pregnancy.

■ Women with chronic high blood pressure are at increased risk of developing pregnancy complications, including placental problems and fetal growth restriction. A change in medications may make it possible for a pregnant woman with chronic high blood pressure to manage her condition without harming her baby.

■ Women with heart disease or kidney problems may require a change of medications as well as careful monitoring throughout their pregnancies.

■ Women with phenylketonuria (PKU)—an inherited body-chemistry disorder in which the body is unable to process a particular type of amino acid (a building block of protein)—must follow a special diet in order to prevent mental retardation and birth defects in their babies.

Have you been immunized against rubella (German measles)?

Exposure to rubella during pregnancy can lead to birth defects or the death of the fetus. Although there was some concern a few years back about the rubella vaccine causing chronic joint or nerve

Unofficially...
Routine vaccinations have reduced the annual toll of rubella-related birth defects from 20,000 in 1964 to only 6 in 1995.
Source: ABCNEWS.com

problems in some women, the *Journal of the American Medical Association* recently came out solidly in favor of the rubella vaccine: "Our findings support the continued vaccination of rubella-susceptible women of child-bearing age as a safe and effective means of preventing congenital rubella syndrome," wrote the authors of a recent study.

Have you been screened for Hepatitis B?

The Centers for Disease Control and Prevention recommend that pregnant women be screened for Hepatitis B—a disease that commonly results in liver disease and cancer in adulthood. Untreated infants of infected mothers have a 50% chance of contracting the virus. Women who are considered to be at high risk of developing the disorder (that is, health-care workers who handle blood) are advised to be vaccinated against Hepatitis B prior to becoming pregnant.

Have you had your flu shot?

A full-blown case of influenza can lead to miscarriage or premature labor. The Centers for Disease Control and Prevention recommend that pregnant women who will reach their third trimester before April consider having a flu shot. The American College of Obstetricians and Gynecologists, however, recommends them only for pregnant women with serious health problems that would place them at risk for flu-related complications.

Is your workplace free of hazards that could jeopardize the well-being of your baby?

If you or your partner is regularly exposed to hazardous substances in the workplace, you may need to consider a job change or job modification before you start your family. Hazardous substances in the workplace can affect both the quality of sperm and the development of the embryo.

Here are some of the types of substances and procedures you should avoid while you're trying to conceive and throughout your pregnancy:

- chemicals such as paints, lacquers, wood-finishing products, industrial or household solvents, and darkroom chemicals

- nuclear medicine testing procedures; X-rays; and anesthesia, which you might be exposed to while working in a hospital, laboratory, or dental office

- lethal and teratogenic gases used in fire-fighting and so on

You can find a chart detailing the various types of toxins you might encounter in the workplace in *Before You Conceive: The Complete Prepregnancy Guide,* by John R. Sussman, M.D., and B. Blake Levitt. (See Appendix C for publishing information.)

Are you more than 20% overweight or 15% underweight?

Women who are overweight are at increased risk of developing gestational diabetes and other problems and giving birth to large babies who can cause a variety of significant obstetrical complications; women who are underweight are at increased risk of giving birth to low-birthweight babies who may have serious health problems.

Are you anemic?

If you are anemic, the hemoglobin in your blood is insufficient to carry the amount of oxygen required to reach all of the cells in your body. This can cause serious problems during pregnancy by reducing the amount of oxygen your baby receives. If anemia is significant, there is an increased risk for intrauterine growth restriction and also fetal hypoxia during labor. In addition, the mother will be less able to handle the blood loss associated with delivery (vaginal or cesarean) if she's already significantly short on blood. Also, anemia that hasn't been adequately evaluated may turn out to be a symptom of a more serious genetic or systemic disease.

Have you ever had problems with your uterus, tubes, or cervix? Have these problems required surgery?

A history of uterine or cervical problems or surgery increases your chances of experiencing a miscarriage or giving birth to a premature baby. Make sure that your doctor is aware of these problems so that he or she can suggest some possible treatments (for example, a cerclage procedure to prevent an incompetent cervix from opening prematurely).

Uterine surgery may increase your likelihood of experiencing a uterine rupture during pregnancy or delivery, and tubal surgery may increase your odds of experiencing an ectopic (tubal) pregnancy—a condition, which is potentially life-threatening and should ideally be ruled out as early as possible in the first trimester.

Did your mother take a drug called DES when she was pregnant with you?

Diethylstilbestrol (DES) was a drug given to many pregnant women in the 1950s and 1960s. It has since been found to be linked to breast cancer and cancer of the vagina in the daughters of women who took the drug. What's more, 90% of these so-called DES daughters have experienced abnormalities of the cervix, vagina, and uterus that make it difficult for them to conceive and carry a pregnancy to term.

Approximately 20% of these women are infertile, and 20% experience repeated miscarriages; but 60% of them are able to carry a pregnancy to term. Just one additional footnote before we move on: The sons of women who took DES also have genital abnormalities, including smaller-than-average testicles and penis, undescended testicles, low sperm counts, poor motility of sperm, cysts, and possibly even testicular and prostate cancer.

Have you had two or more abortions during or after the 14th week of pregnancy?

Although the majority of women who have previously had elective abortions do not have difficulty going on to have children, some women do experience problems. As a rule of thumb, the earlier in your pregnancy the abortion was performed, the better your odds of avoiding future problems. If, however, your abortion was poorly done or you developed a subsequent pelvic infection, you could experience problems conceiving or carrying a subsequent pregnancy to term. Specifically, abortions after the 14th week are more likely to have been associated with cervical trauma and a subsequent increased risk of cervical incompetence.

Have you had three or more miscarriages?

If you have had a large number of miscarriages, you are at increased risk of experiencing another. What's less important than how many miscarriages you've experienced, however, is the number of miscarriages as compared to the number of live births. Consider the numbers for yourself: Women who have had two or more miscarriages and have never given birth to a child have a 40% to 45% chance of experiencing another miscarriage. Women who have had as many as four miscarriages and yet have successfully given birth to a live baby have only a 25% to 30% chance of experiencing another miscarriage. (We will be discussing the issue of pregnancy loss in far greater detail in Chapter 11.)

Have you had five or more pregnancies?

Women who have had five or more pregnancies are at increased risk of developing problems during pregnancy, such as placenta previa (where the placenta partially or fully covers the cervix, sometimes necessitating a cesarean delivery), postpartum hemmorrhage (excessive loss of blood after delivery), intrauterine growth restriction (if the pregnancies are closely spaced and nutrition is not optimal), and rapid labor.

Have you given birth within the previous 12 months?

If your pregnancies are spaced too closely together, your body may not have had a chance to replenish its stores since you gave birth to your previous child. This puts your baby at increased risk for stillbirth, low birthweight, prematurity, and sudden infant death syndrome (SIDS)—although these conditions are thought to be more of a problem in economically disadvantaged groups where nutrition and access to appropriate health care are less than ideal.

Have you ever given birth to a baby who was either less than 5^{1}/$_{2}$ pounds or more than 9 pounds at birth?

If you've previously given birth to a very small or very large baby, you should see your doctor right away to discuss ways of preventing history from repeating itself. Your doctor will make an attempt to identify the underlying cause of the problem (for example, gestational diabetes) and take steps

Watch Out!
If you're planning to travel to third-world countries during your pregnancy, you should plan to be immunized against the following infections, which are thought to cause miscarriages: variola (smallpox), vaccinia (cowpox), and typhoid fever (Salmonella typhi infection).

to try to minimize its affects during subsequent pregnancies.

Have you ever given birth to a stillborn baby?

If your baby was stillborn because of a problem that was preexisting or you developed during your pregnancy (for example, diabetes), careful prenatal management may increase your odds of delivering a healthy baby the next time around. You may want to consider testing for autoimmune disease, reviewing the records relating to your previous pregnancy and birth (including the autopsy and placental pathology reports), having chromosome testing performed, if warranted, and so on.

Have you ever given birth to a baby who died within the first month of life?

You and your doctor will want to know whether there was a preventable cause of death and, if there was, take action to prevent a repeat of this tragedy.

Have you ever given birth to a baby with a birth defect?

Some birth defects are genetically caused; others result from unknown causes. If the birth defect was genetically caused, you may wish to go for genetic counselling before contemplating a subsequent pregnancy.

Have you given birth to a baby who required care in an intensive-care nursery?

Once again, you'll want to discuss your previous experience with your doctor so that your situation can be reviewed and steps can be taken, if possible, to avoid a similar outcome to this pregnancy. In many cases, your doctor will be able to reassure you that the problems your first baby experienced are unlikely to be experienced by your next child.

Bright Idea
Create a detailed health record for yourself and bring it with you to each medical appointment. Start by compiling a complete family medical history. Then, keep a chronological record of information worth noting about your own health: symptoms and illnesses, results of any medical tests you take, a record of prescriptions, and so on.

Have you experienced vaginal bleeding late in pregnancy?

Bleeding in late pregnancy may indicate problems with the position or adherence of the placenta. Women who have experienced a full or partial placental abruption (that is, premature separation of the placenta) or placenta previa (when the placenta implants over the cervical opening) are at increased risk of experiencing similar problems in a subsequent pregnancy.

Do any of the following medical problems run in your family: high blood pressure, diabetes, hemophilia, birth defects, mental retardation, cystic fibrosis, Tay-Sachs disease, sickle-cell anemia, or thalassemia?

If high blood pressure or diabetes runs in your family, you could be at an increased risk of developing pregnancy-induced hypertension or gestational diabetes during your pregnancy—conditions that, if left unmanaged, could affect your baby's well-being as well as your own health.

Genetic disorders such as hemophilia, birth defects, some forms of mental retardation, cystic fibrosis, Tay-Sachs disease, sickle-cell anemia, and thalassemia can be passed from one generation to the next. If these types of medical problems run in your family, you might want to meet with a genetic counselor to discuss your odds of having a child with one of these problems.

Note: It is possible to have a genetic disorder or to carry a gene for a particular disorder without even knowing it. That's why genetic counseling plays an important role in preconception health planning.

As you may recall from your high-school biology class, there are various types of gene disorders:

- Dominant gene disorders (Huntington's disease, for example) are caused by a single abnormal gene from either parent.

- Recessive gene disorders (for example, cystic fibrosis) occur when both parents carry an abnormal gene for a particular disorder.

- X-linked or sex-linked gene disorders (hemophilia, for example) are caused by an abnormal gene on the X chromosome.

- Chromosomal disorders (such as Down syndrome) are caused by problems with the fetus's chromosomes. Chromosomal disorders are sometimes inherited but are more often caused by an error that occurred when the sperm or egg was being formed.

- Multifactorial disorders (such as congenital heart defects) are disorders that are believed to be caused by a mix of genetic and environmental factors.

Some of these diseases—for example, Tay-Sachs disease, sickle-cell anemia, and thalassemia—tend to be particularly problematic for members of certain ethnic groups:

Bright Idea
You can find a directory of genetics centers, clinics, university departments of genetics, and associations of geneticists at www.kumc.edu/gec/prof/genecntr.html.

- Tay-Sachs—a disease that causes fatal brain damage—is more common in people of Central and Eastern European Ashkenazi Jewish descent and in certain French-Canadian subpopulations. It occurs in about 1/3,600 infants born to members of these ethnic groups.

- Sickle-cell anemia—a blood disorder—is more common in African Americans and individuals of Mediterranean, Arab, and Asian Indian origin. Approximately 1/484 infants of African-American descent are born with the disorder.

- Thalassemia—a blood disorder—is more common in people of Mediterranean and Indian origin. Approximately 1/1,600 children born to these ethnic groups is affected by the disease.

If you belong to one of these ethnic groups, you may wish to consult with a genetic counselor to assess your risk of giving birth to a child with one of these diseases.

A genetic counselor will

- provide you with the facts about a particular disease or condition, describe its probable course, and inform you about any available treatments;

- explain how a disease or condition is passed from one generation to the next;

- assess your chances of passing on a serious medical condition to your child;

- advise you whether carrier identification tests are available at genetic clinics within the United States or abroad to detect the types of diseases or conditions you're most likely to pass on to your child;

- advise you whether prenatal diagnostic tests are available at genetic clinics within the United States or abroad to test for these particular diseases or conditions (see Table 1.1).

- let you know if preimplantation diagnosis is available for this disorder (that is, when in vitro fertilization produces several embryos, the one with the best DNA is chosen for implantation—a procedure that costs up to $20,000);

- put you in touch with other families who are dealing with similar conditions;

- refer you to health-care practitioners who specialize in a particular disease or disorder.

Unofficially...
Women who do not obtain adequate prenatal care are twice as likely to give birth to a low-birthweight baby. Source: The Alan Guttmacher Institute

TABLE 1.1: GENETIC DISORDERS FOR WHICH PRENATAL DIAGNOSIS IS AVAILABLE

Disorder	Incidence	Inheritance	Method of Prenatal Diagnosis
Cystic fibrosis	1/2,500 in white population	Recessive	Chorionic villus sampling (CVS); amniocentesis
Congenital adrenal hyperplasia	1/10,000	Recessive	CVS; amniocentesis
Duchenne-type muscular dystrophy	1/3,300 male births	X-linked recessive	CVS; amniocentesis
Hemophilia A	1/8,500 male births	X-linked recessive	CVS; amniocentesis; fetal blood sampling, rarely
Thalassemia	1/1,600 in Mediterranean or Indian population	Recessive	CVS; amniocentesis
Huntington's disease	4–7/100,000	Dominant	CVS; amniocentesis
Polycystic kidney disease (adult type)	1/3,000 by clinical diagnosis	Dominant	CVS; amniocentesis
Sickle-cell anemia	1/484 of African Americans in the U.S.	Recessive	CVS; amniocentesis
Tay-Sachs disease	1/3,600 Ashkenazic Jews; 1/400,000 in other populations	Recessive	CVS; amniocentesis

Adapted from *The Merck Manual*, 16th edition.

What follows is a partial list of genetic disorders for which prenatal diagnosis is available. Because breakthroughs are constantly being made in the field of genetic testing, be sure to ask your genetic counselor whether prenatal testing is available for the particular disease or condition you may be carrying.

There are many other reasons why couples go for genetic counseling prior to attempting a pregnancy. You can find out if you're a good candidate for genetic counseling by answering the questions in our Genetic Counseling Checklist below.

CHECKLIST: GENETIC COUNSELING

Wondering if you and your partner might be good candidates for genetic counseling? If you answer yes to one or more of the following questions, it's an option you might wish to consider.

Note! ➜
The genetic counselor should provide you with details about which medical conditions are genetic and which ones aren't.

- Do you have a genetic disorder?

- Does your partner have a genetic disorder?

- Are you and your partner close relatives (for example, first cousins)?

- Do you, your child, or a close family member have a birth defect?

- Do you, your child, or a close family member have a medical condition that has not been thoroughly diagnosed?

- Are you concerned that you may be a carrier of a genetic disorder which runs in your ethnic group (for example, Tay-Sachs, sickle-cell anemia, or thalassemia)?

- Have you had three or more miscarriages and/or a stillbirth of unknown cause?

- Would you and your partner like more information about your chances of giving birth to a baby with a genetic disorder or birth defect?

There have been some remarkable advances in the field of genetic testing in recent years. Here are just a few examples of what genetic testing can do for you if you are thinking about starting a family:

- **Pre-implantation testing:** New genetic technologies at the molecular level allow the identification of specific mutations known to cause genetic disease. These technologies now make it possible to detect genetic diseases in offspring even as early as before implantation (such as when used as an adjunct to IVF). If multiple embryos are conceived in the laboratory, tests can allow only the embryo(s) without the disease to be implanted. This is a better alternative than delaying the diagnosis until CVS or amnio is done and then facing the potential need for abortion.

- **Carrier testing for members of a particular ethnic group:** Couples of Jewish descent may wish to undergo an Ashkenazi DNA carrier test panel, an all-in-one test that costs approximately $250–$300 per person and that can predict with 95% to 100% accuracy whether a particular person is a carrier for diseases such as Tay-Sachs, cystic fibrosis, Gaucher's disease, Niemann-Pick, Type A, and Canavan disease, all of which tend to be problematic for Jews. The chances that a particular person of Jewish descent carries a gene for one of these diseases ranges from 1/15 for Gaucher's disease to 1/90 for Niemann-Pick disease, Type A. The chances of being a carrier

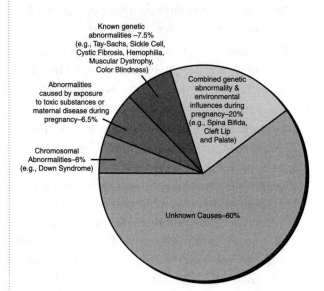

Cause of Birth Defects

Known genetic abnormalities –7.5% (e.g., Tay-Sachs, Sickle Cell, Cystic Fibrosis, Hemophilia, Muscular Dystrophy, Color Blindness)

Abnormalities caused by exposure to toxic substances or maternal disease during pregnancy–6.5%

Chromosomal Abnormalities–6% (e.g., Down Syndrome)

Combined genetic abnormality & environmental influences during pregnancy–20% (e.g., Spina Bifida, Cleft Lip and Palate)

Unknown Causes–60%

of at least one of these mutations are approximately 10% for Ashkenazi Jews.

▪ **Carrier testing for cystic fibrosis:** A case can be made for giving all couples the option of being tested for cystic fibrosis—not just those of certain ethnic groups or who have one or more family members with the disease. Cystic fibrosis is carried by 1/25 Caucasians and 1/80 African Americans. What makes this disease so challenging to predict is the fact that there are more than 600 different mutations worldwide that are known to cause the disease. Although it's not yet possible to test for all of these mutations, couples considering pregnancy can be tested for 64 different mutations for just $125 per person. This test will detect well over 90% of carriers of this relatively common genetic disorder.

Unofficially...
Researchers are in the process of developing a maternal blood test that would enable DNA testing of fetal genetic disorders as early as 8 weeks after conception.

- **Carrier testing for fragile X syndrome:** A similar case can be made for offering a test for fragile X syndrome—a significant cause of mental retardation—to all women who are planning a pregnancy. Fragile X is carried by 1/250–400 women, making it about as common as the risk of a 35-year-old woman having a baby with Down syndrome. Fragile X syndrome affects 1/1,000–1,200 males and 1/1,500–2,000 females. At this point, testing for both female carriers (fragile X is almost always inherited from the mother) and affected fetuses is possible. Though traditionally considered routine only for those with family histories of fragile X or mental retardation in which the fragile X status was unknown, carrier testing is now available to all individuals. Considering the relative frequency with which the fragile X chromosome is carried in the general population, you might want to talk to a genetic counselor about being tested. (See Table 1.2 for detailed information on DNA carrier testing for genetic diseases, and see Table 1.3 for a list of the pros and cons of carrier testing.)

TABLE 1.2: DNA CARRIER TESTING FOR GENETIC DISEASES

Disorder	Symptoms	Prognosis	Carrier Frequency & Disease Incidence	Genetic Testing for Carrier Status
Genetic disorders for which testing is available to all individuals				
Cystic fibrosis	Causes thick secretions that lead to chronic lung disease, gastrointestinal tract problems, and sterility in men. People with cystic fibrosis are of normal intelligence.	Varies considerably. Average life span is now over 30 years.	1/25 whites (Jews and non-Jews) carries the gene; 1/2,500 have the disease. 1/80 African Americans carries the gene; risk of affected child 1/25,000. Both the mother and the father must be a gene carrier for a child to be affected with cystic fibrosis.	DNA tests can detect 97% of European Jewish gene carriers, 90% of northern European non-Jewish gene carriers; 70% or less of carriers from other ethnic groups.
Fragile X syndrome	Causes moderate-to-severe mental retardation in males; autistic-like behavior may be present. 60% of females with the disorder have borderline-to-mild retardation, and 40% have intelligence in the normal range without any recognizable symptoms of the disorder.	Moderate-to-severe retardation may be recognizable during early childhood. Milder cases may not be detected until the child reaches school age.	1/400 women of any ethnic background carries the fragile X premutation (an abnormal gene that predisposes her to having children with fragile X syndrome). 1/1,200 males and 1/2,000 females are affected. Only the mother needs to be a carrier in order for a child to be affected.	A DNA test detects virtually all carriers of the common fragile X mutation.

Recessive gene carrier testing options for individuals of Central/Eastern European Jewish ancestry (Ashkenazi Jewish ancestry)

Disease	Description	Prognosis	Risk	Testing
Tay-Sachs disease	Causes brain cells to die, leading progressively to severe retardation, seizures, and blindness starting at four to six months of age.	Death usually occurs by age six years. No effective treatment is currently available.	1/30 Jews carries the gene. The risk of having an affected child is 1/3,600. 1/300 non-Jews carries the gene. Both parents must be gene carriers for a child to be affected.	DNA tests detect 94% of Jewish gene carriers. Enzyme testing detects almost all carriers of common Tay-Sachs mutations.
Canavan disease	Similar to Tay-Sachs disease.	Death usually occurs by age 10 years, although survival into adulthood occasionally occurs. No effective treatment is currently available.	1/40 Jews carries the gene. The risk of having an affected child is 1/6,400. 1/500 non-Jews in the U.S. carries the gene. Both parents must be gene carriers for a child to be affected.	DNA tests detect 97% of Jewish gene carriers. Carrier testing in other ethnic groups is less accurate.
Niemann-Pick disease, Type A	Causes severe feeding problems and failure to grow with progressive and severe degeneration of brain function in early infancy.	Death usually occurs by age 3. No effective treatment is currently available.	1/90 Jews carries the gene. The risk of having an affected child is 1/32,000. Very rare among non-Jews. Both parents must be gene carriers for a child to be affected.	DNA tests detect 95% of Jewish gene carriers. Carrier testing in other ethnic groups is less accurate.

continues

Disorder	Symptoms	Prognosis	Carrier Frequency & Disease Incidence	Genetic Testing for Carrier Status
Gaucher disease	Causes anemia, bone pain, enlargement of the spleen and liver. People with Gaucher disease are of normal intelligence, and the nervous system is rarely affected.	Disease is usually mild and often not diagnosed until adulthood, if ever. Some suffer from chronic disability starting in childhood or early adulthood. Enzyme treatments are available for those with severe symptoms.	1/15 Jews carries the gene. 1/900 is affected by Gaucher disease. 1/200 non-Jews carries the gene. Both parents must be gene carriers for a child to be affected.	DNA tests detect 97% of Jewish carriers.

Recessive gene carrier testing options for individuals of African, Hispanic, Mediterranean, Asian, and Middle Eastern Ancestry

Disorder	Symptoms	Prognosis	Carrier Frequency & Disease Incidence	Genetic Testing for Carrier Status
Sickle-cell disease	Causes severe anemia, bone pain, damage to major organs, and susceptibility to infection. Individuals with sickle-cell disease are of normal intelligence.	Varies considerably. Severe disease can lead to frequent hospitalization; mild disease may allow for survival to adulthood. Treatments include drugs and transfusions.	1/11 African Americans carries the gene. Risk of having an affected child is 1/484. Less than 1/50 individuals of Mediterranean, Arab, Asian, or Indian ancestry carries the gene. Both parents must be gene carriers for a child to be affected	Hemoglobin electrophoresis finds all carriers of sickle-cell gene.

| Thalassemia | Severe anemia, transfusion dependency, and organ damage. Individuals with thalassemia are of normal intelligence. | Varies. (Depends on specific mutations in family.) In severe cases, complications of disease and treatment lead to death during third and fourth decades. Treatments include transfusions, drugs, and bone-marrow transplants. | 1/20 individuals of Mediterranean or Indian ancestry carries the gene. The risk of having an affected child is about 1/1,600. 1/75 African Americans carries the gene. 1/10 Southeast Asians carries the gene. Both parents must be gene carriers for a child to be affected. | Hemoglobin electrophoresis and complete blood count find almost all carriers of common inherited anemias. |

Note: Carrier frequencies above refer to individuals without a family history of the disorder.
Source: Department of Genetics, Yale University School of Medicine.

TABLE 1.3: PROS AND CONS OF CARRIER TESTING

Pros:

Carrier testing involves a simple blood test.

You'll have your results in one to two weeks.

You will know with certainty what the chances are for having a baby with the disease and what the options are for diagnosing the condition prenatally.

Cons:

Learning that you are a carrier for a particular disease may be a source of worry to you and your partner.

These tests can cost hundreds of dollars per person and may not be covered by your medical insurance.

Although it is unlikely, finding out that you are a carrier of a potentially harmful gene may influence insurance decisions about you or members of your family or influence the way you or others view yourself.

Bright Idea
If you aren't already doing so, start keeping a menstrual calendar. Note the date when your period starts, the number of days it lasts, and anything else your doctor might want to know about. This information could prove helpful if you experience problems in conceiving. It can also prove invaluable in pinpointing the date of conception—and consequently your due date.

As you might expect, the testing of general populations rather than just high-risk populations for carrier states is sometimes a touchy political issue, as can be the testing for disease in the not-necessarily-at-risk fetus or in the preimplantation cell mass in that it can resemble a negative eugenics approach to some. Nevertheless, these technologies are becoming a fact of life for a growing number of couples. Like it or not, "designer babies" are here to stay.

Now that you have an idea of how physically ready you are for pregnancy, it's time to take the next important step by visiting your doctor.

What's up, doc?

Fifteen years ago, women didn't show up on their doctors' doorsteps until they had missed their second period and were 99% sure they were pregnant. Today, most doctors recommend that their patients come in for a checkup before they start trying to conceive.

The reason for the change in thinking is obvious. Recent studies about the benefits of preconception health have served to hammer home an important message: It's not enough to quit smoking, improve your eating habits, and start popping prenatal vitamins the moment the pregnancy test comes back positive. To give your baby the best possible start in life, you need to ensure that you are in the best possible health before you start trying to conceive.

Here's why.

Even though today's pregnancy tests are highly sensitive and allow women to test for pregnancy sooner than ever before, you probably won't know for sure that you're pregnant until at least four weeks after the date of your last menstrual period—perhaps even longer if your cycles are particularly lengthy or irregular. During this time when you're wondering whether you're pregnant, your baby's major organs are being formed—a process that medical science refers to as either organogenesis or embryogenesis. (See Table 1.4.) That's why it's so important to be as healthy as possible before you start trying to conceive. This means setting up an appointment to see your doctor for a preconception checkup.

TABLE 1.4: WHAT HAPPENS WHEN

neural tube: days 19 to 27
heart: weeks 3 to 7
gastrointestinal tract: weeks 4 to 10
kidneys: weeks 5 to 8
limbs: weeks 5 to 8
lungs: weeks 5 to 8
genitals: weeks 7 to 10
hair: weeks 10 to 16

During the preconception checkup, your doctor will

Watch Out!
You and your doctor will have a harder time pinning down your due date if you become pregnant immediately after you stop taking the pill. That's why most doctors suggest that you wait until after your first spontaneous postpill period before you start trying to conceive. (You may be told that you should wait three or more months after stopping the pill. This advice is medically unfounded and may result in a pregnancy sooner than you planned.)

- talk with you about your plans to start a family and answer any questions you might have about fertility, pregnancy, and childbirth;

- tell you what you can do to improve your odds of having the healthiest baby possible (that is, quit smoking, abstain from alcohol while you're trying to conceive and throughout your pregnancy, and so on);

- discuss whether you should attempt to lose or gain weight prior to becoming pregnant;

- provide you with information about how any chronic health conditions you may have—diabetes; cardiac problems; high blood pressure; epilepsy; lung, liver or kidney disorders, and so on—might best be managed before and during pregnancy (see Chapter 10);

- review which medicines you're currently taking (that is, both prescription and over-the-counter medications) and let you know which ones you should stop taking or change once you start trying to conceive (see Chapter 8);

- provide you with some basic information on the time it may take you to conceive, given your age (according to the American Society for Reproductive Medicine, you have a 20% chance of conceiving in any given cycle if you're under 30 but only 5% if you're over 40) (see Chapter 3);

- talk with you about your overall reproductive health and let you know whether it makes sense for you to monitor your basal body temperature (that is, your temperature first thing in the morning—before you even get out of bed), identify changes in cervical mucous, purchase an ovulation predictor kit, and so on, in order to increase your chances of predicting ovulation (see Chapter 2);

■ discuss how any previous miscarriages, abortions, stillbirths, sexually transmitted diseases, and/or venereal infections might impact on either your chances of conceiving or your ability to carry a pregnancy to term (see Chapters 2 and 11);

■ determine whether you should have preconception genetic counseling (that is, if there's a family history of mental retardation, cerebral palsy, muscular dystrophy, cystic fibrosis, hemophilia, or spina bifida; if you are at increased risk of having a child with Tay-Sachs disease, thalassemia, or sickle-cell anemia because of your ethnic background; or if you are either under 18 or over 35);

■ review the importance of healthy eating (see Chapter 8) and/or prescribe a prenatal vitamin supplement so that your body will have the vitamins and minerals it needs during the first few weeks of pregnancy;

■ discuss the role of physical fitness during pregnancy (see Chapter 8);

■ talk about the importance of minimizing stress both when you're trying to conceive and after you become pregnant;

■ inform you about hazards to avoid while you're trying to conceive (that is, exposure to X-rays, toxins, and other substances that could be harmful to your baby);

■ do a pelvic exam and Pap smear to check for symptomless infections, ovarian cysts, and other

Timesaver
Try to book the last appointment of the day for your preconception checkup (as opposed to earlier in the day, when there could be a waiting room full of people). That's when your doctor or midwife is most likely to be able to take the time to answer your questions and address your concerns without feeling rushed to go on to the next patient.

Watch Out!
Contracting rubella while you are pregnant may cause permanent damage to your developing baby. Don't take a chance. If you are not immune to rubella, get immunized and then wait three months before trying to conceive.

conditions that might be difficult or risky to treat during pregnancy;

■ do a blood test to determine if you are anemic or carrying any sexually transmitted diseases;

■ do a urine test to screen for symptomless conditions such as diabetes, urinary tract infections, kidney infections, and asymptomatic infections that may pose a problem during pregnancy;

■ do a rubella test (German measles test) to determine whether you are immune to the disease;

■ check that your immunizations are up-to-date, and screen you for Hepatitis B;

■ talk with you about any hazards you or your partner may face in the workplace, and suggest job changes or job modifications to minimize your exposure to potentially harmful substances;

■ provide your partner with information about the effects of smoking, drinking, and teratogens on both fertility and the developing baby.

By the time you walk out of your doctor's office, you should have a clear idea of what you can do to increase your chances of conceiving quickly and having a healthy baby.

Mom's the word

Up until now, we've been focusing exclusively on the physical aspects of pregnancy. Equally important, however, is how emotionally prepared you and your partner are for the joys and challenges of parenting.

You're most likely to enjoy the experience of parenting if

- you have a realistic idea of what parenting is really like (that is, you don't think it's like something you see on the diaper commercials!);

- you are willing to make the sacrifices required to be a parent, such as putting someone else's needs before your own on a daily basis;

- you and your partner are equally committed to the idea of having a child;

- you and your partner are used to sharing responsibility for a variety of household tasks and intend to share the responsibilities of parenting.

As you no doubt realize, there are almost as many reasons to start a family as there are babies in this world. That said, many men and women are motivated by a powerful emotional pull to become parents. Here are what some of the members of our parent panel had to say about the urge to have a baby:

- "When I decided to have my first baby, it was purely an emotional decision. We did not 'plan our finances,' buy a new house, build our careers, or do anything most other couples do to prepare for their first baby. We simply felt we wanted to bring a child into our family, so we went for it! I think there is really something to be said about women and the urge to have children. It's so hard to explain, but you just 'feel' like you want to have a baby, so you go for it."
—Suzi, 27, mother of two

- "My husband and I had been together for ten years before we married. We met in high school. We traveled, enjoyed ourselves, bought and renovated a house, and then thought that a child was the next logical step. As soon as we started

Unofficially...
Wondering what factors make women in Europe decide that it's the right time to have a baby? Relationship issues are at the top of the list. Between one-half and three-quarters of women who responded to a recent survey said that they waited until "it was the right time in the relationship" before becoming pregnant.

thinking about it, I suddenly couldn't wait."
—Karen, 34, mother of three

- "I hate to admit it, but our main consideration was my age. I was 31 when we got married, and I knew I wanted to have more than one child. I suppose in reality I had many years still to start trying, but my mother died of breast cancer at 32 and my grandmother died of breast cancer when she was very young also. I was scared that I would get breast cancer and die without being able to have a child—or get cancer and not be able to have a child. So although we'd been married less than a year and weren't really financially ready yet, we started trying." —Susan, 33, mother of one

- "My husband and I decided to try to become pregnant after my father passed away from cancer in 1996. I regretted not having given him more grandchildren and I was faced with my own mortality, since he was only 65 years old. My husband and I had been married ten years by that time." —Janet, 33, mother of one

- "We had been married for three years and purchased the house that we wanted kids in. More and more frequently, my husband and I were asking [one another], 'What do you want to do tonight?' The clincher came when I was carrying my sister's very tired two-year-old son. For the first time, he snuggled his head into my neck for a rest. I knew then that I wanted that on an ongoing basis. I told my husband that I was ready and to let me know whenever he was. A few months later he said, 'Okay, let's go for it.'" —Jacqueline, 34, currently pregnant with her second child

The career costs of having a baby

You've no doubt heard all the whispering about the Mommy Track—the idea that having a baby can hold back your career. The argument goes as follows: Women who work and raise children can find themselves being offered fewer opportunities for career advancement than their childless counterparts or are left on the sidelines altogether.

Although this argument may have held true 10 years ago, a recent article on Kiplinger Online casts doubt on the whole idea of the "Mommy Track." The article reports on the findings of a New York–based research firm, Interep Research, which noted that improvements in child care and workplace amenities such as flexible hours, telecommuting, and job-sharing have made it easier for women to balance the competing needs of their families and their careers.

This is not to say that all is rosy on the career front. Although the National Center for Health Statistics reports that approximately 80% of working women will become pregnant at some point during their working lives, the American workforce still hasn't quite come to terms with this simple biological fact. Some companies still penalize "nine to fivers"—employees who must attend to other responsibilities at the end of the working day rather than putting in a few extra hours at the office.

If you work for one of these less-than-enlightened organizations, the onus is on you to blow your own horn on a regular basis, acting as your own lobbyist so that you won't be overlooked when promotions and other perks are being passed around. If you plan to job-share or work part-time hours after the birth of your baby, it will be particularly important for you to maintain a high profile at the office on the days when you're in. That way, coworkers can bring you up to speed on developments that have occurred on your days off.

Here's another development you need to know about: according to a recent article in *Fortune* magazine, some working fathers are being penalized for their involvement with their families. This is what writer Betsy Morris had to say: "Well-educated men with working wives are paid and promoted less than men with stay-at-home wives, probably because they can't clock as much face time. . . . Corporate manuals would do well to carry a warning: Ambitious, beware. If you want to have children, proceed at your own risk. You must be very talented, or on very solid ground, to overcome the damage a family can do to your career."

We'll be tackling this issue in greater detail in Chapter 8, when we talk about working during pregnancy, but for now, you can put your mind at ease by knowing that it's probably neither as good nor as bad as the experts would have you believe. Bottom line? In most cases, having a baby doesn't have to spell doomsday for your career. It isn't easy to juggle the needs of your family with the demands of your job, but it can be done.

A more important issue to consider on the career front is *what it's like* to juggle your family with your career. Most working couples admit to being incredibly busy and constantly tired. It just seems to go with the turf. The secret is to come up with ways of juggling more effectively.

Here are some strategies that have worked for other families:

■ **Telecommuting:** Telecommuting is just the '90s term for working from home. Although only a

Unofficially...
It's not just pin money. According to a recent study by the U.S. Department of Labor, married women who work full-time bring in an average of 41% of family income.

handful of companies allow their employees to work from home on a full-time basis, a growing number have proven willing to allow their employees to telecommute on an occasional or part-time basis. Simply knowing that your boss will be okay with the idea of having you work from home on a day when your child is running a fever can take a lot of the stress out of being a working parent.

- **Job sharing:** Job sharing means splitting a full-time position with another person. Along with the hours, you split the salary and, in some companies, the benefits as well. According to a recent article by Sue Shellenbarger in *The Detroit News,* women who are interested in cutting back on their hours should seriously consider job sharing. "Because most positions are still full-time, job sharers have a better chance of preserving career skills and status—and of advancing—than their part-time counterparts." The secret to successful job sharing is to find a reliable job-sharing partner—someone who is willing to keep up his or her end of the bargain.

- **Flextime:** Flextime means working flexible hours. Although most companies put some types of controls in place (that is, you're required to be at the office during certain core hours), you can adjust your hours of work so that they mesh better with your child-care arrangements, your partner's schedule, and so on.

Although these programs all sound terrific on paper, there's just one downside to these types of work and family programs—one that no one likes to talk about. Parents in many workplaces fail to take advantage of opportunities to telecommute, job-share, or work flexible hours. The reason is simple: although many organizations give lip service to the whole idea of supporting working families, those employees who do decide to take advantage of these types of opportunities are labeled as being less dedicated than their more workaholic counterparts. According to a recent article in *Redbook*, a 1992 study by the Catalyst research group in New York revealed that about 50% of women working flex-time hours have experienced some ill will from their coworkers. What's more, about a quarter of the 45 women who participated in the study had to take a demotion in order to switch to part-time or flex-time hours.

When you're trying to decide how to balance the needs of your family with the demands of your career, don't just go by what's written in the company benefits manual. Get the lowdown from other working parents. Find out what benefits are available, who's taking advantage of them, and what fallout—if any—there has been for their careers. Then you'll be in a better position to decide whether you wish to stick with the status quo, change jobs, start your own business, become a stay-at-home mom, or rethink the timing of having a baby.

Dollars and sense

Now we get down to the real nitty-gritty: what it actually costs to have a child.

As an expectant parent, you need to be concerned about two basic types of costs: the long-term costs of raising a child to age 18 (or later, if your late bloomer takes a little longer to fly the coop) and the short-term costs of giving birth to a child.

What it costs to raise a child

Certain public and private organizations seem to take perverse delight in scaring parents and would-be parents into thinking that no one other than the Kennedys and the Rockefellers can afford to raise a child.

Here are some recent statistics:

- According to New England Financial, the U.S. Department of Agriculture now estimates that an ordinary middle-class family will spend approximately $176,420 to raise a child and pay for her college education. For higher-income families, the total is a wallet-popping $347,000.

- According to Phillip J. Longman, who wrote about the cost of raising children in a recent issue of *U.S. News and World Report*, the cost of raising a single child can easily exceed $1.4 million dollars. (Just a quick note about Longman's method before we move on. He factored in everything but the kitchen sink, including "acquisition costs" of up to $50,000 for couples who undergo infertility treatments in their pursuit of parenthood. It makes for interesting reading, but it hardly reflects the reality of the majority of working Americans. A more realistic approach to calculating the cost of raising a child is to factor in your own lifestyle and do some quick number crunching. Some costs, such as your mortgage, are unlikely to be affected by having one or two children; others, such as your clothing budget, can shoot sky-high when you've got an extra couple of bodies to clothe.)

If you'd like some help, check out the financial tools available online at www.babycenter.com/tools.html.

Moneysaver
If you're worried about the financial hit you might take when it comes to setting up the nursery, start putting money aside as early on in your pregnancy as possible. Have your bank transfer $20 per week into a separate savings account, and you'll have a nice nest egg of $800 to fall back on when it comes time to start shopping for baby.

What it costs to give birth

Ask a dozen new mothers what it cost them to give birth to their babies and you'll likely be hit with three entirely different figures. There is no such thing as an average cost of giving birth in America.

If both you and your spouse have access to HMO plans at work or through the government (because you're on Medicaid), go with whichever one offers the most bang for your buck. You might want to use the checklist below to help you decide which HMO will best meet the needs of your growing family.

CHECKLIST: WHICH HMO IS RIGHT FOR YOU?

Here are some questions to ask when you're shopping for an HMO:

Note! ➜
At least 85% of
HMO specialists
and a majority of
primary-care
physicians are
board certified.

- Is the HMO registered with the American Association of Health Plans (www.aahp.org) or the National Committee for Quality Assurance (www.ncqa.org; 202-955-3500)?

- Is the plan you're considering suited to the needs of young families?

- Are all of the hospitals covered by the plan accredited by the Joint Commission on Accreditation of Healthcare Organizations (www.jcaho.org/; 630-792-5000)?

- Does at least one of the hospitals covered by the plan have an extensive department in any speciality you or your baby might require (for example, a neonatal intensive care unit)?

- How are physicians paid (that is, a salary vs. a flat rate per patient per month)?

- How many of the physicians within the plan are board certified?

- Are the physicians or midwives who are covered by the HMO experienced and highly respected professionals? Do they have specialized train-ing in such areas as infertility and high-risk pregnancy?

■ Are there enough physicians or midwives for you to choose from? (You should think twice before joining a plan that has fewer than three specialists in any speciality or fewer than 10 pri-mary care physicians.)

■ What is the rate of turnover among physicians or midwives?

■ Do the physicians or midwives covered by the plan have offices that are conveniently located?

■ If you decide to use the services of a physician or midwife outside the plan, what percentage of the cost of their services, if any, will be covered by the HMO?

■ What percentage of claims are approved for payment?

■ What is the appeals procedure if a claim is turned down?

■ How are treatment decisions made?

■ Which drugs and treatments are and are not covered by the plan?

■ If experimental treatments are not covered, how does the HMO go about defining what's experimental and what's not?

■ Are there any restrictions on medical coverage? For example, does your primary-care doctor or the HMO administrator have to give the go-ahead before you show up at an emergency room?

■ What type of non-emergency care, if any, is avail-able to you when you travel?

Bright Idea
Ask to have a sneak peak at the HMO's wel-come booklet and list of health-care providers before you sign up for the plan. Evaluate the cov-erage and make a few phone calls to ensure that the doctor or midwife you pre-fer is, in fact, accepting new patients.

- Are the doctors within the plan required to sign a "gag clause" that prohibits them from telling patients about expensive or experimental treatments that aren't covered by the plan?

- Does the HMO dictate standardized procedures for certain diseases or medical conditions (for example, what is its policy regarding vaginal births after cesareans)?

- Is there a cap on the number of referrals to specialists or for expensive tests that a physician can order in a year (or other financial disincentives to utilize services)?

- Does the plan cover the cost of obtaining a second opinion?

- What types of infertility-related services are covered by the plan? How many sessions or treatments are covered?

- Are alternative therapies, such as the services of chiropractors and acupuncturists, covered by the plan?

- Are prenatal visits, well-baby care, and immunizations covered by the plan?

- What is the co-pay (that is, the amount of money you're required to pay out of your own pocket) for prenatal visits, a vaginal or caesarean birth, ultrasounds, prenatal testing, and other types of services?

- What is the deductible you are required to pay for a particular time period (usually per person/per year)?

- What is the grievance procedure in the event that your physician refuses to refer you to a specialist or the HMO refuses to approve your physician's recommended course of treatment?

Unofficially...
According to a survey by California's PacifiCare Health Systems Inc. and Yankelovich Partners Inc., only 17% of employees spend more than one hour reviewing health-plan enrollment materials.
Source: *Business Week*

You can find out more about the ins and outs of managed-care plans at some of the health care Web sites listed in Appendix B.

What every parent-to-be needs to know about taxes

Our discussion of the costs of raising children would not be complete without a mention of three tax breaks that every pregnant woman or new parent needs to know about: the medical expense deduction, the child and dependent care credit, and the child tax credit.

Medical expense deduction

Here's the scoop on the medical expense deduction:

- You are entitled to deduct the portion of your medical and dental expenses that exceeds 7.5% of your adjusted gross income. The IRS defines medical care expenses as "amounts paid for the diagnosis, cure, mitigation, treatment, or prevention of disease, and for treatments affecting any part or function of the body. The expenses must be primarily to alleviate or prevent a physical or mental defect or illness."

- Medical care expenses include the premiums you pay for insurance that covers the expenses of medical care, as well as expenses you pay in getting to and from medical care.

- You are able to deduct expenses that were paid during a particular taxation year. The date of payment is generally considered to be the date when you paid for the medical or dental services—not the date on which they were performed.

Watch Out!
Before you cancel your existing insurance or managed-care coverage, make sure that the other provider is willing to take you on. Difficult as it may be to believe, some companies view pregnancy as a preexisting condition and will not cover maternity costs for pregnant applicants.

- You cannot deduct expenses for which you were reimbursed by a third party (that is, an insurance company or your employer).

- To claim this deduction, you need to use Schedule A of Form 1040. (This means that you can't use Form 1040A or Form 1040EZ.) You simply write in the amount of medical expenses you paid (after deducting the amount for which you were reimbursed by insurance companies and other third parties), enter your adjusted gross income from form 1040, and calculate the amount of your expenses that qualify as a deduction (that is, expenses in excess of 7.5% of your gross adjusted income). You must have records to substantiate your claim. The record should show the name and address of each person you paid, and the amount and date of the payment. Here's another quick tip: If you expect to have significant medical expenses that straddle two tax years—that is, you conceive in September and your baby is due in June—you might consider deferring your initial payments until the new year or prepaying for all of your pregnancy-related services in the first year. This can help to push you over the magic 7.5% threshold. Of course, you'll want to run this by your tax advisor before you get too carried away. We specialize in babies, not bookkeeping!

To find out more about the medical expense deduction, call 800-TAX-FORM (800-829-3676) or visit the IRS Web site at http://ares.fedworld.gov.

Child and dependent care credit

If you need to pay for child care so that you can go to work, you may be eligible for another hefty tax break: the child and dependent care credit.

Moneysaver
If you are an employee of a small business (that is, one that employs fewer than 50 employees) or are self-employed and covered only by a high-deductible health plan, you may be eligible to open a medical savings account (MSA)—an account that allows you to pay for medical expenses in pre-tax dollars. Your employer may also decide to contribute to the plan. *Note:* This is a pilot project of the IRS, and there are limits to the number of dollars available under the program.

Here's how it works.

To be eligible to claim the credit for child and dependent care expenses, you must meet all of the following tests and file either Form 1040 or Form 1040A (not Form 1040EZ):

- The care must be for one or more qualifying persons (that is, children under the age of 13 or older children who are disabled).

- You and your spouse (if you are married) must share your home with the qualifying person or persons and be personally responsible for the costs of keeping up the home (that is, property taxes, mortgage interest, rent utility charges, and so on). If you receive funding from the state (for example, Aid to Families with Dependent Children) that constitutes more than half the cost of keeping up your home, you are not eligible for the Child and Dependent Care Credit. If, however, you share a home with another family, the living spaces of the two families are treated as separate households, so you have to worry only about whether you are providing half (or more) of the funds required to keep up your part of the home.

- You and your spouse (if you are married) must have earned income during the year. (There are exceptions for students and for families in which one or more of the parents were unable to care for himself or herself.)

- You must be paying child-care expenses to enable yourself (or your spouse, if you are married) to work or look for work.

- You must make payments for child and dependent care to someone you (or your spouse) cannot claim as a dependent. This means that you are free to purchase child-care services from relatives who are not your dependents. *Note:* If you are claiming expenses paid to a child-care center, the center must meet all applicable state and local regulations.

Timesaver
You can obtain the tax forms and guides you'll need in order to take advantage of the Child and Dependent Care Credit by calling the IRS at 800-424-FORM or downloading them from the IRS Web site at http://ares.fedworld.gov.

- Your filing status must be one of the following: single, head of household, qualifying widow(er) with dependent child, or married filing jointly. You must file a joint return if you are married, unless you are legally separated or living apart. (It's actually a bit more complicated than that, so call your local IRS office for details if you and your spouse are living apart.)

- You must identify the caregiver on your tax return. You're required to provide the name, address, and taxpayer identification number for anyone who cared for your child during the year. If the caregiver is an individual, the taxpayer identification number is her social security number or individual taxpayer identification number. If the care provider is an organization, then you need to provide the employer identification number (EIN). You don't, however, have to provide the taxpayer identification number if the organization providing care is one of certain tax-exempt organizations (such as, a church or a school). In this case, you simply write "tax-exempt" on the form. If you are unable to provide all of the information required about your caregiver, you must prove to the government that you exercised "due diligence" in trying to obtain the necessary information.

- You may exclude from your income up to $2,400 ($4,800 if two or more qualifying persons were cared for) of dependent care assistance benefits provided by your employer or insurance company.

The credit you are eligible to receive is a percentage of your work-related expenses paid during a given tax year. Regardless of how much you paid out in expenses, however, you cannot receive more than $2,400 for one child (or $4,800 for two or more children).

To determine the amount of your credit, multiply your total eligible work-related expenses by the percentage that applies to your income bracket.

Note: Some benefits plans qualify for this tax break, whereas others do not. Check with your employer to find out whether your plan qualifies.

TABLE 1.5: HOW TO CALCULATE THE CHILD AND DEPENDENT CARE CREDIT

Adjusted Gross Income	Credit Percentage
$0–$10,000	30%
$10,000–$12,000	29%
$12,000–$14,000	28%
$14,000–$16,000	27%
$16,000–$18,000	26%
$18,000–$20,000	25%
$20,000–$22,000	24%
$22,000–$24,000	23%
$24,000–$26,000	22%
$26,000–$28,000	21%
$28,000–no limit	20%

Moneysaver
If you received dependent care benefits from your employer, you may be able to use the Child and Dependent Care Credit to exclude all or part of them from your income. Dependent care benefits include

▪ money your employer pays directly to either you or your care provider for the care of your child while you are working, and

▪ the fair market value of care in a child-care facility that is provided or sponsored by your employer.

If you received dependent care benefits, they should be shown in box 10 of your W-2 form.

Before you get too excited, you'll want to read the fine print on this particular credit: Your tax credit for child- and dependent-care expenses cannot be more than the amount of your tax liability. In other words, you cannot get a refund for any part of the credit that is more than the tax you owe to the government.

Child tax credit

Although it's not specifically tied to child-care expenses, the new Child Tax Credit (introduced under the Taxpayer Relief Act of 1997) may help you put a bit of extra cash in your pocket. Since 1998, there has been a $400 tax credit for each child under the age of 17. The credit will increase to $500 per child in 1999. The credit is phased out at higher income levels, beginning at an adjusted gross income level of $75,000 for single filers and $110,000 for married joint filers. Don't miss out on the tax credit by failing to provide the IRS with all the information it needs. You must provide Social Security numbers for all dependent children who are being claimed as dependents, including those born at the end of the tax year.

Some states offer additional tax incentives as well. Because the situation is tremendously complex and constantly changing, you should consult with your local tax office to get the latest scoop on child-care–related credits. If, however, you want to do a bit of homework before you pick up the phone to make that call, you can get the lowdown on child-care tax credits for your state by reading *Financing Childcare in the United States: An Illustrative Catalog of Collective Strategies* available online in the "Publications" section of the Pew Charitable Trusts Web site: www.pewtrusts.com.

Making a decision you can live with

As you can see, deciding to have a baby is no easy matter. You have to decide whether you're physically and emotionally up to the rigors of pregnancy and the challenges of new parenthood and to assess whether this is the "right time" to have a baby as far as your career and your financial situation are concerned.

Sometimes the decision gets taken out of your hands entirely—something Jim, 37, father of three, discovered when his first child was born nine years ago: "I was not as 'ready' as Sue. My preference was to wait for a time until I had established my career a bit more. But in the end the Final Decision was really quite simple. It happened."

Just the facts

- Schedule a preconception checkup with your health-care practitioner to be certain that your pregnancy gets off to the best possible start.

- Consider how emotionally ready you and your partner are for parenthood before you decide to take the plunge.

- Give some thought to the career implications of starting a family, and start thinking about whether you wish to stay at home following the birth of your child, return to work, or come up with some new type of working arrangement.

- Think about the financial implications of having a baby, but don't make the mistake of postponing parenthood too long. Otherwise, you could end up with tons of money in the bank but no one to spend it on.

- Be sure to take advantage of the tax breaks that are available to families with young children, such as the medical expenses deduction, the child and dependent tax credit, and the child tax credit.

Unofficially...
Six out of every 10 pregnancies are unplanned. Source: *U.S. News and World Report*

GET THE SCOOP ON...
The biggest lies about fertility and infertility ▪
Fertility awareness and other methods of
increasing your chances of conceiving ▪
"Trying" versus letting nature take its course ▪
Ways of protecting your fertility

The Overachiever's Guide to Getting Pregnant Fast

If you've spent the past 10 years or more of your life running to the drugstore at regular intervals in an effort not to get pregnant, it can feel a bit odd to find yourself suddenly engaged in the business of baby making. Even if you are trying to take a rather laid-back approach to conceiving—that is, you're letting passion rather than an ovulation predictor kit determine when you have sex—you probably can't help but think of sex in a whole new way. Rather than merely being an intimate expression of love and passion between you and your partner, it has now become a biological process that is capable of producing the ultimate miracle—another human being.

If, like many couples, you and your partner have been reading up on the art of conceiving, you've probably stumbled across all kinds of contradictory information about getting pregnant. One book will tell you that you can conceive during the days before and immediately after you ovulate; another will tell you that you've missed your chance if you haven't hopped in the sack by the time ovulation occurs. Similarly, one magazine article will suggest that you stand on your head after sex so that you can give the sperm a bit of a boost as they begin their quest to fertilize an egg; another will tell you that you can get up out of bed and do jumping jacks if you'd like, since the sperm are designed to find their way to the egg, gravity be damned.

So why is there such a glut of misinformation about this all-important topic? We think the reason is simple: because there's so much interest in the topic of pregnancy. There are countless old wives' tales and bits of folk wisdom related to pregnancy. What's more, the media tends to give massive amounts of coverage to every new study that promises to shed a bit more light on the mysteries of conception. It doesn't matter if the research sample is overly small, the results are tentative and require further examination, or that the researchers are practicing bad science: news stories about pregnancy make good copy, period.

Because there's so much misinformation, we'll start this chapter by debunking some of the more convincing myths about fertility and conception. Then we'll move on to the length of time it takes to conceive, the pros and cons of "trying" versus letting nature take its course, what you can do to increase your odds of conceiving quickly, and what every man and woman needs to know about preventing infertility.

The biggest misconceptions about fertility and infertility

How many of these common misconceptions about fertility and infertility have you heard?

MYTH: You are most fertile two weeks after your period starts

This rule holds true only if your cycle length happens to be 28 days. However, many women have cycles that are either shorter or longer than this, or are highly irregular. (Just a reminder: The length of your cycle is defined as the length of time between the first day of one period and the first day of the next.) Since ovulation occurs approximately 14 days before the onset of your next period, if your cycle is 35 days long, you can expect to ovulate on or around day 21.

On the other hand, if your cycle is highly unpredictable—that is, 28 days one month and 35 days the next—you could find it a little more challenging to predict your fertile days. We'll be giving you some pointers on predicting your fertile days elsewhere in this chapter.

MYTH: Taking your temperature every morning will tell you when to have intercourse

Many women who are trying to conceive make a point of taking their temperature each morning so that they can track their basal body temperature (BBT), or resting temperature. Although tracking your BBT can provide plenty of valuable information, it won't tell you when to have sex. The reason is simple: by the time your temperature starts to rise, ovulation has already occurred.

What you can learn from tracking your BBT, however, is whether you are ovulating at all, whether

Unofficially...
A recent study by the Opinion Research Corporation in Princeton, New Jersey, revealed that a large percentage of women aren't at all clear about the facts of life. Seventy-six percent of the 477 women who participated in the Unipath Pregnancy Planning Awareness Study admitted that they didn't know everything they needed to know in order to plan for pregnancy.

Bright Idea
Wondering when you have the greatest odds of conceiving? Let the Ovulation Calculator at www.babycenter.com/calculator/2757.html do the number crunching for you. You can find some additional information on predicting your most fertile days at www.babycenter.com/refcap/484.html.

your luteal phase (the second half of your cycle) is long enough for implantation to occur, whether your progesterone levels (the so-called pregnancy hormones) are sufficiently high during your luteal phase, whether you are pregnant (if you have more than 18 consecutive high temperatures), whether you are in danger of having a miscarriage (if your temperature suddenly drops), and whether you were pregnant before having what seemed to be a "late period."

The only way you can use a BBT chart to predict your most fertile days is to look at a few months' worth of charts and try to determine whether your cycle conforms to any repeatable patterns. For example, if your temperature always shoots sky-high on day 14, you'll know that you have a good chance of ovulating in that same time frame during your next cycle.

MYTH: To maximize your chances of conceiving, you should make love during the days leading up to and following ovulation

Although part of this statement is correct, it's living proof that a little bit of knowledge can be a dangerous thing. It's a good idea to time intercourse on the days prior to ovulation, but you've missed your opportunity if you try to conceive more than a day after ovulation has occurred. The reason is simple: the egg is capable of surviving for only 12 to 24 hours after ovulation, so if it hasn't been charmed by a sperm cell by then, it's too late.

A recent study conducted by researchers from the National Institute of Environmental Health Sciences confirmed the importance of timing intercourse prior to or at the time of ovulation: all of the 192 pregnancies that occurred in the 625 couples participating in the study resulted from intercourse the day of ovulation or within five days before it.

MYTH: There's something wrong with you if you don't conceive within the first three months of trying

This is a particularly nasty bit of misinformation because it causes a lot of couples a tremendous amount of anxiety and grief for no good reason. Although some couples do manage to conceive within the first three months of trying, a large number of other highly fertile couples take considerably longer than that. Consider the numbers for yourself:

- Your odds of conceiving in any given cycle are approximately one in four.

- Approximately 60% of couples who are actively trying to conceive (having intercourse two to three times a week) will conceive within the first 6 months of trying, 75% within 9 months, 80% within a year, and 90% within 18 months.

MYTH: Your fertility declines dramatically after age 35

Although it's true that your fertility declines as you age, you still have an excellent chance of having a baby even if you're past the reproductive world's magic age of 35.

According to the National Center for Health Statistics, you have a 96% chance of conceiving within one year if you're under 25, an 86% if you're between 25 and 34, and a 78% chance if you're between the ages of 35 and 44.

MYTH: You can increase your chances of having a boy or a girl by timing intercourse a particular way

Although theories like this abound, there is no scientific evidence to link the timing of conception

> 66
> It took us about six months to get pregnant, but we weren't actually making love on the days we were supposed to until about four months after we stopped using birth control. I think my husband was purposely avoiding the 'right' day because he was feeling ambivalent about the whole thing.
> —Susan, 33, mother of one
> 99

Unofficially...
According to a recent article on Stork Site, an article in the British journal *Nature* claims that the age of your mate may help to determine the sex of your child. Researchers apparently discovered that men with partners at least five years younger than themselves had sons twice as often as daughters, and that women who married younger men produced twice as many daughters as sons. It's an interesting finding, but it's just one study.

and the sex of the baby. (One popular theory claims that you can increase your odds of having a baby girl by making love no closer than two to three days prior to ovulation, and that you can increase your odds of having a baby boy by timing intercourse as close to ovulation as possible.)

Even high-tech methods of sex selection have been branded a failure. A 1996 article in the British newspaper *The Independent* revealed that couples who paid top dollar to a London fertility clinic that claimed to be able to use IVF technology to separate sperm had "an exactly 50-50 chance of getting the sex of their choice."

MYTH: Just relax and you'll get pregnant

If you haven't had anyone pass along this little gem yet, consider yourself blessed. It's one of most pervasive fertility myths out there. Although it's true that a lot of stress can cause your reproductive system to shut down (it's part of the "fight or flight" survival mechanism we all possess), there's no firm evidence that moderate amounts of stress (that is, the running-to-the-bathroom-to-see-if-you're-pregnant-yet kind of stress) affects your chances of conceiving. "This notion implies that only women who can relax can get pregnant—and that's absurd," says Mark Sauer, M.D., director of the division of reproductive endocrinology at Columbia Presbyterian Hospital in New York in an article at http://homearts.com/rb/health/18getpbb.htm.

Here's what a few of the members of our pregnancy panel had to say about that perennial piece of advice:

- "If I had a nickel for every time someone told me to relax and not think about it, I'd be a millionaire." —Rhonda, 30, mother of two

- "I hated hearing, 'Just relax. You're trying too hard.' How can you not try hard when you want a child so badly?" —Randa, 23, mother of one

- "I won't say, 'Don't worry! Relax' to couples who are trying because I always hated it when people said that to me." —Tracy, 31, mother of one

MYTH: Women are the only ones who have to worry about declining fertility. Men can father children well into their seventies

Although it's common knowledge that women are capable of bearing children during only the first half of their adult lives, many people don't realize that men also experience a decline in their fertility as they age. Studies have shown that a man's fertility begins to decline from his late teens onward, and that pregnancy rates for couples in which the man is 40 or older are only one-third those of couples in which the man is 25 or younger. Scientists agree that there is an age-related decline in the production of sperm that leads to a decrease in male fertility.

MYTH: You need to have sex every single day if you want to get pregnant

Although you do boost your odds of conceiving if you have sex every day rather than every other day, the difference is fairly minimal.

Researchers at the National Institute of Environmental Health Sciences recently concluded that couples who had intercourse every other day during their fertile period had a 22% chance of conceiving in any given cycle, as compared to 25% for couples who had intercourse every day. On the other hand, couples who had intercourse only once a week reduced their odds of conceiving in a given cycle to 10%.

Bright Idea
Wondering how long it's taking other couples to conceive? Check out the polls at www. babycenter.com/ poll/all.html. You can check out other couples' responses to a number of pregnancy-related questions, including "Is it taking you much longer than you expected to conceive?" and "How long have you been trying to conceive?"

If your partner's sperm count is low or marginal, you may be advised to have intercourse every other day in order to give his sperm count a chance to build up. Your doctor may even recommend that your partner refrain from ejaculation during the days leading up to your most fertile period. He won't recommend that you limit your sex life to just a few days a month, however: studies have shown that abstaining from sex for more than seven days can decrease your fertility. Any gain in sperm count is more than offset by the increased number of aged sperm cells with lower fertilization potential.

MYTH: To give the sperm a chance to make it through the cervix, you should stand on your head or lie on your back with your knees to your chest for at least half an hour after making love

Although it's not a good idea to dash off to the bathroom and allow all of the semen to dribble into the toilet, you don't have to go to extreme measures to ensure that the sperm make their way past the cervix. For the most part, they know where they're headed and what they're supposed to do when they get there.

"Sperm are like salmon," says Mark Sauer, M.D., a professor of obstetrics and gynecology at the College of Physicians and Surgeons at Columbia University, who was quoted in an article that is available online at http://homearts.com/rb/health/19getpg3.html. "They always seem to swim upstream. A couple shouldn't be concerned about what position they use—the sperm know what direction to head in."

MYTH: Your left ovary releases an egg one month, and your right ovary the next

It's a great theory, but there's very little truth to it. Ovulation is a random event each month, with both ovaries vying for the honor on a first-come, first-served basis. If you have only one ovary, it wins the draw by default.

Fertility awareness and other methods of increasing your chances of conceiving

You can use various methods to increase your odds of conceiving in any given cycle. What they all boil down to, however, are ways of monitoring your fertility signs in order to pinpoint your most fertile days.

Before we get into a detailed discussion of fertility-awareness methods, however, let's quickly review the science behind the process of conception.

The science of sex

During the first half of your menstrual cycle—the so-called follicular, or proliferative, phase—approximately 20 eggs (or ova) begin to ripen and occupy fluid-filled sacks called follicles. At the same time, the level of estrogen in your body continues to rise, causing the endometrial lining in your uterus to thicken, thereby readying it for the possible implantation of a fertilized egg and boosting the production of cervical mucus, the substance that helps the sperm to make their way to the egg.

Just prior to ovulation, rising levels of estrogen trigger a brief but intense surge of lutenizing hormone (LH) from the pituitary gland that causes the dominant follicle to rupture and release its egg. Some women experience pain in the lower abdomen as this is occurring, a sensation the Germans call "mittelschmerz" or "pain in the middle."

During the second half of your cycle—the luteal or secretory phase—the ruptured ovarian follicle (now known as the corpus luteum, or "yellow body") begins to produce progesterone, the so-called "pregnancy hormone." It continues to produce progesterone until the placenta assumes this function some three months down the road.

The rising levels of progesterone cause the endometrial glands to ready the uterus for the arrival of a fertilized egg, which happens some five days later, if conception actually occurs.

When pregnancy occurs, your progesterone levels remain high. If it doesn't occur, the corpus luteum begins to regress; progesterone levels fall; and 12 to 14 days after ovulation, the uterus begins to shed the endometrial layer and your menstrual period begins. (See the following figure.)

Note! ➜ How pregnancy happens. Figure created by Articulate Graphics.

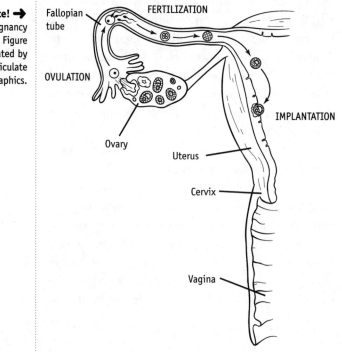

Now that we've completed this brief refresher course on the female reproductive system, let's consider some of the methods you can use to pinpoint the days on which you are most fertile.

Basal body temperature

One of the best ways to figure out what's happening with your menstrual cycle is to take your temperature (with an oral thermometer) at the same time each morning before you get out of bed and record this information on a temperature graph—a reading that is known as your basal body temperature.

BBT CHART INSTRUCTIONS

Starting with the first day of you menstrual period, write the month and day across the top of the graph and keep the chart and thermometer on your night table.

Each morning, as soon as you wake up, place the thermometer in your mouth and take your temperature. Do not eat, drink, smoke, or get out of bed before taking your temperature.

If you are using a digital thermometer, it will beep when it's time to read your temperature. If you're using a mercury thermometer, you should wait a full five minutes before reading your temperature.

Record the temperature reading on your BBT chart by placing a dot in the middle of the appropriate horizontal line in the column underneath the date. (If you forget to take your temperature one day, simply leave that day's column blank.)

If you think your reading may be off because you're ill, you're taking a particular medication, or because of a change in your sleep schedule, be sure to note the reason on your chart. You should also note the days on which you have sexual intercourse by checking off the appropriate boxes in the "coitus" section of the graph and the days on which you are menstruating by checking off the appropriate boxes in the "menses" section of the chart.

Note: You should start a new chart whenever you start a new menstrual cycle.

Example of a BBT Chart

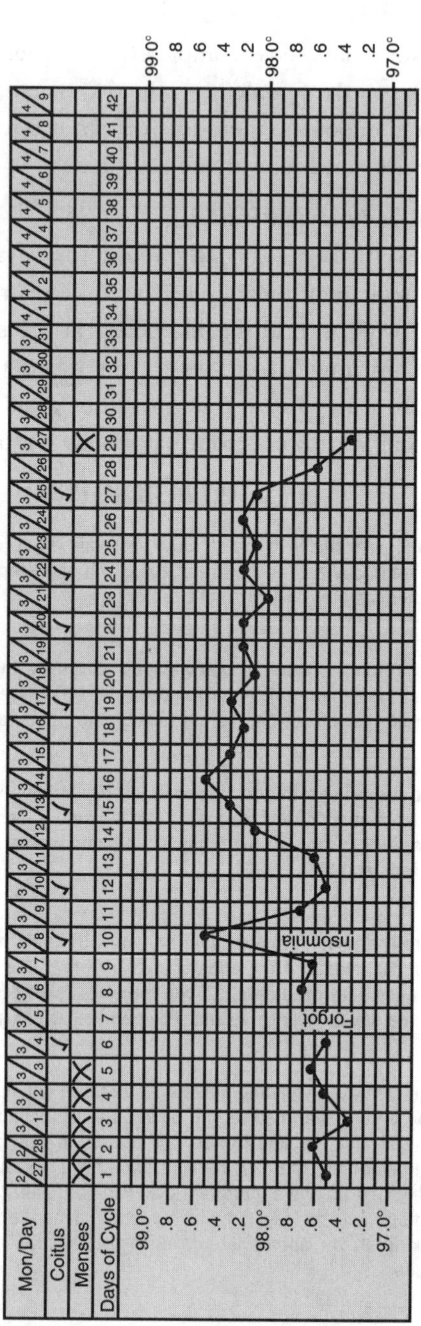

Basal Body Temperature Chart

Mon/Day																																										
Coitus																																											
Menses																																											
Days of Cycle	1	2	3	4	5	6	7	8	9	10	11	12	13	14	15	16	17	18	19	20	21	22	23	24	25	26	27	28	29	30	31	32	33	34	35	36	37	38	39	40	41	42

99.0°
.8
.6
.4
.2
98.0°
.8
.6
.4
.2
97.0°

Bright Idea
Use a digital oral thermometer rather than an old-style mercury thermometer. It's easier to read, it requires no shaking (which can cause your body temp to go up for no good reason), and it even beeps to remind you to record your reading if you accidentally go back to sleep.

If you are ovulating normally, your temperature may dip slightly just prior to ovulation and then shoot upward once you have ovulated. Your temperature will typically range from 97.0 to 97.5 degrees Fahrenheit prior to ovulation, and from 97.6 to 98.6 after ovulation. If you are pregnant, your temperature will remain elevated for the next nine months. If you're not, it will start to drop either close to or on the day your period starts as the level of progesterone in your body drops.

You will probably want to include information on your chart about the days on which you had intercourse. A simple checkmark or circle on the appropriate day is all that is required.

Many women find it useful to include some other types of information on their BBT charts as well, such as any changes to their routines that might have influenced their temperature reading on a particular morning. Something as simple as having a cold or fever, drinking alcohol the night before, getting less than three consecutive hours of sleep before you take your temperature, taking it at a significantly different time than usual, or sleeping under an electric blanket for a change can throw your readings out of whack.

Although BBT charts are a source of much useful information, they aren't a useful tool for everyone. Some women who are ovulating normally don't experience the classic temperature rise upon ovulation. Instead, their basal body temperature remains constant throughout their menstrual cycle. These women often have more luck monitoring the quantity and quality of their cervical mucus.

Cervical mucus

Throughout the course of a woman's menstrual cycle, hormonal changes trigger changes to both the quantity and the quality of her cervical mucus (the substance secreted by her cervix). As ovulation approaches, her secretions change from a thick, opaque texture to a thin, clear, and slippery texture that many women compare to egg white.

Toni Weschler, author of *Taking Charge of Your Fertility*, explains the reason for these changes: "Women are only fertile the few days around ovulation, and therefore only produce the substance necessary for sperm nourishment and mobility during that time."

It's possible to monitor the quality and quantity of cervical mucus by inserting one or two fingers into your vagina daily and noting the characteristics of your cervical mucus on your fingers when you remove them from your vagina. If you notice that you suddenly have an abundance of "egg white"—the type of mucus that is best suited to carrying sperm—you can bet that your fertile time has arrived.

Because you want your vaginal environment to be as sperm-friendly as possible, you will want to avoid

- vaginal sprays and scented tampons (because they can cause a pH imbalance in your vagina);
- artificial lubricants, vegetable oils, and glycerin (because they can kill off sperm);
- using saliva as a lubricant (because saliva can also kill sperm);
- douching (because it alters the normal acidity of the vagina; can cause vaginal infections and/or pelvic inflammatory disease; and may wash away the cervical mucus that is required to transport the sperm).

Watch Out!
Showering, bathing, and swimming can all temporarily alter the quantity and quality of your cervical mucus, so do your checks before you shower, bathe, or swim. You can run into similar difficulty if you attempt to do your checks after you've had intercourse, so it's important to plan ahead.

Position of your cervix

As your body approaches ovulation, your cervix tends to rise up in your vagina, soften, and open slightly. Although it generally feels firm at the beginning of your cycle, like the tip of your nose, it can feel as soft and fleshy as your lips by the time you're ready to ovulate. After ovulation, the cervix changes position, dropping lower in your vagina as estrogen levels fall and progesterone levels rise.

You can check the position of your cervix by washing your hands thoroughly with soap and rinsing well, squatting slightly or sitting on the toilet, and then inserting one finger deep into your vagina and feeling for your cervix. You should try to check your cervix at roughly the same time each day, for the sake of consistency. Just one quick note about this fertility sign: It can take a bit of time to get a sense of what your cervix is like at various times in your cycle. Don't assume that you're hopelessly inept when it comes to predicting your fertility if you can't master this particular technique. At least one obstetrician admits to finding it tricky to use this technique on his own patients!

Ovulation predictor kits (OPKs)

There's no doubt about it: ovulation predictor kits are big business in America today. According to a recent article at Stork Site (www.storksite.com) titled "Pregnancy and Ovulation Test Companies Get Serious," more than $23 million worth of ovulation predictor kits are sold each year.

Although the kits can be expensive—you can expect to pay $30 or more per month if your cycles are regular, a little more if they're not—they are considered to be a highly effective method of predicting ovulation because they are able to detect the

LH surge that typically appears 24 to 36 hours before ovulation.

What they can't do, however, is tell you when to start having sex. Ideally, you should be doing that before the LH surge appears. (You'll recall from our earlier discussion that a recent study indicated that the best time to start trying to conceive is three to five days prior to ovulation.)

One other word of caution before we move on: The fact that you have an LH surge does not necessarily mean you're ovulating. LH can surge with or without the release of an egg. To make matters worse, it's possible to have a series of LH surges prior to the "real" one—something that can throw your timing way out of whack.

Positioning

No chapter on conception would be complete without at least a few words on sexual positions.

As a rule of thumb, the sexual positions that enable the sperm to be deposited high up in the vagina right next to the cervix are thought to provide the best opportunity for baby making. This is why some doctors suggest that couples who are having difficulty conceiving use the so-called missionary position for intercourse (that is, male partner on top) and tuck a pillow under the woman's hips to ensure that the maximum amount of semen reaches her cervix.

This position may be the most conducive to sperm placement, but it can be less than orgasm-friendly for the female partner. Although you might be tempted to forgo your own orgasm for the sake of baby making, don't. Scientists believe that the evolutionary purpose of the female orgasm is to cause the uterus to contract, thereby causing sperm

Moneysaver
If your cycle is irregular and you think you're going to need to purchase more than one ovulation predictor kit per cycle, ask your pharmacist if you can return the additional kits for a refund or credit if you don't end up needing them after all.

to be drawn up into the reproductive tract. Here's another reason not to let your eagerness to conceive get in the way of your ability to enjoy yourself in bed: a single orgasm is thought to be 22 times as relaxing as the average tranquilizer. So if you're finding the process of trying to get pregnant more than a little stressful, an orgasm could very well be just what the doctor ordered.

Some doctors recommend that the female partner remain in bed for at least half an hour following intercourse to provide the sperm with the necessary window of opportunity to make their way past the cervix.

"Trying" versus letting nature take its course

Some couples pull out the thermometers and temperature charts right away. Others prefer to give nature a chance rather than making a conscious effort to time intercourse around the woman's most fertile days.

Which route you decide to go will depend on such factors as

- your age (that is, is your biological clock ticking away nicely or is it about to go off?);

- your eagerness to start a family (that is, how important is it for you to get pregnant right away as opposed to a few months down the road?);

- your personalities (that is, are you a Type A who wants to be in control of everything or a Type B who tends to take things a little more in stride?);

- the likelihood that you or your partner might have an underlying fertility problem and consequently might need a little extra help in conceiving.

As you might expect, there are pros and cons to each alternative.

If you decide to let nature take its course, you don't have to feel obligated to make love just because the ovulation predictor kit gives you the green light. On the other hand, sheer bad luck (for example, one or the other partner working late at the office for too many nights in a row during the woman's most fertile period) could delay your efforts to conceive.

If you decide to make a conscious effort to try to conceive by planning intercourse around your most fertile days, you might manage to conceive sooner. Unfortunately, this particular approach can be hard on both your sex life and your relationship with your partner. (Of course, if you and your partner regularly have sex at least three times a week, you probably won't have to do anything different when you start trying to conceive.)

Here's what some of the members of our parent panel had to say about the whole business of trying to conceive:

- "We had to try for a year to get our daughter. To say the least, trying took all the fun out of sex. Between thermometers, pillows under my hips, and reading every fertility book at Barnes and Noble, the honeymoon was over!" —Randa, 23, mother of one

- "It's a good time to get creative with your sexual routines—whether that means using massage oils or props or your own fantasies. This is probably good practice for the rest of your pregnancy. There will be times in the coming months that you or your partner have a hard time getting in the mood." —Jennie, 30, eight months pregnant with her first child

> 66
> Try to keep sex fun, even if you are scheduling it. Use rooms other than the bedroom, or schedule your rendezvous for an odd time of day.
> —Tracy, 31, mother of one
> 99

■ "When I wasn't pregnant the first month I tried, I started taking my temperature so I would be sure we were timing things as well as possible. It took some of the romance out of it when I would announce to my husband that it was time to 'do the deed.' He had a hard time concentrating. My suggestion is that if you do have to use ovulation predictor kits or you're taking your temperature, when you do know that it's 'the time,' consider keeping this information to yourself. Enjoy the moment. Be romantic. Seduce your husband. Don't make it such a stressful chore. Relax and have fun." —Suzi, 27, mother of two

What women can do to protect their fertility

Whether you're hoping to have a baby in the very near future or a few years down the road, you owe it to yourself to take action today to safeguard your fertility. Following are the major threats you need to know about.

Age

If you're hoping to become a mother some day, it's important to keep an eye on the biological clock. According to the American Society for Reproductive Medicine, a woman's chances of getting pregnant in any given month drop from approximately 20% in women under 30% to 5% in women over 40.

Smoking

Studies have shown that smokers are 30% less fertile than nonsmokers; that they are at increased risk of developing pelvic inflammatory disease (see below); and that women who smoke during their pregnancies are at increased risk of miscarriage, premature

Watch Out!
If you notice any drastic changes in your menstrual cycle (that is, menstrual flow or PMS symptoms), consult your doctor. These types of changes can serve as early warnings that your fertility is on the wane.

birth, and delivering a low-birthweight baby. If there's a baby in your future, the time to quit smoking is now.

Sexually transmitted diseases

Sexually transmitted diseases (STDs) can wreak havoc on your fertility by causing pelvic inflammatory disease (see below). Unfortunately, many STDs are symptomless, and consequently many women aren't aware of the damage that is occurring to their reproductive tracts until it's too late. If you're hoping to have a baby at some point in your life, you should

- be monogamous or limit your number of sex partners;

- use condoms if you're with a new partner or if you have reason to believe that your current partner is not monogamous;

- be alert to the possible symptoms of STDs (that is, unusual vaginal discharges or odors, or pain when you are urinating);

- get tested for STDs regularly, particularly if you change partners.

Pelvic inflammatory disease

Pelvic inflammatory disease (PID) is a general term that refers to the infection or inflammation of one or more of your pelvic organs: your cervix, uterus, fallopian tubes, or ovaries. It occurs when bacteria invade the uterus, and it is typically caused by an untreated STD; an intrauterine device (IUD); douching; infections resulting from abortions, D & Cs (dilation & curettage), and amniocentesis; miscarriages; and even childbirth.

Because the consequences of PID can be so serious, it's important to be aware of the warning signs:

Unofficially...
More than one million North American women are affected by pelvic inflammatory disease each year. The number-one cause is an untreated sexually transmitted disease.

- abdominal pain or tenderness (either sporadic or chronic) that is particularly strong during intercourse, menstruation, or ovulation; and that may worsen when you are active (that is, walking, bicycling, and so on)

- lower back pain

- nausea and dizziness

- a low fever

- chills

- bleeding between periods

- bleeding after intercourse

- heavier menstrual cramps and flows

- frequent urination

- burning during urination or an inability to empty the bladder

- an unusual, foul-smelling vaginal discharge

- a constant urge to defecate

- a general feeling of ill health or abdominal bloating

Intrauterine devices (IUDs)

Women who use IUDs are three to nine times more likely to develop pelvic inflammatory disease than women who use other types of birth control. If you're planning to have a baby in the future, you should seriously consider using another form of birth control.

Infections

Yeast infections and other types of vaginal infections can alter the vaginal environment, making it more difficult for the sperm to survive. If you develop this type of infection, your partner might require treatment as well.

Overexercising

Although it's good to remain active throughout your childbearing years, excessive amounts of exercise can lead to such fertility problems as irregular periods, anovulatory cycles (cycles in which ovulation does not occur), and luteal phase deficiencies (a problem that occurs when the second half of your cycle isn't sufficiently long enough to allow for the proper implantation of the fertilized egg).

Poor eating habits

Starvation diets, purging, bingeing, and yo-yo dieting affect ovulation and consequently your fertility.

Unhealthy weight

If your body weight falls significantly above or below the ideal for someone of your height and body structure, you might want to lose or gain weight in order to increase your chances of conceiving.

A study at the University of South Carolina at Charleston demonstrated that weight may be an underlying cause of infertility in many more women than was previously realized. Ninety percent of underweight women who had previously been unable to conceive managed to become pregnant when they reached their ideal weight. Likewise, 76% of overweight women with fertility problems managed to conceive when they reached their ideal weights.

What men can do

Women aren't the only ones who need to safeguard their fertility. Men who hope to become fathers should make a point of protecting themselves from the following threats to their own fertility.

Bright Idea
Some would have you believe that you can reduce your odds of developing a yeast infection by consuming cranberry juice, yogurt with live cultures, and garlic—and by limiting your consumption of yeast products, refined sugars, carbohydrates, fermented foods, dried fruits, and dry-roasted peanuts. There's no hard scientific evidence to back these claims. That said, these dietary changes do seem to bring some degree of relief to some women.

Watch Out!
According to a recent study at the University of California School of Medicine, men who cycle more than 100 miles per week place their fertility at risk. The repeated banging of the groin against the bicycle seat can damage critical arteries and nerves. If a man experiences numbness in his backside, difficulty getting an erection in the day or two following a bicycling workout, or pain in the genital area, he should consult a doctor immediately.

Injuries to the genitals

Genital injuries can result in a ruptured epididymis, which can prevent sperm from maturing enough to be able to fertilize an egg; a split or torn vas deferens can prevent the transport of sperm; shattered testicles can result in the destruction of both sperm and the male sex hormone testosterone; injured seminal vesicles or an injured prostate gland can lead to ejaculatory problems; bladder damage can harm the muscle that prevents sperm from mixing with urine and that keeps urine from leaking into the urethra and damaging sperm; and back trauma can result in damage to the nerves that control the male reproductive system.

To avoid injury, men should wear protective athletic equipment (athletic cups, jock straps, and/or a padded genital protector) whenever they play sports. If an injury occurs, they should seek medical attention immediately to minimize the long-term repercussions to their reproductive health.

Anabolic steroids

Although the use of anabolic steroids tends to be most prevalent among competitive athletes, other men take them as well. When a man takes anabolic steroids, his testes shrink and his natural testosterone production falls. These changes reverse themselves in many men when they stop taking steroids, but some men continue to experience these changes long after they've discontinued the use of the steroids.

Unhealthy weight

Men who are significantly overweight tend to have an abundance of the female sex hormone estrogen—something that can interfere with communication between the testes and the pituitary gland.

Exposure of genitals to excessive heat

Excessive heat such as what you would experience from a fever, from sitting in hot tubs or excessively hot baths, or from occupations that require long periods of sitting (for example, long-distance truck driving) may reduce a man's fertility by interfering with sperm production.

Toxic chemicals and radiation

Toxic chemicals and radiation can potentially damage sperm production, leaving a man incapable of fertilizing an egg or permanently damaging his genetic material.

Surgery to the urogenital area

Surgery to the urogenital area can cause a buildup of scar tissue that can prevent the passage of sperm. Men who hope to become fathers and who are scheduled to undergo surgery to correct problems such as hernias or undescended testicles may want to consider depositing sperm in a sperm bank before they check into the hospital. Although it's quite possible that they may still be able to father children following the surgery, there's too much on the line to gamble unnecessarily.

Alcohol, drugs, and cigarettes

Alcohol, drugs, and cigarettes can also do their bit to reduce fertility. Heavy alcohol consumption can depress both sperm counts and testosterone levels; recreational drugs such as cocaine and marijuana, and medications such as cimetidine (an antacid), certain antibiotics, chemotherapeutic agents, and anabolic steroids can reduce sperm counts. (In the case of cocaine, the effects can last for up to two years.) What's more, ejaculatory dysfunction can occur with certain blood-pressure drugs. Even a simple cigarette can be bad news because smoking is known to harm sperm motility. Bottom line? You can have the sex and the rock and roll, but skip the drugs.

Just the facts

- There are a lot of fertility myths out there. Make sure you're clear on the real facts of life before you start trying to conceive.

- You can increase your odds of conceiving by paying attention to such fertility-awareness signs as changes to your basal body temperature, your cervical mucus, and the position of your cervix.

- Ovulation predictor kits can alert you to the fact that your body has experienced an LH surge—a biological event that typically precedes ovulation by approximately 24 to 36 hours.

- Although the jury is still out on the issue, certain sexual positions appear to be more baby friendly than others. This is one time in your life when you might want to forgo The Joy of Sex in favor of the missionary position.

- There are both advantages and disadvantages to "trying" versus "letting nature take its course." The factors to consider when you're trying to decide which route to take include your age, your eagerness to start a family right away, your personality, and the likelihood that you or your partner might have an underlying fertility problem.

- Women who hope to have children some day should pay attention to such potential threats to their fertility as age, smoking, sexually transmitted diseases, pelvic inflammatory disease, intrauterine devices, infections, overexercising, poor eating habits, and unhealthy weight.

- Men who hope to become fathers some day should avoid such threats to their fertility as injuries to the genitals, anabolic steroids, excessive heat to the genitals, toxic chemicals and radiation, surgery to the urogenital area, and drug or alcohol use.

GET THE SCOOP ON...
Whether you have a fertility problem ▪ Choosing
a fertility specialist ▪ The fertility workup ▪ The
causes of infertility ▪ The types of treatments
available ▪ The stress of infertility ▪ The truth
about surrogacy ▪ The facts about adoption

When Plan A Fails

If things haven't gone according to plan and you have not yet been able to conceive, you may feel that you are the only person living through the nightmare of infertility. If friends and family members seem to be able to conceive at the drop of a hat, while you continue to try and try and try, you may feel particularly discouraged and alone.

The fact of the matter is that there are far more people with infertility problems than you realize. The problem is that no one wants to talk about it. Because many couples feel embarrassed by their inability to conceive, the subject of infertility tends to get brushed under the carpet. Although it's easy to conclude that you're the only one who's having difficulty getting pregnant, chances are that someone you know is currently going through or has gone through a similar experience.

Consider the numbers for yourself. According to the National Center for Health Statistics

- approximately 2.1 million married couples experienced some type of fertility problem in 1995,

Unofficially...
Medical historian
Robert Marion,
M.D., believes
that George
Washington's fer-
tility problems
changed the
course of
American history.
In an article that
appeared in
Newsday in 1994,
Marion argued
that Washington
turned down the
chance to
become "King" of
the United
States because
of his lack of
heirs to inherit
the throne.

- approximately 1.8 million women used fertility drugs in 1995,

- approximately 9 million American women have used the services of fertility clinics to date.

In this chapter, we tell you how to determine if you have a fertility problem, how to choose a fertility specialist, what to expect from your initial fertility workup, what causes infertility and how it can be treated, how to cope with the stress of infertility, and what you need to know about two other routes to parenthood: surrogacy and adoption.

Do you have a fertility problem?

If you and your partner have been having unprotected intercourse for more than a year yet still haven't managed to conceive, it's possible that you, your partner, or the two of you have some sort of fertility problem.

The American Society of Reproductive Medicine (formerly the American Fertility Society) defines infertility as the inability to conceive after one year of unprotected intercourse. Although it recommends that most couples under age 35 give themselves a full year before seeking treatment, it suggests that couples over 35 as well as those who have some underlying cause of infertility (for example, endometriosis, fibroids, irregular periods, prior abortion, DES mothers, varicoceles, or significant health problems) seek the help of a specialist sooner.

Choosing a fertility specialist

If you suspect that you and your partner may have a fertility problem—or if you're a woman in a lesbian relationship or a single mother considering pregnancy—it's time to start shopping around for a fertility specialist.

You have three basic options:

- an obstetrician/gynecologist (who may or may not specialize in the treatment of infertility),

- a urologist (that is, a medical doctor who specializes in the treatment of disorders of the kidneys, urinary tract, bladder, and male reproductive organs),

- a reproductive endocrinologist (that is, an obstetrician/gynecologist who has completed extra training in the medical and surgical treatments of reproductive disorders).

Here are some questions you'll want to ask:

CHECKLIST: FINDING THE RIGHT SPECIALIST

- What percentage of your practice focuses on the treatment of infertility?

- Are you board certified in reproductive endocrinology?

- What types of treatments do you provide? Do you conduct the full range of infertility tests and treatments yourself, or will you need to refer us to other specialists?

- What are the fees for those treatments? What percentage of these fees is my insurance company or HMO likely to cover?

- What are your success rates for couples with our type of fertility problem? Does that rate refer to the number of pregnancies achieved or the number of live births?

- Will you be available to answer our questions by phone, or will we need to come in and set up an appointment whenever we have any concerns?

Watch Out!
If you or your partner is out of town a lot on work-related matters, it could take you a little longer than average to conceive. The reason is simple: It's hard to get the egg and the sperm to meet if you're on two different continents. Be sure to take these absences into account when you're calculating the length of time you've been trying to conceive.

Timesaver
You can get
the names,
addresses, and
phone numbers
of infertility spe-
cialists in your
area from the
InterNational
Council on
Infertility
Information
Dissemination's
Geographic
Directory of
Physicians,
Therapists, and
Attorneys
(703-379-9178
or 520-544-9548;
www.inciid.org/
webdocs.html).

- Will our questions be answered by you or another person?

- How would you react if, at any point in our treatment, we decided that we wanted to get a second opinion?

Now let's consider what types of answers indicate that you've found the right specialist.

What percentage of your practice focuses on the treatment of infertility?

Look for a specialist whose practice focuses on the treatment of infertility. Wherever possible, choose specialists who are associated with reputable university medical schools or teaching hospitals since they are most likely to be on top of the latest developments in the field. If you do decide to go this route, however, make sure that you're comfortable with the "team approach" to treatment. You're likely to encounter an ever-changing parade of medical students and physicians-in-training.

Are you board certified in reproductive endocrinology?

Since many ob-gyns treat infertility and their expertise varies widely, it will probably be difficult for you to assess their qualifications. If a specialist has been certified in reproductive endocrinology by the American Board of Obstetrics and Gynecology, you can be certain that this physician has the training and expertise to deal with most, if not all, of your infertility treatment needs.

What types of treatments do you provide? Do you conduct the full range of infertility tests and treatments yourself, or will you need to refer us to other specialists?

There are an unbelievable number of fertility treatments available: drug therapy, surgery, and an-ever growing number of methods of assisted reproduction. Make sure you're clear from the outset which types of procedures this particular specialist provides—and which he doesn't. Otherwise, you could find yourself having to hop from one doctor to another over the course of your treatment. Because you're already comfortable with your obstetrician/gynecologist (ob/gyn), he's probably a good starting point. Depending on his experience and expertise, you may, in fact, be able to undergo the majority of tests and treatments for infertility while still under his care.

What are the fees for those treatments? What percentage of these fees is my insurance company or HMO likely to cover?

Although you'll have to check your plan brochure's list of covered services—or, to be sure, call your insurance company or HMO directly to get the specifics on coverage—the specialist should be able to give you an idea of the types of services that most patients are required to pay for out of their own pockets.

What are your success rates for couples with our type of fertility problem? Does that rate refer to the number of pregnancies achieved or the number of live births?

There is a lot of doublespeak when it comes to success rates for fertility treatments. Some fertility specialists consider the achievement of pregnancy to be a measure of success—whether that pregnancy results in a live birth or not. That's why it's important to make sure that you and the specialist are speaking the same language when it comes to the concept of success.

Watch Out!
The expertise of general obstetrician gynecologists varies widely when it comes to infertility. Unfortunately, some fail to either recognize or admit to their own limitations. If your doctor doesn't seem to have a clear idea of what the problems are, perhaps it's time to get a second opinion. Your biological clock is ticking. Don't let anyone waste your time.

Bright Idea
Ask the specialist to give you the billing code and diagnostic code for any procedures you may require. That way, you can find out in advance which ones are covered by your insurance company or HMO—and which ones aren't.

Will you be available to answer our questions by phone, or will we need to come in and set up an appointment whenever we have any concerns?

Make sure that the specialist or another member of the medical team will be available to speak with you by phone or meet with you in person if you experience unusual side effects to any treatments or have any questions or concerns.

Will our questions be answered by you or another person?

Make sure that your questions will be answered by the specialist himself, or at the very least, an equally qualified person. Find out in advance if you are going to be dealing with the physician himself or a nurse or other office worker when you have questions. Some practices have qualified nurses who can address many of your concerns adequately, but others rely on receptionists to relay answers from the busy physician—a process that can make it cumbersome to obtain answers to any follow-up questions.

How would you react if, at any point in our treatment, we decided that we wanted to get a second opinion?

Look for a specialist who will not be threatened by your need to research your options thoroughly, and discuss in advance how your desire to obtain a second opinion will be handled, should it arise.

If you need some help in tracking down a doctor who specializes in infertility, contact RESOLVE Inc., 1310 Broadway, Somerville, MA 02144-1779, phone 617-623-0744, fax 617-623-0252, e-mail resolveinc@ aol.com; or the American Society for Reproductive Medicine (formerly the American Fertility Society), 1209 Montgomery Highway, Birmingham, AL 35216, phone 205-978-5000. RESOLVE can put you in touch with gynecologists who have additional training in infertility, reproductive endocrinologists, and urologists who specialize in male factor infertility. The American Society for Reproductive Medicine can put you in touch with one of its members who is in practice in your area.

The infertility workup

An infertility evaluation is designed to answer four basic questions:

- Is the female ovulating regularly?
- Is the male producing healthy, viable sperm?
- Are the egg and the sperm able to unite and develop normally?
- Is anything preventing the fertilized egg from implanting and developing properly?

Because it's almost impossible to gather all this information in a single session, you will likely to be asked to come for a series of appointments, typically two or more.

During your initial visit, the doctor will take a medical history of both you and your partner. Because you might not have been entirely open with your partner about details of your sexual history, these histories can be taken separately. It's important to level with the doctor and give him information that could be helpful in making a diagnosis: that is, whether you have been treated for an STD (sexually transmitted disease) or had an abortion. If you don't want the doctor to inadvertently share this information with your partner when he is meeting with the two of you together, be sure to let him know that what you have told him is, in fact, privileged information. Your doctor will then conduct a

66
I experienced a lot of stress while we were trying to conceive. I felt abnormal.... I cried frequently when I learned of a friend or acquaintance who was expecting, and it seemed that everywhere I went there were tons of women who were either pregnant or carrying newborns around.
—Christy, 25, former infertility patient, now four months pregnant with her first child
99

detailed physical examination. The results of that examination and the medical history will help to determine what comes next.

If your doctor recommends further testing, non-invasive tests such as bloodwork for you and a semen analysis for your partner will be the likely first steps. There is, after all, little point in subjecting the female partner to surgical investigations if the male partner is, in fact, sterile or what is referred to as "subfertile." If the male partner's test comes back abnormal, a referral to a urologist usually follows. If the semen analysis is normal, a series of tests is then generally performed on the female partner. Here's what you and your partner can expect from a typical fertility workup.

The female partner's infertility workup

Although the fertility workup includes many of the same components as the preconception checkup, it touches on some new areas as well.

Medical history

The specialist will start by taking a detailed medical history that focuses on

- your menstrual history (for example, the age at which you started menstruating, the length of your cycles, your pattern of bleeding, whether you suffer or have suffered from either endometriosis or pelvic inflammatory disease, whether you've had any previous pregnancies including those that resulted in miscarriages or abortions, and whether there's a family history of reproductive difficulties in your family);

- your sexual history (for example, what type of contraception you were using before you started trying to conceive, how long you've been trying, how you've been timing intercourse, whether you've had a large number of sexual partners in the past, and whether you and your partner are using sexual techniques or practices [for example, using lubricants or douching after intercourse] or experiencing sexual difficulties [for example, premature ejaculation or inadequate penetration] that may not be conducive to fertilization);

- your lifestyle (for example, whether you smoke or drink heavily, and whether you suffer from any eating disorders such as anorexia or bulimia);

- your general health (for example, whether you are taking any prescribed or over-the-counter medications, whether you have had any major illnesses in the past, and whether you have had any surgery that might have affected your fertility).

Your doctor will also ask you to share any information you have about your mother's reproductive history, including

- how long it took her to conceive her first child;

- whether she had any miscarriages (and, if so, how many);

- whether she ever experienced an ectopic pregnancy;

- whether she suffered from menstrual irregularities or severe cramping;

- at what age she started menstruating and at what age she started menopause;

- whether she ever took DES to prevent miscarriage.

Timesaver
If your doctor orders baseline testing for follicle stimulating hormone (FSH) and lutenizing hormone (LH), try to schedule your initial appointment during the first week of your cycle so that you don't have to wait until the following cycle to do the necessary blood work or start treatment.

The answers to these questions may help to shed some light on your current reproductive difficulties.

Physical examination

Once the doctor has gathered information about your medical history, she will conduct a detailed physical examination. She will

- note your general health and physical appearance;
- record your height, weight, and blood pressure;
- check the results of a urinalysis test;
- listen to your heart and lungs with a stethoscope;
- note secondary sex characteristics such as breast development, fat distribution, and hair growth around your nipples, on your face, and on your abdomen;
- feel your thyroid gland to see if it is enlarged or of abnormal consistency;
- examine your breasts and squeeze your nipples to see if a milky discharge is extruded;
- check your abdomen by applying pressure and feeling the different areas to check for lumps and painful spots or growths such as uterine fibroids;
- examine your vagina and outer genital organs for structural problems, as well as unusual sores or infections;
- examine your cervix and vaginal walls, looking for signs of infection, sores, growths, or abnormal narrowing or erosion of the cervix;
- do a Pap smear to screen for cancer and sexually transmitted diseases;

Bright Idea
If you are overweight and are experiencing difficulty conceiving, you might want to check out the Infertility FAQ for Women of Size at www.fertilethoughts.net/infertility/index-faq.html. It contains answers to frequently asked questions about being plus-sized and infertile, links to other Web sites, information on mailing lists and newsgroups, and so on. There are even some tips on finding a fat-friendly doctor.

- manipulate your reproductive organs so that she can determine the size, shape, and texture of your uterus, uterine ligaments, and ovaries;

- feel for any unusual lumps, bumps, or enlargements in your reproductive organs;

- examine your rectum for any usual growths, bulging, or pocketing.

Fertility tests

If your partner's semen analysis comes back normal (see below), the doctor may order one or more tests to determine whether ovulation is taking place, whether there are adequate quantities of the hormones required to produce a healthy endometrial lining and healthy cervical mucus, and whether the reproductive tract is free of any scar tissue and anatomical defects that might otherwise prevent fertilization and implantation.

Here's a brief description of the types of tests your doctor might order:

- **Serum progesterone blood test:** This test is done to confirm that you are ovulating. Blood samples are drawn in the middle of the luteal phase (that is, on day 21 of a 28-day cycle). If the progesterone level is significantly elevated, it's likely that you're ovulating. *Note:* If your cycles are irregular, you may have to go in for weekly blood tests starting at day 20 and continuing until you menstruate. More often, however, your doctor will assume that your irregular cycles indicate an ovulation problem, and will order a more extensive blood test (that is, one to check a number of your hormone levels) instead.

66

If you don't get a diagnosis from one doctor, keep looking. It took us two doctors and two years to find a doctor who recognized I had polycystic ovarian syndrome.
—Therese, 31, mother of one

99

- **Prolactin blood test:** Prolactin is a hormone that inhibits ovulation in nursing mothers. If you have excessively high levels of prolactin, you may have a benign (that is, noncancerous) pituitary tumor, in which case your doctor may refer you for further tests, such as a CAT scan.

- **Thyroid hormone blood test:** Abnormal amounts of thyroid hormone can indicate that you have problems with your thyroid. Women with underactive thyroid glands (*hypo*thyroidism) are prone to menstrual and ovulatory disorders. Those with overactive thyroids (*hyper*thyroidism) have more variable menstrual patterns but can become seriously ill if the condition is not recognized and treated during pregnancy.

- **Blood tests for other reproductive hormones:** Depending on the results of your medical history and your physical examination (your degree of menstrual irregularity, if any, or any problems with excessive body hair growth, for example), your doctor may need to obtain specific hormone levels to uncover a variety of endocrinologic conditions. This may involve testing at specific times of the cycle or testing after receiving certain medications.

- **Hysterosalpingogram (HSG):** A hysterosalpingogram is used to determine whether any damage has occurred to your fallopian tubes. It involves filling your reproductive tract with a special type of dye that shows up on X-rays. The test—which is conducted during the follicular phase—involves inserting dye into your uterus through a tube that is placed through your cervix. If one or both of your tubes are blocked, the dye will outline where the obstruction lies. If only one tube appears to be blocked, it may simply be due to the fact that the open tube provided the pathway of least resistance to the dye. (Pregnancy rates aren't very different between women whose HSGs show one tube open to the passage of dye as opposed to both tubes.) An HSG can also be useful in identifying the locations of any scarring or growths such as fibroids in your uterus (see below). Some women—particularly those with blocked tubes—find this procedure to be quite painful, so you might want to talk with your doctor about the advisability of taking a pain medication prior to the procedure. *Note:* The value of HSG as a diagnostic tool is clear. What is more controversial is whether the procedure can actually enhance fertility. There has long been an anecdotal claim among doctors treating infertile patients that there is a blip in the fertility curve in the months following HSG. Studies have demonstrated, however, that this enhancement is seen only with the use of oil-based dyes and not with water-soluble dyes.

▪ **Endometrial biopsy:** An endometrial biopsy can confirm whether you're ovulating and indicate whether your endometrial tissue is sufficiently hospitable to allow a fertilized egg to implant. The biopsy is taken within several days of when you are expected to start menstruating. The doctor inserts a speculum in your vagina and cleanses your cervix, and then a tissue sample is removed from the uterine lining through a combination of suction and gentle scraping. If you're concerned that this procedure may

Watch Out!
If you have a history of pelvic infection, pelvic surgery, or pelvic tenderness, you may be at risk of developing an infection after the HSG. Ask your doctor if it would be advisable for you to take a course of antibiotics before you go in for the procedure.

cause a miscarriage in the event that you have managed to conceive, you may find it reassuring to know that the odds of having an endometrial biopsy cause a miscarriage are extremely small. If you are worried about this possibility, you might choose to use some sort of contraceptive during the cycle in which the endometrial biopsy will be taken or plan to undergo a sensitive blood pregnancy test the day before the procedure.

■ **Laparoscopy:** Like an HSG, a laparoscopy is a test designed to detect obstructions in your fallopian tubes. It's considerably more high-tech and risky than an HSG, however, and can provide more detailed information. The test involves inserting a fiber-optic scope into your abdomen to look for damage caused by endometriosis, pelvic inflammatory disease, or adhesions from any pelvic surgery, and to look for physical evidence that you are ovulating. You need to go under general anesthetic to have the procedure, and you may experience some soreness in your abdomen and shoulders afterward. *Note:* If your doctor suggests that you have a D & C done at the same time as your laparoscopy as part of your infertility workup, get a second opinion. Studies have shown that such D & C procedures provide no more information than what can be obtained through a less-expensive and less-hazardous endometrial biopsy. You should also be prepared to put the brakes on if your doctor wants you to undergo a laparoscopy right away: As a rule of thumb, you should be prepared to wait for six months after your HSG—assuming, of course, that it was normal—so that you can take advantage of the fertility-enhancing effects of HSG. Obviously, if your doctor suspects that you have endometriosis or significant pelvic adhesions—or if you are over 40—a waiting period may not make sense.

- **Hysteroscopy:** A hysteroscopy also involves inserting a fiber-optic scope into the body, but in this case, it is inserted into the uterus through the cervix. It is used to detect abnormal growths or anatomical defects in your uterus when your HSG suggests that these may play a role in your fertility problems. (We'll be discussing these problems elsewhere in this chapter.)

- **Post-coital test:** The post-coital test is used to assess what happens once the sperm make it inside the vagina. You are asked to have sexual intercourse just before you expect to ovulate (when your cervical mucus is at its best) and to show up at your doctor's office at a designated time some 2 to 16 hours later. The doctor then uses a syringe or pipette to extract at least two samples of cervical mucus from the cervical canal, and examines it under a microscope to determine how many sperm are alive and swimming. The test can show whether your mucus is inhospitable to your partner's sperm; it can also suggest whether there are antibodies in either your body or your partner's body that are interfering with sperm production or killing sperm, and whether the root of the problem is the fact that sperm is not being deposited closely enough to the cervix (as can be the case if the male partner experiences premature ejaculation). As you might expect, many couples

Timesaver
Use an ovulation predictor kit to time your post-coital test. You will ensure that it is the optimal time for the test, and you just might find yourself pregnant as a result.

dislike having to have sexual intercourse upon demand and then rush off to the laboratory. That's why many doctors encourage couples to make love the night before and then come into the laboratory the next morning. *Note:* It's possible to fail the post-coital test because you've inadvertently missed your most fertile period (that is, the days prior to ovulation when your cervical mucus is most abundant). If you fail the post-coital test, you will likely be asked to repeat it to ensure that the problem lies with you and your partner, not with the timing.

- **Ultrasound:** Ultrasound is used during the basic infertility evaluation only if the internal or pelvic exam is inconclusive or significant abnormalities are suspected.

The male partner's infertility workup

If your doctor feels that your partner may have a problem with his reproductive functioning, she will refer him to a urologist, ideally one who has particular experience and expertise with fertility-related issues. His doctor will then take a detailed medical history, paying particular attention to

- his sexual and developmental background (whether both of his testicles were descended into his scrotum when he was born, at what age he went through puberty, how many partners he's had, whether he has had any problem with impotence or ejaculatory problems, whether he has ever fathered a child with someone else, whether he's ever been treated for a sexually transmitted disease, and so on);

- his lifestyle (whether he smokes cigarettes or marijuana, whether he takes frequent saunas or

Unofficially...
Fallopian tubes are less than four millimeters wide at their narrowest point and are easily damaged. Almost half of all women seeking infertility treatment have tubal problems.

hot tubs, whether he has gained or lost more than 20 pounds recently, and so on);

- his general health (whether he has been sick or had a fever in the past three months, whether he has ever had the mumps [can result in inflammation of the testes], whether he has had any surgery to the pelvic area, whether he is taking any medications, and so on).

Once the doctor is finished asking the male partner a series of questions, she will conduct the physical examination. She will

- note the male partner's general appearance, paying particular attention to such secondary sex characteristics as facial, chest, and pubic hair; deepness of voice; and physical build;
- record his height and weight;
- note whether he has fat deposits around his breasts (that is, gynecomastia);
- check his blood pressure;
- listen to his chest;
- check his urine;
- check his reflexes;
- examine his head and neck, and check his thyroid for enlargement;
- examine his penis (check the location of the opening of the urethra, note any discharge, investigate any tenderness or unusual firmness, and so on);
- examine both of his testes, noting both their size and their firmness;
- check the epididymis for tenderness or swelling that could indicate an infection;

- search for varicoceles around the testes (similar to varicose veins);

- palpate the prostate and seminal vesicles while the man is sitting and then check the prostate gland for any swelling or inflammation by inserting a gloved finger into his rectum;

- check to ensure that he has full sensation throughout his external genital area.

Watch Out! Make sure that the technician at the lab knows that you're dropping off a sample of semen, not urine. The test results won't be accurate if the sample is allowed to sit around for longer than an hour because the sperm begin to deteriorate rather quickly.

Once the physical checkup has been conducted, the man will be asked to provide a sample of semen, which will then be analyzed in the lab. Because many men feel uncomfortable producing this sample on demand in a clinical setting, most doctors will allow the man to collect the sample at home and then bring it into the lab. He can collect the sample by masturbating or by having intercourse using a special lubricant-free and spermicide-free condom. (If the man decides to go this route, he should ask the doctor to recommend a specific brand of condom. What's more, he should make a point of telling the lab technician how the sample was collected because some of the sample will inevitably be lost as it is poured into the specimen jar—something that could inadvertently skew the results of the test.)

To ensure that the semen analysis provides accurate information about the man's fertility, the man should

- abstain from ejaculating during the two to three days prior to giving the sample,

- collect the sample in a clean container,

- keep it at body temperature,

- deliver it to a designated lab within one hour of collection.

Once the sample has been received at the lab, it will be subjected to a number of different tests. Here are the major ones:

- **Coagulation and liquification:** If a man's semen doesn't coagulate at the time of ejaculation, there could be an underlying problem with the seminal vesicles. If it doesn't reliquify (that is, turn back into liquid approximately 30 minutes after ejaculation), there could be a problem with the man's prostate.

- **Color and appearance:** Semen should be whitish-grey upon ejaculation, and translucent once it has had the chance to reliquify (something that happens approximately 30 minutes later). A yellow hue can indicate infection. A reddish or brownish tinge may indicate the presence of blood.

- **Odor:** An unpleasant odor may indicate infection. A total absence of odor can indicate a prostate problem.

- **Volume:** The normal amount of ejaculate is two to five milliliters (that is, one-half to a full teaspoonful). If there's too little semen, it's possible that some of the semen has been ejaculated backward into the bladder, that the seminal vesicles are missing, that there's an obstruction in a duct, that there's a problem with semen production, or that the man has ejaculated too frequently. Too much semen can indicate a problem caused by overactivity of the seminal or prostate glands—a condition that can affect the quality or motility of the sperm.

- **pH:** Normal semen is just slightly alkaline, ranging between 7.2 and 7.8. If the pH level is too

Bright Idea
Need some laughs? You'll find some terrific one-liners for the "reproductively challenged" at www.mediconsult.com/infertility/shareware/humor/. Here's an example: "You know you're infertile when someone asks you the date and you give them your cycle day."

high or too low, it's possible that the prostate or seminal vesicles are infected or inflamed.

■ **Viscosity:** If the sample is too thick and sticky, an infection may be suspected, in which case antibiotics may be prescribed.

■ **Sperm concentration:** The average sperm count for fertile men is anywhere between 40 and 120 million per milliliter. The World Health Organization (WHO) defines a normal sperm concentration as 20 million/ml or more. There is substantial variation between lab technicians' reading of the same semen specimen and also from one semen sample to the next. As a result, it is often necessary to check two or three semen samples to get a more accurate reading. Sperm counts appear to be declining. A study in 1951 revealed that only 5% of fertile men had sperm counts under 20 million, whereas today 20% to 25% have counts below this level. In Denmark average sperm counts went from 113 million/ml in 1940 to 66 million/ml in 1990. (Scientists believe that toxins in the environment may be to blame.) But before you panic, consider this fact: Fertility rates among couples over similar time spans have not declined, a finding that suggests that this decreasing sperm count is not being reflected in a similar decrease in fertility.

■ **Motility:** The motility test measures the sperm's ability to swim. The lab technician estimates both the percentage of sperm that are moving (for example, 50% to 60%) and the quality of that movement (for example, on a scale of one to four, with grade two or higher being considered normal).

- **Morphology:** Although sperm can have slightly different shapes and appearances, in general, a healthy, mature sperm has an oval head, a cylindrical middle, and a long, tapering tale. If more than 50% of the sperm are abnormal, there may be a fertility problem.

- **Sperm antibodies:** If the sperm clump together, there could be either an infection or antibodies in the semen. Antibodies prevent the sperm from swimming, acting in the same way as an anchor does to a boat, according to Anne Mullins, author of *Missed Conceptions: Overcoming Infertility.*

- **Cultures:** The sample can be cultured and checked for bacteria and sexually transmitted diseases such as chlamydia, gonorrhea, HIV, and so on if infection is suspected.

- **White blood cells:** The presence of significant numbers of white blood cells may indicate inflammation such as prostatitis.

- **Mucus penetration:** If there are concerns about the ability of the man's sperm to make their way through his partner's cervical mucus, a mucus penetration test (sometimes called a sperm invasion test) may be performed as well. In this test, a column of cervical mucus from a cow is placed into a reservoir of sperm. The idea of the test is to see how well the sperm can make it through the mucus.

- **Crossover sperm invasion test:** This test is performed when there's reason to suspect that there's a problem with one partner or another, but it isn't clear whom. In this case, the male partner's sperm is combined with the egg of a

Moneysaver
You can get free advice about insurance-plan coverage and reimbursement for infertility treatments by calling the IVF-PALS Hotline at 800-IVF-PALS (800-483-7257). You can find out more about the service at www. mediaconsult. com/infertility/ shareware/ invpals/.

donor female, and the female partner's egg is fertilized with semen from a donor male. The results can help to determine where the fertility problem lies.

■ **Hamster egg penetration test:** Although this test sounds like something out of a bad science fiction novel, it's for real. In an egg penetration test—sometimes called a sperm penetration assay—a laboratory technician observes how well the sperm are able to penetrate a hamster egg. Although the test is not standardized from lab to lab and its usefulness is widely debated, it may help to identify sperm abnormalities not revealed by the usual measures of count, motility, and morphology in couples with unexplained infertility. It also may be useful in assessing the effects of various sperm treatments and as a preparatory step for in vitro fertilization.

If the results of the semen analysis are abnormal, the test should be repeated at least twice. Fevers, infections, and viruses can affect a man's sperm count for months. If the next round of tests comes back abnormal, he may need to undergo a sperm antibody test (to determine whether his body is producing antibodies to his own sperm), hormonal blood tests (to measure the levels of both male and female hormones in his body), and an exam to check for varicocele. Less frequently, he may need to undergo a testicular biopsy (to determine if his fertility problems are caused by a lack of sperm-generating cells in his testicles, in which case he is permanently sterile), vasography (to check the structure of his duct system and locate any obstructions), and a fructose test (to see if seminal vesicles are adding fructose to semen as they should be).

The causes of infertility

Here are some fast facts on the causes of infertility:

- Approximately 35% of fertility problems are caused by male problems, 35% by tubal and pelvic problems, 15% by ovulatory dysfunction, 5% by unusual causes such as immunological, anatomic, or thyroid problems, and 10% by unknown causes.

- When the problem rests with the woman, it's likely to be caused by either (1) scarring of the fallopian tubes caused by endometriosis, pelvic inflammatory disease, gonorrhea, chlamydia, and intrauterine devices (40%) or (2) irregular ovulation accompanied by poor cervical mucus (40%). The other 20% of fertility problems within the woman result from either unexplained infertility (10%) or other causes (10%).

- Approximately 10% of couples experience infertility problems for which there is no obvious explanation. Nearly half of these couples will, however, go on to conceive within a three-year period.

- Fifty-seven percent of couples become pregnant within three months, 72% within six months, 85% within one year, and 93% within two years.

- The median number of months to conception is three for couples who have at least one child and five for couples who are childless.

Problems with the female partner

Two main types of fertility problems can affect the female partner: (1) hormonal and ovulation problems and (2) structural problems.

Abnormal amounts of FSH, LH, estrogen, and other related hormones can prevent a woman from

Bright Idea
Wondering how to handle thoughtless remarks from family members and friends? You can find some terrific responses at Resolve's "Managing Family and Friends" page at www.resolve.org/famfrend.htm. Included are answers to such perennial favorites as "So when are you going to start a family?"

ovulating, make the vaginal environment inhospitable to sperm, or interfere with the implantation of the fertilized egg. Common fertility problems that fall within the category of hormonal and ovulation problems include

- polycystic ovary syndrome (in which the ovaries develop small cysts that interfere with ovulation and hormone production),

- hyperprolactinemia (in which the secretion of an excessive amount of the hormone prolactin interferes with ovulation),

- deficiencies in gonadotropin-releasing hormone (the hormone responsible for triggering the release of FSH and LH from the pituitary gland),

- a luteal phase deficiency (when insufficient levels of progesterone prevent the fertilized egg from implanting properly).

Structural problems are also a cause of infertility in the female partner. In order for conception and implantation to occur, both the uterus and the fallopian tubes must be in good working order. If you have experienced an ectopic pregnancy, have had a surgical procedure that could have damaged your tubes, or have had an infection such as pelvic inflammatory disease or a sexually transmitted disease, your tubes could be damaged. Similarly, if you were born with a congenital uterine abnormality (for example, septum) or have developed adhesions (bands of scar tissue), polyps, fibroids (noncancerous tumors of the uterine muscle), or endometriosis (a disease in which tissue normally found in the uterine lining grows on nearby surfaces, including the fallopian tubes, ovaries, and inside of the abdomen), your fertility could be similarly compromised.

Problems with the male partner

Various problems can impair fertility in the male partner. Here are some of the most common:

- **Undescended testicles:** One out of every 200 baby boys is born with one or more undescended testicles. The condition can be treated with either hormone therapy or microsurgery before the child is two. If, however, the condition is not treated, sterility can result.

- **Varicocele:** A varicocele is a varicose vein in the spermatic cord. It impairs fertility by increasing the amount of blood circulation to the area, and consequently the temperature, a situation that can kill off sperm.

- **Medications:** Certain medications have been proven to affect fertility. These include corticosteriods (anti-inflammatory agents used to treat ailments including allergies, arthritis, asthma, skin disorders, and chronic athletic injuries such as tennis elbow), antidepressants and antihypertension drugs, large doses of aspirin, and drugs used in chemotherapy. These drugs can affect libido, reduce sperm production, destroy normal DNA production, and alter the hormonal balance, all of which can affect fertility.

- **Sexual problems:** Impotence, premature ejaculation, inability to ejaculate, and sexual problems that restrict full penetration are all problems that can prevent a couple from conceiving.

- **Hypospadias:** Hypospadias is a congenital anomaly in which the urethral opening is found on the underside rather than the tip of the penis. It causes the ejaculate to be deposited too low in the vagina.

- **Retrograde ejaculation:** Retrograde ejaculation is a neurological problem that causes the male partner to ejaculate backward into his bladder rather than forward out through the urethra. It is caused by poor neurological functioning in the nerves that control the muscle at the base of the bladder—a muscle that is supposed to block passage to the bladder during ejaculation. It can be seen in rare severe cases of diabetes, with some neurologic disorders, and as a complication following prostate surgery.

- **Hormonal problems:** Low sperm counts can result when the male partner's pituitary, thyroid, or adrenal glands are not functioning properly.

- **Immunological problems:** When antibodies in a man's body attack his own sperm, a low sperm count can result.

- **Testicular failure:** Testicular failure occurs when semen is produced but contains no sperm. It can be caused by a blow to the testes, exposure to the mumps, or a birth defect.

Fertility treatments

An ever-growing number of fertility treatments are available today: everything from hormone and drug therapy to surgery to the most high-tech conception procedures imaginable.

Let's briefly consider "traditional" fertility treatments for both the female and the male partner, and then take a peek inside the Brave New World of assisted reproduction.

Treatments for female infertility

As you know, female infertility can be caused by two basic types of conditions: (1) hormonal and ovulation problems and (2) structural problems. These conditions can be treated through drug or hormone therapy and surgery.

Drug and hormone therapy is used to treat such conditions as

- polycystic ovary disease
- elevated levels of prolactin (the hormone that inhibits ovulation in breastfeeding women)
- an excess of adrenal androgens (male-type hormones)
- amenorrhea (lack of menstruation)
- anovulation (lack of ovulation) or oligo-ovulation (infrequent ovulation)
- pituitary failure
- endometriosis
- certain glandular disorders
- premature menopause

Clomiphene citrate (Clomid) is one of the most commonly prescribed fertility drugs. Though usually used to stimulate ovulation in women with highly irregular, non-ovulatory cycles, it also is frequently used in cases of luteal phase deficiency (as an alternative to progesterone supplementation) or in cases of unexplained infertility (to give the ovaries a slight "boost" and tip the scales in favor of conception). Women using the drug typically take Clomid from days five to nine of their cycle when they are being treated for ovulation problems. When Clomid is being used to treat other conditions, the drug may be administered on a different schedule. Clomid causes ovulation in approximately 75% of women who take the drug, but only about 35% to 40% actually become pregnant and carry a baby to term. This has been commonly attributed to

Moneysaver
Certain pharmaceutical companies have programs in place to help couples experiencing genuine financial hardship. Be sure to ask your doctor if he knows of any such programs that might be available to you.

adverse effects of Clomid on the uterine lining, cervical mucus, or the ovaries' ability to produce progesterone, but, in fact, it is more likely due to either other causes of infertility or a lack of persistence. Pregnancy rates in patients who ovulate while taking Clomid are the same per cycle and cumulatively as those of fertile patients. In other words, about 60 to 75% are pregnant within six months of cumulative treatment if no other infertility factors are present.

Possible side effects of the drug include hot flashes, bloating, mid-cycle pain or other abdominal discomfort due to the stimulation of the ovaries, breast tenderness, nausea, dizziness, headaches, depression, increased anxiety, insomnia, and tiredness. There is also an increased chance of multiple birth: women who take the drug are five times more likely to conceive multiple fetuses, the vast majority of which are twins.

Treatment with Clomid is relatively inexpensive and usually does not require significant monitoring with blood tests and ultrasound.

Another widely used fertility drug—Pergonal—consists of purified FSH and LH obtained from the urine of postmenopausal women. It is used to stimulate the development of follicles in the ovaries. It is used when anovulatory women don't respond to Clomid or when there are reasons to induce the ovulation of multiple eggs, such as when used in assisted reproductive technologies and as an adjunct to artificial insemination in cases of unexplained infertility (see below). The drug is injected daily until the follicles reach an optimum size, at which point an injection of human chorionic gonadotropin (hCG) is given to trigger ovulation. Women who take the drug must be monitored carefully to ensure that

Watch Out!
If you experience severe abdominal pain during a cycle in which you are using fertility drugs, contact your doctor immediately. You could be experiencing hyperstimulation syndrome—a condition in which the ovaries become enlarged, causing lower abdominal pain and distention, nausea, vomiting, diarrhea, weight gain, cardiovascular and pulmonary disturbances, damage to the ovaries, and even death. Hospitalization may be required.

hyperstimulation does not occur. Other side effects include pain, rash, or swelling at the injection site. About 20% of women who take Pergonal will have a multiple birth.

Newer alternatives to Pergonal consist of purified FSH and genetically engineered FSH, both of which can make the treatment of ovulatory disorders safer and more convenient.

Treatment with Pergonal may cost upward of $1,500 per cycle for the drugs alone, not to mention the considerable costs of frequent blood tests and ultrasound exams.

Other drugs commonly used to treat infertility in women are bromocriptine (Parlodel), a drug that suppresses the pituitary gland's production of prolactin; gonadotropin-releasing hormone (GnRH), which induces ovulation; and Lupron, a drug that enhances the response to Pergonal in selected patients, and is also commonly used to treat endometriosis either instead of or in addition to surgery.

Surgery—the second method of treating infertility in women—is used to repair structural problems and damage to the female reproductive system. It is used to address fertility problems caused by

- pelvic inflammatory disease,
- endometriosis,
- tubal damage and adhesions,
- fibroids,
- endometrial polyps,
- Asherman's Syndrome (when bands of scar tissue in a woman's uterus join one part of the endometrium to another, in some cases cementing the walls together),

- congenital uterine abnormalities (for example, a double uterus, bicornuate uterus, septate uterus, and rudimentary horns),

- uterine abnormalities in DES daughters (that is, daughters of women who took diethylstilbestrol during their pregnancies).

Repairs can often be made to the fallopian tubes, the uterus, and the other female sex organs to increase a woman's chances of conceiving and carrying a baby to term.

Just a few words of caution before we conclude our discussion of surgical solutions to infertility. Some gynecologists—particularly those who don't specialize in the treatment of infertility—are quick to suggest surgery for conditions that are abnormal, but not necessarily the cause of infertility. Three classic cases of this overzealousness are surgeries for pelvic adhesions, fibroids, and mild endometriosis. Not only are some of these procedures unnecessary and inherently risky, but in some cases, they can create additional adhesions, which can add to your fertility problems. Adhesion prevention is the creed of the true infertility specialist, and he will employ surgical techniques to minimize adhesion formation. So before you check yourself into the hospital and sign that patient consent form, make sure you understand what your doctor is doing—and why.

Treatments for male infertility

As you know from our earlier discussions, male infertility problems are also caused by a number of structural and hormonal problems. These conditions can be treated through drug and hormone therapy and surgery.

- **Drug and hormone therapy:** Drug therapy can be used to correct such conditions as antibody problems, retrograde ejaculation, infections of the prostate or seminal vesicle, and low sperm counts. Hormone therapy can be used to treat such conditions as hypogonadotropic hypogonadism (a condition in which low levels of FSH and LH result in a lack of normal testicular function and a lack of masculine characteristics), congenital adrenal hyperplasia (a lack of an enzyme required for the production of male hormones), and hyperprolactinemia (a condition in which there is too much prolactin in the blood).

■ **Surgery:** Conditions such as varicoceles, obstructions in the epididymis, and blockages in the ejaculatory ducts can be repaired through surgery.

■ **Artificial insemination:** Artificial insemination (AI) refers to the introduction of sperm into the female reproductive tract by means other than sexual intercourse. It can be either intracervical (which can use freshly ejaculated semen) or intrauterine (which requires a sperm-washing process prior to depositing sperm into the uterus). AI is typically used when there are problems delivering adequate numbers of sperm high into the vagina (as is the case with premature ejaculation or other ejaculatory dysfunction, hypospadias, and impotence); when there are problems with mucus abnormalities or marginal sperm counts or motility (in which case intrauterine insemination [IUI] may be a better option); or in other situations such as unexplained infertility (where it may be combined with fertility drugs) or when a woman choosing to initiate a pregnancy without a male partner requires donor insemination.

The facts about assisted reproductive technologies

Now we move into the Brave New World of modern fertility treatment—the world of assisted reproductive technologies (ART). A few decades ago, technologies such as in vitro fertilization (IVF), Gamete Intrafallopian Transfer (GIFT), and Zygote Intrafallopian Transfer (ZIFT) were simply the stuff of which science fiction novels were made. Today, they're a fact of life for a growing number of American families.

That's not to say that ART is commonplace—yet. According to a recent article at MSNBC (the online service operated by Microsoft and NBC), only 7% of infertility patients choose to use ART as a means of achieving pregnancy. (As a point of comparison, approximately 21% use drug treatments, and 11% pursue adoption.)

The bottom line

It isn't difficult to figure out why such a small percentage of couples opt to go with ART. The costs are prohibitively high and the odds of success continue to be discouragingly low (see Table 3.1).

Consider these facts for yourself. According to the 1995 Assisted Reproductive Technology Success Rates study conducted by the Centers for Disease Control and Prevention:

- In 1995, 59,142 cycles of ART were carried out in the United States. These cycles resulted in 11,315 live births (that is, deliveries in which at least one infant is born alive).

Watch Out!
Fertility centers measure success in a number of different ways: pregnancy per cycle rates, live birth per egg retrieval rates, live birth per embryo transfer rates, and live birth per cycle rates. The last statistic—the so-called "take-home baby rate"—is the most meaningful one to couples who are trying to start families. It shows the percentage of cycles started that have resulted in a live birth.

- In that same year, 27% of all live births resulting from ART were multiple births (that is, twins, triplets, or higher-order multiples) as compared to 2% in the general population. (Although many infertile couples might initially be delighted at the thought of two or more babies, multiple pregnancies are much riskier than singleton pregnancies, particularly when three or more fetuses are involved. What's more, health-care costs can go through the roof if the mother requires hospitalization during her pregnancy or the babies require weeks—if not months—of care in a neonatal intensive care unit.)

Here's something else you need to know as you go about researching fertility clinics. In recognition of the fact that the odds of ending up with a live baby can be discouragingly low, nearly 20% of fertility clinics nationwide are offering some sort of money-back guarantee to couples who don't get pregnant. Although these offers sound like a win-win venture, as with anything else, you need to read the fine print. Most of these offers don't extend to the cost of diagnostic tests or drugs, nor do they cover patients with extremely poor prognoses.

Choosing an ART program

The American Society for Reproductive Medicine recommends that couples consider such factors as cost and convenience; the quality of care; and the program's track record for success when choosing an ART program.

Here are some questions you might want to ask:

- What is the cost of the entire procedure, including drugs per treatment schedule and the costs of freezing, storing, and transferring embryos, and so on?

Timesaver
The 1995 Assisted Reproductive Technology Success Rates report contains details on the success rates of 281 fertility clinics throughout the United States. You can find the report online at www. cdc.gov/ nccdphp/drh/ arts, or you can order a free copy by phoning 888-299-1585. *Note:* The report is printed in three volumes: Eastern region, Central region, and Western region. Be sure to request the appropriate volume when you call.

TABLE 3.1: ART AT A GLANCE

The Procedure	What It Involves	What It Costs	Your Odds of Success (Live Birth Rate)
In Vitro Fertilization (IVF)	An egg and sperm are combined in the lab, and the fertilized egg is then implanted in the woman's uterus.	$6,000 to $10,000 per attempt	18.6% to 22.3%
Gamete Intrafallopian Transfer (GIFT)	Eggs and sperm are inserted directly into the fallopian tube via a laparoscope.	$6,000 to $10,000 per attempt	26.8% to 28%
Intrauterine Insemination (IUI)	Fresh or frozen sperm is injected into the uterus via a catheter.	$300	10%
Zygote Intrafallopian Transfer (ZIFT)	Eggs are fertilized in the lab, and those eggs that are successfully fertilized (zygotes) are transferred to the fallopian tube.	$8,000 to $10,000 per attempt	24% to 27.7%
Frozen Embryo Transfer (FET)	Surplus embryos from an IVF cycle are frozen and stored for future implantation in the uterus.	$500 to $1,500 per cycle	15.4%

Donor Eggs	Eggs from a donor female are fertilized with the male partner's sperm and then transferred to the infertile woman's uterus.	$9,000 per cycle	46.8% per retrieval
Intracyto-Plasmic Sperm Injection (ICSI)	A single sperm is injected into an egg, and the resulting zygote is transferred to the uterus.	$10,000 to $12,000 per attempt	24%

Sources: 1995 *Assisted Reproductive Technology Success Rates: National Summary and Fertility Clinic Reports*. Atlanta: Centers for Disease Control and Prevention, 1997. Begley, Sharon. "The Baby Myth." *Newsweek*. 4 September 1995: 38; Grady, Denise. "How to Coax New Life." *Time* Canada. Fall 1996 special issue: 28. "Of GIFTS and ZIFTS: A Treatment Glossary." http://homearts.com/depts/health/37upb4.htm.

- What are the costs of cancelling a particular cycle at various stages of the process (such as before egg recovery or before embryo transfer)?

- How much time will my partner and I miss from work?

- Does the program meet the standards of the American Society for Reproductive Medicine (www.asrm.org)?

- Is the lab suitably accredited (by the College of American Pathologists, the Commission on Laboratory Accreditation, and the American Society for Reproductive Medicine)?

- How many physicians will be involved in my care, and what are their qualifications?

Watch Out!
There aren't any federal laws in place to regulate the safety of donor sperm, nor are there any national standards for screening egg donors. Make sure that the clinic you deal with has appropriate health safety measures in place.

- Which of the following types of specialists does your clinic employ: a reproductive endocrinologist; a reproductive immunologist; an embryologist; a reproductive urologist; an andrologist; a geneticist; a genetic counselor; a social worker; one or more surgeons with experience in infertility surgery, including laparoscopy, and the use of the ultrasound; an ultrasound technician or obstetrician gynecologist with specialized training in interpreting ultrasounds; a program director (preferably a medical doctor)?

- What types of counseling and support services are provided?

- Who is available after hours to take my phone call?

- Are there any limitations concerning eligibility for your program (age, reproductive health, and so on)?

- Do you have access to donor eggs or donor sperm?

- Do you freeze embryos?

- How long has the clinic been in operation?

- How many IVF, GIFT, ZIFT, ICSI, and IUI procedures have you performed? How many live births have resulted?

- What is your rate of multiple births for the procedure I am considering?

The emotional aspects of ART

Success rates and costs aren't the only issues that couples contemplating ART have to consider. Following are some other matters you and your partner will need to discuss before choosing ART.

Fetal reduction

Because ART doesn't come cheap—according to some experts, it's not unusual for couples to spend upward of $50,000 in their quest for a baby—some clinics make a point of introducing a large number of embryos into a woman's body in order to increase the odds of at least one of them implanting. If the clinic you choose makes a practice of doing this and a large number of those embryos implant, you and your partner could find yourselves faced with a very difficult choice: to selectively reduce (that is, abort) some of those embryos in order to sidestep the risks of a high-risk pregnancy and possibly increase your odds of walking out with a healthy baby.

What to tell family and friends

Then there's the issue of deciding what to tell family and friends. Should you make it general knowledge that you're using ART in your quest for a baby? Or would you and your partner prefer to keep this information to yourselves? What will you tell your child as he gets older?

Bright Idea
Contact the American Society for Reproductive Medicine to request a list of the organization's patient information booklets.

American Society for Reproductive Medicine, 1209 Montgomery Highway, Birmingham, Alabama 35216-2809. Tel: 205-978-5000, Fax: 205-978-5005, E-mail: asrm@ asrm.com, Web site: www. asrm.org/.

Coping with financial worries

With certain high-tech methods of reproduction ringing in at $10,000 or more per cycle, money worries can also become a major concern for couples who are pursuing other types of fertility treatment. Here are some pointers on minimizing your out-of-pocket expenses when it comes to fertility treatments:

- Find out whether insurance companies in your state are mandated to provide infertility insurance coverage. (In certain states, the legislation also extends to HMOs.) Because the laws are constantly changing—and because we don't want to be accused of practicing law without a degree—we suggest that you do some digging on your own. Before you pick up the phone and call an attorney, get the latest news on State Infertility Insurance Laws at www.asrm.org/patient/insur.html.

- Shop around for the best possible policy. Some policies cover a greater range of infertility-related treatments than others. If possible, ask your doctor or a friend who has been through infertility treatments to recommend an HMO or insurance company.

- Know your policy inside out. Find out which procedures are covered—and which ones aren't. You might start by writing to your insurance company to inquire about what types of treatments are covered, whether there's a cap on the amount of money that can be paid on an individual claim or a limit to the number of cycles of assisted reproduction you can attempt, and so on. You can find an excellent sample letter at www.fertilitext.org/sample.htm. *Note:* To avoid any nasty surprises down the road, be sure to submit this predetermination-of-benefits letter before you start treatment.

- If your insurance company fails to underwrite the costs of your fertility-related treatments, ask the company to respond in writing with details explaining why your claim for coverage was denied. You may wish to use this information when registering a complaint with your state insurance commission. You can find the contact information for each state insurance commission at www.fertilethoughts.net/infertility.

- If you find yourself stuck with a lot of drug expenses, you might want to ask your doctor whether you can switch to a less-pricey generic brand of prescription drug or see if he has any pharmaceutical company samples he would be willing to pass your way; see if your company benefits package allows you to purchase drugs at a discount; or use the services of a discount pharmacy such as Action Mail Order (800-452-1976), Family Pharmaceuticals (800-922-3444), or Medi-Mail (800-331-1458).

- Keep in mind that your financial worries won't necessarily end once you conceive. A recent article in the *New England Journal of Medicine* revealed that whereas the hospital charges for a single birth in 1991 were approximately $9,845, they were $37,947 for twins, and $109,765 for triplets. The authors of the article concluded that more attention needs to be paid to approaches to infertility that reduce the likelihood of multiple gestations.

Moneysaver
"Expect to pay for all aspects of IVF, but work with the office manager of your IVF clinic to see if some of the charges associated with IVF will be covered within your plan. For example, your plan may cover all prescription drugs, blood work, and ultrasound monitoring for any medical condition. The costs of these procedures add up to the majority of costs for a typical IVF cycle."
—From the Insurance Information FAQ at www.fertilethoughts.net.

Bright Idea
Want expert advice on fertility-related issues? You can e-mail questions to specialists in the field of reproductive medicine by visiting the following Web page: www. fertilitext.org/ Question.htm.

What to do if you don't conceive

It's critical that you and your partner agree in advance about the number of cycles you're willing to try and what types of high-tech procedures you are and aren't willing to consider. Once you get involved in treatment, you can become obsessed with the idea of continuing with treatment until you end up with a baby—no matter what the physical, emotional, or financial costs may be.

Here's what writer Sharon Begley had to say about this phenomenon in an article in *Newsweek:* "Some [couples] seem trapped in their own private Vietnams: having spent $10,000 and with nary a swollen abdomen to show for it, they can't quit until they have a victory—a baby." Begley goes on to quote Valerie Hendy, a 44-year-old woman who describes what it's like to go through ART: "You almost feel like you've got a bug for gambling. You say, 'What else is there to try, what else have you got?'"

The problem becomes immeasurably more complex if one of you wants to continue and the other feels that it's time to call it quits. In an article in *Psychology Today* magazine, psychologist Susan McDaniel told writer Virginia Rutter why men and women often feel differently about this issue: "As much as men are invested in having children, they don't have to think about it, or perhaps be as conscious of it—because women are so focused on the problem. It makes sense, then, that . . . men will often be the ones to put on the brakes. . . . So what happens—largely because of sex roles—is [that] women become advocates of the process, and men, who may be more ambivalent, question it and wonder if it's time to stop."

Assuming that you do decide to call it quits, you'll have to grapple with another complex issue: what to do with the sperm, eggs, and embryos you and your partner have stored. Depending on the laws in your state, you might choose to donate them to another couple, have them destroyed, or continue to store them in case you have a change of heart.

If, on the other hand, the stress of infertility has taken its toll on your relationship and you and your partner decide to go your separate ways, the situation becomes even more complex. The New York Court of appeals recently ruled, for example, that five frozen embryos belonging to a divorced couple must be donated to research despite the female partner's desire to use them to have children. The reason? The man involved in the case did not wish to father any children with his former partner.

What to do if you do manage to conceive

Other emotional issues are involved, even if you do manage to conceive. Some couples using donor eggs or donor sperm have to struggle to come to terms with the fact that they weren't able to conceive naturally. Sometimes the infertile partner can have a particularly difficult time accepting the fact that someone else's egg or sperm was used to conceive his or her child. Not all couples struggle with this issue, however. Here's what Lorna, 33, has to say about her experiences with donor insemination: "We wanted a child and this was the best option for us. My husband and I chose the donor and went to all the appointments together. The clinic we chose was wonderful—very helpful and supportive. As far as we're concerned, this baby is 'all ours.' We just needed a little help with the biology!"

Bright Idea
Dozens of infertility-related newsgroups and mailing lists are available online: groups devoted to DES daughters, secondary infertility (that is, infertility after you've had one or more children), donor insemination, surrogate mothers, infertility in general, and much more (see Appendix B, "Resource Directory," for Web addresses).

Unofficially...
According to the Centers for Disease Control and Prevention, the primary causes of infertility in couples using ART procedures in 1995 were tubal factors (32%), male factors (20%), endometriosis (16%), unexplained causes (16%), ovarian factor (9%), and other causes such as structural problems with the uterus and fibroid tumors (9%).

Some couples find that it is possible to reduce some of the stress of trying to conceive artificially if they make an effort to humanize the process as much as possible.

Couples who are attempting artificial insemination by donor sperm can often choose to do the insemination themselves at home, rather than under the bright lights of an examining table. Victoria and Dawn, a lesbian couple who are expecting their first child, decided to go this route: "We did it when we had a lot of time and weren't rushed. After the insemination, we cuddled and talked." Lorna and her partner had the procedure done at the doctor's office but managed to humanize it nonetheless: "While they did the procedure, my husband sat beside me and held my hand. He continued to do so during the resting period which followed."

Is ART the right choice for you?

Your doctor will provide you with the medical information you will need in order to assess whether ART is a good choice for you, physically speaking. Only you can decide whether it's the best choice for you and your partner from an emotional standpoint. Here are some questions the two of you should probably discuss before pursuing these types of high-tech infertility treatments:

- If you decided to proceed with a technique that uses donor sperm or eggs, would you or your partner be upset by the fact that the child is not genetically your own?

- Would you or your partner feel jealous or inadequate if a donor was able to conceive a child with one of you but the other partner wasn't?

- Would you and your partner tell your child the truth about how she was conceived, or would you try to keep it a secret?

- Would you and your partner tell friends and family the truth? What about casual acquaintances or people at work?

- How many attempts would you and your partner be prepared to make? What would you do if one partner wanted to continue trying but the other did not?

- What would you and your partner do with any frozen sperm, eggs, or embryos you did not end up using? Donate them to another couple? Allow them to be used for genetic research? What would happen to the frozen sperm, eggs, or embryos if you and your partner separated?

- What percentage of the costs of infertility treatments, if any, would your insurance company cover? How much money would you and your partner be prepared to spend out of your own pockets?

- Are you and your partner prepared to assume the risk of having twins or other multiples? How would you cope if one or more of the babies died?

Timesaver
If your doctor prescribes fertility drugs that must be injected, ask him to train your partner to administer the shots for you. This will help cut down on the number of trips you have to make to the doctor's office.

The stress of infertility

Although couples who go through ART have a lot of complex issues to deal with, they aren't the only ones who experience the stress of infertility.

Regardless of the type of infertility treatment you and your partner are receiving, you may find yourself on a roller-coaster ride that follows the pattern of your menstrual cycle: During the first part of the cycle, you are fueled by hope that this could be the cycle in which you conceive. As ovulation approaches, you may become obsessed with timing intercourse to maximize your chances of getting pregnant. Once ovulation occurs, you're left in a two-week-long holding pattern that could try the patience of a saint. You wonder if the symptoms you're experiencing are caused by PMS, whether they're due to the hormonal treatments or fertility drugs you're taking, or whether in fact you're pregnant. If your period shows up again, you may feel hopeless and depressed, wondering if you'll ever be able to conceive.

Part of the stress of infertility stems from the fact that it's one area of your life over which you have little or no control. As much as you'd like to, you can't just block off some time to conceive in your Daytimer. (Well, actually, you can; there's just no guarantee that it will actually happen!)

Not surprisingly, those of us with Type A tendencies tend to find it particularly difficult to relinquish control over the whole business of baby making, and may become quite depressed or discouraged as the months drag on and on.

Here are some tips on coping with the stress of infertility:

- Don't let your fertility treatments take over your entire life. Try not to lose sight of all the good things that may be happening at home and at work.

- Keep yourself healthy. Feelings of stress can be worsened if you're not sleeping well, eating properly, or exercising enough.

- Watch your intake of alcohol. It's not just bad for the baby you're hoping to conceive; it's also bad for you. Because alcohol is a depressant, it will only add to your feelings of depression.

■ Talk about your feelings with your partner, and accept the fact that you may not always be on the same wavelength. Although you both need to have the opportunity to express all of the powerful emotions you may be feeling—hope, disappointment, excitement, frustration, guilt, and so on—it's important to realize that you may experience conflicting emotions from time to time. If this becomes a problem for you and your partner, the two of you may wish to seek the services of a therapist who can help you work through your feelings about one another and the baby you hope to conceive.

■ Try to keep your sex life separate from your reproductive life. If you're finding that there's no joy left in sex, you might want to think about taking a break from trying to conceive for a cycle or two. Although it may delay your plans to have a baby, a brief time-out could help keep your relationship with your partner on track. Odd as it may sound, some infertile couples who decide to go this route make a point of using birth control during their nontrying cycles so that they don't spend the entire second half of the cycle trying to guess whether this was their lucky month.

The facts about surrogacy and adoption

Although most people think of the Baby M case when they think about surrogacy, the heart-wrenching custody battle fought and lost by surrogate mother Mary Beth Whitehead is far from the norm today.

Whereas the first generation of surrogates were genetically related to the babies they carried—a situation that led to more than a few cases of the Baby M variety—more often than not, today's surrogates are more like human incubators than parents to the babies they carry. The reason is obvious. Advances in assisted reproduction techniques have made it possible for the so-called "gestational surrogate" or "carrier" to carry someone else's sperm and egg—either the intended couple's sperm and eggs, or a combination of donor egg and donor sperm—rather than conceiving a child with the male partner and then relinquishing parental rights to him and his partner. According to psychologist Andrea Braverman, chief psychologist at Pennsylvania Reproductive Associates, these changes to the nature of surrogacy have led to much happier outcomes for all concerned: "It is a very different psychological hurdle to navigate if you are genetically related to the child you're carrying," she recently told MSNBC. Because they have no genetic link to the child they are carrying, today's surrogates can tell themselves, "Hey, it's her egg and his sperm."

This is not to say that surrogacy has become a run-of-the-mill process complete with guaranteed happy endings, however. Would-be parents who choose surrogacy as their route to parenthood are still forced to confront some mind-bogglingly complex legal, financial, and psychological hurdles.

Just a couple of quick footnotes before we plunge into our discussion of these important issues related to surrogacy:

- The terms "full surrogate" and "traditional surrogate" are used interchangeably to describe situations in which the surrogate conceives and carries the child of an infertile woman's partner. This form of insemination can be either direct (that is, through intercourse) or indirect (using ART).

- The terms "partial surrogate," "gestational surrogate," and "carrier" are used to describe situations in which an egg from a woman who is unable to conceive is fertilized with her partner's sperm, and the resulting embryo is implanted into the surrogate mother's uterus.

Although we're fairly consistent with our terminology—we tend to use "traditional surrogate" and "gestational surrogate"—you're likely to find a mix of terms in other sources.

Legal hurdles

The legal status of surrogacy varies from state to state. The situation is so complex that the American Surrogacy Center (www.surrogacy.com) uses seven different categories to define the legal status of surrogacy in various states.

Regardless of what state you're in, you'll need to formalize your arrangement with your surrogate by having your attorney draft a surrogacy contract which specifies

- the purpose and intent of the arrangement (that is, that you and your partner will be considered to be the child's parents at the end of the period of surrogacy);

- some guidelines regarding the selection of physicians and a counselor/mediator to resolve any disputes that may arise between you and the surrogate;

- what fees you are responsible for paying to the surrogate;

Unofficially...
According to the Center for Surrogate Parenting and Egg Donation Inc., a typical surrogate mother is a woman in her twenties or thirties who is married with two children of her own. She is motivated to become a surrogate because she enjoys being pregnant, has a history of uncomplicated pregnancies, and feels empathy for childless couples. She may also be motivated by a desire to contribute to her family's well-being by earning an income as a surrogate.

- what medical tests the surrogate must take (for example, a full prenatal blood workup, ultrasounds as required, amniocentesis if the intended parents wish to go that route, testing for HIV, and so on) and what lifestyle restrictions she must follow (for example, she will be expected to go on bed rest if her physician recommends it, and she will be expected to refrain from smoking, drinking, and taking drugs of any kind, except those specifically prescribed by her physician);

- what specific rights and responsibilities each party has under the law;

- the intended parents' and the surrogate's expectations of one another (for example, how regularly they will be in contact with one another both prior to and after the birth);

- under what terms the agreement may be terminated (for example, if the surrogate does not become pregnant within a specific period of time);

- under what terms the pregnancy may be terminated (for example, if the surrogate's life is at risk due to complications of pregnancy or if it is necessary in a multiple pregnancy);

- where and how the birth will take place (for example, what role you and your partner will play at the birth; what rights you will have in ordering medical care for the child after the birth; and so on);

- how many counseling sessions the surrogate will be required to participate in over the course of her pregnancy;

- to what extent the agreement is considered to be confidential (for example, is the surrogate free to tell other people whose child she is carrying);

■ what life insurance the intended parents and the surrogate are carrying, and what would happen to the child if either or both of the intended parents were to die prior to the birth of the child.

You can find a sample surrogacy agreement in Appendix D.

Financial hurdles

Hiring a surrogate to carry your child is quite an expensive proposition. You can expect to be approximately $50,000 poorer by the time you walk out of the hospital with a baby in your arms—assuming, of course, that you're fortunate enough to have that ultimate of happy outcomes. Obviously, your chances of success will be determined in part by which route to surrogacy you choose—high-tech fertility methods will result in rates of success similar to those shown in Table 3.1, whereas traditional methods of conceiving will give you success rates similar to those experienced by fertile couples.

Here's a breakdown of costs, based on information posted at the Center for Surrogate Parenting and Egg Donation Inc., Web site at www. creatingfamilies.com/Costpg.HTML.

Bright Idea
Compare notes with other parents who have been through surrogacy by participating in one of the numerous online surrogacy information and support groups. You can find out more about these groups in Appendix B.

TABLE 3.2: SURROGACY: WHAT IT COSTS

Fee to agency	$18,000
Fee to surrogate	$15,000
Surrogate's out-of-pocket expenses	$4,750
Surrogate's medical expenses	$6,420
Miscellaneous expenses (for example, life insurance)	$550
Counseling fees	$4,600
Total	$49,320

Although these costs are daunting enough in and of themselves, they often follow closely on the heels of pricey fertility treatments. That's why surrogacy continues to be an option that is open primarily to America's wealthiest families.

Emotional hurdles

Most couples find the emotional hurdles of surrogacy to be far more difficult than the legal and financial obstacles. There's the stress of finding a surrogate. (It's illegal to use an agency in some states, so would-be parents have to be extremely creative—and careful.) There's the worry that something will go wrong with the pregnancy. And then there's the biggest fear of all: that she won't be willing to give up the baby in the end.

According to the Organization of Parenting Through Surrogacy (OPTS), the last possibility is extremely unlikely: only 17 of the more than 8,000 recorded surrogacy births have resulted in a custody battle. Still, it's the stuff of which nine-month-long nightmares are made, and an issue that would-be parents ignore at their own peril.

As if these issues weren't difficult enough to contend with, parents who use surrogates must also accept the fact that they may experience interpersonal conflicts with the surrogate or grow very attached to her over the course of the pregnancy. Either scenario can add to the stress of an already emotionally draining time.

Last but not least, there's the matter of bonding with a baby who's been gestating in someone else's womb—and figuring out what to tell family members, friends, and the child himself about his unconventional conception.

As you can see, surrogacy isn't an arrangement to be entered into on a whim. It's an option that needs to be researched fully. We've given you the basic facts, but you need to decide whether it's the right option for you. We've included some suggested resources for more information in Appendix B.

The facts about adoption

Adoption is an option that approximately 11% of infertile couples choose to pursue, but before you pick up the phone to call the domestic or international adoption agency of your choice, give some serious thought to whether adoption is right for you.

Chris Adamec, author of *The Complete Idiot's Guide to Adoption,* agrees that couples need to decide for themselves whether adoption is, in fact, the right choice: "Here's [a] tough issue that most people don't like to think about. Is adoption good enough for you? You may have wanted a biological child but couldn't have one, so you decide to adopt. . . . If you feel that what is most important is to have a child who resembles you or carries forth your genes, then adoption wouldn't be right for you. If you feel that the primary reason to adopt is to become a parent, a role you strongly want, then adoption might be right for you."

Here are some basic facts on adoption you will also want to consider as you make this important decision:

- In 1992, there was a total of 51,157 domestic adoptions of nonrelatives, according to the National Council on Adoption. Approximately half of the children involved were infants. Thirty-nine percent of these adoptions were

Watch Out!
Make sure that you understand the difference between an open adoption (when the birth mother chooses the adoptive family) and a closed adoption (when the adoptive and birth parents never meet, and all records are sealed after the adoption is finalized). An open adoption typically allows for some contact between the child and the birth mother as the child grows up—something you may or may not be comfortable with.

Unofficially...
In 1996, a total of 11,316 American families adopted children from countries such as China (3,318), Russia (2,328), Korea (1,580), Romania (554), and Guatemala (420). The remaining 3,116 children placed through foreign adoption came from other countries. Sixty-four percent of these children were female, and 36% were male. Fifty-four percent were under one year of age, and 35% were between the ages of one and four.

handled by public agencies, 29% by private agencies, and 31% by private individuals.

■ According to a recent article at Family.com, eligibility requirements for adoption are becoming much less rigid, even for couples who wish to adopt infants. However, you'll still be required to go through a home study (a tool that the child welfare authorities use to assess the suitability of prospective parents). You can get a sense of what adoption agencies are looking for these days by reading our Agency Checklist.

CHECKLIST: AGENCY

You increase your odds of being approved by an adoption agency if

■ you are married rather than single, and have been with your partner for a minimum of three years,

■ you are no more than 40 years older than the child you wish to adopt,

■ you are in good health,

■ you are infertile,

■ you have fewer than two children of your own,

■ you or your partner is able to be at home with the child you adopt for a minimum of six months,

■ you are financially stable and capable of paying the agency's fee,

■ your home is safe, clean, and child-friendly,

■ your background check doesn't turn up any disturbing information about you,

■ your home study goes well.

- Contrary to popular belief—to say nothing of media hype—the majority of adoption stories have happy endings. According to a recent report at Family.com, approximately 80% of adoptions are completed successfully. This means that such factors as birth mother change of heart, birth father intervention, and breakdown of communication and trust between birth parents and adopting parents become an issue only in approximately one out of every five adoptions.

- Foreign adoption is becoming an increasingly popular option for American couples, mainly because the waiting lists for foreign-born children are considerably shorter than those for American children. As a rule of thumb, prospective adoptive parents who are accepted into foreign adoption programs can expect to have a child within a year to 18 months, whereas those who choose to participate in domestic adoption programs can expect a wait of approximately $2^{1}/_{2}$ years.

- According to the National Adoption Information Clearinghouse, domestic adoptions cost up to $30,000 but may, in fact, be free if you're adopting a child who is in the care of the state. Foreign adoptions, on the other hand, typically cost anywhere from $12,000 to $25,000.

Moneysaver
If you are determined to adopt a child but don't have sufficient funds sitting in the bank, you might want to turn to one or more of the following sources of financial assistance: family and friends, bank loans, employee benefit packages, home-equity loans, retirement funds, and/or life insurance policies.

They don't call him "Uncle" Sam for nothing!

Although the costs of adopting a child can be more than a little daunting, there is some good news, courtesy of none other than Uncle Sam. Adoptive parents are able to take advantage of a significant tax break, courtesy of the federal government.

Here's the scoop. If your modified adjusted gross income is less than $75,000:

- You are eligible for a $5,000 federal tax credit per child for certain types of adoption-related expenses: court costs, adoption fees, legal fees, traveling expenses, and so on. (*Note:* If you adopt a child from a foreign country, this is the only adoption-related tax windfall that the federal government is willing to throw your way.)

- If you receive adoption assistance as a benefit of your employment, you are able to exclude up to $5,000 of these funds from your federal taxable income.

- If you adopt an American child who has special needs, you are eligible for $6,000 in tax credits or income exclusions.

- If your efforts to adopt a child in the United States fail, you can still write off your expenses.

- If your modified adjusted gross income is more than $75,000 but less than $115,000 you are eligible for some of these credits or exclusions. If your income exceeds this level, however, you're out of luck. Remember, the taxman giveth and the taxman taketh away. . . . You can read the fine print for yourself at http://ares.fedworld.gov/prod/forms_pubs/pubs/p968toc.htm.

Adoption is a complex issue, so you'll want to do some additional research to determine if it's the right choice for your family. You'll find a number of very useful resources in Appendix B.

Just the facts

- If you and your partner have been having unprotected intercourse for more than a year

Watch Out!
If you apply for the adoption credit on your income tax return, the IRS may ask you to provide the name of the agent who assisted with the adoption. If you aren't able to supply this information, your credit could be disallowed.

and still haven't managed to conceive, it's possible that you have a fertility problem.

■ When you're shopping around for a specialist, look for a doctor who devotes a significant percentage of her medical practice to the treatment of infertility.

■ Make sure that you are clear about both the costs of treatment and your odds of having a healthy baby before you agree to any type of fertility treatment.

■ Your fertility workup will consist of a medical history, a physical examination, and possibly some additional tests. As a rule of thumb, the male partner should be tested first because tests of the male reproductive system are considerably less invasive than those of the female reproductive system.

■ A range of infertility treatments are available, including hormone therapy, drug therapy, and surgery.

■ There are also a number of high-tech methods of conceiving, including IVF, GIFT, ZIFT, IUI, and ICSI, and the use of donor sperm and donor eggs.

■ Infertility can be extremely stressful for couples who are affected by it. You may want to consider going for therapy or taking a break from the Baby Olympics for a while.

■ The laws concerning surrogacy vary from state to state. Be sure to get professional legal advice before you embark on any type of surrogacy arrangement.

■ Most surrogates today have no genetic link to the babies they are carrying. They are simply acting as human incubators for the couples who have contracted their services.

■ If you decide to adopt a child, be sure to take advantage of the adoption tax credit when you file your income tax.

Decisions, Decisions

PART II

Finding Out You're Pregnant

Chapter 4

If you and your partner have been trying to conceive for some time, you may strongly suspect that you are pregnant even before the pregnancy test actually comes back positive. Part of this is clearly wishful thinking: you're hoping like crazy that this is the cycle when you've actually managed to conceive. But at least a part of this feeling may be based in biological fact. Studies have shown that some women are able to detect hormonal changes, however slight, from the time that the body begins to produce human chorionic gonadotropin (hCG)—about seven days after conception. If you don't notice anything particularly out of the ordinary until you've missed your first period, you're certainly in good company. Most women don't experience any of the classic symptoms of early pregnancy—morning sickness, fatigue, and tender breasts—until after their first missed period.

If, on the other hand, you aren't consciously planning a pregnancy, it may take you even longer to consider the possibility that you might be pregnant. If you aren't on the lookout for possible symptoms of early pregnancy, the milder symptoms may actually go unnoticed. You may explain away your feelings of fatigue by thinking about how hard you've been working lately and wonder if the touch of nausea you experienced when you woke up this morning was caused by something you ate for dinner last night. Because these symptoms can be mild or even nonexistent, you could be well into your third month of pregnancy before you decide that it's time to dash down to the drug store to purchase a home pregnancy test.

In this chapter, we discuss the symptoms of early pregnancy, how pregnancy tests work, what your due date really means, and what to expect when you share your news with others in your life—your partner, friends, family, and employer. We also briefly touch on your rights as a pregnant employee—something you'll want to know all about before you start spreading your news at work.

> The moment I discovered I was pregnant, I began a nine-month-long research project. I read everything I could get my hands on regarding pregnancy, labor and delivery, and raising babies and children.
> —Jennifer, 21, mother of one

The symptoms of early pregnancy

Despite what some pregnancy books would have you believe, there's no such thing as a one-size-fits-all pregnancy. You may experience a lot of early pregnancy symptoms, or none at all. What's more, the fact that you felt perfectly well during your first pregnancy is no guarantee that you'll be quite that lucky during the next. It's the ultimate crapshoot.

That said, you are likely to experience at least one of the following common signs of pregnancy. Just one word of caution before we plunge into the list: If you wait for each and every pregnancy symptom to appear—or if you expect them to appear in a predesignated order—you could be in labor before you believe that you're actually having a baby!

- **A missed period:** Although missing a period is one of the most frequently cited symptoms of pregnancy, it's by no means a clear indicator that you are, in fact, pregnant. Although pregnancy is the most common explanation for missing a period, you can miss a period for many other reasons: low estrogen birth control pills, jet lag, severe illness, surgery, shock, bereavement, or other causes of stress. And as if that weren't enough to muddy the waters, some women continue to have menstrual-like bleeding throughout at least part of their pregnancies.

- **A need to urinate more frequently:** As your progesterone levels rise and your body begins to produce hCG (something that typically happens about a week after conception), blood flow to the pelvic area increases. This can cause you to feel as if you need to urinate more frequently than usual, even if you're passing only small quantities of urine at a time.

- **Fatigue:** Here are two good reasons why you may feel tired during the early weeks of pregnancy: your body increases its production of progesterone, a natural sedative, and it increases your metabolism so that it will be able to support the growth of an embryo as well as your own vital organs.

- **A heightened sense of smell:** Strong odors such as cigarette smoke, coffee, or perfume may make you feel sick. Some scientists believe that this aversion to unhealthy substances is nature's way of protecting the baby you are carrying.

Bright Idea
Compare pregnancy symptoms with other moms-to-be by participating in online pregnancy chat groups, such as the ones at www. storksite.com.

- **Food aversions and cravings:** Hormonal changes can cause your mouth to take on a metallic taste—something that can dramatically affect your enjoyment of certain foods and beverages, such as coffee. You may find that you start to crave certain foods—maybe even the proverbial pickles and ice cream!

- **Morning sickness:** The term *morning sickness* is used to describe everything from a mild feeling of nausea to vomiting to the point of dehydration. Although the condition can occur at any time of day, it tends to be worse when your blood sugar is at its lowest level, as is the case first thing in the morning.

- **Breast changes:** Your breasts may become fuller and feel achy or tender. The areola may begin to darken, and tiny glands on the areola may begin to enlarge.

- **Cramping:** You may feel period-like cramping in the lower abdomen and pelvis, or you may feel bloated and gassy.

In this chapter, we've focussed only on the symptoms you're likely to experience around the time that your pregnancy is confirmed. We'll be discussing other first-trimester symptoms in Chapter 14.

Pregnancy tests

If you suspect that you're pregnant, you should arrange to take a pregnancy test as soon as possible. That way, you can ensure that both you and your baby receive the best possible care during the months ahead.

You have two basic choices when it comes to confirming pregnancy: using an over-the-counter home pregnancy test or making an appointment to have your pregnancy confirmed by your doctor or midwife.

Home pregnancy tests

Gone are the days when you had to pace nervously, waiting for a call from the doctor to confirm your suspicion that you were, in fact, having a baby. Rather than using the lab-based tests of yesterday—tests that required hours if not days to conduct—most American women today turn to home pregnancy tests, a habit that translates into $206 million a year in sales for the companies that manufacture them.

Home pregnancy tests are designed to detect the presence of hCG, the hormone manufactured by the blatocyst (the name for the hollow clump of cells resulting from the meeting of sperm and egg) following implantation. Enough hCG is present in the urine to allow a pregnancy to be confirmed as soon as two weeks after conception, although it takes some pregnant women a little longer to test positive.

Although home pregnancy tests are proven to be about 97% accurate, false positives and false negatives can occur. Consequently, to ensure that you obtain the most accurate results possible, you should

- check that the test has not yet passed its expiration date;

- follow the test results to the letter, paying particular attention to the amount of time you have to wait before you read the results of the test and at which point the test results lose their validity (for example, a pregnancy test can

Moneysaver
You can save yourself the cost of a home pregnancy test if you're tracking your basal body temperature. If your period is late, you simply need to note whether your luteal phase— the number of days since you ovulated—is longer than normal. If you have 18 consecutive elevated temperatures or your temperature remains elevated for at least three days longer than your longest luteal phase to date, you're probably pregnant.

change from negative to positive if you leave it sitting around long enough);

▪ make sure that you use your first morning urine (it has a higher concentration of hCG than the urine you pass later in the day);

▪ if you use a test that requires that you collect a sample rather than test your urine while you urinate, be sure to use a clean, soap-free container.

Although the latest generation of home pregnancy tests highly accurate, it's still possible to get a false positive or negative. Your test results could be inaccurate if

▪ the urine has been improperly collected or stored,

▪ the urine and the test kit are not at room temperature at the time you conduct the test,

▪ there is blood or protein in your urine,

▪ you have a urinary tract infection,

▪ you're approaching menopause.

Note: Contrary to popular belief, taking contraceptive pills, antibiotics, and analgesics such as acetaminophen should not affect the results of your pregnancy test.

If you get a positive test result, you're probably pregnant. When errors occur during testing, they are most likely to result in false negatives.

If your test comes back negative but your period still hasn't arrived a week later, test again. It's possible that you ovulated a few days later than usual during this particular cycle.

If your test shows only a very faint positive, test again a few days later to see if your hormone levels have begun to increase.

If your test is initially positive but a subsequent pregnancy test comes back negative, it's possible that you have experienced an early miscarriage. (See Chapter 11.)

Having your doctor or midwife confirm your pregnancy

If you decide to have your doctor or midwife confirm your pregnancy, she will likely order a urine test or blood test.

The urine test you take at the lab is virtually identical to the urine test you can find in any home pregnancy test kit. You either urinate directly on the test stick or dip the test stick into a sample of urine. If your doctor wants you to bring in a sample of first morning urine, remember to keep it at room temperature.

The blood test you take to confirm pregnancy can be either qualitative (that is, a test that merely confirms whether you are pregnant) or quantitative (that is, a test that provides your health-care practitioner with a reading of the level of hCG in your blood). Your health-care practitioner is more likely to order a quantitative blood test if he has reason to believe that your pregnancy may be in jeopardy, if you've experienced a series of first-trimester miscarriages in the past, if ectopic pregnancy is a concern, or if he intends to start you on progesterone in an effort to prevent you from miscarrying (see Chapter 11). Quantitative blood tests are sometimes referred to as beta hCG tests, quantitative beta hCG tests, quantitative serum beta-hCG tests, human chorionic gonadotropin-quantitative, and beta-hCG-quantitative. You may be asked to take a series of these tests to determine that the hCG levels are rising appropriately (doubling every 48 hours) and

Timesaver
Here's a quick way to get the lowdown on home pregnancy tests. The Home Testing for Pregnancy Web page, http://kerouac.pharm.uky.edu/hometest/Pregnant/ptoc.html, contains detailed information about 10 different home pregnancy tests, as well as 800 numbers for their manufacturers.

that your pregnancy is a viable, intrauterine pregnancy. The series of tests is known as serial beta-hCG
tests or repeat quantitative hCG tests.

What your due date really means

One of the first things you'll want to know once your
pregnancy is confirmed is when your baby is due. To
calculate this date—a date your doctor or midwife is
likely to refer to as your estimated date of confinement (EDC)—you simply add 266 days or 38 weeks
to the date when you conceived or, assuming that
your menstrual cycles are 28 days in length, you add
280 days or 40 weeks to the first day of your last menstrual period. If your cycles are slightly longer, your
doctor or midwife may knock a few days off your due
date. Likewise, if your cycles are slightly shorter, she
may add a few days to your due date. If your cycles
are highly irregular—or if you conceived before having your first post-pill period—your due date may be
adjusted as your health-care practitioner is better
able to track your baby's development. Any information you may have about the timing of conception can be extremely valuable to your doctor or
midwife. Be sure to share anything that might prove
useful: ovulation predictor kit results, basal body
temperature charts, records of the dates on which
you had intercourse, and so on. (You should, of
course, make a point of recording the dates of the
first day of your menstrual periods whenever you're
trying to conceive.)

You can get an idea of when your baby will make
his or her grand entrance by using the following
table.

The first row of numbers refers to the date of
your last menstrual period (LMP). The second row
of numbers refers to your baby's estimated due date.

Your Estimated Date Of Delivery

Month	1	2	3	4	5	6	7	8	9	10	11	12	13	14	15	16	17	18	19	20	21	22	23	24	25	26	27	28	29	30	31
January *October*	8	9	10	11	12	13	14	15	16	17	18	19	20	21	22	23	24	25	26	27	28	29	30	31	1	2	3	4	5	6	7
February *November*	8	9	10	11	12	13	14	15	16	17	18	19	20	21	22	23	24	25	26	27	28	29	30	1	2	3	4	5			
March *December*	6	7	8	9	10	11	12	13	14	15	16	17	18	19	20	21	22	23	24	25	26	27	28	29	30	31	1	2	3	4	5
April *January*	6	7	8	9	10	11	12	13	14	15	16	17	18	19	20	21	22	23	24	25	26	27	28	29	30	31	1	2	3	4	
May *February*	5	6	7	8	9	10	11	12	13	14	15	16	17	18	19	20	21	22	23	24	25	26	27	28	1	2	3	4	5	6	7
June *March*	8	9	10	11	12	13	14	15	16	17	18	19	20	21	22	23	24	25	26	27	28	29	30	31	1	2	3	4	5	6	
July *April*	7	8	9	10	11	12	13	14	15	16	17	18	19	20	21	22	23	24	25	26	27	28	29	30	1	2	3	4	5	6	7
August *May*	8	9	10	11	12	13	14	15	16	17	18	19	20	21	22	23	24	25	26	27	28	29	30	31	1	2	3	4	5	6	7
September *June*	8	9	10	11	12	13	14	15	16	17	18	19	20	21	22	23	24	25	26	27	28	29	30	1	2	3	4	5	6	7	
October *July*	8	9	10	11	12	13	14	15	16	17	18	19	20	21	22	23	24	25	26	27	28	29	30	31	1	2	3	4	5	6	7
November *August*	8	9	10	11	12	13	14	15	16	17	18	19	20	21	22	23	24	25	26	27	28	29	30	31	1	2	3	4	5	6	
December *September*	7	8	9	10	11	12	13	14	15	16	17	18	19	20	21	22	23	24	25	26	27	28	29	30	1	2	3	4	5	6	7

Don't forget that your due date is only an estimate. A healthy pregnancy can last anywhere from 38 to 42 weeks. Although it's impossible to exactly pinpoint your baby's due date, you can feel relatively confident about the timing of his or her arrival. Even though your chances of delivering on your due date are relatively slim—5%—your chances of giving birth during the week prior to or following your due date are approximately 85%.

Bright Idea
Keep a running list of questions to ask your doctor or midwife at your first appointment.

How you may feel about being pregnant

How you feel about being pregnant will obviously be determined in part by whether your pregnancy was planned. If you've been trying to become pregnant for some time, you may be positively elated that you've finally managed to conceive. If, on the other hand, you already have three children, you've been using birth control, and you discover that a surprise set of triplets is on the way, you may be panicked or outright horrified!

You can expect to experience some—or all!—of the following reactions when you discover that you are pregnant:

- **Elation.** Assuming that you are eager to become a parent, there are few things as exciting as discovering that you are going to have a baby. You may feel giddy and euphoric and unable to focus on anything else but your wonderful news.

- **Pride.** You may feel proud that you are carrying a baby. You may gain new respect for your body and what it is capable of producing. Even those women who have had a love-hate relationship with their bodies for most of their adult lives usually manage to call a truce for at least nine months.

- **Shock.** If your pregnancy was unplanned, you may find it difficult to accept that you are actually pregnant. Even if you were actively trying to conceive, you may find it difficult to believe that the biology of sex actually works and you are really going to have a baby.

- **Fear.** If you have previously experienced a miscarriage or stillbirth, you may be afraid that you may lose this baby too. (You will find more detailed discussion of what it is like to experience pregnancy after loss in Chapter 11.)

▪ **Worry.** If you're like most pregnant women, you're probably carrying around at least a few of the following worries: Will my baby be alright? Will I be able to cope with the pain of childbirth? Will I be a good enough parent? Will having a baby ruin my relationship with my partner? Will it derail my career? (You can find out about these and other common pregnancy worries in Chapter 14 when we discuss "The Top 10 Worries of Expectant Parents.")

▪ **Guilt.** Pregnant women tend to carry around a lot of guilt. If you wanted this baby but your partner didn't, you may feel guilty for forcing the issue. If your children are going to be spaced closely together, you may feel guilty about forcing your older child to share you and your partner with the new baby. If your pregnancy is going to require that you take some time off work during your company's busy season, you may feel guilty for letting your employer down. If your previous pregnancy ended in miscarriage, stillbirth, or neonatal death, you may feel like you are being disloyal to the baby you lost if you dare to love the new baby. Guilt, like its twin sister, worry, seems to go along with the experience of motherhood.

As you can see, it's possible to experience a whole kaleidoscope of emotions—sometimes simultaneously. Here's how some of the members of our parent panel reacted when they first discovered that they were pregnant:

▪ "On Christmas Eve 1992, I did the home pregnancy test. I was so excited I could barely contain myself. Finding out on Christmas Eve was so wonderful. I remember that night every year: the feelings I had inside—scared, excited, nervous. I was in heaven!" —Amie, 38, mother of two

■ "Even though I very much wanted to get pregnant, it was still difficult to accept the reality, when I did conceive, that I would be host to a fetus for nine months, and then have to give birth to it!" —Tracy, 31, mother of one

■ "Since I had just suffered a miscarriage and my period hadn't resumed, neither my husband nor I thought I was pregnant. I was over nine weeks pregnant when I finally took a blood test. The pregnancy didn't seem real until we saw our baby move her tiny arms and legs on ultrasound. Seeing a living, moving baby filled us both with incredible joy and awe and brought tears to our eyes." —Dawnette, 28, mother of one

■ "Our second pregnancy was the closest thing we had to having an unplanned pregnancy. It wasn't really, as we weren't taking precautions, but it did happen a little sooner than I expected. I struggled with coming to terms with being pregnant for the first few months." —Jacqueline, 34, pregnant with her second child

■ "We weren't planning this one. It just happened. We had previously discussed waiting until we were in a house and financially sound. It was stressful when we discovered we were pregnant." —Andrea, 34, mother of one

■ "Our pregnancy was unplanned—the result of failed contraception. It was a surprise and initially not a welcome one. We had been married two-and-a-half years, but had recently moved to New York City and were living in a tiny studio apartment. On top of that, I was five months into a new job. We were panicked and afraid at first, and briefly and irrationally considered not going forward with the pregnancy. After a couple of days, we had come to terms with the fact that we were going to be parents many years earlier than expected or planned. Now was as good a time as any, and fate brought us here." —Jennifer, 27, mother of one

▪ "The last pregnancy was unplanned. I conceived while using an IUD. I took the pregnancy test because I was four days late, and just wanted to rule out the possibility of pregnancy so that I could relax. Well, the test came back positive and I was in shock. This may sound horrible, but I bawled for almost an hour afterwards." —Erika, 25, pregnant with her third child

If you're like most women, you can expect your feelings about your pregnancy to fluctuate over the course of your pregnancy. The initial feelings of euphoria may ebb a little as reality kicks in and you stop to consider what taking a maternity leave may do to the household budget or your career. Likewise, your initial dismay at finding out that you are pregnant may start to lessen as you stop to consider all of the wonderful things that go along with having a baby.

If you're having difficulty adjusting to the idea of being pregnant, it's important to seek the services of a therapist. Your midwife or doctor should be able to put you in touch with someone who can help you or your partner work through your emotions.

Bright Idea
Get the scoop on working during pregnancy from women who've been there. Call the free job problems hotline operated by 9 to 5, the National Association for Working Women, at 800-522-0925. Write to 9 to 5, the National Association for Working Women, 614 Superior Avenue NW, Cleveland, OH 44113-1387, or call the Membership Hotline at 216-566-9308.

Telling your partner

You've no doubt seen the commercials on TV: a pregnant woman shows her partner the positive home pregnancy test result, and the two of them dance around the room.

Although scenes like this do get played out in some bedrooms across the country, in at least as many homes the scene is less than a scriptwriter's dream: for one reason or another, the partner is less than pleased by the fact that a baby is on the way.

Here are some examples of the types of reactions women on our parent panel encountered when they shared the news of their pregnancy with their partners—the good, the bad, and the ugly!

- "Finding out we were pregnant was not unlike the typical TV commercial. My partner [a woman] went and bought the pregnancy test. After being fully educated on all the different types of tests by the pharmacist—who, ironically, was male!—she chose one and we took our first test. It went according to script from there as we watched a pink line appear after two minutes. We were both ecstatic, with it being our first time with artificial insemination and our first child."
  —Michelle, 28, pregnant with her first child

- "I was late, but I also had a pretty irregular cycle, so when I saw two lines on the little stick, one of which was pretty pale, I wasn't sure I really was pregnant. I showed my husband and he said, 'You're definitely pregnant.' I think we were both pretty shocked and amazed for the next couple of hours." —Jennie, 30, pregnant with her first child

- "I told my husband when we went out to dinner. I had a pair of knit booties wrapped up in a small gift box, hoping he would understand without me having to say anything. I was so nervous. He opened the box, looked at it, and started to cry. Then he smiled." —Colleen, 29, mother of three

- "My husband was very hesitant to believe the news, based on a home pregnancy test, which was disappointing to me because at that point I was sure. However, when the doctor told us that they take positive home pregnancy tests as a 'yes,' he finally jumped for joy." —Wendy, 30, pregnant with her first child

- "He was out of town and I called him at 6:00 a.m. to tell him. He was very sleepy and kept saying, 'Are you sure? Maybe it's wrong.' I was very frustrated because I wanted him to be excited and he didn't believe it was real. He finally believed the test from the doctor's office, which was done about three days later." —Laura, 31, mother of one

- "I showed him the faint line. I had to convince him that it was positive. Then he asked to see the instructions to make sure I did it right! He was a lot more convinced two days later when he watched me take a test first thing in the morning and it showed a definite positive. He was very enthusiastic and has been ever since." —Melissa, 24, pregnant with her first child

- "All in all, I'd have to say that my husband was much more excited than I. Our doctor had indicated that it would probably take about three months to get pregnant, and I was counting on that time to adjust to the idea of being a mom." —Susan, 29, pregnant with her first child

- "My husband was home the morning I took the pregnancy test, eating breakfast and reading the newspaper. I tried to show him the stick, and he said, 'You peed on that, and I'm eating so keep it away.' He didn't even get up to hug me until I asked him to. He kept telling me not to get my hopes up, that it might be a false positive. He didn't see any reason to get excited or happy until the pregnancy was confirmed with a blood test." —Tracy, 31, mother of one

If your partner's reaction leaves you shaking your head, don't despair. As the months go on and your pregnancy begins to feel more "real," your partner will likely start to come around. It's quite common for men in particular to go through a bit of a crisis when their partners are pregnant.

If you'd like to share a lighter moment with your partner—not a bad idea if you're both feeling totally stressed by your impending parenthood!—check out BabyCenter's "Birth and Labor Conflict Catcher" at www.babycenter.com/conflicts/. This one-of-a-kind interactive pregnancy calendar allows sports fanatics to determine what athletic events they're likely to miss when their partner goes into labor. There's even a link to an interactive map so that your partner can plot out the shortest possible route between the hospital and the baseball stadium. If your partner ends up missing the World Series while you're in labor, don't be surprised if you find him using the conception planner to fine-tune the timing of your next round of baby making!

Telling friends and family

The first major pregnancy-related decision you and your partner will have to make is when to share your

Unofficially...
According to an article at thrive@ passion, found at www. thriveonline.com /sex/sheet. smarts.html, more than 114 million sex acts are performed each day around the world.

news with family and friends. Whereas pregnant women were once advised to keep their news to themselves until they were into their second trimester and had passed the peak risk period for miscarriages, most couples today choose to share their news shortly after the pregnancy test comes back positive.

Here's what some of the members of our parent panel had to say about announcing their pregnancies to family and friends. As you will see, some decided to announce their pregnancies right away; others chose to keep their news to themselves for a while:

- "The pregnancies were so much on my mind that it felt weird to be talking to a good friend or my sister and not tell her the most important thing that was happening in my life." —Johnna, 33, mother of three living children and a baby who was stillborn

- "We told everyone very early on and I regretted it. Problems of bleeding and threatened miscarriage were made worse by all the phone calls of concern. Of course, if anything tragic had happened, we would have needed their support, but the added stress of them worrying too made it harder on me." —Debbie, 38, mother of six

- "The first time around, I told everyone right away. I figured if anything went wrong, I'd want their support. When I had a miscarriage during my second pregnancy, I was glad of their kind words when things ended. When I got pregnant the third time, I told all my close friends right away but held off on telling casual acquaintances, whom it would be more awkward to 'untell.'" —Sarah, 31, mother of two

▪ "At first I was paranoid about telling before
three months, but the best advice came from my
midwife. She said that women who tell people
they're pregnant and then miscarry feel terrible
because people say insensitive things. And people who don't tell, and then lose the baby, feel
terrible because they don't have anyone to
mourn with. Either way, losing a baby is a terrible thing." —Jennie, 30, pregnant with her first
child

Once you tell one family member, you had better plan to hang up and hit speed-dial for the next
person on your list. News of pregnancies spreads
like wildfire in most families, and you don't want
the grandparents-to-be (particularly first-time
grandparents-to-be!) to hear the news from anyone
but you.

How to tell your boss

Telling family and friends is the easy part. The
toughest thing for many women is breaking the
news to their boss. Although there's no "right time"
to share your news, you increase your chances of
meeting with a positive response if you plan your
announcement carefully. Here are some tips on
deciding when—and how—to announce your pregnancy at work:

▪ Share your news with your boss before she hears
it from someone else. This doesn't mean that
you can't tell anyone else first: you just have to
be discreet. In fact, you may want to make a
point of getting the lowdown from coworkers
who have had babies recently. They should be
able to tell you how well or how poorly your boss
is likely to react and provide you with tips on

Bright Idea
Meet with your
supervisor or the
manager of
human resources
to find out what
pregnancy-
related benefits
are provided by
your company.
You may find
that the com-
pany designates
certain plum
parking spots for
women in their
third trimester of
pregnancy or
that the group
health insurance
plan covers the
services of a
doula (a profes-
sional labor-
support person).

breaking the news to her. They should also be able to give you the inside scoop on what concessions, if any, they were able to negotiate with the company (for example, a partially paid maternity leave or the ability to work part-time hours upon their return).

- If you think your boss will react negatively to your news, you might want to wait until you have passed the highest-risk period for miscarriage before announcing your pregnancy. That way, you won't end up causing waves at the office only to discover that you aren't going to need a maternity leave after all. Of course, if you are suffering from severe morning sickness or other pregnancy-related complications, you may have to spill the beans a little sooner that you had hoped in order to explain why you are late coming in each morning or why you have been taking so much time off for medical appointments.

- If you are expecting a performance or salary review in the near future, keep your news to yourself until it has been completed. That way, if the results of your review are less than what you'd hoped for, you won't have to wonder whether you're the victim of a subtle form of pregnancy discrimination.

- Time your announcement to coincide with a major achievement at work (such as the completion of a major project). That way, you can show your boss through actions rather than words that you are as productive and committed to your job as ever—thereby addressing a perennial fear of many employers.

■ Don't be afraid to postpone your announcement if your boss is having a bad day. If she is in a particularly foul mood or is scrambling to meet an important deadline, hold off on sharing your news until she's in a more receptive frame of mind.

■ Be prepared for a lukewarm reaction. Although your boss may be genuinely happy for you, she may be concerned about what your pregnancy may mean to the company. If yours is the first pregnancy she has had to deal with on the job, she's likely to be particularly apprehensive.

■ Be ready to talk about what work modifications, if any, may be required during your pregnancy. If you work in a hazardous environment—for example, an X-ray laboratory or a chemical manufacturing plant—you may need to ask to be reassigned to a different type of work for the duration of your pregnancy.

■ Don't make promises you can't keep—such as when you plan to take your maternity leave and how quickly you will return to work. Instead, simply agree to discuss these plans when your pregnancy is a little further along. (We'll be providing you with some pointers on planning your maternity leave in Chapter 15.)

Here's what some of the members of our parent panel had to say about how they handled announcing their pregnancies at work:

■ "I told my assistant and close friend at work right away, but waited until I was three months along before I told my boss. I just wanted to make sure that everything was okay before I let the cat out of the bag." —Kim, 35, mother of one

■ "I had just accepted a job offer the week before I found out I was pregnant. I kept the news to myself for about two months, until it started becoming obvious. I felt uneasy at first because I was pregnant when I was hired, even though I did not know it at the time. My employer took it well, but I had worked very hard for those two months to prove myself." —Jennifer, 28, mother of one

■ "I was scheduled to start a year-long project at work, so I had to tell my boss early on so that we could make some decisions about the project." —Anne, 33, pregnant with her first child

■ "I knew I would have to tell my staff as soon as I felt that the pregnancy was safe because they were beginning to pick up on some of my symptoms and were wondering why I was going to the doctor so often. I wanted to tell my boss before I told them, so I broke the news to him on a Monday and asked him to keep my secret until the following Friday so no one would have to find out through the grapevine. After telling my staff, I shared the news with my coworkers." —Susan, 29, pregnant with her first child

■ "I had to tell people at work as soon as I knew in order to avoid doing any X-rays." —Karen, 34, mother of three

■ "I was in the army during both pregnancies, and I told my supervisor immediately both times. There are certain things a soldier is not allowed to do when she is pregnant, and I wanted the baby and me to be safe." —Melanie, 39, mother of two

If you are self-employed, it's your clients rather than your boss that you have to share your news

Bright Idea
Compare notes with other self-employed moms in the "Work From Home Mothers" chat forum at www. ivillage.com.

with—something that can be scary, to say the least. Here's some advice from Suzi, 27, a self-employed mother of two:

"With my first baby, I told my clients right away. My thought was that if they had a problem with the fact that I was expecting, then I didn't need to be working with them. I also thought that it was the nineties and people didn't have a problem with a career woman having a baby. Unfortunately, I experienced a lot of problems by being so open about it with my professional contacts. I found that if clients knew, they thought that I was falling off the planet or something. They worried about their accounts, and if I was unavailable for a meeting or something fell through the cracks, they blamed it on the pregnancy—even though that was never a problem for me.

"With my second baby, I didn't tell a soul. Some of my clients to this day don't know that I had a baby last November! After the resistance I experienced with this first baby, I decided to keep my personal and professional lives completely separate."

Your rights as a pregnant employee

Although the days when you were expected to announce your pregnancy and hand in your resignation on the same day are long since gone, pregnancy discrimination is still alive and well in America. In 1994, the U.S. Equal Employment Opportunity Commission received 4,170 complaints of pregnancy discrimination—up from 3,000 in 1990.

Your employer is unlikely to fire you outright, but you could face subtler forms of discrimination in the workplace. You might, for example, be passed over for a promotion because someone in management thinks that you are unlikely to return to your job after your maternity leave. That's why you owe it to yourself to understand your rights under the law. That means familiarizing yourself with the provisions of the Pregnancy Discrimination Act and the Family and Medical Leave Act.

The Pregnancy Discrimination Act

The federal Pregnancy Discrimination Act of 1978 (an amendment to the Civil Rights Act of 1964) prohibits any type of discrimination on the basis of pregnancy in companies that have 15 or more employees. (Don't panic if you work for a two-person shop. In most cases, state legislation kicks in to provide similar protection to employees of smaller companies.)

Here's a brief summary of what the Pregnancy Discrimination Act means to you:

- **Hiring:** An employer cannot refuse to hire a woman solely because she is pregnant, provided that she is capable of fulfilling the major requirements of the job.

- **Pregnancy and Maternity Leave:** An employer may not introduce special procedures that in any way single out pregnant women. If, for example, a pregnant woman is temporarily unable to fulfill the requirements of her job due to her pregnancy, the employer must treat her in the same manner as any other temporarily disabled employee (provide modified tasks, alternative assignments, disability leave, or leave without pay—whatever the case may be). Pregnant women are also entitled to continue working as long as they are able to perform their jobs.

Watch Out!
If your employer's health insurance plan does not cover any preexisting medical conditions, you could be denied benefits for any medical costs arising from a pregnancy that occurred before the policy went into effect.

▪ **Health Insurance:** Any health insurance provided by an employer must treat expenses for pregnancy-related conditions in the same manner as costs for other medical conditions. In other words, pregnancy-related expenses should be reimbursed using the same formula used to calculate reimbursement for other types of medical expenses. What's more, employers must provide the same level of health coverage for spouses of male employees as they do for spouses of female employees.

▪ **Fringe Benefits:** Pregnancy-related benefits cannot be limited to married employees. What's more, any benefits provided to employees with other types of medical conditions must be extended to women with pregnancy-related conditions. Employees who are off work because of pregnancy-related disabilities must be treated in the same fashion as other temporarily disabled employees when it comes to such matters as the accrual and crediting of seniority, vacation calculations, pay increases, and temporary disability benefits.

If you think that you are being discriminated against because of your pregnancy, you should

▪ keep detailed notes on everything that happens, and keep copies of any e-mail messages or other correspondence that might support your claim;

▪ ask to review the contents of your personnel file, and make copies of anything that might help you make your case (for example, copies of particularly glowing performance appraisals);

▪ follow appropriate channels as much as possible, but be prepared to go to your company's human resources department or the U.S. Equal Employment Opportunity Commission (800-669-4000; www.eeoc.gov) if that's what it takes to ensure that your complaint is handled appropriately.

You can learn more about the provisions of the Pregnancy Discrimination Act of 1978 at www.eeoc.gov/facts/fs-preg.html or by calling 202-663-4900.

The family and medical leave act

The Family and Medical Leave Act (FMLA) of 1993 requires employers covered by the legislation to provide up to 12 weeks of unpaid, job-protected leave to employees for certain family and medical reasons.

The FMLA applies to all

- public agencies (including state, local, and federal employers, and schools) and

- private-sector employers who have (or had) 50 or more employees for 20 or more workweeks in either the current or the preceding calendar year and who are engaged in commerce.

To be eligible for benefits under the Act, you must

- work for an employer who is covered by the Act,

- have been employed by this employer for a total of at least 12 months,

- have worked at least 1,250 hours over the previous 12 months,

- have worked at a location that is either inside the United States itself or any of its territories or possessions, and where at least 50 employees are employed within a 75-mile area.

Bright Idea
Call the U.S. Equal Employment Opportunity Commission at 800-669-3362 to request your copy of *Facts About Pregnancy Discrimination,* and the Department of Labor at 800-827-5335 to request your copy of *Don't Work in the Dark,* a pamphlet that outlines your rights under the Family and Medical Leave Act (FMLA).

Timesaver
Some employers allow new parents to take their FMLA intermittently (for example, a few weeks now and a few weeks later) or use their FMLA entitlement to cut back on their usual daily or weekly working hours.

Eligible reasons for leave include

- giving birth to a baby,

- adopting a child,

- providing foster care to a child,

- caring for an immediate family member (your spouse, child, or parent) who has a serious health condition (that is, one requiring hospitalization or bedrest at home), or

- having a serious health condition (for example, complications of pregnancy).

In order to take the leave, you must

- provide your employer with 30 days' notice of your intention to take FMLA leave (assuming that it is possible to provide such notice),

- supply a medical certificate supporting the reason for your leave (if your employer requests it),

- obtain second and third medical opinions (if your employer requests it),

- have your doctor or midwife periodically report to your employer about your ability and intention to return to work (if your employer requests it).

Here's some additional fine print you need to know about:

- If you and your partner share the same employer, you are entitled to a combined total of 12 workweeks of family leave for the birth and care of a newborn child, to welcome an adopted or foster child, or to care for a parent who has a serious health condition.

- You must take your leave within 12 months of the birth, adoption, or foster-care placement of your child.

- During your leave, your employer is required to maintain your group health insurance coverage on the same terms as when you were at work. If you were required to pay for a portion of your insurance costs prior to your leave, you may still be expected to cover those costs while you are on leave. This could mean that you might be expected to fork over some hefty premiums during a period of time when you're not actually receiving a paycheck. What's more, if you decide not to return to work following FMLA leave, your employer could decide to recover the cost of any health-care premiums it paid while you were on leave.

- In most situations, when you return from leave, your employer must give you back your original job or an equivalent job with equivalent pay, benefits, and other terms and conditions of employment. What's more, you can't lose any employment benefits that you were entitled to prior to leave, nor can the time you took be counted against you under the provisions of the company's attendance policy.

- If you are deemed to be a "key" employee (that is, a highly paid employee whose reinstatement at the company following a period of leave may cause "substantial and grievous economic injury to its operations"), your employer may not be required to hire you back following your leave. If this provision applies to you, your employer must notify you in advance of your status as a "key" employee; inform you that it will not restore you to your original position, should you decide to take FMLA leave; explain the reasons for its decision; offer you a reasonable period of time in which to return to work (assuming that you're already on leave at the time the company designates you as a "key" employee); and make a final decision about whether you will get your old job back if you request such reinstatement in writing.

You can find more information about the provisions of the FLMA at www.dol.gov/dol/esa/fmla.htm.

Just the facts

- You may experience all—or none—of the following pregnancy symptoms: a missed period, an increased urge to urinate, fatigue, a heightened sense of smell, food aversions and cravings, morning sickness, breast changes, and cramping.

- Your due date is simply your doctor or midwife's best estimate of your baby's estimated time of arrival. You have about a 5% chance of actually delivering on your due date.

- Urine and blood tests for pregnancy detect the presence of human chorionic gonadotropin—a substance that is produced once the embryo implants in the uterus.

- You may experience a kaleidoscope of emotions when you discover that you are pregnant: elation, worry, and everything in between. Your emotions may fluctuate over the course of your pregnancy.

- Your partner may have similarly mixed feelings about the idea of becoming a parent.

- You may decide to share your news with family and friends right away—or keep it under wraps for a while.

- It's important to plan how—and when—to announce your pregnancy at work. As a rule of thumb, you should make sure that your boss hears the news from you rather than via the office grapevine.

- Bring yourself to speed about your rights as a pregnant employee by familiarizing yourself with the provisions of both the Pregnancy Discrimination Act and the Family and Medical Leave Act.

GET THE SCOOP ON...
Finding the caregiver who is right for you ▪
Choosing the birth environment that's right for
you ▪ Setting up your first prenatal appointment ▪ What to expect from the prenatal
workup

Choosing a Caregiver and a Place to Give Birth

N ow that you've had a chance to get used to the idea of being pregnant, you need to start making some important decisions about your pregnancy—such as finding a caregiver and deciding where you would like to give birth.

You have three basic options when it comes to choosing a caregiver: an obstetrician (a general obstetrician or one who has specialized training in high-risk pregnancy), a family physician (your family doctor), or a midwife (a certified nurse-midwife, a certified midwife, or a lay midwife). Although 80% of American women continue to turn to obstetricians for care during pregnancy, a growing number are using the services of certified nurse-midwives (CNMs). In fact, according to the U.S. Department of Health and Human Services, the number of CNM-attended births has grown from 19,686 in 1975 to 196,977 in 1994.

The growing interest in midwifery reflects a new view of birth as a natural process rather than an illness requiring a lot of medical intervention. In recent years, even the medical establishment itself has changed its way of managing low-risk pregnancy, recognizing that pregnant women and their partners want to play a more active role than ever before in planning the births of their babies.

Some women are choosing to give birth in places other than hospitals—the setting of choice since the end of World War II. Some are seeking birth centers (family-friendly facilities designed to meet the needs of laboring women and their families); others are choosing to give birth at home (the norm in America prior to World War II, but something that was almost unheard of during the years after the war).

Unofficially...
Midwives attend 5% of births in the United States and 75% of births in Europe.

In this chapter, we talk about the pros and cons of each of these options and give you the inside track on choosing both a caregiver and a birthing environment that are right for you. Then we tell you what to expect from your first prenatal appointment.

Finding the caregiver who is right for you

There are three basic options when it comes to caregivers: family physicians, obstetricians, and midwives.

Family physician

A family physician is a medical doctor who has had several years of specialized training in primary care, including obstetrics. He is interested in all aspects of your health and well-being, not just your obstetrical health.

Obstetrician

An obstetrician is a medical doctor who has received specialized training in obstetrics. Obstetricians typically handle high-risk pregnancies but are also the caregiver of choice for many women who are having low-risk pregnancies.

Midwife

The term *midwife* is an old Anglo-Saxon word meaning "with woman." That, in a nutshell, describes what midwives do: they are "with women" throughout pregnancy, labor, delivery, and the whole postpartum period.

Although midwives have been practicing for thousands of years in Europe and played a major role in birthing in America until the turn of the century, they've been relegated to the sidelines in America for the past 100 years. It was only in the late 1970s that midwifery care became an option once again.

It has taken even longer, however, for midwives to gain acceptance from the medical establishment: despite evidence to the contrary, some doctors continue to believe that midwives provide an inferior form of care. The facts speak for themselves. In 1992, the U.S. Department of Health and Human Services declared that the quality of care provided by midwives is "equivalent to physicians' care within their area of competence" and that midwives are "better than physicians at providing services which depend on communications with patients and preventative action."

Part of the image problem that midwifery faces is caused by the fact that the three types of midwives who practice in America—certified nurse-midwives (CNMs), certified midwives (CMs), and lay midwives—have varying degrees of expertise.

Consider the facts for yourself.

Certified nurse-midwives are registered nurses who have been specially trained to care for women

Timesaver
You can get the lowdown on state-specific laws concerning certified nurse-midwives at www.acnm.org/press/stfacts.htm or by calling the American College of Nurse Midwives at 202-728-9860.

with low-risk pregnancies. To earn the designation CNM, a nurse must have received additional training in midwifery and passed a national certification examination administered by the American College of Nurse-Midwives Certification Council (ACC). She must also have met strict requirements established by state and health-regulatory agencies. Here's what you need to know about clinical nurse-midwives:

- CNMs can practice legally in all 50 states and the District of Columbia.

- Their services are covered by Medicaid, and 31 states have laws that require that private insurance companies pay for their services.

- They have prescription-writing authority in 41 states.

- The majority of CNMs work in hospitals or birth centers, but a few attend home births: in 1993, approximately 95% of CNM-attended births took place in hospitals, 3% at birth centers, and 1% at home.

- Many midwives also provide "well-woman" care: gynecological services such as pelvic and breast exams and Pap smears; family-planning assistance; and lifestyle counselling.

A certified midwife, on the other hand, is someone with a background in a health-related field other than nursing who has received specialized training through a midwifery education program accredited by the American College of Nurse-Midwives Division of Accreditation. She is required to pass the same national certification exam as a CNM but receives the professional designation certified midwife instead. Certified midwives are not allowed to practice in certain states.

Lay midwives (also called independent midwives or direct entry midwives) are midwives who have learned their skills by apprenticing with other midwives. They have not received any formal training in midwifery. Lay midwives are illegal in certain states. (You can get an update on the latest changes to state laws concerning direct entry midwives at www.mana.org/region.html; or 888-923-6262.)

Once you've decided on the type of caregiver you would like to have, it's time to find the person who is right for you. If you're sticking with your present family physician or obstetrician, your search is over. If you intend to change doctors or use the services of a midwife, you will need to do some further research.

You might wish to consult the following sources as you begin your search for a family physician, obstetrician, or midwife:

- your insurance company or HMO (to find out which doctors and midwives in your community are fully covered, partially covered, or not covered at all under the plan);

- other women you know who have recently given birth and who have birthing philosophies similar to your own;

- your family doctor, pediatrician, or gynecologist (if she does not do deliveries);

- an obstetrical nurse, childbirth educator, lactation consultant, or other person who knows many of the doctors and midwives in practice in your community;

- the county medical society;

- the staff of the birthing unit at the hospital at which you would like to deliver;

Unofficially...
According to a recent study reported in the *American Journal of Public Health*, women with low-risk pregnancies experience fewer medical interventions when they are in the care of a midwife than when they are being cared for by either an obstetrician or a family physician.

- the staff of your local birth center (if you have one);
- the American College of Obstetricians and Gynecologists (202-638-5577; www.acog.org);
- the American College of Nurse-Midwives (888-MIDWIFE or 202-728-9860; www.acnm.org/);
- the Association for Childbirth at Home International (213-667-0839) or the Midwives' Alliance of North America (lay midwives) (615-964-2394; www.mana.org/).

Once you've settled on a doctor or midwife, you should set up an appointment to meet with this person and decide whether, in fact, his birthing philosophy and approach to care are compatible with your own. Be sure to bring a list of questions with you to the appointment. (See the following checklist.)

CHECKLIST: WHAT TO ASK A DOCTOR OR MIDWIFE

About the practice

- How long have you been in practice? How many babies have you delivered?
- Are you certified by the American Board of Obstetrics and Gynecology, the American Board of Family Practice, or the American College of Nurse-Midwives?
- Do you have

    ___ a solo medical practice (a single doctor or midwife plus her support staff);

    ___ a partnership or group medical practice (two or more doctors share patients, costs, and space);

    ___ a combination practice (one or more obstetricians and one or more midwives and other specialists work cooperatively);

Note! ➜
You won't have time to ask all these questions, so just zero in on the ones that are most important to you and that can be answered only by the doctor or midwife herself. You can always follow up with members of the doctor's or midwife's support staff to ask the nuts-and-bolts questions later.

___ a maternity or birth-center practice (certified nurse-midwives provide majority of care, but physicians are available if they are needed); or

___ an independent certified nurse-midwife practice (midwives work on their own but have a physician backup available for consultation and emergency care)?

- Who other than you might be present at the birth? Will I have the opportunity to meet the backup caregiver before I go into labor?

- How will I get in touch with you in an emergency? Are there times when you are unavailable? If so, whom would I call in that situation?

- Will you be available to take my non-emergency phone calls during working hours? If you are not available, who will be able to answer my questions or address my concerns?

- What is your call schedule? Will you be available around the time I am due to deliver my baby?

- What percentage of your patients' babies do you deliver yourself?

- Do you use residents or interns as part of your practice?

- What hospital(s) and/or birth center(s) are you affiliated with?

- Do you attend home births?

- What proportion of your fees are likely to be covered by my insurance company or HMO?

Approaches to pregnancy

- What is your recommended schedule of prenatal visits? How long do you set aside for each appointment?

- What tests will you order during my pregnancy (ultrasound, amniocentesis, genetic screening, and so on)? What if I have a concern about a certain test?

- Under what circumstances, if any, would you need to transfer me into the care of another health-care practitioner? (That is, if you develop certain types of complications, will the caregiver be able to manage these complications, or will you be transferred to someone else?)

- Under what circumstances do you induce labor?

Approaches to birth

- How do you feel about the fact that we intend to prepare a birth plan? Will you set aside time to review our birth plan before the onset of labor?

- How much time will you spend with me when I'm in labor?

- Do the majority of women in your practice have medicated or nonmedicated births? What percentage have epidurals?

- What are your thoughts on natural childbirth?

- How would you feel if I wanted to use the services of a doula or other support person?

- In what positions do most of the women in your practice labor and give birth?

- What percentage of women are induced?

- Do you routinely use electronic fetal monitoring during labor?

- What percentage of women in your practice have episiotomies?

- What percentage of women in your practice have cesareans?

- What percentage of women attempting a VBAC (vaginal birth after cesarean) manage to deliver vaginally?

- Do you allow labor support people other than the father to be present at the birth?

- Will my baby and I be separated after the birth?

- Do you provide breastfeeding support and/or postpartum care?

Choosing the birth environment that's right for you

If you have your heart set on giving birth in a particular setting—that is, in a birth center, at a specific hospital, or at home—you will need to decide on the birthing environment before you finalize your choice of a caregiver. This is because most caregivers have privileges only at a particular hospital or birth center, and the majority are unwilling to attend home births at all.

You have three basic choices of location for giving birth: a hospital, a birth center, and your own home. Let's quickly run through the pros and cons of each of these options.

Hospital

Not all hospitals are created equal. Some are extremely family-friendly; others are not. Some boast state-of-the-art obstetrical facilities; others do not. That said, it's important to consider the basic pros and cons of giving birth in a hospital when weighing various options.

Pros:

- All the high-tech bells and whistles are there if you or your baby needs them, and you can be prepped for an emergency c-section in a matter

Unofficially...
Prior to 1900, 95% of Americans were born at home. Today, only 2% to 3% of women give birth at home.

Bright Idea
The Coalition for Improving Maternity Services (CIMS) has a Web site (www.healthy. net/cims) and guidelines for mother-friendly birth locations and services.

of minutes. Most doctors and midwives agree that a hospital is the safest place to give birth if your pregnancy is considered high-risk because of a pre-existing medical condition, complications of pregnancy, or previous birth-related complications. There's just one small caveat: complications can develop—sometimes within a matter of minutes. When one of these unanticipated emergencies arises, the best place to be is in a hospital. That's why most doctors argue that the safest place to give birth is in a hospital, period.

- You have more options for pain relief with a hospital birth than with a birth-center delivery or home birth.

- A growing number of hospitals are introducing family-friendly birthing facilities that allow women to labor, deliver, and receive postpartum care in the same room (as opposed to laboring in one room, delivering in another, recovering in a third, and then moving to the postpartum floor for the duration of your stay—the norm in days gone by). Some hospitals have even introduced alternative birth centers (also called family birth centers or 24-hour suites); these consist of a group of rooms for the family's use during labor: living room, small kitchen, private bath, birthing room.

Cons:

- Despite efforts to create a warmer, more intimate setting, many labor and delivery wards continue to have a sterile, clinical atmosphere.

- Rigid or archaic hospital policies may leave you and your partner feeling as though you have little or no control over the process of giving birth.

- If the technology is there, it may be used, whether you need it or not. Studies have shown that women giving birth in a hospital can be subjected needlessly to such interventions as artificial rupture of membranes (AROM), fetal monitoring, augmentation of labor, and cesarean sections.

- A hospital delivery is more expensive than a birth-center delivery or home birth, averaging $8,000 for an uncomplicated birth. You pay for all that high-tech equipment even if you have a low-tech delivery.

If you think you would like to give birth in a particular hospital, arrange to take a tour before you make up your mind. Sometimes hospitals that claim to be family-friendly are anything but. Our Hospital Checklist will give you an idea of what to look for—and what to ask—while you take your tour. (Once again, you may not wish to ask all the questions on the checklist. Ask as few or as many as you wish—and don't be afraid to follow up with a phone call after your visit if there are some points you wish to clarify with hospital staff.)

CHECKLIST: HOSPITAL

Location

- Is the hospital located relatively close to your home?

- How long would it take you to get there during rush-hour traffic?

- Is the parking lot designed to allow laboring women and their partners easy access to the building?

> **"**
> I got a detailed list of my in-hospital charges after my first delivery and was shocked to see that a pad cost $10 and Tylenol was $3 per dose! With my second baby, I packed my own pads, Tylenol, and diapers for the baby.
> —Suzi, 27, mother of two
> **"**

Costs

- What percentage of costs are covered by your insurance company or HMO?

- What are the payment terms for your portion of the costs?

- Does the hospital have a written description of its services and fees?

- Are staff members available to help you obtain financial assistance if you need it?

Expertise/accreditation

- Is the hospital

  ___ a level I facility or primary-care center (a hospital that provides services to low-risk clients);

  ___ a level II or secondary-care center (a hospital that is able to provide care to both low-risk clients and clients with about 90% of maternal or neonatal complications); or

  ___ a level III facility or tertiary-care center (a hospital that provides care to high-risk clients who require highly sophisticated types of medical and technical interventions)?

- Do the services and specialties of the hospital meet your specific medical needs? (In other words, if yours is a high-risk pregnancy, are the staff up to the challenge of meeting the needs of you and your baby?)

- Is the hospital accredited by a nationally recognized accrediting body such as the Joint Commission on Accreditation of Healthcare Organizations (630-792-5800; www.jcaho.org)?

Hospital staff

- Are the staff on the labor and delivery floor friendly and willing to answer your questions?

- Do they seem to be genuinely interested in helping you to have the type of birth experience you want, as specified in your birth plan?

- How receptive are they to any special requests you may have (bringing a doula or other support person with you to the birth, for example)?

- Are they comfortable dealing with any special circumstances related to your situation (if you're a single mother or part of a lesbian couple, for example)?

- Is the labor and delivery floor adequately staffed? How many laboring women does each nurse care for?

- Is there an anesthetist at the hospital 24 hours a day, or does someone have to be called if an emergency occurs in the middle of the night?

- Are midwives available?

- What is the hospital's cesarean rate? (This may not be relevant if you are under the care of a physician whose own rate varies significantly from the hospital average.)

- What are the policies that promote nonseparation of mother and baby after the birth?

- Is an anesthesiologist available around the clock in case you need an emergency cesarean section?

Labor policies and procedures

- Does the hospital offer its own childbirth preparation classes to parents who will be delivering

← Note!
Certain states, including Massachusetts and New York, require that hospitals provide consumers with information on their cesarean rates upon request. You can find out if such a law exists in your state by contacting the Public Citizen's Health Research Group at 202-833-3000.

there to familiarize them with hospital policies and procedures?

- Does the hospital invite you to prepare an individualized birthing plan that specifies your hopes and desires for the birth and your thoughts on such issues as medication, epidurals, and episiotomy? (You can find the template for a birth plan in Appendix D, "Important Documents.")

- Does the hospital have facilities for water birth?

- Are there limits on the number of labor support people who are allowed to be present at the birth?

- Are children permitted to be present at the birth? If so, does the hospital offer any special sibling preparation classes?

- Can photos and videos be taken during the birth?

- Are women in labor encouraged to walk around or to try other labor positions in an effort to help nature along?

- Are you allowed to eat or drink once you are in labor?

- Under what circumstances might your labor support person be required to leave the room (if fetal distress necessitates an emergency cesarean, for example)?

- Are labor support people allowed to be with you in the operating room and the recovery room if you have a cesarean?

- What are the hospital's policies toward active management of labor (for example, interventions in the event that labor doesn't progress at the hospital's prescribed rate)?

■ What procedures are performed routinely during labor?

___ Enemas?

___ IVs?

___ Pubic shaving?

___ External and/or internal fetal monitoring?

___ Artificial rupture of membranes (AROM)?

■ What are the hospital's policies regarding the use of intravenous lines? Can the IV unit be converted to a heparin lock (a device that allows you to be temporarily disconnected from the IV unit to allow you more freedom to move around)?

■ What are the hospital's policies regarding the use of epidurals and pain medications during labor?

■ Does the hospital offer so-called "walking epidurals" (that is, the use of narcotic pain medication through the epidural catheter as opposed to anesthetic, so as not to cause numbness or weakness in the legs)?

■ What is the hospital's cesarean rate? How does this compare to the national average of 25%–30%? Under what circumstances are cesarean sections performed at this hospital?

■ Under what circumstances might you be required to be moved from a labor room to a delivery room? Does the hospital require that all women move from labor rooms to delivery rooms as their labor progresses, or does the hospital use birthing rooms (that is, rooms that

← Note!
More important by far than the hospital's cesarean rate, of course, is the cesarean rate of the attending obstetrician, but even that stat isn't as clear-cut as you might think. An obstetrician's cesarean rate is as much determined by the nature of his practice—that is, the number of high-risk patients that he takes on—as by his individual tendency to resort to cesareans.

are designed to be used for both labor and delivery)?

■ Will the baby be given to you immediately after birth (assuming, of course, that the baby doesn't require any special care)?

■ Who is responsible for examining the newborn upon delivery?

____ The midwife or doctor delivering the baby?

____ The pediatrician of your choosing?

____ The pediatrician who happens to be on call at the time?

■ What procedures are performed on the baby shortly after birth?

____ Apgar testing?

____ Vitamin K injections?

____ Placing antibacterial drops into the baby's eyes?

____ Suctioning of the baby's nose and throat?

■ Which of these procedures are required by the state or province?

■ What are the hospital's policies in the event that you and your partner decide to decline procedures, such as vitamin K injections or antibacterial drops in the baby's eyes?

■ Can the newborn examination be conducted in the birthing room while the baby is resting on his mother's breast, or does the baby have to be taken somewhere else? If the baby needs to be moved, can one or both of the parents accompany the baby?

- Can any of these procedures be delayed until after the parents have had some time to bond with the baby?

- If you are choosing to breastfeed, will you be encouraged to breastfeed your baby as soon as possible following the birth?

Birthing facilities

- Does the hospital have birthing rooms, or labor, delivery, recovery rooms (LDR, a room where the mother labors, gives birth, and recovers for an hour so after the delivery)? (The two terms are often used interchangeably.)

- Does the hospital have labor, delivery, recovery, postpartum (LDRP) rooms (that is, a room in which the mother labors, gives birth, recovers, and then remains throughout her hospital stay)?

- Does the hospital have an alternative birth center (ABC) (that is, a homelike suite of rooms for the use of the woman and her family)?

- Are the birthing rooms fully equipped to handle any emergencies that may arise?

- Are the birthing rooms designed to give you and your partner as much privacy as possible? Is there more than one bed in each room? Is it possible that you will have to share your room with another laboring woman? Is there a place where your partner can rest (a bed or pull-out cot)?

- Will you have your own bathroom, or will you have to share one with another laboring woman?

Watch Out!
The most progressive hospital policies in the world mean nothing if your caregiver doesn't choose to follow them. Make sure you and your caregiver are on the same wavelength when it comes to issues such as having other people present at the birth and your desire to remain mobile during labor.

- Are the birthing rooms attractive and homelike, or clinical and sterile? Do they look like a place where you would want to give birth?

- Are the rooms large enough for you to be able to move around while you're in labor?

- Do the birthing rooms have any amenities, such as birthing stools, squatting bars, showers, over-sized bathtubs, or Jacuzzis you can use while you are in labor?

- Are all birthing rooms in the unit equally well equipped, or are there a few older rooms that lack some of these amenities?

- Is there a phone you can use to call family and friends during labor or after the birth?

Nursery facilities

- How extensive are the hospital's intensive care facilities?

- If your baby was born with a serious birth defect or develops respiratory or other problems after delivery, would he have to be transported else-where to receive specialized care?

- What safety procedures does the hospital have in place to ensure that your baby is released only to you and your partner?

Postpartum floor

- How many private rooms are available?

- What are the costs of private, semiprivate, and ward rooms?

- Is rooming-in available (that is, the baby stays with the mother)?

- Can your partner stay at the hospital overnight if the two of you want to spend some time together with your new baby?

- Is there a shower in each room, or do you need to use shared shower facilities down the hall? Who will watch your baby while you're in the shower?

- What are the hospital's policies regarding visiting hours? Are there different hours for members of your immediate family as opposed to other relatives and friends?

Postpartum care

- What will the hospital do to support your decision to breastfeed your baby? Do they follow "baby-friendly" guidelines?

- If you choose to bottle-feed, will this choice be respected as well?

- Are lactation experts available to help troubleshoot any breastfeeding problems?

- How much instruction on newborn care is provided to new moms? Are you allowed to phone the postpartum floor after discharge to ask any questions that might occur to you once you're home?

Birth center

Birth centers (also called childbearing centers, birthing centers, or alternative birth centers) are homelike facilities that provide care during pregnancy, labor, birth, and the first few hours postpartum. The birth-center movement started in the 1970s, when women began to demand more control over the process of giving birth.

Unofficially...
At New Milford Hospital in Connecticut, new mothers are offered a complimentary full-body massage to soothe aching postpartum muscles and, with their partners, an elegant, private candelit dinner for two on their final night at the hospital.

Bright Idea
Read up on
birth centers
at www.
BirthCenters.org.

Pros:

- Birth centers provide a relaxed, family-friendly setting. You can wear your own clothing, eat and drink when you're hungry, have a shower or bath if you'd like, and have friends and family present for the birth if that is your choice.

- Many birth centers offer such amenities as whirlpool baths and special birthing chairs.

- You're less likely to end up with a c-section if you deliver in a birth center. According to the National Birth Center Study, the cesarean rate for mothers using birth centers is 4.4% as opposed to the national average of 25%. Although most of the low rate can be explained by the fact that women with high-risk pregnancies are not permitted to use birth centers, it's an impressive statistic nonetheless.

Cons:

- Birth centers aren't available in all communities, so you might not even have the option of using one.

- If you run into an unexpected emergency during your delivery, you will have to be transported to a nearby hospital. The time you lose in transit could adversely affect the well-being of you or your baby, which explains why many caregivers believe that birth centers don't provide as safe an option as hospitals.

- Birth centers are not equipped to care for women with high-risk pregnancies. The definition of high risk is often very broad and may prevent you from delivering in a birth center, even if you and your baby are perfectly healthy. If you pass the center's initial screening process but pregnancy complications do arise, you may be required to give birth somewhere other than at the center.

- Most birth centers are unable to offer their clients any type of pharmacological pain relief. Analgesics are a rare commodity, and epidurals are non-existent. However, the staff will focus on a variety of other non-interventive methods of pain relief.

- You will be expected to leave the birth center shortly after you give birth. Birth-center clients are expected to do their recuperating at home.

- Some insurance companies and HMOs refuse to cover the costs of birth-center deliveries. This means that you could be out of pocket to the tune of $3,000.

Assuming that you're fortunate enough to have the option of giving birth in a birth center, you will want to conduct a tour of the facility before settling on this particular birthing environment. You can find some suggested questions in our Birth-Center Checklist.

Timesaver
Don't waste your time checking out a birth center if you have a serious health condition or a history of pregnancy complications (other than miscarriage) or birth-related problems. You're unlikely to be given permission to give birth at the center.

CHECKLIST: BIRTH CENTER

If you ask the birth center to mail you information before you go on your tour, you'll be able to answer many of these questions for yourself.

Administrative issues

- How close to your home is the birth center?

- How long would it take you to get there during rush-hour traffic?

- Is the parking lot designed to allow laboring women and their partners easy access to the building?

- In the event that you required an emergency cesarean section or you or your baby required other emergency care, how long would it take for you to be transported by ambulance to the closest hospital? What might the risks be to you and your baby?

- What is the birth center's rate for transfer of care? (A rating of 5% or higher may suggest that the center isn't screening its clients carefully enough.)

- What percentage of costs is covered by your insurance company or HMO? What are the payment terms for your portion of the costs?

Birth-center credentials

- Is the birth center licensed by the state or province? (Check with your state department of health, or your provincial health ministry if you're in Canada.)

- Is the center a member of the National Association of Childbearing Centers (215-234-8068)? Has it been accredited by the Commission for the Accreditation of Birth Centers (an independent accrediting authority established by NACC)?

- Is the center affiliated with any hospitals? If so, which ones?

Birth-center staff

- What are the professional credentials of the birth-center staff? Who will actually deliver your baby?

- Are the birth-center staff friendly and willing to answer your questions?

- Do they seem to be genuinely interested in helping you have the type of birth experience you want, as specified in your birth plan?

- How receptive are they to any special requests you may have (bringing a doula or other support person with you to the birth, for example)?

- Are they comfortable dealing with any special circumstances related to your situation (if you're a single mother or part of a lesbian couple, for example)?

- Is the birth center adequately staffed?

Birthing policies and procedures

- What policies are in place to ensure that you're a good candidate for a birth-center delivery rather than a hospital delivery?

- Does the birth center offer its own childbirth preparation classes to familiarize parents who will be delivering there with birth-center policies and procedures?

- Are there limits on the number of labor support people who are allowed to be present at the birth?

- Are children permitted to be present at the birth? If so, does the birth center offer any special sibling preparation classes?

- Can photos and videos be taken during the birth?

- Are women in labor encouraged to walk around or to try other labor positions in an effort to help nature along?

- Do you have facilities for water births?

- Under what circumstances would you and/or your baby be transported to a nearby hospital?

- What types of procedures are performed routinely during labor?

- What diagnostic equipment is available?

- Are any pain medications available to laboring women? What about anesthesia?

- Will the baby be given to you immediately after birth (assuming, of course, that the baby doesn't require any special care)?

- Who is responsible for examining the newborn upon delivery?

- What procedures are performed on the baby shortly after birth?

  ___ Apgar testing?

  ___ Vitamin K injections?

  ___ Placing antibacterial drops into the baby's eyes?

  ___ Suctioning of the baby's nose and throat?

- Which of these procedures are required by the state or province?

- Can the newborn examination be conducted in the birthing room while the baby is resting on her mother's breast, or does the baby have to be taken somewhere else? If the baby needs to be moved, can one or both of the parents accompany the baby?

- Will you be encouraged to breastfeed your baby as soon as possible following the birth?

- How soon after the delivery will you be encouraged to go home? What is the maximum period of time you will be allowed to stay there?

Birthing rooms

- Are the birthing rooms fully equipped to handle any emergencies that may arise?

- Are the birthing rooms designed to give you and your partner as much privacy as possible? Is there more than one bed in each room?

- Are the birthing rooms attractive and homelike, or clinical and sterile? Do they look like a place where you would want to give birth?

- Are the rooms large enough for you to be able to move around while you're in labor?

- Will you have your own bathroom, or will you have to share one with another laboring woman?

- Do the birthing rooms have any amenities, such as birthing stools, squatting bars, and Jacuzzis, you can use while you are in labor?

- Are all birthing rooms in the unit equally well equipped, or are there a few older rooms that lack some of these amenities?

- Is there a phone you can use to call family and friends during labor or after the birth?

Home birth

There's no denying it: women have been giving birth at home for thousands of years, and the majority of babies born in the world today are born at home. If you are in the care of a qualified doctor or midwife and you are able to get to a hospital quickly, a home birth is no more dangerous than a birth-center delivery, but it isn't as safe as a hospital delivery, given the fact that unexpected complications can and do arise. Although some women choose to have their babies at home, home birth isn't the best option for everyone. You should consider a home birth only if

- you are in good overall health;

- your pregnancy can be characterized as low risk (that is, your baby is neither premature nor postmature; you haven't developed any complications of pregnancy, such as preeclampsia or gestational diabetes; your baby is in a head-down position; and you are giving birth to one baby rather than multiples);

Note! ➜
The fact that previous pregnancies have been problem free is no guarantee that subsequent pregnancies will be risk free. There is always an element of risk with any delivery, regardless of the setting in which you choose to give birth.

- there are no red flags in your obstetrical history (for example, you don't have a history of difficult delivery of the baby's shoulders or one that required the use of forceps or vacuum extraction; or a history of cesarean section, maternal hemorrhage, or stillbirth);

- you are willing to take the responsibility for the full range of home birth preparations, from buying all the supplies needed for labor and delivery to priming yourself physically and mentally for the birth itself;

- you have a doctor or certified nurse-midwife who is willing to attend a home birth and who has access to the appropriate emergency medical supplies (oxygen, resuscitation equipment, and so on);

- your home is reasonably close to a hospital, given road conditions (for example, about 10 minutes away);

- you are prepared to head to the hospital immediately if any sort of complication arises;

- your partner and/or children are comfortable with the idea of a birth at home;

■ you have support people available to help before, during, and after the birth.

Even if you're an ideal candidate for a home birth, unexpected complications can and do arise. Here are some situations that might necessitate a trip to the hospital:

■ a prolapsed cord (an emergency situation in which the umbilical cord precedes the baby's head in the birth canal, potentially leading to severe brain damage or death);

■ undetected placenta previa (when the placenta blocks all or a portion of the cervix, preventing the baby from exiting) or a placental abruption (when the placenta detaches from the uterine wall prematurely, potentially causing fetal death or maternal hemorrhage);

■ poor fetal heart rate (when the baby's heart rate is too slow—under 100 beats per minute—or too fast—over 180, something that may indicate fetal distress);

■ your amniotic fluid is greenish or brownish when your membranes rupture—a sign that your baby has passed her first stool (meconium) and could be in distress;

■ you are experiencing a prolonged labor that doesn't appear to be going anywhere or it's been more than 18 hours since your membranes ruptured;

■ your baby has moved into a breech position (bottom first) or transverse position (across your middle) and will need to be either turned or delivered by cesarean section;

■ your newborn is blue, limp, and not breathing, and requires specialized medical attention in a

Moneysaver
Insurance companies and HMOs do not generally cover the costs of home births. Make sure that you understand in advance what type of fee you will be required to pay to the person attending your birth. It could be as much as $2,000—possibly even more.

neonatal intensive care unit after being revived at home by the attending doctor or midwife;

■ the placenta has not been delivered within an hour of the birth of the baby, or your body has retained pieces of the placenta;

■ you have received some tears to the perineum, vagina, or cervix that cannot be repaired at home;

■ you experience a maternal hemorrhage after birth (either a great gush or a continuous flow of blood).

Now that we've considered who's a good candidate for home birth, and who's not, let's quickly run through the pros and cons of giving birth at home:

Pros:

■ A home birth tends to be a more intimate experience than a hospital birth. You give birth in the privacy of your own home surrounded only by those people you invite to the birth.

■ There's no need to drive to a hospital or birthing center while you're in labor.

■ You're in control of your birth experience. You can move around and labor in any position that feels comfortable, and you can follow your body's own schedule when it comes to eating and sleeping.

■ Because you are likely to be more relaxed laboring in your own home than in a hospital or birth center, you may be able to work with your body, thereby enabling your labor to progress more efficiently and with less pain, even though you don't actually have access to medical pain relief.

Note! ➜
Don't assume that you have to give birth at home in order to be in control of your birth experience. Many birth centers and even hospital birthing units can offer this kind of freedom and flexibility.

- You avoid the possibility of being infected by the types of highly resistant germs that live in hospitals and other health-care facilities.

- You are less likely to be subjected to unwanted interventions such as intravenous feeding, electronic fetal monitoring, and hormonal augmentation of labor if you don't give birth within a certain time frame.

Cons:

- If a rare but critical emergency arises during the delivery, you or your baby could be at risk. It may not be possible to transport the two of you to the hospital in time, even if the hospital is just minutes away.

- Home birth is meant for women with low-risk pregnancies, and it's impossible to guarantee in advance that a particular pregnancy and delivery will remain low-risk. If you develop pregnancy- or birth-related complications, you may have to abandon your plans for a home birth—possibly at the eleventh hour.

- You need to equip your home with the necessary supplies to give birth—something that a hospital or birthing center will do for you. Although you're likely to have many of these supplies in your home anyway, you will have to spend a bit of money on a few odds and ends. (See the Home Birth Supplies Checklist.)

CHECKLIST: HOME BIRTH SUPPLIES

If you decide to have a home birth, you will need to have the following supplies on hand:

- two sets of clean sheets (one for during the birth and one for after the birth)

Note! ➜
Shower curtains or large plastic tablecloths make excellent water-proof sheets.

- a waterproof pad or sheet to prevent the mattress from being damaged

- disposable absorbent pads or large diapers to place underneath the mother

- clean towels and washcloths

- sterile gauze pads

- a dozen pairs of sterile disposable gloves

- umbilical-cord clamps

- a three-ounce bulb syringe for suctioning mucus from the baby's mouth and nose

- a large bowl to catch the placenta

- receiving blankets for the newborn baby

- sanitary napkins

If you are planning a water birth at home (see Chapter 17), you will also need

Watch Out!
An unplanned home birth is not a safe option. If you're planning to give birth at home, you need to hire a competent caregiver and devote the time and effort necessary to prepare for the birth. That means getting the necessary prenatal care and ensuring that you are, in fact, a good candidate for home birth.

- a suitable birthing tub (a hot tub, Jacuzzi, bathtub, or portable tub)

- an accurate water thermometer (to ensure that the temperature stays between 99°F and 101°F

- an underwater flashlight to allow the caregiver to view the birth

- an inflatable plastic pillow so that you can stay comfortable

- a fish net to catch any remnants from the birth or other debris

- clean towels

When to set up your first appointment

Up until quite recently, pregnant women were not seen by their health-care providers until the end of the first trimester (approximately 12 weeks after the start of their last menstrual period). It was argued that there was no point in scheduling that initial visit until the risk of miscarriage had passed.

Today we know better. Study after study has demonstrated the benefits of first-trimester prenatal care. That's why most doctors and midwives recommend that you be seen as soon as you realize that you are pregnant—typically 6 to 10 weeks after the start of your last menstrual period. This is particularly important if you haven't been in to see your doctor or midwife for a prepregnancy consultation.

Timesaver
Phone your doctor's or midwife's office before you leave home to find out if he is running on schedule.

What to expect from your prenatal workup

During your first prenatal checkup, your doctor or midwife will

- confirm your pregnancy with a urine test, blood test, and/or physical examination;

- estimate your due date by considering such factors as the types of pregnancy symptoms you are experiencing and when they first occurred, the date of your last normal menstrual period, the results of ovulation predictor tests you used or any temperature charts you kept, and changes to the cervix and uterus;

- take a general medical history or review the findings from your preconception checkup (see Chapter 1);

- take an obstetrical history (assuming, of course, that you have had other pregnancies);

- conduct a general physical exam (heart, lungs, breasts, abdomen, and so on);

- conduct a pelvic exam (a visual examination of your vagina and cervix, as well as a bimanual exam of your pelvic organs);

- do a blood test to check for anemia, hepatitis B, HIV, syphilis, and antibodies to rubella, as well as certain genetic diseases (for example, sickle-cell anemia or Tay-Sachs disease), if your history warrants it;

- take a vaginal culture to check for the presence of infection, if warranted;

- do a Pap smear to check for cervical cancer or potential pre-cancer;

- check your urine for infection, sugar, and protein;

- weigh you to establish a baseline weight;

- take your blood pressure;

- provide you with advice on nutrition and lifestyle issues;

- answer any questions you may have;

- talk to you about how you are feeling about being pregnant.

You can expect to see your doctor or midwife again in about a month's time. You'll continue to see her at monthly intervals until you reach week 28, at which point you'll start coming for checkups every two to three weeks. Once you reach week 36, you will generally be seen weekly.

Your prenatal record

Doctors and midwives are required by law to keep detailed records for their maternity patients. Each time you go for a prenatal visit, your doctor or midwife records the pertinent facts about your pregnancy on your prenatal record. (See the following table.)

Here are some of the terms and abbreviations that may turn up on your prenatal record:

Watch Out!
Your weight can fluctuate significantly if you wear different amounts and types of clothing to subsequent prenatal check-ups. Try as much as possible to wear the same type of clothing to each appointment. Sudden weight gain can indicate that you are retaining fluid and possibly developing a condition called preeclampsia.

DECODING YOUR PRENATAL RECORD

Your obstetrical history

Para 1011   This is your doctor's or midwife's way of summarizing your obstetrical history. The first digit (in this case "1") represents the total number of full-term births. The second digit ("0") indicates the number of preterm births. The third digit ("1") represents the total number of miscarriages, abortions, and ectopic pregnancies. The fourth digit ("1") indicates the total number of living children. Therefore, a woman who is para 1011 has had one full-term birth; has had one miscarriage, abortion, or ectopic pregnancy; and has one living child.

Gravida 31011   This is another method of summarizing your reproductive history. In this case, the first digit ("3") represents your total number of pregnancies, including the present one; the second digit ("1") represents the total number of full-term births; the third digit ("0") represents the number of preterm births; the fourth digit ("1") represents the total number of miscarriages, abortions, and ectopic pregnancies; and the fifth digit ("1") represents the total number of living children. Therefore, a woman who is gravida 31011 is in her third pregnancy and has had one full-term birth; has had one miscarriage, abortion, or ectopic pregnancy; and has one living child.

Primigravida   You are pregnant for the first time.

Primipara   You are giving birth for the first time.

Multigravida   You are pregnant for the second or subsequent time.

Multipara   You've given birth one or more times.

The dating of your pregnancy

LMP   The first day of your last menstrual period.

EDC/EDD   Estimated date of confinement, or estimated date of delivery (that is, your due date).

Bright Idea
If you will be traveling out of town during your pregnancy, ask your doctor or midwife if you can take a copy of your prenatal record along. That way, if you run into complications, the attending physician will have some idea of how your pregnancy has been progressing to date.

Prenatal tests

AFP   Alpha-fetoprotein test (also a component of what is called triple screen or maternal serum screening). An AFP test is designed to tell you whether you are at increased risk of giving birth to a child with either Down syndrome or a neural tube defect such as spina bifida. (See Chapter 7.)

BP   Blood pressure. There are two readings: the systolic pressure (the upper figure) and the diastolic pressure (the lower figure). You are generally considered to have high blood pressure if the reading exceeds 140/90.

Hb/Hgb   Level of hemoglobin, an oxygen-carrying substance present in red blood cells; anything less than 10.5% or so indicates that you are anemic.

Blood group   Your blood type and whether you are Rh positive or Rh negative.

Rh antibodies   Indicates whether you have any anti-Rh antibodies, which are capable of crossing the placenta and destroying the baby's red blood cells.

VDRL test   Test for syphilis (also referred to as RPR).

HIV test   Test for the presence of the AIDS virus.

hCG   Refers to the blood level reading of human chorionic gonadotropin (hCG).

CBC   Complete blood count: hemoglobin, red and white cells (RBCs and WBCs respectively), and blood platelets.

Your physical health

Edema   Swelling or the retention of water.

Fe   Iron. Indicates that you have been prescribed iron.

Watch Out!
If you are a plus-sized woman, make sure that your caregiver notes in your prenatal record that all blood pressure readings have been taken with the large-sized blood pressure cuff. This is because there may be a discrepancy in readings if someone subsequently checks your blood pressure with the regular-sized cuff since a blood pressure cuff that is too small will give falsely elevated readings.

Your baby's well-being and position

FH or FHR   Fetal heart or fetal heart rate.

FM   Fetal movement.

Eng/E   Engaged. The baby's head has dropped into the bony pelvis.

Floating   The baby's head is not yet engaged.

Presenting part   The part of the baby's body that is likely to come through the cervix first.

0, -1, -2, -3, +1, +2, +3   The baby's station (an indicator of how high or low in the pelvis the presenting part is). Generally, negative numbers mean the presenting part is unengaged, and positive numbers mean it is engaged.

Vertex   Baby is head-down.

Breech   Baby is bottom-down.

LOA, LOP, ROA, ROP   Left occipito-anterior, left occipito-posterior, right occipito anterior, right occipito posterior. These terms refer to the position of the crown of the baby's head (that is, occiput) in relation to your body (right or left), and anterior (toward your front) or posterior (toward your back).

Fundal height   The measurement of fundal height (distance in centimeters from the upper edge of the pubic bone to the top of the uterus) is used to give a rough idea of the growth of the fetus and the amount of amniotic fluid at any given point in pregnancy after about 20 weeks. On average, the measurement is equal to the number of weeks of pregnancy, but it may vary by as many as three to four centimeters or more, depending on the person's height, weight, and body shape; the position of the baby; and, of course, the size of the baby and the amount of amniotic fluid. The measurement technique is subjective to some degree, and different caregivers can get different measurements on the same day.

Typically, over time, the fundal height increases about one centimeter per week from about 20 to 36 weeks, but this is also variable, especially in the short run (that is, from week to week) and near term.

Unofficially...
There are more certified nurse-midwives in practice in California than in any other state. Other states with a large number of midwives in practice include New York, Florida, Pennsylvania, Illinois, and Massachusetts.

Just the facts

- You have three basic choices when it comes to caregivers: a family physician, an obstetrician, or a midwife.

- Make sure you understand the difference between a certified nurse-midwife, a certified midwife, and a lay midwife. A certified nurse-midwife is a nurse who has received special training in midwifery and who has passed a national certification examination. A certified midwife is a health-care worker with a non-nursing background who has received special training in midwifery and who has passed a national certification examination. A lay midwife is a midwife who has acquired her skills through informal apprenticeship rather than formal education.

- Hospitals are the safest place to give birth if you have a high-risk pregnancy or if an emergency situation arises during labor.

- Birth centers provide a homelike atmosphere to families who are seeking an alternative to both home birth and hospital birth.

- Home births may be the norm worldwide, but they are far from mainstream in America.

- A home birth must be carefully planned and attended by a skilled doctor or midwife.

- You should set up your first prenatal checkup as soon as you discover that you're pregnant—typically 6 to 10 weeks after the start of your last menstrual period, and even earlier if you haven't had a prepregnancy consultation.

GET THE SCOOP ON...
What a childbirth education class can do for
you—and what it can't ▪ The different types of
childbirth classes ▪ What to look for in a class ▪
What a typical class is really like

Chapter 6

Finding the Childbirth Education Class That's Right for You

There's no doubt about it: parents are passionate when it comes to the subject of childbirth classes. They either love 'em or hate 'em; there's no in-between. Some couples swear by them, insisting that they're every bit as important a part of having a baby as choosing a good caregiver and finding the right place to give birth. Others view them as a complete waste of time.

You've no doubt got your own ideas about what childbirth classes are like. If your knowledge of childbirth classes is based on what you've seen on TV, you could be in for a pleasant surprise. Although the sitcom writers seem to take perverse delight in portraying childbirth classes as a form of boot camp for pregnant women and their partners, they can actually be fun and informative—provided, of course, that you choose the right class.

205

In this chapter, we give you the facts you need to do just that. We give you some good reasons for attending childbirth classes, discuss the philosophies behind the most popular types of classes, tell you what to look for in a class, and then wrap up our discussion by giving you the lowdown on what childbirth classes are really like.

Why bother?

You're exhausted after a day at the office, and nothing looks halfway near as appealing as your very own couch. Why on earth would you want to head out the door to spend the evening at childbirth class?

Here are six good reasons why you might want to make the effort:

- Childbirth classes can help reduce your anxiety about giving birth by giving you an idea of what to expect—whether you end up having a vaginal or cesarean delivery.

- They educate you about various birthing options so that you have the facts you need in order to plan for the birth you want.

- They give you the opportunity to make friends with other expectant couples—contacts that can be pure gold if you find yourself housebound with a colicky baby a few months down the road.

- They can help you master breathing, relaxation, and coping techniques designed to reduce your perception of pain during labor.

- They give your partner the chance to play an active role in your pregnancy while familiarizing him with his role during the delivery: that is, providing you with support and encouragement and acting as your advocate.

Unofficially...
When a baby is born at Peterborough Civic Hospital, Brahms's Lullaby is played over the hospital PA system. "All you ever hear over the PA is code blue, code red, code yellow, or a request for a doctor," a hospital spokeswoman explained to the *Peterborough Examiner.* "This is a reminder that exciting things are happening in maternity."

- They give you the opportunity to ask questions about pregnancy, labor, childbirth, breastfeeding, and life after baby, and help draw your attention to issues that you need to be thinking about (for example, the pros and cons of episiotomy, circumcision, rooming in, "drive-through deliveries," and more).

Will that be Bradley, Lamaze, or something else entirely?

It's time we let you in on a little secret: there's no such thing as a "typical" childbirth class. Childbirth classes can be taught by highly trained instructors who provide you with an in-depth look at the wonders of birth—or by shockingly incompetent instructors who haven't had any experience with childbirth at all, firsthand or otherwise. They can be fun and informative—or deadly boring and completely useless. They can have you eagerly anticipating the birth of your baby—or leave you paralyzed with fear at the thought of the pain that will accompany that first contraction.

Although there's no such thing as a single Good Housekeeping seal of approval when it comes to childbirth classes, a few organizations do offer the next best thing: certification programs that require childbirth instructors to meet at least minimal standards before they are set loose on innocent pregnant couples! The American Academy of Husband-Coached Childbirth (the Bradley Method), Lamaze International Inc. (ASPO/Lamaze), and the International Childbirth Education Association (ICEA) have certification programs for childbirth educators. (You can find the contact information for these organizations in Appendix B.)

66
Having a baby is not like passing an exam or winning a race. You are not expected to come out 'on top' with a two-hour labor, or no pain-relieving drugs, or whatever. It is much more a question of learning how to adapt your responses—mainly those of breathing and relaxation—to the particular challenges of your own labor.
—Sheila Kitzinger, *The Complete Book of Pregnancy and Childbirth*

Bright Idea
Having a hard time deciding which childbirth class is right for you? Here's an online tool that can help. Go to www.babycenter.com/calculator/2874.html, choose the four factors that are most important to you in a childbirth class, click on "evaluate," and you'll find out which of the three most popular types of childbirth classes—Bradley, Lamaze, or ICEA—is most likely to be right for you.

Philosophies unlimited

We've already identified the three big players in the American childbirth education arena, but you'll also find classes that support the Dick-Read, Leboyer, Odent, and Kitzinger philosophies—to say nothing of "Heinz 57" classes that beg, borrow, and steal from all of the above. Let's briefly consider what these childbirth philosophies are all about.

Dick-Read

Dr. Grantley Dick-Read is credited with being the father of modern-day childbirth education. At the end of the World War II, when war-weary couples started giving birth to the Baby Boomers, Dr. Dick-Read was busy making baby-related waves of his own. He and his assistant, registered nurse Margaret Gamper, began teaching pregnant women that they could break the so-called fear-tension-pain cycle of childbirth by educating themselves about what childbirth involved and learning techniques to manage the pain. The technique—often called the Gamper method—was considered revolutionary at the time because it brought American fathers into the laboring process for the very first time. These types of classes continue to be available in America today and are delivered by someone who has been trained in the Gamper method.

The Bradley method

The Bradley method—also called "husband-coached childbirth"—was developed by Denver obstetrician Robert Bradley. The method promotes the husband's active participation in the process of giving birth and the benefits of natural childbirth as opposed to medicated deliveries. The classes cover a lot of ground, running for approximately 12 weeks, starting in the fifth or sixth month of pregnancy.

Bradley classes are ideal for couples who are aiming for drug-free deliveries but not for those who are considering epidurals or analgesics. Many people believe that Bradley classes are the best option for couples contemplating a home birth. Check out the facts for yourself. You'll find a detailed version of the course outline online at www.bradleybirth.com/cc.htm.

Timesaver
You can obtain a free information package on the Bradley Method by filling out the form at www.bradleybirth.com/tbm5.htm or by calling 800-4A-BIRTH.

ASPO/Lamaze (now called Lamaze International, Inc.)

The so-called Lamaze method was developed after a French physician named Dr. Ferdinand Lamaze was inspired by some of the teachings of Dr. Ivan Petrovich Pavlov, of salivating dog fame. Lamaze believed that just as dogs could be conditioned to salivate at the sound of a bell, women in labor could be conditioned to alter their responses to the pain of labor.

The Lamaze method is based on the philosophy that birth is a normal experience that profoundly affects both women and their families. It is rooted in the idea that a woman's internal wisdom provides her with the resources needed to get through the rigors of childbirth, and that women have the right to give birth without needless medical intervention. The Lamaze method—also called the ASPO method after the American Society for Psycho-prophylaxis, which popularized the method in America—used to focus on techniques (complex breathing exercises) designed to take a laboring woman's mind off the pain of labor. Although these techniques are still a part of the modern Lamaze program, they are complemented by other methods designed to heighten a pregnant woman's awareness of what is happening to her body. The classes also provide a frank discussion of the pros and cons

Bright Idea
Use the online directory at www.icea.org/cb.htm to find out whether there are any International Childbirth Education Association certified instructors offering childbirth classes in your community.

of medicated pain relief. Most Lamaze classes take place in hospital settings and require 12 to 16 hours of instruction time.

International Childbirth Education Association

Many childbirth classes are taught by members of the International Childbirth Education Association—a nonprofit organization that seeks to promote "freedom of choice through knowledge of alternatives." The ICEA offers certification programs for childbirth educators, postnatal educators, and doulas (that is, women who provide support during labor, childbirth, and the postpartum period). There's no standard party line to follow—as is the case with some other childbirth certification programs—so you'll want to find out where an ICEA-certified childbirth educator stands on any birthing issues of particular concern to you before you sign up for her class.

Other types of childbirth classes

Now let's quickly run through the other types of childbirth classes that may be offered in your community:

- **Leboyer:** Childbirth classes that are based on the theories of Frederick Leboyer look at the experience of birth from the baby's—rather than the mother's—perspective. These classes stress the importance of giving birth in a peaceful environment—that is, a room with soft lighting and little noise or movement—and of providing the new baby with plenty of opportunity for skin-to-skin contact with his mother.

- **Odent:** Childbirth classes that follow the teachings of French physician Dr. Michel Odent (for example, BirthWorks) are based on Odent's theory that women in labor enter a primitive biological state that should be respected rather than interfered with. He argues that when laboring women are allowed to follow their natural instincts (assume positions that are comfortable to them), natural narcotics called endorphins kick in to help ease the pain of childbirth.

- **Kitzinger Psychosexual Approach:** Classes that follow British childbirth educator Sheila Kitzinger's so-called psychosexual approach to childbirth operate on the assumption that women are active—not passive—participants in the births of their babies, and that they have every right to negotiate to obtain the type of birth experience they want.

- **Other childbirth classes:** Some of these classes serve up a smorgasbord of childbirth philosophies that might include a main course of Lamaze accompanied by a side dish of Bradley—or vice versa. By the way, these "Heinz 57" classes are far more prevalent than any of the pure-bred classes we described above.

What to look for in a childbirth class

Now that you've got a basic feel for the types of philosophies behind the various types of childbirth classes out there, it's time to hone in on the one that's right for you.

What to look for in an instructor

The most important factor in the childbirth education equation is the instructor. You and your partner are going to be spending a lot of time with this person and will share details about some of the most

Watch Out!
Be sure to scrutinize the credentials of a childbirth educator before you sign up for her class. The fact that a woman has experienced childbirth herself doesn't necessarily mean that she's qualified to teach you anything useful about giving birth.

intimate aspects of your lives with her. That's why it's important to choose this person wisely.

Basically, you should look for someone who

■ has the necessary training and experience;

■ has a realistic idea of what childbirth classes can and can't do for you (regardless of what some folks would have you believe, childbirth classes don't guarantee you a quick or painless labor);

■ has given birth herself or, in the case of a male instructor, has played an active role in someone else's birth and therefore has firsthand knowledge of the joys and challenges of giving birth;

■ is familiar with the routines at the hospital or birth center where you plan to deliver your baby or understands the steps involved in planning a home birth;

■ is willing to tolerate a variety of viewpoints on such perennially hot topics as pain relief during labor, episiotomy, and circumcision.

Other factors to consider

The teacher isn't the only factor you need to consider when you're weighing the pros and cons of your various childbirth education options. You also need to consider factors such as

■ the location of the classes (Are they offered in a pregnancy-friendly setting, or do you have to cram your blossoming belly into an impossibly small desk? Is the room well-ventilated and kept at a comfortable temperature, or does it bring to mind a 17th-century sweatshop?);

■ the size of the group (no fewer than 5 and no more than 10 couples) is ideal;

■ the composition of the group (married couples versus single women, first-time mothers versus women having their second baby or subsequent babies, women having planned c-sections versus those planning vaginal deliveries, women who have experienced pregnancy loss versus those who haven't, women planning home versus hospital versus birth-center deliveries, and so on);

■ the cost of the classes (typically $100 or so for a series of Lamaze or other childbirth classes, or $200 or more for Bradley classes);

■ the format of the classes (Does the class seem to have the right blend of hard facts and touchy-feely stuff? Is a hospital or birthing-center tour included?);

■ who is offering them (the hospital where you will be giving birth, an independent childbirth educator, and so on);

■ whether or not there's an early-bird class (a class offered during your first or second trimester that covers important pregnancy-related lifestyle issues such as nutrition and exercise), in addition to the regular classes that are offered later in your pregnancy;

■ what your caregiver thinks of these classes (assuming that he has some knowledge of the course content or the instructor's style);

■ whether there is an adequate number of hours of instruction (a minimum of 10 hours of instruction, ideally spread out over a period of weeks so that you have time to absorb and practice what you've learned).

Here's an idea you might want to consider. If you don't have the time or the inclination to attend regular childbirth education classes, hire a childbirth educator to come to your home to offer private classes for your and your partner. This is the ideal

Moneysaver
Before you fork over your own cash, be sure to ask whether the cost of childbirth classes is covered by your HMO, insurance company or benefits package at work.

Bright Idea
Be sure to schedule your childbirth classes so that they end around your 37th week of pregnancy. If they finish much earlier than that, you might forget what you've learned when the big moment arrives. If they go much later, you could end up giving birth before you "graduate."

situation for couples who have busy schedules or who have special circumstances (for example, a previous stillbirth or neonatal death) that might make it difficult for them to feel comfortable in a regular childbirth education class. This is also a popular choice for women who are on bedrest and consequently are unable to leave their homes to attend childbirth education classes.

What childbirth education classes should cover

Make sure that the childbirth education class you sign up for covers as many of the following topics as possible:

- the physiology of pregnancy (how your body changes and why, and how you can cope with some of the common discomforts of pregnancy);

- the basic elements of prenatal care (your caregiver's role in caring for both you and your baby and the role of tests and technology during both pregnancy and labor);

- the psychological and emotional experience of giving birth;

- what's involved in delivering both vaginally and through cesarean section;

- relaxation techniques and/or breathing techniques;

- laboring positions that can reduce pain or help your labor to progress;

- the role of pain relief during labor;

- tips on getting breastfeeding off to the best possible start (assuming, of course, that you choose to breastfeed your baby);

- advice on caring for a newborn—ideally from couples who recently gave birth themselves;

- advice on choosing a pediatrician;

- the lowdown on what the postpartum period is really like;

- the pros and cons of giving birth in various childbirth settings (in a hospital, in a birth center, or at home).

The classes should also include

- the opportunity to view films or videos of actual vaginal and cesarean births so that you and your partner will be prepared for either alternative;

- the chance to tour the hospital or birth center at which you will be giving birth (assuming, of course, that you've decided to give birth in a place other than home);

- the opportunity to ask questions or express concerns you may have about pregnancy or childbirth;

- time at the end so that you can chat informally with other couples and cement friendships that could be real sanity savers during the weeks and months ahead.

Childbirth education classes should provide as much information and as little propaganda as possible. Rather than shoving her own views down your throat, the childbirth educator's role is to provide you with the facts and let you and your partner make your own decisions about various birthing options. Bottom line? You shouldn't be left feeling that your baby's birth was a failure because it didn't follow the childbirth educator's script to a tee.

Just one more quick bit of advice before we move on: Don't decide against a particular childbirth education class simply because the instructor has chosen to de-emphasize breathing techniques.

> 66
> My spouse and I took a Bradley class. The emphasis was on having a natural, medication-free delivery. I was wonderfully prepared to deal with pain, I was well informed—but when labor didn't go as planned, I was very disappointed. I still deal with deep feelings of failure—of not being a 'real' mom because my daughter was not born 'naturally,' because I had what the class workbook calls a 'drugged delivery,' not a birth.
> —Leila, 33, mother of one
> 99

Watch Out!
Make sure that the childbirth philosophies of your childbirth educator mesh with those of your doctor or midwife. Otherwise, you could find yourself dealing with contradictory information and conflicting advice. The last thing you need is to have the childbirth educator undermining your confidence in your caregiver.

Although breathing techniques were once regarded as the key to childbirth preparation, they are now regarded as just one of many tools a pregnant woman and her partner should have in their labor bag. An understanding of relaxation techniques, the support of a caring partner, and an overall feeling of confidence in her ability to give birth are every bit as important as breathing techniques to a woman in labor.

So what are the pillows for?

As we mentioned earlier in this chapter, there's no such thing as a "typical" childbirth education class— just as there is no such thing as a "typical" birth.

That said, you can expect each class to be structured something like this:

7:00 p.m.   Each couple arrives, carrying the pillows they were instructed to bring with them to class. They grab a bottle of juice and a pregnancy-friendly snack from the snack table, and take a seat.

7:05 p.m.–8:00 p.m.   The instructor uses flip charts and a series of visual aids to cover a particular aspect of pregnancy or childbirth, setting aside time to answer questions and address any areas of concern. She also reminds the group about the upcoming tour of the birthing unit at the local hospital and asks if any siblings will be on hand for the siblings tour.

8:00 p.m.   The class takes a break so that everyone can hit the washrooms or the snack table again.

8:15 p.m.   The instructor has everyone get down on the floor and practice various relaxation and breathing techniques and laboring positions. (This is where the pillows come in!)

9:00 p.m.   The formal instruction portion of the evening wraps up, but a few couples stick around to chat over a cup of coffee—decaffeinated, of course!

Don't be surprised if your partner is less than enthusiastic about attending childbirth classes. For whatever reason, the average father-to-be finds childbirth classes to be about as fulfilling and exciting as a typical bridal shower.

Even fathers-to-be who are totally involved in their partners' pregnancies can find the classes a little hard to take: "The classes were a little too touchy-feely, and it sometimes became more of a support group than a way to gather information," admits John, 44, a second-time father.

Not all fathers feel this way, however. Some actually get more out of the classes than their partners: "We took childbirth classes once a week for six weeks. I didn't think they were worthwhile, but my partner thinks he definitely got something out of them," says Molly, 29, who recently gave birth to her first child.

Many couples have fond memories of the times they spent at their childbirth education classes: "My husband and I took childbirth classes together," recalls Brenda, 34, a mother of one. "Because of the classes, we had a better idea of what to expect, and my husband was able to coach me through labor with the breathing techniques we learned."

"The best thing about Lamaze class is meeting other parents-to-be. We exchange information about pediatricians and plan to spend some park

Bright Idea
When you're signing up for a childbirth class, be sure to ask whether it includes instruction on breastfeeding techniques, a father's-only session, or a sibling-preparation class. These additional bells and whistles are proving to be popular with many pregnant women and their families.

time together when our babies are born. And it's great to have others to commiserate with!" adds Jennie, 30, who is pregnant with her first child.

The classes definitely have their lighter moments too. This is what Lisa, 27, had to say about the classes she and her husband took before their baby was born eight months ago: "At one point, the instructor asked everyone in the class to lie down on the floor with their partners, and then she turned out the lights. She played a record of what was supposed to be relaxing music with a commentator's voice explaining the breathing techniques. My husband and I could not stop laughing. We were trying so hard not to disturb the other people in the class, but we just couldn't help ourselves. Before long, we had everyone in class cracking up."

Some couples report less-than-glowing experiences: "My husband and I took the childbirth classes that were offered through our doctor's office," recalls Amy, 31, a mother of two. "I was very disappointed. The course was taught by a nurse who basically assumed that we would all just end up getting epidurals anyway—even though many of us were planning to try to avoid taking drugs."

Other couples see the benefits of the classes in retrospect. "I wish I had paid more attention to the c-section details that were discussed in my Lamaze class," confesses Jennifer, a 25-year-old mother of one. "I really didn't think I would ever need to pay attention to that stuff."

If there's a universal benefit to attending childbirth classes, it's this, says Allison, 27, a mother of one: "Childbirth classes helped me to realize that the birth was coming soon, and that I'd better get to planning. They helped my husband because it made it seem more 'real' to him that we were actually having a baby."

If you'd like to do some additional reading on childbirth classes, you'll find some leads on the hottest childbirth Web sites and the addresses of the best-known childbirth education organizations in Appendix B.

Just the facts

- Childbirth classes can help reduce your anxiety about giving birth; educate you about various birthing options; give you the opportunity to meet other expectant couples; teach you breathing, relaxation, and coping techniques; encourage your partner to become involved in your pregnancy and the birth of your child; and give you the opportunity to ask questions about pregnancy, labor, childbirth, breastfeeding, and life after baby.

- There is no such thing as a Good Housekeeping stamp of approval when it comes to childbirth classes. Buyer beware!

- Childbirth classes should provide as much information and as little propaganda as possible. What matters is your health and your baby's well-being, not the childbirth educator's personal agenda.

- Don't let breathing techniques make you crazy. They're just one of many tools in your labor bag.

Unofficially...
According to a recent article in *USA Today,* some companies offer workers incentives for attending childbirth education classes. At Haggar Clothing Company, for example, women who attend five childbirth education classes are given a free infant car seat by the company.

GET THE SCOOP ON...
Screening tests versus diagnostic tests ▪ The
pros and cons of prenatal testing ▪ Why the age
argument doesn't hold water ▪ Alpha-fetoprotein
(AFP) ▪ The different types of prenatal tests ▪
What to do if the test brings bad news

To Test or Not to Test?

To our mothers' and grandmothers' generations, modern prenatal tests must sound like the stuff of which science fiction novels are made. Miniature cameras inserted right into the uterus allow doctors to assess the well-being of the developing baby. Samples of amniotic fluid, umbilical cord blood, and fetal tissue provide expectant parents with a genetic and chromosomal fingerprint of their unborn child. And a simple blood test can be used to predict the probability that a particular woman will give birth to a child with either a neural tube defect or Down syndrome.

Although prenatal tests have proven beneficial to large numbers of pregnant women, the information they provide doesn't come without a price. Prenatal tests can cause unnecessary stress to couples who might otherwise be enjoying problem-free pregnancies and, in a small percentage of cases, can lead to complications that may result in the loss of an otherwise healthy baby.

221

In this chapter, we provide you with the facts you need in order to make informed choices about prenatal testing. We discuss the pros and cons of prenatal testing, the risks and benefits of the various types of tests, and the options you have in the event that the test brings bad news rather than good.

Tests, tests, and more tests

Prenatal tests fall into one of two basic categories: screening tests and diagnostic tests.

Prenatal screening tests are designed to do what their name implies—to screen a large number of women in order to identify those who have a higher-than-average risk of giving birth to a child with a serious or life-threatening health problem (in the case of the alpha-fetoprotein, or AFP, test) or of developing gestational diabetes (in the case of the glucose tolerance test—a test we'll discuss in Chapter 15). Screening tests are not designed to say definitively that there is a problem. Their job is simply to alert a pregnant woman and her caregiver to the possibility that there could be a problem.

Diagnostic tests, on the other hand, pick up where screening tests leave off. They are used to determine whether there is, in fact, a problem. Diagnostic tests that are commonly used in pregnancy include amniocentesis, chorionic villus sampling, level 2 or targeted ultrasound, and the three-hour glucose tolerance test.

Unfortunately, screening tests tend to get an undeservedly bad rap because pregnant women or their caregivers sometimes expect them to do more than what they're designed to do.

This is where all the controversy about the high level of false positives fits in. In order to ensure that as many problems are detected as possible, screening tests inevitably end up generating a certain percentage of so-called false positives (that is, cases in which a pregnant woman is identified as being at risk of having a particular problem when, in fact, she and her baby are perfectly healthy).

As you can see, there's an art to designing a good screening test. You need to strike a balance between maximizing the rate of detection and minimizing the rate of false positives. Here's the difficulty: the only way to eliminate all false positives is to make the testing criteria so rigid that the test ignores any results that are less than clearcut (that is, situations in which there may or may not be a problem, but it isn't obvious which is the case). This results in an increased number of false negatives—situations in which problems are missed.

Let's take a moment to consider where the most maligned screening test of them all—the AFP, or triple screen test—fits into the picture. If the AFP screening test were designed to be a diagnostic test, its track record would be horrendous: 95% of women who receive a positive result on the test are, in fact, carrying perfectly healthy babies. But since it's designed to be a screening test, it makes sense to assess its effectiveness on that basis (that is, how good it is at identifying women who are at risk of giving birth to a baby with a serious birth defect).

Consider the numbers for yourself. AFP testing results from the University of Connecticut show, for example, that the AFP test has a respectably high detection rate: approximately 82.1% of cases of neural tube defects and 73.7% of cases of Down syndrome in women under age 35 are picked up by the test.

There's just one other point we want to make before we get down off the screening-test soap

Moneysaver
Although most insurance companies and HMOs will cover the cost of prenatal testing that is medically necessary, there are exceptions. That's why it's a good idea to find out up front which tests you may be required to pay for out of your own pocket.

box—something that makes perfect sense but that isn't intuitively obvious. Screening tests such as the AFP have a very important role to play in prenatal testing because they alert pregnant women who, for age or other reasons, might not otherwise have considered diagnostic testing for the possibility that there could be problems in their pregnancies.

Unfortunately, the reverse assumption cannot be made. The AFP is not capable of providing women in so-called high-risk categories (for example, women in their forties) with sufficient reassurance to enable them to decline more invasive procedures such as amniocentesis or chorionic villus sampling just because their AFP results look promising. There simply isn't enough data to support this assumption—at least in our opinion.

The prenatal testing merry-go-round: do you really want to get on?

66
I wanted to know if my child was going to be healthy and to be able to prepare myself if my baby was going to be less than healthy.
—Helena, 42, mother of one
99

The sheer number of prenatal tests is enough to make any expectant parent feel uneasy. After all, the fact that these tests even exist is proof positive that some babies are born with serious—even fatal—birth defects, something that most pregnant women don't even want to think about. Although the odds of having a healthy baby are extremely high—even for women in their forties—a growing number of expectant couples are choosing to undergo prenatal testing.

Here are the pros and cons of deciding to go that route.

Pros

Prenatal testing allows you to find out if there's a problem with your baby before you give birth. This may allow you to

- treat your baby's condition during pregnancy (for example, provide blood transfusions to a baby with Rh incompatibility problems);

- make appropriate choices for the delivery (for example, scheduling a cesarean delivery to minimize birth-related injuries to a baby with spina bifida or avoiding an emergency cesarean for fetal distress if it's known in advance that your baby will be born with a fatal birth defect);

- prepare to give birth to a baby who has special needs (for example, ensure that you give birth in a hospital with top-notch neonatal care facilities or have time to prepare emotionally for a mentally retarded child) or a baby who may be stillborn;

- choose to terminate the pregnancy.

Cons

Prenatal testing also has its downside. Here are some points you need to consider:

- Prenatal tests can't detect all problems. They're able to test for only a limited number of conditions. No prenatal test can guarantee that you're going to give birth to a perfectly healthy baby. There are simply too many unknowns.

- Prenatal tests often can't tell you how severe your child's disability may be—something that can make it difficult for you to determine what kind of quality of life your child can expect to experience.

- Once you get on the prenatal testing merry-go-round, it can be hard to get off. A positive test result on an AFP test, for example (a test result that indicates that you are at increased risk of

> 66
> We decided to proceed with amniocentesis because of my age and because my brother had a child born with Down syndrome. My partner and I decided that if there was a problem with the baby-to-be, we would consider abortion because neither of us wanted to care for a child with such special needs. It sounds selfish, but we both had careers and other children to think about.
> —Anne, 39, mother of three
> 99

having a baby with either an open neural tube defect or Down syndrome), can lead to a follow-up AFP test, an ultrasound, an amniocentesis, and possibly even riskier and more invasive procedures. If you take the AFP without giving much thought to the consequences of a positive test result, you could end up subjecting yourself to a series of follow-up tests and invasive procedures that might ultimately serve only to prove that the baby is perfectly healthy. That's why you need to understand the reasons for agreeing to a particular test, the possible outcomes, what course of action would be advised in the event that the test came back positive (and the risks of those next steps), and so on. Bottom line? Never consent to a prenatal test just because your doctor or midwife routinely orders one for every pregnant woman.

Why the age argument doesn't hold water

Typically, the medical profession routinely recommends that women over 35 be tested for chromosomal anomalies such as Down syndrome by using diagnostic procedures such as amniocentesis or chorionic villus sampling. However, many caregivers question this inflexible approach, preferring instead to counsel their patients about the pros and cons of the tests and then reach a decision together with their patients that takes into account the patient's values about things such as abortion, her tolerance for risks of various types, and even her intuition about her body and her pregnancy.

Although the all-too-common obsession with a pregnant woman's age might lead you to conclude that the risk of giving birth to a baby with a chromosomal anomaly increases dramatically with age, this is simply not the case. As Table 7.1 demonstrates, your risk of giving birth to a baby with a chromosomal anomaly does increase as you age, but the increase is gradual rather than sudden.

What's behind this move to routine diagnostic tests for pregnant women over age 35 is what can at best be described as flawed logic. You've no doubt heard someone argue the case that diagnostic procedures such as amniocentesis and chorionic villus sampling are justified only when the risk of miscarriage (as a result of the test) is less than the risk of giving birth to a child with a birth defect—something that typically happens, statistically speaking, at around age 35.

Unfortunately, this argument fails to take into account that three distinctly different issues are involved: (1) a woman's odds of giving birth to a child with a chromosomal anomaly (for example, Down syndrome); (2) her desire to know for certain whether her baby has a chromosomal anomaly; and (3) her willingness to accept the risks involved with the tests that will give her that answer.

A 25-year-old woman might decide, for example, that she wants to know for certain whether she is carrying a child with a particular birth defect—even though the risks involved in obtaining that information (she has a 1/250 chance of miscarriage if she chooses to undergo amniocentesis) may be significantly higher than her actual risk of having a baby with such defects (1/476—see Table 7.1). (Of course, if she's had the AFP test, she should have a clearer idea of her risks, but even that may not be enough information to satisfy her need to know.) She may decide that she is willing to pay any price— including inadvertently miscarrying a healthy

TABLE 7.1: RISK OF HAVING A LIVEBORN CHILD WITH DOWN SYNDROME OR ANOTHER CHROMOSOMAL ANOMALY

Maternal Age	Risk of Down Syndrome	Total Risk for Chromosome Abnormalities
20	1/1667	1/526
21	1/1667	1/526
22	1/1429	1/500
23	1/1429	1/500
24	1/1250	1/476
25	1/1250	1/476
26	1/1176	1/455
27	1/1111	1/455
28	1/1053	1/435
29	1/1000	1/417
30	1/952	1/384
31	1/909	1/384
32	1/769	1/323
33	1/625	1/286
34	1/500	1/238
35	1/385	1/192
36	1/294	1/156
37	1/227	1/127
38	1/175	1/102
39	1/137	1/83
40	1/106	1/66
41	1/82	1/53
42	1/64	1/42
43	1/50	1/33
44	1/38	1/26
45	1/30	1/21
46	1/23	1/16
47	1/18	1/13
48	1/14	1/10
49	1/11	1/8

Source: *The Merck Manual*, 16th edition.

baby—in order to avoid giving birth to a child with a chromosomal anomaly. She may argue that whereas a miscarried pregnancy can be replaced (in most cases, at least), a child with a severe disability may require a greater commitment that she and her partner are prepared to make.

A 40-year-old woman who has had a great deal of difficulty becoming pregnant may be unwilling to risk miscarrying her baby (once again, a 1/250 chance) even though the odds of having a baby with a chromosomal anomaly are considerably higher (1/66—see Table 7.1)—even if forgoing that test means that she may end up giving birth to a child with a chromosomal anomaly.

This is why any "across the board" policy about prenatal testing is a bad idea. It fails to take into account the varying circumstances of people in a particular age category. You don't listen to the same music or read the same books as everyone else your age; why, then, should medical science assume that you'll make the same choices as your peers when it comes to an issue as important as prenatal testing?

There's one other important fact about chromosomal disorders and aging that seems to get lost in all the media hype about older women having babies. Even if you give birth at age 45, you still have an excellent chance of having a healthy baby. In 31 cases out of 32, for example, you will not give birth to a child who has Down syndrome. That puts the odds decidedly in your favor, at about 97%.

Who's a good candidate for prenatal testing . . .
Although the decision to proceed with prenatal testing is a highly personal one, you may want to consider prenatal testing if

- you have a family history of genetic disease or you know that you are a carrier of a particular disease;

- you have been exposed to a serious infection during pregnancy (for example, rubella or toxoplasmosis);

- you have been exposed to a harmful substance that could cause a birth defect;

- you have had one or more unsuccessful pregnancies or have previously given birth to baby with a birth defect;

- you feel a need to know with certainty whether your baby has a detectable abnormality, even though you are not considered at particularly high risk.

. . . and who's not . . .

You might choose against prenatal testing if

- you have concerns about the accuracy of certain tests;

- taking the test would increase your anxiety rather than alleviating it;

- you are opposed to abortion and wouldn't consider terminating the pregnancy even if the news was bad;

- you don't want to take the risk of inadvertently harming a perfectly healthy baby—something that can be a concern with certain types of prenatal tests.

What to do before you sign the consent form

Before you agree to take any type of prenatal test, you should make sure that you have a clear understanding of both the risks and the benefits of having the test performed. Our Prenatal Test Checklist (see below) will give you some ideas about the types of questions you may want to ask your doctor or midwife.

CHECKLIST: PRENATAL TEST

- What are the benefits of taking this test?
- What does the test involve?
- Will it be painful?
- What risks, if any, does the test pose to me or my baby?
- Where will the test be performed? How experienced is that person/facility in performing this particular test?
- How accurate is this test? Is it meant to be a screening test or a diagnostic test? What is the rate of false positives or false negatives?
- How quickly will I receive the results?
- What would happen if I decided not to have this test performed? Are there any other ways of obtaining the same information?
- What is the cost of this test? Will the cost be covered by my insurance company or HMO?
- What kind of follow-up tests will be recommended if the test results are abnormal or nonreassuring?

The last question on our checklist is particularly important. You need to know what other testing options will be available to you, should you choose to proceed with the test.

Now that we've talked about the factors that should be taken into account when weighing the pros and cons of taking a particular test, let's consider the various types of tests that are available to you and your baby. The first four tests we'll discuss—alpha-fetoprotein, amniocentesis, chorionic villus sampling, and ultrasound—are widely used. The remaining tests—percutaneous umbilical blood sampling (PUBS) (or cordocentesis) and fetoscopy—are used far less frequently because they pose greater risks to the developing baby.

Alpha-fetoprotein

66

My doctor gave me the option of having the AFP, but we declined. We knew that no matter what, we would not terminate the pregnancy, so we didn't want to have to go through any unnecessary stress, thinking that something might be wrong when it really wasn't.
—Beth, 27, mother of one

99

The alpha-fetoprotein test (also called Trisomy 21) is a blood test that is used to assess the likelihood that a pregnant woman is carrying a child with a neural tube defect or Down syndrome. It can also pick up evidence of other problems, including Trisomy 13, Trisomy 18, and a variety of other birth defects including omphalocele and absence of the kidneys. A high level of alpha-fetoprotein (a substance produced in the fetal liver) may indicate that a woman is carrying a child with a neural tube defect such as spina bifida or anencephaly, whereas a low level may indicate a higher than expected chance that she is carrying a child with Down syndrome. (*Note:* You will screen positive for an open neural tube defect if your AFP level is twice the mean level for all women who are the same number of weeks pregnant. If you are known to be carrying multiples, your test results will be interpreted accordingly.)

The results of the test are plugged into a formula that takes into account such factors as gestational age at the time of the test, and maternal age, to produce a probability that the fetus begin carried is affected by Down syndrome.

The AFP test is often combined with tests of human chorionic gonadotropin (hCG) and unconjugated estriol, in which case it is called the triple screen test, or referred to simply as Maternal Serum Screening (MSS). If it's combined with a fourth measurement—inhibin-A, a chemical produced by the ovaries and the placenta—it is known as the quad-screen test.

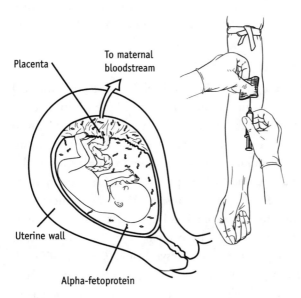

Placenta

To maternal bloodstream

Uterine wall

Alpha-fetoprotein

← Note!
Maternal Serum Alpha-Fetoprotein Screening Test. Figure created by Articulate Graphics.

The AFP test is usually done between the 15th and 18th weeks of pregnancy, and it takes anywhere from a couple of days to a week to get the results.

The benefits

The AFP test can be used to identify women who are at risk of giving birth to children with so-called open neural tube defects, severe kidney or liver disease, esophageal or intestinal blockages, Down syndrome and other chromosomal anomalies, urinary obstructions, and osteogenesis imperfecta (that is, fragile bones). Women who have elevated levels of AFP not associated with any identifiable birth defect are at

Unofficially...
The AFP test was initially designed to screen for open neural tube defects. It was only after scientists began analyzing the data that they discovered its capability to screen for Down syndrome as well.

increased risk for preterm labor, intrauterine growth restriction, and stillbirth and therefore are watched particularly closely for problems in their third trimester.

As a rule of thumb, screening for chromosomal anomalies is of greatest value to younger women who might not otherwise choose to pursue diagnostic testing such as amniocentesis and chorionic villus sampling.

The risks

Although the AFP test itself doesn't pose any real risks to the mother or fetus, a false positive result may lead a woman to subject herself and her baby to other riskier prenatal tests such as amniocentesis. Consequently, the key problem with this test is the high number of false positives: 40 out of every 1,000 women who take this test will be told that their readings have come back as higher risk, but only one or two will actually be carrying a child with a neural tube problem or Down syndrome. (As you will recall from our earlier discussions, this high rate of false positives helps to ensure that fewer false negatives occur.)

Who's a good candidate for this test?

The test is increasingly becoming a routine part of prenatal care across the United States, although it's technically optional in the majority of states. Women in California and New York are, however, legally required to have an AFP.

The fine print

The AFP test can't tell you whether you are carrying a child with a birth defect; it can only give you a risk assessment. It's considered to be highly accurate in predicting your risk of giving birth to a child with a neural tube defect (95% accuracy) but less accurate in predicting your risk of giving birth to a child with Down syndrome (60% accuracy).

A false positive can be caused by either a miscalculation in the dating of your pregnancy or the presence of twins, so an ultrasound is typically the next step if your initial AFP (and a follow-up AFP test if you and your caregiver choose to do one) indicates that there could be a problem. If an earlier ultrasound has been done, or if your caregiver feels there is adequate evidence of good pregnancy dating and the lack of twins, this extra step can be omitted.

If your AFP levels are low, indicating a risk of Down syndrome, your caregiver may suggest an aneuploidy screen and a fetal echocardiogram (ultrasound procedures designed to detect particular abnormalities in babies with Down syndrome). If none of the markers (abnormal features) for Down syndrome is detected during the aneuploidy screen and none of the heart problems characteristic of babies with Down syndrome is detected by the fetal echocardiogram, it is less likely that you are carrying a baby with Down syndrome. (*Note:* Although some caregivers routinely tell their patients that their AFP-derived risk of having a child with Down syndrome is cut in half if nothing unusual is detected during the aneuploidy screen or the fetal echocardiogram, there is no hard science to back this claim.) If you absolutely want to know for certain whether your child has Down syndrome, you may choose to proceed with amniocentesis and forgo ultrasound testing.

If your AFP levels are high, suggesting a risk of having a baby with an open neural tube defect, you will also be given the option of having a level II ultrasound. If your level II ultrasound doesn't reveal

Watch Out!
Some doctors have taken a leap of faith by assuming that a reassuring result on the AFP test is reason enough for a woman over 35 to call off further diagnostic testing. Unfortunately, the AFP test was designed for younger women, and there simply isn't enough hard data about women over 35 to encourage women in this age bracket to forgo further testing on the basis of a reassuring AFP test result.

Bright Idea
Arrange to have your triple screen test done as early as possible (that is, at 15 weeks, 0 days if possible). This will ensure that you receive the results early and have the maximum amount of time to consider your options and pursue whatever course of action you ultimately choose.

anything unusual, you can feel about 90% certain that you are not carrying a child with a neural tube defect. If, however, you want to know for certain, you will need to proceed with amniocentesis.

Amniocentesis

Amniocentesis involves inserting a fine needle through a pregnant woman's abdomen and into the amniotic sac and withdrawing less than an ounce of amniotic fluid for analysis. (See the following figure.) Ultrasound is used to locate the pocket of fluid and to minimize the risk to the fetus and the placenta. Although local anesthetic is frequently used to numb the area in which the needle is inserted and the majority of women find the procedure to be at most mildly uncomfortable, some women do find amniocentesis to be painful. (*Note:* Some doctors will encourage you to skip the anesthetic, arguing that the needle prick required to numb the area is every bit as painful as the needle prick required to do the amnio. If you have strong feelings about this either way, make your feelings known. This particular issue should be open to negotiation.)

Amniocentesis is typically done at 15 weeks of pregnancy, although some health-care practitioners perform it at 12 to 14 weeks (early amnio). This practice, though initially promising an alternative to the extra heartache and complications associated with the mid- to late-second-trimester results from standard amniocentesis, has already been abandoned by many reputable academic centers because of unacceptably high miscarriage rates.

It takes approximately 10 to 14 days to get the test results. If the test is done prior to 20 weeks or so,

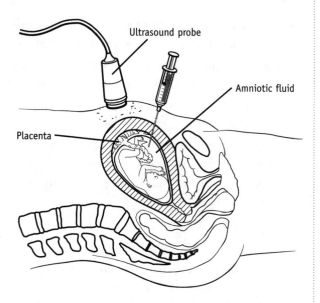

Ultrasound probe

Amniotic fluid

Placenta

← Note!
Amniocentesis.
Figure created by
Articulate
Graphics.

the woman can get the results back in time to terminate her pregnancy, if she chooses.

The benefits

Amniocentesis is used to detect

- chromosomal defects (for example, Down syndrome or Turner's syndrome)

- neural tube defects (for example, spina bifida)

- genetic diseases (for example, cystic fibrosis)

- skeletal diseases (for example, achondroplasia)

- fetal infections (for example, herpes or rubella)

- central-nervous-system disease (for example, Huntington's disease)

- blood diseases (for example, sickle-cell anemia)

- chemical problems or deficiencies (for example, Tay-Sachs disease)

It can also be used to

- determine the sex of the baby (important in the case of sex-linked diseases such as hemophilia)

- assess the lung maturity of the baby closer to term (important when premature labor is threatened or a decision has to be made about inducing labor in a high-risk pregnancy)

- measure the bilirubin count of the amniotic fluid (an indicator that a baby with Rh disease may need a blood transfusion) during the second half of pregnancy.

The risks

In a very small percentage of cases, amniocentesis results in injury to the fetus, placenta, or umbilical cord. Approximately 1 out of every 200 to 500 women who have amniocentesis will miscarry or go into premature labor as a result of the procedure. Those who undergo early amniocentesis (that is, during the late first trimester) are at an even greater risk of experiencing a miscarriage than women who have the procedure during their second trimester.

In most cases, amniocentesis isn't performed until well into the second trimester. Given the length of time it can take to receive the test results, a pregnant woman who receives abnormal results from amniocentesis may decide to terminate her pregnancy in the middle of her second trimester, an experience that can be both physically difficult and emotionally traumatic.

The fine print

Amniocentesis is recommended for couples with a history of certain genetic diseases and birth defects affecting themselves, their prior offspring, or members of their families; or who have been shown to be

Watch Out!
Contact your caregiver immediately if you experience any bleeding or watery discharge following either amniocentesis or chorionic villus sampling. There is a small risk of pregnancy loss with each procedure.

high risk for chromosomal anomalies on their triple screen test.

Chorionic villus sampling

Chorionic villus sampling involves passing a catheter through the cervix (see the first of the following two figures) or a needle through the abdomen (see the second of the following two figures) to obtain a sample of chorionic villus tissue (the tissue that will eventually become the placenta). Because this tissue comes from the baby, it is able to provide information about the baby's genetic makeup.

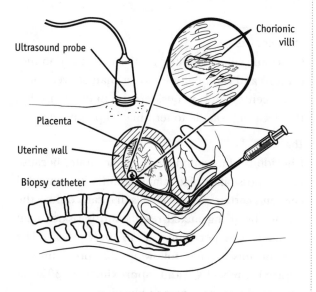

← Note!
Chorionic villus sampling—transcervical. Figure created by Articulate Graphics.

Some women find the procedure painful, but most describe it as merely uncomfortable.

Chorionic villus sampling is typically done at 10 to 12 weeks. It can take anywhere from a few days to a few weeks to get the results, depending on the extent of the testing performed.

Note! ➜
Chorionic villus
sampling—
transabdominal.
Figure created by
Articulate
Graphics.

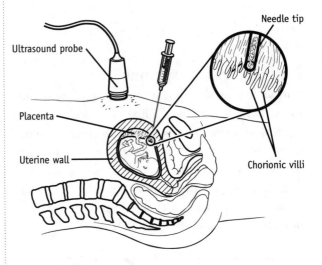

Bright Idea
CVS is a tricky
procedure that
should be per-
formed by a
skilled practi-
tioner. Don't just
settle for a refer-
ral to a particu-
lar facility—ask
to be referred to
a specific person
who has a
proven track
record with CVS
(that is, some-
one with accept-
ably low miscar-
riage rates when
performing the
procedure).

The benefits

Chorionic villus sampling is safer than early amniocentesis and can be done sooner than conventional
amniocentesis, a key consideration in the event that
the decision is made to terminate a pregnancy.

The risks

Chorionic villus sampling is less accurate, because
of the possibility of contamination with maternal
cells and certain placental cells that can confuse the
picture by giving mixed results and is riskier than
amniocentesis performed at 16 to 18 weeks. The
rate of miscarriage following the procedure is
approximately 1%, and approximately 30% of
women report some type of bleeding.

Note: Early concerns about limb reduction
abnormalities in babies whose mothers underwent
chorionic villus sampling during pregnancy have
not been borne out by the evidence, so this is one
less thing to worry about.

The fine print

Chorionic villus sampling is often recommended to
women who are at risk of giving birth to a baby with

Down syndrome; those with sickle-cell disease or thalassemia; those who are at risk of giving birth to a baby with cystic fibrosis, hemophilia, Huntington's disease, or muscular dystrophy; and those who prefer to get an answer by the end of the first trimester.

Unlike amniocentesis, chorionic villus sampling can't be used to detect neural tube defects.

Ultrasounds (sonograms)

Although the American medical establishment has yet to prove that routine ultrasounds result in better outcomes for mothers and babies, the majority of pregnant women continue to receive at least one ultrasound during their pregnancies. This is one testing procedure that most pregnant women enjoy, because it gives them the opportunity to "meet" their babies—if only on-screen.

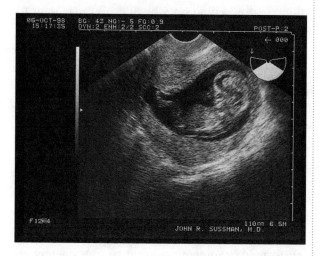

← Note!
Sonogram. Image courtesy John R. Sussman, M.D.

An ultrasound involves bouncing high-frequency sound waves off the fetus to create a corresponding image on a computer screen. It can be done either by rubbing a transducer on a pregnant woman's abdomen or by inserting an ultrasonic probe in her vagina.

If you're having a transabdominal ultrasound, you may be required to have a full bladder. This is because a full bladder helps to push the uterus out of the pelvic cavity and into full view of the ultrasound equipment. You will be asked to consume 32 ounces of liquid before the test. You can best accomplish this by drinking 32 ounces of liquid an hour before your test. You'll find it easier to get the liquids down if you consume a variety of beverages: herbal tea, fruit juice, clear soup, club soda, and so on. Just be sure to avoid beverages that are overly filling (for example, milkshakes) or you'll never manage to get 32 ounces of liquid down.

Before you start downing a tray full of drinks, call your doctor's office to make sure that everything is proceeding on schedule. You may want to delay your intake of fluids by a quarter-hour or so if the doctor is falling behind schedule.

If, on the other hand, you're having a transvaginal ultrasound, you will need to have an empty bladder. Be sure to allow enough time to go to the bathroom right before you have your ultrasound.

Ultrasounds can be performed at any stage of pregnancy. Some women will have a series of ultrasounds during their pregnancies; others will have one or none. The results will be conveyed either immediately (if the ultrasound is being conducted by your doctor) or later (if the ultrasound is being performed by someone other than your doctor).

You can find some detailed information about ultrasound, including some actual ultrasound images, at the Obstetric Ultrasound Web site: http://home.hkstar.com/~joewoo/joewoo2.html.

> **❝**
> I did not have any early ultrasounds done. My midwife's attitude was that unless there was a problem, a routine ultrasound wasn't necessary, and David and I agreed.
> —Leila, 33, mother of one
> **❞**

The benefits

Ultrasound can be used to

- confirm your due date by measuring the size of the fetus at 16 to 20 weeks' gestation or earlier (a measurement that is accurate within plus or minus 5 to 10 days at that stage of pregnancy);

- check for the presence of an intrauterine device if that was the method of birth control you were using at the time you became pregnant;

- check for multiples;

- monitor the baby's growth and assess her well-being;

- detect certain fetal abnormalities;

- locate the fetus, the umbilical cord, and the placenta during amniocentesis and chorionic villus sampling;

- measure the amount of amniotic fluid;

- determine the cause of any abnormal bleeding;

- assess the condition of the placenta if it appears that the baby is developing slowly or is in distress;

- determine the condition of the cervix (for example, whether it has begun to open prematurely);

- check for miscarriage, an ectopic pregnancy, a hydatidiform mole (that is, "molar pregnancy"), or fetal demise (a concern if no fetal movement has been detected by week 22 or if movements appear to cease at any time thereafter);

- determine the baby's sex (the accuracy of which depends both on the baby's position and the skill of the person conducting the ultrasound);

Bright Idea
If you have an ultrasound—particularly a screening ultrasound at 18-20 weeks—find out if you can have it done at a facility that allows you to take home a video of your baby. While most facilities will give patients still pictures of their babies, many are now equipped to make a video as well—a wonderful keepsake for our high-tech times.

- decide which delivery method to use (vaginal versus cesarean) based on the baby's size and position, the position of the placenta, and other factors;

- reassure the mother that the pregnancy is proceeding well (a valid use of ultrasound in cases in which the mother has a history of pregnancy loss or appears to need reassurance).

The risks

Although there are no known risks to ultrasound, it is still a relatively new technology. That's why the American College of Obstetricians and Gynecologists does not recommend its routine use during pregnancy. If your caregiver recommends that you have an ultrasound, make sure that you find out whether he routinely sends all of his patients for ultrasounds or whether an ultrasound is warranted in your case.

The fine print

Some doctors and ultrasound technicians will allow you to tape your ultrasound—and others won't. Some will provide you with one or more still photos of your baby, either free or for a nominal charge.

Although partners and support people are welcome to be present at most ultrasounds, the situation varies from facility to facility. Make sure that you understand the policies at a particular facility up front and plan accordingly.

Percutaneous umbilical blood sampling (PUBS)

Percutaneous umbilical blood sampling, also called cordocentesis, involves taking a sample of fetal blood from the umbilical cord by using an

Watch Out!
Some insurance companies and HMOs do not cover the cost of ultrasound. Others require that pregnant women be pre-approved for the procedure. Make sure that you know who's picking up the tab before you consent to the procedure.

amniocentesis-like needle inserted through the maternal abdominal wall into the baby's umbilical cord near its junction with the placenta, with ultrasound for visual guidance. The sample is then analyzed for blood disorders and infections.

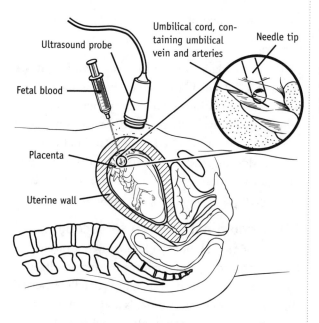

Ultrasound probe

Umbilical cord, containing umbilical vein and arteries

Needle tip

Fetal blood

Placenta

Uterine wall

← Note! Percutaneous Umbilical Blood Sampling. Figure created by Articulate Graphics.

The procedure is generally performed after 16 weeks' gestation and is typically offered at larger medical centers that has staff with specialized expertise in PUBS. It is rarely necessary to perform except in cases in which additional fetal cells are necessary to clarify genetic results from CVS or amniocentesis or when needed to assess for fetal anemia in conditions in which the baby is at high risk.

The benefits
Percutaneous umbilical blood sampling can be used to detect

- Rh incompatibility problems (to see if a fetal blood transfusion is warranted)
- blood disorders
- infections (for example, rubella, toxoplasmosis, and herpes)
- chromosomal problems

The risks

PUBS is a riskier procedure than amniocentesis: between 1/50 and 1/100 babies are lost due to complications resulting from the procedure. Consequently, it is typically reserved for cases in which the test results are needed right away (that is, if you are considering the possibility of terminating the pregnancy, and time is running out) or if there is no other method of obtaining the same information.

Transabdominal embryo fetoscopy

A transabdominal embryo fetoscopy is a rarely performed procedure that involves passing an ultrafine scope into the uterus via a tiny needle inserted through the pregnant woman's abdomen. It can be used to diagnose a potentially lethal skin disorder, multiple Ptyerigium syndrome, and another called Epidermolysis Bullosum by skin biopsy. It is typically performed after 10 weeks' gestation.

The benefits

A transabdominal embryo fetosocopy allows the doctor to observe the fetus, placenta, and amniotic fluid. The procedure can also be used to take blood samples from the junction of the umbilical cord and placenta and to remove small amounts of fetal or placental tissue.

The risks
Transabdominal embryo fetoscopy has a miscarriage rate of 3% to 5%.

The fine print
Transabdominal embryo fetoscopy is recommended for couples who have previously given birth to a child with a condition that cannot be detected by using any other prenatal diagnostic technique.

The future of prenatal testing
So what lies ahead in the Brave New World of prenatal testing? Plenty, it would appear.

There are a few developments that appear to have particular promise: a new chemical marker for Down syndrome that would enable a maternal blood test to be conducted at as early as 10 weeks' gestation, and a high-resolution ultrasound technique that would make it possible to conduct an accurate aneuploidy screen at 10 weeks' gestation. Also on the horizon is a way of gathering fetal cells from the maternal blood, allowing for fetal diagnostic tests of a wide variety to be done with a sample of the pregnant mother's blood.

There are also, of course, a growing number of genetic tests available to couples who wish to obtain detailed information on their risks of giving birth to a child with a birth defect prior to planning a pregnancy. (As you may recall, we discussed this issue in greater detail in Chapter 1.)

What to do if the test brings bad news
Although the odds of receiving good news from any of the prenatal tests that we have just discussed are decidedly in your favor, sometimes the news you receive is nothing short of devastating. If you find out that you are carrying a child with a severe—even

fatal—condition, you will be forced to make some very difficult decisions concerning your pregnancy.

You may decide to carry your pregnancy to term if

- you are prepared to raise a child with a severe disability or give birth to a baby who either is stillborn or dies shortly after birth;

- you are morally opposed to abortion under any circumstances;

- you feel more comfortable carrying your baby to term and then letting nature take its course;

- you want to cherish the remaining time with your baby, even if much or all of the time you are able to spend together takes place during your pregnancy rather than after the birth.

On the other hand, you may decide to terminate your pregnancy as soon as possible if

- you are not prepared emotionally or financially to raise a child with a severe disability;

- you are not willing to carry a child to term, only to watch him or her die during or shortly after birth;

- you are not morally opposed to abortion;

- you are concerned that your baby is suffering and do not wish to prolong his suffering any longer than necessary;

- you are concerned that your baby will be subjected to painful and costly interventions if he is born alive and that you will not be legally permitted to refuse those interventions;

- you wish to put this painful experience behind you as soon as possible.

Some parents choose to proceed with their pregnancies, even if that means facing life with a severely disabled child, giving birth to a stillborn child, or giving birth to a child who may live for only a few hours or days. Others choose to terminate their pregnancies.

Here are some factors you may wish to weigh as you go about making this incredibly difficult decision:

- What chance does the baby have of being born alive? Of leading a "normal" life?

- How much would the baby suffer physically and emotionally?

- Would the baby be able to live at home? If so, who would be prepared to care for her? You? Your partner?

- Is your marriage strong enough to survive the strain of caring for a severely disabled child? How might it affect your relationships with your other children?

- Are the baby's disabilities treatable? If so, how many and what types of surgeries would be required?

- What are the odds that these treatments would be successful? What quality of life could your baby expect to enjoy after these treatments?

- Would you be able to find the funds to pay for these treatments?

- What are your feelings about abortion?

As you can see, there are no easy answers to these questions. Deciding whether to proceed with your pregnancy or terminate it at this stage is probably one of the most difficult choices you will ever have to make. You and your partner may find it helpful to sit down with a therapist who has experience in helping families to work through these issues. If you don't know whom to turn to for support, ask your doctor to recommend someone who will treat you with sensitivity and compassion regardless of what option you ultimately choose.

Because you may have to come to a decision fairly quickly, you may find that you have a tendency to second-guess your decision after the fact. This reaction is perfectly normal, according to Deborah L. Davis, Ph.D, author of *Empty Cradle, Broken Heart,* who offers these words of wisdom: "It is important to remember that whether you had two minutes or two years, emotional turmoil would accompany whatever decision you made. After all, you had to make an impossible choice between 'terrible' and 'horrible.'"

Preparing for the birth of a child with a severe disability

If you will be giving birth to a child who will be severely disabled, you need to find out as much as you can about the challenges of raising a child with this particular disability and then spend some time planning for your child's birth. It's important to find out from your caregiver what medical interventions may be necessary following the birth and what role you can expect to play during your baby's first few hours of life. You might find it helpful to write a birth plan that specifies which interventions you would like your child to receive—and which ones you would prefer to decline (assuming, of course, that you have that choice).

Just the facts

- Although prenatal tests can be a source of valuable information about the health of the baby, they are not the best choice for everyone.

- Alpha-fetoprotein is used to screen for neural tube defects and Down syndrome.

- Amniocentesis is used to diagnose chromosomal defects, neural tube defects, genetic defects, and other problems. The miscarriage rate following the procedure is approximately 1/200 or less.

- Chorionic villus sampling (CVS) can be used to detect a number of disorders, but not neural tube defects. It is riskier than amniocentesis: the miscarriage rate is approximately 1/100.

- Ultrasound is one of the most common types of prenatal tests. It is widely believed to be safe during pregnancy, but the American College of Obstetricians and Gynecologists argues against its routine use at the present time.

- Percutaneous umbilical blood sampling (PUBS) involves taking a sample of fetal blood from the umbilical cord. The sample is then analyzed for blood disorders, infections, and a range of other problems. It has a miscarriage rate of 1% to 2%.

- Transabdominal embryo fetoscopy is used to observe the fetus, placenta, and amniotic fluid in utero or to take blood or tissue samples. It has a miscarriage rate of 3% to 5%.

- Tests that are currently under development include a new chemical marker for Down syndrome that would enable a maternal blood test to be conducted at as early as 10 weeks' gestation and a high-resolution ultrasound technique that would make it possible to conduct an accurate aneuploidy screen at 10 weeks' gestation. Both would be used for the diagnosis of chromosomal anomalies. Also on the horizon is a way of gathering fetal cells from the maternal blood, allowing for fetal diagnostic tests of a wide variety to be done with a sample of the pregnant mother's blood.

- If prenatal testing reveals that you are likely to give birth to a baby with a severe—or even fatal—disability, you may decide to terminate the pregnancy.

GET THE SCOOP ON...
Weight gain during pregnancy ▪ Nutrition during
pregnancy ▪ Exercising during pregnancy ▪
Medications during pregnancy ▪ Other hazards
to avoid ▪ Sex during pregnancy ▪ Working
during pregnancy

Lifestyle 101: Making the Best Choices for Your Baby

Chapter 8

Think it's tough being pregnant today? Imagine what it was like to be an expectant mother 100 years ago. You were not merely expected to protect your baby's physical well-being by eating well, exercising, and leaving your corset unlaced. You were also expected to begin to educate your child from the moment of conception and to think pure thoughts that would encourage your child to develop into a morally upstanding citizen. Sex was obviously out of the question, according to the author of this particular marriage manual, who took great pains to remind his readers that having sex during pregnancy wasn't merely unnecessary; it was also morally wrong: "Impregnation is the only mission of intercourse, and after that has taken place, intercourse can subserve no other purpose than sensual gratification."

Although attitudes about pregnancy have changed a great deal in the past 100 years, the

Victorians did manage to get one fact straight: a pregnant woman's lifestyle has a major impact on her baby's well-being.

In this chapter, we provide the facts you'll need to make the best possible lifestyle choices when it comes to eating, exercising, taking medications, avoiding hazards to your baby, remaining sexually active, and working during pregnancy.

Weight gain during pregnancy

It takes approximately 80,000 calories to grow a baby. That amounts to approximately 300 extra calories per day. So although you are technically "eating for two" during your pregnancy, you certainly don't need to consume enough food to feed yourself and a 250-pound trucker!

Before we get into a detailed discussion about what foods your body needs during pregnancy, let's stop to consider how much weight your body needs to gain and why.

Bright Idea
If you're con-
cerned that you
are gaining
weight too
quickly, measure
the circumference
of your upper
thighs weekly. If
the weight you're
gaining is within
the normal range,
the measurement
should stay
about the same.

Your gain plan

Take a look around the waiting room the next time you're sitting in your doctor's or midwife's office, and you'll see that pregnant women come in all shapes and sizes. Some start out overweight and some start out underweight. Some gain large amounts of weight during their pregnancies; others gain only a little. That's why health-care practitioners are steering away from the conventional wisdom that states that all pregnant women need to gain a certain amount of weight, period. Instead, many are choosing to come up with a customized weight-gain plan for each woman. Here are some of the factors that are generally considered:

- **Your prepregnancy weight:** If you start your pregnancy at a normal weight (see Table 8.1), you will likely be encouraged to gain between 25 and 35 pounds during pregnancy, a figure recommended by the National Academy of Sciences/Institute of Medicine (NAS/IOM). If you are underweight, you'll be encouraged to gain a little more—28 to 40 pounds—and if you are overweight, you'll be encouraged to gain a little less—15 to 25 pounds.

- **Your age:** Because their own bodies are still developing, adolescent women are encouraged to gain more weight than women in their 20s, 30s, and 40s: 28 to 40 pounds.

- **Your height:** Short women are often encouraged to gain slightly less than their taller counterparts: 18 to 30 pounds.

- **The number of babies you are carrying:** If you are carrying twins, you will need to gain between 35 and 45 pounds during your pregnancy. If you are carrying triplets or other high-order multiples, you will need to gain even more.

You should aim for slow, gradual weight gain during pregnancy. Although you may not gain any weight during the first trimester (and, in fact, may lose a few pounds if you're having particular difficulty with morning sickness), you should plan to gain one pound a week during your second and third trimesters—slightly less if you're overweight, and slightly more if you're underweight. You may not gain any weight during the last four weeks of pregnancy. In fact, you may even lose a pound or two.

This means that you can expect to gain approximately 25% of your weight between weeks 12 and 20, another 50% between weeks 20 and 30, and the remaining 25% between weeks 30 and 36.

> **66**
> If you have an eating disorder like I have, ignore all that sanctimonious preaching in certain pregnancy books about how if you eat a donut you're a bad pregnant lady. Getting stressed out about food is bad anytime, and it's worse when you are pregnant.
> —Laura, 31, mother of one
> **99**

TABLE 8.1: WHERE DOES YOUR WEIGHT FIT IN?

Height	Underweight	Normal	Overweight	Obese
5'	< 102	102–132	133–147	≥ 148
5'2"	< 107	107–141	152–157	≥ 158
5'4"	< 116	116–152	153–170	≥ 171
5'6"	< 123	123–161	162–180	≥ 181
5'8"	< 130	130–171	172–191	≥ 192
5'10"	< 138	138–181	182–202	≥ 203

Source: National Academy of Sciences

Unofficially...
Maternal fat stores are deposited early in pregnancy in anticipation of the rapid fetal growth that occurs during the last 10 weeks of pregnancy.

Why it's important to gain weight during pregnancy

Many women find it hard to believe how much weight gain is required to support a healthy pregnancy. After all, if the baby weighs in at $7^1/2$ pounds, where does the other $22^1/2$ pounds of a 30-pound weight gain end up?

As you can see from the following table, you gain far more weight during pregnancy than your baby. If you keep your weight gain within the recommended range, you can expect to lose most of this weight within the first few months after birth. So even though you may worry that all 30 pounds are going to end up on your hips or thighs, you could be pleasantly surprised by how easy it can be to lose this "baby fat" after the delivery.

TABLE 8.2: WEIGHT GAIN: WHERE THE POUNDS GO

Maternal stores of fat, protein, and other nutrients (for both pregnancy and lactation)	7 lbs.
Increased body fluid	4 lbs.
Increased blood	4 lbs.
Breast growth	2 lbs.
Enlarged uterus	2 lbs.
Amniotic fluid	2 lbs.
Placenta	$1^1/2$ lbs.
Baby	$7^1/2$ lbs.
Total	30 lbs.

Nutrition during pregnancy

Contrary to what some pregnancy books would have you believe, you don't have to have a Ph.D in nutrition sciences or a personal chef to have a baby. Although it's important to understand some basic facts about nutrition—what nutrients your baby needs and why—no one expects you to analyze every bite you eat to determine its nutritional composition.

What's more, it's perfectly okay to "fall off the wagon" from time to time. In fact, we'd prefer it if you didn't feel as if there was a wagon to fall off in the first place! If you feel as though you're on some sort of diet—that you're depriving yourself of the foods you enjoy for the good of your baby—you're probably attempting to change your eating habits too quickly, something that in all likelihood will lead you to more than one secret rendezvous with a few Twinkies at some point during your pregnancy. If you're trying to reform your eating habits, don't go "cold turkey" overnight. Make gradual changes to your eating habits—ones you can sustain during your pregnancy and beyond. One book that can help you to make some permanent lifestyle changes, *Tailoring Your Tastes,* by Linda Omichinski, RD, and Heather Wiebe Hildebrand, RN, BSN, shows you how to train your taste buds to enjoy foods that are lower in sugar and fat and higher in fiber.

The foods your body needs

You've no doubt heard of the Food Pyramid, the U.S. Department of Agriculture's guidelines for healthful eating. Just to refresh your memory, the pyramid shows which foods you should be eating a lot of (breads and cereals) and which you should be

Watch Out!
Gaining too little weight can put you at risk of giving birth to a low-birthweight baby (that is, a baby who is 5.5 pounds or less at birth), who may experience developmental delays, and increases your chances of experiencing stillbirth or neonatal death. Gaining too much weight during pregnancy increases your chances of experiencing back strain, high blood pressure and preeclampsia, gestational diabetes, macrosomia (an excessively large baby), weight problems after your baby is born, and stillbirth or neonatal death.

eating less frequently (fats, oils, and sweets). (See the following figure.)

The American College of Obstetrics and Gynecologists (ACOG) recommends that pregnant women consume the following foods each day:

- nine servings from the bread, cereal, rice, and pasta group;
- four servings from the vegetable group;
- three servings from the fruit group;
- three to four servings from the milk, yogurt, and cheese group;
- two to three servings from the meat, poultry, fish, dry beans, eggs, and nuts group;
- fats, oils, and sweets in moderation.

Servings are defined in the following ways:

- Bread, cereal, rice, or pasta: one slice of bread; one cup of ready-to-eat cereal; one-half cup of cooked cereal, rice, or pasta; or five or six small crackers
- Vegetables: one cup raw, leafy vegetables; one-half cup of cooked or chopped raw vegetables; or three-quarters cup of vegetable juice
- Fruit: one medium apple, banana, or orange; one-half cup of chopped, cooked, or canned fruit, or 1 cup of berries; or one-half to three-quarters cup of fruit juice
- Milk, yogurt, and cheese: one cup of milk or yogurt, 1.5 ounces of natural cheese, or two ounces of processed cheese
- Meat, poultry, fish, dry beans, eggs, and nuts: two to three ounces of cooked lean meat, poultry, or fish (this portion is about the size of your

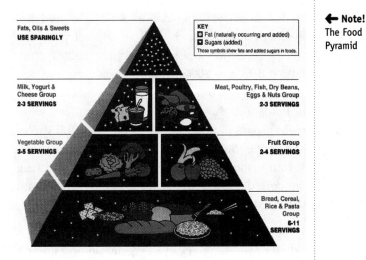

← Note!
The Food
Pyramid

palm or a deck of cards); one-half cup of cooked dry beans; one egg; two tablespoons of peanut butter; or one-third cup of nuts.

Each of these foods plays an important role in your diet. (See Table 8.3.)

TABLE 8.3: THE FOODS YOUR BODY NEEDS

Food Group	Why Your Body Needs These Foods
Bread, iron-fortified cereals, rice, and pasta	Provide complex carbohydrates, an important source of energy, vitamins, minerals, and fiber
Vegetables	An excellent source of vitamins A and C, fiber, folic acid, and minerals such as iron and magnesium
Fruit	An excellent source of vitamins A and C, potassium, and fiber
Milk, yogurt, and cheese	A major source of protein, calcium, phosphorus, and vitamins
Meat, poultry, fish, dry beans, eggs, and nuts	An important source of the B vitamins, protein, iron, and zinc

If you follow the guidelines set out by the Food Pyramid, approximately 50% to 60% of your diet will come from carbohydrates, 20% to 30% from fats, and 15% to 20% from proteins.

There's one other thing your body needs: plenty of fluids. You should plan to consume at least six to eight glasses of water per day. You can tell if you're drinking enough by noting the color of your urine. If your urine is light yellow or clear, you're drinking enough; if it's dark yellow, it's too concentrated and you need to increase your fluid intake.

Following a vegetarian diet

Whether you are a vegan (a vegetarian who doesn't consume any animal products), a lacto-vegetarian (a vegetarian who consumes dairy products), a lacto-ovo vegetarian (a vegetarian who eats dairy and eggs), or a semivegetarian (a vegetarian who consumes dairy products, eggs, fish, and chicken), you will need to pay careful attention to your diet to ensure that you're getting adequate levels of nutrients. Specifically, you will want to maximize your iron absorption by combining iron-rich foods with foods that help with the absorption of iron (that is, those that are rich in vitamin C) and ensure that you are obtaining an adequate number of complete protein exchanges—either from legumes and grains or from legumes, grains, and dairy foods.

Vegetarians are also at risk of developing deficiencies in vitamins B12, B2, and D, and in calcium, iron, and zinc.

Make sure that your doctor or midwife is aware that you are following a vegetarian diet. She may want to check your hemoglobin regularly during your pregnancy and recommend a vitamin B12 supplement.

Bright Idea
For more information on the Food Guide Pyramid, contact the Center for Nutrition Policy and Promotion, 1120 20th Street N.W., Suite 200, North Lobby, Washington, DC 20036; phone 202-606-8000; Web site www.usda.gov/fcs/cnpp.htm.

Lactose intolerance

If you are someone who is lactose intolerant (that is, someone who has difficulty digesting the sugar in milk), you may have difficulty getting enough calcium in your diet. Here are some tips on maximizing your intake of calcium-rich foods:

- Get your calcium from other sources, such as tofu (specifically, calcium-fortified soy milk), calcium-fortified bread or juice, dark-green leafy vegetables, sardines, and salmon.

- Drink milk at mealtimes rather than on its own.

- Try lactose-reduced cottage cheese and yogurt.

- Experiment with smaller portion sizes (such as one-half cup of milk rather than a full glass).

- Choose low-fat cheeses (because a large percentage of the lactose is removed during processing) and hard cheeses such as Swiss and cheddar (because they are naturally lower in lactose).

- Eat yogurt that contains acidophilus or active cultures (because these active cultures can actually help you to digest lactose).

- Drink lactose-reduced milk or add over-the-counter enzyme drops (for example, Lactaid) to your milk to help break down the lactose. You may also opt to take a Lactaid pill with dairy foods.

Morning sickness

Morning sickness affects approximately 80% of pregnant women at some point during the first four months of pregnancy, although only 50% actually experience vomiting.

Unofficially...
In an effort to give vegetarians a sexier new image, the British vegetarian society has produced a movie-theater commercial that is so steamy that it's been given an "over 15" rating. The controversial commercial—aptly named "hot dinner"—includes an asparagus tip that drips melted butter suggestively and a pea being fondled in its pod.

Watch Out!
If your intake of calcium is inadequate, your baby may draw calcium from your bones, something that can put you at increased risk for osteoporosis later in life. If you are concerned that you are not getting enough calcium in your diet, talk to your caregiver about the possibility of taking a calcium supplement. If you are taking prenatal vitamins, make sure that they contain calcium.

If you are experiencing morning sickness, you may be concerned that your baby is missing out on important nutrients because you're feeling too sick to eat much of anything. Fortunately, morning sickness is rarely severe enough to harm the developing fetus. What's more, it usually doesn't last much past the end of the first trimester.

Unless you are experiencing a severe form of morning sickness known as hyperemesis gravidarum—a condition that is characterized by dehydration, weight loss, acid-base imbalance, and electrolyte deficiencies, and that generally requires hospitalization—you can feel confident that your baby is not being unduly harmed by your inability to stomach anything other than soda crackers.

You can find some tips on managing morning sickness in Chapter 14.

Vitamins and minerals: where do they fit in?

Although the American College of Obstetricians and Gynecologists does not formally endorse the routine use of prenatal multivitamins during pregnancy, they do advise daily supplementation with 0.4 mg of folic acid both before and during pregnancy to reduce the risk of neural tube defects such as spinda bifida. Most doctors and midwives however, recommend that pregnant women do take some sort of multivitamin supplement. The reason is simple. It's almost impossible for pregnant women to meet their bodies' demands for iron and folic acid during pregnancy through diet alone. As the following table illustrates, your body's demand for these and other nutrients increases dramatically during pregnancy.

Table 8.4 shows how much more of each of the following nutrients your body needs during pregnancy.

TABLE 8.4: NUTRIENT WATCH

Calories	14%
Protein	20%
Vitamin D	100%
Vitamin E	25%
Vitamin K	8%
Vitamin C	17%
Thiamin	36%
Riboflavin	23%
Niacin	13%
Vitamin B6	27%
Folate	122%
Vitamin B12	10%
Calcium	50%
Phosphorus	50%
Magnesium	14%
Iron	100%
Zinc	25%
Iodine	17%
Selenium	18%

Source: National Academy of Sciences

The problem with choosing a prenatal vitamin is that it's sometimes difficult to know what you're getting. Because neither the Food and Drug Administration nor the American College of Obstetricians and Gynecologists has established any clear standards for prenatal vitamins, you could find yourself paying top dollar for a so-called "prenatal" vitamin that is virtually identical to your standard run-of-the-mill multivitamin.

Here's some more vitamin-related info for you to chew on.

Despite the pretty packages, there is no evidence that prenatal supplements (both over-the-counter and prescription) have anything more to offer the

Unofficially...
A pregnant woman absorbs twice as much iron from foods as a nonpregnant woman.

majority of pregnant women than a standard multi-vitamin formulation containing at least 0.4 milligrams of folic acid.

If you are in the habit of eating healthful foods before you become pregnant, you probably don't need to worry about taking a prenatal vitamin. Chances are your diet will give you all of the nutrients you and your baby need—if not more. The secret is to let your hunger be your guide and to reach for healthful foods most of the time. (You'll note that we said "most of the time." Although some pregnancy books will leave you feeling like an unfit mother if you occasionally indulge your Twinkie habit, we'd rather see you treat yourself occasionally than turn your pregnancy into a nine-month-long exercise in junk-food deprivation.)

Although there is no proof that vitamin supplementation is necessary in pregnancy (other than to ensure an adequate amount of folic acid), many women take supplements to cover any possible deficiencies in their diets, recognizing that in real life it is difficult, at best, to eat the recommended foods in the recommended amounts. If you choose to pay more for a specially formulated prenatal vitamin (as opposed to a store-brand multivitamin) be sure to look for one that contains

- between 4,000 and 5,000 I.U. (International Units) of vitamin A
- between 800 and 1,000 mcg (1mg) of folic acid
- no more than 400 I.U. of vitamin D
- at least 200 to 300 mg of calcium
- at least 70 mg of vitamin C
- at least 1.5 mg of thiamine
- at least 1.6 mg of riboflavin

Moneysaver
The top four vitamin money-wasters according to *Good Housekeeping* magazine: "Natural" formulations that are chemically identical to their synthetic counterparts; multivitamins that are supposedly designed to meet the unique nutritional needs of women, but that are no different than any other multivitamin; brand-name vitamins that are chemically identical to generic brands; and "high potency" multivitamins that give you higher doses of nutrients you don't need.

- at least 2.6 mg of pyridoxine
- at least 17 mg of niacinamide
- at least 2.2 mg of vitamin B12
- at least 10 mg of vitamin E
- approximately 15 mg of zinc
- approximately 30 mg of iron

Note: Some prenatal supplements also contain magnesium, copper, biotin, or pantothenic acid.

If you are still unsure about what brand to choose, ask your doctor or midwife for a recommendation.

You are what you eat

Although prenatal supplements can play an important role during pregnancy, they are no substitute for healthful eating. That's why it's important to know which types of nutrients come from which types of foods—and what they can do for you and your baby. (See Table 8.5.)

Before we wrap up our discussion of vitamins and minerals, we'd like to pass along the latest news on vitamin A, calcium, and zinc-three nutrients that have been getting a fair bit of press in recent years.

The truth about vitamin A

There's been enough flip-flopping on the vitamin A issue to make anyone but a confirmed vitaminophile lose track of the debate. Although a recent study by the National Institute of Child Health and Human Development (NICHHD) seemed to pooh-pooh the link between high doses of vitamin A during pregnancy and birth defects, the American College of Obstetricians and Gynecologists continues to urge caution. ACOG recommends a maximum daily dosage of vitamin A

Timesaver
The interactive food finder at Fast Food Facts, www.olen.com/food/, allows you to search the menus of well-known restaurant chains and find out how various fast foods measure up. Just choose the restaurant and enter your criteria (for example, "maximum 10 grams of fat"), and you will be presented with a list of menu options. (or, use the USDA Nutrient Database at www.nal.usda.gov/fnic/cgi-bin/nut_search.pl.)

TABLE 8.5: VITAMINS AND MINERALS FROM A TO Z

What It Is	What It Does	Where to Find It
Vitamin A (retinol and carotene)	Maintains skin, body tissues, and vision; helps your body to respond to infection. Necessary for the growth of fetal tissue as well as bone formation and growth.	Liver, fortified milk, carrots, tomatoes, cantaloupe, whole milk, butter, cheese, egg yolk, cod, and other fatty fish
Vitamin B1 (thiamine)	Helps your body to digest carbohydrates. Needed for normal functioning of nervous system.	Whole grains, enriched grains, legumes, nuts, beans, organ meats, pork, brewer's yeast, wheat germ
Vitamin B2 (riboflavin)	Promotes tissue growth and regeneration and enables your body to use carbohydrates, fat, and protein.	Brewer's yeast, wheat germ, whole grains, green leafy vegetables, milk, cheese, other milk products, eggs
Vitamin B3 (niacin)	Helps to release energy from food and plays a role in DNA synthesis and the maintenance of healthy skin, nerves, and digestive system.	Whole grains, wheat germ, organ meats, green vegetables, oily fish, eggs, milk, poultry, cereals, legumes
Vitamin B5 (pantothenic acid)	Aids in metabolism of food, especially proteins.	Organ meats, eggs, peanuts, cheese, cereals, milk, vegetables
Vitamin B6 (pyridoxine)	Enables your body to make use of protein. Essential to the formation of all tissues, including the brain, nervous	Brewer's yeast, whole grains, soy flour, organ meats, wheat germ, mushrooms, potatoes

Nutrient	Function	Food Sources
	system, and muscles, as well as hormones, enzymes, red blood cells, and neurotransmitters (brain chemicals that relay messages).	
Vitamin B12 (cyanocobalamin)	Used to form hemoglobin and the baby's central nervous system. Helps your body to make use of protein, folic acid, and fatty acids. Also plays a role in the correct replication of the genetic code within each cell, and the formation of body tissues.	Kidney, fish, milk, eggs, meat
Vitamin C (absorbic acid)	Helps with the formation of connective tissue and the absorption of iron. Assists with both healing and the formation of bones.	Citrus fruits, strawberries, dark-green leafy vegetables, tomatoes
Vitamin D (calciferol)	Helps with the formation and maintenance of bones. Necessary for the growth of fetal tissue.	Fortified milk, oily fish, eggs, butter, liver
Vitamin E	A potent antioxidant. Protects cells from damage and degeneration. Necessary for the growth of fetal tissue.	Wheat germ, egg yolks, peanuts, seeds, vegetable oils
Vitamin K	Aids in blood coagulation. Necessary for the growth of fetal tissue.	Leafy green vegetables

continues

What It Is	What It Does	Where to Find It
Calcium	Strengthens bones and teeth, promotes blood clotting, and regulates nerve and muscle function.	Milk, cheese, sardines, salmon, oysters, shrimp, tofu, kale, and broccoli
Chromium	Strengthens your bones and the baby's skeleton, and helps to regulate your blood sugar levels.	Whole-grain breads and cereals, wheat germ, orange juice
Copper	Helps body to use iron and aids in energy metabolism. Aids in the development and maintenance of your baby's heart, arteries, blood vessels, and skeletal and nervous systems.	Chicken, fish, meat, avocado, potatoes, soybeans
Folic acid	Assists with cell division and the development of the baby's central nervous system.	Raw leafy vegetables, soy flour, oranges, bananas, walnuts, brewer's yeast, legumes
Iodine	Strengthens your bones and the baby's skeleton.	Iodized table salt, shellfish, seaweed
Iron	Necessary for the formation of red blood cells, which carry oxygen to your tissues and the baby.	Kidneys, fish, egg yolks, red meat, cereals, molasses, apricots, shellfish, dried fruits
Magnesium	Works with calcium to build bone. Aids in muscle contraction and relaxation and plays a role in energy metabolism, blood sugar regulation, nerve transmission,	Low-fat milk, peanuts, bananas, wheat germ, dark-green leafy vegetables, and oysters

	and the removal of toxic waste products from the body.	
Phosphorus	Needed for fetal skeletal and tooth formation.	Milk and milk products, meat, poultry, fish, whole-grain cereals, legumes
Potassium	Maintains proper muscle tone and fluid balance. Regulates blood pressure and aids in the transmission of nerve impulses and muscle contractions.	Fruits, vegetables, fish, peanuts, potatoes
Selenium	Strengthens the immune system.	Whole grains, seafood, lean meat
Zinc	Strengthens the enzymes that drive the metabolic system; may play a role in strengthening the baby's immune system. Needed to produce insulin.	Wheat bran, eggs, nuts, onions, shellfish, sunflower seeds, wheat germ, whole wheat, lean meat, turkey, dried beans and peas

Sources: Dr. Miriam Stoppard. *Conception Pregnancy and Birth*. Toronto: Macmillan Canada, 1993. Sheila Kitzinger. *The Complete Book of Pregnancy and Childbirth*. London: Dorling Kindersley Limited, 1989. And various online nutritional Web sites.

of 5,000 I.U. during pregnancy—about what you'll find in a standard prenatal vitamin, but significantly less than what you may find in some over-the-counter vitamin cocktails, some of which have been found to contain as much as 25,000 I.U. per daily dosage.

The facts about calcium and preeclampsia

Calcium does your body and your baby a lot of good during pregnancy, but according to a recent study by researchers at the National Institute of Child Health and Human Development, it doesn't prevent preeclampsia. Although previous studies had concluded that calcium supplementation could reduce the risk of preeclampsia by as much as 62%, the NICHHD study—which monitored the pregnancies of 4,589 first-time mothers—concluded that calcium supplementation is ineffective in preventing this serious pregnancy complication. What's more, high doses of calcium may actually cause problems in certain women with kidney disease or a history of kidney stones.

Something to zinc about

Pregnant women who take zinc supplements may deliver bigger, healthier babies, according to a study at the University of Alabama at Birmingham. Women in the study who received 25 milligrams of zinc along with their regular prenatal vitamins went on deliver babies with higher birthweights, larger head sizes, and fewer infections than women who didn't take zinc during their pregnancies. The findings were particularly pronounced for underweight women: those who took zinc delivered babies who were nearly a pound heavier than their nonzinc-consuming counterparts.

More food for thought

Here's the latest on caffeine, artificial sweeteners, and food-borne illness.

Caffeine update

The medical profession has done a fair bit of flip-flopping about caffeine over the years. Although some studies have demonstrated a link between caffeine consumption and miscarriage or Sudden Infant Death Syndrome (SIDS), others have failed to prove that caffeine is harmful to the developing baby.

That issue aside, you may want to limit your consumption of caffeine during pregnancy for the following reasons:

- Caffeine tends to act as a diuretic, drawing both fluid and calcium from the body.

- It can interfere with the absorption of iron.

- It can heighten mood swings.

- It can cause insomnia.

Caffeine is found in more foods than you may realize. If you want to cut back your consumption of caffeine, it's important to know which foods to avoid (see Table 8.6).

The facts about artificial sweeteners

In the United States, three artificial sweeteners are approved for use in foods and as sugar replacements: aspartame, saccharin, and acesulfame K. All three are considered to be safe for pregnant women (except for aspartame, which is unsafe for pregnant women who have phenylketonuria—PKU—and must restrict their intake of phenylalanine, an amino acid from all sources). To be on the safe side, however, it is probably a good idea to limit your

Watch Out!
Milk, tea, coffee, and antacids inhibit the absorption of iron. Try to avoid ingesting them at the same time as iron-rich foods.

Unofficially...
More than three-
quarters of preg-
nant women
experience crav-
ings during preg-
nancy, and more
than half have at
least one food
aversion. Some
experience a
strange phenome-
non known as
pica, in which
they crave
unusual sub-
stances such as
soil and laundry
starch. Now
there's some food
for thought!

TABLE 8.6: THE CAFFEINE CONTENT OF FOOD AND BEVERAGES

Item	Milligrams of Caffeine	
	Average	Range
Coffee (5 oz. cup)		
Brewed, drip method	115	60–180
Brewed, percolator	80	40–170
Instant	65	30–120
Decaffeinated, brewed	3	2–5
Decaffeinated, instant	2	1–5
Tea (5 oz. cup)		
Brewed, major U.S. brands	40	20–90
Brewed, imported brands	60	25–100
Instant	30	25–50
Iced (12 oz. glass)	70	67–76
Some soft drinks (6 oz.)	18	15–30
Cocoa beverages	4	2–20
Chocolate milk beverages (8 oz.)	5	2–7
Milk chocolate (1 oz.)	6	1–15
Dark chocolate, semi-sweet (1 oz.)	20	5–35
Baker's chocolate (1 oz.)	26	26
Chocolate-flavored syrup (1 oz.)	4	4

Source: U.S. Food and Drug Administration and National Soft Drink Association

intake of artificial sweeteners (even the sanctioned ones) during pregnancy.

Avoiding food-borne illness

Although food-borne illness is bad news at any time, it can be particularly harmful to a pregnant woman and her baby. Be on the lookout for improperly canned or preserved food that may lead to botulism; raw or undercooked pork or steak that may lead to toxoplasmosis; raw eggs, undercooked eggs, or chicken that may lead to salmonella; and soft cheeses (feta, brie, and Camembert), unpasteurized milk, and improperly cooked meat that may be a source of listeriosis (a food-borne illness that can be particularly harmful to the developing baby).

Exercising during pregnancy

The benefits of exercise during pregnancy are enough to make even a card-carrying coach potato head for the gym. Prenatal exercise can

- boost your energy

- help you to keep your weight gain within the target range

- contribute to an overall sense of well-being

- help to regulate your blood glucose levels, something that may help to reduce your chances of developing gestational diabetes

- prevent or relieve backache, leg cramps, and constipation

- help you to get the sleep your body needs

- get your body ready for childbirth and reduce your recovery time

Of course, prenatal exercise isn't for everyone. Your doctor or midwife will likely advise against a prenatal fitness program if

Bright Idea
Call the American Dietetic Association/ National Center for Nutrition and Dietetics Consumer Nutrition Hot Line at 800-366-1655 for general food and nutrition information or a referral to a registered dietitian in your area, or visit the American Dietetic Association Web site at www.eatright.org.

- you are experiencing pregnancy-induced high blood pressure

- you are having problems with persistent bleeding in the second or third trimester

- you have had preterm rupture of the membranes (PROM) or preterm labor in either your current pregnancy or a previous pregnancy

- your baby is experiencing intrauterine growth restriction

- your cervix is weak

- you have a history of second-trimester miscarriage

- you are carrying more than one baby

- you have a pre-existing medical condition such as heart disease or diabetes

- you are underweight

Choosing an activity

When it comes to prenatal fitness, all activities are not created equal. Some types of exercise may do you and your baby more harm than good.

The following types of exercise are generally considered to be good choices for pregnant women:

- walking,

- swimming,

- riding a stationary bicycle,

- participating in a prenatal fitness class that emphasizes stretching and low-impact aerobics. (See our Prenatal Fitness Class Checklist for tips on finding the class that's right for you.)

CHECKLIST: PRENATAL FITNESS CLASS

- Is the class held at a convenient location?

> 66
> Swimming is great. Don't worry about how you look in a bathing suit. You get bathing suit amnesty when you're obviously pregnant!
> —Laura, 31, mother of one
> 99

- Is the class held at a convenient time?

- Is it affordable?

- Is the class leader a certified fitness instructor?

- Does he have any specialized training in prenatal fitness?

- How long has he been teaching prenatal fitness classes?

- Does he encourage each participant to modify the workout to suit her own fitness level and stage of pregnancy?

- Is there a warm-up period at the beginning of the class?

- Is the workout designed to be low-impact?

- Is there a cool-down period at the end of the class?

- Are pillows or mats available for extra cushioning?

- Is the exercise room kept at a comfortable temperature?

- Are there showers available?

← Note!
Find out if you are required to produce a certificate from your doctor or midwife to prove that it is safe for you to exercise during pregnancy.

On the other hand, the following types of exercises are generally not recommended for pregnant women—especially in the later stages:

- contact sports such as football, basketball, and volleyball

- adventure sports such as parachuting, mountain climbing, and scuba diving

- sports with a high risk of trauma, such as skiing, horseback riding, surfing, and ice skating

- high-impact, weight-bearing sports such as running or jogging

Watch Out!
Avoid weight-
bearing exercises
such as running
or high-impact
aerobics if you
are having prob-
lems with sciat-
ica (pain in the
sacroiliac joints).
You may further
stress the joints
and add to the
amount of pain
that you are
experiencing.

Exercise and your changing body

Although it is generally safe to exercise during pregnancy, it's important to be aware of the ways in
which normal body changes during pregnancy may
impact your workout.

Here are a few important points:

- Your respiratory rate increases during pregnancy. This is your body's way of ensuring that
  the baby receives adequate amounts of oxygen.
  This tends to reduce the amount of oxygen
  available for exercise, however, and can result in
  both breathlessness and decreased endurance.

- Your growing uterus causes your center of gravity to change, which can cause you to lose your
  balance more easily and put strain on your
  lower back muscles.

- During pregnancy, your body releases a hormone called relaxin. Its function is to relax your
  joints and ligaments to make it easier for your
  body to give birth. Because relaxin loosens up
  all of the joints in your body—not just those in
  the pelvic region—you are more susceptible to
  spraining or straining your muscles and joints.

- Your metabolism speeds up during pregnancy.
  Because exercise also increases your metabolism, it's possible to experience low blood sugar
  during exercise.

- To speed up the delivery of oxygen to your baby,
  your blood volume increases by approximately
  40% during pregnancy, and your heart rate
  increases by approximately 15 beats per minute.
  This can result in occasional lightheadedness—
  particularly if you're anemic.

- When you exercise, your body releases a neuro-
  transmitter called norepinephrine. It increases

smooth muscle contractions, including painless uterine contractions.

- Your core body temperature increases when you exercise. Because an elevated core body temperature can be harmful to the fetus, it's important to consume adequate quantities of fluids when you are exercising—particularly if you're exercising in very hot weather.

Getting started

Here are some tips on getting started on a prenatal fitness program:

- Always consult your doctor or midwife before starting a prenatal fitness program. (If you're already active, you should also ask your doctor or midwife if you should modify your existing fitness program.)

- Start slowly and pay attention to your body's signals. If you're huffing and puffing, you're working too hard. Rather than making exercise an unpleasant experience (and one you're unlikely to stick with), gradually increase the length and intensity of your workouts as your strength and endurance increase.

- Plan to exercise for 20 to 30 minutes at least three times per week.

- Drink plenty of water while you are exercising to prevent overheating and dehydration. As a rule of thumb, you should limit strenuous exercise to 30 minutes (or less in humid weather) and then skip the post-exercise hot tub or sauna (to avoid potential damage to the fetus).

- Ensure that your workout includes both a warm-up and a cool-down.

Bright Idea
Although it's not generally a good idea to start running during pregnancy, you may be able to continue with an existing running program during pregnancy—assuming, of course, that you get the go-ahead from your doctor or midwife. You can read all about running during pregnancy at Running On Full at http://lifematters.com/rofintro.html.

Unofficially...
A recent study at
the University of
Michigan con-
firmed that per-
forming Kegel
exercises both
during and after
pregnancy reduces
your chances of
experiencing
incontinence both
in late pregnancy
and after birth.
Pregnant women
should practice
their Kegels by
starting and stop-
ping the flow of
urine. (Once you
have the hang of
things, though,
you can do
your Kegels
anywhere—in
your car or sitting
at your desk at
work. Starting
and stopping the
flow of urine may
have harmful
effects, so don't
do your Kegels
while you're
urinating.)

- Wear a bra that provides adequate support.

- Use an abdominal support for more strenuous exercise.

- If you find that exercising on your back makes you feel lightheaded or nauseated, then avoid this position. (When you are lying on your back, the weight of your pregnant uterus is placed on the inferior vena cava—the vein responsible for returning blood from the lower body to the heart. This can cause dizziness.)

- Avoid deep knee bends, full sit-ups, double-leg raises, and straight-leg toe touches.

- Make sure that your workout includes the four most important prenatal exercises: squatting, pelvic tilting or rocking, abdominal curl-ups, and pelvic floor exercises (also called Kegels). (See Table 8.7.)

- Remember that pregnancy alters your center of gravity, so it may be easier for you to lose your balance.

- Never exercise to the point of exhaustion.

- Stop exercising immediately if you experience vaginal bleeding or uterine contractions, or if your membranes rupture.

Taking medications during pregnancy

Nearly 2,500 years ago, the Greek physician Hippocrates warned that for the safety of the developing baby, drugs should be administered to pregnant women only from the fourth to the seventh month. Three millennia later, we're continuing to heed his warnings about the dangers of using medications during pregnancy—although we now realize that the period of greatest risk is during the earliest weeks of pregnancy.

TABLE 8.7: THE BIG FOUR: PREPARING YOUR BODY FOR LABOR

The Exercise	The Benefits	How to Do It
Squatting	Stretches the legs and opens the pelvis; a useful position for laboring, provided you have the leg strength and balance down pat.	Stand straight. Place your feet a shoulder's width apart and hold onto the back of a chair or your partner for balance. Bend your knees and lower your body as far as is comfortable while keeping your heels firmly on the floor. Hold this position for a few seconds, and then gradually rise to a standing position.
Pelvic tilting and rocking	Strengthens the muscles in your abdomen and back; helps to prevent or relieve backache while improving your overall posture.	Stand with your legs a comfortable distance apart. Breath out and tilt your pelvis forward and upward by simultaneously pulling in your abdominal muscles and bringing your buttocks forward. Hold this position for a few seconds and then release while breathing in.

continues

The Exercise	The Benefits	How to Do It
Abdominal curl ups	Strengthens the abdominal muscles that support the uterus.	Lie on your back and bend your knees. Raise your head and shoulders until your neck is about eight inches from the floor. Cross your hands over your abdominal area and gently pull yourself upward. Breath in and lower your body gently.
Pelvic floor exercises (Kegels)	Strengthens the muscles that support the abdominal organs. Can help prevent pregnancy incontinence and make birth easier.	Exercise these muscles by tightening them the way you would if you were trying to stop yourself from urinating. hold for three seconds and then release gradually.

The period of greatest vulnerability for the developing baby is when you are approximately 4 to 10 weeks from the first day of your last menstrual period—the period during which the baby's major organs are being formed. Exposure to a harmful substance during this period can result in either birth defects or miscarriages. If the fetus is exposed to a harmful substance prior to this—that is, during the first two weeks after conception—either it will be unaffected by the exposure or the cells will die and the pregnancy will not continue. A drug taken during the second and third trimesters may alter the growth and physiological and biochemical functioning of the developing baby.

Depending on the fetal age, drug potency, and dosage taken, a medication may

- be toxic to the developing baby;
- cause a variety of birth defects;
- interfere with placental functioning, thereby affecting the flow of oxygen and nutrients from the mother to the baby;
- alter the mother's biochemistry, something that indirectly affects the baby as well.

There are three basic categories of drugs you need to be concerned about during pregnancy: lifestyle drugs, over-the-counter products, and prescription medications.

Lifestyle drugs

When we talk about lifestyle drugs, we are referring to alcohol, tobacco, and so-called recreational drugs (illegal drugs). None of these substances has a place during pregnancy. Here's why.

Alcohol has been proven to cause serious birth defects. Babies born to mothers who drink heavily

Unofficially...
According to the U.S. Department of Health and Human Services, American women take an average of four prescription or over-the-counter drugs during pregnancy, plus vitamin and mineral supplements.

Watch Out!
The best time to talk about the risks of taking certain medications during pregnancy is before you conceive. If you become pregnant unexpectedly, contact your doctor's office immediately to talk about which medications you can continue to take safely and which you should avoid.

during pregnancy can be born with Fetal Alcohol Syndrome (FAS)—the leading known cause of preventable mental retardation. Babies with FAS typically suffer from prenatal and postnatal growth deficiency, facial malformations, central nervous system dysfunction, and varying degrees of major organ system malfunction. A related syndrome—Fetal Alcohol Effect—is a milder version of FAS.

Tobacco can have equally disastrous effects on babies. It is widely believed that nicotine constricts blood vessels and may consequently reduce the amount of oxygen and nutrients the baby receives via the placenta. Despite the fact that smoking during pregnancy has been linked to miscarriage, stillbirth, preterm birth, low birthweight, and sudden infant death syndrome, in 1995, 14% of pregnant women continued to smoke during pregnancy.

Illegal drugs are also dangerous to the developing baby. They have been proven to cause physical malformations including cleft palate, heart murmurs, eye defects, facial deformities, central nervous system problems, damage to major organs, withdrawal effects at birth, and low birthweight. Cocaine has been proven to cause both miscarriage and placental abruption, and marijuana is thought to be responsible for a range of neurobehavioral abnormalities in the newborn.

Over-the-counter products

The fact that a particular drug is available over-the-counter (or that it's sitting in your own medicine cabinet) is no guarantee that it's safe during pregnancy. As Table 8.9 shows, even a seemingly harmless product such as aspirin poses particular risks during pregnancy. You'll note that each of the drugs in this table has been assigned a particular risk factor using a rating system designed by the FDA to classify drugs for use during pregnancy. (See Table 8.8.)

Just one quick caution before we get into a detailed explanation of what each rating means. As helpful as these ratings can be to caregivers and pregnant women, they tend to oversimplify the highly complex issues involved. That's why it's so important for caregivers to review the sources of information available to them when recommending or prescribing medications. They should consult sources such as *Drugs in Pregnancy and Lactation*, make use of teratogen/pregnancy risk-lines (that is, hotlines), tap into the PDR (*Physician's Desk Reference*—the "bible" of FDA-approved information about prescription and nonprescription drugs, as well as a compendium of the package inserts that manufacturers are required to package with their products), and so on. Decisions about the use of medications during pregnancy must take many factors into account, including the specific individual circumstances that necessitate the use of a medication, the dose and method of administration, the timing and duration of exposure in the pregnancy, and the simultaneous use of other drugs. All factors being equal, it is generally best to use drugs that have been available longer and therefore have more of a track record in pregnancy.

That said, here's what the ratings actually mean.

Prescription drugs

Over-the-counter drugs aren't the only drugs that can be harmful to the developing baby. Some of the most harmful drugs are those used to treat such serious medical conditions as epilepsy, heart disease, and cancer.

Watch Out!
Douching during pregnancy isn't merely unnecessary, but can actually be harmful to both you and your baby. Women who douche during the period between conception and implantation are twice as likely to experience an ectopic pregnancy as women who don't douche. What's more, some douche preparations contain substances that could harm your baby.

TABLE 8.8: FDA RISK-FACTOR RATINGS FOR DRUGS USED DURING PREGNANCY

- Category A drugs have demonstrated no fetal risks in controlled human studies.

- Category B drugs are believed to be without significant risks to the fetus based on what researchers have learned from animal or human studies. In some cases, animal studies have indicated no risk to the fetus, but no human studies have been done. In other cases, animal studies show a risk to the fetus, but human studies do not.

- Category C drugs may or may not be harmful during pregnancy (the data is inconclusive). Either no adequate studies, human or animal, have been done, or adverse fetal effects have been seen in animals, but no testing has been done in humans.

- Category D drugs are known to pose a threat to the well-being of human fetuses, but they may be used if the benefit of using the drug (such as preventing an epileptic woman from experiencing seizures) outweighs the risks to the baby.

- Category X drugs have been proven to cause fetal abnormalities. The benefits of these drugs do not justify the risk of taking them. They should not be used under any circumstances.

If you take prescription drugs regularly, it's important to find out whether it's safe to continue taking these medications during your pregnancy. In some cases, your doctor will advise you to stop taking the drug because the risks to the fetus are greater than the benefits the drug provides. In other situations, she may advise you to continue taking the drug because the developing baby is more likely to be harmed by the condition the drug is treating (for example, epileptic seizures) than the medication itself.

Although there is still a great deal we don't know about the effects of drug use during pregnancy, the Food and Drug Administration (FDA) rates drugs on the basis of their safety during pregnancy.

Prescription drugs are assigned to one of the previous five categories, based on their relative safety during pregnancy, as previously discussed earlier in this chapter.

As you can see from Table 8.10, only a handful of prescription drugs are considered absolutely safe to take during pregnancy.

Other hazards to avoid

We don't want to make you totally paranoid about all the things that might possibly affect your baby, but there are a few other hazards you need to know about. These are radiation, toxins, and infectious disease.

Radiation

Diagnostic X-rays to areas other than the abdomen pose little threat to the developing baby, provided that appropriate radiation shields are used. On the other hand, CAT scans that involve multiple X-rays are believed to be harmful to the fetus and consequently are used only rarely during pregnancy.

Radioactive dyes are not used at all during pregnancy because of the risk of damage to the fetal thyroid.

Bright Idea
You can find out more about the safety of medications by contacting the March of Dimes Birth Defects Foundation, National Office: 1275 Mamaroneck Avenue White Plains, NY 10605 914-428-7100 www.modimes.org

TABLE 8.9: ACTIVE INGREDIENTS IN COMMON OVER-THE-COUNTER MEDICATIONS

Active Ingredient	Risk Factor	Where You Can Find It	Possible Problems
Acetaminophen	B	Used in aspirin substitutes such as Actifed Cold and Sinus; Alka-Seltzer Plus; Comtrex; Contac Cold and Flu; Coricidin; Dimetapp Cold and Fever; Drixoral Cold and Flu; Excedrin; Multi-Symptom Formula Midol; Panadol; Robitussin Cold, Cough, and Flu; Sinarest; Sine-Aid; Sine-Off; Sinutab; Sudafed Cold; Sudafed Sinus; TheraFlu; TYLENOL; Vicks Nyquil	No apparent link to birth defects. Possible association with fetal renal failure.
Aluminum hydroxide	Not rated (NR)	Used in antacids such as Gaviscon, Maalox, Mylanta	No apparent link to birth defects. Chronic or excessive use may be associated with neonatal calcium or magnesium imbalance.
Aspirin (acetylsalicylic acid)	C D (if full dosage is used in third trimester)	Used in aspirin compounds such as Alka-Seltzer, Ascriptin, Genuine Bayer, Bufferin, Ecotrin, St. Joseph, Vanquish	No apparent link to birth defects, though some studies disagree. In large doses close to term, causes - clotting disorders with possible fetal and maternal hemorrhage. Other possible effects are low birthweight, prolonged gestation and labor, and neonatal cardiac problems.
Attapulgite	NR	Used in antidiarrheals such as Donnagel and Kaopectate	

Bacitracin Zinc	C	Used in antibiotic ointments such as Mycitracin, Neosporin, and Polysporin	No apparent link to birth defects.
Benzocaine	NR	Used in topical anesthetics such as Americaine, Cepacol, Hurricaine, Chloraseptic	No reports of use during pregnancy available.
Bisacodyl	NR	Used in laxatives such as Correctol, Dulcolax	No reports of use during pregnancy available.
Bismuth Subsalicylate	C	Used in products for upset stomach, indigestion, and so on, such as Pepto-Bismol	Because of aspirin-like effect with salicylates, use in pregnancy should be restricted to the first five months in amounts that do not exceed the recommended dosages.
Brompheniramine Maleate	C	Used in antihistamines such as Dimetapp, Vicks DayQuil	Possible association with birth defects. Use of antihistamines in last two weeks of pregnancy increases the risk of a neonatal eye problem known as retrolental fibroplasia.
Caffeine	B	Used in Excedrin, Maximum Strength Midol, No Doz, Vanquish	No apparent link to birth defects.
Calcium carbonate	NR	Used in antacids such as Ascriptin, Bufferin, Caltrate, Di-Gel, Mylanta, Rolaids, Tums	No adverse effects proven with usual dosages.
Camphor	C	Used in anti-itch and local anesthetic products and nasal inhalers such as Afrin, Mentholatum, Vicks VapoRub	No adverse effects from topical use.

continues

Active Ingredient	Risk Factor	Where You Can Find It	Possible Problems
Chlorpheniramine Maleate	B	Used in antihistamines such as Alka-Seltzer Plus, Chlor-Trimeton Allergy, Comtrex Maximum Strength, Contac, Coricidin, PediaCare, Sinarest, Sine-Off, Sinutab, TheraFlu, Triaminic, TYLENOL Allergy	No apparent link to birth defects. See brompheniramine.
Clotrimazole	B	Used in antifungal/yeast infection products such as Mycelex-7	No apparent link to birth defects.
Dexbrompheniramine	C	Used in antihistamines such as Drixoral	No apparent link to birth defects. See brompheniramine.
Dextromethorphan	C	Used in cough suppressants such as Alka-Seltzer Plus Cold and Cough, Cheracol D Cough, Comtrex, Contac Cold, Dimetapp Cold, Robitussin, Sudafed Cold and Cough, TheraFlu, Triaminic, TYLENOL Cold, Vicks 44	No apparent link to birth defects.
Dimenhydrinate	B	Used in antinausea products such as Dramamine	May be responsible for cardiovascular defects and hernias in the fetus, but research inconclusive.
Diphenhydramine	C	Used in antihistamines such as Actifed, Benadryl, Contac, Sine-Off Night Time, TYLENOL Allergy, TYLENOL PM, Unisom Sleepgels, Unisom	May be responsible for cleft palate and other birth defects, but research inconclusive.
Docusate	C	Used in laxatives such as Colace, Dialose, Peri-Colace, Senokot-S	Chronic use may cause fetal magnesium imbalance.

Doxylamine	B	Used as a sleep aid in products such as Alka Seltzer Plus Night-Time Cold, Robitussin Night-Time Cold, Unisom Nighttime, and Vicks Nyquil	May be responsible for skeletal, limb, cardiac defects; cleft palate; and gastrointestinal malformations. Research inconclusive.
Ephedrine	C	Used in decongestants such as Primatene Tablets	May be responsible for heart-rate disturbances, minor birth defects, hernias, and clubfoot, but research inconclusive.
Guaifenesin	B	Used in expectorants such as Benylin, Novahistine, Primatene Tablets, Robitussin, Sudafed Cold, Vicks 44E	No apparent link to birth defects.
Hydrocortisone (topical)	C	Used in topical and hemorrhoid sprays and ointments such as Anusol HC-1 Hydrocortisone, Cortaid, Cortizone, Nupercainal Hydrocortisone, Preparation H Hydrocortisone 1%	No reports of use in pregnancy available.
Ibuprofen	B D (if used in third trimester)	Used in aspirin substitutes such as Advil, Motrin IB, Nuprin	No apparent link to birth defects, but third-trimester use can cause fetal cardiac malfunction.
Lactase	NR	Used in products for lactose intolerance such as Lactaid	No reports of use in pregnancy available.
Magnesium Carbonate Magnesium Hydroxide Magnesium Trisilicate		Used in antacids such as Ascriptin, Bufferin, Di-Gel, Gaviscon, Maalox, Mylanta, Phillips' Milk of Magnesia, Rolaids, Vanquish	No adverse effects proven with usual dosages. Chronic or excessive use may be associated with neonatal calcium or magnesium imbalance.

continues

Active Ingredient	Risk Factor	Where You Can Find It	Possible Problems
Meclizine	B	Used in antinausea products such as Bonine, Dramamine	Causes birth defects in some animals, but no apparent link to birth defects in humans.
Menthol	NR	Used in cough and sore throat preparations and in soothing ointments such as Afrin, BenGay, Cepacol, Eucalyptamint, Gold Bond, Hall's Cough Drops, Listerine, Mentholatum, Vicks Chloraseptic, Vicks Cough Drops	No reports of use in pregnancy available.
Miconazole	C	Used in products used to treat yeast/fungal infections such as Lotrimin, Monistat	No apparent link to birth defects.
Oxymetazoline	C	Used in nasal decongestant sprays such as Afrin, Neo-Synephrine, Vicks Sinex	No apparent link to birth defects, but excessive use could impair uterine blood flow.
Phenolphthalein	C	Used in laxatives such as Dialose, Ex-Lax, Phillips' Gelcaps	No apparent link to birth defects.
Phenylephrine	C	Used in nasal decongestant sprays and hemorrhoid creams such as Afrin, 4-Way Fast Acting Nasal Spray, Hemorid, Neo-Synephrine, Preparation H, Vicks Sinex	Causes birth defects in animals. May be responsible for minor birth defects: hernia and clubfoot. (These studies do not apply to topical creams.) Excessive use could impair uterine blood flow.
Phenylpropanolamine	C	Used in decongestants and appetite suppressants such as Acutrim, Comtrex, Contac, Dexatrim, Dimetapp, Robitussin-CF, Tavist-D, Triaminic, Vicks DayQuil Allergy	May cause eye and ear defects and other anomalies, but research inconclusive. Excessive use could impair uterine blood flow.

Drug	Rating	Used in	Comments
Pseudoephedrine.	C	Used in decongestants such as Actifed, Advil Cold and Sinus, Alka-Seltzer Plus, Allerest, Benadryl Allergy/Cold, Comtrex, Contac, Dimetapp, Robitussin Cold, Sine-Off, Sinutab, Sudafed, TheraFlu, Triaminic, TYLENOL Allergy, TYLENOL Cold, Vicks 44D, Vicks DayQuil, Vicks NyQuil	May be responsible for heart rate disturbances, minor birth defects, hernias, and clubfoot, but research inconclusive.
Psyllium (a natural fiber that promotes normal bowel movements)	NR	Used in laxatives such as Metamucil	No reports of use in pregnancy available. Since it is not absorbed into the bloodstream, it is felt to be safe to use.
Simethicone	C	Used in antiflatulents such as Di-Gel, Gas-X, Maalox, Mylanta, 3M Titralac, Tums	Possible association with cardiovascular birth defects, but cause and effect not likely.
Sodium Bicarbonate	NR	Used in antacids such as Alka-Seltzer, Arm and Hammer Pure Baking Soda	No adverse effects proven with usual dosages.
Sodium Chloride (table salt)	NR	Used in nasal sprays such as Afrin, Ocean Nasal Mist	Safe for use during pregnancy.

Note: Some drugs have more than one rating. This is because they may be more dangerous at certain parts of the pregnancy, in certain dosages, or in combination with other drugs. Consult your physician for details.

Sources: *Before You Conceive* by John R. Sussman, M.D., and B. Blake Levitt. New York: Bantam Books, 1989. *Drugs in Pregnancy and Lactation* (Fourth edition, 1994) by Gerald G. Briggs, Roger K. Freeman, and Sumner J. Yaffe. Baltimore: Williams and Wilkins, 1994. (Plus Updates Volume 7 Number 1, March 1994 through Volume 11 Number 2, June 1998). *Physician's Desk Reference for Non-Prescription Drugs.* Oradell, NJ: Medical Economics Publishers, 1998. *Drugs and Pregnancy* by Larry C. Gilstrap III and Bertis B. Little. New York: Elsevier Science Publishing Co., Inc., 1992.

TABLE 8.10: FDA RATINGS FOR PRESCRIPTION DRUG USE DURING PREGNANCY

Drug	Risk Factor	Possible Problems	Comments
A. Antihistamines			
Allegra (fexofenadine)	C	No reports of use during pregnancy available.	Too new to evaluate. Use over-the-counter product like chlorpheniramine if treatment necessary.
Claritin (loratadine), Zyrtec (lefrizine)	B	No reports of use during pregnancy available.	Too new to evaluate. Use over-the-counter product like chlorpheniramine if treatment necessary.
B. Antibiotics/Anti-infectives			
1. Antifungals			
Terrazol (terconazole)	C	No known link to birth defects.	Use as directed by your physician for vulvo-vaginal yeast infections.
Diflucan (fluconazole)	C	Possible birth defects with continuous use at higher doses.	Should be avoided in pregnancy, if possible.
Fulvicin (griseofulvin)	C	Possible association with conjoined twins.	Avoid.
Mycostatin (nystatin) oral or cream	B	No apparent link to birth defects.	A possible alternative to terconazole.

2. Antimalarials

Aralen (chloroquine)	C	May be responsible for various birth defects. Research inconclusive.	A safer alternative than quinine.
Paludrine (proguanil)	B	No apparent link to birth defects.	May be best choice for malaria prophylaxis in pregnancy.
Quinine	D	Possible birth defects.	Use alternatives if possible.

3. Antituberculosis

Isoniazid (INH)	C	Toxic in animal embryos; may cause neurological abnormalities.	Use as directed by your physician.
Myambutol (ethambutol)	B	No apparent link to birth defects.	Use as directed by your physician.
Rifampin (antituberculosis)	C	Possible increase in fetal anomalies.	Use as directed by your physician.

4. Antivirals

Famvir (famciclovir)	B	No reports of use during pregnancy available.	For treatment of recurrent genital herpes. Should be avoided in pregnancy if possible.
Retrovir (zidovodine-AZT)	C	No apparent link to birth defects.	Effective in preventing maternal-fetal transmission of HIV.
Valtrex (valcyclovir)	B	No reports of use during pregnancy available.	For treatment of recurrent genital herpes. Should be avoided in pregnancy if possible.
Zovirax (acyclovir)	C	No apparent link to birth defects.	For treatment of geintal herpes. Should be avoided in pregnancy.

continues

Drug	Risk Factor	Possible Problems	Comments
5. Cephalosporins			
Keflex (cephalexin), Ceclor (cefaclor), Duricef (cefadroxil), Suprax (cefixime), cephradine	B	No apparent link to birth defects.	Use as directed by your physician.
6. Fluoroquinolones			
Cipro (ciprofloxacin)	C	No apparent link to birth defects.	Should be avoided in pregnancy unless no safer alternatives exist.
Floxin (ofloxacin)	C	No apparent link to birth defects.	Should be avoided in pregnancy unless no safer alternatives exist.
Noroxin (norfloxacin)	C	Possible association with birth defects.	Should be avoided in pregnancy unless no safer alternatives exist.
7. Penicillins			
Amoxicillin, ampicillin, cloxacillin, dicloxacillin, penicillin	B		Use as directed by your physician.
8. Sulfonamides (Sulfa Drugs)			
Bactrim, Septra (sulfamethoxazole)	B	Possible association with birth defects. Not confirmed. If administered near term, may cause neonatal jaundice.	Use as directed by your physician.

9. Antitrichomonas

Flagyl, Protostat (metronidazole)	B	Controversy regarding safety during pregnancy.	Should be avoided in first trimester and used only if absolutely necessary in second and third trimesters.

10. Urinary Antibiotics

Macrodantin/Macrobid (nitrofurantoin)	B	No apparent link to birth defects.	Avoid usng near term or with suspected G6PD deficiency (a genetic disorder that weakens red blood cells).
Monurol (fosfomycin)	B	No reports of use during pregnancy available.	Taken as a single dose.

11. Other

Augmentin (clavulonate/ amoxicillin)	B	Possible association with spina bifida. Not confirmed.	Use as directed by your physician.
Cleocin (clindamycin)	B	No apparent link to birth defects.	Use as directed by your physician.
Biaxin (clarithromycin)	B	No apparent link to birth defects.	Related to erythromycin, but newer.
Erythromycin	B	No apparent link to birth defects. Possible maternal liver toxicity with certain forms (estolate or ethylsuccinate esters).	Preferred drug in pregnancy for chlamydia.
Vibramycin, Doryx (minocyclin), tetracycline, (doxycycline), Minocin	D	May cause various birth defects, tooth discoloration, and possible bone damage.	Avoid during pregnancy.
Zithromax (azithromycin)	B	No apparent link to birth defects.	Related to erythromycin, but newer.

continues

Drug	Risk Factor	Possible Problems	Comments
C. Antilipemics (Cholesterol-Lowering Drugs)			
Lipitor (atorvastatin), Mevacor (lovastatin), Lescol (fluvastatin), Pravachol (pravastatin), Zocor (simvastatin)	X	Theoretically toxic to fetal development.	Do not use during or prior to pregnancy.
Lopid (gemfibrozil)	C	Possible association with birth defects.	Rarely necessary during pregnancy.
Questran (cholestyramine), Colestid (colestipal)	B	No apparent link to birth defects.	Has limited use during pregnancy.
D. Cancer Drugs			
Adriamycin (doxorubicin), fluorouracil, methotrexate, Cytoxan (cyclophosphamide), Idamycin (idarubicin), Novantrone (mitoxantrone), Oncovin (vincristine), Platinol (cisplatin), Vesanoid (tretinoin Oral)	D	Highly toxic. Multiple birth defects, neonatal bone-marrow suppression, and intrauterine growth restriction.	Benefits must clearly outweigh the risks. Occupational exposure to these agents by pregnant women is potentially toxic in the first trimester.
Novadex (tamoxifen)	D	Toxic in animal studies. Possibly carcinogenic as well.	Avoid in pregnancy and for at least two months before conceiving.

E. Muscle Relaxants

Drug	Category	Effects	Advice
Flexeril (cyclobenzaprine)	B		Use as directed by your physician.
Parafon Forte (chlorzoxazone), Robaxin (methocarbamol), Norflex (orphenadrine)	C	No apparent link to birth defects.	Avoid during pregnancy.

F. Cardiovascular Drugs

1. Angiotensin-Converting Enzyme Inhibitors (ACE Inhibitors)

Drug	Category	Effects	Advice
Capoten (captopril), Vasotec (enalapril), Zestril (lisinopril)	D	Toxic to fetus. Causes birth defects even in second and third trimesters.	Avoid during pregnancy.

2. Antihypertensives (Blood Pressure Medications)

Drug	Category	Effects	Advice
Aldomet (methyldopa)	C	No apparent link to birth defects.	Discuss switching from your current antihypertensive to methyldopa or labetolol with your caregiver.
Inderal (propranolol)	C	Decreased heart rate, low blood sugar, possible growth restriction.	Consider switching to methyldopa or labetalol.
Lopressor (metoprolol)	C	First-trimester reports lacking; mild neonatal hypotension and decreased heart rate a possibility.	Consider switching to methyldopa or labetalol.
Normodyne (labetalol)	C	First-trimester reports lacking; mild neonatal hypotension and decreased heart rate a possibility.	Preferred to methyldopa by some maternal-fetal medicine specialists.
Tenormin (atenolol)	C	Possible association with birth defects. Otherwise similar to labetalol.	Consider switching to methyldopa or labetalol.

continues

Drug	Risk Factor	Possible Problems	Comments
3. Calcium Channel Blockers			
Calan (verapamil), Norvasc (amlopidine), Procardia (nifedipine)	C	Not proven to be safe during pregnancy. Possible temporary fetal/neonatal cardiovascular functional abnormalities.	Consult your cardiologist.
4. Cardiac Drugs			
Lanoxin (digoxin)	C	Maternal overdose may be toxic to developing baby.	Consult your cardiologist.
5. Vasodilators			
Nitroglycerin	B	No apparent link to birth defects.	Also used for treatment of excessive uterine contractions/premature labor.
G. Central Nervous System (CNS) Drugs			
1. Analgesics (Pain Relievers)			
Darvon, Darvocet (propoxyphene)	C	Possible association with multiple birth defects. Not confirmed.	Narcotic analgesics are generally preferred for occasional use in pregnancy when acetominophen is not effective.
	D	Neonatal withdrawal symptoms if used for prolonged periods.	
2. Anticonvulsants (Epilepsy Drugs)			
Depakene (valproic acid), Depakote (sodium valproate)	D	High incidence of cranial, facial, and limb defects, including cleft lip and palate, and underdeveloped fingers. Impaired physical and mental development, congenital heart defects.	Untreated epilepsy poses a greater risk than valproic acid. The minimum effective dosage should be used.

Dilantin (phenytoin, diphenylhydantoin)	D	Fetal Dilantin syndrome. High incidence (2%–26%) of cranial, facial, and limb defects, including cleft lip and palate, and under-developed fingers. Impaired physical and mental development, congenital heart defects.	Untreated epilepsy poses a greater risk than phenytoin. The minimum effective dosage should be used.
Mysoline (primidone)	D	High association with birth defects.	Untreated epilepsy poses a greater risk than primidone. The minimum effective dosage should be used.
Phenobarbital	D	Barbiturates cross the placenta and are stored in higher concentrations in the fetus than in the mother. Possible effects include fetal addiction, fetal bleeding and coagulation defects, and possible malformations.	Avoid except in cases in which seizure disorders can't be treated with safer medications.
Tegretol (carbamazepine)	C	Possible birth defects.	Preferred drug for grand mal seizures. Discuss medication strategy with your neurologist.
Zarontin (ethosuximide)	C	Possible birth defects.	Preferred drug for petit mal epilepsy, especially during first trimester.
3. Antidepressants			
Effexor (venlafaxine)	C	Limited reports of use during pregnancy available.	Unrelated to other antidepressants.
Luvox (fluvoxamine)	C	No reports of use during pregnancy available.	A selective seritonin re-uptake inhibitor (SSRI) used to treat obsessive-compulsive disorder (OCD).

continues

Drug	Risk Factor	Possible Problems	Comments
Paxil (paroxetine)	B	Limited reports of use during pregnancy available.	An SSRI.
Prozac (fluoxetine)	B	Limited reports of use during pregnancy available.	Because there is longer follow-up data for this drug than for newer SSRIs, this is probably the best choice of antidepressant for use during pregnancy.
Remeron (mirtazapine)	C	No reports of use during pregnancy available.	A tetracyclic antidepressant chemically unrelated to tricyclics, SSRIs, and monamine oxidase (MAO) inhibitors.
Serzone (nefazodone)	C	No reports of use during pregnancy available.	An SSRI.
Sinequan (doxepin)	C	Possible association with birth defects.	When antidepressants are needed in pregnancy, the SSRI drugs appear to be the safest.
Tricyclics including Elavil (amitriptyline), Surmontil, (trimipramine), Tofranil (imipramine)	D	Possible facial, head, limb, and central nervous system defects; possible neonatal withdrawal symptoms.	Avoid in pregnancy if possible.
Wellbutrin (bupropion)	B	No reports of use during pregnancy available.	Mechanism of action unrelated to other antidepressants.
Zoloft (sertraline)	B	No reports of use during pregnancy available.	An SSRI.

4. Narcotic Analgesics

Codeine	C	Possible association with multiple birth defects. Not confirmed.	Use only as directed by your physician.
	D	If used for prolonged periods or in high doses at term.	
Dilaudid (hydromorphone), OxyContin, Percodan, Tylox, (oxycodone), Synalgos-DC (dihydrocodeine), Vicodin, Lortab (hydrocodone)	B	No reports of use during pregnancy available.	Use only as directed by your physician.
	D	If used for prolonged periods or in high doses at term.	
Demerol (meperidine)	B	Possible association with hernias.	Use only as directed by your physician.
	D	If used for prolonged periods or in high doses near term, baby may experience withdrawal, respiratory depression, growth restriction, and neonatal death.	
Heroin (diacetylmorphine)	B	Possible chromosome damage.	Do not use.
	D	If used for prolonged periods or in high doses near term, baby may experience withdrawal, respiratory depression, growth restriction, lagging intellectual development, and neonatal death.	

continues

Drug	Risk Factor	Possible Problems	Comments
Methadone	B D	If used for prolonged periods or in high doses near term, baby may experience withdrawal, respiratory depression, growth restriction, and neonatal death.	Use only as directed for treatment of narcotic addiction.
Morphine	B D	Possible association with hernias. If used for prolonged periods or in high doses near term, baby may experience withdrawal, respiratory depression, growth restriction, and neonatal death.	Use as directed by your physician.
Talwin (pentazocine)	B D	If used for prolonged periods or in high doses near term, baby may experience withdrawal, respiratory depression, growth restriction, and neonatal death.	Use as directed by your physician.

5. Nonsteroidal Anti-inflammatory Drugs (NSAIDs)

Drug	Risk Factor	Possible Problems	Comments
Anaprox (naproxen), Ansaid (flurbiprofen), Clinoril (sulindac), Motrin (ibuprofen), Ponstel (mefenamic acid), Voltaren (diclofenac)	B D	No apparent link to birth defects. If used in the third trimester or near delivery, this drug can cause neonatal pulmonary hypertension.	Should not be used by women trying to conceive. May impair implantation.
Relafen (nabumetone), Daypro (oxaprozin)	C D	No apparent link to birth defects. If used in the third trimester or near delivery, this drug can cause neonatal pulmonary hypertension.	Should not be used by women trying to conceive. May impair implantation.

6. Sedatives and Hypnotics

Ambien (zolpidem)	B	No reports of use during pregnancy available.	Relatively new, so if sleeping pill is absolutely needed, most doctors will prescribe a barbiturate, narcotic, or antihistamine for occasional use only.
Benzodiazepines such as Valium (diazepam), Xanax (alprazolam), Klonipin (clonazepam), Ativan (lorazepam)	D	Possible birth defects, neonatal depression, "floppy baby" syndrome, neonatal withdrawal.	Avoid, especially in first trimester. Severe panic disorders may need to be treated in the second and third trimesters.

7. Stimulants/Appetite Suppressants

Fastin, Adipex-P (phentermine)	C	Possible association with stillbirth.	Avoid during pregnancy and preconceptionally.
Meridia (sibutramine)	C	No reports of use during pregnancy available.	Avoid during pregnancy.

8. Tranquilizers

Lithium	D	Possible changes in newborn heart rhythms and thyroid function; possible goiter, jaundice, electrolyte imbalance. Possible birth defects, especially of the heart.	Avoid during pregnancy.
Phenothiazines such as Trilafon (perphenazine), Compazine (prochlorperazine), fluphenazine	C	Research regarding birth defects is inconclusive. Possible neurological effects on fetus when taken close to term.	Avoid using these drugs near term. It may be safe to use some of these drugs for the treatment of severe nausea and vomiting in the first trimester.

continues

Drug	Risk Factor	Possible Problems	Comments
H. Anticoagulants (Blood Thinners)			
Coumadin (warfarin)	D	High incidence of birth defects (for example, "Fetal warfarin syndrome"); may lead to fetal hemorrhage or death.	Do not use these drugs during pregnancy. Heparin is the drug of choice when anticoagulation is necessary.
Heparin	C	Fetal and maternal complications possible with prolonged use.	Generally preferable to Coumadin (warfarin) when anticoagulation is needed in pregnancy.
I. Diuretics			
Lasix	C	Possible electrolyte imbalance, increased fetal urine output.	Should be used only in cases of severe hypertension and other cardiovascular disorders.
Thiazides such as Dyazide, Maxzide, Aldactazide (hydrochlorthiazide), Diuril chlorothiazide)	D	Bone-marrow depression, possible birth defects, decreased platelet count (poor blood clotting), electrolyte imbalance.	Should be used only in cases of severe hypertension and other cardiovascular disorders.
J. Gastrointestinal Drugs			
1. Antidiarrheal			
Immodium (loperamide)	B	No apparent link to birth defects.	Use as directed by your physician.
Lomotil (diphenoxylate)	C	No apparent link to birth defects.	Related to narcotic meperidine.. (Demerol).

2. Anti-emetics (Antinausea)

Phenergan (promethazine), Tigan (trimethobenzamide), Compazine (prochlorperazine)	C	No apparent link to birth defects. Frequent use in later part of pregnancy may be associated with neonatal jaundice, depression, and withdrawal symptoms.	An option for severe morning sickness (hyperemesis gravidarum).
Reglan (metoclopramide)	B	No apparent link to birth defects.	Also used when needed to stimulate breastmilk production in nursing mothers.

3. Antisecretory Drugs

Cytotec (misoprostil)	X	Causes miscarriage and birth defects.	Do not use during pregnancy.
Pepcid (famotidine)	B	No reports of use during pregnancy available.	Use as directed by your physician.
Prilosec (omeprazole)	C	No birth defects in animals, but effects unclear in humans.	Avoid during pregnancy, especially prior to week 20.
Prevacid (lansoprazole)	B	No reports of use during pregnancy available.	Structurally similar to omeprazole. Avoid during pregnancy, especially prior to week 20.
Zantac (ranitidine)	B	No apparent link to birth defects.	Use as directed by your physician.

K. Hormones

1. Adrenal

Cortisone	D	Possible birth defects. Possible neonatal adrenal suppression and electrolyte imbalance.	Switch to prednisone if necessary.

continues

Drug	Risk Factor	Possible Problems	Comments
Dexamethasone	C	Birth defects in animals; no observed birth defects in humans. Possible neonatal adrenal suppression and electrolyte imbalance.	Switch to prednisone if necessary.
Prednisone	B	No apparent link to birth defects. Possible neonatal adrenal suppression and electrolyte imbalance.	Preferred adrenal steroid during pregnancy. Should be used instead of other corticosteriods whenever possible.
2. Antidiabetic Drugs			
Diabinase (chlorpropamide)	D	Suspected birth defects, low blood sugar, fetal death.	Change to insulin if your diabetes cannot be controlled by diet alone.
Glucophage (metformin)	B	Appears to be the safest of the oral diabetes drugs.	Though insulin is the drug of choice for the treatment of diabetes during pregnancy, this drug may be preferred for women of childbearing age who are not planning a pregnancy.
Glucotrol (glipizide)	C	No apparent link to birth defects.	Change to insulin if your diabetes cannot be controlled by diet alone.
Glynase (glyburide)	D	Possible birth defects with first trimester use.	Change to insulin if your diabetes cannot be controlled by diet alone.
Insulin	B	Low blood sugar. Maternal insulin shock can result in fetal death.	Your dose may have to be adjusted during pregnancy. Consult your physician.
Orinase (tolbutamide)	D	Possible birth defects, low fetal platelet count, low blood sugar, fetal death.	Change to insulin if your diabetes cannot be controlled by diet alone.

3. Antiprogesterone Drugs

RU486 (mifepristone)	X	Causes abortion.
4. Antithyroid		
Propylthiouracil (PTU), Tapazole (methimazole)	D	May cause various birth defects and fetal/neonatal hypothyroidism.
		PTU is the drug of choice for treatment of hyperthyroidism during pregnancy.
Radioactive Iodine	X	Causes birth defects.
		Do not use during pregnancy.
5. Estrogens		
Clomid, Serophene (clomiphene)	X	Though rated X by manufacturer, no birth defects are proven.
		A fertility drug. Should be used only after possibility of pregnancy has been ruled out.
DES (diethylstilbestrol)	X	Reproductive organ defects and future reproductive problems.
		Should not be used during pregnancy.
Oral contraceptives including the morning-after pill (contain Estrogen and progestogen)	X	Possible genital anomalies like with DES. Possible advanced neonatal bone age with resulting short stature.
		Stop taking your oral contraceptives as soon as your pregnancy is confirmed. (You should take a pregnancy test as soon as possible if you suspect that you may be pregnant.)
6. Progestogens		
Crinone, Prometrium, Micronized progesterone (progesterone)	Not rated	No animal reports and no apparent link to birth defects.
		Used for the treatment of infertility, luteal phase deficiency, and assisted reproductive technologies in first 10 weeks of pregnancy.
Provera (medroxyprogesterone)	D	Possible birth defects.
		When used to treat abnormalities or absence of menstruation, pregnancy must be ruled out first.

continues

Drug	Risk Factor	Possible Problems	Comments
7. Thyroid			
Synthroid (levothyroxine), Armour thyroid (thyroid hormones)	A	No adverse effects with appropriate doses.	Use as directed by your physician. Dose may need to be adjusted during pregnancy.
L. Asthma Drugs—Bronchodilators			
1. Sympthomimetics			
Alupent (metaproterenol), Max air (pirbuterol), Ventolin, Proventil (albuterol), Serevent (salmeterol)	C	No apparent link to birth defects in normal inhaled doses.	Generally available as inhalers. Use as directed by your physician in minimum effective doses.
2. Antispasmodics			
Aminophyllin, TheoDur (theophyllin)	C	Possible association with birth defects.	One of a number of acceptable treatments for chronic asthma during pregnancy.
M. Other			
1. Acne			
Accutane (isotretinoin)	X	Increased risk of miscarriage and birth defects.	Stop using the drug at least one month prior to attempting pregnancy.
Retin-A (tretinoin)	C	No proven adverse effects when used topically.	Not to be confused with Accutane.

2. Antimigraine

Imitrex (sumatriptan)	C	No apparent link to birth defects, but data lacking. Possible increase in risk of miscarriage.	Discontinue use two to three months prior to conception.
Midrin (isometheptene)	C	No reports of use during pregnancy available.	Use as directed by your physician.

Note: Some drugs have more than one rating. This is because they may be more dangerous at certain parts of the pregnancy, in certain dosages, or in combination with other drugs. Consult your physician for details.

Sources: *Before You Conceive* by John R. Sussman, M.D., and B. Blake Levitt. New York: Bantam Books, 1989. *Drugs in Pregnancy and Lactation* (fourth edition, 1994) by Gerald G. Briggs, Roger K. Freeman, and Sumner J. Yaffe. Baltimore: Williams and Wilkins, 1994. (Plus updates Volume 7 Number 1, March 1994 through Volume 11 Number 2, June 1998). *Physician's Desk Reference*. Oradell, NJ: Medical Economics Publishers, 1998. *Drugs and Pregnancy* by Larry C. Gilstrap III and Bertis B. Little. New York: Elsevier Science Publishing Co., Inc., 1992.

Watch Out!
Make sure that
your immuniza-
tions are up-to-
date before you
become preg-
nant. Although
tetanus, diphthe-
ria, and rabies
shots are consid-
ered to be safe
during preg-
nancy, live vac-
cines such as the
MMR (measles,
mumps, rubella),
the primary vac-
cine against
polio, and the
yellow-fever
vaccine are not
recommended.

Toxins

Your baby's immature liver and kidneys can't process and eliminate toxins as quickly as your organs can. That's why substances that are hazardous to you are many times more hazardous to your developing baby. Consequently, it's a good idea to avoid exposing yourself to cleaning products with powerful odors (such as chlorine and ammonia-based products), paints, solvents, lawn-care products, and other powerful chemicals.

Just one small footnote before we move on. Although research into the effects of hair dye during pregnancy has been largely inconclusive, why tempt fate? If you don't want to postpone dyeing your hair until after your baby is born, you might consider waiting until the end of the first trimester, the point at which your baby's vital organs, head, body, and limbs are fully formed.

Infectious disease

You should also make a conscious effort to minimize your exposure to infectious diseases—something that's easier said than done if you've got older children who subscribe to the virus-of-the-month club.

Although it's unlikely that a common cold or even a bad case of the stomach flu will do your baby any harm—unless, of course, you come down with a very high fever—various infectious diseases can be harmful to the fetus. Here are some examples:

- **Measles:** Measles can lead to fetal loss and prematurity. Fortunately, because most pregnant women have been immunized against the disease, it is extremely rare for a pregnant woman to contract the disease.

- **Chickenpox and shingles:** Chickenpox and shingles can cause prematurity, skin lesions, neurologic anomalies, eye anomalies, skeletal abnormalities, gastrointestinal and genitourinary anomalies, limb deformities, low birthweight, meningoencephalitis, miscarriage, or stillbirth in the babies of pregnant women who are not immune to the virus. Fortunately, 85% to 90% of pregnant women are immune to the disease.

- **Toxoplasmosis:** Toxoplasmosis is an infection that can result from eating raw or insufficiently cooked meat, coming into contact with cat feces or cat litter, or eating foods that have come into contact with the feces of animals carrying the disease. If a pregnant woman is exposed to this infection during the first half of pregnancy, her baby could be affected with hydrocephalus, eye problems, psychomotor retardation, convulsions, microphthalmia, and intracerebral calcification (calcium deposits in the brain). If a pregnant woman is exposed to toxoplasmosis during the second half of pregnancy, the damage is likely to be less severe. Toxoplasmosis can be treated with antibiotics.

- **Cytomegalovirus (CMV):** Cytomegalovirus is a virus that can cause miscarriage, mental retardation, psychomotor retardation, developmental abnormalities, progressive hearing impairment, respiratory illness, jaundice, intrauterine growth restriction, failure to thrive, and eye infections. Cytomegalovirus is the most common cause of congenital viral infections in the United States, with approximately 0.2%–2.2% of liveborn infants acquiring the virus perinatally. Ninety percent of infected newborns do not show symptoms of the virus at birth, but many subsequently demonstrate some form of impairment (deafness, mental retardation, or delayed psychomotor development).

■ **Mumps:** Mumps can also be hazardous to the developing baby. One study showed that babies who are exposed to mumps are 15 times as likely to suffer from adult onset diabetes as babies who were not exposed to the mumps in utero.

You can find out more about avoiding hazardous substances during pregnancy by calling the Reproductive Technology Center, 202-293-5137; Care Northwest, 900-225-2273; or, in Canada, the Motherisk Clinic at the Hospital for Sick Children, 416-813-6780.

Sex during pregnancy

Pregnancy may change your feelings about sex entirely—or it may have no effect on your sex life. Whereas some couples find that their sex lives improve tremendously during pregnancy, others find that the flames of passion all but disappear.

Some women find that their interest in sex diminishes during the first weeks of pregnancy, when fatigue, morning sickness, and tender breasts can make sex sound considerably less than appealing. "My interest in sex decreased. I didn't even want my husband touching me. I was just too uncomfortable," admits one first-time mother.

Others find that their interest in sex goes through the roof, even during the first trimester. "My interest in sex really increased at the beginning of this pregnancy, my third. I felt very sexy and always in the mood, even before I knew that I was pregnant. I think we had sex more often during the first trimester than at any time other than our newlywed stage," says one woman who is currently pregnant with her third child. "My appetite for sex was voracious the whole nine months," admits one first-time mother. "So was my husband's. He thought my pregnant body was very sexy, although he did laugh at some of my attempts to be the pregnant sex kitten."

Sometimes it's the partner's feelings about sex that puts out the flames: "My husband wanted nothing to do with me sexually. After he saw the ultrasound picture, he thought that sex with a pregnant woman was disgusting," insists one mother of one.

If there's been a history of pregnancy loss, both partners may be afraid about having sex—even though sex is considered to be perfectly safe for women with low-risk pregnancies: "The interest in sex was certainly there, but we were both overcome with fear," recalls one first-time mother. "We had a miscarriage with our previous pregnancy, which had us too scared to have sex for the entire subsequent pregnancy!"

Many women find that their interest in sex picks up once morning sickness begins to wane and fatigue begins to lift. "During the second trimester of each pregnancy, my sex drive definitely increased," recalls one third-time mother. "I felt very sexy, even as my tummy expanded. Actually, it was wonderful to have an excuse for my tummy to stick out, and for the first time in my life, I was totally unselfconscious about my husband stroking it," admits one first-time mother.

Although many couples find that their interest in sex begins to taper off as the birth of their baby approaches—one study showed that one-third of couples were abstaining by the time the ninth

Unofficially...
The top four sex-related concerns of expectant fathers, according to *Parenting* magazine:

1. Fear of hurting the baby.
2. Feeling like a third wheel.
3. Feeling uncomfortable about having sex when the baby is right there.
4. Changing feelings about his partner's increasingly maternal shape.

month rolled around—others manage to enjoy moments of sexual intimacy right up until the very end—blossoming belly and all. "You just have to get creative with positioning," confides one first-time mother.

Some women report that sex is more pleasurable than ever during pregnancy as rising estrogen levels cause the vagina and labia to become slightly swollen and increasingly sensitive. Others find this increased sensitivity to be uncomfortable or irritating. "I don't have a problem achieving orgasm, except during pregnancy," admits one third-time mother.

Not everyone is a good candidate for sex during pregnancy, however. Your doctor or midwife is likely to advise you to forgo intercourse or orgasm, or both, for at least part of your pregnancy if

- you have a recurrent history of first-trimester miscarriage;

- you have been diagnosed with placenta previa (that is, the placenta is blocking all or part of the cervix);

- you have been diagnosed with a placental abruption (that is, the placenta is prematurely separating from the uterine wall);

- you are carrying more than one baby;

- you have a history of premature labor or are showing signs that you may be about to go into premature labor;

- you or your partner has an untreated sexually transmitted disease;

- your membranes have ruptured.

There's probably no need to panic if you experience a small amount of spotting after intercourse. A

"

I have a wonderful husband, and as my body grew—I gained 60 pounds in total—he continually told me how beautiful I was and tried to make me feel as though all the added weight was a good thing and not to feel ugly because of it. This helped with sex because it made me feel a little less self-conscious about my body and about being naked in front of him.
—Anonymous, mother of one, 25

"

small amount of spotting can occur if your cervix gets bumped with your partner's penis during intercourse. Because it's difficult to differentiate between harmless bleeding and bleeding that may indicate a problem with your pregnancy, some caregivers will suggest that you hold off on intercourse until your cervix becomes a little less prone to this type of bleeding—typically after the first trimester. Of course, if it can be determined that the pregnancy is not threatened and the bleeding is simply coming from these small cervical blood vessels, then intercourse is harmless. If, on the other hand, you think that you will be excessively worried about the bleeding, should it occur (or recur), then abstinence during this time frame may make sense for you.

Working during pregnancy

Women a generation or two ago were expected to resign from their jobs the moment the pregnancy test came back positive, but today pregnant working women are every bit as much a part of the modern office as the computer and the fax machine. Most women experiencing low-risk pregnancies are able to work throughout their entire pregnancies.

When you shouldn't work during pregnancy

There are, of course, some situations in which you may want to consider leaving work early or requesting some modifications to your working environment. You might choose to go this route if

- you are exposed to infectious diseases, chemicals, or toxic substances at work;

- your job requires that you stand for more than three hours per day;

Unofficially... During pregnancy, your body will produce as much estrogen as a nonpregnant woman's body would make in 150 years—at mid-pregnancy, as much in a single day as a nonpregnant woman's ovaries produce in three years.

- your work is highly strenuous or physically demanding;

- your job involves a lot of repetitive work that could increase your chances of developing carpal tunnel syndrome (repetitive stress syndrome);

- your job involves a lot of bending, stooping, stair- or ladder-climbing, or heavy lifting;

- you work in an extremely hot, cold, or noisy environment;

- you work long hours or rotating shifts.

Staying comfortable on the job

Your biggest challenge during your nine months on the job will be staying comfortable as you find yourself battling morning sickness, fatigue, and an ever-changing lineup of pregnancy-related aches and pains. Here are some tips on maximizing comfort at the office:

- Put your feet up on a stool or an open desk drawer to relieve pressure on your lower back. Your boss may not approve, but your chiropractor will.

- Wear comfortable shoes and loose clothing. (See Chapter 13 for some tips on maternity clothing.)

- Keep a glass of cold water on your desk so that you'll remember to drink frequently, and do not—we repeat, do not—skip meals, no matter how hectic things may be at the office.

- Take 5- or 10-minute catnaps on your break or over your lunch hour. You can either hit the couch in the company nurse's office or put your head on your desk for a couple of minutes.

Watch Out!
Although there's no hard evidence that working in front of a computer screen is harmful to your baby, working at a computer all day can be harmful to your health. Pregnant women are at increased risk of suffering from carpal tunnel syndrome—a painful condition that can affect the wrist and lower arms if you spend a lot of time typing. If you work in such an environment, check out the preventive exercises at www.bham.net/aosc/aosc2.html.

- Keep stress to a minimum and accept any and all offers of help. People love to help pregnant women. You'll never have it this good again!

Fear of flying

It's one thing to stay comfortable in the office. It's quite another to stay comfortable if you're packed into an airline seat like an over-stuffed sardine. Here are some tips on coping with airline travel during pregnancy:

- Call the airline ahead of time to inquire about its policies on travel during pregnancy. Here are the numbers of the major carriers:

Alaska	800-426-0333
American	800-433-7300
America West	800-247-5692
Continental	800-231-0856
Delta	800-221-1212
Northwest	800-225-2525 (domestic)
	800-447-4747 (international)
Southwest	800-435-9792
TWA	800-221-2000 (domestic)
	800-892-4141 (international)
United	800-241-6522
USAirways	800-428-4322

- Try to book an aisle seat so that you can stretch your legs and make those inevitable treks to the washroom as easily as possible.

- Drink plenty of fluids to avoid dehydration.

- Carry a copy of your medical records with you, and keep your doctor's name and telephone number handy.

- Avoid flying during the last month of pregnancy, when the risk of labor is greatest (and when many airlines may refuse to allow you to travel, with or without a doctor's certificate).

- Avoid traveling to areas where it may be difficult to obtain proper medical care.

- Don't travel to destinations that involve a significant change in altitude, or in which good, clean drinking water is in chronically short supply.

- Ensure that your immunizations are up-to-date—or talk to your doctor about what you should do if they're not (see www.travelhealth.com/preg.htm for details).

- Ask to be hand-searched by a female security officer at the airport if you'd rather not walk through the metal detector (which, by the way, is actually perfectly safe).

- Cancel your trip if you are experiencing cramping or bleeding, unless your caregiver is aware of your symptoms and has given you the go-ahead to travel anyway.

Although there's no guarantee that leading a healthy lifestyle will result in the birth of a healthy baby, you will feel better knowing that you have put the odds in your favor. Besides, the good habits you develop during your pregnancy may stick with you after your baby is born—something that's good news for you and your growing family.

Just the facts

- You should plan to gain approximately 25 to 35 pounds during pregnancy—a little more if you're underweight when you become pregnant, and a little less if you're overweight when you become pregnant. This translates into about 300 extra calories per day.

- You should eat a well-balanced diet: one made up of nine servings from the bread, cereal, rice, and pasta group; four servings from the vegetable group; three servings from the fruit group; three servings from the milk, yogurt, and cheese group; and three servings from the meat, poultry, fish, dry beans, eggs, and nuts group.

- Exercising during pregnancy is safe for most women and can bring tremendous rewards for both the pregnant woman and her baby. Walking, swimming, riding a stationary bike, and participating in low-impact prenatal fitness classes are excellent ways of staying fit during pregnancy.

- You should avoid smoking, drinking, and consuming illegal drugs during pregnancy. Be sure that any over-the-counter drugs or prescription drugs you take are safe to use during pregnancy.

- You should also do your best to avoid radiation, toxic chemicals, and infectious diseases during pregnancy.

- Sex is considered to be safe for most couples with low-risk pregnancies. Certain complications such as preterm labor, placenta previa, or a partial abruption may necessitate that you abstain from sex for all or part of the pregnancy.

Bright Idea
If you end up traveling to a third-world country, drink bottled water (and cook with boiled water) rather than gambling on the safety of the local water supply. You should even use bottled water to brush your teeth.

- If your job is physically strenuous or involves a lot of standing, you might want to meet with your employer to discuss job modifications.

- Although flying is generally considered to be safe during pregnancy, most airlines require a doctor's certificate from women flying during the late third trimester.

What Other Pregnancy Books Won't Tell You

GET THE SCOOP ON...
What causes a multiple birth • What it's like to
be pregnant with multiples • The facts about
selective reduction • What you should do now
to prepare for your babies' arrival • How to
shop for your babies without going broke

PART III

Carrying Multiples

I f you've just discovered that you're carrying multiples, you are probably experiencing a mix of emotions. On the one hand, you may feel very special to be carrying two or more babies— particularly if you had a great deal of difficulty conceiving. On the other hand, you may feel concerned about what this pregnancy may mean to your physical health, and worried about what giving birth to more than one baby may mean to your finances and your relationship with your partner or other children.

Once you and your partner have had a chance to absorb the news, you will probably find that you have a million questions about being pregnant and giving birth to multiples. You may be wondering what causes a multiple pregnancy, how a multiple pregnancy differs from a singleton pregnancy, what can go wrong and why, what you should do to prepare for your babies' arrival, and what to expect during the first few weeks. These are just some of the issues we address in this chapter.

Why the number of multiple births is on the rise

The latest figures from the National Center for Health Statistics show a remarkable increase in the number of multiple births in America. Since 1980, the number of twins has increased by 37%, and the number of triplets and other "higher-order multiples" (the trendy term these days is "supertwins") has increased by an astounding 312%. This translates into 100,750 babies born as twins, 5,298 as triplets, 560 as quadruplets, and 81 as quintuplets or other higher-order multiples per year.

Two key factors are responsible for the increasing numbers of multiples, according to the National Center for Health Statistics: the fact that an increasing number of women in their late thirties are giving birth and the growing popularity of fertility treatments such as ovulation-inducing drugs and in vitro fertilization.

Scientists believe that women between the ages of 35 and 39 are more likely to give birth to multiples than women in other age groups because the body begins to produce higher levels of gonadotropin hormones, which cause more eggs to mature and be released from the ovaries. The National Center for Health Statistics attributes one-third of the rise in multiple births to this age factor.

The second factor—the growing popularity of fertility treatments—is credited with the other two-thirds of the increase in multiple births. About 20% of women undergoing fertility treatments have multiple births, as opposed to approximately 1.5% of all women giving birth in the United States.

Fertility drugs used to induce ovulation frequently cause more than one egg to be released.

The rate of multiple pregnancy among women using Clomid is less than 5%, whereas the rate for women using gonadotropins is between 10% and 20%.

Assisted reproductive technologies (ART) are also responsible for many multiple births. Because in vitro fertilization techniques are so costly— $20,000 a cycle for some types of treatments—and only a fraction of implanted embryos survive, many fertility specialists try to tip the odds in their patients' favor by implanting a large number of embryos at a time (for example, four). If an unusually high number of these embryos manage to "take," the couple can end up being pregnant with a large number of babies.

Can you have too much of a good thing? Some people think so. In fact, many in the medical community feel that reproductive medicine needs to find ways of reducing the odds that a woman undergoing fertility treatments will end up with triplets or quadruplets—or even more babies. Multiple pregnancies are, after all, far riskier than pregnancies that involve single babies, and they can be financially ruinous to families that lack the funds to foot the necessary bills for three, four, or five babies. "It's a burden for the parents, it's a burden for the extended family. Certainly, to health-care providers and insurance carriers, it's a nightmare," said Dr. Andrew Toledo of Reproductive Biology Associates, an Atlanta fertility clinic, during a recent interview with CNN Interactive.

What causes a multiple birth

Twin pregnancies result from either the fertilization of two separate eggs by two separate sperm (a process that results in dizygotic, or fraternal, twins)

Unofficially...
Twins occur naturally in 1 out of every 90 births; triplets in 1 out of every 10,000 births; and quadruplets in 1 out of every 650,000 births.

or the separation of a single fertilized egg into two fetuses (a process that results in monozygotic, or identical, twins). Higher-order multiple pregnancies involve fraternal twins, identical twins, or a combination of both types of twins.

Here are some basic facts about multiples:

- Fraternal twins occur more often in certain families and in certain ethnic groups (the rates are 1/70 in African Americans and 1/300 for women of Chinese descent with whites falling in between). The incidence of fraternal twins also increases with maternal age, weight, height, and parity (that is, the number of pregnancies a woman has had).

- Identical twins occur in approximately 4 out of every 1,000 births and are unrelated to maternal age, race, or parity.

- Fraternal twins typically look no more alike than any other pair of siblings. They can be either of the same sex or one of each sex.

- Identical twins have identical features: hair, eye color, blood type, and so on. If, however, one twin developed more rapidly in utero than the other one, they may not look identical at birth.

- Identical twins have similar handprints and footprints, but they do not share the same fingerprints. (This was good news to one family of identical twins who had to rush their babies off to FBI headquarters to get them refingerprinted so that they could figure out who was who!)

- Some identical twins are known as "mirror twins" because one is virtually a mirror image of the other (for example, a birthmark that appears on the left arm of one appears on the

Bright Idea
Find out if special prenatal classes are offered in your community to couples who are expecting multiples. If you can't find specialized classes in your community, you might consider hiring a childbirth educator or a doula with expertise in multiple birth to conduct private classes in your home.

right arm of the other, one is left-handed and the other is right-handed, and so on).

- Identical triplets can also occur, but they are extremely rare.

- It is possible for fraternal twins to be conceived by two different fathers, a process known as superfecundation. In some cases, the second egg is fertilized in a different reproductive cycle than the first egg. This rare phenomenon occurs when low hormone levels in pregnancy fail to suppress ovulation.

- Scientists believe that approximately one in eight natural pregnancies starts out as a twin pregnancy—even though only 1 out of every 90 births results in the birth of twins. This is one reason why many caregivers routinely do ultrasounds to confirm that there are no other viable fetuses left in the uterus when they suspect that a patient is miscarrying.

- It is possible to miscarry one multiple and go on to carry the others to term. It is also possible to have a combination ectopic and uterine pregnancy (that is, one or more babies implant in the fallopian tubes and the others in the uterus). Fortunately, this is rare.

- Although most twins are born within minutes of one another, sometimes days—even months—can elapse between the births of twins.

- Often, it isn't immediately obvious at birth whether same-sex twins are identical or fraternal. If the parents want to know for medical reasons, blood from the umbilical cord is drawn and analyzed for type, Rh factor, and so on. If the results are still inconclusive, parents can

Watch Out!
If your first pregnancy resulted in a twin birth, you are five times more likely to have a twin or multiple birth occur with your next pregnancy than a woman who hasn't previously given birth to multiples.

choose to opt for DNA testing—a little pricey at $600 or more, but highly accurate.

How a multiple pregnancy is diagnosed

The increased use of ultrasound has made it possible for the vast majority of parents to find out in advance that there's more than one baby on the way. This wasn't the case a decade or two ago, when it wasn't unusual for as many as 40% of multiple pregnancies to be undiagnosed prior to labor and delivery.

Even if you haven't had an ultrasound, certain red flags may alert you and your caregiver to the possibility that you may be carrying twins. These are the warning signals:

- Fraternal twins tend to run in your family.
- You have been taking fertility drugs.
- You experienced excessive nausea and vomiting during the first trimester.
- Your uterus is growing more quickly or is larger than what would be expected at a particular point in your pregnancy.
- You notice more fetal movement in this pregnancy than in previous pregnancies (assuming, of course, that this is your second or subsequent pregnancy).
- More than one fetal heartbeat is heard.

If your caregiver suspects that you may be carrying multiples, he will likely send you for an ultrasound. Ultrasound can detect more than 95% of multiple pregnancies.

What it's like to be pregnant with multiples

There are significant differences between pregnancies that involve one baby and those that involve two or more babies. If you are carrying multiples, you may experience

- heightened symptoms of early pregnancy (for example, morning sickness, breast enlargement, fatigue) due to the high level of pregnancy hormones in your body;

- a range of discomforts caused by the pressure of your heavy, stretched uterus on surrounding organs (for example, shortness of breath, heartburn, constipation, pelvic discomfort, urinary leakage, back pain, and hemorrhoids);

- a range of other discomforts that are often associated with multiple pregnancies (for example, insomnia, water retention, difficulty walking, abdominal itching, and anemia);

- increased fetal movement;

- substantial weight gain (you should consume an extra 300 calories per day per baby and should aim for a weight gain of 1.5 pounds per week— or more—during the second and third trimesters);

- a shorter pregnancy than what you would expect if you were carrying a single baby (40 weeks). The mean pregnancy length is 37 to 38 weeks for twins and 34 weeks for triplets.

You may also need to abstain from sex or vigorous exercise during your pregnancy; leave work weeks or months earlier than originally planned, if you develop any serious complications; or have a

Unofficially...
Twins Restaurant in New York City is owned and operated by identical twins Debra and Lisa Ganz. The restaurant—located at 54th and Broadway—is staffed by 37 sets of identical twins, and it caters to twins and other multiples.

planned or emergency cesarean section, depending on how your pregnancy progresses.

Prenatal care

A woman who is carrying multiples needs to be monitored more closely than a woman who is carrying a single baby. This is because more things can go wrong in this situation than during a single pregnancy.

As a result, your caregiver will probably want to see you every two weeks (rather than once a month) until week 28, and then weekly thereafter. During that time, you will probably receive one or more of the following tests:

- **Ultrasound:** Ultrasound is used to check on fetal growth, to detect abnormalities, and to determine what position the babies are in before you go into labor.

- **A nonstress test (NST):** A nonstress test involves strapping fetal monitors—one for each baby—to your abdomen and then monitoring your babies' heartbeats to determine whether they are reactive (which indicates that the baby is doing well) or nonreactive (which indicates that there could be a problem such as cord entanglement, oxygen deprivation, pregnancy-induced hypertension, and intrauterine growth restriction).

- **A contraction stress test (CST):** A contraction stress test is similar to a nonstress test except that your nipples are stimulated (either manually or by using a breast pump) to cause uterine contractions. Your babies' response to the stress of contractions is then monitored.

- **The oxytocin challenge test (OCT):** The oxytocin challenge test is similar to the contraction stress test except that Pitocin (a synthetic form of oxytocin) is used to stimulate contractions.

- **A biophysical profile (BPP):** The biophysical profile is a detailed ultrasound used to assess your babies' overall well-being by looking at such factors as heart-rate activity, body movements, muscle tone, and amniotic-fluid volume.

- **Fetal movement counting:** Fetal movement counting may be a low-tech approach to assessing your baby's well-being, but it can be quite useful. You are asked to lie on your side and count fetal movements. A count of 10 movements per baby over a two-hour period is considered to be a sign that all is well. (You don't have to lie there for the whole two hours if your babies are active; you stop counting once you get to 10 movements per baby.) If you notice a decrease in movement—that is, if it usually takes 30 minutes to get 10 kicks, but one day it takes 90 minutes—you should report your findings to your caregiver.

If complications arise during your pregnancy, your caregiver may suggest bed rest (to improve uterine blood flow) or prescribe contraction-stopping drugs (tocolytics). She may also suggest home monitoring (hooking yourself to an electronic monitoring device for an hour or more per day to record uterine activity and hopefully detect premature-labor contractions before you go into active labor).

Note: Although the jury is still out on the effectiveness of bed rest in preventing preterm labor, most doctors agree that bed rest combined with

Timesaver
You can track down the contact information for a twins club or other multiple-birth association in your area by contacting the National Organization of Mothers of Twins Clubs at 800-243-2276. Canadian parents should call the Parents of Multiples Birth Association at 519-272-2203.

tocolytics is effective in reducing or stopping contractions. You can get some practical tips on coping with bed rest in Chapter 10.

Problems that can arise in a multiple pregnancy

There's no doubt about it: your risk of experiencing pregnancy-related complications increases with the number of babies you are carrying. Studies have shown that women carrying multiples experience far more problems than women carrying a single baby.

Here are some other points worth noting:

- According to the National Center for Health Statistics, the rate of complications for a woman who is pregnant with twins is eight times that of a woman who is carrying a single baby.

- Whereas just 6% of single births result in low-birthweight babies (that is, babies who weigh less than 5.5 pounds), 53% of twins and 93% of triplets are classified as low birthweight.

- Fifty-three percent of twins and 92% of triplets are born prematurely, as compared to 8% of single babies.

The following are some of the pregnancy complications that can occur during a multiple pregnancy.

Anemia

The increased blood volume during pregnancy puts any pregnant woman at risk of anemia, but women carrying multiples are particularly susceptible to this problem. In fact, one study showed that women who are pregnant with twins are 2.4 times as likely to develop anemia as women who are carrying single-tons. If blood tests indicate that you are becoming anemic, your caregiver will likely prescribe an iron supplement.

Miscarriage and stillbirth

Women who are pregnant with multiples are at increased risk of losing one or both of their babies. Although most pregnancy losses occur in the first trimester, they can also occur in the second or third trimesters as a result of such factors as placental abruptions, cord accidents, toxemia, and twin-to-twin transfusion syndrome.

When a baby dies after the 20th week of pregnancy, the loss is classified as a stillbirth. Twins are four times as likely to be stillborn as singletons, and triplets are four to six times as likely to be stillborn as singletons.

Pregnancy-induced hypertension

Pregnancy-induced hypertension (high blood pressure) is approximately 2½ times more likely to occur when a woman is carrying multiples as when she is carrying a single baby.

Women with mild pregnancy-induced hypertension before 36 weeks are usually placed on bed rest and monitored closely. If both the mother and the baby appear to be doing well, delivery may be delayed until fetal lung maturity is achieved. If the situation worsens, however, it may be necessary to deliver the baby as soon as possible. Amniocentesis can be performed to assess lung maturity if the fetal age is in question.

Preeclampsia

Women carrying multiples are twice as likely as women carrying single babies to develop preeclampsia—a potentially life-threatening condition characterized by a rise in blood pressure, fluid retention, and the leakage of protein into the urine. If you experience the following symptoms of preeclampsia, be sure to report them to your caregiver immediately:

- sudden weight gain
- swelling of your hands, face, or feet
- headaches
- dizziness
- seeing spots before your eyes
- nausea, vomiting, and abdominal pain (particularly severe pain in the upper abdomen) during your second or third trimester of pregnancy.

Problems with the placenta

Three major types of problems with the placenta can occur during a multiple pregnancy:

- a placental abruption, when the placenta partially or fully detaches itself from the uterine wall, causing bleeding and endangering the lives of the pregnant woman and her babies;
- placenta previa, when the cervix partially or fully blocks the cervical opening, something that can lead to complications during pregnancy or necessitate a cesarean delivery;
- intrauterine growth restriction, caused by the inadequate flow of nutrients through the placenta to the baby.

Polyhydramnios

Polyhydramnios occurs when there is an excessive amount of amniotic fluid. It is usually associated with fetal problems (for example, congenital abnormalities) or maternal problems (for example, gestational diabetes), but in some cases it occurs for no apparent reason.

Bright Idea
Subscribe to one of the many online discussion groups for parents of multiples. You can find the listings for many such groups at www.owc.net/ ~twins/resource. htm.

Polyhydramnios can cause extreme discomfort and, in some cases, premature labor. In certain circumstances, the condition is treated by removal of excess fluid through amniocentesis.

Growth discordance

Growth discordance occurs when one of the babies grows more slowly or more quickly than the others. Growth discordance can be caused by either placental problems (such as twin-to-twin transfusion syndrome) or crowded conditions in the uterus.

Intrauterine growth restriction

Intrauterine growth restriction occurs in 12% to 47% of multiple pregnancies, as opposed to 5% to 7% of singleton pregnancies. It is widely believed that intrauterine growth restriction in a multiple pregnancy is caused by fetal competition for the available nutrients—just one more reason to make sure that you're eating ample quantities of nutritious foods.

Preterm birth

Preterm birth is the leading cause of neonatal death in multiples. Although the mere fact that you are carrying multiples puts you at increased risk of experiencing a preterm birth, there are other factors that add to your risk. You're at increased risk if

- you have had abdominal surgery during the current pregnancy (for example, an appendectomy)

- you have an abnormal uterine structure

- you have fibroids (benign uterine tumors)

- you are experiencing emotional or physical stress

- you have high blood pressure

Watch Out!
Nearly half of multiple pregnancies are complicated by preterm birth. If you experience any of the following symptoms, you could be experiencing premature labor: a watery, mucus, or bloody discharge; pressure in the pelvic area or lower abdomen; a low, dull backache; abdominal cramps with or without diarrhea; or regular contractions or uterine tightening, whether painful or not.

- you develop a high fever during pregnancy
- you have a kidney infection
- you are outside of the optimal age range (that is, if you are under 16 or over 35)
- you are a DES daughter (your mother took diethylstilbestrol (DES) when she was pregnant with you)
- you have been diagnosed with placenta previa
- you have been diagnosed with polyhydramnios
- you haven't gained enough weight
- you have previously experienced premature labor or delivery
- you have been experiencing unexplained vaginal bleeding
- you are a smoker

66
Always repack the change bag the moment you get home.
—Cindy, 39, mother of four-year-old twins
99

Although cerclage (a surgical procedure in which the cervix is stitched shut to prevent it from dilating prematurely) was once considered to be an effective means of preventing premature labor, most doctors no longer agree with its routine use in women carrying multiples. These days, cerclage is performed only on women with weak cervixes—a condition that the medical profession charmingly refers to as cervical incompetence. (As you probably realize, this is just a less-than-diplomatic way of saying that the cervix is unable to withstand the weight of the developing fetus, or fetuses, and opens prematurely.)

Birth defects and complications
Multiples are twice as likely to be born with birth defects as singletons. What's more, there is a higher percentage of malformations in identical twins than in fraternal twins.

Consider these facts:

- Although most malformations occur early in pregnancy, some—such as twin-to-twin transfusion syndrome or problems resulting from compression of the fetuses—can occur later in the pregnancy.

- Heart anomalies occur in approximately 1 of every 50 twin pregnancies. Either one or both twins may be affected.

- Acardia—absence of the fetal heart—occurs in 1% of identical-twin pregnancies.

- Conjoined twins (that is, Siamese twins) occur approximately once in every 100,000 births.

You may want to consider prenatal testing to determine whether your baby has a serious genetic or chromosomal birth defect. If conditions such as conjoined twins or fetal acardia (the absence of a fetal heart) are detected, you may wish to consider terminating the pregnancy. The issues of prenatal testing and pregnancy termination are discussed in greater detail in Chapter 7.

Complications in identical twins

Women carrying identical twins are two to three times as likely to experience problems as women carrying fraternal twins. The types of problems that can occur when a woman is carrying identical twins include

- miscarriage, since identical twins are miscarried more often than fraternal twins;

- twin-to-twin transfusion syndrome, a disorder in which there is an unequal sharing of nutrients from the shared placenta between identical twins. The blood-deprived "donor" twin may become anemic and be smaller than the "recipient" twin, who may experience jaundice, respiratory problems, or heart failure due to excessive blood flow;

- complications that can arise when two babies share the same amniotic sac (that is, monamnionic twins). There is a 50% mortality rate in such cases because of the high risk of problems with cord entanglement and the possibility that the two babies will be conjoined. Fortunately, monamnionic twins occur in only 1% to 2% of identical twins.

Presentation problems

Unofficially...
Triplets have a median weight of four pounds.

Another possible complication in a multiple pregnancy concerns the position the babies assume at the time of birth.

- In 43% of cases, both twins are vertex (head down). A vaginal delivery is considered to be a good option in 70% to 80% of so-called vertex-vertex cases. In most cases, the second twin is born shortly after the first. The second twin is carefully monitored during this period before its birth.

- In 38% of cases, the first twin is in a vertex position and the other twin is in a breech (foot or bottom down) or transverse (sideways) position. If a vaginal delivery is planned, external version (a procedure in which the doctor or midwife places her hands on the pregnant woman's abdomen and gently turns the baby) may be attempted. There is a success rate of 70% for version. If the procedure is unsuccessful, the baby is usually delivered by cesarean section, although some doctors feel comfortable delivering the second baby as a breech vaginally.

- In 19% of cases, the first twin is in a breech or transverse position and the second twin is in a vertex position. A cesearean delivery is the best option in this situation.

Low birthweight

Approximately half of twins are classified as low birthweight (that is, they weigh less than 5.5 pounds at birth). Even those multiples who are carried to term may have low birthweights because of both crowded conditions in the uterus and the need to share nutrients with one or more babies. Fraternal twins tend to weigh more than identical twins.

Postpartum hemorrhage

Women who give birth to multiples are at increased risk of experiencing a postpartum hemorrhage (that is, loss of a significant amount of blood following the delivery). This is because the uterus has been severely stretched and may have difficulty contracting after the babies are born.

Perinatal mortality

Twins are three to five times more likely to die within the first 28 days of life as singletons. The most common cause of death among twins born before 36 weeks is respiratory failure, whereas the most common cause of death in twins born after 36 weeks involves problems with the placenta.

Sudden infant death syndrome (SIDS)

Sudden infant death syndrome (SIDS) is believed to be twice as common in twins as in singletons—not surprising given that SIDS is more likely to occur in babies with low birthweight than babies of average weight.

If one twin dies, the second twin is closely monitored during the month following the loss because the other twin is believed to be at risk.

The facts about selective reduction

Selective reduction involves selectively aborting one or more fetuses. It is typically performed when a couple wishes to terminate the pregnancy of a fetus that has birth defects or to reduce the total number of fetuses being carried.

During the first trimester, the fetus that has been terminated can be removed through the cervix. During the second and third trimesters, the fetus that has been terminated is carried along with the live one.

There is an element of risk involved in selective reduction. The procedure can result in the inadvertent loss of both babies due to miscarriage, infection, premature labor and birth, or the need to terminate the entire pregnancy because of complications that arise as a result of the procedure.

Couples who decide to reduce the total number of fetuses in order to increase their odds of ending up with at least one healthy baby often find it extremely difficult to selectively reduce other healthy fetuses. They may experience the same type of grief as other parents experience upon the loss of a pregnancy.

What you should do now to prepare for your babies' arrival

There's no way around it: giving birth to more than one baby is going to throw your life into upheaval for at least the foreseeable future. That's why it's a good idea to do as much as you can ahead of time to prepare for Life After Babies.

Get ready to take care of yourself

By the time you walk out of the hospital with your babies, you will have been through a lot. Even if your pregnancy was relatively straightforward, you've been carrying around a heavy load for many months and subletting your uterus to some very demanding tenants. If it was complicated, you may have spent months on bed rest—which, ironically, tends to be anything but restful—or had a cesarean delivery. Add that to the fact that you're not likely to get a whole lot of sleep for at least the foreseeable future, and you can see why it pays to pamper thyself during the postpartum period.

To help make things as stress-free as possible after the births of your babies, consider doing a few of the following things before they arrive:

- Make extra batches of soup, casseroles, stews, meatballs, and other entrees that freeze well (just remember to go lightly on the spices; some babies don't appreciate garlic-flavored breast-milk).

- Pay as many of your bills ahead of time as possible so that you don't forget to make the car payment or pay credit card bills as a result of the postpartum chaos.

- Address your birth announcements before the babies arrive.

- Join a club or online newsgroup for parents of multiples, and ask experienced mothers of multiples for tips on surviving the postpartum period.

- Prepare your older children for the disruption that is likely to accompany the babies' arrival (for example, arrange for them to take a

Bright Idea
Dress each twin in his or her own color if you have difficulty telling them apart. If you're worried that the color-coding system might fall apart in your sleep-deprived state, paint their toe-nails instead!

hospital tour or to participate in a sibling-preparation class—ideally one that is targeted at siblings of multiples).

- Spend some quality time with your spouse and talk about ways you can try to stay connected during the crazy weeks and months ahead.

Ask not what you can do for your community . . .

"There are times in your life when you have to ask for help, and this is one of them," says Cheryl McInnes, founder of Parents of Multiples Birth Association of Canada, Inc., and the mother of 18-year-old twins. McInnes suggests that couples who are pregnant with multiples spend some time lining up as much help as they can for the period right after their babies arrive.

Here are some tips on lining up some extra sets of hands:

- Let everyone in your circle of friends know that help is welcome, and encourage them to spread the word.

- Make a list of jobs you wouldn't mind delegating to someone else (making a salad, picking up a package at the post office, and so on), and ask one of your volunteers to serve as a volunteer coordinator. (Having a volunteer coordinator was a lifesaver for one family when their quadruplets arrived. At one point they had 32 volunteers working around the clock caring for the new arrivals.)

- Invite a much-loved family member to move in for a couple of weeks to help with meals, laundry, housework, and child care.

- If you can't line up enough volunteers, resort to paying someone to help you. Neighborhood teenagers can be had for a fairly decent hourly rate—particularly if you hire them on a regular basis (such as two or three days a week after school).

How to shop for your babies without going broke

Equipping a nursery for one baby is expensive enough. Equipping one for two or more babies can be enough to bankrupt a family—or so you might think.

Although there's a real temptation to run out and buy your babies matching brand-name gear, there are cheaper ways to acquire what your baby needs. Here are some tips from parents who've been there:

- Borrow as much baby gear as you can. Just make sure that whatever you borrow meets current safety standards.

- Shop second-hand. You can find nearly new brand-name baby products at most consignment stores for half their original price or less. Although the top second-hand stores don't carry cribs or car seats that don't comply with current safety standards, mistakes can and do happen. Therefore, the onus is still on you to make sure that what you're purchasing is up to snuff.

- Don't scrimp on the double (or triple or quadruple) stroller. It's the one thing that will keep you mobile. *Note:* You might want to consider purchasing two doubles rather than one quadruple stroller if someone else will always be with you when you're out with the babies. They're easier to maneuver and easier to pick up second-hand.

> 66
> A lot of parents have to get past the idea that everything has to be new for the babies. It's safety and practicality you're after, not the most beautiful crib in the store window.
> —Childbirth educator and mother-of-twins Joyce MacKenzie
> 99

- If your friends are planning to have a baby shower for you and they ask what you want, suggest a car seat or other big-ticket item. Your friends can pool their funds and buy you something you really need, rather than a lot of cutesy frilly dresses or sailor suits!

- See if a local baby store or department store would be willing to give you a break if you bought all of your baby gear through them. If you're purchasing two or more cribs, car seats, high chairs, and so on, you represent a lot of purchasing power. Don't be afraid to bargain a little.

- If you prefer to shop online, be sure to find out if the company offers a discount to parents of multiples. InternetBABY, at www.iBaby.com, offers parents of multiples a 5% discount on the second and subsequent units of a particular product.

- See if you can solicit some outright donations. One family was able to convince the owner of a local pharmacy to let them have every seventh bag of diapers free.

- Save money on baby wipes either by making your own (fill a squirt bottle with a mixture of liquid baby soap and plain water, and then buy some inexpensive washcloths) or by making a box of wipes go further by cutting the wipes in half (one family swears that an electric knife works like magic).

- You can save on disposable diapers by using high-quality brand names during the night (when you really want the babies to stay dry!) and lower-quality generic brands during the day.

Another good strategy is to start buying diapers when you're pregnant: one couple expecting triplets had 1,600 diapers stockpiled by the time their babies came home.

- Save items such as used baby bottles, nipples, caps, lids, and acetaminophen samples from the hospital if your children spend some time in the NICU (neonatal intensive care unit). Otherwise, these items are thrown away by hospital staff.

- Don't overspend in the clothing department. As a rule of thumb, twins need 1½ times rather than 2 times as much clothing as single babies.

- See if your children's pediatrician will reduce the copay per visit given that you're buying his services in bulk! Also, don't be embarrassed to ask for any free coupons and baby-product samples that he may be able to pass your way.

- Give your weekly cash flow a boost by changing the federal withholding rate on your Form W-4 to reflect the fact that you will receive additional personal exemptions and credits in the year your babies are born. Visit the IRS Web site for details: www.irs.ustreas.gov.

- Find out if you qualify for the Women, Infants, and Children (WIC) program, which provides nutritional assistance during pregnancy and lactation and during infancy and early childhood. Because family size is factored into the program eligibility criteria, many families of multiples qualify for assistance. You can find the phone number of your local WIC office in your phone book.

You'll find plenty of other money-saving ideas in Chapter 13.

Moneysaver
Some companies provide free coupons or samples to parents who have multiples. You can get the scoop on the latest offers at the Mothers of Super Twins Web site, at www.MOSTonline.org/free/company.htm, or phone Mothers of Super Twins at 516-434-MOST. Other Web sites with leads on freebies include www.thebabynet.com/babytalkpages/messages/multiples/62.html and www.owc.net/~twins/freebie.htm.

Just the facts

- The number of twins has increased by 37% since 1980, and the number of triplets and other higher-order multiples has increased by 312%.

- Twin pregnancies result from either the fertilization of two separate eggs by two separate sperm (a process that results in dizygotic, or fraternal, twins) or the separation of a single fertilized egg into two fetuses (a process that results in monozygotic, or identical, twins). Higher-order multiple pregnancies involve fraternal twins, identical twins, or a combination of both types of twins.

- You will likely experience increased pregnancy symptoms (such as nausea, fatigue, and morning sickness) due to the high level of pregnancy hormones in your body. You are also likely to experience a range of discomforts caused by the pressure of your heavy, stretched uterus on surrounding organs (shortness of breath, heartburn, constipation, pelvic discomfort, urinary leakage, back pain, and hemorrhoids).

- You should plan to consume an extra 300 calories per baby per day and aim for a weight gain of 1.5 pounds or more per week during the second and third trimesters.

- You should be prepared for the possibility of a preterm birth. The average length of pregnancy for a woman carrying twins is 37 to 38 weeks; for triplets, 34 weeks.

- Your caregiver may monitor the well-being of your babies through ultrasound, a nonstress test

(NST), a contraction stress test (CST), an oxytocin challenge test (OCT), and a biophysical profile (BPP). You may also be encouraged to do fetal movement counting.

- You and your babies are at increased risk of experiencing complications during pregnancy. According to the National Center for Health Statistics, a woman carrying multiples is eight times as likely to experience complications as a woman who is carrying a single baby.

- Some pregnant women choose to undergo selective reduction to either terminate a fetus with severe anomalies or reduce the total number of babies in order to lower the risk of losing all of the babies to pregnancy-related complications.

- Look for prenatal classes specifically designed for parents of multiples, or hire a childbirth educator or doula to give you private classes at home.

- While you're expecting, stock your freezer with easily reheated meals to make life a little less stressful after the babies arrive.

- Accept any and all offers of help. If you don't get enough offers, ask people to help.

- Negotiate bargains and freebies whenever you can to reduce the cost of parenting multiples.

Coping with a High-Risk Pregnancy

There's nothing warm and fuzzy about the term *high-risk pregnancy*. In fact, it can be downright scary. What many people don't realize, however, is that the term *high-risk pregnancy* is a catch-all term that's used to describe women who are on the risk continuum at any point during their pregnancy: women who are at a slightly higher-than-average risk of experiencing complications during pregnancy or birth, or giving birth to a baby with a minor birth defect; and those who have the odds of a happy outcome firmly stacked against them, but who are willing nonetheless to take their chances at starting a family.

If you are at the low end of the risk continuum, your pregnancy may be, for all intents and purposes, perfectly normal. If, on the other hand, you're at high risk of experiencing complications, your pregnancy will be a major commitment—one that will change virtually every aspect of your life during the months ahead.

349

Chapter 10

In this chapter, we talk about what being high risk is likely to mean to you and your baby. Then we discuss both chronic conditions that require special management during pregnancy and conditions that can arise during pregnancy and plunge a low-risk pregnancy into the high-risk category in the blink of an eye. We wrap up the chapter by discussing what it feels like to experience a high-risk pregnancy and offering some practical tips on staying sane during bed rest—one of the biggest challenges many women face during a high-risk pregnancy.

What being high risk means to you and your baby

The term *high risk* is used to describe pregnancies in which the mother, the baby, or both are at higher-than-average risk of experiencing complications. You are likely to be classified as high risk if you have

- a chronic medical condition that may affect your pregnancy,

- a history of previous pregnancy-related complications or pregnancy-related complications during your current pregnancy,

- a history of pregnancy loss.

Note: We discuss chronic medical conditions and pregnancy-related complications in this chapter, and pregnancy loss in Chapter 11.

As you can see from the following checklist, there are a number of reasons why your pregnancy may be classified as high risk.

CHECKLIST: IS YOUR PREGNANCY HIGH RISK?

Your pregnancy may be treated as high risk if

- you are over 35 years old and are therefore at increased risk of giving birth to a child with a chromosomal anomaly;

- you are under 17 and are therefore at increased risk of experiencing intrauterine growth restriction;

- you are carrying more than one baby and are therefore at risk of experiencing a number of pregnancy-related complications, including preterm labor;

- you have a chronic health condition such as diabetes, heart problems, or a blood-clotting disorder that has the potential to affect your pregnancy;

- you have a history of gynecological problems such as pelvic inflammatory disease (PID), endometriosis, or large symptomatic fibroids;

- you have a history of pregnancy loss (miscarriage, ectopic pregnancy, or stillbirth) or premature birth;

- you have an STD, including HIV, that could be transmitted to your baby during pregnancy or at the time of birth;

- you are pregnant as a result of assisted reproductive technologies (something that may put you at increased risk of having a multiple pregnancy);

- you have had two or more second-trimester abortions (which may increase your chances of having problems with an incompetent cervix);

- your mother took DES during her pregnancy (which may increase your chances of having difficulty carrying a pregnancy to term);

- you conceived while using an IUD (something that increases your chances of experiencing a miscarriage);

Watch Out!
Any pregnancy can become high risk. Although the occurrence of any of the following symptoms may not necessarily indicate a problem, you should call your caregiver immediately if you experience
- vaginal bleeding or spotting
- swelling in the face or fingers
- a leakage of fluid or increased vaginal discharge
- severe or persistent headaches
- pain in the abdomen or shoulder
- persistent vomiting that is not related to morning sickness
- chills or a fever
- a noticeable change in the frequency or strength of your baby's movements
- painful or urgent urination
- dizziness or faintness

- you have a child with a genetic disorder or are a carrier for a genetic disorder (something that may increase your risk of giving birth to a child with that particular genetic disorder).

If your doctor or midwife lacks the specialized expertise to deal with someone with your particular risk factors, you may need to switch to a high-risk-pregnancy specialist. You may find this upsetting if you've established a good rapport with your current caregiver, but switching caregivers is probably the best option for you and your baby. Candace Hurley, the founder of Sidelines (a national support group for moms on bed rest) put it this way in a recent interview with the *Los Angeles Times:* "You're not a Ford anymore, you're a Ferrari. You need a mechanic who works on Ferraris."

Regardless of who your caregiver is, however, your pregnancy will be more closely monitored than it would be if your pregnancy were classified as low-risk. Consequently, you may be required to make more frequent visits to the doctor, and your doctor may recommend additional tests. If complications do arise—or seem likely to arise—your doctor may prescribe certain types of medications or bed rest.

Chronic conditions that place a pregnancy at risk

Advances in obstetrical medicine have made motherhood a possibility for large numbers of women who might have been discouraged from starting a family a generation ago. Not everyone, however, is able to have a baby. Some chronic conditions place such a tremendous burden on the body that pregnancy is unlikely to occur in the first place, or if it does, the odds of miscarriage, stillbirth, or neonatal loss are extremely high. In certain situations, a

woman with a serious medical condition who manages to beat the odds and become pregnant will be
encouraged to terminate her pregnancy because
the risks to herself or her baby, or both, are simply
far too high.

If you are dealing with such a condition, the
time to weigh the risks and benefits of a pregnancy
is before you become pregnant. Set up an appointment with your doctor to discuss how your
pregnancy may affect your condition, how your
condition may affect your pregnancy, how past treatments (chemotherapy, radiation therapy, surgery,
and so on) for your condition may affect your pregnancy and delivery, what warning signs you need
to be aware of, what prenatal tests you may wish to
consider, and what—if anything—can be done to
minimize the risks to you and your baby.

High blood pressure

There's high blood pressure—and then there's
really high blood pressure.

If you have mild or moderate hypertension (that
is, your blood pressure is from 140/90 to 160/105)
and it is not complicated by other factors such as
kidney disease or heart disease, your odds of developing preeclampsia are just 10%, and your chances
of having a healthy baby are excellent.

If, however, you suffer from severe chronic
hypertension (that is, your blood pressure is over
160/105 or your condition is complicated by either
kidney disease or heart disease), having a baby will
be a fairly risky venture for you. You have a 50%
chance of developing preeclampsia and a 10%
chance of experiencing a placental abruption,
and you are at increased risk of intrauterine
growth restriction, premature delivery, and maternal

Bright Idea
If you are at risk
of experiencing
blood-pressure
problems during
pregnancy, pur-
chase a blood-
pressure gauge at
your local drug-
store or medical
supply store so
that you can
keep track of
your blood pres-
sure between
prenatal check-
ups.

complications such as stroke and cardiovascular problems.

You are at highest risk of experiencing blood-pressure-related problems during your pregnancy if

- you are over 40;

- you have a lengthy history of hypertension (you've had problems with your blood pressure for more than 15 years);

- your blood pressure is higher than 160/110 early on in your pregnancy;

- you have diabetes, cardiomyopathy (a disease of the heart muscle caused by either hypertension or other problems), kidney disease, or connective tissue disease (for example, lupus);

- you have previously experienced blood-clot complications;

- you developed severe preeclampsia early on in a previous pregnancy;

- you experienced a placental abruption in a previous pregnancy.

Women with extremely complicated cases of hypertension typically spend 15 days in the hospital during their pregnancies. What's more, they have a 50% chance of requiring a cesarean section, a 50% chance of experiencing major complications such as deteriorating kidney function, and a 50% chance of developing preeclampsia—with a 25% chance that the baby will die.

Heart disease

The increased blood volume during pregnancy means that your heart already has to work 50% harder than usual. That's why women with pre-existing heart problems can run into difficulty during pregnancy.

Watch Out!
Don't stop taking your medications without talking to your doctor first. Although certain medications (for example, epilepsy drugs) may be harmful to your baby, the risks of not taking your medications may be even higher. Only your doctor can help you decide whether it's safe to discontinue your medications during pregnancy and, if so, how you can safely wean yourself off them.

Here are the facts on some common types of heart disease and pregnancy:

Unofficially...
Heart disease is the third-leading cause of maternal death during pregnancy, exceeded only by hemorrhage and infection.

■ **Rheumatic heart disease:** Rheumatic heart disease is caused by rheumatic fever—an autoimmune response to an infection (typically, untreated strep throat). If it results in mitral stenosis—a particular form of heart-valve damage—the rate of maternal mortality during pregnancy is high. Women affected by this condition require intensive monitoring and multiple cardiac drugs during labor.

■ **Congenital heart diseases:** Although the majority of congenital heart defects are mild or repair themselves spontaneously during childhood, some more serious types of congenital heart diseases can endanger a pregnant woman and her baby. Some of these diseases have maternal mortality rates of 50% and fetal mortality rates of 25% to 50%. What's more, babies who survive are also at increased risk of developing congenital heart defects themselves. Women with Eisenmenger's syndrome and primary pulmonary hypertension are advised to avoid pregnancy because of the high rates of maternal mortality associated with these problems. Women with mitral valve prolapse (a disorder in which the heart valve clicks and murmurs) don't face any significant risk during pregnancy, although some caregivers will prescribe antibiotics during labor to prevent potential complications.

Lung disorders

Like the heart, the lungs have to work harder during pregnancy. Although most pre-existing lung diseases (for example, tuberculosis and sarcoidosis) don't cause problems during pregnancy, asthma warrants special monitoring and care.

According to the U.S. Department of Health and Human Services, approximately 1% of pregnant women have chronic asthma, and another 1% will develop the disease as a complication of pregnancy.

Some women with asthma will experience an improvement (25%), others will experience a deterioration (25%), and others will find that their condition remains stable (50%). Unfortunately, there's no way to predict in advance what will happen to any particular woman.

If you are asthmatic and become pregnant, you should

- avoid substances that tend to trigger asthma attacks,

- minimize your exposure to colds, flus, and respiratory infections,

- consider having a flu shot (particularly if you will be pregnant during flu season),

- continue to take your allergy shots (with your doctor's approval),

- continue to use your asthma medications (with your doctor's approval),

- treat asthma attacks immediately to avoid depriving your baby of oxygen.

Kidney disease

The kidneys—which are responsible for filtering the blood—are also required to work harder during pregnancy because they must contend with the waste products that the baby releases into the mother's blood stream, as well as the increased volume of blood.

Here are the facts on kidney disease and pregnancy:

- Women with mild kidney disease experience very few problems during pregnancy, but those who have more severe forms of the disease are at risk of developing pyelonephritis (an acute kidney infection that can cause permanent damage), experiencing a premature delivery, or having a baby with intrauterine growth restriction.

- Women who have both chronic kidney disease and high blood pressure have a 50% chance of developing severe hypertension during pregnancy.

- Women who are on dialysis prior to pregnancy will require dialysis treatments more frequently during pregnancy.

- Women who are pregnant after a kidney transplant will continue to require medications to prevent rejection of the kidney. They have a 33% chance of developing preeclampsia, a 50% chance of experiencing a premature delivery, an increased risk of having a baby with intrauterine growth restriction, and a higher risk of cesarean due to pelvic bone disease or narrowing of the birth canal.

Note: To maximize their chances of giving birth to a health baby, women who have had a kidney transplant should wait two to five years before attempting a pregnancy. Women who have minimal protein in their urine, normal blood pressure, and no evidence of kidney rejection are considered to be the best candidates for a pregnancy.

Watch Out!
An untreated urinary-tract infection can spread to the kidneys, causing kidney damage or premature delivery.

Liver disorders

The liver plays a role in a number of important bodily functions. It produces substances the body needs in order to metabolize fats, vitamins, minerals, proteins, and carbohydrates; it controls blood sugar level and lipids; it stores essential vitamins, minerals, and glucose; and it detoxifies substances such as drugs, alcohol, and chemicals.

Although most forms of hepatitis do not appear to worsen during pregnancy and therefore don't appear to pose a significantly increased risk to the mother, certain liver disorders can endanger the fetus (for example, it's possible that a woman with hepatitis B or C could transmit the disease to her baby).

Some women develop a particular form of jaundice during pregnancy (intrahepatic cholestasis). It tends to develop during the third trimester, and it results in severe itching and mild jaundice. It disappears spontaneously within two days of delivery. *Note:* Some studies have shown that women who experience jaundice during pregnancy may be at increased risk of experiencing a premature delivery or a stillbirth.

Diabetes mellitus

Pregnancy can be risky for a woman with diabetes. Hormonal changes cause an increase in insulin requirements that a diabetic woman's body can't meet. If a pregnant woman does not manage to keep her blood sugars under control, she is at increased risk of experiencing miscarriage, stillbirth, or fetal death, or of giving birth to a baby with heart, kidney, or spinal defects. She is also more likely to give birth to an extremely large baby—something that can lead to problems during the delivery or necessitate a cesarean section.

> 99
> If you have previously given birth to a premature baby, make sure you see a high-risk-pregnancy specialist during your next pregnancy. Ask for every test available, particularly if they don't know the cause of your first premature labor.
> —Susan, 33, mother of two boys who were each premature
> 66

A diabetic woman is likely to experience the best possible outcome if she manages to tightly control her blood sugars during the two months prior to becoming pregnant, as well as through her pregnancy. Blood sugar levels of 70 to 140 milligrams/deciliter in the months prior to pregnancy and an average of 80 to 87 milligrams/deciliter during pregnancy are associated with positive pregnancy outcomes. A diabetic woman can find out how well her blood sugars are under control by taking a glycosylated hemoglobin (hemoglobin A_{1c}) test at two to three months of pregnancy. A favorable result on the test indicates that she is at no greater risk of giving birth to a baby with birth defects than any other pregnant woman.

Most of the damage that causes birth defects occurs during the first trimester. Some of the problems that can result are minor and correctable; others can be fatal. That's why it's important for a diabetic pregnant woman to check her blood levels up to six or seven times daily using a home glucose monitor and to report any problems in controlling her blood sugar levels to her caregiver. If blood sugar levels cannot be controlled through diet alone, insulin doses may be required. (Women with pre-existing diabetes—as opposed to gestational diabetes—always need insulin.)

A diabetic woman may require additional tests during pregnancy to check on the status of her eyes, her kidneys, the placenta, and the baby. What's more, her baby may need to be checked over in the neonatal intensive care unit after delivery to be observed for both respiratory problems and hypoglycemia.

Watch Out!
A family history of diabetes is one of the factors that increases your risk of developing gestational diabetes during your pregnancy.

Watch Out!
The leading
cause of mater-
nal death during
pregnancy is
motor-vehicle
accidents.

Thyroid disorders

The thyroid is responsible for regulating the body's metabolic processes.

If it is overactive—a condition known as hyperthyroidism—the metabolism speeds up; the heart rate increases; and such symptoms as muscle weakness, nervousness, anxiety, heat sensitivity, flushed skin, bulging eyes, weight loss, and goiter are experienced. Pregnant women with hyperthyroidism can develop thyroid storm—a severe form of the disorder—during pregnancy. Thyroid storm is associated with an increased risk of premature delivery and low birthweight.

If the thyroid is underactive—a condition known as hypothyroidism—the metabolism slows down, causing lethargy, aching muscles, intolerance to cold, constipation, weight gain, voice deepening, facial puffiness, and dry skin.

Thyroid function needs to be monitored closely in pregnant women with either type of disorder, and where appropriate, medication should be prescribed.

Parathyroid disorders

The parathyroid is located behind the thyroid gland. It plays a role in regulating calcium levels in the body.

Too much parathyroid—a condition known as hyperparathyroidism—results in fatigue, muscle weakness, abdominal pain, bone pain and fractures, frequent urination, thirst, kidney stones, pancreatitis, stomach ulcers, and constipation. Pregnant women with this disorder are at slightly increased risk of experiencing a stillbirth or neonatal death or of giving birth to a baby with tetany (severe muscle spasms and paralysis caused by inadequate levels of calcium).

Too little parathyroid—a condition known as hypoparathyroidism—can cause bone-weakening disorders in the developing baby. Consequently, women with this disorder will be prescribed calcium and vitamin D supplements.

Pituitary disorders

The pituitary gland is responsible for regulating the flow of hormones in the body. A couple of pituitary-related disorders can cause problems during pregnancy:

- **Pituitary tumors:** Some women have undetected pituitary tumors. Pregnancy hormones can cause these tumors to grow, causing severe headaches and visual-field disturbances (that is, spots before the eyes or obstructions to vision). If this occurs, the pregnant woman will need to be monitored by a team of specialists, including an obstetrician, an endocrinologist, and an opthamologist.

- **Diabetes inspidus:** Diabetes inspidus is a rare condition caused by a deficiency in an antidiuretic hormone manufactured by the pituitary gland. This disorder causes increased thirst and a correspondingly increased output of urine. The condition tends to get worse during pregnancy but can be controlled through medication.

- **Pituitary insufficiency:** Pituitary insufficiency— a deficiency in overall pituitary function—can be caused by damage from a tumor, surgery, radiation, or complications from a previous pregnancy. If the condition is not corrected during pregnancy, a woman has only a 54% chance of having a healthy baby. Women who have had previous surgery or radiation in the pituitary region or who have experienced a severe hemorrhage during a previous pregnancy—particularly if the hemorrhage was followed by an inability to lactate—should be tested for pituitary insufficiency.

Adrenal gland disorders

The adrenal glands are responsible for maintaining the correct levels of salt in the body, for producing sex steroids (hormones), and for manufacturing other hormones known as glucocorticoids. Two types of adrenal gland disorders tend to cause problems during pregnancy:

Bright Idea
Read up on high-risk pregnancy at the Johns Hopkins Health Information Web site: www. intellihealth.com

- Cushing's syndrome—the result of too much cortisone—is associated with a high rate of premature delivery and stillbirth. The syndrome is characterized by muscle weakness and wasting; thinning and reddening of the skin; an accumulation of excess fat on the face, neck, and torso; and excessive hair growth. Later stages of the syndrome may also result in high blood pressure, diabetes mellitus, and an increased susceptibility to various infections. It is difficult to diagnose during pregnancy because many of the symptoms are also associated with pregnancy: weakness, weight gain, edema, stretch marks, high blood pressure, and diabetic tendencies.

- Addison's disease—the result of inadequate adrenal production—can result in life-threatening infections. It is characterized by fatigue, loss of appetite, nausea, dizziness, fainting, skin darkening, and abdominal pain.

Blood disorders

The following five blood disorders can cause problems during pregnancy:

- **Anemia:** Anemia—a blood disorder that is caused by deficiencies in iron, vitamin B12, and folic acid—can result in fatigue; weakness; shortness of breath; dizziness; tingling in the hands and feet; a lack of balance and coordination; irritability; depression; heart palpitations; a loss of color in the skin, gums, and fingernails; jaundice of the skin and eyes; and—in particularly serious cases—heart failure. Because many women become anemic during pregnancy, you're at increased risk of experiencing these types of difficulties if you are anemic prior to pregnancy.

- **Sickle-cell anemia:** Sickle-cell anemia is a hereditary blood disease. Women with sickle-cell anemia who become pregnant have a 25% chance of miscarriage, an 8% to 10% chance of stillbirth, and a 15% chance of neonatal death. They have a 33% chance of developing high blood pressure and toxemia and also tend to have problems with urinary tract infections, pneumonia, and lung tissue damage. Sickle-cell crises—painful episodes that can lead to organ damage due to the lack of proper blood flow into the fine capillaries—are more likely to occur during pregnancy. As if that weren't enough, a pregnant woman runs the risk of passing along sickle-cell anemia to her baby if her partner also happens to carry the gene for the disease.

- **Thalassemia:** Thalassemia is another hereditary blood disease. Although most people with Cooley's anemia (alpha-thalassemia) die before they reach childbearing age, the handful of women who do live long enough to become pregnant often suffer severe anemia and congestive heart failure requiring blood transfusions. Those pregnant women who have the less-severe form of thalassemia (beta-thalassemia) may require blood transfusions during pregnancy and run the risk of giving birth to a baby with the disease if their partner is also a carrier.

- **Thrombocytopenia:** Women with thrombocytopenia—a deficiency of blood platelets—are at increased risk of requiring a cesarean section. Babies born vaginally to mothers with severe thrombocytopenia may have decreased platelet counts and problems with hemorrhaging—particularly around the brain.

- **Von Willebrand's disease:** Von Willebrand's disease is an inherited disorder that affects the blood's capability to clot. It can lead to severe blood loss during surgery, accidents, or delivery, which is why pregnant women with this disease need to be treated with intravenous clotting factors.

Autoimmune disorders

Autoimmune disorders occur when the body's immune system develops antibodies to its own body tissue, resulting in damage to its own major organs.

Here are the facts on four of the most common autoimmune disorders and pregnancy:

- **Lupus:** A generation ago, women with lupus were advised not to have any children because of the risks to both the mother and the baby. Today, a growing number of women with the disorder are trying to have children. This is not to say that it's an easy journey to make: according to the Lupus Foundation of America, although 50% of women with lupus can expect to enjoy a normal pregnancy, 25% will experience either stillbirth or a miscarriage, and another 25% will experience preterm labor. What's more, 20% of women with lupus develop preeclampsia, and 3% give birth to babies with "neonatal lupus"—a form of the disease that lasts until the baby is six months old and that may cause a permanent heart abnormality. Women with moderate-to-severe involvement of the central nervous system, lungs, heart, kidneys, or other internal organs are advised to avoid pregnancy.

- **Rheumatoid arthritis:** Rheumatoid arthritis is a common form of arthritis. Its symptoms include joint pain and swelling, and stiffness (especially in the morning). Almost all women with rheumatoid arthritis go into remission during pregnancy. Unfortunately, the disease recurs in 90% of women after they give birth—25% within a month of the delivery.

- **Scleroderma:** Scleroderma is a progressive connective tissue disorder that can cause lung, heart, kidney, and organ damage and that is characterized by both joint inflammation and reduced mobility. In 40% of cases the disease worsens during pregnancy, in another 40% there is no change, and in the remaining 20% of cases the condition actually improves. Pregnant women with the disorder face an increased risk of premature delivery and

Unofficially...
Babies born before 25 weeks who weigh more than two pounds have a 50% chance of survival if they're born in a hospital that is equipped to deal with a baby who is this premature. On the other hand, babies who weigh in at three pounds or more have a 95% chance of survival.

stillbirth, but the majority of babies born to mothers with scleroderma are born healthy.

■ **Myasthenia gravis:** Myasthenia gravis is an autoimmune disease that causes skeletal muscle weakness and easy fatigability. Thirty percent of women with the condition experience no change to their condition during pregnancy, 40% experience a worsening of symptoms, and 30% go into remission. There is a 25% rate of premature delivery associated with the disorder and a 10% to 20% chance that the baby will experience a temporary case of myasthenia gravis within two days of delivery.

Gastrointestinal disorders

Here's what you need to know about chronic gastrointestinal disorders and pregnancy:

■ **Peptic ulcers:** Peptic ulcers are chronic sores that protrude through the gastrointestinal tract lining and can penetrate the muscle tissue in the duodenum, stomach, or esophagus. Forty-four percent of women with peptic ulcers experience an improvement during pregnancy because the high levels of progesterone in the body stimulate the production of mucus, which can help to provide a protective shield in the stomach lining. Another 44% experience no change in their condition, however, and the remaining 12% actually report a deterioration.

■ **Ulcerative colitis:** Ulcerative colitis is an inflammatory disease of the colon and rectum. It can lead to bloody stools, diarrhea, cramping, abdominal pain, weight loss, and dehydration. It can also be linked to fever, anemia, and a high white-blood-cell count. A woman whose colitis is inactive when she becomes pregnant has a 50% to 70% chance of having it remain inactive during pregnancy—good news for both her and her baby. The condition tends to be a significant problem only if emergency surgery is required, because this type of surgery can cause premature labor or necessitate a cesarean delivery.

- **Crohn's disease:** Crohn's disease is similar to ulcerative colitis, but it affects the entire gastrointestinal tract (that is, from the mouth to the anus), although it tends to be focused in the intestines. If Crohn's disease is active at the time of conception, a pregnant woman faces 50% odds of miscarrying. If, however, she is in remission, she has an 85% chance of having the remission continue during her pregnancy.

Neurological disorders

Here's what you need to know about neurological disorders and pregnancy:

- **Epilepsy and seizure disorders:** Pregnancy is risky business for a woman with epilepsy. Many of the drugs used to control the disorder are linked to birth defects; facial, skull, and limb deformities; fatal hemorrhages in newborns; unusual childhood cancers; cleft palate or lip; congenital heart disease; spina bifida; intrauterine growth restriction; and fetal death. Women with epilepsy also have a 1 in 30 chance of giving birth to a child with a seizure disorder. Not everyone faces an equal risk of running into problems; however: women who experience frequent seizures prior to becoming pregnant are four times as likely to experience problems during pregnancy as women who don't.

Bright Idea
You can reduce the likelihood of experiencing problems with your epilepsy if you take your medications as prescribed. Studies have shown that women who take their epilepsy medications as directed have an 85% to 90% chance of giving birth to a healthy baby. If morning sickness is making it difficult for you to keep your medications down, try taking them at times when your nausea is less severe or with plain crackers and a drink of milk.

Watch Out!
If you're subject to migraines, don't allow yourself to get too hungry. Low blood sugar can trigger migraines.

- **Migraines:** Nearly one in five pregnant women suffers from migraine headaches. Fortunately, 80% find that their condition improves during pregnancy, and others are able to avoid problems by avoiding such dietary triggers as MSG (found in Chinese food), sodium nitrates and nitrites (found in cured meats), and tyramine (found in strong cheese).

- **Multiple sclerosis:** Multiple sclerosis is a disease in which the insulating material covering the body's nerve fibers is destroyed, causing weakness in the legs, vision problems, poor coordination and balance, spasticity or trembling in one hand, loss of bladder control, and other difficulties. Women with multiple sclerosis are able to give birth to perfectly healthy babies since there is only a 1% to 5% chance that the baby will develop the disease. Women with a lack of sensation in their lower bodies are monitored closely during the ninth month in case they are unable to detect the onset of labor. They also may require a forceps or vacuum-assisted delivery since the disorder can affect their ability to push.

Cerebrovascular disease

Pregnancy can pose a significant risk to women with a history of strokes, hemorrhages, and blood clots. If a pregnant woman has a known blood-vessel disorder of the brain, such as an arteriovenous malformation, she has a 33% chance of dying during pregnancy.

Malignant diseases

As a rule of thumb, women with cancer should delay becoming pregnant until they are reasonably sure that a recurrence won't occur during pregnancy. This is because women who are diagnosed with cancer during pregnancy are often advised to terminate their pregnancy so that they can obtain the medical treatment they need. Delaying treatment can, in many cases, reduce their odds for long-term survival.

Phenylketonuria (PKU)

Phenylketonuria is a genetically transmitted disorder that can cause severe mental retardation in the newborn if it is undetected within two days of birth. People with PKU are deficient in a particular liver enzyme needed to metabolize phenylalanine, an amino acid found in most foods. Pregnant women with PKU face a higher risk of miscarriage and tend to give birth to more children with microcephaly, heart defects, mental retardation, growth restriction, and low birthweight. Women with PKU must follow a special diet during pregnancy. Studies have shown, however, that women who begin following the diet prior to becoming pregnant have better outcomes.

Group B beta-hemolytic strep

Group B Beta-hemolytic strep is a strain of bacteria that is carried by somewhere between 20% and 40% of pregnant women. Two percent of babies born to women who are infected with the bacteria develop Group B strep disease—a serious condition with a 6% mortality rate. Group B strep is more likely to be a problem if a baby is premature, if the membranes have been ruptured for more than 30 hours when labor commences, or if the woman had a previous baby who contracted a Group B strep infection. Most caregivers screen for Group B strep when a woman is 35 to 37 weeks' pregnant and prescribe

Bright Idea
You and your doctor can obtain the latest information on the effects of chemotherapeutic agents on pregnancy through the Registry of Pregnancies Exposed to Chemotherapeutic Agents. The database contains details on the known effects of cancer drugs during specific stages of pregnancy. Contact the Department of Human Genetics, University of Pittsburgh, Pittsburgh, PA 15261, 412-624-9951, bgettig@helix.hgen.pitt.edu.

antibiotics during labor to women who are carriers or who have other risk factors. (See Chapter 16).

Sexually transmitted diseases

Nearly two million pregnant women experience STDs each year. (See Table 10.1.) If you or your partner has had unprotected sex with someone since your last STD screening, you should be retested. STDs can occur at any time—even during pregnancy—and can be harmful to the unborn baby. Fortunately, there are treatments available to minimize the risk to the baby. Consider the facts for yourself:

Unofficially...
According to a recent study in the *British Journal of Obstetrics and Gynaecology,* women with hepatitis C have an excellent chance of giving birth to perfectly healthy babies. Pregnancy doesn't worsen the disease, and it has not been linked with any pregnancy-related complications.

- Babies of HIV-positive mothers who have been treated with AZT prior to birth and who are delivered by cesarean section have, for example, a less than 1% chance of developing HIV, according to the National Institute for Child Health and Human Development. Babies born to women who do not receive any form of treatment, on the other hand, have a 20% to 32% chance of developing the disease.

- Babies whose mothers test positive for hepatitis B can usually avoid developing the disease if they are given hepatitis B vaccine and immune globulin within 12 hours of birth. These treatments are repeated one month and six months later.

TABLE 10.1: THE NUMBER OF PREGNANT WOMEN IN THE U.S. WITH STDS EACH YEAR

STD	Estimated Number of Pregnant Women Who Get the Disease Each Year
Bacterial vaginosis	800,000
Herpes simplex	800,000
Chlamydia	200,000

Trichomoniasis	80,000
Gonorrhea	40,000
Hepatitis B	40,000
HIV	8,000
Syphilis	8,000
Total	1,976,000

Source: Goldenberg et al., 1997

Psychiatric illness

Psychiatric illness is relatively common in women of reproductive age. Between 8% and 10% of women of childbearing age experience depression and approximately 1% are schizophrenic.

Although certain drugs used to treat psychiatric illness have been linked with birth defects, others are considered to be relatively safe for use during pregnancy (although, ideally, you will want to avoid taking any drug during your first trimester). Your obstetrician or your psychiatrist will be able to provide you with information on the use of your medication during pregnancy.

If you suffer from an eating disorder, you may find it difficult to allow yourself to gain weight during pregnancy. You may wish to continue with an existing treatment program or seek the services of a professional to ensure that you are able to give your baby the best possible start in life.

Conditions that can develop during pregnancy

As we mentioned earlier, any pregnancy can change from low risk to high risk in the blink of an eye. That's why it's important to be prepared to spot the warning signals of the most common pregnancy-related complications. (See Table 10.2.)

Unofficially...
Pregnant women are particularly susceptible to diabetes because the placenta produces hormones that counteract the effects of insulin. As a result, a pregnant woman's body needs to produce 30% more insulin than normal.

TABLE 10.2: CONDITIONS THAT CAN ARISE DURING PREGNANCY

Condition	What Can Happen	Risk Factors and Warning Signs	Treatment
Hyperemesis gravidarum (severe morning sickness)	Can lead to malnutrition and dehydration.	Occurs in 1/200 pregnancies. More common in first-time mothers, women carrying multiples, and mothers who have experienced the disorder during a previous pregnancy.	You will usually be hospitalized so that intravenous drugs and fluids can be administered.
Chorioamnionitis (an infection of the amniotic fluid and fetal membranes)	Can lead to premature rupture of the membranes or premature labor.	Occurs in 1/100 pregnancies. Often there are no symptoms early on except a rapid heartbeat and a fever over 100.4° F.	Treatment options include antibiotics and/or prompt delivery.
Gestational diabetes	Can lead to excessive fetal growth. An overly large baby may have to be delivered by cesarean section and may have difficulties at birth. The diabetes may continue after delivery or recur later in life.	Risk factors: —subsequent pregnancy, —family history of diabetes, —have previously given birth to a baby over 9 lbs., —have experienced unexplained pregnancy losses, —overweight, —high blood pressure, —recurrent yeast infections.	You may be admitted to a hospital if your blood sugar remains high despite efforts to control your sugar levels through diet. You may require insulin injections.
Preeclampsia (also known as toxemia)	Associated with increased risk of placental abruption and fetal distress. In severe forms, it can cause a life-threatening condition that includes blood	Symptoms of early-stage preeclampsia include swelling of hands and feet, sudden weight gain, high blood pressure (140/90 or higher), increased protein in the urine, and headaches. Most likely to occur in:	Mild cases can be treated through bed rest. Severe cases require hospitalization for treatment with antihypertensive drugs. The condition is cured when the baby is born, although the danger period extends to approximately 24 hours after

	clotting problems, liver dysfunction, stroke, and possibly even the death of the mother or baby. When seizures are present, it is known as eclampsia.	—first-time mothers, —women carrying multiples, —women with chronic high blood pressure, diabetes, kidney disease, or a family history of preeclampsia.	delivery. Labor may be induced or cesarean performed if the condition progresses to a certain point.
Intrauterine growth restriction (IUGR) (also known as intrauterine growth retardation)	Can result in low-birthweight babies or infants who are less alert and responsive.	Diagnosed when the developing baby consistently measures small for dates. Most likely to occur in: —women with chronic health problems or an unhealthy lifestyle, —women with high blood pressure, —women carrying multiples, —woman having first or fifth (or later) pregnancy, —a fetus with chromosomal abnormalities.	Bed rest and/or hospitalization. Labor may be induced if it is felt that the baby will do better in the nursery than in the relatively hostile uterine environment.
Amniotic fluid-level problems: polyhydramnios (too much fluid) or oligohydramnios (too little fluid)	Polyhydramnios may indicate Rh-incompatibility problems, diabetes, or the presence of multiple fetuses. Oligohydramnios may indicate a malfunction or absence of fetal kidneys or leakage of amniotic fluid due to premature rupture of the membranes.	Suspected when a woman measures too large or too small for dates; diagnosed via ultrasound.	Polyhydramnios: If severe and causes significant symptoms or fetal compromise, can be treated by removing excess liquid through amniocentesis. Oligohydramnios: This is a serious condition that is generally treated by delivering the baby as soon as it is considered safe to do so.

continues

Condition	What Can Happen	Risk Factors and Warning Signs	Treatment
Premature labor	Health of premature newborn is determined by week of gestation, type of neonatal care available, birthweight, and general health.	Contractions accompanied by cervical dilation, vaginal bleeding or discharge, or vaginal pressure between the 20th and 37th week of pregnancy. Other symptoms include menstrual-like cramps, with possible diarrhea, nausea, or indigestion. Risk factors include smoking, urinary tract infections, poor general health, diabetes or thyroid problems, bacterial infections or STDs, placental problems, physical trauma (car accident, spouse abuse), a history of premature labor, multiple fetuses, abdominal surgery during pregnancy, or a history of two second trimester miscarriages.	Bed rest, intravenous fluids, and/or the prescription of drugs to prevent labor. *Note:* Medications are generally effective only if your cervix is dilated less than three centimeters and is not yet effaced.
Placenta previa (placenta covering the cervical opening)	The baby cannot pass out of the mother's body without dislodging the placenta and disrupting its own blood supply. A postpartum hemorrhage may occur after the birth of the baby.	Bleeding can be triggered by coughing, straining, or sexual intercourse. More common in women who have had several children. Occurs in 1/200 pregnancies.	Bed rest, monitoring, and/or hospitalization. A cesarean section may be required.*Note:* If placenta previa is diagnosed n 2nd trimester, the condition may correct itself by the time you deliver.

Placental abruption (placenta prematurely separates from uterus, either partially or wholly)	Can be harmful—even fatal—to mother and baby.	Warning signs include heavy vaginal bleeding, premature labor, contractions, uterine tenderness, and lower back pain. More common in women who have had two or more children, who smoke, who have high blood pressure, or who have had a previous placental abruption. Sometimes caused by the trauma of an automobile accident. Occurs in 1/150 pregnancies.	Bed rest and careful monitoring. If fetus goes into distress, an emergency cesarean section may be necessary.
Placental insufficiency	Can result in a low-birthweight baby.	Can be caused by abnormal development, restricted blood flow due to a clot, a partial abruption, a placenta that is too small or poorly developed, a pregnancy that is postdate, or maternal diabetes.	Sometimes warrants the delivery of the baby before term.

☼

Bright Idea
Check out the online guide to gestational diabetes at www. mediconsult. com/pregnancy/ shareware/gest/.

Unofficially...
A recent study in the *New England Journal of Medicine* indicated that a daily dose of baby aspirin during pregnancy does not reduce a woman's chances of developing preeclampsia.

Coping with the stress of a high-risk pregnancy

Nine months can seem like an impossibly long time when you're dealing with the stress of a high-risk pregnancy. If your pregnancy has been categorized as high risk, you may be dealing with a lot of conflicting emotions. "At some point during your confinement, you can expect to feel angry at your baby (for keeping you in bed), your husband (for getting you into bed in the first place), your doctor (for not fixing the problem), and everyone else you can think of," explains Laurie A. Rich, author of *When Pregnancy Isn't Perfect: A Layman's Guide to Complications in Pregnancy.*

Here are some of the types of emotions you may be experiencing:

- **Guilt:** You may be wondering if you are somehow responsible for the fact that you and your baby are at risk. Did you overdo things at work? Did you fail to follow your doctor's orders to the letter? It's easy to beat yourself up after the fact.

- **Anger and sadness:** If your pregnancy necessitates bed rest, you may feel angry about your lack of control over your life and sad and lonely at being cut off from the rest of the world.

- **Resentment:** You may find yourself feeling resentment toward those women who seem to sail through pregnancy with nothing more significant to worry about than whether they're getting stretch marks.

- **Helplessness:** If your pregnancy becomes complicated and you are put on bed rest or hospitalized, you may feel helpless because you have to rely on other people to make your meals, take care of your other children, and so on. You may actually find it difficult to ask friends and family members for favors, assuming that you'll never in a million years be able to repay them for all the help you need right now.

- **Fear:** You may be afraid that despite everything you're doing to increase your odds of having a healthy baby, something could still go wrong.

Because there are so many emotions to deal with in a high-risk pregnancy, many women find it helpful to find someone who will take the time to talk to them about their worries and concerns. If your caregiver doesn't have the time, training, or bedside manner necessary to talk with you about your concerns, you may wish to see a therapist—ideally one who has experience in dealing with clients experiencing high-risk pregnancies. You may also want to hook up with a local or national support group specializing in your particular type of pregnancy complications. (See Appendix B.)

The facts about bed rest

Bed rest sounds like a wonderful thing until you're sentenced to it 24 hours a day. The novelty of surrounding yourself with pillows and junky novels wears off fairly quickly for most women, who then find themselves facing weeks—if not months—of bed rest.

How bed rest feels

Crazy as it sounds, bed rest can be exhausting. When you're on bed rest, you tire more easily and feel tired more often. You may feel achy and sore from spending so much time lying in the same position. You may feel stiff when you get out of bed, and you may actually find it painful to walk if you've been on

Bright Idea
Ask your doctor or a social worker at the local hospital if they can recommend a therapist who specializes in working with women who are experiencing high-risk pregnancies.

bed rest for some time. (This is because lying in bed with your legs relaxed for an extended period can cause the Achilles tendon to tighten.)

You can help minimize some of the effects of bed rest by getting your doctor's go-ahead to do some exercises in bed. (*Note:* Not all women on bed rest are good candidates for exercise, so don't do as much as a single leg-lift without checking with your doctor first.) A well-designed exercise program can help you prevent muscle weakness, limit the loss of your range of motion, prevent lung congestion, minimize the effects of bed rest on the heart, and help you maintain sufficient muscle tone to be able to walk without assistance after delivery.

Assuming that you get the nod of approval from your caregiver, you may be able to do pelvic tilts; Kegels; gluteal sets; leg, ankle, and heel raises; knee extensions; arm raises; shoulder shrugs; wrist circles; and neck circles.

How to survive it

Here are some tips on staying sane while you're on bed rest:

- Arm yourself with facts. Find out exactly what you can and cannot do. (See the following checklist.)

Watch Out!
If you suspect that you are experiencing premature labor, drink several glasses of water and lie down on your side. This will often stop the contractions.

CHECKLIST: QUESTIONS TO ASK YOUR DOCTOR ABOUT BED REST

- Are you allowed to sit up in bed, or do you have to lie on your left side (the side that allows for maximum blood flow to the baby) all the time?

- Are you allowed to get out of bed to go to the bathroom, or do you need to use a bedpan?

- Do you need to eat your meals lying down?

- Can you take a shower, or do you have to have a sponge bath?

- Are you allowed to work while you're lying down?

- How long will you be on bed rest?

- Are you allowed to exercise?

- Are you allowed to have sex?

- Are you allowed to sleep on the sofa, or do you have to stay in bed?

- Are you allowed to lift anything? If so, how heavy an object are you allowed to lift?

There are other issues to consider before you go on bed rest:

- Give your notice at work. Because the need for bed rest can arise virtually overnight, you may not be able to give your employer much notice of your need to leave work. Try to pull your thoughts together before you call your employer. Be sure to let him know how long you're likely to be on bed rest (for example, for a week or two, or for the rest of the pregnancy); what type of work, if any, you could do from home; who might be able to assume responsibility for any projects that are in progress; and so on.

- Be creative when it comes to choosing where to spend your bed rest. "If it's nice outside, have someone set up a table for you outside with your favorite books, a radio, a cooler filled with fruit, drinks, and food," suggests Stephanie, 26, mother of one and veteran bed rester. If your doctor gives you the go-ahead to set up camp somewhere other than in your own bed, go for it. A change of scene will do you good.

Moneysaver
Don't forget to make a call to human resources. Your company maternity-leave or disability-leave program may cover part or all of your salary while you're on bed rest.

- Organize your environment so that you'll be less tempted to get out of bed and go searching for something you need. Here are some things you'll want to keep within reaching distance: a phone, a telephone book, a radio, the remote control for the radio or TV, tissues, a cooler (packed with cold beverages, healthy snacks, and your lunch), craft supplies, a laptop computer with Internet access ("I spent three hours a day on the Internet, and it literally kept me sane," says one former bed rester), a cassette tape player and books on tape, photo albums to work on, and plenty of reading materials.

- Come up with a routine to prevent yourself from going stir-crazy. Pencil in the times of your favorite TV shows, arrange to meet another pregnant woman on bed rest online in one of the bed rest chat forums, plan when you're going to make phone calls to friends and family members, and so on.

- Reach out to other moms on bed rest by phone or via the Internet. You can either get in touch with Sidelines (www.sidelines.org/ or 949-497-2265) or ask your doctor if he knows of a local support group for moms on bed rest.

- Stay connected with people. "Have a friend come over and just talk—or make you lunch—as often as possible. It will make the whole day better," says Heather, 22, mother of one, who spent three weeks on bed rest during her pregnancy.

- Make suitable child-care arrangements for any other children. If you're a stay-at-home mother with young children, you may need full-time child care.

- Call your insurance company or HMO to find out if it will cover the costs of a personal care attendant while you're on bed rest. Some companies do and some don't. Sometimes all it takes to sway the claims department is a phone call or letter from your doctor, so don't be afraid to ask him to intervene on your behalf if you run into difficulty.

- Reassure your children that it won't be like this forever. Your stint on bed rest will be over as soon as the baby is born—sometimes sooner.

- Spend some time alone with your partner each day, and keep the lines of communication open. This is a stressful time for both of you.

- If you can afford it, arrange for a childbirth educator or doula to give you childbirth classes at home. If possible, find someone who is familiar with the particular medical conditions or pregnancy-related complications you are dealing with and who understands how they may affect on the birth.

Just the facts

- The term *high risk* is used to describe pregnancies in which the mother, the baby, or both are at higher-than-average risk of experiencing complications.

- You are likely to be classified as high risk if you have a chronic medical condition that may affect your pregnancy, a history of pregnancy-related complications, or pregnancy loss.

- If your doctor prescribes bed rest, it's important to find out exactly what you are and aren't allowed to do.

66

If you end up on bed rest in the hospital, be sure to bring snacks. I got supper at 5:00 p.m. and no more food until 8:00 a.m. I was starving by then since I was used to supper at 6:00 p.m., a snack in the evening, and breakfast at 6:30 a.m.
—Susan, 33, mother of two

99

- Connecting with other moms on bed rest can help you to stay sane. Either ask your obstetrician to recommend a local support group or get in touch with Sidelines (www.sidelines.org/ or 949-497-2265).

GET THE SCOOP ON...
Miscarriage ▪ Ectopic pregnancy ▪ Molar
pregnancy ▪ Stillbirth ▪ Intrapartum death ▪
Important decisions you will have to make ▪
Grieving ▪ Trying again

What Every Pregnant Woman Needs to Know About Pregnancy Loss and Neonatal Death

L osing a baby can be an incredibly painful experience. Regardless of when your baby dies, you lose all of the hopes and dreams you have invested in that child from the moment you first found out you were pregnant.

Although you may feel, initially, that you are the only person in the world to experience this heartbreak, you will discover—as you begin talking about your loss—that miscarriage, stillbirth, and neonatal death happen far more frequently than most of us are led to believe.

The problem is that there continues to be a conspiracy of silence when it comes to talking about these types of losses—a strange holdover from the Victorian era, given that we're now "out of the closet" on so many other matters. Although most childbirth classes give you some basic facts about

Chapter 11

miscarriage, they tend to ignore stillbirth, intra-partum loss, and neonatal death altogether. This is true of most pregnancy books. Is it any wonder that the majority of women who experience these types of losses feel terribly alone?

This chapter wasn't much fun for us to write, and it might not be much fun for you to read, either. Indeed, you may find it extremely difficult to even think about the possibility that something could happen to the baby you are carrying. But things can and do go wrong during pregnancy, and that's why it's important to arm yourself with the facts about pregnancy loss and neonatal death.

(Just a quick note before we plunge into the rest of the chapter. Ann Douglas, one of the authors of this book, lost her fourth child, Laura, to stillbirth. Laura died at 26 weeks due to a knot in her umbilical cord. Ann has chosen to share her experience at selected points in this chapter.)

The facts about miscarriage

As you no doubt realize, miscarriages are extremely common, occurring in approximately 15% to 20% of all confirmed pregnancies (that is, pregnancies that have been confirmed via a home pregnancy test or visit to the doctor). Although the majority of miscarriages occur during the first 13 weeks of pregnancy (with the lion's share occurring before a woman even suspects that she is pregnant), miscarriages can and do occur up to the 20th week of pregnancy. (A pregnancy loss after that point is classified as a stillbirth.)

The causes of miscarriage

Certain factors are known to cause miscarriages. These factors include

- **Chromosomal abnormalities:** More than half of miscarriages are caused by chromosomal abnormalities—problems with the structure or number of chromosomes in the embryo or with the genes that the chromosomes carry. Many of these embryos would not have developed normally: scientists believe that the high rate of miscarriage helps to ensure that only 2% to 3% of babies are born with congenital anomalies rather than 12%, as would be the case if these miscarriages didn't occur. Miscarriages caused by chromosomal abnormalities are random occurrences and consequently are less likely to recur during subsequent pregnancies than other causes of miscarriage.

- **Maternal disease:** Conditions such as lupus and other autoimmune disorders, congenital heart disease, severe kidney disease, uncontrolled diabetes, thyroid disease, and intrauterine infection are associated with higher-than-average miscarriage rates—just one more reason to make sure that any chronic health conditions that you have are under control before you become pregnant.

- **Hormonal imbalances:** Hormone imbalances (for example, progesterone deficiencies) are known to cause miscarriages.

- **Immune system disorders:** Women with high levels of antiphospholipid antibodies (APA)— substances that increase the clotting tendencies of blood—are at increased risk of miscarriage. This is because the small blood vessels leading to the placenta can become clogged, resulting in fetal death.

Watch Out!
If your blood is Rh negative (and the baby's father is Rh positive) and you experience a miscarriage, you will need an Rh immune globulin shot to prevent you from developing antibodies that could affect a future Rh-positive baby.

- **Allogeneic factors:** Some women develop anti-bodies to their partner's leukocytes (white blood cells)—something that increases the chances of miscarriage.

- **Anatomical factors:** Anatomical problems of the uterus and cervix (for example, uterine adhesions, abnormal uterine structure, uterine fibroids, and incompetent cervix) are known to cause miscarriages.

- **Viral and bacterial infections:** Viral and bacterial infections are thought to play a role in miscarriage, although the cause-and-effect relationship is not 100% clear.

- **Recreational drug and alcohol use:** Using recreational drugs and consuming large quantities of alcohol increase your chances of suffering a miscarriage.

- **Environmental toxins:** Exposure to environmental toxins such as arsenic, lead, and formaldehyde can lead to miscarriage.

- **Age:** Your chances of having a miscarriage increase as you age. Whereas women in their twenties have a 10% risk of experiencing a miscarriage during any given pregnancy, the rate for women in their forties is 50%.

How to tell if you're experiencing a miscarriage

You could be having a miscarriage if you experience

- spotting or bleeding without pain,

- heavy or persistent bleeding—with or without clots—with abdominal pain or cramping,

- a gush of fluid from your vagina but no pain or bleeding—an indication that your membranes may have ruptured,

Unofficially...
Twenty percent of miscarriages are associated with gestational sacs in which there is no apparent embryo, yolk sac, or umbilical cord. This type of non-viable pregnancy is sometimes referred to as a "blighted ovum"—a term that we detest but that is still widely used in obstetrical circles.

- a sudden disappearance of pregnancy symptoms such as morning sickness or breast enlargement.

Note: Not all first-trimester bleeding is an indication that you are having a miscarriage. See Chapter 14 for details.

How miscarriages are classified

Your doctor may use the following terminology when describing your miscarriage (or "spontaneous abortion"—the medical term for miscarriage):

- **Threatened abortion:** Threatened abortion means that a miscarriage is possible but not inevitable. You are probably experiencing bleeding and possibly pain.

- **Inevitable abortion:** Inevitable abortion means that your cervix has begun to dilate and it's only a matter of time until you miscarry.

- **Incomplete abortion:** An incomplete abortion occurs when some of the products of conception (for example, gestational sac, fetus, umbilical cord, placenta) are left in the uterus after the miscarriage. A dilation and curettage (D & C) or suction curettage (a form of D & C where the contents of the uterus are removed through a tube using suction) is usually performed if an incomplete abortion has occurred.

- **Complete abortion:** A complete abortion occurs when all of the products of conception are expelled from the uterus during the miscarriage.

- **Missed abortion:** A missed abortion occurs when the fetus and placenta die but remain in the uterus. Even though pregnancy symptoms may disappear almost immediately, many

Watch Out!
Try to save any fetal or other tissue (other than blood clots) that passes out of your body when you are having a miscarriage. Your caregiver may wish to examine it.

women do not realize that they have experienced a missed abortion until a few weeks later in their pregnancy—typically when a doppler or ultrasound fails to detect a fetal heartbeat. Still, there's no reason to go into panic mode if your pregnancy symptoms disappear overnight—something that often occurs toward the end of the first trimester in a perfectly healthy pregnancy.

Blighted ovum, an old-fashioned and medically inaccurate term, is a form of missed abortion that generally refers to the earliest pregnancies (that is, pregnancies in which a fetus is not yet evident at the time of diagnosis).

Recurrent miscarriage

Doctors used to wait for a woman to have three consecutive miscarriages before attempting to determine if there were any underlying medical problems causing her to miscarry, but studies in recent years reveal that it doesn't make any sense to wait until a woman has had a second miscarriage to determine the causes—particularly if she's approaching the end of her reproductive years.

Unfortunately, the cause of recurrent miscarriage remains a mystery in as many as 50% of cases. Still, couples who experience miscarriage from unknown causes have a 52% to 61% chance of giving birth to a live baby in their next pregnancy—lower-than-average odds, but still significantly high enough to encourage many couples with a history of miscarriage to pursue their dream of having a baby.

Part of the difficulty in pinpointing a cause for recurrent miscarriages, of course, is the fact that a series of miscarriages may be caused by a number of different factors (for example, one may be caused

Unofficially...
Although it's theoretically possible to become pregnant within two weeks of experiencing an early miscarriage, most caregivers recommend that you wait until after you have had two to three normal menstrual cycles before trying to conceive. Some researchers suspect that waiting this additional time may give your uterus time to heal and your endometrial lining time to build back up to healthy levels.

by a chromosomal abnormality and a second by a viral infection).

A recent study reported in *Obstetrics and Gynecology* revealed that a number of different factors need to be considered when assessing a woman's chances of having a successful pregnancy after one or more miscarriages. The researchers found that a woman under the age of 25 who has no anticardiolipin antibodies (a type of antiphospholipid antibody), a regular menstrual cycle, and one previous live birth has an 88% chance of experiencing a live birth during her next pregnancy. On the other hand, a woman who is over the age of 30, has irregular periods, has had more than four previous miscarriages, has elevated anticardiolipin antibodies, and has had no previous live births has a 60% chance of having a successful outcome in her next pregnancy.

Searching for clues

If you experience three miscarriages in a row, you will be classified as a "habitual aborter" (a dreadfully insensitive term that simply means that you have a history of recurrent miscarriage), and you may be given one or more of the following tests:

- blood tests (to detect any hormonal or immune-system problems),

- genetic tests of you and your partner and/or chromosomal testing of tissue from a miscarriage (to determine if you or your partner is a carrier of a disorder that could be causing you to miscarry repeatedly—something that's a problem for approximately 2% to 3% of couples),

- genital-tract cultures (to look for the presence of infection),

Bright Idea
If you've had two or more miscarriages, you should plan to have a complete preconception workup before you try to get pregnant again. If you unexpectedly find yourself pregnant again before you have a chance to have a full medical workup, see your doctor or midwife right away so that appropriate treatments can be considered.

- endometrial biopsy (the removal and analysis of a sample of endometrial tissue to determine if the tissue that lines the uterus is sufficiently hospitable to allow the embryo to implant and grow),

- a hysterosalpingogram (HSG) (an X-ray of the uterus and fallopian tubes that is used to look for blockages and other problems),

- a hysteroscopy (an examination of the inside of the uterus using a telescope-like instrument inserted through the vagina and cervix that is ordered if the HSG is abnormal),

- a laparoscopy (an internal examination of the pelvic organs using a slender light-transmitting instrument),

- ultrasound or sonohysterogram (to detect structural problems with the uterus, as well as fibroids or adhesions that could be causing you to miscarry).

Treatment options

Depending on the suspected cause of your recurrent miscarriages, your doctor may recommend

- surgery to correct any uterine abnormalities (something that gives you a 70% to 85% chance of having a live baby in your next pregnancy) or to remove large fibroids,

- a cerclage procedure around week 14 of your next pregnancy (to stitch the cervix shut so that it won't open prematurely),

- antibiotics to cure any infections,

- improved management of any chronic diseases,

- hormone therapy (prescribing progesterone supplements to create a more embryo-friendly uterine environment),

- treatment for immune-system problems (prescribing prednisone with low doses of aspirin or heparin with or without low doses of aspirin—treatment methods that boast success rates of 55% to 85%),

- treatment for allogeneic factors (one experimental treatment involves injecting the female partner with leukocytes—white blood cells—from the male partner).

Ectopic pregnancy

Approximately 1% of pregnancies are ectopic, meaning that the fertilized egg implants somewhere other than inside the uterus—most often in the fallopian tube.

An embryo that implants in the fallopian tube cannot develop normally. It can only grow to about the size of a walnut before it causes the tube to burst, causing a medical emergency that can result in major bleeding or even death.

Ectopic pregnancies are classified as either unruptured or ruptured:

- An unruptured (also known as subacute) ectopic pregnancy is one in which the fallopian tube has not yet burst. It is characterized by pain on one side of the abdomen and in the shoulder region (as a result of blood pooling under the diaphragm), vaginal bleeding, and fainting (if the blood loss has been substantial). If an unruptured ectopic pregnancy is detected soon enough, it may respond to medication, or if surgery is needed, it is often possible to save the tube.

- A ruptured (also known as acute) ectopic pregnancy is one in which the fallopian tube bursts,

Watch Out!
There's more in that glass of tap water than you might realize. A recent study of 5,000 pregnant women in California revealed that in certain locales, those who drank five or more glasses of tap water each day were more likely to experience miscarriages than women who drank bottled water.

Unofficially...
Scientists theorize that nicotine's effect on estrogen is responsible for the increased risk of ectopic pregnancy in women who smoke. Reduced levels of estrogen affect the fallopian tube's ability to contract and transport the embryo to the uterus.

causing pain and shock, a weak but rapid pulse, paleness, and falling blood pressure. Treatment for a ruptured tube typically involves removal of the tube and possibly a blood transfusion.

You are at increased risk of experiencing an ectopic pregnancy if

- you smoke (women who smoke more than 30 cigarettes per day are five times as likely to experience an ectopic pregnancy);
- you have previously experienced pelvic inflammatory disease (PID), STDs such as gonorrhea and chlamydia, endometriosis, or salpingitis (inflammation of fallopian tube);
- you have already had an ectopic pregnancy (even though you still have an 88% chance of not experiencing another ectopic pregnancy);
- you have been treated for infertility;
- you have had pelvic or abdominal surgery (for example, an appendectomy);
- you were using an intrauterine device (IUD) at the time you became pregnant;
- you became pregnant despite the fact that you had a tubal sterilization.

An ectopic pregnancy is typically diagnosed through a pelvic exam, blood tests, ultrasound, or a combination of these methods. In some cases, it is necessary to perform a D & C (to check for signs of an early miscarriage).

Once the diagnosis has been confirmed, your doctor will recommend either surgery (to remove the pregnancy or all or part of the fallopian tube) or drug treatment (to stop the growth of the tissue and allow it to be reabsorbed over time). Drug treatment is an option only if the pregnancy is small, the tube has not yet ruptured, and there is no internal bleeding.

You will need to go for a series of blood tests in the weeks following treatment. These blood tests are to check for escalations in hCG, which may indicate that some tissue was left behind and that it is growing.

Molar pregnancy

A molar pregnancy (also known as gestational trophoblastic disease, or GTD) is a rare disease of pregnancy, occurring in just one 1 of every 1,500 to 2,000 pregnancies in the United States. The incidence of molar pregnancy varies with ethnicity and is far more common in Asians.

It occurs when a pregnancy results in the growth of abnormal tissue rather than an embryo, and it typically results in miscarriage before the fourth month of pregnancy.

In a complete molar pregnancy, there is a mass of abnormal cells that—in a normal pregnancy—would have become the placenta.

In a partial molar pregnancy, there is a mass of abnormal cells that would have become the placenta and an abnormal fetus as well.

The symptoms of a molar pregnancy include

- vaginal bleeding during the first trimester,
- a uterus that grows too quickly,
- enlarged ovaries (detected through ultrasound),
- extremely high levels of hCG (detected through a blood test).

A molar pregnancy is removed by suction curettage. Follow-up is required for six months to a year to ensure that no abnormal cells have been left

Bright Idea
Being bombarded with baby-related junk mail? Write to the Mail Preference Service, Direct Marketing Association, P.O. Box 9008, Farmington, NY 11735-9008, or the Mail Preference Service, Direct Marketing Association of Canada, 1 Concord Gate, Suite 607, Don Mills, Ontario M3C 3N6, and indicate that you don't wish to receive any mail from its members.

behind (a condition known as persistent GTD—something that happens in 10% of molar pregnancies). It is sometimes necessary to resort to chemotherapy to treat persistent GTD.

In 2% to 3% of cases, a cancerous form of GTD develops. This disease—known as choriocarcinoma—can spread to other parts of the body, including the lungs. That's why it's necessary for women who have had a molar pregnancy to postpone any subsequent pregnancy until such a possibility has been ruled out, since the rising hCG levels of a normal pregnancy would be difficult to distinguish from the rising levels of persistent GTD.

Women who have experienced one molar pregnancy have a 1.3% to 2.9% chance of experiencing another molar pregnancy.

Stillbirth

Stillbirth—the death of a baby before birth—occurs in approximately 1% of births.

A stillbirth is typically diagnosed when the mother reports a cessation of fetal movements or when the doctor or midwife is unable to detect a fetal heartbeat during a routine prenatal checkup.

Most pregnant women find the experience of losing a baby to stillbirth to be utterly devastating. This is what one grieving mother had to say about her experiences in a recent article in the *Daily Telegraph:* "A stillbirth robs you, as a parent, of part of your future. That child is so wanted and is suddenly taken away. It is so difficult leaving a child behind in the maternity ward when all the other mothers are leaving with their babies."

What makes it even more difficult is that many people—even family members and very close friends—may fail to understand what this baby

Unofficially...
According to the Wisconsin Stillbirth Service Program at the University of Wisconsin, 68 babies are stillborn each day in the United States—approximately 1 in every 115 births.

meant to you. Many women find their grief after stillbirth to be a very lonely experience, as C. Elizabeth Carney writes in *The Miscarriage Manual:* "I thought that if my baby had lived for a while, if people had gotten to know and love her, maybe then I would have been given the affirmation to grieve the way I needed to. But I was the only one with any memory of her, the only one who had the chance to love her. I had no one to share her with, not even my husband."

The causes

Although researchers have identified a number of causes of stillbirth, it is possible to come up with a firm explanation of what led to a particular baby's death only in approximately 40% to 50% of cases.

When a cause is identified, it is usually one of the following:

- a problem with the umbilical cord (for example, a knot);

- a problem with the placenta (for example, a placental abruption);

- maternal disease (chronic hypertension, preeclampsia, metabolic diseases, Rh incompatibility, and certain viral and bacterial infections);

- congenital abnormality (responsible for approximately 25% of stillbirths).

Note: Some doctors attribute any unexplained stillbirth to either a cord accident or a problem with the placenta. In fact, only a relatively small number of stillbirths involve these particular problems.

Intrapartum death

Intrapartum death occurs when a baby dies during labor, typically due to a lack of oxygen. Fortunately, intrapartum death is relatively rare today—small consolation, however, for the families who lose much-wanted babies due to accidents during birth.

Studies have identified a number of factors associated with an increased risk of intrapartum death: preeclampsia (toxemia/pregnancy-induced hypertension), intrauterine growth restriction, prolonged pregnancy (more than two weeks beyond the due date), vaginal breech delivery, previous perinatal death, and even physician (or other caregiver) inexperience.

If your baby dies during labor, you will need the support of family, friends, your caregiver, and a social worker or therapist to help you work through your shock and grief.

Waiting to go into labor versus being induced

When you find out that your baby has died, you must decide whether you would prefer to go into labor naturally—something that occurs within two weeks of fetal death in 80% to 90% of cases—or be induced as soon as possible. There are risks associated with carrying a dead fetus for longer than four weeks (maternal blood coagulation problems, for example), so your doctor or midwife will encourage you to consider induction if you don't go into labor naturally within the allotted time period.

If you choose to be induced—as the majority of women who find themselves in this situation do—your doctor will use either laminaria (a seaweed product that dilates the cervix mechanically), vaginal prostaglandin supplements, or pitocin (an artificial form of oxytocin) to get labor started.

(A quick comment from Ann: You may want to request pain relief during labor. I remember telling my midwife and the attending obstetrician that I didn't want to feel anything during the delivery since I didn't think I could cope with the pain of labor as well as the overwhelming feelings of grief I was experiencing. In fact, I asked to be put under general anesthetic at one point so that I could be completely unaware of what was going on, but my midwife convinced me that it would be better for me both physically and emotionally if I chose another alternative. In the end, I opted to be awake and alert during a vaginal delivery. While I did receive pain relief throughout the delivery, it wasn't enough to eliminate all of the sensations of pain, however—just enough to make the pain bearable and to allow me to be alert enough to spend some very precious time with my daughter—the only time we would ever have together after she was born.)

Some women choose to give birth by cesarean section rather than vaginally, although many caregivers will discourage this choice given the increased risks involved. If you feel quite strongly that this is the route you would like to go, you will need to discuss this issue with your caregiver.

Preparing for the birth of a child who will be stillborn

If you will be giving birth to a child who will be stillborn, you will need to decide whether you and your partner would like to spend some time with your baby after the birth. Although you may think that the experience of spending some time with your baby's body might be tremendously upsetting, most families who go through this experience actually find it to be incredibly comforting. "I spent a few moments with my son after delivery," recalls Johnna, 33, whose son was stillborn at 27 weeks. "It was the most precious time."

> 66
> When you experience a loss, your naivete is gone. You are suddenly acutely aware of the fact that all kinds of things can go wrong, and that pregnancy is indeed a very fragile thing.
> —Johnna Horn, 33, mother of three living children and a baby who was stillborn
> 99

Here's another reason to spend some time with your stillborn baby, according to one obstetrician: "I've always encouraged patients to spend enough time with their stillborn baby to see how normal it appears otherwise, because if the mother never allows herself the chance to see her stillborn baby, her fantasies of it may be far more morbid than the reality of its appearance, even if the baby is severely discolored and has macerated [that is, peeling] skin."

Neonatal death

If you know (from the results of amniocentesis, for example) that you will be giving birth to a child who is likely to live for just a short time after birth, you need to decide how you want to spend that time with your child. Here are some questions to ask yourself: Do you want to spend that time alone with your baby and your partner? Would you like your other children or your baby's grandparents to be present as well? Do you want to hold your baby as she passes away? Would you like some time alone with your baby after her death?

You will also need to consider whether you would like your baby to receive pain relief and whether you wish to donate the baby's organs to another child—a decision that allows many families to make something good come of an otherwise nightmarish experience.

Although the U.S. infant mortality rate has been declining steadily throughout this century, it is still unacceptably high. (The United States ranks 25th among industrialized nations, despite all the high-tech bells and whistles at our disposal. In 1996, the U.S. infant mortality rate was 7.2 per thousand live births. The top 10 causes of infant mortality in 1996

66

The fullness of motherhood was compressed into that day. A mother's deep love for her son, her tender concern, her exquisite pain of separation, her comforting touch for a lifetime's scraped knees, her worry for a lifetime's dangers, her peace in their inseparable bond, all came together in that rich moment as she gazed upon her precious little boy. —pediatrician Dr. Alan Greene of www.drgreene. com recalling the experience of a patient who lost a baby to Trisomy 13 shortly after birth

99

(ranked in order of frequency) are shown in Table 11.1.

TABLE 11.1: TEN LEADING CAUSES OF INFANT DEATH IN THE UNITED STATES IN 1996

Cause	Number of Babies
Congenital anomalies	6,463
Preterm/low birthweight	3,706
Sudden infant death syndrome (SIDS)	2,906
Respiratory distress syndrome (RDS)	1,368
Problems related to complications of pregnancy	1,212
Complications of the placenta, cord, and membranes	892
Accidents	772
Perinatal infections	747
Pneumonia/influenza	469
Intrauterine hypoxia and birth hypoxia	429

Important decisions

While you are trying to come to terms with the loss of your baby, you will need to make a number of important decisions—such as whether you wish to have an autopsy performed, what—if anything—you would like to do to create memories of your baby, and what type of funeral arrangements you would like to make.

Deciding whether to have an autopsy performed

Most couples who lose a baby have very strong feelings about having a detailed physical examination performed on their baby after the delivery. Such an examination typically involves

- an extensive physical evaluation
- an internal postmortem examination (autopsy)
- photographing the baby's face, body, and unusual features

- taking X-rays

- performing genetic tests on some of the baby's tissues

If the cause of death is not obvious and the couple hopes to have other children, they may request an autopsy in the hope that they will gain some information that may be helpful to them as they plan a subsequent pregnancy. These results are usually available within a few weeks, but sometimes it can take as long as a few months to get the full autopsy report back from the coroner's office.

Some couples choose not to proceed with an autopsy because they are concerned about how their baby's body will be treated during the procedure. If you are struggling with this issue, you may find it helpful to know that the majority of medical examiners treat the bodies that have been entrusted to them with the utmost respect and dignity.

Making funeral arrangements

If your baby is born any time after 20 weeks' gestation, you may be required to have your baby's remains buried or cremated. (The laws are slightly different in each state or province, so ask your caregiver or hospital social worker to clarify your legal and financial obligations.)

In many communities, there are one or more funeral homes that waive the majority of their fees as a service to bereaved parents. If you're not up to researching funeral homes on your own, have a trusted friend or family member make some initial phone calls for you to help narrow down your options. Then, once you've made a few phone calls of your own and have zeroed in on a particular funeral home, you can arrange to meet with the funeral director and finalize the arrangements.

Unofficially...
Although traditional Jewish law doesn't allow mourning rituals for a baby who lived less than 30 days, a growing number of Jewish families are choosing to have funerals or memorial services to mark the loss of a child in the perinatal period.

Just a word of caution to parents who will be giving birth to stillborn babies. You may be shocked to learn that your life-insurance policy won't cover the cost of burying a child who is stillborn, and that you cannot claim a stillborn child as a dependent on your tax return (something you would be permitted to do if your child was born alive and then died). Many parents of stillborn children consider these policies to be a slap in the face at a time in their lives when they are at their most vulnerable.

Creating memories

As you begin the grieving process, you may find yourself struggling to come to terms with the fact that you and your baby didn't have the chance to share the lifetime of memories you had dreamed about. Many parents find that it helps to ease their grief if they make a conscious effort to create memories that will allow them to remember and honor their baby.

Here are a few suggestions:

- Name your baby.

- Announce your baby's birth and death to family and friends, either by placing an advertisement in the newspaper or by sending out announcements.

- If possible, take photos of your baby and store the negatives in a safe-deposit box.

- Create a memory box and fill it with memorabilia from your pregnancy: for example, the positive home pregnancy test, photos of your blossoming belly, cards and letters you sent to friends describing your excitement at being pregnant, anything special you bought for the baby, your prenatal and birth records, and so on.

Watch Out!
Well-meaning people in your life may want to protect you by making funeral arrangements and other decisions on your behalf. Remind them that making these choices is your way of caring for and saying goodbye to your baby.

Unofficially...
Most hospitals routinely photograph babies who are stillborn or who die during labor—even if the grieving parents are certain they do not wish to have a photograph of their baby. These photographs are kept on file in case the parents change their mind after the fact—a reaction that is not at all unusual.

- Write about your pregnancy: describe how you felt when the pregnancy test came back positive, how you shared your news with family and friends, how excited you were the first time you heard the baby's heartbeat or felt him move.

- Write a letter to your baby expressing your love for him and, if applicable, explaining why you made the choices you made.

- Make a donation to a charity in your baby's memory.

- Set up an appointment with your caregiver so that you can discuss the circumstances surrounding your baby's birth and death.

Coping with grief

Grief is a powerful emotion, one that can rob you of your interest in life and leave you feeling as if you've been run over by a truck. It's no wonder therapists refer to the process of coming to terms with a loss as "grief work"—it's probably the hardest thing you'll ever have to do.

You may experience headaches, a loss of appetite, and extreme fatigue, and have trouble concentrating or sleeping. (A comment from Ann: During the days after I lost my baby, I was physically exhausted but unable to sleep for more than two to three hours at a time. As soon as I got enough sleep to take the edge off my exhaustion, I would wake up crying and be unable to get back to sleep.)

During the weeks following the loss of your baby, you may experience some of the following reactions:

- Anger toward your partner. You may feel angry with your partner if he doesn't appear to be grieving as deeply as you are. More often than not, the other partner is grieving too—just in a different way. Sometimes one parent feels obligated to hold things together for the sake of the other—something that can be misinterpreted as a lack of compassion.

- Feelings of hurt or frustration at the reactions of family members and friends. If your family and friends fail to acknowledge your loss, or pressure you to "pull yourself together" while you're still grieving deeply for your baby, you may feel hurt and frustrated.

- A need to connect with other women who have experienced this type of loss. Sharing your experiences with other women who understand what you're going through can be tremendously healing. If you don't know anyone personally who has been through a loss of this kind, you might want to contact one of the many pregnancy-loss organizations or tap into one of the many online support groups listed in Appendix B.

- A feeling that you're never going to be happy again. In the days following the loss of your baby, you may be convinced that you will never be happy again. If you work through your grief and give yourself time to heal, you will feel happy again. That's not to say that you ever "get over" your loss, or that you will ever forget your baby (something many women agonize about as they begin to feel better). You will just find new ways of feeling happy despite the tiny piece of your heart that will always be broken.

- A strong need to become pregnant right away or a fear of never being pregnant again. Some women need to become pregnant right away; others need time to come to terms with their

> ❝
> I once read that the grief a mother feels when she has lost a baby is so intense that it would be considered psychotic at any other time. It is important to remember that you will never "get over" this, but that you can accept it and feel more at peace about it.
> —Johnna, 33, mother of four children, including a little boy who was stillborn at 27 weeks
> ❞

Unofficially...
University of Florida obstetrician Dr. Kenneth Kellner recently reviewed the cases of 800 families who lost babies to stillbirth. He discovered that 80% of the mothers saw their babies and 55% held them; 72% of the fathers saw their babies and 39% held them. He also learned that 75% of the stillborn babies were named, and that private memorial services were held for 30% of the babies.

loss before they even contemplate another pregnancy. Although many caregivers will advise you to postpone your next pregnancy for six months to a year (in order to give yourself time to grieve and to avoid giving birth to another baby around the anniversary of the loss of the first), only you know what's best for you. (Ann's comment: I needed to become pregnant so that I would have something to look forward to again—a reason to go on. I knew that I would have nine months to work through my grief before my subsequent baby arrived, and by the time he was born, I had done the bulk of my grief work.)

Although it's easy to get caught up in your own grief, it's important not to forget that your other children may need to grieve the loss of their baby brother or sister. Even very young children can be encouraged to express their grief by

- talking about how they are feeling
- helping to pick out flowers for the baby's grave
- drawing a picture to express how they are feeling
- writing a letter to the baby
- participating in a family memorial service

Pregnancy after loss

Whether you decide to become pregnant as soon as possible after the loss of your baby or to postpone it for a while, it's never easy to go through another pregnancy. Your joy at being pregnant may be overshadowed by fears about what might happen to this baby, grief about the baby you lost, and guilt about "being disloyal" to her because you are going ahead with another pregnancy.

It's important to choose a caregiver who will help you cope with so many conflicting emotions and will understand your need for ongoing reassurance. "My obstetrician was extra sensitive to my need for reassurance that things were going well with my pregnancy," says Cindy, 34, who experienced three consecutive miscarriages prior to the birth of her first child. "She did ultrasounds for me when there wasn't any other medical reason except to reassure me."

During your initial prenatal visit, you should have a frank discussion about what—if anything—can be done to maximize your chances of experiencing a happy outcome this time around. For example, are there any tests that can be done to reduce your anxiety? Would your doctor or midwife be prepared to teach you how to use a fetoscope or doppler so that you could monitor your baby's well-being at home in between appointments?

You may find it helpful to connect with other women who are pregnant after a loss—either by seeking this type of support group in your own community or by joining an online support group such as Subsequent Pregnancy After Loss (SPALS). (You can find the information on subscribing to this e-mail list in Appendix B.)

If you are planning to deliver in the same hospital or birthing center in which you lost your previous baby, you may find it helpful to plan a return visit to the facility before you arrive there in hard labor. While you're there, give some thought to whether you'd like to deliver your new baby in the same—or another—birthing suite you had the last time around, assuming that you have that choice.

> 66
> Don't feel as if you are being unfaithful to the baby you lost if you are happy about the new pregnancy.
> —Dawnette, 28, mother of one who had a miscarriage prior to the birth of her first child
> 99

Just the facts

- Miscarriage occurs in approximately 15% to 20% of pregnancies that have been confirmed through a pregnancy test.

- Most miscarriages occur during the first trimester.

- Miscarriages can be caused by chromosomal abnormalities, maternal disease, hormonal imbalances, immune-system disorders, allogeneic factors, anatomical problems of the uterus and cervix, viral and bacterial infections, recreational drug and alcohol abuse, environmental toxins, and age.

- Approximately 1% of pregnancies are ectopic.

- A molar pregnancy occurs in 1 in 1,500 to 1 in 2,000 pregnancies.

- Stillbirth occurs in approximately 1% of pregnancies.

- The 10 leading causes of infant death in the United States in 1996 were congenital anomalies; preterm or low birthweight; sudden infant death syndrome (SIDS); respiratory distress syndrome (RDS); problems related to complications of pregnancy; complications of the placenta, cord, and membranes; accidents; perinatal infections; pneumonia/influenza; and intrauterine hypoxia and birth hypoxia.

- You may wish to have an autopsy performed on your baby if the cause of death is not obvious.

- You may require additional reassurance if you choose to proceed with a subsequent pregnancy.

GET THE SCOOP ON...
Pregnancy after infertility ▪ Pregnancy after
abortion ▪ Pregnancy after giving up a child for
adoption ▪ Being pregnant with a disability ▪
Being pregnant and 40-plus ▪ Being pregnant
and single ▪ Being pregnant and lesbian ▪ Being
pregnant and in an abusive relationship ▪ Being
pregnant and plus-sized

Special Circumstances

As you've no doubt noticed, there's a bit of a conspiracy taking place at your local bookstore. Most of the pregnancy books seem to be intended for some mythical pregnant woman who actually lives the 1990s version of the American dream: she has a fabulous career, a wonderfully supportive husband, and no complicated health problems or messy psychological baggage.

If you don't happen to fit that dubious profile, it's easy to fall through the cracks, which is why we've chosen to include a chapter on a few not-so-unusual circumstances, such as what it's like to finally get pregnant after being infertile; how to cope with giving up a child for adoption, or have an abortion after experiencing sexual abuse; and what it's like to be pregnant if you're disabled, over 40, single, gay, or larger than size 18.

Pregnancy after infertility

If you've struggled with infertility, you may find it hard to believe your good fortune when the pregnancy test finally comes back positive. In fact, you may rush out to buy another test or two before you allow yourself to believe that the good news could actually be true.

Once you accept the fact that you are really pregnant, you may find yourself dealing with a whole list of pregnancy-related worries: Does the spotting you're experiencing mean that you're having a miscarriage? Does the disappearance of your nausea mean that you've experienced a missed abortion? Does the fact that your baby isn't moving around as much as usual mean that there's some kind of serious problem?

Such anxiety is natural and understandable, given what you've been through to get across the starting line in the Baby Olympics. Here are some tips on coping with it:

- Find a doctor you respect and trust. "You have enough worries when you're pregnant," says Molly, 29, a first-time mother and former infertility patient. "You don't need to be worrying about the competency of your doctor."

- Don't be afraid to turn to your caregiver for reassurance and information whenever the need arises, adds Heather, 31, who also experienced infertility prior to the birth of her first child. "You will enjoy this pregnancy more than you imagined, but you will also be very worried about everything. That is very normal. You can never ask too many questions during your prenatal visits."

- If you find yourself rushing to the bathroom every five minutes to check for signs of bleeding, try to focus on something other than the possibility of miscarriage. Remind yourself that you have an 80% or greater chance of carrying your baby to term.

- Hook up with other mothers who are experiencing pregnancy after infertility. If you can't find such a group in your community, seek support online.

Pregnancy after abortion or giving up a child for adoption

Sometimes a pregnancy brings painful memories to the surface—such as your decision to have an abortion or to give up a child for adoption. If you have not yet come to terms with the choice you made, you may find it helpful to seek the services of a therapist who can help you to work through these issues. But even if you have come to terms with your choice, you should anticipate the occasional difficult moment during your pregnancy.

Kate, 33, who gave up her first child for adoption when she was a teenager, explains: "Almost sixteen years ago, I become pregnant and chose to have the baby," she explains. "After a lot of soul-searching, I gave her up for adoption. Not everyone knows this piece of my history, but my doctor needed to know, so I told him."

Although Kate believes that being open with her doctor about her situation was the best way to go, she did run into some awkward moments during her pregnancy: "The codes the doctor used on my chart were pretty universal, so most of the health-care professionals I saw knew that I'd had a previous pregnancy. There were an awful lot of embarrassing silences after people asked me, 'So what do you have at home?'"

> "
> I got a lot of comments from well-meaning individuals about this being my first child. I got around the question, 'Is this your first?' with 'Yes, this is our first,' meaning my husband's and my first baby.
> —Kate, 33, who gave up her first child for adoption 16 years ago
> "

Unofficially...
Take a moment to thank your lucky stars you're not a TV mom. Jamie Buchanan on "Mad About You" was pregnant for 12 months. Lucy Ricardo of "I Love Lucy" got left behind when Fred, Ethel, and Ricky went to the hospital without her. And Murphy Brown's water broke on-air.

If there's something from your reproductive past that you'd prefer not to have broadcast to the four corners of the earth, ask your doctor if it would be possible to omit some of this information from the medical record that will be used at your delivery.

Here's what one prominent obstetrician has to say about the issue: "I think that doctors often *don't* need to know everything their patients think they need to know, especially about previous abortions that were uncomplicated. Even if they *do* know, they're not obligated to put the information onto forms that are circulated to other health-care personnel, who may not have been briefed on the patient's need for discretion."

Pregnancy after sexual abuse

Survivors of sexual abuse often find that pregnancy or childbirth can be difficult because of their history.

"Pregnancy whacks your hormones and opens up all sorts of hidden things," explains Heather, 32, a mother of one and sexual-abuse survivor. "Memories may come up, or old feelings of body-shame and fear may come back full force. You'll need help dealing with these."

Here are some tips on coping with pregnancy if you've experienced sexual abuse:

- Bring up your history with your caregiver. If you don't feel comfortable enough to share this information with your current doctor or midwife, change caregivers.

- Write a birth plan that includes a stress reaction list so that the members of your labor support team and the hospital staff will know how you may react to the pain of labor and what you would like them to do to help you work through it. You should be aware that it's not uncommon for a sexual-abuse survivor to experience abuse flashbacks or to begin to disassociate (that is, psychologically withdraw) during labor.

■ Make sure that your caregiver is aware of potential triggers that may cause anxiety or body memories of childhood sexual abuse to surface during labor.

■ Decide whom you do—and don't—want to have present at the birth. Many abuse survivors bring in close friends or hire doulas so that there will be plenty of people to provide support and encouragement when the going gets tough.

■ Have confidence in your body's ability to give birth and your own personal strength. "If you survived the abuse, you can survive anything," Heather stresses. "Remember that you are strong, able, and creative. You managed to get through something very nasty, and pregnancy and childbirth isn't nasty—just difficult—so you can do this too. Put your faith in yourself and allow yourself to be astonished, amazed, and awestruck at your own strength."

■ Above all, stay focused on the positive, most-important outcome of labor—your baby!

Pregnant with a disability

Depending on the nature of your disability, your pregnancy may be no different than that of any other pregnant woman, or it may require a great deal of monitoring by a high-risk-pregnancy specialist.

Here are some tips on coping with pregnancy if you have a disability:

Unofficially...
The state of Georgia plans to give out 110,000 classical musical tapes and CDs each year to newborn babies. The program— which is being sponsored by Sony Music Entertainment— is designed to capitalize on research that demonstrates a link between classical music and enhanced brain development.

- Find a caregiver who supports your decision to start a family and who feels confident that he has the necessary expertise to manage your pregnancy.

- Ask your caregiver how your disability is likely to affect your pregnancy—and how your pregnancy is likely to affect your disability. For example, if your pregnancy puts you at increased risk of developing a urinary tract infection, should you be put on antibiotics as a preventive measure?

- Find out what types of positions you can safely adopt during labor, whether you're a good candidate for a vaginal birth versus a cesarean, whether there are any drug-interaction issues to be considered if you opt for medications during labor, and so on.

- Remind yourself that you're a pregnant woman first and a woman with a disability second. This is how Rhonda, 30, a mother of three who is confined to a wheelchair, puts it: "When you see your baby on the ultrasound screen for the first time or your baby smiles at your for the first time, you don't feel like someone with a disability. You feel like every other mother does."

Pregnant and 40-plus

Bright Idea Compare notes with other pregnant older moms at www. midlifemommies. com.

Over the past 20 years, the number of women in their 40s having babies has increased by more than 50%. In 1996, 71,663 babies were born to American women between the ages of 40 and 44; 2,980, to American women between the ages of 45 and 49.

This 40-something baby boom has been explained by a number of factors, including the growing tendency of women to postpone childbearing until their careers are well-established and they are on a solid footing financially; the decision to start "second families" (that is, having additional children with a new partner); and the fact that assisted reproductive technologies have helped make pregnancy an option for more older mothers than ever before.

Here are the facts on becoming pregnant when you're 40 or older:

- You are at increased risk of experiencing a high-risk pregnancy because of either pre-existing conditions (for example, cardiovascular, neurologic, connective-tissue, renal, and pulmonary disorders) or conditions that can occur during pregnancy (for example, placenta previa, placental abruptions, preterm delivery, and intrauterine growth restriction).

- You are twice as likely to need a cesarean as a woman under the age of 35, according to the *New England Journal of Medicine*.

- You are at greater risk of experiencing miscarriage, stillbirth, or neonatal death, and of giving birth to a baby with an anomaly.

As if these physical factors weren't enough to contend with, you'll likely have to deal with some emotional and career issues as well. People may question your decision to start a family so late in life or heighten your anxiety about the odds of giving birth to a baby with a birth defect by pointing out scary newspaper headings. At the same time, you may find yourself experiencing a tug of war between the demands of your job and your need to care for yourself during pregnancy—something that's more likely to be a problem if you have a particularly high-stress administrative or managerial position.

"
Many older women show no greater signs of problems than younger women. . . . Age need not be a barrier to the enjoyment of a safe, happy experience.
—*Later Childbearing,* a brochure published by the American College of Obstetricians and Gynecologists
"

Although these facts may have you second-guessing your decision to start a family, many of the physical risks and emotional challenges can be minimized if you receive proper care during your pregnancy and make the best possible lifestyle choices for you and your baby.

Being pregnant and single

Although some single women become pregnant by accident, a growing number of women are choosing to become pregnant by choice, either because they have no interest in becoming part of a couple or because their ideal partner has yet to come along and their biological clock is ticking loudly.

Whether you find yourself pregnant and single by choice or circumstance, you should plan to line up as much support as possible for the period leading up to and following the birth. As much as you may be looking forward to the birth of your baby, it's never easy to go it alone.

"I found the hardest part of being pregnant and single was not having any emotional support from the baby's father," says Helena, 42, a single mother of one. "It's hard enough dealing with a pregnancy, but to have the added stress of feeling alone in something so life-altering and miraculous is rough."

One of the most important decisions you will have to make is whom to invite to be present at the birth. You might consider inviting

- your mother, sister, or other close relative
- your best friend
- a professional labor support person (for example, a doula)

Moneysaver
The Special Supplement Nutrition Program for Women, Infants, and Children (WIC) provides low-income pregnant women with access to food, nutrition counseling, and health services. You can find out more about the program by calling 703-305-2286 or by writing to the USDA Food and Nutrition Service Public Information Staff, 3101 Park Center Drive, Room 819, Alexandria, VA 22302.

Being pregnant and lesbian

If you are pregnant and in a lesbian relationship, it's important to find a caregiver who isn't homophobic and who will make an effort to make your partner feel welcome.

"We kind of lucked out on this one," admits Michele, 31. "Our general practitioner made the referral to a particular obstetrician/gynecologist. We were one of the first—if not the first—lesbian couple he'd worked with. We like to think we blazed a trail through his office, but we can't take that credit. He went to bat for us on more than one occasion and prepared the hospital staff before we delivered. He warned everyone on staff that if they had any problems with our situation, they were to stay away from our room. He didn't want them assisting him or taking care of Beth. It helped tremendously, and we were treated no differently than a heterosexual couple."

Being pregnant and in an abusive relationship

According to a recent study reported in *Obstetrics and Gynecology,* one in five pregnant teens and one in six pregnant women can expect to experience physical or sexual abuse during her pregnancy. The abuse puts them at increased risk of experiencing miscarriage or giving birth to a low-birthweight baby.

Some pregnant women report an escalation of abuse during pregnancy, whereas others indicate that they only feel safe while they are carrying a child because they feel confident that their partner won't do anything to hurt the baby—something that

"
Make sure that you and your partner are clear about who will carry the child, who will take turns staying home with a sick child (assuming that you both work), what legal paperwork will be required (for second-parent adoption or other safe-guards), what the child will call the nonbiological mom, how you will explain arti-ficial insemina-tion to your child, etc."
—Krista, 27, pregnant with her first child
"

can lead to repeated pregnancies as a way of escaping abuse.

Many women who have been putting up with abuse decide to make the break during pregnancy or shortly after the birth, fearing that the abuser may harm the baby. Their concern about their baby's well-being is justified, since studies have shown that more than 50% of men who abuse their female partners also abuse their children and many others threaten to abuse their children.

"It took me nine months after my son was born to finally leave an abusive relationship," says Janna, a 35-year-old mother of two. "When I realized that my partner would be abusing my son, I realized I'd had enough."

If you are in an abusive relationship and have made the decision to leave, here are some steps that can help you and your children get out as safely as possible:

- Pack a suitcase and leave it in the care of a trusted friend or neighbor. Include clothing for yourself and your children, prescription medicines, toiletries, and an extra set of car keys.

- Set up your own bank account and leave the passbook in the care of a friend.

- Make sure that all of the important records you might need are in a place where you can find them quickly. These include birth certificates, social security cards, your voter registration card, your driver's license, medical records, financial records, and documents proving ownership of the house and car.

- Know exactly where you're going and how to get there. If you will be staying with a friend or family member, make sure that person is prepared for the fact that you could show up at their doorstep at any time.

■ Call the police if you need help leaving or if you wish to press charges against your partner.

■ Arrange for counseling for yourself and/or any children you already have.

Being pregnant and plus-sized

Studies have shown that 40% of American women wear size 14 or larger. If you fall into the plus-sized category, here are some tips on managing your pregnancy:

■ Choose a caregiver who will treat you with respect rather than fixating on your weight, and who will provide you with useful information on nutrition and exercise during pregnancy.

■ Prepare yourself for the possibility that complete strangers may make rude comments about your weight. Although all pregnant women tend to run into this situation, the comments can be particularly hurtful if you're already sensitive about your weight.

■ Try to find ways to exercise without feeling uncomfortable. "Consider swimming—even if you hate the way you look in a bathing suit," suggests Heather, 32, a plus-sized mother of one. "Swimming—or even just floating in the pool—helps take the weight off your back and reduces sciatica."

■ Accept the fact that you don't exist—at least in the eyes of most maternity stores. For whatever reason, the fashion world hasn't caught on to the fact that large women actually have sex, let alone get pregnant. The few stores that do carry

Bright Idea
Find a way to get some time alone or spend time with people you trust and can talk to. Having a sounding board can be very helpful.

plus-sized maternity clothes tend to charge top dollar for them, which is why Debbie, a 31-year-old plus-sized mother of three, suggests that you bypass these stores entirely: "Just say no to maternity stores. You can save large amounts of money by avoiding the word 'maternity' altogether."

- Pull together a maternity wardrobe of your own: buy leggings that are two sizes larger than what you usually wear, and top them off with oversized T-shirts or baggy sweaters. Dress up the look with an oversized men's blazer—something you can usually pick up second-hand for just a few dollars.

- If you're planning to give birth somewhere other than at home, be sure to bring a couple of old pairs of underwear with you to the hospital or birthing center; the bizarre mesh underwear they tend to give you after the delivery is at best one-size-fits-some.

- Don't be afraid to insist that your weight be kept private if that's important to you. One plus-sized mom in labor didn't want to tell the nurse her weight while her partner was in earshot, so she wrote down the figure on a piece of paper.

- Compare notes with other plus-sized moms who've given birth. They may be able to pass along some valuable tips.

Just the facts

- If you've had difficulty conceiving, you may find it hard to believe that you're really pregnant, and you may be extremely worried about the possibility of experiencing a miscarriage.

- If you have experienced an abortion, given up a child for adoption, or experienced sexual abuse, pregnancy and labor may bring up difficult issues for you.

- If you are pregnant with a disability, it's important to choose a caregiver with experience in dealing with women with your condition.

- Although your odds of experiencing pregnancy-related complications increase as you get older, women in their forties still have an excellent chance of taking home a healthy baby.

- If you are pregnant and single—whether by choice or by circumstance—make an effort to surround yourself with caring and supportive people, especially during the birth.

- If you are pregnant and in a lesbian relationship, seek a caregiver who will be sensitive to you and your partner's needs.

- If you are pregnant and in an abusive relationship, you should consider the fact that the majority of men who abuse their partners also abuse their children.

- If you are pregnant and plus-sized, seek a caregiver who won't keep obsessing about your weight.

GET THE SCOOP ON...
Having a baby on a budget ▪ The essentials ▪
The frills ▪ Baby clothes ▪ Maternity and nursing
wear ▪ Where the bargains are ▪
Tips on shopping second-hand

The Dirt on Diapers and Other Baby Gear

Chapter 13

The U.S. juvenile products business manages to rack up $3.7 billion in sales each year. It's no wonder that the industry's sales figures are so healthy. Their marketing messages are everywhere. You'll find baby-product catalogs tucked in the prenatal magazines you pick up in your doctor's office, and you'll probably leave the hospital or birthing center with even more slick marketing materials designed to put a dent in your dwindling baby-equipment budget.

If you've got the financial means to buy one of everything in the FAO Schwartz catalog, then you might as well skip this chapter; it's not for you. If, however, you are looking for some guidance on what is and isn't essential before you hit the baby-gear smorgasbord at Toys R Us, then read on. We'll tell you what's essential, what's not, and what items you might like to have, budget permitting. Then we'll tell you where to find the bargains and what you need to know about shopping second-hand.

Having a baby on a budget

It's easy to drop a bundle of cash when you're shopping for your baby. According to Denise and Alan Fields, authors of the best-selling book *Baby Bargains*, it's not unusual for parents to spend $6,400 on baby-related expenses during baby's first year. (See Table 13.1.)

TABLE 13.1: THE AVERAGE COST OF BABY'S FIRST YEAR—TAKE ONE!

Crib, mattress, dresser, and rocker	$1,500
Bedding/decor	$300
Baby clothes	$500
Disposable diapers	$600
Maternity/nursing clothes	$1,200
Nursery items, high chairs, toys	$400
Baby food	$100
Bottle-feeding	$1,000
Stroller, car seat, baby carrier	$300
Miscellaneous	$500
Total	$6,400

Source: Industry estimates as quoted in *Baby Bargains* by Denise and Alan Fields. Boulder Creek, CO: Windsor Peak Press, 1997.

Does this mean that you should rush out and see your banker as soon as the pregnancy test comes back positive? That you should resign yourself to the fact that you're going to be saddled with a baby-equipment loan that may still be hanging around when it's time for junior to head off to college?

Hardly.

If you look at this table carefully, you'll see that there are some items that can come right off the top, if you've got a little less cash to spend on baby than the average Fortune 500 company executive but still want to buy everything new:

■ **Crib, mattress, dresser, and rocker:** The only items in this category that are really essential are the crib and the mattress—unless, of course, you decide to have your baby sleep with you. The dresser is nice to have, but you can probably get away with some other method of storage (for example, a plastic container with a lid that slides under your baby's crib, an old desk, or even a laundry basket). The rocking chair is another frill—something that's nice to have, but not essential. Assuming that you decide to stick with the crib and the mattress and forgo the other two items for now, you've chopped your expenditure down to under $300.

■ **Bedding/decor:** Babies don't care if they are sleeping on Winnie the Pooh sheets or if they have a Mickey Mouse wallpaper border. You can save a bundle by purchasing solid-color sheets rather than their designer equivalents and coming up with creative and inexpensive ways to decorate your baby's room (for example, decorating the baby's room with handprints signed and dated by special people in your baby's life—grandparents, aunts, uncles, cousins, and so on). If you settle for a couple of sets of decent-quality sheets and blankets and a couple of gallons of paint, you can chop this budget line down to about $150.

■ **Baby clothes:** The amount of money you spend on baby clothes will be determined by (a) how important it is to you that your baby wears designer togs and (b) how often you want to do laundry. If you're willing to pass on the name brands and do laundry every other day, you can probably chop this budget line down to about $300—and still have enough room in your budget to splurge on one or two really special outfits.

Bright Idea
Resist the temptation to buy everything your baby might need during his first year of life before he's even born. All you really need to have on hand when he arrives are some clothing, a car seat, a stroller, a baby carrier, and a safe place for him to sleep. The rest can come later—assuming that you actually need it at all.

- **Disposable diapers:** If you decide to use disposable diapers, you may be able to chop about 20% off this figure by shopping sales, buying non-name brands, and buying in bulk. The best way to save money on diapers, however, is to go with a good-quality cloth alternative. Either way, you should be able to bring your costs down to about $480.

- **Maternity/nursing clothes:** Although we don't know very many women who are willing to fork over a minimum of $1,200 or more for a wardrobe that will last for only a year or two at most, there are, no doubt, plenty of women out there who fit the bill. You can save a bundle on maternity clothes by shopping in plus-size or men's clothing stores instead. And you can eliminate the need for over-priced nursing clothes by looking for regular clothing that does the job just as well (for example, soft, oversized tops that can be lifted out of the way to allow you to nurse your baby). Allowing for a few new bras—something you will need both during your pregnancy and after the baby is born—you can probably bring this figure down to about $500.

- **Nursery items, high chairs, toys, and so on:** The only item in this category you may wish to purchase right away is a baby monitor ($50 or so). The high chair ($75) won't be needed until your baby starts solid food (around six months). You can probably get away with a first-year toy budget of about $150 without feeling that you're sacrificing your child's intellectual development for the sake of the almighty dollar. Your newly adjusted total for this line: $275.

- **Baby food:** You can eliminate this line entirely by making your own baby food. There are tons of excellent baby food cookbooks, but many families simply run bits of their own meals through a blender or food grinder instead. (Obviously, you'll need to do some reading on infant nutrition to ensure that you don't make any nutritional faux pas, but you get the basic idea.) Write in a zero on this line.

- **Bottle-feeding:** If you're in budget mode, breastfeeding is your best option. There's nothing to purchase other than an extra 500 calories per day's worth of food for yourself and a package of washable breast pads. (You may also need to pick up a breast pump and some bottles if you're planning to return to work while your baby is nursing, but we'll defer that discussion until Chapter 18.) Set aside $100 for breastfeeding-related expenses.

- **Stroller, car seat, baby carrier:** This is where we hit the big bucks, unfortunately. All of these items are necessary, and you will do well to pick up the lot for $300 or less.

- **Miscellaneous:** We also won't fiddle with the $500 miscellaneous figure because a lot of items fall into this category: the $5 bathtub, the $10 digital thermometer, the $2 pair of nail scissors, and so on.

As you can see from Table 13.2, we've managed to cut the baby budget by more than half by whittling down the unnecessary expenses. If you decide to shop second-hand or are able to borrow some or all of these items from friends or family members, your bottom line will be even less. (We'll give you some pointers on shopping for second-hand baby gear elsewhere in this chapter.)

Moneysaver
Form a purchasing co-op with other members of your childbirth class, and negotiate the best possible deal on cribs, car seats, and so on.

TABLE 13.2: THE UNOFFICIAL BUDGET FOR BABY'S FIRST YEAR

Crib, mattress, dresser, and rocker	$300
Bedding/decor	$150
Baby clothes	$300
Disposable diapers	$600
Maternity/nursing clothes	$500
Nursery items, high chairs, toys	$275
Baby food	$0
Bottle-feeding	$100
Stroller, car seat, baby carrier	$300
Miscellaneous	$500
Total	$3,025

66

Although change tables are great for holding supplies, they're completely unnecessary. I change my babies on the floor or on the bed and rarely use the change table.
—Suzi, 27, mother of two

99

The baby equipment you need

No matter how lean-and-mean your budget may be, there are four pieces of baby equipment that most parents consider to be essential: a safe place for baby to sleep, a car seat, a stroller, and a baby carrier. Because these purchases are so important, let's briefly discuss what features to look for when you're shopping for each of these items.

A safe place for baby to sleep

Some parents use a crib right from the beginning, others opt for a cradle or bassinet until the baby gets a little older, and still others choose to take their babies into their own beds.

If you're shopping for a crib, look for one that

- conforms to current government safety standards (you can find out if a particular juvenile product is affected by a recall by phoning the U.S. Consumer Product Safety Commission at 800-638-2772; by writing to the U.S. Consumer Products Safety Commission, Washington, DC

20207; or by visiting the Commission's Web site at www.jpsc.gov. Canadian parents should contact Consumer and Corporate Affairs, Canada's Product Safety Department, at 819-953-8082);

- has been certified by the Juvenile Products Manufacturers Association (call 609-231-8500; write to JPMA, 236 Route 38 West, Suite 100, Moorestown, NJ 08057; or visit the organization's Web site at www.jmpa.org);

- has a tight-fitting mattress (that is, there is no more than two fingers' width of space between the edge of the mattress and the side of the crib);

- has slats that are no more than 2⅜" apart;

- is height adjustable (so that you can lower the mattress as your baby learns to stand and climb);

- is painted with nontoxic paint;

- has a teething rail (to prevent your baby from chewing the finish off the crib rails);

- has a railing that can be dropped or raised using one hand and that doesn't make a loud noise that could wake a sleeping baby;

- has a firm mattress (because soft mattresses are dangerous for babies);

- has metal rather than plastic casters (they wear better).

Watch Out!
More than 70,000 children are injured by juvenile products each year.

Never purchase a crib that has corner posts that are more than one-sixteenth of an inch above the end panels. Babies can strangle themselves if their clothing gets caught on a corner post.

Here are few money-saving tips on shopping for a crib:

- You can save about $50 by purchasing a crib with a single drop railing rather than double drop railings.

- Cribs that convert to toddler beds (also called junior beds) are the biggest rip-off going. You often pay more for this feature than you would pay for a crib and a single bed combined. What's more, if you have your next child before the first child is finished with the bed, you'll need to purchase another crib.

- Three to four fitted sheets, two or three cotton blankets, and a simple set of bumper pads are all your baby needs for bedding.

Here are some pointers on shopping for a cradle or bassinet:

- Make sure that the mattress is firm and fits the bassinet snugly so that your baby can't get caught between the mattress and the sides.

- Make sure that the cradle or bassinet is sturdy and stable—particularly if there are other children in your home.

- Follow the manufacturer's guidelines for weight and size. Most babies outgrow cradles and bassinets by the time they are three to four months of age.

- You can get more mileage out of a portable playpen with a built-in bassinet (for example, the Fisher Price model) than a standard bassinet or cradle. Whereas the bassinet or cradle will be gathering dust in the basement within a matter of weeks, you can get two or more years' worth of use out of a portable playpen. Just one quick word of caution: Not all portable playpens are designed to be used for sleeping. Check with the manufacturer.

- If you decide to go with a bassinette or cradle, try using pillow cases for bedding rather than paying for custom-fitted linens.

A car seat

A car seat is one product you should probably purchase new. Otherwise, you're that a chance that the seat may have been in a car accident—something that can damage the seat and make it unsafe to use.

There are three basic choices when it comes to a car seat:

- an infant seat (designed for infants up to 20 lbs.)

- a toddler seat (designed for children over 20 lbs.)

- a convertible seat (designed to be used in the rear-facing position by babies who weigh less than 20 lbs. and in the front-facing position by babies who weigh more than 20 lbs.)

Although some parents choose to purchase the convertible seat because it eliminates the need to buy an infant seat, which is used only for about six to nine months, there are some disadvantages to going this route. First of all, you could find yourself shopping for a second car seat if you space your children too closely together—something that eliminates the advantages of purchasing a convertible seat. Second, it's virtually impossible to remove a sleeping baby from a convertible seat without waking him or her up. Most parents feel that this is enough justification for going with an infant seat that can be carried into the house, baby and all.

Moneysaver
Here's how to get an infant car seat free! Pay the wholesale price for a car seat ($44) through your local Midas dealer and then return it when you're finished with it. The company will give you a $44 credit, which you can then apply to automotive repair services. Find out more about this program—called Project Safe Baby—at www.midas.com/about/safebaby.htm.

Watch Out!
Convertible car seats are not recommended for premature or very small babies who may slump over and possibly suffocate. The American Academy of Pediatrics recommends that infant seats be used instead— and that they be used in the reclined position.

Timesaver
You can obtain a list of current car-seat models, including prices, by writing to The American Academy of Pediatrics, Shopping Guide, 141 Northwest Point Boulevard, P.O. Box 927, Elk Grove Village, IL 60009

Here are some tips on shopping for a car seat:

- Before you reach for your wallet, make sure that you actually need to buy a car seat. Certain HMOs provide free car seats to their clients.

- Assuming that you do need to purchase one, look for a model that has a handle that makes the seat easy to carry and that can be folded back to make it easier to get your baby in and out of the seat; a seat-belt system that can be adjusted easily as your baby grows; and a car-seat cover that can be removed easily and that is fully washable.

- Numerous car seats have been recalled in recent years. You can get the scoop on the problems with various makes and models by contacting the National Highway Traffic Safety Administration (NHTSA) at 800-424-9393 or 202-366-0123 and asking to have a list of car-seat recalls faxed to you or by downloading the information yourself from the NHTSA Web site at www.nhtsa.dot.gov.

- NHTSA can also tell you whether a particular car seat will fit into your make and model of vehicle. (This can be more of a problem than you might think.)

A stroller

Shopping for a stroller is not unlike shopping for a car at a dealership: you have an enormous range of makes and models to choose from. Here's what you can expect to see on the showroom floor:

- **Umbrella strollers:** As the name implies, umbrella strollers fold up like an umbrella. They're lightweight and inexpensive ($25 to

$35), but they don't last very long and don't provide much back support for your baby.

- **Carriages:** Carriages (also called prams) look like bassinets on wheels. They are the aristocratic-looking contraptions pushed by the Mary Poppinses of the world. The only disadvantage to one of these is the price: $500 to $1,500 for a piece of equipment your baby will outgrow in a matter of months.

- **Carriage/strollers:** As the name implies, carriage/strollers are hybrids. They can function either as a carriage (when the seat is fully reclined) or as a stroller (when the seat is partially or fully lifted). Typically, they can be had for $100 to $300, although some name brands will set you back more than that.

- **Jogging strollers:** Jogging strollers have big wheels and lightweight frames that make it easy for a new mother or father to take baby along for a run. They tend to come in at about $200 to $300.

- **All-terrain strollers:** All-terrain strollers are sturdy contraptions designed for off-road strollering—the baby world's equivalent of the ATV. They have oversized tires and better undercarriage clearance than other models, and they typically ring in at about $100.

- **Lightweight strollers:** Lightweight strollers are souped-up versions of your basic umbrella stroller. Their frames are a bit sturdier, but they're nowhere near as heavy to lug around as full-blown carriage/strollers. They ring in at about $200 to $300.

■ **Car seat/strollers:** Combination car seat/strollers are a perfect example of what happens when an idea that looks good on paper gets tested in the real world. Most of these units are more expensive than the two separate components (that is, a stroller and a car seat), and they tend to be quite cumbersome to use. You can expect to pay well over $200 for a name-brand combination car seat/stroller.

Here's what to look for in a stroller:

■ a strong but lightweight frame (aluminum)

■ a stable design (that is, securely balanced and not prone to tipping)

■ a handle that is reversible (that flips from one side of the stroller to the other so that you can keep the sun and wind out of baby's face, regardless of what direction it's coming from)

■ a handle that is the right height for you (tall people can find it particularly difficult to find a stroller that is comfortable to push)

■ a fully reclining seat so that baby can nap on the run

■ fabric that is stain resistant

■ a pad that can be removed for washing

■ a broad base, for added stability

■ secure and easy-to-use restraining straps

■ sun and rain shields

■ a model that can be folded with one hand while you're holding a baby

■ a lightweight construction

■ storage space underneath so that you won't be tempted to hang grocery bags from the handle of the stroller

> 66
> A good-quality stroller will see you through all your children, whereas a cheapie will cost you again and again.
> —Karen, 34, mother of three
> 99

- an adjustable footrest

- a removable front bar (to make it easier for your child to get in and out of the stroller when he reaches toddlerhood)

- lockable wheels (to make it easier to travel in a straight line)

A baby carrier

There are two basic types of baby carriers: ones that are worn on the front of your body and ones that are worn on your back.

Some carriers position the baby vertically against your chest (Snugli and other similar types of baby carriers), whereas others allow the baby to assume a number of different positions, depending on how you adjust the carrier (baby slings). Some families swear by Snuglis; others wouldn't be caught dead without their slings. It all boils down to a matter of personal preference.

Whatever type you decide to choose, make sure that it

- is constructed from a sturdy; washable fabric;

- has some type of support for baby's back and neck;

- has leg holes that are small enough to prevent the baby from slipping through, yet not so small that they are tight and uncomfortable.

Back-pack carriers typically incorporate some type of aluminum frame. A back-pack carrier should be

- stable enough to stand up on its own so that you can put the baby in and take her out without needing help from another adult,

Bright Idea
Check out the cost and availability of replacement parts for your stroller before you decide which brand to purchase. Some brands are extremely expensive to repair—assuming that parts are even available.

- sufficiently padded to ensure that both you and the baby are comfortable,

- made of stain-resistant fabric.

The frills

Now that we've discussed the items you absolutely need to purchase, let's talk about some items that, though hardly essentials, can certainly make a new parent's job a whole lot easier.

A baby swing

You've been pacing the floor with an unhappy baby for the past eight hours, and you're about to collapse from exhaustion. What would you be willing to pay to have the baby lulled to sleep by someone—or something—else?

As much as $100, if the marketing gurus at the brand-name baby equipment manufacturers have it right. That's about what you can expect to pay for a top-quality battery-operated baby swing. It's a small price to pay for peace of mind and a break from a fussy baby—or at least that's how some parents feel.

"After her early morning feeding, Chelsea went in the swing and I went to sleep on the couch, sometimes for as long as three or four hours," recalls Ellen, 29, a mother of one. "I owe almost all the sleep I got during her early infancy to that beautiful swing."

If you decide to purchase a baby swing, be sure to look for a battery-operated model. The wind-up swings tend to make enough noise to wake a sleeping baby—something that defeats the whole purpose of owning a baby swing. Here are some other features to look for:

- two speeds (slow for young babies and faster for bigger babies),

- seat adjustability (the seat moves from upright to reclining),

- a model without an overhead bar (so that you don't have to worry about banging your baby's head as you take him in and out of the swing),

- thick padding for comfort,

- washable fabric.

A playpen

Although a playpen was considered to be a necessary piece of equipment for parents a generation ago, most parents today choose to baby-proof the environment rather than to confine baby to a playpen. Here's what Stephanie, a 25-year-old first-time mother, had to say about the playpen she purchased for her baby: "For me, the playpen was a complete waste of money. Isabel won't sit in it. She likes to be seen and held and does not want to be confined to a playpen. It has just become a very large toy-storage container in the living room."

Playpens still have their place, however, particularly if you're traveling. That's why a growing number of parents are choosing portable playpens (that is, playpens that collapse into a carry bag that is roughly the size of a gym bag and that function as cribs-away-from-home).

When you're shopping for a portable playpen, look for a model with

- mesh sides (fine enough to prevent baby's fingers and toes from getting trapped),

- walls that are at least 19 inches tall,

- a sun canopy (if you intend to use it outside).

Although all portable playpens claim to be easy to fold, some require a postgraduate degree in

Bright Idea
If you're traveling out of town and you don't want the bother of dragging along the high chair, the stroller, the portable playpen, and so on, find out if there's a Baby's Away store close to your destination. The chain specializes in renting baby supplies and has stores in nearly 30 locations in the United States and Canada. Call 800-571-0077 for details.

mechanical engineering. Test-drive this feature of the playpen before you agree to purchase it.

Note: If you intend to use your portable playpen as a crib for your baby to sleep in, make sure that it's designed for this use. Some are and some aren't.

A baby monitor

Many parents rate baby monitors as nothing short of essential—even those who initially saw no use for them.

"I highly recommend a baby monitor," says Tracy, 31, mother of one. "I didn't think I'd need one, but whenever I put Ben down for a nap, I'd be terrified to go too far from his room for fear that I wouldn't hear him when he woke up. We got a monitor when he was three months old, and I suddenly felt so free!"

Here are some features to look for in a baby monitor:

- a model that provides for maximum flexibility by allowing you to use a battery or an AC adaptor at both the sending and the receiving ends,

- a monitor with a sturdy AC adapter that looks as though it will withstand a fair amount of wear and tear,

- a monitor that has more than one channel (so that you can switch channels if you're picking up the sounds of your neighbor's baby rather than your own).

The only downside to baby monitors is that they have an annoying habit of interfering with cordless phones—and vice versa. Even if you have a cordless phone that operates on the 900 MHz frequency and a baby monitor that works on the 46 to 49 MHz frequency, you could run into problems—particularly

Watch Out! Don't have a heated discussion with your partner when the baby monitor is turned on. You could be broadcasting your dirty laundry to the entire neighborhood.

if your neighbor uses a bargain-basement baby monitor. Be sure to keep your receipt until you're sure that all systems are go on the baby-monitor front.

An exersaucer

As you're probably aware, the American Academy of Pediatrics strongly urges parents not to use baby walkers. Here's what the latest edition of *Caring for Your Baby and Very Young Child* has to say about them: "Walkers eliminate the desire to walk since they allow the baby to get around too easily. To make matters worse, they present a serious safety hazard because they can easily tip over when the child bumps into an obstacle such as a small toy or a throw rug. Children in walkers also are more likely to fall down stairs and get into dangerous places that would otherwise be beyond their reach."

An exersaucer is a safer alternative to a walker. Unlike walkers, which have wheels that allow them to move, an exersaucer has a saucer-like base designed to stay in one place.

Here's what pediatrician Dr. Alan Greene (www.drgreene.com) has to say about them: "For children who want to be upright, an exersaucer can be a nice alternative. These look like walkers, but without the wheels. They allow children to bounce, rock, spin, and sit upright—without satisfying the urge to move across the floor. They are safe and developmentally appropriate."

If you're looking for a way to keep a young baby entertained and happy while you eat your dinner, an exersaucer might be the way to go. Many parents swear by them. Just one word of caution: Some babies don't want anything to do with exersaucers, so let your baby try the floor model in the store before you buy.

A diaper bag

You're going to need to use something to tote around diapers, baby wipes, diaper cream, spare clothing, and so on. Whether you decide to go with a bona fide diaper bag or something else depends entirely on both your budget and your sense of style.

Up until quite recently, most diaper bags were covered with pink bunnies, pastel-colored teddy bears, and other juvenile prints. Fortunately, a few manufacturers have clued into the fact that it's Mom or Dad who carries the diaper bag—not baby.

Although some high-quality diaper bags, such as the ones Land's End produces, are designed to look more like a piece of carry-on luggage than a diaper bag, you don't necessarily have to spend a lot of money to avoid carrying a pink bunny bag along with your leather briefcase. A gym bag, canvas tote bag, knapsack, or almost any other bag you already own will do the trick. Still, if you've got the budget to pick up a Land's End bag, you might want to go for it. It's the one to have—or at least that's the buzz in the online chat rooms.

Baby clothes

As we mentioned earlier, how much you spend on baby clothes will be determined by your budget and your eagerness to avoid doing laundry every day. "If you don't mind doing laundry every day, you can get by with half a dozen outfits," says Dawnette, 28, mother of one.

Although it's impossible to predict how much laundry a particular baby will generate—some babies leak poop all over their clothes a couple of times a day, whereas others somehow manage to confine the mess to their diapers; and some babies spit up so much that they have to be changed after every feeding—you should expect to change your baby's clothes approximately three to six times each day.

The list of items shown in Table 13.3 would be enough to survive on for the first six weeks, assuming that you plan to do laundry every other day.

TABLE 13.3: THE UNOFFICIAL BABY LAYETTE

12 newborn nighties @$5/each	$60
3 sleepers	$30
2 baby towel-and-washcloth sets	$30
3 sets of fitted crib sheets	$20
12 extra-large receiving blankets	$30
3 pairs of socks	$5
1 sweater (depending on season)	$10
2 cotton hats	$30
1 snowsuit or bunting bag (if you live in a cold climate)	$20
4 large bibs (snap or velcro) if you are formula-feeding or your baby spits up a lot	$20
Total	$255

Here are some tips on picking out baby clothes:

- Don't buy too many clothes in the newborn size. Some babies are born too large to wear them or can wear them only for a couple of weeks. Although some books advise you to bypass the newborn size entirely, we don't go quite that far. Because there's no way of telling in advance whether you're going to be having a 7- or 10-pound baby, you should plan to have at least one outfit in the newborn size on hand. Then, if you need more, you can send a friend or relative out to buy more.

- Keep your baby's initial wardrobe as simple as possible. You might be tempted to buy all kinds of cute frilly dresses or adorable sailor suits, but keep in mind that these types of outfits can be a royal pain to get on and off your baby. You may find newborn nighties (hospital-style nighties for babies) to be your best bet during the first few weeks. They make diaper changes easy, and they're easy to take on and off as they become soiled.

- Don't even think about buying a sleeper that doesn't have crotch snaps. These poorly designed items are such a pain to use that you simply won't be bothered.

- Look for clothing that's designed to grow with your baby (for example, sleepers with adjustable foot cuffs).

- Keep your baby's comfort in mind at all times. Believe it or not, many baby clothes are designed for fashion rather than comfort. Outfits with poorly positioned buttons or zippers can be uncomfortable for baby to sleep in, and frilly dresses are about as much fun to sleep in as a wedding dress.

- Baby booties are almost impossible to keep on tiny little feet. Look for miniature stretch socks instead.

- Stick to unisex colors as much as possible. That way, you don't have to go out and buy a second wardrobe if your next baby happens to be of the opposite sex.

- Buy clothing only as your baby needs it. That way, you can factor in what other people lend or give you and avoid having more size six-month booties than even Madonna's child could wear.

- Don't buy too far ahead. Although it's tempting to pick up next year's snowsuit during this year's winter sales, it's hard to predict what size your baby will be wearing a year from now. That $30 bargain could end up being a $30 waste of money.

- If you intend to use cloth diapers and are prepared to do a load of diapers every two to three days, you will need 36 fitted or contoured diapers or 48 square diapers, six to seven pairs of waterproof pants, and 30 cloth wipes.

Maternity clothes

Maternity clothing has come a long way since it hit its ugly peak during the 1960s and 1970s. Gone are the days when being pregnant meant wearing dresses that looked like oversized versions of what you might find in the toddler fashions section at JCPenney.

The only downside to today's maternity fashions is their price. Although you will find a few bargains out there, far too many maternity clothing manufacturers take advantage of the fact that pregnant women need to wear *something*. (Think *captive market*.)

Here are some tips on shopping for maternity wear:

- Purchase just a few items at a time. It's hard to predict how your belly will grow during the months ahead. Besides, it's nice to have something new to wear during the never-ending third trimester.

- Think comfort. You've got the rest of your life to be a fashion queen. Look for fabrics that breathe rather than fabrics that are high on glitz—and leave your high heels in the back of the closet for now. Remember, your metabolic

Bright Idea
Presoak stained clothing in a pail full of water and laundry detergent before you wash them. Then, check that the stains have come out before you throw everything in the dryer.

rate increases by about 20% when you're pregnant, and your feet may grow a full size!

- Avoid anything that cuts or binds. Although Victorian women were encouraged to wear corsets throughout much of their pregnancies, you're free to wear whatever you want. Pass on tight belts, girdles, and waistbands.

- If you make a habit of wearing bikini underwear, you'll be able to continue to wear them through most—if not all—of your pregnancy. If, however, you wear hip or waist-height underwear, you're going to have to search out some oversized briefs. If you're not already in the habit of wearing cotton underwear, switch now. Pregnant women are more susceptible to yeast infections, so spending nine months in polyester undies is a recipe for disaster.

- Pick up a pair of maternity support hose. They can help prevent or minimize varicose veins.

- You can't scrimp on bras during your pregnancy or you'll be downright uncomfortable. As a rule of thumb, you will need two bras in each size as your bustline expands—and expand it may: some women increase by three cup sizes during pregnancy. You'll be more comfortable with cotton, but make sure that whatever type of bra you purchase provides adequate support. *Note:* You can save yourself a bit of cash by making your last set of bras nursing bras since you'll still be able to wear them after baby arrives.

- Don't make this mistake when it comes to the rest of your wardrobe, however. You're not likely to want to wear anything from your maternity wardrobe while you're nursing. In fact, most women avoid their maternity clothing like the plague once the baby has arrived, both because they're sick of wearing the same old thing and because they don't want anyone to think that they're still pregnant.

- Go for the layered look. Rather than buying long-sleeved dresses, pair up a short-sleeved top with a cardigan. That way, you can peel off the cardigan if you start to feel too hot.

- Casual maternity clothing doesn't have to come from a maternity store. Shop in the plus-sized section of your local department store or hit a plus-sized retailer, and you'll find leggings, shirts, jackets, empire-style dresses, and other oversized garments galore. (These stores are also a great source of comfortable, over-sized cotton underwear, by the way.) You might also try raiding your husband's side of the closet—assuming, of course, that he's larger than you—or hitting a quality second-hand boutique. You can find some more wardrobe-stretching points in *Pregnancy Chic* by Cherie Serota and Jody Gardner (see Appendix C).

- If you have to look professional at the office, you'll probably have to break down and purchase at least two or three maternity suits. Instead of spending $200 or more to purchase each outfit new, see if there's a second-hand clothing store in your community that specializes in maternity wear. You could save yourself a bundle.

- If you need a dress for a highly formal occasion, see if you can rent it rather than buying it. Maternity-clothing rental boutiques are springing up in many large U.S. cities. (*Note:* Some of these boutiques also specialize in career wear. Check your local Yellow Pages.)

Shopping second-hand

Although you will probably want to purchase certain items new—a car seat and crib, for example—you can stretch your dollars a lot further if you pick up other baby items second-hand. You'll probably be able to borrow a lot of second-hand baby equipment from family members and friends, but you may still find it necessary to purchase some of the items you'll need.

You can find second-hand baby equipment

- by shopping at consignment stores (particularly those that specialize in children's clothing and baby equipment)

- by visiting second-hand clothing stores operated by charitable organizations

- by hitting garage sales

- by reading the classified ads

- by checking out bulletin boards at the grocery store or community center or by hanging up a "baby equipment wanted" ad of your own

- by contacting the local twins club and finding out when its annual garage sale will be held

Although you can save a lot of money by shopping second-hand, you also run certain risks. Some of the most unsafe juvenile products ever made— baby walkers, for example—regularly crop up at garage sales.

Here are some questions to ask when you're shopping second-hand:

Watch Out!
Don't fill your closet with polyester maternity wear. Not only can it be ugly (think 1970s stretch pants!), but it also can be darned uncomfortable when your temperature is shooting sky-high.

- Who manufactured this product and when was it made?

- What is the model number?

- Where is the instruction manual?

- How many families have used it?

- Has it ever been repaired?

- Are any of the parts missing? (If the missing parts are essential to the functioning of the product, call the manufacturer to confirm that parts are still available before you buy the product.)

- Does the product conform to current safety standards? (The vendor may or may not be able to answer this question accurately, so you'll have to do some research yourself. See Appendix B for leads on organizations that can provide you with information on safety standards.)

Just the facts

- Resist the temptation to buy out Toys R Us before your baby is even born. All you really need to have on hand are some clothing, a car seat, a stroller, a baby carrier, and a safe place for baby to sleep.

- If you buy everything new, you can expect to spend at least $3,200 on equipment, clothing, and diapers for baby's first year.

- The U.S. Consumer Product Safety Commission and the Juvenile Product Safety Commission are good sources of information on baby equipment for American parents. Canadian parents may wish to contact Consumer and Corporate Affairs, Canada's Product Safety Department.

Bright Idea
If you misplace the manual from your car seat, try getting a replacement copy from the manufacturer. If that fails, try contacting the Infant and Toddler Safety Association (ITSA) at 519-570-0181. ITSA keeps a number of car seat manuals on file and charges only a small photocopying fee for duplicating the materials and mailing them to you.

- You can save money on a crib by passing on models with two rails that drop and ones that convert to junior beds.

- You can get a car seat free by participating in the Project Safe Baby program at your local Midas dealer.

- Purchase a good-quality stroller the first time, and you won't have to purchase another one six months down the road.

- Some parents swear by Snuglis; others couldn't live without their slings. Test-drive before you buy.

- A baby swing, a portable playpen, a baby monitor, and a good-quality diaper bag are nice to have, budget permitting.

- When you're shopping for clothing for your baby, consider comfort and practicality before fashion.

- You should also put comfort first when you're shopping for your own maternity wardrobe.

The Whole Nine Months

PART IV

GET THE SCOOP ON...
How you may be feeling ▪ The emotional challenges of the first trimester ▪
The top 10 worries of expectant parents ▪ How your baby is growing

Ready or Not: The First Trimester

Chapter 14

Perhaps you have known a Ms. Perfect Pregnancy—a friend or coworker who felt so well during her pregnancy that she never missed a single aerobics class, got grumpy with her partner, or bolted out of an important meeting because she couldn't stomach the smell of coffee. Although women like these do exist—and heaven knows they make their presence known to the rest of us—most pregnant women feel somewhat less than euphoric about the mind- and body-morphing that occurs during the first few weeks of pregnancy.

As you've no doubt discovered by now, pregnancy is one of life's greatest levelers. No matter how fit you are, how painstakingly you planned your pregnancy, or how much you want to be a mother, you could very well find yourself being sideswiped by the powerful hormonal cocktail your body needs in order to grow a baby.

That doesn't mean, however, that you have to be a slave to your pregnancy, abandoning your career aspirations or your relationship with your significant other in favor of sleep and soda crackers. In this chapter, we'll show you how to manage the smorgasbord of pregnancy symptoms that usually make their presence known just about the time your pregnancy test comes back positive, confirming in pink and white that you're on the road to motherhood, ready or not.

How you may be feeling

Although the symptoms of early pregnancy vary tremendously from woman to woman—and even from pregnancy to pregnancy—most women can expect to experience one or more of the signs of early pregnancy listed below.

Note: It's possible that you may be experiencing some aches and pains that are normally associated with the second or third trimester. If you've got a particular complaint that isn't listed here, you'll probably find it discussed in one of the following two chapters.

Cessation of menstrual periods

As we mentioned in Chapter 4, a missed period is often the first sure sign of pregnancy for women with highly regular menstrual cycles. Although it's possible to miss a period for other reasons—in times of high stress, for example—the most common reason for a woman of childbearing age to miss a period is pregnancy.

Spotting

Spotting is common after an internal exam—a reason why many health-care practitioners are reluctant to perform internal examinations during the early weeks of pregnancy when the cervix is most prone to bleeding. It can also occur after intercourse if the

> **"**
> All of the pregnancy books I read described the early signs of pregnancy as being much more prominent than mine were. I searched book after book to find one that said, 'Some people don't have any early symptoms.' As a result, I didn't really believe I was pregnant until I saw the first ultrasound of my baby.
> —Susan, 29, pregnant with her first child
> **"**

penis happened to bump against the cervix, causing the tender cervix to bleed slightly.

Cervical bleeding in pregnancy, whether caused by an internal exam or sexual activity, is absolutely harmless. Therefore, your caregiver shouldn't hesitate to do an exam if the information obtained from that exam will make a difference in her ability to provide you with good health care. Similarly, if you want to have sex and your caregiver has determined that any bleeding you are experiencing is cervical in nature, then you should be reassured that there is no increased risk of miscarriage. If, however, you can't stop obsessing about the bleeding, despite your caregiver's reassurances, you might want to postpone the romance for now.

Spotting can also occur shortly after conception. In this case, it's known as implantation bleeding—bleeding that occurs approximately seven days after conception when the fertilized egg attaches itself to the uterine wall. Many women mistake this light amount of bleeding for a menstrual period—an error that can wreak havoc on their ability to calculate their due dates. Heavy bleeding during pregnancy, however, is cause for concern and may indicate that you are having a miscarriage.

You should call your doctor immediately if you experience any of the following symptoms:

- heavy vaginal bleeding or clotting
- lighter bleeding that lasts for more than one day
- the passage of greyish or pinkish tissue
- any amount of bleeding that is accompanied by cramps, fever, chills, or dizziness
- severe pain in abdomen or in your shoulder area

Moneysaver
Ask your doctor if he has any pharmaceutical-company samples you can try before you go out and buy a super-sized bottle of prenatal vitamins that your stomach may or may not be able to keep down.

- dehydration
- a fever of more than 101°F
- painful urination
- a watery discharge from the vagina

Morning sickness

Morning sickness is a catchall term used to describe everything from a hypersensitivity to odors or an aversion to certain foods to severe vomiting. And despite what the name implies, it can cause misery at any time of day—not just in the morning.

Morning sickness is thought to be caused by the hormonal, metabolic, and chemical changes of early pregnancy. Kicking in around six weeks after the first day of your last menstrual cycle, and lasting until well into the second trimester, nausea can strike at any time of day or night and affects between 60% and 80% of pregnant women. It is more likely to be a problem for women who are carrying twins or other multiples or who are feeling somewhat rundown.

66

People ask me how it's been to be pregnant, and I have to say I've enjoyed it. Even with the stress, sickness, aches, and pains, it's all part of the pregnancy experience, in my opinion. —Marie, 28, pregnant with her first child

99

Although you may be feeling anything but grateful about experiencing this classic symptom of pregnancy, scientists feel that there's something good to be said about morning sickness. Studies have shown that women with little or no nausea or vomiting are two to three times more likely to miscarry because their levels of pregnancy-related hormones may not be sufficiently high to support a pregnancy. So there you go—some good news to take to the bathroom with you.

You can minimize nausea at home and at work by

- eating something before you get out of bed in the morning

- keeping crackers in your desk so that you can eat before you get really hungry

- eating only those foods that genuinely appeal to you rather than limiting yourself to vegetables and other nutritionally rich foods

- avoiding foods that are likely to trigger nausea (fried foods, greasy foods, high-fat foods, sausages, fried eggs, spicy foods, foods containing monosodium glutamate (MSG), onions, sauerkraut, cabbage, cauliflower, and beverages that contain caffeine)

- seeking out foods that are less likely to cause your stomach to do flip-flops (potatoes, soda crackers, applesauce, and so on)

- chewing gum or sucking on mints or hard candy

- sniffing or sucking on slices of lemon

- eating neither too much nor too little food at a time (either can make you feel rather queasy)

- drinking plenty of water and fruit juices if you can't stomach milk

- taking a vitamin B6 supplement if you're experiencing particularly severe symptoms of nausea

- avoiding cigarette smoke and other strong odors

- wearing loose-fitting garments and avoiding pants that are too tight and belts that dig into your waist

- getting as much rest as possible

Here's an additional tip. Some women swear by antinausea wristbands that apply constant pressure to the acupressure points on the wrists that control

Unofficially...
Some scientists suspect that morning sickness may serve as a defense mechanism, encouraging pregnant women to avoid alcohol, tobacco, coffee, and other substances that could be harmful to their developing babies. There's just one small problem with this theory: human genetic evolution has occurred over a period of many thousands of years, but most of the substances that make pregnant women feel queasy have been around for only the past few hundred years. After all, the caveman lifestyle didn't exactly lend itself to leisurely after-dinner cigars!

nausea and vomiting. They're inexpensive enough ($10) to be worth a try if you're feeling particularly miserable.

About 1 out of every 300 pregnant women develops a severe form of morning sickness known as hyperemesis gravidarum (Latin for "excessive vomiting in pregnancy"). This condition occurs when the body is unable to compensate for the relentless vomiting and loses valuable body salts (electrolytes) and body fluids. The disorder is thought to be linked to higher-than-usual levels of the hormones hCG and estrogen, and it is more common in first pregnancies, young women, and women carrying multiples.

If you are experiencing the following symptoms, you may be developing hyperemesis gravidarum:

- excessive vomiting (you haven't been able to keep any food or drink down for 24 hours)
- reduced frequency of urination (particularly if your urine appears darker in color and consequently is becoming more concentrated)
- dryness of the mouth, eyes, and skin
- extreme fatigue, weakness, or faintness
- confusion

If you develop hyperemesis gravidarum, you will probably be hooked up to an IV (either in a hospital or at home) and given the salts and fluids necessary to rehydrate your body. Your doctor may also decide to prescribe an antinausea medication.

A bloated, heavy feeling

Many women report that in the first few weeks of pregnancy, they have a bloated, heavy feeling that is not unlike what they experience around the time that their periods are due. Headaches and

Bright Idea
Many pregnant women can't stomach their prenatal vitamins. To increase the chances of keeping your prenatal vitamin down, try taking it in the middle of a meal rather than on an empty stomach, switch to a less troublesome brand, use liquid vitamins instead of a tablet, or just take folic acid until the nausea subsides.

irritability may accompany these PMS-like symptoms, as can some minor cramping.

Note: Sharp, one-sided pain is not normal and should be reported to your caregiver immediately. Such pain may indicate that your pregnancy is ectopic. (See Chapter 11 for details.)

Constipation

Many pregnant women experience problems with constipation—and for good reason. Increased levels of progesterone can make the muscles of the small and large intestines rather sluggish. Although laxatives are not thought to be harmful during pregnancy, it's best to find natural ways of improving your bowel function, such as exercising regularly; adding more fruits, vegetables, grains, and fluids to your diet; and reducing your consumption of dairy products, fatty foods, and processed sugar. You could also try the tried-and-true method that probably worked for your grandmother: two tablespoons of unsulphured blackstrap molasses dissolved in a glass of warm water.

Gas

Gas is a common complaint throughout pregnancy, but it can be particularly problematic during the first trimester, when there is a tendency to swallow a lot of air in an effort to relieve feelings of nausea. Gas then has to make the 22-foot trip through the intestines—no small feat, given that the high progesterone levels of pregnancy and the expanding uterus make it difficult for the intestines to do their job.

Here are some tips on minimizing your problems with gas:

- Avoid the so-called gassy foods (beans, cabbage, and so on).

Timesaver
If you're worried about missing time from work due to morning sickness, ask your boss if you can either telecommute or shift your working hours to a time of day when nausea is less of a problem for you.

- Avoid sipping hot drinks and soups, consuming carbonated beverages, and talking while you are chewing, because all of these habits can cause you to swallow air.

Breast changes

Some of the most dramatic changes in early pregnancy are the changes that occur to the breast. Many women go up a bra size or two overnight—a situation that can be either disconcerting or delightful, depending on how you feel about your breasts.

The hormones at work behind this sudden increase in breast size are also responsible for other changes in the appearance of your breasts. Your nipples sometimes become enlarged and erect, the areola broadens and becomes darker, and the increased blood flow through your body causes the veins in your breasts to become more visible.

Many women also experience a certain amount of breast discomfort during this stage of pregnancy. The swelling, tingling, throbbing, and aching that you may be feeling are indications that your body is getting ready to go into the milk-production business a few months down the road.

Increased vaginal secretions

Moneysaver
Increased vaginal secretions combined with a growing belly can wreak havoc on your designer panties. Invest in cheap cotton undies instead.

An increase in the amount of leukorrhea (the odorless white mucousy discharge that your body produces throughout your childbearing years) is triggered by hormonal changes and is perfectly normal during pregnancy. If, however, you experience a vaginal discharge that is greenish-yellow, foul-smelling, or watery, you should contact your health-care provider immediately.

Shortness of breath

This particular pregnancy symptom is one of the medical world's greatest mysteries. Your uterus and your baby haven't grown enough to start compressing your lungs—something you can look forward to a little further down the road—but you're likely to find yourself huffing and puffing at the top of each flight of stairs. Some doctors believe that dyspnea (the medical term for shortness of breath) is caused by increased levels of progesterone. It's not likely to be a cause for concern for you unless you're asthmatic, in which case you may need to have your medications adjusted.

Faintness

In the days before home pregnancy tests, a sudden episode of fainting was a sure-fire indication of pregnancy. As is the case with many other pregnancy-related complaints, progesterone is to blame. It dilates the smooth muscle of the blood vessels and causes a pooling of blood in the legs. Most pregnant women can minimize their dizziness problems by shifting their weight from foot to foot. Those who experience faintness due to hypoglycemia (low blood sugar) simply need to eat better-quality foods at more regular intervals.

Here are some other ways to cope with the faintness you may be experiencing:

- Drink more fluids.

- Rise more slowly after sitting or lying down.

- Avoid hypoglycemia and its resulting dizziness by minimizing your intake of sweets and not going more than two hours without eating something.

Insomnia

If you haven't already kicked the caffeine habit, now's the time to do it. Many women experience insomnia at various points in their pregnancies, and caffeine will only add to the problem. If you find

66
Be practical and helpful to your partner when she's pregnant. If the laundry's overflowing, someone's going to have to do it, so do it.
—Jim, 36, father of three
99

yourself wide awake in the middle of the night—even though your body is begging for sleep—a cup of warm milk or chamomile tea may help you get the rest that you and your baby need.

Nasal congestion

A stuffy nose is a common complaint during pregnancy. Congestion in the nasal passages is caused by the increased blood supply to the mucus membrane. The condition does not require any treatment and will disappear automatically after your baby is born.

Nosebleeds

Bleeding from the veins in your nose may be an indicator of high blood pressure (hypertension), but more often than not it's simply caused by the very same increase in blood flow that is responsible for so many other pregnancy-related symptoms. If you have recurrent nosebleeds, however, you should mention this problem to your health-care provider so that he can rule out the possibility of hypertension.

Increased frequency of urination

Another classic symptom of early pregnancy is the need to run to the bathroom at frequent intervals throughout the day and night. The cause of increased frequency of urination is obvious: as your uterus expands, it begins to put pressure on your bladder. The hormonal changes of early pregnancy are also thought to play a role.

Urinary tract infections (UTIs)

If you experience burning while you urinate or feel a constant urge to urinate (even if you've just gone to the bathroom), you could be suffering from a urinary tract infection. Your doctor will treat the infection with an antibiotic such as ampicillin, amoxicillin, or sulfamethoxazole/trimepthoprim, all of which are thought to be safe during pregnancy. Because UTIs tend to recur, you'll need to have your urine checked at regular intervals throughout the remainder of your pregnancy.

You may be able to head off a urinary tract infection by consuming one to two cups of cranberry juice each day. Studies have shown that cranberry juice helps reduce the number of bacteria in urine and may actually prevent the bacteria from sticking to cells in the bladder.

Fatigue

Most women start feeling extremely tired shortly after their first missed period, and their energy levels don't return to normal until well into the second trimester (weeks 14 to 20 on average). Although it's hard to get enough rest when you're working full-time, at least you can try to

- take a power nap at your desk during your lunch hour or during your morning and afternoon breaks,

- flop out on the couch as soon as you get home from work,

- head to bed earlier than usual so that you can get the 10 hours of sleep per night that is recommended during pregnancy.

It's also important to eat as well as possible and get some form of regular exercise. (See Chapter 8 for additional tips on nutrition and exercise during pregnancy.)

Headaches

Headaches are also common during pregnancy. If you're reluctant to take acetaminophen (for

Watch Out!
Not all urinary tract infections are symptomatic. That's why it's important to ensure that your health-care provider tests your urine at each prenatal visit. Untreated urinary tract infections have been proven to cause premature labor.

Bright Idea
Apply an ice pack to your forehead, or to the source of the pain, as soon as a tension headache sets in. The ice will cause your blood vessels to contract, eliminating the cause of your headache. You should feel better within 20 minutes— roughly the amount of time it takes for a painkiller to work.

example, Tylenol), which is generally considered to be perfectly safe to take during pregnancy, you might want to try a few other techniques for getting rid of a headache:

- Lie down with a cool cloth on your head.

- Eat more frequently to keep your blood sugar on an even kilter.

- Ask your partner to massage your feet. (The big toe is the acupuncture point for the head.)

Yeast infections

Severe itching or burning and a curdlike or cottage cheese–like discharge from the vagina are classic symptoms of a vaginal yeast infection. Other symptoms include painful urination (due to irritation to the urethra); painful intercourse; and swelling, redness, and irritation of the outer and inner lips of the vagina.

Yeast infections are usually caused by candida albicans, a type of fungus that tends to run rampant during pregnancy for three key reasons: hormonal changes make your vaginal environment less acidic; increased amounts of sugar are stored in the cell walls of the vagina; and your immune system is less effective during pregnancy, making you more susceptible to infection.

Yeast infections tend to be a particular problem for women who require antibiotics to treat UTIs or other bacterial infections during their pregnancies. Although there are numerous over-the-counter medical and herbal remedies for yeast infections, you should not use any of these products until your health-care provider both confirms that you do, in fact, have a yeast infection and recommends an appropriate treatment.

This is definitely one of those situations in which an ounce of prevention is worth a pound of cure. You can help prevent yeast infections by

- eating two small containers of unflavored yogurt with acidophilus (active yogurt cultures) each day,

- avoiding tight clothing around your vagina,

- choosing clothing made from natural rather than synthetic fibers,

- wiping from front to back when you go to the bathroom,

- making sure that your vagina is well-lubricated before intercourse,

- reducing the amount of time you spend sitting on vinyl seats in your home, car, or office.

Weight gain

During the first trimester, you should expect to gain approximately two to four pounds. If you have had particular difficulty with nausea, you may actually lose weight during the first few months of pregnancy—a situation that generally isn't cause for concern because your body simply draws upon its prepregnancy stores. (For additional information on weight gain during pregnancy, see Chapter 8.)

Skin changes

Skin changes during pregnancy vary from woman to woman. Some take on that much-talked-about maternal glow; others break out in acne. If you tend to break out in pimples right before your period, you're likely to be a candidate for complexion problems during pregnancy.

Timesaver
Delegate jobs to other people if all you want to do is hit the couch. There's no reason why you need to be the one who is running all over town, paying bills, picking up dry cleaning, and so on.

The emotional challenges of the first trimester

Up until now, we've been talking about all the nitty-gritty physical changes. Equally important, however, are the emotional changes you are likely to experience as your body chemistry undergoes the most radical changes you'll encounter in your lifetime. One moment, you may feel totally euphoric about the idea of being pregnant. The next, you may feel weepy, sad, irritable, or anxious. You're not going crazy, although you may find that difficult to believe if you just burst into tears while watching a long-distance telephone commercial.

"My frustration tolerance was very low," recalls Jennie, 30, who recently gave birth to her first child. "I'd cry if the mailman was mean to me or if someone told me I couldn't park my car where I want to park it. One of the hardest things about being pregnant is the feeling of being out of control."

Even those women who wanted desperately to become pregnant can find themselves feeling somewhat less than elated when the event actually occurs. That letdown feeling is natural. You're no longer fantasizing about being pregnant; you're now coping with the less-than-delightful realities of morning sickness, constipation, and overwhelming fatigue. "I had this feeling, like I'd gotten on a roller coaster but couldn't get off," says Laura, a 31-year-old mother of one.

The first-trimester reality check can also be a difficult one for partners, says Troy, 30, a first-time father. "During the first trimester, Yvonne was extremely ill with morning sickness. In fact, it was so bad that she was off work for almost two months. I ended up having to do everything around the house—after working for about nine hours in front of a computer. It wasn't too bad at first, but after a while it started to really wear on me. All our friends would ask, 'How's Yvonne?' but no one would ask, 'How are you?' The truth was I was very tired and feeling alone, neglected, and somewhat dumped on."

The top 10 worries of expectant parents

As if the raging hormones and other pregnancy symptoms weren't enough to contend with, many women find that they spend a lot of time worrying during pregnancy.

Here are some of the most common pregnancy-related worries.

Will I lose the baby?

Although the odds of carrying your baby to term are decidedly in your favor, many women spend their first trimester fearing that they are going to have a miscarriage.

"During the first trimester, I had some bleeding on and off for about two weeks," recalls Jennifer, 21, a mother of one. "I was terrified that I was going to lose the baby. I remember walking into our bedroom once and my husband asked me what was wrong, and all I said was, 'I'm bleeding' and I just cried all night long. I was put on a few days of bedrest and had a couple of ultrasounds and, in the end, everything was okay."

Even women who are not experiencing complications may worry that they have experienced a missed abortion (a situation in which the fetus dies but is not expelled from the uterus until weeks later). Part of the problem is that most pregnancy books neglect to mention that you can have a symptom-free first trimester and still walk away with a healthy baby some nine months down the road.

Women who have previously lost a baby are particularly vulnerable to feelings of anxiety during the first trimester, notes Julie, a 45-year-old mother of six. "The biggest emotional challenge of the first trimester for a mom who has lost a baby through miscarriage is worry. Pregnancy is no longer a simple, natural process. It's as if someone has stolen your naivete. Along with the massive hormonal changes of early pregnancy, you're faced with a nagging doubt that something will go wrong this time too. You don't want to tell anyone you're pregnant, and every little twinge is a reason to panic."

You can review the facts about pregnancy loss by reading Chapter 11.

Will my baby be healthy?

The fear of giving birth to a baby who is less than healthy is also a very common pregnancy-related worry. "My biggest concern during pregnancy was always the health of the baby. I was constantly worried about his development," says Kim, 35, a mother of one.

Although it's difficult to eliminate this fear entirely until after the birth, you may find it reassuring to learn as much as you can about fetal development so that you can make the best possible lifestyle choices during the critical first trimester. (See Table 14.1).

Here are some of the highlights of your baby's development during the first trimester:

> 66
> A pregnant woman and her spouse dream of three babies—the perfect four-month-old who rewards them with smiles and musical cooing, the impaired baby, who changes each day, and the mysterious real baby whose presence is beginning to be evident in the motions of the fetus.
> —pediatrician T. Berry Brazelton in *Touchpoints*
> 99

TABLE 14.1: ON THE GROW

Week	Developmental Highlights
3	On the day of conception, your ovum and your partner's sperm unite to form a barely visible single cell known as a zygote. It takes the zygote the better part of a week to make the journey to your uterus. Because pregnancy is typically dated in relation to the woman's last menstrual period (LMP), you're already two weeks' pregnant by the time you actually conceive.
4	During the fourth week of pregnancy (approximately one week after conception), the tiny cell ball (.004 of an inch) implants itself in the lining of your uterus. It then divides into two parts, which will ultimately become the placenta and the embryo. By the end of this week, amniotic fluid will begin to form.
5	At the start of this week, the embryo is as large as an apple seed, and the beginnings of its major organs are present.
6	The embryo is now approximately $^1/_4$-inch long. Its heart—which is no larger than a poppy seed—has begun to beat, and other major organs such as the kidneys and the liver have begun to develop. The neural tube, which connects the brain and the spinal cord, closes.
7	The embryo is now about $^1/_2$-inch long about — the size of a kidney bean. At this stage of development, its head is much larger than the rest of its body. This is because of the rapid brain growth that has been occurring. The embryo has visible nostrils, lips, and tongue, and the buds of its first teeth are present. The heart has four clearly recognizable chambers. The limb buds have grown into arms and legs, but the hands and feet are mere ridges.
8	The fetus is now $1^1/_4$ inches long—the size of a large grape. It has distinct, slightly webbed fingers and toes, and its veins are clearly visible through its parchment-like skin. The teeth, palate, and larynx are beginning to form, and the ears are starting to assume a more human shape.
9	The fetus continues to grow, and its organs, muscles, and nerves start to function. Sometime during week nine, it begins to make its first spontaneous movements. You won't be able to feel these movements yet, of course, because the fetus is so tiny and rarely comes into contact with the uterine wall.

Bright Idea
You can track your baby's development by visiting the interactive pregnancy calendar at www.olen.com. Simply type your baby's due date, conception date, or the date of your last menstrual period, and you can print a detailed calendar that highlights key milestones in your baby's development.

continues

Week	Developmental Highlights
10	The fetus now weighs about $1/3$ of an ounce. By the end of week 10, the umbilical cord is fully formed and blood is circulating along its arteries and veins. The chorionic villi are growing and maturing over the area of implantation, and they will eventually become part of the placenta. If the fetus is a boy, this is the week when his scrotum will form.
11	The fetus is now about two inches long and weighs about half an ounce. Its head is approximately half of its length. The ovaries or testicles are fully formed and the external genitalia are developing; but it's still too early to distinguish the sex of the fetus.
12	The fetus is now about $2\frac{1}{2}$ inches long and is fully formed. During the second and third trimesters, it will grow and mature. The urine produced by the fetus's kidneys is excreted into the amniotic fluid. (Don't worry; the urine is sterile and is carried away as the fluid is replaced.) Your baby's face is now properly formed and eyelids are present. The umbilical cord has started to circulate blood between the embryo and the placenta.
13	The fetus is now about three inches long and weighs about $1\frac{1}{2}$ ounces. Its internal organs are up and running: the liver is manufacturing bile, and the kidneys are secreting urine into the bladder. This is the week when its intestines migrate from the umbilical cord to the abdomen. The fetus has already acquired some reflexes, and its eyes and ears have almost assumed their permanent positions.
14	By the end of week 14—the last week of the first trimester—the fetus is $3\frac{1}{2}$ inches long and weighs up to two ounces. Its hands are functional and it is able to "breathe" amniotic fluid in and out of its lungs. The internal organs are fully formed, although the lungs, liver, kidney, and intestine will continue to grow and mature.

How will I cope with the pain of labor?

Many women worry about labor from the moment they find out that they are pregnant. Others don't start worrying until their pregnancies are further along.

Tracy, 31, remembers being frightened throughout her entire pregnancy: "One of the first thoughts that went through my head when I read that positive on the pregnancy test was, 'Oh no. Now I have to give birth!' My fear of giving birth was pretty steady throughout the pregnancy. Whenever I'd read birth stories or the chapters on birth in my pregnancy books, or watch a birth video, my hands would shake and I'd feel myself turn hot and cold. I was afraid that I wouldn't be able to handle it; that I'd fall apart, that I'd panic."

Johnna found that she became more anxious over time. "My biggest concern during the pregnancy was labor. It was such a big unknown and you hear so many scary stories from other moms. The books make it sound like if you just breathe right, it will be manageable, but you know from talking to others that is sometimes really difficult. It was hard to sit and wonder what it would be like."

Fear of labor can also be a big issue for partners, as first-time father Troy, 30, explains: "One of my concerns was what would labor be like and would I be up to the challenge. All the pregnancies I'd ever seen were on TV shows. You know—first the mother's water breaks and then within about three minutes she goes into extreme contractions, but of course it's all over in ten minutes! Lastly—and this is selfish—I was hoping her water would not break while riding in our new car. I just kept thinking about all this amniotic fluid running over my leather seats. Yuck!"

What's going to happen to my body?
Many women worry about how pregnancy is going to affect their bodies. Tracy, a 31-year-old first-time mother, explains: "In the beginning of my

Bright Idea
Have someone take a photo of you each month so that you will have a record of how your body changed during pregnancy.

pregnancy, I was fearful of the changes my body was going to have to go through. My body was no longer familiar to me, and it was no longer my own."

Although your body will undergo tremendous changes during pregnancy, most tend to be gradual and the majority will reverse themselves shortly after you give birth. You can get an idea of how your body will change during the months ahead by looking at the illustrations in the following figures.

Note! ➡
How your body changes during pregnancy.

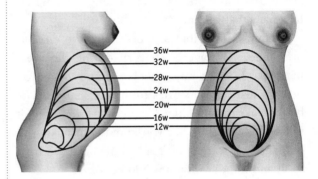

Note! ➡
Fetal development (12 weeks). Figure created by Articulate Graphics.

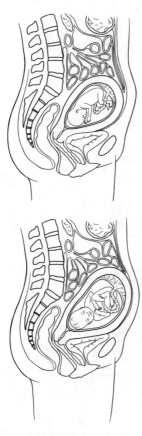

← **Note!**
Fetal develop-
ment (16 weeks).
Figure created
by Articulate
Graphics.

← **Note!**
Fetal develop-
ment (20 weeks).
Figure created
by Articulate
Graphics.

← **Note!**
Fetal develop-
ment (24 weeks).
Figure created
by Articulate
Graphics.

Note! ➜
Fetal development (28 weeks). Figure created by Articulate Graphics.

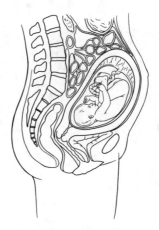

Note! ➜
Fetal development (32 weeks). Figure created by Articulate Graphics.

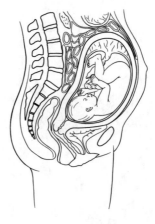

Note! ➜
Fetal development (36 weeks). Figure created by Articulate Graphics.

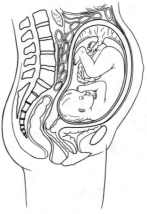

Will I be a good parent?

Many expectant couples worry about whether they've got what it takes to be a good parent. Tracy, 31, had no experience with infants until her son was born, and she spent a good part of her pregnancy worrying about how she would care for him while he was an infant. "I was worried that I wouldn't know how to dress him, how to bathe him, how to diaper him."

Other parents find it rather humbling to consider the responsibility that they have assumed by choosing to have a baby. "The hardest part was the overwhelming sense of responsibility," admits Heather, a 32-year-old first-time mother. "Suddenly, I was carrying another life—one that had no say in what happened. If I made a mistake and crashed my car, I could live with me paying for it with injuries, and so on, but I couldn't imagine the guilt of having injured my child."

How will having a baby affect my relationship with my partner?

It's also common for pregnant women to worry about how having a baby will change their relationships with their partners. "I kept wondering if I'd ruined a perfectly good relationship by deciding to have another baby," recalls Ann, a 34-year-old mother of four.

Anne, 39, had similar feelings: "My first marriage broke up after the birth of a child, so I was worried that history might repeat itself when my new partner and I were awaiting the birth of our daughter."

If your pregnancy was unplanned and your partner is less than thrilled about the whole idea, this may be a particularly difficult issue for you, and you

> **"**
> Having a child is so irreversible. Any other decision you make in life can be changed. You can quit a job, grow out a bad haircut, drop out of school, or get a divorce, but nothing stops you from being a parent. I often felt like I was trapped on a speeding train, destination unknown, and I just hoped I'd like where I was when the train finally stopped.
> —Tracy, 31, mother of one
> **"**

may wish to consider individual or couples therapy during pregnancy.

How will having a baby affect my relationship with my other children?

Pregnant women with other children at home frequently wonder whether they will, in fact, have enough love for another baby. "I loved my first child so intensely that I couldn't imagine loving another baby that much again," admits Marie, 34, a mother of four. "Of course, I've since learned that I have more than enough love for four kids—and maybe even more."

Could I be carrying more than one baby?

Comments from well-meaning and not-so-well-meaning strangers are often responsible for causing a pregnant woman to worry that she might be carrying more than one baby. It only takes a few comments such as, "Are you sure there are not twins in there?" to make you start wondering if, in fact, there's more than one baby on board.

Fortunately, this is one of the most easily resolved pregnancy worries. Your caregiver should be able to reassure you that you are, in fact, carrying one baby—or break the news to you gently if it turns out that you're not.

Am I gaining too much or too little weight?

It's a rare pregnant woman who doesn't obsess from time to time about how much weight she is gaining during her pregnancy.

If you're gaining too much weight, you may wonder whether you'll be left with a horrific amount of weight to lose after the delivery.

If you're gaining too little, you may worry that you're depriving your baby of the nutrients he needs in order to grow.

If you are worried about your weight gain, talk to your caregiver. She will be able to provide you with feedback on your weight gain to date.

How will having a baby affect my career?

If you decide to continue working after your baby arrives, you may worry about how you will manage to juggle the needs of your family with the demands of your career. If you decide to stay at home with your baby for a few years, you may worry about the long-term impact of your decision on your career.

The best way to resolve this particular worry is to speak with women within your company or your profession who have made the same choice you are intending to make, and to find out what, if anything, they would do differently if they had the chance to do things over. You might not necessarily decide to make the same choices they did—but at least you'll be able to benefit from what they learned through the school of hard knocks.

Just the facts

- You can eliminate many of the most common complaints of early pregnancy by eating properly, keeping your stress level down, and getting enough rest. You just have to live with the others.

- Pregnancy is also a time of tremendous emotional change for pregnant women and their partners.

- It's normal to worry about everything from the well-being of your baby to your fitness for motherhood.

- Throughout the first trimester, your baby is growing and developing at a remarkable rate. By week 14, your baby's major organs are all fully developed.

Unofficially...
The Greek physician Hippocrates believed that it was possible to tell the sex of a developing child by looking at a pregnant woman's eyes and breasts. If the right eye was brighter or the right breast was firmer, she would have a boy. If the left eye was brighter or the left breast was firmer, she would have a girl.

Unofficially...
Back in the 17th century, it was believed that a woman could tell if she was pregnant if she saw her reflection in her boiled urine. (*Note:* Don't try this at home.)

- Heavy bleeding (or lighter bleeding that lasts for more than one day), a watery vaginal discharge, the passage of dark red clots or grayish or pinkish tissue, cramping, abdominal or shoulder pain, fever, weakness or dizziness, and vomiting are indications that you could be experiencing a miscarriage or an ectopic (tubal) pregnancy (see Chapter 11). Call your health-care provider immediately.

GET THE SCOOP ON...
How you may be feeling ▪ The emotional challenges of the second trimester ▪
How your baby is growing ▪ Screening tests for
gestational diabetes, anemia, and premature
labor ▪ Planning your maternity leave ▪ Writing
a birth plan ▪ Hiring a doula

The Golden Age of Pregnancy: The Second Trimester

Chapter 15

The second trimester is often referred to as the Golden Age of pregnancy. For most women, the nausea and extreme fatigue of the first trimester are but a memory (albeit a powerful one!), and the third-trimester aches and pains have not yet had a chance to set in. The risk of miscarriage declines significantly at this point in the pregnancy, something that may add to your enjoyment of this trimester if you spent the first trimester running to the bathroom every 10 minutes, looking for any tell-tale signs of bleeding.

This is also the trimester when you get to experience those exciting first flutters sometime between weeks 16 and 20—something that, for the majority of women, makes all the aches and pains of pregnancy suddenly seem worthwhile.

Many women take advantage of the increased energy levels that tend to coincide with the second trimester, using this time to make some important decisions concerning the birth: when to start their maternity leave, whether to hire a doula, and whether to write a birth plan.

Aches and pains: the sequel

Of course, this isn't to say that the second trimester is entirely blissful. Aches and pains are, after all, part of the pregnancy turf. Although you'll likely lose a few of the more distressing symptoms of the first trimester (for example, nausea and extreme fatigue), your constipation and breathlessness may hang around for a while and be joined by a few new complaints.

Just a reminder: if you can't find the particular pregnancy complaint you're looking for in this chapter, we've probably covered it in either Chapter 14 or 16.

Feeling fat rather than pregnant

Many women at this stage of the game worry that they look fat rather than pregnant. You're probably too big for your regular clothes—particularly the more tailored garments—but too small for tent-style maternity fashions. (Of course, if this is your second or subsequent pregnancy, you may have been wearing your maternity clothes for a while by now since you seem to show sooner if you have been pregnant before.)

If you're worried that you look fat rather than pregnant, take heart. By the end of this trimester, there will be no question about the fact that you're pregnant. During weeks 12 to 27, your uterus will quadruple in height and rise out of your pelvis, causing your body to take on those classic curves of pregnancy.

Back pain

Look at any cartoon of a pregnant woman and you'll see someone with two hands on her back, leaning into the classic swayback position. You don't have to be pregnant for very long to figure out why pregnant women do this. They're supporting their aching backs!

Back pain during pregnancy occurs for a number of reasons. First of all, progesterone—the so-called "pregnancy hormone"—causes the ligaments and connective tissue holding the bones in the pelvic region together to soften so that they can open up during the birth, something that frequently causes pain around the pubic bone as well. Second, the heavier uterus throws off a pregnant woman's center of gravity, something that can lead to a change of postures that can cause back pain. Third, the rectus abdominis muscles—the muscles that run along the front of the abdomen from the rib cage to the pubic bone—can separate during pregnancy, a condition that tends to worsen back pain.

Although it's useful to know what causes back pain, it's more important to know how to prevent or manage it. Here are a few tips:

- Wear low-heeled (but not flat) shoes with good arch support.

- Ask for help when you are lifting heavy objects, and lift by bending your knees rather than your waist.

- To reduce your chances of injury, make gentle rather than jerky motions when you are reaching or stretching.

- Sit in chairs that provide adequate back support or place a small pillow between the chair and your lower back.

Bright Idea
Exercise regularly to keep your abdominal muscles strong and reduce your chances of experiencing back pain.

- Pay attention to posture. Keep your pelvis tucked in and your shoulders back when you are sitting or standing.

- Place one foot on a step stool if you're going to be sitting or standing for long periods of time.

- Get up and walk around every half-hour if your job requires that you sit for long periods of time.

- Take the pressure off your lower back when you are sleeping on your side by placing one pillow under your abdomen and another between your knees.

Watch Out!
Abdominal pain can also be caused by appendicitis, a gallbladder attack, the stretching of adhesions from previous abdominal surgery, an ectopic pregnancy, or preterm labor. If the pain you are experiencing is particularly severe or lasts for an extended period of time, call your caregiver immediately.

Round ligament pain

Round ligament pain is the shooting pain in the lower abdomen that many women experience when they change position suddenly. It is caused by the sudden stretching of the ligaments and muscles that support the expanding uterus. It tends to be at its worse between weeks 14 and 20, when the uterus is big enough to exert its pressure on the ligaments, yet not big enough to rest some of its weight on the pelvic bones.

You may be able to minimize the amount of round ligament pain if you move slowly and carefully when you are changing position. Some women find it helpful to support their belly from below when they rise to a standing position. Others find that warm baths help to ease some of the discomfort of round ligament pain.

Leg cramps

It's not unusual to experience painful leg cramps during the second and third trimesters. These cramps—which occur most often while you are sleeping—are believed to be caused by the pressure of the uterus on the nerves in the legs or by a calcium deficiency.

Here are some tips on preventing and managing leg cramps in your calf muscles:

- Stretch your calf muscles before you head to bed. Pull your toes up toward your knee while pushing your heel away from you. You should repeat this exercise at least 10 times for each leg to really stretch the muscles out.

- Ask your partner to massage your calf muscles.

- As soon as a cramp starts, point your toes downward toward your knees. Whatever you do, don't point your toes. The pain will only intensify.

- If you're not already taking a calcium supplement, ask your caregiver to recommend one.

Heartburn

Heartburn—a burning sensation in the middle of your chest or upper digestive tract—is another common complaint during pregnancy. It occurs because progesterone (1) relaxes the muscle that is responsible for controlling the opening at the top of the stomach and (2) causes the stomach to empty more slowly so that as many nutrients as possible can be absorbed from the food you eat.

Here are some tips on preventing heartburn:

- Avoid fatty and greasy foods, carbonated drinks, processed meats, and junk food.

- Eat slowly. The more slowly you eat, the more time the enzymes in your saliva have to break down the food before it reaches your stomach.

- Eat less. Heartburn is more likely to flare up if you overfill your stomach, particularly if you're eating a lot of carbohydrates.

- Don't eat too close to bedtime.

66

I had terrible heartburn during all three of my pregnancies. It started at about five months with my second and third children. I tried papaya enzyme, which tasted great but didn't do much. Then my midwife recommended Gaviscon tablets. They foam in your mouth like a butterscotch-flavored fire extinguisher, but they really work. The only good thing about heartburn is that within minutes of giving birth, you realize you don't have it anymore."
—Karen, 34, mother of three

99

- Avoid lying flat on your back when you are resting or sleeping because this will only intensify your heartburn. Try propping yourself up with pillows instead.

- If you're feeling particularly miserable, ask your caregiver if you can take an antacid.

Low blood pressure

Many women experience low blood pressure during pregnancy. This can lead to dizziness and feelings of faintness—particularly if you're standing in one spot for a prolonged period of time (for example, when you're waiting in line at the grocery store or the bank). If you find yourself in this situation and you feel as though you're going to faint, you should

- shift your weight from foot to foot, or

- sit with your head between your knees.

Don't worry about looking silly if you have to sit down on the floor in the middle of the grocery store or bank. Anyone who has been pregnant before will understand what you're going through. As for anyone who hasn't been pregnant before—who really cares what they think anyway?

Carpal tunnel syndrome

Bright Idea
Use a bag of frozen vegetables or a bag of chilled, uncooked rice to ease the pain of carpal tunnel syndrome.

Carpal tunnel syndrome is another common complaint in pregnant women—particularly those who work on computers all day or do work that involves repetitive hand and wrist motions. It is caused when the nerves in the wrist become compressed by fluids being retained by the surrounding tissues.

The symptoms of carpal tunnel syndrome include numbness, tingling, or shooting or burning pain in the middle and index fingers and thumb; cramping or stiffness of the hands; weakness in the thumb; and a tendency to drop objects. Some pregnant women report numbness as far up their arm as their elbow.

If you develop carpal tunnel syndrome, your caregiver will likely recommend that you wear a splint at night to reduce your discomfort and pain. (A steroid injection is rarely needed). Although the condition usually corrects itself spontaneously after delivery, minor surgery may be required if it persists.

Hip pain

One of the most aggravating pregnancy complaints for many women is hip pain and stiffness. Unfortunately, it's hard to avoid when your growing belly pretty much limits you to sleeping on one side or the other.

Some women find that putting a pillow between their knees and tucking another pillow under their abdomen provides at least a measure of relief.

Fortunately, hip pain quickly disappears after the baby is born.

Edema (fluid retention)

Edema occurs during a normal pregnancy for two reasons: the growing uterus places pressure on the veins carrying blood back from the lower extremities, forcing water into the tissues around your feet and ankles; and the increased levels of progesterone in your body encourage fluid retention.

You will know if you are retaining extra fluids if your feet feel swollen and uncomfortable or your fingers start to feel puffy.

Here are some tips on coping with edema:

■ Lying on your side helps reduce fluid retention by allowing gravity to pull fluid from your tissues back into your bloodstream so that it can be passed out of your body through your

66
The extra weight really makes whatever side you are lying on ache. Really ache. I would flip to the other side, but eventually that side would hurt too.
—Molly, 29, mother of one
99

kidneys. If you can't lie down, sit and put your feet up.

- Warm—not hot—baths can help to reduce swelling.

- Avoid diuretics ("water pills"). Not only are they ineffective, but they affect your body's fluid balance and can be dangerous during pregnancy.

- Increase your fluid intake. Believe it or not, this can have a diuretic effect and help reduce water retention and swelling.

- Watch your salt intake but don't eliminate salt from your diet entirely. You need salt to maintain your normal fluid balance.

- Remove your rings before they start getting tight so that you won't have to have them cut off.

Note: If you experience edema and high blood pressure, and your caregiver detects protein in your urine, you could be developing preeclampsia—a serious pregnancy-related condition. (See Chapter 10 for more information on preeclampsia, and see the following table for other symptoms to watch for during the second trimester.)

TABLE 15.1: WHEN TO CALL YOUR CAREGIVER

You should call your doctor immediately if you experience any of the following symptoms:

- heavy vaginal bleeding or clotting;
- lighter bleeding that lasts for more than one day;
- any amount of bleeding that is accompanied by pain, fever, or chills;
- severe abdominal or shoulder pain;
- a severe or persistent headache—particularly one that is accompanied by dizziness, faintness, or visual disturbances;
- dehydration;

- a fever of more than 101°F;
- painful urination;
- a watery discharge from the vagina;
- sudden swelling of the face, hands, or feet;
- the signs of premature labor: regular uterine contractions (a tightening feeling in your abdomen that you may be able to feel with your fingertips but that won't necessarily be accompanied by any significant pain, lower back pain, a feeling of heaviness in the lower pelvis or abdomen, diarrhea, slight spotting or bleeding or a watery fluid or mucus discharge;
- a significant decrease in fetal movement after the 24th week of pregnancy.

Skin problems

Some women find that their skin improves during pregnancy and they acquire that much-lauded maternal glow. Others experience a number of skin-related problems.

Here are some common complaints:

- **Mask of pregnancy (chloasma):** Some women experience a darkening of the skin on their face because increased levels of estrogen and progesterone stimulate production of melanin (skin pigment). The so-called "mask of pregnancy" is a butterfly-shaped darkened area that extends around the eyes and across the nose and cheeks. Because chloasma is made worse by exposure to sunlight or other sources of ultraviolet light, be sure to use a sunblock with an SPF of at least 15 when you are outdoors.

- **Increased pigmentation:** Ninety percent of pregnant women experience some sort of increased pigmentation. This skin darkening occurs on the nipples or areola (the area around the nipples), on the perineum, and on

Timesaver
If you will be returning to work after the birth of your baby, start looking for child-care now. You can get the scoop on finding quality, affordable childcare in *The Unofficial Guide to Childcare,* by Ann Douglas.

the line that runs from the navel to the pubic bone (the linea nigra).

- **Changes to moles:** Some women find that their moles become darker and larger during pregnancy. Because these types of changes can also be a sign of cancer, it's important to report them to your doctor.

- **Red and itchy palms and soles:** Some women find that the palms of their hands and the soles of their feet become extremely itchy during pregnancy. These symptoms can usually be relieved by a moisturizing cream.

- **Skin tags:** Some pregnant women develop skin tags—small, loose growths of skin under the arms or breasts. These are painless and usually disappear after your baby is born. If they persist, however, you can arrange to have them removed through minor surgery.

- **Rashes:** Some pregnant women develop a heat rash during pregnancy. The best way to cope with this particular problem is to use cornstarch (rather than scented baby powders) after bathing and to keep the skin cool and dry.

- **Acne:** Some women find that their skin breaks out during pregnancy. Here's what Jennifer, 25, had to say about the skin problems she experienced during pregnancy: "The absolutely worst aspect of my entire pregnancy was how terrible my skin broke out. I had no idea this would happen. I assumed pregnant women got wonderful skin—you know, 'the glow.' By my fifth month, I was so broken out on my back, chest, shoulders, and all over the sides of my face, forehead, and chin that there wasn't a spot you could touch without pimples."

Although your skin may be in for a rough ride during pregnancy, you're likely to have a healthy head of hair. Pregnancy hormones reduce the rate at which hair falls out, something that can leave you with a thick head of hair until at least a few months after the delivery.

Bleeding gums (pregnancy gingivitis)

During pregnancy, your gums are softer, more swollen, and more sensitive than usual. Consequently, they are more likely to bleed when you are brushing and flossing.

You can minimize the problems you experience by

- brushing and flossing more often than usual
- using a softer bristle than you normally use and brushing gently
- eating foods that are rich in vitamin C and calcium
- rinsing with an antiseptic mouthwash

Dry eye

Some women find that their eyes become light-sensitive, gritty, and dry during pregnancy. If you experience these symptoms, you might want to try using an artificial-tears product to add moisture to your sore, irritated eyes. This condition usually disappears after the birth.

Vision problems

Fluid retention can cause changes to the shape of your eyeball and consequently your vision. This is why some pregnant women find that they become more far-sighted or near-sighted during pregnancy or notice that their contact lenses no longer feel comfortable. Vision problems caused by fluid retention disappear after the delivery.

The emotions of the second trimester

Many women report that the second trimester is a time of tremendous joy. The peak risk of miscarriage is behind them, and they are feeling more stable now that their bodies have had a chance to adjust to the powerful hormonal cocktail of pregnancy. "The second trimester was great," recalls Beth, 27, who recently gave birth to her first child. "I was starting to show, and I felt really wonderful."

Other women report that it is during the second trimester that the pregnancy starts to feel "real." Jennifer, a 28-year-old mother of one, explains: "I heard my baby's heartbeat during the second trimester, and things really hit home that I was having a baby."

Although most pregnant women enjoy the second trimester, it's not a cakewalk for everyone. Some women—like Christy, a 25-year-old first-time mother—find themselves feeling out of control: "During the second trimester, the hormone attacks began to hit. The slightest thing would set me off. When it did, I'd bawl for hours, uncontrollably for no reason at all. I didn't have anything bad happening, I wasn't afraid of things, I just felt like crying and couldn't stop. I hated it."

Other women, like Wendy, a 30-year-old first-time mother, find the second trimester more difficult than the first. "For me, the first trimester was a total breeze—a fact that I wasn't expecting because everyone told me it's one of the most difficult. So when I was barely into the second trimester, I wasn't expecting to suddenly be hit with such a big physical change. I kept trying to do everything like I always had, assuming I had the energy reserves I've always had, and that I could handle the massive stress of work, get seven hours of sleep, keep my house clean during the week, and still be a nice spouse (oh yeah, and keep up a regular exercise schedule). I pretty much worked myself up into a state of panic before my doctor told me to get more sleep and lay off the exercise for a few weeks."

If you're feeling less than euphoric about being pregnant, you may worry that there's something wrong with you. As one woman put it, "The hard thing about having doubts and not being sure you want to be pregnant is that there really isn't anyone you can talk to about it. People view pregnancy as this wonderful event you should be unconditionally happy about. It's not okay to be unhappy or to wonder if you really want a baby."

A small number of women develop full-blown depression during pregnancy. If you experience such symptoms as a loss in appetite, a loss of interest in activities you usually enjoy, extreme fatigue, feelings of guilt and inadequacy, or sleep disturbances, you could be suffering from prenatal depression. Talk to your caregiver about your feelings, or seek the services of a therapist.

The incredible growing baby

You aren't the only one going through massive changes. Your baby is growing at an incredible rate. Table 15.2 describes some of the key changes your baby will experience during this trimester. Here are some of the highlights of your baby's development during the second trimester:

When I was pregnant with my daughter, I was in a car accident. Every part of my body was bruised and cut and battered except my tummy where the baby was. I had an ultrasound to make sure everything was okay. It was. I saw two arms, two legs, and a heartbeat. I didn't know who she was yet, but it was a great relief to see that she was fine.
—Nancy, 31, mother of three

TABLE 15.2: ON THE GROW

Week	Developmental Highlights
15	At this stage of pregnancy, the fetus is covered with lanugo—ultra-fine, downy hair that usually disappears before birth. It has already mastered the art of facial expressions and has probably added frowning, squinting, and grimacing to its repertoire. If you have an ultrasound from this point onward, you might even catch your baby sucking its thumb!
16	The fetus is about 4½ inches long and weighs about 5½ ounces. By the end of this week, its limbs will be formed and all of its joints will be fully functional. The fetus is now sensitive to light. Sometime over next four weeks, you will probably be able to feel your baby's movements. (You'll recognize them sooner if you've been pregnant before.)
17	The fetus is now about 5 inches long and weighs about 6 ounces.
18	The fetus is now about 5½ inches long and weighs about 7 ounces. The bones in its skeleton continue to be extremely soft.
19	The fetus has as many nerve cells as an adult. Connections between the nerves and the muscles are being established.
20	The fetus is now 6½ inches long and weighs about 9 ounces. Its senses of taste and smell are fully developed.
21	The fetus is gaining weight quickly because it needs to have a layer of fat to keep itself warm. It is covered in a slick, fatty substance—vernix caseosa—that is designed to protect the baby's skin while it floats in the amniotic fluid.
22	The fetus now weighs about three-quarters of a pound and measures in at about 7½ inches. Its eyebrows and eyelids are fully developed, and its fingernails are present as well. The fetus's skin is now sensitive to touch, and the fetus is likely to respond to pressure placed on the abdomen.
23	The fetus weighs approximately one pound and is eight inches long. Although its head-to-body proportions resemble those of a newborn, it is still extremely thin. Its lips are present and its eyes are developed (although there is still no pigment in the iris). The fetus's lungs are starting to develop surfactant—the substance that enables the lungs to expand easily when the baby is born.

24	The fetus's vital organs have developed to the point that they are sufficiently mature for the fetus to survive for a short period of time if it happens to be born prematurely. If treated by neonatal specialists, the baby has a chance of survival if it is born at this stage of pregnancy.
25	The fetus now weighs approximately 1½ pounds and is about 9 inches long. If you feel any rhythmic jerking, your baby might have a case of the hiccups. Fetal hiccuping is fairly common during the second half of pregnancy.
26	The fetus's brain waves resemble those of a newborn baby. The fetus has now developed distinct patterns of sleeping and waking.
27	The fetus now weighs approximately 2 pounds and is approximately 11 inches long. It passes a full pint of urine into the amniotic fluid each day. This fluid is then carried out to the mother's body for elimination.

Bright Idea
Be sure to note the date on which you first feel fetal movement. This can help your caregiver to accurately date your pregnancy and will prove valuable in timing your alpha-fetaprotein test and 18 to 20 week ultrasound, should you decide to have these screening tests. (See Chapter 7 for further details.)

Screening tests for gestational diabetes

As you will recall from Chapter 10, gestational diabetes—also known as gestational glucose intolerance—is caused by the hormonal and metabolic changes of pregnancy. It occurs in 2% to 10% of pregnant women.

Some caregivers routinely screen all pregnant women for gestational diabetes because the screening test is readily available and the disease can be difficult to diagnose without the test; others choose to screen only those women who have one or more of the following risk factors:

- age 30 or older
- family history of diabetes
- previous macrosomic (that is, overly large), malformed, or stillborn baby
- obesity

Watch Out!
Half of pregnant women with gestational diabetes don't exhibit any of the classic risk factors.

The glucose screening test is usually performed between 24 and 28 weeks of pregnancy. It involves drinking a glucose solution (a super-sugary drink that tastes like an overly sweet bottle of orange soda or cola). After an hour, a blood sample is taken and your glucose level is measured.

Approximately 15% of pregnant women who take the glucose screening test obtain an abnormal result on the test. Because it is a screening test rather than a diagnostic test, an abnormal result merely indicates that you are at increased risk of having gestational diabetes. (You might want to review our discussion of the differences between screening tests and diagnostic tests back in Chapter 7.) To find out whether you do, in fact, have the disease, you will need to take an oral glucose tolerance test.

Only about 15% of women who obtain an abnormal result on the glucose screening test and go on to take the oral glucose tolerance test are found to have gestational diabetes.

If you are sent for an oral glucose tolerance test, you will be asked to fast the night before the test (that is, not eat or drink anything for at least eight hours prior to the test). Then, after a blood test to measure your fasting level of blood sugar is obtained, you'll drink a beverage with an extremely high concentration of glucose. (Not surprisingly, a fair number of pregnant women report that drinking such a beverage on an empty stomach leaves them feeling somewhat queasy. A handful of pregnant women are unable to stomach the beverage at all.) There are alternatives using food services (e.g., chocolate bars) of sugar in these cases.

Once you've swallowed the beverage, the clock starts ticking. A series of blood tests will then be taken over a three-hour period to measure your blood sugar. Generally, if the fasting blood sugar level is high or two out of three of the post-glucose-drink blood sugars are high, the test is considered abnormal.

If you are diagnosed with gestational diabetes, you will need to follow a special diet (typically 2,200 to 2,400 calories per day, made up of 45% carbohydrates, 25% protein, and 30% fat) and have frequent blood tests to monitor your blood sugar levels. Your doctor may also decide to perform non-stress tests (see Chapter 16) during your last few weeks of pregnancy to monitor your baby's well-being and one or more ultrasound tests to assess fetal growth. You can find out more on gestational diabetes in Chapter 10.

Screening for anemia

Your caregiver may decide to screen you for anemia at the same time that the glucose screening test is performed. It is fairly common practice to test for iron deficiency at this stage of pregnancy. Although you might have entered pregnancy with healthy hemoglobin (the substance that carries oxygen in the blood) and hematocrit readings (the concentration of red blood cells in the blood), you could be anemic by now. This is because anemia can be caused by either (1) the dilutional effect of the expanded blood volume that can outpace the growth of red blood cells in a pregnant woman's body or (2) an inadequate intake of iron.

Screening for preterm labor

Preterm birth—the birth of a baby before the start of the 37th week of pregnancy—occurs in approximately 10% of all pregnancies and accounts for 60% to 75% of all infant health problems and deaths.

Unofficially...
According to a recent article in *Midwifery Today* magazine, premature birth costs the U.S. health-care system an estimated $2 billion per year.

Studies have shown that 50% of cases of preterm birth are caused by premature rupture of the membranes and 20% by other maternal fetal complications.

If you've previously given birth to a premature baby, you are three times as likely to give birth to another premature baby as someone who hasn't previously given birth to a premature baby. (Your risk factor is 15% rather than 5%. If you have experienced two premature births in a row, your risk factor increases to 32%.)

Four types of tests are used to predict which pregnant women are at increased risk of going into labor prematurely: cervical length, bacterial vaginosis, the fetal fibronectin (fFN) test and the salivary estriol test.

Cervical length

Your caregiver may order an ultrasound or manual exam to measure the length of your cervix. Women with shorter than average cervixes are at increased risk of experiencing premature labor.

Bacterial vaginosis

Women who have bacterial vaginosis (the predominance of an assorted variety of anerobic bacteria in the vagina that is often—but not always—associated with a thin, milky discharge and fishy odor) are at increased risk of experiencing preterm labor, premature rupture of membranes, and/or preterm delivery. That is why a growing number of caregivers are choosing to screen pregnant women for bacterial vaginosis and treat those affected with oral antibiotics.

Fetal fibronectin (fFN)

The fetal fibronectin test (fFN) is a diagnostic test used to predict a woman's risk of experiencing

preterm labor. Similar to a pap smear, the test is performed when a woman is 24 to 34 weeks pregnant
and experiencing some of the symptoms of preterm
labor. The test can be performed if a woman's
membranes are still intact and cervical dilation is
minimal (that is, less than 3 cm). Because the test is
relatively expensive ($200), it is not routinely
offered to every pregnant woman.

Salivary estriol

The salivary estriol test—its brand name is SalEst—
is a saliva test performed between 22 and 36 weeks
of pregnancy. It is primarily used to rule out the
likelihood of premature labor in women who would
otherwise be considered high risk. It is considered
to be 98% accurate in identifying those who are not
at high risk for delivering prematurely but only 9%
to 20% accurate in pinpointing those who are. The
test recently received approval from the Food and
Drug Administration; it is available for under $100.

As exciting as these tests may be, there is still no
proven way to prevent preterm labor.

Maternity leave

The second trimester is the ideal time to plan your
maternity leave. Your pregnancy is now well established, but your due date is still several months away.

When you start planning for your maternity
leave, you should have two alternative scenarios in
your head: what you will do if everything goes
according to plan, and what you will do if complications arise and it is necessary for you to leave your
job sooner than originally planned.

Even if you're used to being a bit of a loner, you
should make an effort to keep colleagues apprised
of your progress on various projects. That way, if

Watch Out!
The United
States Public
Health Service
recommends that
women who are
at increased risk
of experiencing
preterm labor be
screened for
and/or treated
for bacterial
vaginosis.

> **❝**
> I wish someone had told me how unrealistic it was to work up until the baby was born. My thinking was that as long as I felt good, I should keep working so that I could spend my maternity leave with the baby. I worked up until the day I gave birth, went home from work, stopped at the store, and my water broke. So it was off to the hospital. I wish I had taken a week off to rest.
> —Kim, 35, mother of one
> **❞**

your baby decides to make its grand entrance before opening night, you won't be caught off guard.

Something else you need to give some serious thought to is the sheer timing of your maternity leave. Although the conventional wisdom says that you should work up until the moment the contractions kick in, there's something to be said about taking some time off before the baby arrives.

Here are some words of wisdom from Debby, a 37-year-old first-time mother: "I had planned to work until a week or two before my due date. On the advice of a friend, however, I stopped working almost two months before I delivered. It was a very good decision. I enjoyed the summer, took long walks, read a lot, and prepared myself emotionally for having the baby. I was very rested by the time I delivered the baby. It was tempting to keep working to get ahead financially, but I'm very happy I made the decision to stop working early."

If you don't want to stop working very far in advance of your due date, you might consider asking your boss if you can arrange to work part-time during your last few weeks on the job. You might, for example, choose to arrange to put in a solid morning's work and then hit the couch in the afternoon when the urge to nap is at its strongest.

Much ado about doulas

A growing number of couples are choosing to use the services of doulas—women who specialize in providing support and care to laboring and postpartum women.

A doula's services—which typically run between $250 and $550—usually include

- holding one or more meetings with you and your partner to talk about your plans for the birth;

- helping you to draft your birth plan;

- making herself available by telephone to address any concerns about the birth;

- providing continuous support during labor (for example, suggesting different positions and breathing techniques that may help ease the pain);

- providing support during the first hours or days postpartum and offering assistance with breast-feeding, if required.

Note: Doulas do not perform clinical tasks such as monitoring blood pressure, conducting fetal heart checks, and so on; nor are they trained to serve as professional birth attendants in either a home or a hospital setting.

A growing number of HMOs are starting to insure their services, and some hospitals provide them, if requested, free of charge.

If you are thinking of hiring a doula, call Doulas of North America (DONA) at 206-324-5440, or the National Association of Postpartum Care Services at 206-672-8011 or 800-45-DOULA.

Just one quick footnote before we move on: Although many partners welcome the presence of a doula at the birth, some partners (particularly men) feel threatened by their presence. If your partner reacts negatively to your interest in hiring a doula, be sure to stress that the doula is there to supplement—not replace—his support. By delegating the coaching role to someone else, your partner frees himself up to provide you with the emotional support you are likely to need as the two of you weather the challenges of labor together.

Writing a birth plan

The key advantage of writing a birth plan is that it encourages you to think about your various birthing options and to discuss them with your caregiver.

Despite what you might have heard from other people, writing a birth plan doesn't have to be a difficult or time-consuming process. You don't need a formal document—just a simple letter from you to your caregiver that spells out your hopes and dreams for the birth of your baby. (See Appendix D for a sample birth plan.)

Depending on what is important to you and your partner, you may wish to include in your birth plan a discussion of such issues as

- where you would like to give birth (in a hospital, in a birthing center, or at home);

- your feelings about the use of medications during labor;

- whom you would like to have present at the birth, and what each person's role will be;

- what clothing you would like to wear while you're in labor (your own street clothes versus a hospital nightie);

- the atmosphere you would like to have while you are in labor (for example, dim lights and quiet music);

- where you would like to labor (for example, in the Jacuzzi or the shower) and in what positions (sitting, standing, squatting, or leaning against your partner);

- under what circumstances, if any, you would agree to such procedures as episiotomies, inductions, and internal examinations;

- whether you are willing to permit medical students or residents to be present during the birth;

- what birthing equipment you would like to use (for example, a birthing stool, a birthing bed, a beanbag chair, a squatting bar, or a birthing tub);

- whether you would like the newborn examination to be performed in your presence to avoid separation from your baby.

It's important to keep reminding yourself that your birth plan is not a blueprint for labor. Neither you nor your caregiver can predict in advance whether it will be possible to follow your birth plan to the letter. That's why it's important to be flexible and to understand that you and your caregiver may have to scrap the birth plan entirely if a medical emergency arises.

"Our birth plan was very simple," says Jacqueline, 34, who recently gave birth to her second child. "Deliver a healthy baby from a healthy mom. It didn't matter to us how we got there."

Don't assume that you don't need a birth plan if you've given birth before. That's a lesson that Anne, 39, a third-time mother, learned the hard way. "I wish we had written a birth plan. The nurses were about to change shift at the hospital and took sort of a kamikaze approach to the birth—fast and furious. In retrospect, I wish we had more control and had taken a bit more time with the birth. They were so anxious to get the baby out. If we had a birth plan, my partner (a first-time father) would have felt more confident stepping in and taking charge."

Likewise, don't assume that you don't need a birth plan if you're having a planned cesarean. If you feel strongly about how you would like the birth to be handled, spell it out in black and white. Here's what Heidi, a 27-year-old mother of three, had to say about her and her partner's decision to write a birth plan for their planned c-section: "I never thought you could have a birth plan with a planned c-section, but my midwife set me straight. It was wonderful having things written down: that is, the fact that I wanted my husband to be in the operating room when they gave me the spinal. I did not have to fight with anyone about what I wanted because it was all there in writing."

Once you've finished writing your birth plan, review it with your caregiver and then make several copies. Keep one at work and one at home, and give two copies to your caregiver. (Your caregiver should keep one copy with your prenatal records and forward the second copy to the hospital or birthing center where you plan to deliver.)

You probably won't need to use your birth plan for at least another few months, but it's one less thing for you to think about as you enter those exciting but exhausting final weeks of pregnancy.

Just the facts

- Although you'll likely lose a few of the more distressing symptoms of the first trimester (for example, nausea and extreme fatigue), your constipation and other symptoms may be joined by a few new complaints, such as round ligament pain, heartburn, and edema.

Unofficially...
Parents who give birth at South Nassau Communities Hospital in Oceanside, New York, can celebrate baby's safe arrival by dining on chateaubriand and drinking fine wine at the hospital's aptly named in-house restaurant, The Stork Club.

- Most women find the second trimester to be a joyous time—the most enjoyable period in their pregnancies.

- Your baby continues to grow at a phenomenal rate during the second trimester. By the end of the trimester, he will weigh approximately two pounds and be approximately 11 inches long.

- Depending on your caregiver's policies and your own individual risk factors, your caregiver may choose to screen you for gestational diabetes, anemia, or preterm labor. You will also be offered the AFP (triple screen) test and possibly a screening ultrasound.

- When you're planning your maternity plan, be sure to develop both Plan A (what you will do if you deliver on your due date) and Plan B (what you will do if baby comes early).

- Doulas are an excellent source of labor support. Their services typically cost between $250 and $550—a fee that may or may not be covered by your HMO.

- It's important to keep in mind that your birth plan is a wish list—not a blueprint—for labor. There's no way to predict how a particular labor will go.

GET THE SCOOP ON...
How you may be feeling ▪ The emotional chal-
lenges of the third trimester ▪
How your baby is growing ▪ The group B
strep test ▪ Choosing your baby's doctor ▪
Breastfeeding versus bottle-feeding ▪
The circumcision decision ▪ Going past
your due date

The Good, the Bad, and the Ugly: The Third Trimester

Chapter 16

B y the time you reach the third trimester, the novelty of being pregnant is starting to wear off. You're sick of wearing the same three mix-and-match maternity outfits, and you wish that friends and strangers alike would keep their comments on your size and shape to themselves. The only good thing to be said about the third trimester is that by the time you've lived through it, you're more than ready to give birth. Even if you've been dreading labor up until now, you may suddenly find that you're eager to get the whole show on the road. After all, the pain of giving birth is a small price to pay if it means that you don't have to be pregnant any longer.

If, on the other hand, you aren't troubled by many of the infamous third-trimester aches and pains, you may still be enjoying pregnancy as much as you did during the second trimester. You may love feeling your baby's movements and spend a lot of time looking forward to the day when you finally get to meet him or her.

As you've probably gathered, this chapter focuses on the highs and lows of the third trimester. We talk about the physical and emotional challenges, tell you what you need to know about your baby's position prior to labor, and give you the facts on group B strep—an important but admittedly scary topic. We then pass along some pointers on choosing your baby's pediatrician, deciding whether to breastfeed or bottle-feed, and making the circumcision decision. We then wrap up the chapter by giving you some pointers on staying sane if your due date comes and goes and you're still pregnant.

The complaint department

By the start of the third trimester, your uterus is large and hard, your baby's movements are visible, and you may be experiencing Braxton-Hicks contractions (the so-called practice contractions that prepare your body for labor). You may continue to experience some of the aches and pains that you experienced during the first and second trimesters, but you will likely experience a few other complaints as well. Here are some of the most common third-trimester aches and pains.

Shortness of breath

Like the majority of other third-trimester complaints, the breathlessness you may be experiencing is caused by your growing uterus. During the third trimester, the diaphragm—the broad, flat muscle that lies underneath your lungs—is pushed out of its place by a good 1½ inches, decreasing your lung capacity. You'd be feeling even more breathless if it

> **"**
> My husband had to endure our air-conditioning going full blast all the time during heat waves. We even had to install ceiling fans in the hallway and our bedroom because I was just too hot.
> —Jacqueline, 34, mother of two
> **"**

weren't for the fact that the high levels of progesterone in your body trigger the respiratory center in
your brain, causing you to breathe more deeply.
This helps to ensure that your baby receives plenty
of oxygen, despite your diminished lung capacity.

Although there's no cure for breathlessness
other than giving birth, you can do a few things to
minimize your discomfort. To reduce the feeling of
breathlessness, you should make a habit of sitting
and standing with your back straight and your
shoulders back. To ensure that you can breathe
comfortably when you are lying down, either prop
yourself up with a pile of pillows or lie on your side
so that some of the pressure will be taken off your
diaphragm.

Sciatica

Sciatica is the name given to pain, tingling, or
numbness that runs down the buttock, hip, and
thigh. It is typically caused by the pressure of the
pregnant uterus on the sciatic nerve. (Just a quick
refresher course in biology: you have two sciatic
nerves, which run from your lower back down your
legs to your feet.)

Sciatic pain can be excruciatingly painful—even
immobilizing. As painful as it may be to move
around, it's important to get up and walk around at
least every half hour during the day or the sciatica
will worsen. Some pregnant women report that
floating in a swimming pool provides tremendous
relief because it helps take the weight of the uterus
off the sciatic nerve.

Note: Applying hot or cold compresses or rub-in
lotions to the affected area can help manage the
pain, but check with your caregiver first.

Unofficially...
Prior to preg-
nancy, your
uterus weighed
two ounces and
was capable of
holding half an
ounce of liquid.
By the time you
deliver, it will
weigh over two
pounds and hold
a quart of amni-
otic fluid.

Sleeping problems

Just when you'd do just about anything for a good night's sleep, the sandman is strangely elusive. Mechanics have a lot to do with your sleeping problems, of course, because it isn't easy to get comfortable when you've got a uterus the size of a watermelon. Then there are the metabolic changes that can have you burning up in bed when your partner is huddled under a down comforter. Those midnight treks to the washroom don't help either, nor does your growing preoccupation with what lies ahead—labor, delivery, and life after baby.

Here are some tips on coping with sleeping problems:

- Surround yourself with pillows. The more the merrier. (Your partner might not agree, but this is one time in your life when you get to pull rank. The pregnant woman's comfort comes first.) You can either load up on everyday pillows or purchase one of those oversized body pillows that are specially designed for sleeping during pregnancy. (You'll probably be able to find one at your local home-health-care products store or maternity boutique.)

- Sleep on your side with your legs and knees bent. Tuck one pillow under your abdomen and put another pillow between your knees. If you're experiencing a lot of achiness in your hip, tuck a pillow underneath the side you're sleeping on to take some of the pressure off your hip.

- Don't exercise too close to your bedtime. Although exercise will ultimately help you get a better night's sleep, a late-evening walk may actually keep you awake.

- Don't eat a heavy meal within two to three hours of going to bed. Your metabolism will go into overdrive, something that can keep you awake.

- Pass on the midnight snack if heartburn and indigestion are causing you grief. Otherwise, you could be up a good part of the night dealing with these particular discomforts. See Chapter 15 for some additional tips.

- Stretch your calves before you go to bed if leg cramps are waking you up in the middle of the night. (See Chapter 15 for additional information about this troublesome pregnancy complaint.)

- Make yourself a batch of bedtime tea by mixing together a pinch each of lavender, lemon balm, linden, and chamomile leaves. If it tastes like something out of your flower garden, cut back on the lavender.

- Drink a cup of warm milk. If it tastes too bland on its own, add a small amount of cinnamon and honey or sugar.

- Have a warm bath.

- Practice relaxation breathing in bed. Not only is it a great opportunity to do your homework from your childbirth class, but it also may help put you to sleep.

- Get up and do something rather than tossing and turning in bed. Then, hit the sack again once you start feeling sleepy.

Itchy abdomen

As your skin stretches to accommodate your growing uterus, it can become dry and itchy. Although

Watch Out!
Severe shortness of breath, chest pain, rapid breathing, or pain when taking a deep breath are not normal third-trimester complaints. If you experience any of these symptoms, call your caregiver or head for the emergency room immediately.

it's difficult to eliminate this particular pregnancy complaint until after the birth, a good-quality moisturizing cream can provide a certain degree of comfort.

Varicose veins

Varicose veins are the fine bluish, reddish, or purplish lines that show up under the skin (most often on the legs, ankles, and vulva). They are caused by a weakness in the small veins that carry blood back to the heart.

You are more likely to develop varicose veins if

- you have gained a lot of weight during your pregnancy,
- you have a family history of varicose veins,
- this is your second or subsequent pregnancy. (*Note:* varicose veins tend to become worse with each pregnancy.)

Varicose veins tend to be a particular problem during pregnancy because the weight of the growing uterus places pressure on the veins passing through the pelvic region and the legs. This, combined with the fact that progesterone causes the walls of the blood vessels to relax, spells trouble for any pregnant woman with a predisposition to varicose veins.

You can prevent or ease the discomfort of varicose veins by

- not standing for prolonged periods of time;
- not sitting with your legs crossed;
- elevating your legs whenever you can;
- avoiding underwear with tight elastic around the legs or abdomen, because this may interfere with blood flow and contribute to varicose veins;

Watch Out! Most of the time, varicose veins are harmless, but in a very small number of cases, they can cause blood clots that can cause potentially serious medical complications, though this is much more of a problem when the deeper veins of the leg are involved. If you have a tender, reddened area on the surface of a varicose vein that is accompanied by fever or leg pain, call your caregiver for advice. If you experience shortness of breath or a rapid heartbeat, contact your caregiver immediately or head for the emergency room.

- exercising regularly to improve your overall circulation;

- wearing support stockings to help to improve the circulation in your legs. (Support stockings are designed to be tight at the ankle. They prevent the blood from pooling in your ankles and lower calves and lend support to the veins in these areas.)

In most cases, varicose veins improve after delivery when the uterus returns to its normal size, the progesterone level is no longer high, and the weight you've been carrying is reduced. If they don't improve to your satisfaction, minor surgery will correct them.

Vascular spiders

Vascular spiders—also known as spider veins—are tiny red raised lines that branch out from a particular spot on the skin in a spider-like fashion. Appearing most often on the upper body, face, and neck, they are caused by the effects of hormones on the circulatory system. They don't cause any pain or discomfort, and they usually disappear after delivery.

Stretch marks

Stretch marks are reddish streaks caused by the stretching of skin. Many pregnant women get them on their breasts and abdomen. Because stretch marks develop deep within the connective tissue, they can't be prevented by any lotions or creams.

Although stretch marks tend to fade from reddish to silver after the delivery, if you're not happy with the way they look, you can have them removed with a pulse-dye laser treatment that burns off the top layers of scarred skin with minimal pain and no bleeding.

> **"**
> The worst ache I've been dealing with—besides my back, of course!—is my pubic bone. My doctors say it is normal and it has to do with both my weight and the stretching of ligaments, but it was scary at first. None of the books I read mentioned this ache, and I thought something was wrong.
> —Barbara, 26, pregnant with her first child
> **"**

Increased frequency of urination

Remember all those jaunts you made to the bathroom when you first found out you were pregnant? Well, as Yogi Berra said, it's déjà vu all over again. Back in the first trimester, it was pregnancy hormones that had you urinating so frequently. This time, it's the position of your baby's head that's to blame. To put it simply, your baby's head and your bladder are having a turf war, and your bladder is losing.

In addition to increased frequency of urination, you may experience increased urgency (that is, you have to go now!) or stress incontinence (a lack of bladder control that can happen if the baby gives the bladder a powerful kick, or if you cough, sneeze, laugh, or strain).

You can minimize problems with stress incontinence by

- emptying your bladder more frequently,

- practicing your Kegel (pelvic floor) exercises,

- wearing a panty liner to keep yourself dry.

Stress incontinence occasionally continues after the delivery. If this happens, it can usually be corrected through postnatal exercise—especially by working those muscles that control the pelvic floor.

Restless legs syndrome

Restless legs syndrome is an aptly named disorder that affects 15% of Americans but that tends to be more common during pregnancy. It consists of unpleasant sensations in the limbs—creeping, crawling, tingling, burning, or aching in the calves, thighs, feet, or upper portions of the legs. RLS occurs when you are resting and is relieved if you get up and walk around.

RLS symptoms tend to be particularly trouble-some at night, so the syndrome is often accompa-nied by insomnia. It is also sometimes associated with nighttime leg twitching —a condition that is formally known as periodic limb movements of sleep.

If you suffer from RLS, you can minimize your symptoms by

- taking a warm bath,

- massaging your legs,

- exercising regularly (but not too late at night),

- avoiding alcohol and caffeine, which tend to make the condition worse.

You may also require some form of pain relief if your RLS symptoms are particularly severe.

Pruritic urticarial papules and plaques of pregnancy (PUPP)

Pruritic urticarial papules and plaques of pregnancy is a condition characterized by itchy, reddish, raised patches on the skin. Occurring in approximately 1 in every 150 pregnancies, the condition tends to run in families and usually occurs in first pregnan-cies. It can be treated with oral medications, anti-itching creams, and oatmeal or baking-soda baths.

Intertrigo

Intertrigo is the name given to a red, irritating skin rash caused by a fungal infection that occurs when folds of skin are in close contact, preventing the normal evaporation of sweat. It is more common in women who are overweight, and it tends to be local-ized to the area under the breasts and the groin area. It is treated with anti-fungal cream

Woman can prevent intertrigo by washing the above areas frequently and powdering them with talcum powder or cornstarch. If significant itching occurs, it can be controlled with either calamine lotion or hydrocortisone ointment, in addition to the anti-fungal cream.

Hemorrhoids

Watch Out!
Consult your doctor before using any over-the-counter treatments for hemorrhoids.

Hemorrhoids—firm, swollen pouches that are formed underneath the mucus membranes both inside and outside of the rectum—are experienced by half of pregnant women. Some suffer from them throughout their pregnancies; others develop them only during the pushing stage of labor.

Hemorrhoids are caused by

- straining to empty the bowel—something that can be caused by either constipation or uncontrolled diarrhea;
- the effects of the high levels of progesterone in your body on the veins in the anal canal;
- the pressure of the baby's head in the pelvis during late pregnancy, which can interfere with the flow of blood to and from the pelvic organs.

You can lessen the likelihood that you will develop hemorrhoids by

- preventing constipation: ensure that your fluid intake is adequate,
- eating plenty of high-fiber foods to keep your stools soft,
- exercising regularly,
- not straining during bowel movements.

If you do develop hemorrhoids, you can ease your pain and itching by

- keeping the area around the anus clean by gently washing it after each bowel movement using either soft, undyed, unscented toilet paper or hygienic witch-hazel pads);

- soaking in a sitz bath (a shallow basin that fits over the toilet);

- soaking in a bathtub containing oatmeal bath formula or baking soda;

- not sitting for long periods of time, particularly on hard surfaces.

Although most hemorrhoids go away on their own, some become filled with blood clots and require minor surgery.

Aching in the perineum

At some point during late pregnancy (possibly not until labor), your baby will descend into the pelvis. This descent (known as engagement or lightening, and often referred to as dropping) can occur a week or two before labor starts in a first pregnancy. In subsequent pregnancies, it doesn't tend to happen until labor actually starts. However, there is significant variation in this phenomenon, and many women don't experience it at all.

As the baby's head moves lower, you will experience increased pressure or even sharp twinges as it presses against the pelvic floor. The only upside is that women who experience lightening find it easier to breathe now that their babies have shifted position.

Braxton Hicks contractions

Braxton Hicks contractions—the so-called practice contractions—are most commonly felt during the third trimester, but some women feel them during the second trimester too. They are mild and irregular contractions that last 20 to 30 seconds, and usually stop after a period of one to two hours.

When you first start having Braxton Hicks contractions, you probably won't even feel

Unofficially...
Braxton Hicks contractions are named after Dr. John Braxton Hicks, the English doctor who first described them back in 1872.

Bright Idea
A lack of adequate fluids can make your uterus more irritable. If you are experiencing a lot of uncomfortable Braxton Hicks contractions, try drinking a couple of glasses of water and lying on your side.

them—unless, of course, you have your hand on your uterus and happen to notice the periodic tightening and hardening. You might also notice them if you are exercising. By the end of your pregnancy, these Braxton Hicks contractions may be becoming quite painful. In fact, they are often mistaken for labor contractions.

Some doctors believe that Braxton Hicks contractions prepare the cervix for the process of effacement and dilation.

It can be difficult to differentiate between Braxton Hicks contractions and the real thing. If you are concerned that you could be experiencing premature labor, contact your caregiver for advice. (See the following table for further information.)

WHEN TO CALL YOUR CAREGIVER

You should call your doctor immediately if you experience any of the following symptoms:

- heavy vaginal bleeding or clotting;
- lighter bleeding that lasts for more than one day;
- any amount of bleeding that is accompanied by pain, fever, chills, or severe abdominal or shoulder pain;
- a severe or persistent headache—particularly one that is accompanied by dizziness, faintness, or visual disturbances;
- dehydration;
- a fever of more than 101°F;
- painful urination;
- a watery discharge from the vagina;
- sudden swelling of the face, hands, or feet.

  - the signs of premature labor: regular uterine contractions (a tightening feeling in your abdomen that you may be able to feel with your fingertips but that won't necessarily be accompanied by any significant pain, lower back pain, a feeling of heaviness in the lower pelvis or abdomen, diarrhea, slight spotting or bleeding or a watery fluid or mucus discharge;

- a significant decrease in fetal movement after the 24th week of pregnancy.

Fetal movement counting

You've no doubt heard a lot of talk about the value of fetal movement counting in assessing fetal well-being. Unfortunately, it isn't quite as simple as some people would have you believe. Here are the three key problems:

- Some pregnant women don't experience fetal movement as consistently as other women (or even as they themselves experience on other occasions), either because the baby's movements aren't consistent or because their perceptions of those movements aren't consistent.

- The quality and strength of fetal movements vary as pregnancy progresses and as the relative ratios of amniotic fluid to baby size change.

- Studies using ultrasound to observe the movements of fetuses have shown that women typically feel fewer than half of these movements despite the fact that they are consciously trying to feel them and the baby is awake and actively moving.

- The third-trimester sleep-wake cycle of the fetus (30 minutes awake and 30 minutes asleep) makes it easy for an expectant mother to miss her baby's active time. If she is working, if she is busy with other children, or if her attention is otherwise diverted during her baby's active period, she may fail to perceive any movement. Likewise, if she does her fetal movement counting when the baby is sleeping, she won't detect any movement.

Fetal Movement Counting Chart

Day of the Week	Start Time	1	2	3	4	5	6	7	8	9	10	Finish
Monday												
Tuesday												
Wednesday												
Thursday												
Friday												
Saturday												
Sunday												

Despite these limitations, fetal movement counting does have a role to play in prenatal care.

If you are concerned that you are not feeling enough fetal movement, you might want to practice fetal movement counting at the start of the day (see the previous figure).

Count fetal movements from the time you wake up in the morning until you have experienced 10 movements. Then, record the time at which the 10th movement is felt each day on the chart. This will help you to determine what pattern is normal for your baby and to notice if there is a significant deviation from that pattern—in which case, you would want to notify your caregiver that there could be a problem.

Even if you don't want to practice fetal movement counting on a daily basis (either because it's a chore or because you're concerned that it might make you worry too much), you can still use fetal movement counting as a tool to detect potential problems. Here's how: If you feel less than two fetal movements within an hour, you should spend the next hour lying on your side or sitting in a recliner with a glass of fruit juice and focusing on your baby's movements. If there are still fewer than two movements in the subsequent hour, then your caregiver should be notified—even though it's highly likely that the baby is fine, just sleepy.

Unofficially...
Studies have shown that girls tend to have longer gestations than boys, and that pregnancies that end in the summer typically last longer than those that end in the winter.

The emotions of the third trimester

By the time the last trimester rolls around, you may be bored of being pregnant and eager to meet your new baby.

Don't be surprised if you find yourself feeling absentminded and preoccupied during the final weeks of pregnancy. You may be spending a lot of time and energy thinking about what lies ahead—when you will go into labor, how the birth will go, whether you will end up with a healthy baby, and how your life will change after the birth.

Here's how Heather, a 32-year-old mother of one, recalls this period of pregnancy: "In the third trimester, the reality set in and I thought, 'Oh my God. What were we thinking? We are about to have a baby. There is no way out. Now what? How do we raise it? How do we keep it safe? What do I do if it gets sick? How do I make sure that I don't smother it with love and protection? What if it hates me? How do I deal with the fact that this child will someday be a teenager? Will it love me or will it spend years in therapy recovering from my stupid mistakes?'"

If you have older children, you may feel guilty because you'd rather rest than play with them, and you may worry about how they will react to the new baby.

"The third trimester with my second child was a big emotional challenge. It was hard dealing with a two-and-a-half-year-old who wanted mommy to play when I just felt too hot and tired to do it. There was a lot of guilt during this trimester," says Lisa, a 27-year-old mother of two.

"During my second pregnancy, I worried how the new baby would affect my firstborn," adds Debbie, a 39-year-old mother of two. "He was still a baby himself."

You may feel distant from your partner at the very time when you need his or her support most. "My husband didn't really understand a lot of what I was going through," says Mary, a 27-year-old mother of one. "From a medical standpoint, he knew a lot about pregnancy, but he couldn't understand how it affected my perspective on life. I had

> **66**
> I am still concerned that I'll be discounted when I return to work because I'm a mother. It wouldn't be the first time in my field either. The life of a lawyer at a big law firm is judged solely by how many hours you work.
> —Kathi, 31, pregnant with her first child
> **99**

new and intense emotions to figure out: fears about myself and the baby to understand, concerns about my changing body and my changing relationship with my husband, changes in the future to deal with."

Many fathers-to-be experience a range of emotions as they consider what lies ahead. Rather than expressing any feelings of anxiety about the well-being of their partner or the baby, many men tend to fixate on more concrete concerns, such as whether they and their partner can really afford to have a baby. Here's how Armin A. Brott and Jennifer Ash, co-authors of *The Expectant Father: Facts, Tips, and Advice for Dads-to-Be,* describe this phenomenon: "American society values men's financial contributions to their families much more than it does their emotional contribution. And expressing strong feelings, anxiety, or even fear is not what men are expected to do when their wives are pregnant. So, as the pregnancy progresses, most expectant fathers fall back on the more traditionally masculine way of expressing their concern for the well-being of their wives and little fetuses: they worry about money."

Don't be surprised if you feel a little crazy as your due date approaches—or, heaven help you, if it comes and goes. We'll talk more about the emotions of the third trimester further on in this chapter when we talk about going overdue.

Your incredible growing baby

Your baby continues to grow and develop during the third trimester. Here are some of the highlights of your baby's development during the third trimester:

Bright Idea
If you have to change caregivers during pregnancy, arrange to have your prenatal records forwarded to the new caregiver prior to your next appointment. Better yet, offer to hand-deliver them to the new caregiver yourself.

ON THE GROW

Week	Developmental Highlights
28	The fetus weighs between $2\frac{1}{2}$ and 3 pounds and is somewhere between 12 and 15 inches long.
29	The head of the fetus is only slightly out of proportion to the body because the body has grown more quickly than the head in recent weeks.
30	The fetus weighs approximately 3 pounds and is about 17 inches long. Nearly all babies react to sounds by this stage of pregnancy.
31	The fetus's lungs and digestive tract are almost mature. From this point onward, the baby will grow more in weight than in length.
32	The fetus now weighs approximately 4 pounds. Although its movements may be less noticeable because of the cramped quarters, you should still be feeling fetal movement on a regular basis.
33	The fetus now weighs approximately $4\frac{1}{2}$ pounds and is approximately 19 inches long. The fetus's skull bones are not yet joined—something that makes it easier for you to give birth.
34	The fetus weighs approximately 5 pounds and is approximately $19\frac{1}{2}$ inches long. Its skin is pink rather than red because of the layers of white fat that are being deposited under the skin. These fat deposits will help your baby regulate her temperature after birth.
35	By this stage of pregnancy, the fetus has usually settled into a head-down position but may change positions again before you actually go into labor.
36	The fetus weighs approximately 6 pounds and is approximately 20 inches long. Its home—the uterus—has now expanded to 1,000 times its original volume. The lungs are busy producing surfactant—the substance that will allow your baby to take his first breath.
37	The fetus now weighs approximately $6\frac{1}{2}$ pounds and is roughly 21 inches long.
38	The fetus continues to gain about 1% of its weight each day during this stage of pregnancy. Males tend to be slightly heavier than females.
39	The fetus's adrenal glands are busy producing cortisone—the hormone that some researchers believe gives the signal for labor to begin. The baby's intestine is filled with a dark green, almost black, substance called meconium—the baby's first stool.

40   Lanugo—the fine layer of hair that covers the fetus's body—has virtually disappeared but may still be visible on shoulders, arms, legs, and sometimes forehead. Vernix—the creamy white paste that protects the baby's skin—is mainly confined to the skin creases of the groin, the elbows, under the armpits, and behind the knees.

Screening for group B strep

Group B streptococcus (GBS) is a type of bacteria that causes particular problems for pregnant women and newborn babies. It is carried by 10% to 30% of pregnant women. It is found most often in the vagina and the rectum.

Here are some important facts on group B strep:

- A pregnant woman with group B strep may either experience no complications at all or develop bladder infections, amnionitis (an infection of the amniotic fluid and membranes), or endometritis (an infection of the uterus that generally occurs postpartum).

- A pregnant woman can pass group B strep on to her baby during pregnancy, during delivery, or after the birth. This happens in approximately 1 to 2 of every 100 babies born to women who are group B strep carriers. A baby may also be infected through contact with other people who are group B strep carriers.

- A baby who is infected with group B strep may end up with blood, lung, brain, and spinal-cord infections. Five percent of babies who are infected with group B strep die.

- The American Academy of Pediatrics recommends that all pregnant women be screened for group B strep bacteria between 35 and 37 weeks

Unofficially...
Think nine months is too long to be pregnant? Elephants are pregnant for 21½ months.

Bright Idea
Find out if the hospital where you intend to give birth rents beepers to expectant couples. A beeper will make it easier for you to get in touch with your partner when you go into labor.

of pregnancy, and that all women who have risk factors prior to being screened for group B strep (for example, women who have preterm labor beginning before 37 completed weeks' gestation) be treated with IV antibiotics during their labors or after their membranes have ruptured until it is determined whether they are group B carriers.

■ According to the Centers for Disease Control, if all pregnant women were screened for group B strep at 35 to 37 weeks' gestation and all women who tested positive were treated with antibiotics during labor, 75% of cases of group B strep that appear during the first week of life could be prevented.

The group B strep test involves taking a culture from the vagina, perineum, and rectum during pregnancy. The results of the culture are available within two days. If your test comes back positive (meaning that you are carrying group B strep), you should strongly consider taking antibiotics during your labor to minimize the risk of passing on group B strep to your baby. Only a very small percentage of babies whose mothers take antibiotics during labor end up being infected with group B strep.

The group B strep test is typically performed at 35 to 37 weeks of pregnancy—although there is some controversy concerning the timing of the test. A woman who tests negative at week 37 (meaning that she doesn't have group B strep) may, in fact, be group B strep positive by the time she goes into labor. This is why some caregivers choose to forgo the screening and decide instead to treat any pregnant woman who has the following risk factors with antibiotics during labor:

- preterm labor (labor before 37 postmenstrual weeks),

- preterm rupture of membranes (membranes rupture before 37 weeks LMP),

- prolonged rupture of membranes (membranes have been ruptured for more than 18 hours before the baby is born),

- having previously given birth to a baby with GBS infection,

- a fever during labor.

Because approximately 310 U.S. babies die each year during the first 90 days of life after being infected with group B strep, scientists are hard at work developing a vaccine to protect unborn babies. The vaccine—which is still years away— would create an immunity in adult women that, during pregnancy, could cross the placenta and protect the baby.

Choosing your baby's caregiver

Although you might feel a little odd interviewing caregivers for your baby before she arrives, this is one task that needs to be handled before the birth. You need to know who will be responsible for performing the newborn examination and healthy-baby checkups during your child's first few weeks of life. Besides, if a medical complication arises that needs immediate attention, you will want to have had the opportunity to begin to establish some rapport with the person who will be caring for your baby.

Here are some tips on choosing a caregiver for your baby:

- Decide whether you would like to have your baby cared for by a doctor with training in

Unofficially...
According to the American College of Obstetricians and Gynecologists, approximately 7,600 infants in the United States are infected with group B strep each year— approximately 2 out of every 1,000 births.

Bright Idea
Ask if the doctor has a separate waiting area for children who have infectious diseases (for example, chickenpox) or who are seriously ill. There's nothing worse than bringing your baby in for a well-baby checkup when the waiting room is full of sick kids.

pediatrics or family medicine or by a pediatric nurse practitioner (an RN who has specialized training in caring for children and who often practices alongside a physician).

- Ask your insurance company or HMO for a list of doctors who are covered by the plan.

- Ask other parents with young children to pass along the names of doctors whom they and their children like.

- Look for a doctor who has been board-certified and who has received at least three years of specialized training in pediatrics or family medicine. (You can get this information from the receptionist at the doctor's office or by calling your state medical society.)

- Set up an initial interview with at least one doctor so that you can find out about her child-rearing and health-care philosophies and decide whether this is the right caregiver for your child.

- Look for a doctor with a waiting room that is clean, bright, pleasant, and safe for crawling babies.

- Note how friendly and helpful the office staff appears to be. It doesn't matter how wonderful the doctor may be if the Receptionist from Hell won't put your call through.

- Find out how difficult it is to get an appointment. If you call first thing in the morning, how likely is it that the doctor will be able to see your child the same day? Does the doctor or one of his associates have any evening or weekend office hours?

- Find out how much time the doctor sets aside for each appointment. If it's less than 15 minutes, you and your child may not get the attention you both need and deserve.

- Find out how quickly the doctor is able to return phone calls both during and after office hours, and who will care for your child when she is not on call. Make sure that you understand whether there is a charge for telephone consultations.

Breast or bottle?

Few decisions are as emotionally charged as whether you should breastfeed or bottle-feed your baby. Some people in your life may try to influence your decision either way—arguing that you'll be too tied down if you breastfeed or implying that your baby will be plagued with allergies and ear infections if you decide to bottle-feed.

It's hard to take the emotion out of this whole debate, but we're going to do our best. Here are some hard facts about the pros and cons of breastfeeding and bottle-feeding.

The pros and cons of breastfeeding

A generation ago, only one-third of American women chose to breastfeed their babies. Today, that figure has nearly doubled. And if the American Academy of Pediatrics (AAP) gets its way, even more women will be breastfeeding their babies during the years ahead. (The AAP recommends that women breastfeed their babies exclusively for at least the first six months of a baby's life, and that they continue to breastfeed throughout the first year—longer if mother and baby are willing.)

That said, breastfeeding isn't for everyone. Here's a quick look at the pros and cons.

Unofficially... Breastfeeding may make babies smarter. One study of a group of premature babies showed that those who were tube-fed breast milk as opposed to formula performed better on intelligence tests when they were seven years of age.

Pros:

- Breastfeeding is good for babies. There are 400 nutrients in breast milk (including hormones and growth factors) that are missing in formula. Clearly, these "secret ingredients" deliver a lot of benefits. Breastfed babies have 5 to 10 times fewer stomach infections; they have 50% fewer ear infections; they are less likely to become diabetic; they are protected from bronchitis, bronchiolitis, and pneumonia; they get fewer diaper rashes; and they are leaner.

- Breastfeeding is good for mothers. Breastfeeding triggers the release of oxytocin, a wonder hormone that helps the uterus to contract to its prepregnancy size and can give you a natural high. (Don't believe us? Watch how many breastfeeding mothers drift off to sleep while nursing their babies.) Because it requires 500 or more calories a day to breastfeed even the youngest of babies, breastfeeding can also help promote weight loss. (Remember: One of the reasons your body packed on some extra pounds during pregnancy was so that it would have some food stores to draw upon during lactation.) What's more some studies have also shown that women who breastfeed for at least three months may be less likely to develop premenopausal breast cancer, ovarian cancer, or osteoporosis.

- Breastfeeding is convenient. There are no bottles to prepare and no nipples to sterilize, and you can feed your baby at 3:00 a.m. without having to fully wake up. What's more, you can feed your baby anywhere, anytime.

- Breastfeeding is inexpensive. In fact, it's practically free. Other than having to consume a few extra calories each day and possibly purchase some breast pads or a breast pump, there's nothing else to buy.

- Breast milk is designed for babies. It contains the right balance of nutrients such as proteins, fats, and carbohydrates. Both the composition and the quantity of breast milk changes as the baby matures. It's the perfect supply-and-demand production system.

- Breastfeeding promotes closeness and intimacy with your baby. This isn't to say that you can't feel close to your baby when you're bottle-feeding. It's just that there's something particularly warm and intimate about having your baby's cheek tucked up against your breast.

Cons:

- Unless you decide to supplement with a bottle, you need to be available for all of your baby's feedings.

- You may not be a good candidate for breastfeeding if you take medications that could be harmful to a breastfeeding baby if transmitted through breast milk.

- If your baby is born with one of several genetic diseases, such as PKU, intestinal lactase deficiency, or galactosemia, he will require a modified diet that may not allow breast-milk intake.

The pros and cons of bottle-feeding

Despite what the more zealous breastfeeding advocates would have you believe, there's nothing inherently evil about bottle-feeding. It's just another way of nourishing your baby.

Bright Idea
Take a breastfeeding class or sit in on a La Leche League meeting before your baby arrives. There's no better way to learn the art of breastfeeding than by picking up tips from experienced breastfeeding moms.

Consider the facts for yourself.

Pros:

- Formula is designed to meet the nutritional needs of growing babies. Although it can't deliver all of the benefits of breast milk (increased immunity to disease, for example), it certainly comes close.

- Bottle-feeding allows other people in your life to share responsibility for feeding the baby.

Cons:

- Your breasts will be tender and sore after the delivery when your milk comes in. A generation ago, you would have been given a shot of estrogen to dry up your milk and minimize your discomfort. Today, most doctors prefer to let nature take its course, encouraging you to rely on ice packs, pain relievers, and a tight-fitting bra to cope with your engorgement.

- Bottle-feeding isn't nearly as convenient as breastfeeding—particularly at 3:00 a.m. Instead of rolling over and plunking a breast in a howling baby's mouth, you have to make your way to the kitchen and warm up his bottle. There's also the business of mixing up formula, sterilizing bottles, and so on.

- Bottles of formula can't be stored as conveniently when you're on the run. You either have to drag along a cooler bag or opt for pricier ready-to-serve cans of formula.

It's not all or nothing

A message that often gets lost in the breastfeeding-versus-bottle-feeding debate is the fact that you can, in fact, do both. If you would like to breastfeed but are unwilling or unable to do so on a full-time basis, you might choose to combine bottle-feeding and breastfeeding. Although there are risks involved in going this route—your baby may decide to go with the bottle exclusively because it's less work!—if you were going to bottle-feed anyway, you've got nothing to lose by giving breastfeeding a shot. Bottom line? Any amount of breast milk is better than none.

You can find some practical tips on combining breastfeeding and bottle-feeding in Chapter 18.

Preparing to breastfeed

Despite what you might have heard, there's no need to toughen up your nipples to prepare them for breastfeeding. (Some books will tell you to rub them with a washcloth daily during pregnancy.) Although there is a certain amount of wear and tear on the nipples during the first few days of breastfeeding, most pain and discomfort can be eliminated through proper positioning, so this is one less thing you need to worry about while you're pregnant.

The only women who need to prepare for breastfeeding are those who are likely to experience nipple problems. If, for example, your nipples are flat or inverted (that is, the nipple is depressed inward), you may need to massage your nipples regularly to encourage the nipple to protrude or consider wearing breast shields (flexible, dome-shaped devices with a small hole in the center that is used to pull retracted nipples outward).

Note: Some women with protruding nipples can experience breastfeeding difficulties if their nipple has a tendency to invert when the baby latches on. You can tell if this is likely to be a problem for you and your baby by trying this simple test. Place your thumb and forefinger above and below the nipple

on the areola—the pigmented skin surrounding the
nipple—and squeeze gently. The nipple should
move outward. If it goes inward, you may need to
wear breast shields or to manually extract the nipple
regularly in order to prepare for breastfeeding.

The circumcision decision

Another hot topic—particularly with fathers-to-be—
is the whole issue of circumcision. This surgical procedure, which involves removing the sheath of tissue
covering the head of the penis, is performed on
approximately 70% of U.S. boys, making it the most
commonly performed surgical procedure on males.
(As a point of comparison, only 48% of Canadian
boys, 24% of those living in the United Kingdom,
and 15% of boys worldwide are circumcised.)

Although the American Academy of Pediatrics
came out strongly against circumcision back in
1975, stating, "There are no valid medical indications for circumcision in the newborn period," it has
since softened its position. This is what it is telling
parents today: "The American Academy of
Pediatrics believes that circumcision has potential
medical benefits and advantages, as well as inherent
disadvantages and risks. Therefore, we recommend
that the decision to circumcise is one best made by
parents in consultation with their pediatrician.
Factors affecting the decision include medical conditions, aesthetics, religion, cultural attitudes, social
pressures, and traditions."

Here are the pros and cons of circumcision from
a medical standpoint.

Pros:

■ Males who are circumcised are only one-tenth as
   likely to experience urinary tract infections as
   their noncircumcised counterparts.

- Circumcised men are less likely to pick up sexually transmitted diseases such as syphilis, genital herpes, genital warts, and AIDS.

- Males who are circumcised as newborns almost never develop cancer of the penis and are unlikely to experience problems with phimosis (the inability to retract the foreskin by approximately five years of age).

- Circumcision prevents paraphimosis—an emergency situation that occurs if the foreskin gets stuck when it is first retracted.

- Circumcision reduces the incidence of balanoposthitis (inflammation of the skin of the penis caused by either trauma or poor hygiene).

- It is easier to practice good hygiene on a circumcised rather than uncircumcised penis.

- Circumcision during the newborn period is far less risky and expensive than circumcision later in life.

Cons:

- Circumcision is painful. Studies have shown that circumcision is a stressful event for the newborn—one that affects the baby's behavior both during and for as long as 24 hours after the procedure.

- Complications—primarily bleeding problems—occur in approximately 1 in 1,000 procedures. In very rare circumstances, severe penile damage does occur. Circumcision is not recommended for a baby who is sick, who is premature, or who has any penile abnormality.

- Circumcision is expensive. It costs the American health-care system an estimated $140 million per year.

- Circumcision may not be necessary. Proper penile hygiene and safe sexual practices can prevent phimosis, paraphimosis, balanoposthitis, penile cancer, sexually transmitted diseases, and many other health problems associated with the uncircumcised penis.

As you can see, there are no easy answers to the circumcision decision. Here are some parting words from pediatrician Dr. Alan Greene of Parent Soup fame: "To me, the risks and benefits of circumcision are very evenly balanced. Don't be misled by anyone who tells you that one option is clearly better than the other. It comes down to a matter of personal preference."

If you do decide to opt for circumcision, be sure to talk to your doctor about what pain relief options are available. He will probably recommend a dorsal nerve block (an injection of anesthetic at the base of the penis that numbs the pain impulses that travel to the brain), a topical anesthetic (a cream or gel that is applied to the foreskin before the procedure to numb the area), or both (a topical anesthetic followed by a dorsal nerve block). *Note:* Topical anesthetics are less effective than dorsal nerve blocks.

Going overdue

You feel as though you've been pregnant forever. You can hardly remember the last time you sipped a glass of wine, slept on your stomach, or ran up a flight of stairs without huffing and puffing. Is it any wonder you're feeling ready to give birth?

The overdue blues

If your due date comes and goes, you could find yourself feeling a little crazy. You may actually start to believe that you're going to be pregnant forever, and find yourself feeling really depressed.

Debbie, 31, a mother of three, found it difficult to cope when her due date for her third baby came and went. "My youngest daughter was two weeks overdue, something that was especially torturous because my other two children were two and three weeks early. I cried everyday, was a real jerk to be around, and tried every old wives' tale to bring on labor. None of them worked. I became depressed, withdrawn, and obsessed with the calendar. I would wake up every morning disappointed again."

Carrie, a 31-year-old first-time mother, experienced similar emotions: "My baby arrived ten days late. What made it really bad was the doctor told me I would probably go in labor early, so I was expecting that and she ended up being ten days late. I tried to stay sane, but it was really hard. I worked all the way up until I had her, and the worst part was walking into work everyday and having everyone say, 'You haven't had that baby yet? When is that baby coming?' I was ready to strangle someone. I felt like making an announcement over the intercom each morning that I was still here and had not had the baby yet."

You may be tempted to try anything and everything to get labor started. Danielle, a 27-year-old mother of three, recalls how impatient she was to get labor underway: "I did aerobics, I jogged up and down my street, I massaged buckets of essential oils into my tummy, and I even did the castor-oil and juice thing—the worst idea in the world. None of these tactics worked. I still had to be induced."

> 66
> One thing nobody talks about is the depression that can come with being overdue.
> —Melissa, 24, mother of two
> 99

Unofficially...
According to obstetrician and author Gordon Bourne, it takes an average of 150 contractions to deliver a first baby, 75 for a second or third child, 50 for a fourth or fifth child, and 30 to 40 for subsequent children.

One first-time mom—32-year-old Heather—took things a step further: "I drove over a bumpy road (my mom drove), I ate a spicy Mexican meal, I drank a glass of red wine (okay, it was actually ruby port because I didn't want to open a whole bottle!), and I spent three hours belly-dancing. This didn't start things right away, but by the middle of the night I was in early labor."

Of course, not everyone finds it stressful to be overdue. Mary, a 27-year-old first-time mother, was happy to see her pregnancy go on a little longer: "My son was due on Labor Day but arrived seven days late. I was glad for each extra day I had to get used to the idea of having a baby."

If, like the majority of pregnant women, you're feeling less than grateful about having your pregnancy drag on, here are some tips on staying sane:

- Keep yourself busy. Jennifer, 27, whose daughter was three weeks late, remembers taking lots of walks and spending hours at the movies while she waited for her daughter to arrive. Jessica, a 32-year-old second-time mom, took up a new hobby: "I learned how to knit and made a few sweaters and a blanket for the baby."

- Meet a friend for lunch. It's easy to go stir-crazy if you're home alone. (*Note:* Don't be afraid to make plans because you might have to cancel them. Going into labor is the ultimate excuse for getting out of anything!)

- Pamper yourself. Enjoy all those special indulgences that you'll find it hard to fit in after your baby arrives. Soak in a bubble bath, spend an afternoon reading magazines, or treat yourself to a new hairdo.

- Let your answering machine screen your calls. Better yet, let it run interference for you. Here's what Jennie, a 30-year-old first-time mother, did: "In response to all the phone messages that said, 'Oh, you're not home. You must be out having your baby,' we finally changed our answering machine message to say, 'We're just out, we're not having our baby.' (Of course, we had to change the message when my water broke and we really were out having our baby!)"

- Realize that your caregiver doesn't have a crystal ball and can't pinpoint the day and hour of your delivery. "The doctors have no idea exactly what day the baby is coming," confirms Jackie, 34. "With my first, I went for my 38-week checkup and was told, 'See you next week,' but ended up seeing my doctor in the delivery room the very next day."

There's overdue, and then there's really overdue . . .
Ten percent of babies don't arrive until at least two weeks past their due date, at which point they're described as being postdate or post-term.

You've probably heard a common pregnancy myth, which states that you're more likely to experience a postdate pregnancy if you're having your first baby. Despite what other pregnancy books may tell you, the studies in the medical literature on this subject are contradictory, at best. You are, however, more likely to experience a longer-than-average pregnancy if you have a history of postdate pregnancies.

Some babies who are classified as post-term are, in fact, right on schedule; it's the due date that's out of whack. These types of due-date miscalculations are more common in women who have irregular

> 66
> To pass the time, we went to lots of movies. When we ran out of movies to see, we rented videos. We actually watched three videos during the early stages of my labor. After the delivery, we had to ask the video store to forgive our late fee!
> —Jennie, 30, mother of one
> 99

menstrual cycles or who were using oral contraceptives prior to the pregnancy. Your caregiver will attempt to verify that the due date is, in fact, accurate by reviewing your prenatal record. She will begin to suspect that it's inaccurate if

- your baby's heart beat wasn't heard as early as usual (10 to 12 weeks with a Doppler device or 18 to 20 weeks with a fetoscope)

- the measurements taken during any ultrasounds (especially those taken before 20 weeks) seem to call your due date into question

Although many babies actually do need to "cook" a little longer, there is cause for concern if a pregnancy continues too long. Postdate babies are at increased risk of becoming too large for a safe delivery or of experiencing fetal postmaturity syndrome (which occurs if the deteriorating placenta is no longer functioning as well as it did earlier in the pregnancy). At 43 weeks, it is five times riskier for a baby to remain inside the womb than to be born. At 44 weeks, this figure rises to seven times.

If your pregnancy goes beyond 42 weeks but your baby appears to be doing well, your caregiver may give you the choice of either waiting it out a little longer or being induced. (Recent studies suggest that routine induction of labor at 41 weeks may result in healthier babies and fewer cesareans.) If you decide to let nature take its course, your caregiver will want to monitor your baby closely to ensure her continued well-being by performing one or more of the following types of tests—although some caregivers advise beginning testing at 41 weeks just in case the due date is off by a week and you're really further along than was thought):

- a nonstress test (NST) (the baby's heart rate is monitored via external monitoring equipment for up to 40 minutes to look for the reassuring accelerations that occur in reaction to fetal movements);

- a biophysical profile (an NST plus a detailed ultrasound that assesses the baby's breathing movements, his body or limb movements, his fetal tone, and the quantity of amniotic fluid);

- a contraction stress test (the baby's response to uterine contractions is monitored, looking for potentially worrisome decelerations in the heart rate).

Based on what the tests reveal, you and your caregiver may decide to continue to play the waiting game or to opt for induction. Either way, you can feel confident that your baby's birthday is fast approaching. Believe it or not, you won't be pregnant forever. Honestly.

Just the facts

- By the time the third trimester rolls around, you may be sick of being pregnant—tired of dealing with all the aches and pains and eager to meet your baby. On the other hand, if you aren't experiencing many of the classic third-trimester pregnancy complaints, you may continue to enjoy your pregnancy right until the very end.

- Your baby gains approximately half a pound a week during much of the third trimester.

- Group B strep is a bacteria that can be harmful—even fatal—to newborn babies. Your caregiver may recommend that you be screened for it during your last few weeks of pregnancy.

Watch Out!
If you notice a significant decrease in fetal movement, contact your caregiver promptly. Although usually a false alarm, it could indicate that your baby is in distress.

- The third trimester is the ideal time to start shopping around for a doctor for your baby.

- If you're planning to breastfeed, you might want to take a breastfeeding class or sit in on a La Leche League meeting before your baby arrives.

- Don't leave the circumcision decision until after your baby is born. Talk things through with your partner now, and get your prospective pediatrician's opinion as well.

- Going past your due date will drive you insane if you let it. Keep yourself busy and let your answering machine field all those dreaded "haven't you had your baby yet?" calls.

What It's Really Like to Give Birth

PART V

GET THE SCOOP ON...
What happens to your body before labor starts ▪
True versus false labor ▪ Pain-relief options during labor ▪ When to leave for the hospital or
birthing center ▪ What to expect during each
stage of labor ▪ Getting to know your new baby

Labor and Delivery

D espite what some childbirth instructors
would have you believe, there's no such
thing as a textbook delivery. Birth experiences are every bit as individual as the babies they
produce.

This may come as a tremendous relief to you if
you've been listening to birth-related horror stories
for the past nine months, or as a bit of a shock if
you've been counting on having the intense but satisfying birth experience like the woman in the labor
video.

The best way to prepare for what lies ahead is to
learn as much as you can about giving birth and to
spend some time anticipating virtually every possible scenario—a long labor and a short labor; a labor
that requires fetal monitoring and one that doesn't;
a pushing stage that warrants an episiotomy and one
that doesn't; a planned vaginal delivery, a planned
cesarean delivery, and an emergency cesarean delivery; and so on. It's important to have at least some
idea of how you would handle the situation if it
became necessary to deviate from your birth plan,
however slightly.

What happens to your body before you go into labor

Just when you think you're going to be pregnant for-ever, some tell-tale signs cue you to the fact that your baby's birth is fast approaching.

You may experience one or all of the following symptoms during the weeks and days leading up to your baby's birth:

- **Lightening ("dropping"):** The term *lightening* refers to a descent into the pelvis that causes the abdomen to protrude at a lower position than before, resulting in a sense of reduced pressure and crowding in the upper abdomen. What most pregnancy books fail to tell you is that it is a very subjective phenomenon and not experienced by all women, first-time mothers or otherwise, to the same degree—or even at all. Once lightening has occurred (be it a few weeks prior to the onset of labor or as labor starts), you will carry your baby differently: your breasts will probably no longer touch the top of your abdomen, and you may find it easier to breathe. On the other hand, because the baby is now being carried in a much lower position than previously, you may experience an increased urge to urinate. *Note:* The term *lightening* is often used interchangeably with the term *engagement*—even though the two terms mean totally different things. Engagement is a mea-surable and detectable event that occurs when the leading bony edge of the fetal head descends into the pelvis and reaches the level of the ischial spines (at which point the baby is said to be at zero station).

- **Increasing pressure in the pelvis and rectum:** You may experience crampiness, groin pain, and persistent lower backache. These symptoms are likely to be more pronounced if this is your second or subsequent birth. One fourth-time mother describes the sensation as being not unlike carrying a bowling ball around in a sling—the sling, of course, being your just-plain-weary levator sling—a collection of muscles that support the pelvic organs.

- **Slight weight loss or reduced weight gain:** Your weight gain may taper off at the end in spite of adequate nutrition and continuing fetal growth. This is because of the complex interaction of a number of factors, including varying rates of water retention.

- **Fluctuating energy levels:** Some pregnant women feel fatigued to the point of exhaustion during the last few weeks of pregnancy. Others get a sudden burst of energy (often referred to as the "nesting instinct") that makes them want to clean out closets, organize the baby's room, and otherwise prepare for baby's arrival. Just a quick word of wisdom from all the mothers who have been there: Even if it kills you, force yourself to rest and relax. You don't want to be feeling burned out and exhausted by the time the first contraction hits.

- **Passage of mucus plug:** Either a few days before or at the onset of labor, the mucus plug—the wad of thick, sticky mucus that seals off the cervix during pregnancy and protects your baby from infection—will become dislodged as your cervix begins to dilate. Despite what other pregnancy books may tell you, the loss of your

Unofficially... In 18th-century Russia, it was customary for the midwife to ask the laboring woman and her husband to list all the people they had slept with. It was believed that if they each told the truth, the labor would be easy; if one of them lied, the labor would be difficult.

mucus plug is not helpful in predicting with any accuracy the onset of labor.

- **Pink or bloody show:** As the cervix effaces and dilates, capillaries on the surface of the cervix may rupture, causing a small amount of bleeding. This is a strong indication that labor is hours—or at most a few days—away for the majority of women.

- **Increasingly painful Braxton Hicks contractions:** The so-called "practice contractions" of pregnancy become stronger and more frequent. Some women find that they are every bit as painful as real labor contractions.

True versus false labor

It's one of those classic nightmare scenarios that run through your mind when you're pregnant: you'll have your doctor or midwife racing across town at 3:00 a.m., convinced that you're about to deliver your baby, when in fact you're not really in labor at all.

Or, even worse, you'll ignore your labor contractions, mistaking them for a particularly persistent bout of Braxton Hicks contractions, and then suddenly deliver your baby while you're standing in the checkout line at the grocery store.

Although a fair number of women find it extremely difficult to differentiate between true and false labor, only a handful actually end up delivering their babies in supermarkets. If your false labor contractions are intense enough that you have to resort to labor breathing to cope with them, you may not be 100% sure that you're experiencing "the real thing" until your doctor of midwife confirms that your cervix has started to dilate.

Unofficially... Only 10% of women experience premature rupture of membranes (PROM)— that is, having your water break before labor has actually started. Therefore, your chances of having your water break in the middle of a restaurant are decidedly slim— unless, of course, you plan to dine out while you're in active labor.

The majority of women are able to tell the difference between true and false labor, however, even though it may take them a while to be sure. Here are some facts that may help you figure out whether the moment of truth has arrived—or whether you're dealing with a most unwelcome false alarm.

Why do they call it false labor?

If false labor kept you from getting a good night's rest last night—and false labor does tend to happen more often at night—you're probably cursing the person responsible for coining the term "false labor." Although there is nothing false about the contractions, which can in fact be extremely painful, false labor is false in the sense that it does not dilate the cervix or result in the birth of a baby.

Still, some practitioners recognize that the term "false labor" can be extremely discouraging to some women, and prefer, instead, to call it "prelabor" in recognition of the fact that these contractions help prepare a woman's body for labor. You may not end up with your baby right away, but your false labor is helping you inch toward that goal.

How is false labor different from true labor?

Just as no two pregnancies are the same, no two labors are the same. No one can tell you any hard-and-fast rules that will allow you to definitely differentiate between true and false labor, but there are some general characteristics that may help you distinguish between the two.

You can be fairly confident that you are experiencing false labor as opposed to true labor if

- your contractions tend to be irregular and are not increasing in either frequency (the interval in minutes from the start of one contraction to the start of the next is decreasing) or severity

> **66**
> During the false labor, I questioned if this was the real thing; during the real labor, there was no doubt in my mind.
> —Nicola, 35, mother of four
> **99**

Watch Out!
Some pregnancy
books may sug-
gest that you
consume an alco-
holic beverage to
see if the con-
tractions you are
experiencing are
real. We don't
agree with this
advice. Not only
is alcohol known
to be harmful to
developing
babies, but it's
not likely to
have any effect
on your contrac-
tions. Back in
the day when
alcohol was used
to stop prema-
ture labor, it was
administered
intravenously
(although in
much larger
doses than what
you would
receive in a
single drink).

(when the contractions are sufficiently severe that you need to use breathing techniques or other methods of relaxation to cope with them). As a rule of thumb, if your contractions are becoming difficult to cope with and they're coming at four- to five-minute intervals, you're probably in labor;

- the contractions subside altogether if you change position or have two large glasses of any non-alcoholic beverage;

- the pain is centered in your lower abdomen rather than your lower back;

- your show (that is, blood-tinged mucus), if any, is brownish (most likely the result of either an internal examination or intercourse within the previous 48 hours).

On the other hand, you can be fairly confident that you are experiencing true labor as opposed to false labor if

- your contractions tend to be falling into some type of regular pattern, and they are getting longer, stronger, more painful, and more frequent;

- the contractions intensify with activity and are not relieved by either a change of position or two large non-alcoholic drinks;

- the pain begins in your lower back and spreads to your lower abdomen and may also radiate to the legs. It may feel like a gastrointestinal upset, and may be accompanied by diarrhea;

- show is present and either pinkish or blood-streaked;

- your membranes have ruptured.

Although these characteristics may hold true for the majority of women, some women experience false labor that is virtually indistinguishable from true labor. Likewise, some women have true labors in which the contractions fail to fall into any recognizable pattern, and that may initially seem to be a bout of false labor.

If you fall into this category, the only way you'll know for sure if you're actually in labor is to have your practitioner conduct an internal exam.

Are some women more likely to experience false labor?

Although women who are expecting their first child tend to spend a great deal of time worrying about false labor, those who tend to be most likely to experience it are women who are expecting second or subsequent babies. This is because a uterus that has previously been through labor is more easily stimulated to contract during subsequent pregnancies.

What if I rush to the hospital, only to find out that it's false labor?

First of all, try not to be too discouraged. You aren't the first pregnant woman to make this mistake, and you certainly won't be the last. Besides, it's far wiser to check things out with your caregiver than it is to give birth in the car just because you wanted to wait "a little longer" to make sure that the labor pains you were experiencing were, in fact, "the real thing."

To try to avoid false alarms, call your practitioner before you head for the hospital. Be prepared to describe the length of the contractions and their frequency, and to comment on any other significant occurrences (for example, Have your membranes ruptured? Did you have any bloody

Bright Idea
Make sure that you know where you're supposed to park your car and what entrance you're supposed to use at the hospital or birth center. You don't want to be trying to figure this out when your contractions are two minutes apart.

show?). Try not to minimize your discomfort or hide how you're feeling as you talk through a contraction. Your doctor or midwife will be trying to assess whether you are in active labor. If he or she isn't sure either, you may be asked to come in for an examination. (For additional information on when to call your caregiver, see the following table.)

Timesaver
Tape to your phone a list of the names and phone numbers of people who have volunteered to care for your older children while you're in labor. That way, you can find someone quickly when the contractions start coming.

TABLE 17.1: WHEN TO CALL YOUR CAREGIVER

You should call your caregiver if

- your contractions are strong and regular (5 minutes apart for most women, but 6 to 10 minutes if you have a history of rapid labors, you have a long trip into the hospital or birth center, or your doctor or midwife has indicated that she would like to have you evaluated earlier than usual during your labor, perhaps to rule out the possibility that you are having an active herpes outbreak, or when a cesarean is planned);

- your past experience with labor tells you that this is the real thing, and your gut instinct says that it's time to call your caregiver;

- your membranes have ruptured or you suspect that they may have ruptured.

Note: **You should call your caregiver immediately if**

- you experience a lot of bleeding (something that can indicate premature separation of the placenta or placenta previa, both of which require special care);

- you notice thick, green fluid coming from your vagina (an indication that your baby has passed meconium into the amniotic fluid and may be in distress);

- you see a loop of umbilical cord showing at your vaginal opening, or you think you feel something inside your vagina (an indication that the umbilical cord may have prolapsed, blocking the flow of oxygen to your baby). While you are waiting for the ambulance to arrive, lie with your head and chest on the floor and your bottom in the air. This will help prevent the weight of your baby from interrupting the flood of oxygen through the umbilical cord. (Fortunately, this type of obstetrical emergency is rare.)

Now let's consider a few issues you need to think about before you find yourself in the heat of labor: namely, pain relief, episiotomy, fetal monitoring, and the presence of other people at the birth.

Pain relief during labor

During labor, you can expect to experience a combination of sensations: a tightening of the uterus that feels as if someone has put a blood pressure cuff around your abdomen and pumped it up it too tightly, a pulling sensation as your cervix stretches open, and a stretching sensation as your baby's head makes its way through your vagina and perineum.

Some women find the pain of labor to be bearable; others do not. If you are finding labor difficult to cope with, you are perfectly justified in requesting pain relief. Here's what the American College of Obstetricians and Gynecologists has to say about this issue: "The pain of labor varies and can be severe for many women. . . . Maternal request is sufficient justification for pain relief during labor. The full range of pain relief should be available and should not be denied because of an absence of other 'medical indications.'"

That said, it's important to understand the pros and cons of using pharmacological pain relief during labor. Table 17.2 briefly summarizes your various options:

Watch Out!
Keep the vaginal area as clean as possible once your membranes have ruptured. Don't take a bath, have sexual intercourse, use a tampon to absorb the flow of amniotic fluid, or attempt to conduct an internal exam on yourself to assess your progress.

TABLE 17.2: PAIN RELIEF DURING LABOR AND DELIVERY

Type of Pain Relief	How It Works	Risks to You or Your Baby	Other Considerations
Demerol and other narcotics and narcotic-like medications, such as Nubain and Stadol	Administered intravenously or via injection into a muscle. Effective within 15 minutes and lasts for two to four hours.	Can cause drowsiness, nausea, vomiting, respiratory depression, and maternal hypotension (low blood pressure). Will be present in the newborn if injected within 5 hours of delivery and can result in breathing difficulties.	The small doses that are typically given to laboring women often don't provide sufficient pain relief, particularly during advanced labor.
Inhaled analgesics (for example, nitrous oxide)	A mix of gas and oxygen that is inhaled via a face mask. You administer the gas yourself when needed. Numbs the pain center in the brain.	May cause drowsiness and nausea. Some studies have shown problems with pulmonary aspiration of gastric contents.	Not widely available.
Epidural (lumbar epidural)	An anesthetic and/or narcotic is injected into the space between the sheath surrounding the spinal cord and the bony vertebrae of your spine. An epidural numbs you from the waist down, providing complete relief in 85% of women, partial relief in 12%, and no relief in 3%.	Maternal hypotension (low blood pressure), difficulty in urinating, and severe postpartum headache (in 2% of cases). Not appropriate for women with certain neurological disorders. Can slow labor if given before the cervix is 5 cm dilated. May also diminish ability to push, necessitating forceps	Most widely used form of regional block for pain relief during labor. A continuous low-dose epidural (the so-called "walking epidural") injects enough anesthesia into the back to block the pain sensations but doesn't immobilize your legs (a key disadvantage to a regular epidural). The

	Takes effect within 15 to 20 minutes.	delivery. Baby's heartbeat may also drop when an epidural is being used.	lower dosage decreases the likelihood of side effects.
Spinal	Injected into the spinal fluid in the lower back. Numbs you from the waist to your knees. Takes about four minutes to take effect. You may have to lie flat on your back for several hours after delivery to avoid developing a postspinal headache, though new technology in spinal needles has made this complication rare.	Can cause maternal hypotension (low blood pressure), severe postdelivery headache, temporary impairment of bladder function, nausea, and (in rare cases) convulsions or infections.	Used as anesthetic for cesarean, not for labor. Not recommended for women with severe preeclampsia.
Paracervical block	Local anesthetic is inserted into the tissues around the cervix to numb the pain caused by cervical dilation.	Can slow baby's heartbeat. Should be avoided if caregiver feels that baby's health would be compromised.	Lasts only 45 to 60 minutes. Additional injections can be given if necessary.
Pudendal block	Anesthetic is injected into the nerves of the vaginal area and perineum. Does not reduce uterine discomfort.	Provides rapid pain relief in the perineum for the actual delivery. No ill effects on baby.	Not effective for all women. Can't be used if the baby's head is too far down the birth canal. Sometimes used when an episiotomy is being performed.

continues

Type of Pain Relief	How It Works	Risks to You or Your Baby	Other Considerations
Caudal block	Anesthetic is injected into the spinal area around the sacrum, numbing the vagina and perineum.	Can inhibit labor.	Used when short-term relief is needed (for example, for a forceps delivery or vacuum extraction). A less popular option today than in the past.
Local anesthetic	Anesthetic is injected into the tissues of the perineum in preparation for episiotomy or is given prior to placing sutures after delivery.	No significant risks except rare allergic reactions and inadvertent intravascular injections.	Some believe injection may weaken perineal tissue and increase the likelihood of tearing if episiotomy is not needed.

Nonmedicinal pain relief

There are also a number of nonmedicinal forms of pain relief that may be available to you, including the following:

- **Acupuncture:** Needles are inserted in your limbs or ears to block pain impulses.

- **Hypnosis:** A woman who has been trained in self-hypnosis may be able to use these techniques to relax herself during labor.

- **Transcutaneous electronic nerve stimulation (TENS):** A battery-powered stimulator is connected by wires to electrodes placed on either side of your spine. You can use the accompanying handset to regulate the amount of stimulation your lower back receives to block the transmission of pain impulses to the brain.

- **Laboring in water:** According to childbirth educator Penny Simkin, the relief that women get from laboring in warm water is second only to that provided by an epidural. Laboring in water helps counteract the effects of gravity, something that can make labor less painful. We'll be talking more about the benefits of laboring in water in our section on water birth below.

- **Relaxation and positive visualization:** Women who have been trained in relaxation methods and positive visualization are able to put these techniques to work during labor. Most childbirth classes include this type of training.

- **Other:** The use of music, massage, position change, heat or cold application, counterpressure, reassuring touch from a caring support person, and adequate hydration can also provide relief.

Unofficially...
According to a recent article in *U.S. News and World Report*, 80% of women in the United States receive some form of medication during childbirth. What's more, 33% use epidurals—nearly twice as many as 15 years ago.

Making up your mind

As you no doubt realize, the issue of pain relief during labor continues to be a hot topic. Some women are clamoring for medication by the time the first heavy-duty contraction hits; others are determined to do everything they can to avoid it.

"I knew before I had the baby that I was going to get an epidural," says Carrie, a 31-year-old mother of one. "I received it about two hours into labor. It was the best thing I ever did. It allowed me to rest. I will definitely have an epidural again."

"I had planned a labor with no drugs or interventions, but never imagined that labor would be so excruciatingly painful," confesses Susan, a 33-year-old first-time mother. "Labor started at 7:00 a.m. and I ended up having the first epidural at about 4:00 p.m. or so. It didn't numb me as it was supposed to, so I ended up having a second one at 11:00 p.m. I would make the same choice again because I was practically hallucinating from the pain by the time I got it—not to mention all of the throwing up I had done! They let the epidural wear off in time to push, and I would do that again too. I think it helped me have the motivation to push and to better feel when to push."

Although it helps to think through the issue of pain relief during labor in the weeks and months before the birth, it's important to keep an open mind about this issue. After making your caregiver promise that you will be able to have an epidural as early on in your labor as possible, you may decide that the contractions are far more bearable than you had anticipated, and that you don't really need one after all. Similarly, you may be opposed to any kind of medication during labor—until your labor drags on for more than 24 hours and exhaustion begins to set in.

What's important about the whole issue of pain relief is not whether you use any form of medication. It's whether you feel comfortable with those choices. It doesn't matter if your childbirth educator thinks you were crazy because you chose to have an epidural or if your mother thinks you were crazy because you didn't; what matters is how you feel about those choices.

Fetal monitoring

Fetal monitors are used to monitor the baby's response to contractions. Although some hospitals and caregivers monitor all patients routinely, you are more likely to be monitored if your pregnancy is high risk, if your amniotic fluid was stained with meconium, if you're having an especially difficult labor, or if your labor is being induced.

Fetal monitors record both the baby's heartbeat and the mother's contractions. Each of these functions can be monitored either "internally" or "externally." In other words, it's possible to obtain these two measurements by using an internal monitor, an external monitor, or one of each. An external fetal monitor consists of devices worn on elastic belts fastened around your abdomen or held on by elasticized panties, an ultrasound transducer designed to pick up your baby's heartbeat, and a pressure-sensitive gauge designed to monitor your contractions (though it is not reliable for assessing their strength). With both internal and external monitoring, the reading is displayed or printed out, and your baby may be monitored either continuously or intermittently, depending on your situations. If your hospital has a portable fetal monitor, you will be

> **66**
> About a week before my son was born, a peace and calm came over me, and I actually looked forward to experiencing the power and beauty of giving birth. Perhaps that was my hormones kicking in, in preparation for the coming birth. And I did have a wonderful birth experience—one where I was in control and not panicky or upset.
> —Tracy, 31, mother of one
> **99**

able to remain active during your labor; if it doesn't, you may find that you are confined to the area where your monitor is plugged into the wall while you are being monitored—but you may not necessarily be confined to bed.

An internal fetal monitor consists of devices inserted through the vagina to monitor the baby's heartbeat and the mother's contractions. The electrical impulses of your baby's heartbeats are detected by an electrode attached to your baby's scalp via the cervix. It is used when a particularly accurate reading is required. The actual pressure generated by your uterine contractions can be measured with a pressure transducer attached to the end of a fine catheter inserted through the vagina and cervix into the inside of the uterus alongside the baby. It is sometimes necessary to know the exact strength of the contractions when the caregiver is concerned about a lack of progress during the labor or needs to make decisions about stimulating the contractions with medications. Though insertion of these devices can be temporarily uncomfortable or even painful, once they are placed you will not be aware of their presence. In order for an internal fetal monitor to be put into place, your membranes will have to be ruptured (if they haven't ruptured by this point), and your cervix will need to be at least one to two centimeters dilated. There is a small risk of infection associated with the use of an internal fetal monitor. On rare occasions, use of the scalp electrode may cause your baby to develop a rash, an abscess, or a permanent bald spot.

If you're being monitored and an alarm goes off, try not to panic. False alarms are common with fetal monitors and more often than not simply indicate an interruption in the heartbeat signal being detected by the device due to a loose connection or the fact that you're in a certain position. If, on the other hand, a true abnormal reading is obtained, you will probably be asked to change positions and/or you will be given IV fluids and oxygen.

If you change position and the reading continues to provide cause for concern, your caregiver may decide to test your amniotic fluid for the presence of meconium (a possible sign of fetal distress) by breaking your water (if your membranes are still intact), assess fetal responsiveness to sound and pressure, and take a fetal blood sample from the scalp to measure your baby's pH levels (which assesses the oxygen and carbon-dioxide content in the baby's blood). If these measures fail to produce reassuring results, you may require an emergency cesarean section, though cesareans for fetal distress are not very common.

Episiotomy

An episiotomy is a surgical incision made in the perineum to enlarge the vaginal opening before the birth of the baby's head. It is generally needed in cases of fetal distress, shoulder dystocia (that is, when the shoulders are stuck), a vaginal breech delivery, an especially fragile baby being delivered, and a forceps delivery. It is also done as a preventive measure by many caregivers if it appears that without one a potentially serious laceration may occur. Most caregivers agree that it should be used when warranted, but not routinely.

Two types of cuts are made when an episiotomy is performed:

- **Medio-lateral:** This is an episiotomy that slants away from the rectum.

Unofficially...
The episiotomy was invented in Ireland in 1742 as a means of assisting with difficult births. It was not, however, widely performed until the mid–20th century. Today, 80% to 90% of first-time mothers and 50% of women having subsequent births can expect to have an episiotomy.

▪ **Median:** A median cut is made directly back toward the rectum.

There are both pros and cons to each type of incision. You might want to ask your caregiver which type he performs and why.

Your episiotomy will be performed under local anesthetic injected into the perineum at the height of a contraction (when pressure from the baby's head is numbing the area). The incision is also timed to take advantage of this natural pain relief.

An episiotomy can occasionally lead to a lot of postpartum discomfort and possible complications such as rectal problems, so it's in your best interests to avoid one, if at all possible. You can reduce chances of tearing or needing an episiotomy if you listen to your caregiver's instructions during this time because she will tell you to stop pushing when the head is almost born so that the final delivery of the head can be gently guided rather than explosive. Your caregiver can then support the perineal tissue and gently ease the baby out.

IVs: what you need to know

Bright Idea
A few weeks before you're due to deliver, test-drive the route to the hospital. Try taking different routes at different times of day so that you'll know what route to take when the big moment arrives.

Some caregivers routinely insert intravenous (IV) needles connected either to continuous IV fluids or to heparin locks into all laboring women. The heparin lock (a device that keeps the blood in the needle from clotting while fluids are not flowing) allows for instant intravenous access yet does not limit a laboring woman's mobility by tying her to an IV pole and a bag when continuous IV fluids are not needed.

Other caregivers prefer to reserve IVs for only those women who have a known increased risk of postpartum hemorrhage, fetal distress, or cesarean section, or who have a particular need for intravenous medications during labor.

Because caregiver and institutional policies about the use of IVs vary considerably, you may want to broach this subject with your caregiver at the same time you're discussing such other interventions as fetal monitoring and episiotomies.

Once you and your caregiver have come to an agreement about the use of IVs during your labor, be sure to note your preferences in your birth plan.

The pros and cons of inviting other people to the labor

Another issue you'll need to consider before you go into labor is whether you would like to have anyone other than your partner present at the delivery.

As we mentioned earlier, some parents-to-be choose to hire doulas to provide professional labor support. Others invite family members or friends to witness the birth.

"I think that having a couple of people with you is a good idea so that your partner can have a break and you don't have to be alone," explains Danielle, 27, a three-time mother.

Not everyone feels this way, however. Some couples feel quite strongly that they want to be alone. "We didn't invite anyone to either labor or delivery," explains Suzi, a 27-year-old mother of two. "We felt it was a private thing and wanted to use the moment to be close to one another and experience the miracle together. I'm glad we did. It was the most romantic experience of our lives to bring our children into this world together."

Some couples who wouldn't dream of having strangers present at the birth of their baby feel quite strongly that their baby's siblings should be present.

If you decide to have children present at the birth, you should

- have a frank discussion with your caregiver about the extent to which you would like your children to be involved in the delivery;

- make sure that your children want to be there and mentally prepare them for what they are likely to witness;

- give some thought to whether your child is old enough to handle the situation (that is, will he understand why he can't have a cuddle from mommy during the peak of a contraction?);

- bring along an extra support person for each child—someone who can take them outside for a walk if they need a break;

- talk to other families who've had their older children present at their baby's birth and see if they have any words of wisdom to share.

When to head for the hospital or birthing center

If you're planning to give birth somewhere other than at home, make sure that you and your caregiver are in agreement about when you want to head for the hospital or birthing center.

As with anything else in life, timing is everything. You don't want to arrive at the hospital or birthing center too soon, or you will find yourself pacing the hall for hours. (Even worse, your labor could grind to an absolute halt—something that's more likely to occur if you make the move while you're still in early labor.) On the other hand, you don't want to leave things too long and risk having your picture on the front page of your local newspaper under a headline that reads: "Woman gives birth on freeway."

Unofficially...
Among certain tribes in Guatemala, it is customary for the midwife, both grandmothers, the husband, and sometimes the father-in-law to attend the birth.

Although there's an art to timing your departure, most women instinctively know when it's time to toss their labor bag in the car and go. As a rule of thumb, you should wait until you're in active labor (when your contractions are intense but not unbearable) but not until you're in transition. Your caregiver can help you to assess how far your labor has progressed and when it's time to leave home.

Here's a quick rule of thumb: If this is your first baby, you should plan to head to the hospital when your contractions are four minutes apart, lasting one minute, and occurring consistently for one hour or more; if they are so painful that you cannot talk during them or require that you use your relaxation breathing; or if you instinctively feel that it's time to go. If this is your second or subsequent baby, you may wish to head to the hospital a little sooner because your labor is likely to progress more quickly. (Just a brief footnote: One of the authors of this book waited a little too long before heading to the hospital to deliver her third child and ended up going through transition on the bumpiest road in town. Her water broke in the admitting area of the hospital, and her son was born 20 minutes later. Needless to say, she decided not to cut things quite so close the next time around!)

What to bring with you

Even if you're planning a so-called drive-through delivery (that is, you intend to be back home within 24 hours of giving birth), you should pack as if you're staying for a week. Some of these extra garments could come in handy.

> 66
> My contraction, weren't coming at textbook intervals, so it was hard for me to know if it was time to go to the hospital. After listening to me dealing with two contractions while we were talking on the phone, my midwife decided it was time for me to go to the hospital. When I got there, I was already at eight centimeters.
> —Tracy, 31, mother of one
> 99

CHECKLIST: WHAT TO TAKE TO THE HOSPITAL OR BIRTHING CENTER

Your labor kit:

- your health-insurance card and proof of insurance

- sponges that your partner can use to help cool you off in between contractions

- snacks and drinks for your partner

- magazines or books to read (for both you and your partner)

- a picture or other object you can use as your focal point during labor (assuming that you choose to use a focal point)

- a camera or video camera plus spare batteries and spare film (and perhaps even a spare disposable camera in case your usual camera or video camera won't function properly)

- pillows in colored pillowcases (so that they don't get mixed up with the hospital or birth center's pillows)

- a portable stereo and music to listen to during labor

- massage oil or lotion

- a hot water bottle

- lip balm or petroleum jelly

- cornstarch or other nonperfumed powder to reduce friction during massage

- a notebook and pens

- change or a prepaid phone card and a list of phone numbers

- your hospital preregistration forms

- one or more copies of your birth plan

Watch Out!
Test your camera or video camera long before you go into labor. You don't want to miss out on the most exciting photo opportunity of your baby's life.

- a tennis ball or rolling pin

- a frozen freezer pack (small) wrapped in a hand towel

- your partner's or labor support person's bathing suit (so that he can accompany you in the shower and help you work through contractions)

- a change of clothes and a few basic toiletries for your partner (in case labor is particularly prolonged)

Your hospital suitcase:
Clothing

- at least two nightgowns and two nursing bras (front-opening style if you're planning to breastfeed)

- five or more pairs of underwear (ideally ones you don't care about in case your pad soaks through)

- two pairs of warm socks

- a bathrobe

- a pair of slippers

- a going-home outfit for you (something that fit when you were five months pregnant)

- a going-home outfit for the baby (ideally a sleeper or newborn nightie and a cotton cap)

- a receiving blanket

- a bunting bag and heavy blanket if it's cold outside

- a couple of diapers you can use when it's time to take your baby home (in case the hospital uses cloth rather than disposables)

Timesaver
Preregistering at the hospital or birthing center will reduce the amount of paperwork you'll have to fill out when you arrive in active labor. You may even be able to complete the paperwork at your caregiver's office.

Toiletries

- a hairbrush, shampoo, soap, toothbrush, tooth-paste, deodorant, and other personal-care items

- some super-absorbent sanitary pads (unless you know for a fact that the hospital will provide these free of charge)

Etc.

- small gifts for baby's siblings

- books and magazines (including a good breast-feeding book if you intend to breastfeed your baby)

- birth announcements

- earplugs (so that you can get some rest in what is likely to be a noisy maternity ward)

What will happen once you arrive

Once you arrive at the hospital or birthing center, you will be taken to the birthing unit, where you will probably be asked

- when your contractions started

- how far apart they are now

- whether your membranes have ruptured (and, if so, when)

- when you last ate or drank

- whether you have a birth plan

- whether you intend to have an epidural or med-ications during labor

Once you've changed into your hospital nightie (or your own nightgown and housecoat, if that's your preference), the nurse will

- take your vital signs (pulse, respiration, and temperature) and record this information on your chart;

Bright Idea
Bring along a bottle of witch hazel lotion to apply to your stitches or your hemorrhoids. Some women swear by this stuff.

- perform an internal examination to see if your cervix has begun to dilate (unless, of course, your caregiver or an intern or a resident is on hand to perform the exam);

- monitor the frequency and duration of contractions, as well as your baby's heart rate, by using an external fetal monitor (an oversized stethoscope-like contraption that is strapped around your lower abdomen) either for a few minutes at a time or continually throughout your labor.

What to expect during each stage of labor

Now that you've wrestled with the issue of pain relief during labor, figured out what interventions you do and do not want, and decided whom you do and do not wish to have present at the birth, it's time to consider what the experience of labor is actually like.

As you probably know, labor consists of three distinct stages:

- the first stage, which ends when the cervix is fully dilated;

- the second stage, which ends with the birth of the baby;

- the third stage, which ends once the placenta has been delivered.

The three stages of labor typically last for 12 to 14 hours for first-time mothers and 7 hours for women who have previously given birth.

The following figures illustrate what happens from prelabor through to delivery.

66
I didn't find childbirth to be painful. It was, however, overwhelmingly uncomfortable— the most intense physical experience I've ever had in my life. I remember it as powerful and amazing. Immediately after my son slid out of my body, I said to my husband, 'If childbirth is like this for every woman, I don't know why anyone uses drugs.'
—Tracy, 31, mother of one
99

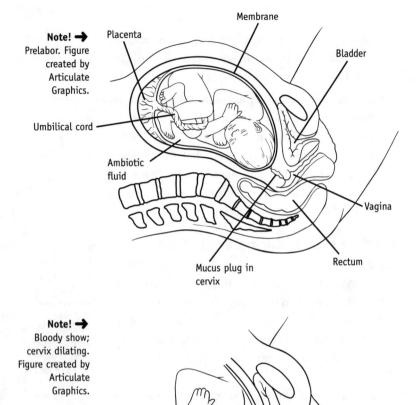

Note! ➡
Prelabor. Figure created by Articulate Graphics.

Placenta

Membrane

Bladder

Umbilical cord

Ambiotic fluid

Vagina

Mucus plug in cervix

Rectum

Note! ➡
Bloody show; cervix dilating. Figure created by Articulate Graphics.

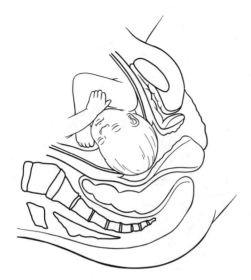

← **Note!**
Membranes
bulging; cervix
effaced. Figure
created by
Articulate
Graphics.

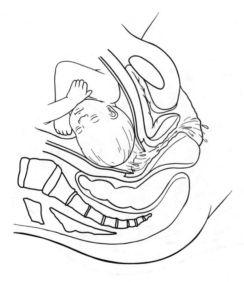

← **Note!**
Membranes
ruptured. Figure
created by
Articulate
Graphics.

Note! ➔
Transition; dilation complete; pushing. Figure created by Articulate Graphics.

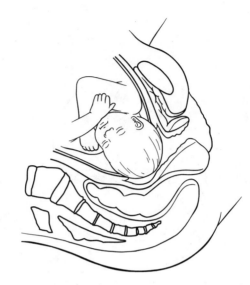

Note! ➔
Crowning. Figure created by Articulate Graphics.

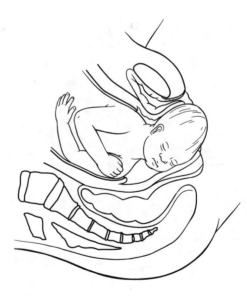

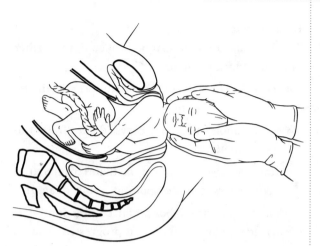

← **Note!**
Delivery. Figure
created by
Articulate
Graphics.

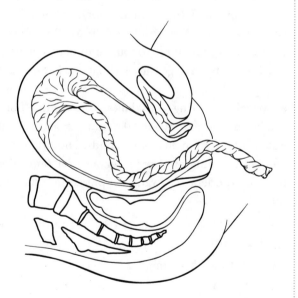

← **Note!**
Afterbirth. Figure
created by
Articulate
Graphics.

The first stage

The first stage of labor can be broken down further into three distinct phases:

- early or latent labor, when your cervix dilates from 0 to 3 centimeters;

- active labor, when your cervix dilates from 4 to 7 centimeters;

- transition, when your cervix dilates from 8 to 10 centimeters (at which point it is fully dilated).

You are in early labor when contractions start occurring regularly and there is progressive dilation and effacement of the cervix. Any contractions you experience prior to that point are classified as false labor or prelabor (prodromal labor). By the end of early labor, your cervix will be 50% to 90% effaced (thinned out) and three to four centimeters dilated.

If you happen to go into early labor while you are asleep, you might not wake up until you are in more active labor. During early labor, your contractions can be anywhere from 5 to 30 minutes apart and will last anywhere from 30 to 45 seconds. They will probably start coming at closer intervals over time. You may be experiencing a range of physical sensations, including

- backache (either constant or just during contractions),

- menstrual-like cramping,

- indigestion,

- diarrhea,

- a feeling of warmth in the abdomen,

- bloody show (the blood-tinged mucus discharge that occurs when your mucus plug becomes dislodged),

- a trickling or gushing sensation if your membranes have ruptured. (They may have ruptured by now, or they may remain intact until you are in more active labor, until your caregiver ruptures them, or even until the baby is being born.

You may be feeling a range of emotions: excitement, relief, anticipation, uncertainty, anxiety, and fear. You may be tempted to phone up all your friends to let them know that you're in labor, or you may want to withdraw into yourself and prepare for the challenges that lie ahead.

During this phase of labor, you should

- eat lightly;

- either continue with your normal activities as long as you want or are able, thereby keeping your mind off the early contractions, or rest up so that you'll have some energy reserves to call upon when it's time to face the rigors of the later stages of labor;

- ask your partner or labor support person to help you pack any last-minute things (assuming that you're going to a hospital or birth center) and to help you time contractions;

- alert your caregiver to the fact that you are in labor.

The next phase of labor is active labor. It lasts 2 to 3½ hours on average, with contractions coming at 3- to 5-minute intervals and lasting from 45 to 60 seconds. By the end of the active phase, your cervix will be approximately 7 centimeters dilated.

During this stage of labor, you may experience

- increased discomfort from contractions (for example, you may no longer feel like talking or

walking through them)

■ pain and aching in your back and legs

■ fatigue

■ increased quantities of bloody show

You may be concerned about what lies ahead, or you may be totally absorbed in what is happening right now. If labor is taking longer than you had hoped it would, you may be starting to feel discouraged.

During the active phase of labor, you should

■ remain upright and active for as long as you can;

■ experiment with positions until you find the one that works best for you when a contraction hits (see the following figure), since changing positions every 30 minutes or so may help the baby descend;

Note! ➡
Laboring position (slow dancing). Figure created by Articulate Graphics.

← **Note!**
Laboring position (dangling squat). Figure created by Articulate Graphics.

← **Note!**
Laboring position (supported squat). Figure created by Articulate Graphics.

Note! ➜
Laboring position (squatting down). Figure created by Articulate Graphics.

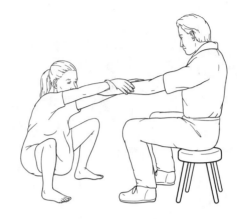

Note! ➜
Laboring position (using a squat bar). Figure created by Articulate Graphics.

Note! ➜
Laboring position (on hands and knees). Figure created by Articulate Graphics.

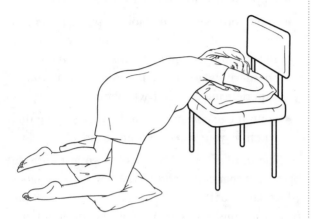

← Note!
Laboring position (leaning on a chair). Figure created by Articulate Graphics.

← Note!
Laboring position (leaning on a table). Figure created by Articulate Graphics.

Unofficially...
Your body releases endorphins—natural pain relievers—during labor. These endorphins are morphine-like substances that block the pain receptors in your brain.

- rest in between contractions;

- empty your bladder at least once an hour;

- allow your partner or labor support person to help you with your labor breathing or any other relaxation techniques and ask her to apply firm counterpressure to your lower back if you're experiencing a lot of back labor;

- continue to consume light fluids (assuming that you have your caregiver's go-ahead).

The third phase of labor is known as transition because it marks the end of the first stage of labor (the dilation of the cervix) and the beginning of the next (the pushing stage). It is the most intense phase of labor, with contractions occurring two to three minutes apart and lasting for 60 to 90 seconds. The only good thing to be said about transition is that it doesn't tend to last very long: 15 minutes to an hour, on average.

During this phase of labor, you may experience

- an increased amount of show as more capillaries in your cervix burst

- pressure in your lower back

- perineal and rectal pressure

- hot and cold flashes

- shaky legs

- an intense aching in your thighs

- nausea or vomiting

- belching

- heavy perspiration

During this stage of labor, it's common to feel as though you've reached the end of your rope. You may feel discouraged, irritable, disoriented, restless, and frustrated. You'd gladly call the whole birth off, if only you knew how to tell your uterus to stop contracting.

It's difficult to find a comfortable position during this stage of labor, but many women find that soaking in a bath or taking a shower helps ease the pain. Have your partner or labor support person hop in the shower with you so that he can provide counterpressure to your lower back, if required.

If you're having a particularly painful episode of back labor (that is, severe pain in your lower back), you might want to try one or more of these coping techniques:

- walk, crouch, squat, get down on your hands and knees, or lie on your side with your back well rounded—whatever it takes to relieve some of the pressure you are feeling in your back;

- apply a hot water bottle or a cold pack to your lower back—whichever provides the most relief;

- have your partner or labor support person apply firm counterpressure on the part of your back that is hurting by pushing with either a rolling pin, a tennis ball, or the palm of his hand;

- put strong finger pressure below the center of the ball of the foot (an acupuncture technique that many laboring women swear by).

The second stage

Just when you've reached your wit's end, your caregiver will announce that you're fully dilated and will give you the go-ahead to start pushing. The pushing stage typically lasts from ½ to 1½ hours. You'll experience a series of 60- to 90-second-long contractions at two- to five-minute intervals, but these

Watch Out!
If you experience an overwhelming urge to push during transition, have your caregiver examine you to determine if your cervix is fully dilated. Pushing against a less-than-fully dilated cervix can cause swelling, something that can prolong your labor.

contractions will likely be much less painful than what you experienced during transition.

Don't be alarmed if you don't feel the urge to push right away. (You'll know you're experiencing it when you get an overwhelming desire to bear down, as if you needed to have the world's largest bowel movement.) Some women experience a 10- to 20-minute lull between transition and the start of the second stage. The urge to bear down is triggered as the baby's head (or buttocks, if it's a breech birth) stretches the vaginal and pelvic-floor muscles. Microscopic receptors in the area both trigger the Ferguson reflex (that is, the urge to push) and signal your brain that it's time to increase the production of oxytocin (the hormone that causes your uterus to contract). Pushing before the urge is there may actually be counterproductive according to some studies. According to one recent report the need for operative deliveries may be decreased if women delay pushing for 30 minutes after reaching full dilation.

During this stage of labor, you may experience

- a renewed burst of energy
- strong rectal pressure
- an increase in bloody show
- the desire to grunt as you bear down
- a tingling, stretching, burning, or stinging sensation as your baby's head crowns in the vagina
- a slippery, wet feeling as the baby suddenly emerges

You may feel relieved that the difficult contractions of transition are now behind you and that you're finally able to start pushing your baby out, exhilarated and excited about your baby's impending birth, or discouraged and overwhelmed at how difficult it can be to push a baby out. "Pushing was a frustrating phase for me," admits Beth, a 27-year-old first-time mom. "I wasn't progressing on getting the baby out, and I was becoming angry, tired, and very upset."

During this phase of labor, you should

- allow your partner or labor support person to help you into a semisitting or semisquatting position—a position that helps gravity work for, not against, you;

- push when you feel the urge, taking several short breaths and making several short pushes during each contraction rather than trying to hold your breath and push throughout the duration of an entire contraction;

- stop pushing, pant, or blow if your caregiver tells you to stop pushing in order to give your perineum a chance to stretch gradually (you might end up avoiding an episiotomy or a bad tear).

Don't be alarmed if you pass small amounts of urine or feces during the pushing stage. Many laboring women do; it kind of goes with the turf and indicates that you are pushing effectively.

Once your baby's head starts to emerge, your caregiver will

- suction the baby's nose and mouth and help the shoulders and torso to come out;

- check to see if the umbilical cord is wrapped around the baby's neck and either lift it over your baby's head or cut and clamp it, if necessary;

Bright Idea
Put gravity to work for you. Pushing in a semisitting or semisquatting position may make it easier for your pelvis to open up and allow your baby to be born.

- lay the baby across your abdomen, if that's your preference (unless the baby appears to be having difficulty breathing, in which case it may be necessary to place the baby in the isolette, suction out any meconium, stimulate respiration, and give the baby oxygen before she is returned to you);

- gently rub the baby's back to stimulate her (the days of upside-down spankings have gone the way of the dinosaur);

- cut and clamp the umbilical cord (before or after the cord has stopped pulsating or the placenta has been delivered, depending on how you and your caregiver feel about the timing of the cutting of the umbilical cord);

- perform the Apgar test (see Table 17.3);

- wrap the baby to keep her from losing too much body heat.

TABLE 17.3: APGAR TEST

	0	1	2
Appearance (skin color); shows how well the lungs are working to oxygenate the blood	Pale or blue	Body pink, extremities blue	Pink
Pulse (heart rate); measures the strength and regularity of the heart beat	No pulse	Below 100	Over 100
Grimace (reflex irritability)	No response to grimace stimulation		Lusty cry
Activity (movements); an indication of the baby's muscle tone	No activity or weak activity	Some movement	Active movement
Respiration (breathing)	None	Slow, irregular	Crying

The Apgar test is performed twice: once when your baby is one minute old and again when your baby is five minutes old. A baby with a one-minute combined score of seven or over is doing well; a baby with a score of five or six may require resuscitation; a baby with a score of four or less may be in serious trouble.

Because newborns are particularly alert right after birth, you might want to take advantage of this opportunity to try breastfeeding your baby. (Your baby may be much sleepier in a few hours, and you may find it difficult to get the baby to wake up enough to nurse.) There's an added bonus to breastfeeding at this stage of the game: the nipple stimulation that occurs as your baby nurses will help release oxytocin, which will help your uterus contract, expel the placenta, and stop bleeding. (*Note:* You will experience these contractions—so-called afterpains—each time you nurse during the first week postpartum. These contractions aren't overly uncomfortable after the birth of your first baby, but they can be downright excruciating after the birth of a subsequent child. Ask your caregiver to prescribe an analgesic if you're finding it difficult to cope with these afterpains. You suffered enough during labor; there's no point in being a martyr now.)

Although you and your partner may want to spend some time alone with your new baby after the placenta has been delivered (see below), the baby may need to be taken to the nursery at some point, so that a full newborn exam can be performed. (This isn't the case in all hospitals and birthing centers, so be sure to ask about these policies ahead of time.) If you do not want to be separated from your baby, find out if you or your partner, or both of you, can accompany the baby to the nursery.

Unofficially...
The Apgar test is named for pediatrician Dr. Virginia Apgar, who developed it. A memory device that many caregivers find helpful when assessing a newborn is to assign the terms "appearance, pulse, grimace, activity, and respiration" to the letters of "APGAR."

Unofficially...
Squatting widens your pelvic outlet by 20% to 30% and provides your baby with the path of least resistance for exiting the uterus.

The third stage

The third stage of labor—the delivery of the placenta—will take place while you're busy admiring your new baby. You may be so distracted that you may hardly even notice the massive one- to two-pound placenta—your baby's life-support system for the past nine months—making its way out of your body. This stage typically lasts anywhere from five minutes to half an hour and involves mild contractions that typically last for one minute or less. These contractions tend to be so mild that you might not even feel them. In an effort to avoid any possible problems with postpartum hemorrhaging, your caregiver may give you a shot of oxytocin or methylergonovine, which will cause the uterus to contract for a prolonged period of time, minimizing bleeding from the former site of the placenta. Once the placenta has been delivered, your caregiver will examine it to make sure that it's complete (retained placental fragments can cause hemorrhaging) and then do any stitching required to repair your perineum.

During this stage, you may feel either tired or bursting with energy, thirsty and hungry, or cold. You will be bleeding quite heavily from the vagina. This blood flow, known as lochia, tends to be heavier than even the heaviest of menstrual periods. You may even find that you gush slightly if you stand up while your uterus is contracting. You may also pass some fairly large blood clots when you go to the bathroom. You will want to alert your caregiver if they are the size of a lemon, or larger.

Why labor sometimes stops

Up until now, we've been talking about textbook labors—the kinds that follow the prenatal class handouts to the tee. Unfortunately, not all labors are quite that straightforward. There are a number of reasons why labor can stop. Here are a few of the more common:

- **Failure to dilate:** If your uterine contractions are ineffective, your cervix will not be able to dilate.

- **Fetal obstruction:** If your baby is too large for your pelvis to accommodate (a problem that is medically termed cephalopelvic disproportion); is in a transverse or oblique position; has a breech, face, or brow presentation; has a congenital abnormality such as hydrocephalus; or is wrapped around another twin, your baby may not be able to be born vaginally.

- **Maternal causes of obstruction:** If you have a deformity or disproportion of the bony pelvis; pelvic tumors such as exceptionally large fibroids or a very large ovarian cyst; abnormalities of the uterus, cervix, or vagina; or a tight band of muscle around your uterus that prevents a contraction from being transmitted all the way down the uterus, your labor may fail to progress.

Your caregiver will begin to suspect that there's a problem if

- during active labor, you are dilating at a rate of less than 1 centimeter per hour (if you're a first-time mom) or 1.5 centimeters per hour (if this is your second or subsequent baby) or

- the pushing stage lasts for more than two hours.

Depending on the stage at which your labor stalls and the suspected causes, your caregiver may decide to augment your labor with Pitocin, attempt to deliver your baby with forceps or a vacuum

Bright Idea
To keep your uterus firm and minimize the amount of blood loss you experience following the birth, you should periodically attempt to feel the height of your fundus (the top of your uterus), which will be located somewhat below your navel. (If you have trouble finding it, your caregiver or nurse can help you.) It should be firm to the touch. If it is squishy rather than firm, vigorous massage will help it contract.

Bright Idea
If your labor stalls during the early or latent phase, you may be able to get things going again by walking, resting, or stimulating your nipples.

extractor, prep you for a cesarean, or wait things out a little longer to see if the problem resolves itself.

What it's really like to be induced

You've no doubt heard the horror stories about what it's really like to be induced—about how the contractions come on top of one another, leaving some laboring woman gasping for air. Not all induced labors are this horrific—something you'll be glad to hear if your baby is late (or might benefit from delivery before you go into labor naturally) and your caregiver is talking induction. Here are the facts on being induced.

Reasons for an induction

The decision to induce is not made lightly. If your caregiver decides that your labor should be induced, it will likely be for one of the following reasons:

- there are signs of placental insufficiency (the placenta may not be getting sufficient nutrients and oxygen from the placenta);

- you are post-term (42 weeks plus), although recent studies suggested better outcomes and fewer cesareans if induction is done routinely at 41 weeks;

- the fetus is no longer thriving in the uterus (due to suspected postmaturity syndrome, poor placental function, maternal disease, or other problems);

- a stress test or nonstress test reveals that the placenta is no longer functioning properly, and the baby would be better off being born than remaining in the uterus any longer;

- your membranes have ruptured but labor has not yet started spontaneously within 12 to 24 hours;

- you have developed preeclampsia or another serious medical condition that cannot be controlled with bed rest and medication, and delivery is necessary for the sake of your own health as well as that of the baby.

Sometimes labor is induced for reasons that are not purely medical. Your caregiver may recommend an elective induction if

- you have a prior history of rapid labor that puts you at risk of having an unplanned home birth;

- you live a considerable distance from a hospital;

- your caregiver will be unavailable for a certain period of time (for example, if your high-risk-pregnancy specialist is about to head out of town for a conference and you're due to deliver any day);

- your family circumstances warrant it (for example, if your partner is able to get only a short period of military leave and would like to be present at the birth).

- you are within one week of an accurate established due date, your cervix is favorable (see below), and you desire a scheduled delivery for significant personal emotional reasons. Because there is always the risk that an induction may fail, necessitating a repeat attempt at induction or a cesarean section, be sure to ask your caregiver about the pros and cons of going this route before you agree to an induction. Generally, the more favorable your cervix is, the less likelihood of a failed induction. Favorable means that your cervix is already starting to soften, dilate, and efface, and the baby's head is relatively low in the pelvis.

One tool your physician may use in assessing your body's readiness for labor is the so-called Bishop scoring system, in which a score of 0 to 3 is given for each of the following five factors:

- dilatation
- effacement
- station
- consistency
- position of cervix

If your score exceeds 8 (see Table 17.4), your cervix is considered to be favorable for induction.

Note: If your labor starts but is weak, is erratic, or stops, your caregiver may augment your labor by using some of the techniques that are used to induce labor.

There are certain circumstances in which labor should not be induced, however. These include pregnancies in which either vaginal delivery is excessively risky or where additional stimulation of the uterus could add unacceptable risk, such as those pregnancies in which

- the placenta blocks the cervix (placenta previa);
- the placenta is prematurely separating from the uterine wall (placental abruption);
- there is an usual presentation of the baby that would make vaginal delivery dangerous or impossible;
- the baby is believed to be too large for your pelvis to accommodate (cephalopelvic dispro-portion);
- you have an active genital herpes infection;
- you are carrying multiples;
- there is evidence of fetal distress;

TABLE 17.4: BISHOP SCORING SYSTEM

	0	1	2	3
Dilatation (cm)	Cervix is closed	Cervix is 1 to 2 cm dilated	Cervix is 3 to 4 cm dilated	Cervix is more than 5 cm dilated
Effacement (%)	Cervix is 0% to 30% effaced	Cervix is 40% to 50% effaced	Cervix is 60% to 70% effaced	Cervix is more than 80% effaced
Station (an estimate of the baby's descent into the birth canal)	-3	-2	-1, 0	+1, +2
Consistency of the cervix	Firm	Medium	Soft	
Position of the cervix	Posterior (pointing backward)	Midposition	Anterior (pointing forward)	

- the uterus is unusually large (due to the increased risk of uterine rupture if you have polyhydramnios or are carrying multiples).

Methods of induction

If your caregiver decides to induce or augment labor, he will probably use one or a combination of the following methods:

Watch Out!
Some caregivers will rupture your membranes to speed up a sluggish labor. Once your membranes have been ruptured, your labor will become faster and more intense. Make sure that you're psychologically prepared for these more intense contractions.

- **Artificial rupture of membranes (AROM):** The caregiver ruptures the membranes using a device that looks like a crochet hook. The procedure will be virtually painless if your cervix has already begun to dilate but can be quite painful if it is only one centimeter or less. If this procedure—known as an amniotomy—fails, your labor will have to be induced using other, more invasive methods. Once your membranes have been ruptured, you've reached the point of no return: you're going to have your baby; it's simply a matter of time.

- **Prostaglandin E suppositories or gel:** Prostaglandin E suppositories or gels help ripen the cervix (make it more favorable for induction). According to the American College of Obstetricians and Gynecologists, 50% of women will go into labor spontaneously and deliver within 24 hours with just a single application of the gel; others will require some other method of induction.

- **Misoprostol:** Misoprostol tablets placed high in the vagina can also help to ripen the cervix and induce labor. This new technique is still considered experimental and the drug is not approved by the FDA for this purpose. However, many caregivers are impressed by its safety, effectiveness, and ease of use compared to Prostaglandin E

■ **Pitocin:** Pitocin is the synthetic form of oxytocin—a hormone that is produced naturally by your body and that is responsible for causing your uterus to contract during labor. If it is used when your cervix is already ripe, a Pitocin-induced labor won't be all that different from a natural labor. If, on the other hand, your cervix isn't ripe, it may take several hours of exposure to Pitocin in a series of separate attempts over a period of two to three days to get labor started. This is why many caregivers use Prostaglandin E or Misoprostal as a warmup to Pitocin. When you are first hooked up to an intravenous drip, a small amount of Pitocin will be injected. This is because your caregiver will want to monitor the strength of your contractions and your baby's response to them before upping the dosage. It's very difficult to predict how a particular mother and baby will react to the drug. Sometimes, contractions caused by a Pitocin drip can be stronger, longer, and more painful than non-Pitocin-induced contractions, and there are shorter breaks between them. You may require pain medication to help you cope with the contractions, and you will probably need to be hooked up to a fetal monitor for the majority of your labor. In some cases, however, a small dose of Pitocin (especially if the membranes are ruptured) is all that is required to get labor started, and, once started, your contractions will continue on their own without any further need for Pitocin.

Despite all the scary stories you might have heard to the contrary, an induced labor does not have to be any more painful than any other labor. Since the dose of Pitocin can be precisely controlled and adjusted up or down in small increments, the contractions you experience in a labor that has been triggered with Pitocin need not be any stronger or closer together (or consequently more painful) than what would be seen in a spontaneous labor. About the only thing that is different with an induced labor in which the Pitocin is administered appropriately is that the early phase of labor may be shortened and the active phase may be reached more quickly than they might otherwise have been.

- **Cervical dilators:** Cervical dilators are a mechanical method of dilating the cervix. Laminaria (sticks of compressed and dried seaweed or synthetic materials) are placed in the cervix. As they absorb water and swell, they force your cervix to dilate. Cervical dilators are considered to be approximately as effective as Prostaglandin E; in other words, they are able to get labor started within a 24-hour period in about 50% of women.

Note: Some pregnancy books may recommend nipple stimulation as a means of getting labor started. This technique is not only unproven, but it's potentially harmful in that the amount of oxytocin being released by your body when your nipples are stimulated cannot be controlled and in rare cases could lead to excessive uterine stimulation (hyperstimulation, or tetanic contractions) that could impair fetal/placental blood flow and cause distress.

Not everyone is a good candidate for induction. Your caregiver will probably suggest other alternatives (for example, a cesarean section) if

Unofficially...
Some parents are choosing to store the blood from their child's umbilical cord and placenta in a cord blood bank so that it will be available in the event that their child someday needs a bone-marrow transplant. Cord blood banks charge approximately $1,500 for the initial deposit and $95 per year for storage—either the bargain of the century or the ultimate rip-off, according to the two sides on this controversial issue.

- your baby needs to be delivered quickly (for example, he is in distress or the placenta is starting to separate);

- it isn't clear whether your baby will be able to fit through your pelvis;

- you have been diagnosed with placenta previa (that is, the placenta is blocking the cervix);

- you have had five or more previous births;

- you have a vertical uterine (not skin) scar from a previous cesarean section;

- you are carrying more than one baby;

- your baby is in the breech position.

If your caregiver believes that either you or your baby is not up to tolerating the stresses of labor, she will recommend that a cesarean be performed instead.

What to expect if you have a breech delivery

Although 97% of babies move into the head-down (vertex) position before labor starts, 3% remain in the breech position. You are at increased risk of having a breech birth if

- you have had more than one pregnancy;

- you are carrying more than one baby;

- you have too much or too little amniotic fluid;

- your uterus is an abnormal shape due to a congenital anomaly;

- you have a number of large fibroids;

- the placenta partially or fully covers the opening of the uterus (placenta previa);

- your baby is premature (due to the shape of the uterus and the shape of the baby's head and

66

The night before our 8:00 a.m. scheduled c-section, we simply spent time hanging out in the nursery. We folded never-worn baby clothes and set up the crib. We watched the "lullaby light show" which attached to the baby's crib and projected little sky scenes onto the ceiling. It was a wonderful night. It felt like a closing to our life together as it had been so far.
—Jennifer, 25, mother of one

99

body at this stage of development and the fact that premature babies are more likely to have birth defects that may predispose them to assuming the breech position).

There are three main types of breech positions, as you will see from the following figure.

- the frank breech (when the baby's legs extend straight upward),
- the complete breech (when the baby is sitting cross-legged on top of the cervix),
- the footling breech (when one or both of the baby's feet are pointing downward).

Assuming that your baby's presentation is detected prior to labor (and most breech babies' presentations are detected ahead of time), your caregiver may wish to try turning the baby before you go into labor. This procedure—known as external version—is typically performed after the 36th week of pregnancy. An ultrasound will be performed to assess the condition and position of the baby, locate the placenta, and measure the amount of amniotic fluid. Your caregiver will place her hands on your abdomen and try to gently coax your baby to change position—kind of like performing a slow-motion somersault in utero. You may be given a

Note! ➜
The three main types of breech presentations: frank (left); complete (middle); and footling (right). Figure by Articulate Graphics.

  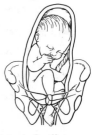

Frank   Complete   Footling

drug to relax your uterus before the procedure is attempted, and your baby will be monitored throughout the procedure in case complications arise and he goes into distress. The key drawbacks to this procedure are the fact that the procedure can be painful, it can be unsuccessful, and—even if it is successful—your baby may revert to the breech presentation between the time when the version is performed and labor commences. There's also an element of risk—which is why the American College of Obstetricians and Gynecologists states that caregivers must be prepared to do an immediate cesarean section if complications arise during a version.

If you're lucky, you may not even need a version: some babies spontaneously turn from a breech or transverse lie (sideways) into the vertex (head down) presentation after the 36th week.

Your chances of being able to deliver a breech baby vaginally are greatest if your baby is a frank breech—but there are still no guarantees that you will be able to avoid a cesarean. Your caregiver may rule out the possibility of a trial vaginal delivery entirely if

- the baby is very large
- your pelvis is small
- your baby is premature
- your baby is exhibiting signs of fetal distress

Assuming that you are able to deliver your baby vaginally, your caregiver may have to use forceps to deliver the baby's head. The baby's head is the largest part of its body, so it's possible for the baby's head to momentarily get stuck when the baby is born feet and buttocks first.

What to expect if you have a cesarean delivery

A cesarean section involves delivering a baby through an incision in a woman's abdomen and uterus. Approximately 15% to 20% of U.S. babies are born by cesarean section—a significant increase from the 3% to 5% rate of 25 years ago. Although the media likes to put a negative spin on this increase by focusing on the number of unnecessary cesareans, what often gets left out of the discussion is the number of babies whose lives have been saved or improved because of this increase in the cesarean rate.

This isn't to say that the 25% or higher cesarean rate at some institutions is something to cheer about, however. Cesareans continue to be four times riskier than vaginal deliveries (at least according to oft-quoted studies; in some patient populations, however, the difference in risk appears to be significantly smaller). Potential complications include

- infections (particularly of the uterus, the nearby pelvic organs, and the incision)
- excessive blood loss
- complications from the anesthesia
- blood clots due to decreased mobility after surgery
- bowel and bladder injuries

You may have heard a common myth about cesareans: that the baby misses out on the squeezing motion of a vaginal delivery—a process that helps clear amniotic fluid from the lungs and stimulate the circulation. There's no evidence showing that babies delivered through cesarean section are at a disadvantage because of this so-called lack of squeezing. In truth, a fair bit of squeezing does occur as the doctor guides your baby out through the incision he or she has made in your uterus.

Still, most caregivers agree that cesareans should be planned only when there's a solid medical reason for avoiding a vaginal delivery. Here are some common reasons:

- The baby is predicted to be too large to pass through your pelvis.

- The baby is in a breech or transverse position.

- You have placenta previa.

- You have an active genital herpes infection.

- You have previously had a cesarean section.

Note: Not all women who have previously had a cesarean section are candidates for a repeat cesarean. The cause of your previous cesarean (for example, a one-time emergency versus a chronic problem), the type of uterine incision used, and your obstetrical status during your subsequent pregnancy will determine whether another cesarean will be necessary. We'll be discussing this issue further on in this chapter.

What a cesarean birth is like

If your section is planned rather than the result of an obstetrical emergency, you can expect your birth to proceed something like this:

- You will be given medication to dry the secretions in your mouth and upper airway. You may also be given an antacid. (In the event that you vomit and then inhale some of the contents of your stomach, the damage that your lungs sustain will be reduced if you have taken an antacid.)

- The lower part of your abdomen will be washed and possibly shaved as well.

Watch Out!
Be sure to find out if your caregiver and the hospital allow partners or labor support people to be present at a cesarean birth—and under what circumstances. (Some hospitals won't allow anyone to be present if an emergency cesarean section needs to be performed.)

- A catheter will be placed in your bladder to keep it empty and to reduce the chances of injury.

- An intravenous needle will be inserted into a vein in your hand or arm to allow for the administering of fluids and medications during your surgery.

- You will be given an anesthetic (typically an epidural or spinal, but general anesthesia may be used in certain circumstances).

- Your abdomen will be washed with antiseptic solution and covered with a sterile drape.

- A screen will be placed in front of your face to keep the surgical field sterile, blocking your view of the delivery.

- Once the anesthetic has had an opportunity to take effect, an incision will be made through the wall of your abdomen and then the wall of your uterus. You will probably feel slight pressure at the incision site, but not any pain. Although your caregiver will attempt to use a so-called bikini cut (a horizontal cut that is low on your abdomen), a vertical skin incision is sometimes made in an emergency.

- Regardless of the type of skin incision, the uterine incision is made horizontally and low down on the uterus unless the position of your baby or the placenta demands a vertical cut instead.

- The amniotic sac will be opened and the amniotic fluid will pour out.

- Your baby will be eased out manually or, on occasion, with the aid of forceps or a vacuum extractor. You may feel a slight tugging sensation as well as feelings of pressure, if you've had an epidural. You probably won't feel anything, if you've had a spinal, except pressure on your upper abdomen if the doctor needs to apply pressure to push the baby out through the incision.

- Your baby's nose and mouth will be suctioned. The umbilical cord will be clamped and cut, and the placenta will be removed. The doctor will hand the baby to the nurse or other caregiver responsible for suctioning the baby.

- The baby's caregiver will assess the baby and perform the Apgar test.

- Your uterus and abdomen will be stitched up. The stitches in your uterus will dissolve on their own. Depending on your doctor's preference, your abdominal incision will be closed with stainless-steel staples or nonabsorbant sutures, which can be removed anytime after three or four days, or absorbable sutures below the skin surface, which dissolve on their own.

- If you feel up to it, you may have the opportunity to hold your baby in the delivery room.

- You will be taken to the recovery room, where your blood pressure, pulse rate, and respiratory rate will be monitored, and you will be watched for excessive bleeding and other potential complications. You may be given antibiotics to minimize your chances of infection and will be offered pain medication either through the IV or in an injection after the anesthetic wears off.

- You will be moved to a room on the postpartum floor. If you are intending to breastfeed, your nurse will show you how to position yourself and your baby to ensure that you are as

Bright Idea
If you know ahead of time that you will be having a cesarean section, look for childbirth classes that are tailored to couples who are planning cesareans.

comfortable as possible, despite your incision. (You will want to either place a pillow over your incision and rest your baby on that while you sit up straight in a chair, or feed your baby when you are lying on one side.)

■ Six to eight hours after your surgery, your catheter will be removed and you will be encouraged to get out of bed and move around.

■ You will require intravenous fluids for a day or two until you're able to start eating and drinking.

■ Your doctor will probably prescribe an analgesic to help you cope with the discomfort and pain that typically accompany a cesarean recovery.

■ You will be discharged from hospital three to five days after your surgery, and you will be able to resume your normal activities four to six weeks after your baby's birth.

Up until now, we've been talking about planned cesarean sections. An emergency cesarean section may be required if, during the course of labor,

■ the baby's heart rate becomes irregular, indicating that she may be in distress and may not be able to withstand the stress of continued labor;

■ the flow of blood and oxygen through the umbilical cord is being excessively restricted because of the position of the cord or the baby;

■ the placenta has started to detach from the uterine wall (placental abruption);

■ the baby is not moving down into the birth canal because the cervix has stopped dilating or the baby is too large for the mother's pelvis, or because of some other obstetrical complication.

Once a cesarean, always a cesarean?

Although the conventional wisdom stated that a woman who had previously had a cesarean was destined to have another cesarean during her next delivery, that is not necessarily the case. Although some women will always require cesareans, others may be good candidates for a vaginal birth after cesarean (VBAC). Your caregiver may recommend that you consider a VBAC if

- you are carrying only one baby
- your baby is neither breech nor transverse
- your baby is full-term
- the baby isn't too big and your pelvis isn't too small
- you are delivering in a setting where an anesthetist is on call and a cesarean can be performed on short notice
- your baby doesn't show any signs of distress.

Here are just a few of the benefits of trying for a VBAC:

- Vaginal deliveries are less risky than cesareans. As is the case with all major types of surgery, it's possible to develop postoperative complications, including infection, bleeding, and reaction to the anesthetic.
- It takes less time to recover from a vaginal delivery than a cesarean.
- A woman who is having a vaginal delivery can play a more active role in the birth and, in general, has more options concerning the birth (who will be present in the delivery room and so on).

The primary concern posed by a trial of labor (a VBAC attempt) is the fact that it may not be

Unofficially...
A recent study of 6,000 first-time mothers indicated that women carrying male fetuses were 50% more likely to require a cesarean than women carrying female fetuses. Bernard Harlow, Ph.D., a reproductive epidemiologist at the Obstetrics and Gynecology Epidemiology Center at Brigham and Women's Hospital in Boston explained the results by noting that male babies tend to be heavier at birth and to have broader shoulders than their female counterparts.

"
Remove your nail
polish before you
go to the hospi-
tal. I didn't know
that most hospi-
tals require that
you remove nail
polish before
surgery, and I
had just redone
my nails—deep
red, three coats.
Needless to say,
the little one-
inch-square pads
of polish remover
that the nurses
provided were
almost useless. I
ended up with
icky, red-stained
fingers.
—Elaine, 29,
mother of two
"

successful and a cesarean will have to be performed again. Depending on the reason the first cesarean was done, the success rate for VBAC may vary by 50% to 80%. Another risk is the possibility of splitting of the uterine scar tissue from your previous incision. You're less likely to experience this rare but potentially life-threatening complication if you received a transverse uterine incision rather than a vertical incision. Note that the type of skin incision you had does not indicate what type of uterine incision you may have had. Although the vast majority of modern cesareans are done through low uterine horizontal (transverse) incisions, your caregiver will probably check your previous records to verify what type of uterine incision you had before recommending an attempt at VBAC.

How you may be feeling about having a cesarean

When you first found out you were pregnant and started thinking about the birth of your baby, you may have envisioned giving birth peacefully in the birthing suite at your local hospital or birthing center. Finding out midway through your pregnancy—or in the heat of labor—that you're going to require a cesarean section can be a bit of a shock.

Part of the problem stems from the fact that cesarean births are stigmatized as being less intimate and meaningful to laboring women and their partners than vaginal deliveries. This attitude angers women like Andrea, 27, a first-time mother. "Women need to realize that having a cesarean birth makes them no less of a mother than women who have vaginal deliveries," she insists.

Sometimes all that is required is a shift in mindset, says Jennifer, a 25-year-old mother of one: "I had to plan a c-section when my baby was found to be breech two weeks before my due date. I was very disappointed not to be able to experience labor and delivery as I had envisioned, but I quickly convinced myself that this could be a wonderful thing as well—to be able to relax and enjoy my baby's entrance into the world without even thinking about my performance and my breathing techniques."

If you continue to feel disappointed about your inability to deliver your baby vaginally, you may wish to share your feelings with your caregiver or talk with a therapist.

Water birth

Most caregivers agree that there are a number of advantages to laboring in warm water. Laboring in warm water promotes relaxation and a more efficient labor while reducing the perception of pain.

Where most caregivers tend to draw the line, however, is when it comes time to actually deliver the baby. There is conflicting evidence about the safety of delivering under water, and many caregivers have particular concerns about the possibility of respiratory complications in the event that the baby inhales water.

A recent article in the British medical journal *Lancet* recommended that those women who do choose to give birth under water get out of the tub as soon as the baby is born and clamp the cord within a minute or two rather than delaying the clamping until after the delivery of the placenta. Staying in the warm water allows the blood vessels in the umbilical cord to stay open much longer than they normally would—something that can contribute to postdelivery complications for both the mother and the baby.

Unofficially... Maternity centers have reported no increased rate of infection in women laboring in appropriately sanitized tubs after their membranes have ruptured.

Meeting your baby

The hard work of labor and delivery are behind you, and the time has come to savor your reward. It's time to meet your baby.

You probably realize that newborns bear only a passing resemblance to those adorable eight-month-old cherubs pictured in Anne Geddes photographs. What you might not realize is how very odd newborn babies can look—particularly if you've never seen one before. Here's a brief description of what your newborn may look like:

- **Irregular head shape:** If you delivered your baby vaginally, he might have a molded or conelike shape to his head. If your baby's head was jammed against an inadequately dilated cervix, it may have an alarming lump known as a caput succedaneum. Although the molding may last for up to two weeks, the caput will likely disappear within a day or two.

- **Hair:** Some babies are born with a full head of hair; others are virtually bald. Regardless of what amount of hair your baby arrives with, her hair will soon fall out. As this newborn hair is shed, it will be replaced with new hair.

- **Vernix caseosa coating:** Vernix is the protective coating that covered your baby's skin while he was in utero. Your baby will probably have traces of vernix in his folds of skin. A premature baby may be heavily coated in vernix, whereas a post-term baby may have virtually none.

- **Lanugo:** Lanugo is the fine downy hair found on a full-term newborn baby's shoulders, back, forehead, and temples. (As is the case with vernix, lanugo is more abundant in premature babies.)

- **Genital swelling:** Your baby's genitals and breasts may be swollen as a result of maternal hormones crossing the placenta. A baby girl may even pass a milky-white or blood-tinged secretion from her vagina. These signs will disappear within a week to 10 days.

- **Birthmarks:** Reddish blotches are most common in Caucasians, whereas bluish-gray pigmentation on the back, buttocks, arms, or thighs is more common in babies of Asian, south European, or African American ancestry.

- **Neonatal urticaria:** Your baby may have a series of red spots with yellow-white centers. These typically appear during the first day of life, but they disappear by the time your baby is one week old.

- **Red marks on the skin or broken blood vessels in the skin or eye:** Your baby may have red marks on her skin or broken blood vessels in her skin or eye. These marks—which are caused by pressure during birth—typically vanish within a few days.

How you may be feeling about becoming a mother

Some women experience an instant bond with their babies after they give birth; others take a little longer to warm up to the pint-sized strangers in their arms.

Suzi, a 27-year-old mother of two, recalls the feelings of joy she experienced after the births of each of her sons: "Once I had my babies, I was truly overwhelmed with joy. It was an experience and feeling that you cannot explain to anyone because it is so miraculous and beautiful."

Ann, 34, experienced similar emotions: "I was on a high from the moment my daughter was born.

I was so thrilled that I was finally able to meet my baby."

Nancy, 31, couldn't believe how quickly she fell in love with her babies: "As soon as I set eyes on them, I fell head over heals for them. I couldn't get enough of them. I loved looking at those sweet little faces that I had been waiting so long to see."

Other women are surprised by their lack of emotion during those first few moments.

"I had anticipated throughout my pregnancy that holding my baby for the first time would be wondrous," admits Tracy, a 31-year-old mother of one. "I expected that I would be weeping with joy and love for my baby, that I would feel an instant connection. But when he was born and they put him, bloody and naked, up on my chest, I felt like I was being handed a stranger."

Stephanie, a 25-year-old first-time mother, echoes those feelings: "I did not feel an instant bond at all and actually remember thinking, 'What's wrong with me? I'm supposed to be loving this child right away, and all I want to do is go to sleep.'"

Marilyn, 43, who is currently pregnant with her third child, admits to feeling totally detached from her first baby immediately after the birth. "I kept thinking that her mother was about to come and fetch her at any moment and I was just minding her until then. It was perhaps a few hours later that I began to fall in love with her."

Some women gain a newfound respect for their bodies in the moments after giving birth. Heather, a 32-year-old first-time mother, describes it this way: "I felt powerfully connected to all my ancestries down through all time. I could literally see the echoes of every woman who ever labored to give forth a new life. I felt triumphant; filled with grace; utterly humbled by my own body and by the miracle that lay wet and sweet and messy on my belly. I was full to the skin with welcome for the new life that so suddenly became real to me."

Others are surprised to find themselves experiencing feelings of regret that their pregnancy has come to an end: "I was relieved that it was all over, but also a little sad," confesses Erika, 25, a mother of two. "Being pregnant and giving birth is such a miraculous experience that part of me didn't want it to end."

Just the facts

- You may experience lightening, increased pressure in the pelvis and rectum, weight loss or reduced weight gain, fluctuating energy levels, the passage of your mucus plug, some pink or bloody show, and increasingly painful Braxton Hicks contractions in the days and weeks leading up to labor.

- It can be extremely difficult to distinguish between true and false labor. Don't be embarrassed if you experience at least one false alarm.

- While many women opt for unmediated births, epidurals have become the pain-relief option of choice among American women.

- Make sure that your caregiver knows how you feel about fetal monitoring and episiotomy and other interventions.

- You may wish to use some of the nonpharmaceutical methods of pain relief before resorting to pharmacologically based methods.

- Be sure to have an extra support person lined up for each of your children if you intend to have them present at the birth.

- Assuming that your caregiver agrees, time your departure for the birth center or hospital so that you arrive when you're in active labor rather than early labor or transition.

- Pack both a labor bag and a hospital bag at least three weeks prior to your due date. You don't want to be searching for a spare tube of toothpaste in between contractions.

- Make sure that you know what's involved in an induction, a breech delivery, and a cesarean delivery so that you'll be prepared if any of them happen to you.

- Although most caregivers will encourage you to labor in water if that's an option in the birthing facility you've chosen, the majority will encourage you to hop out of the tub when it's time to start pushing.

- Don't be concerned if you're too exhausted to bond with your baby right away. There will be plenty of time to enjoy your precious newborn during the days and weeks ahead.

Food for Thought: Breastfeeding and Bottle-Feeding

In 1995, approximately 60% of new mothers in the United States were breastfeeding their infants either exclusively or in combination with formula feeding at the time they were discharged from the hospital, but only 21.6% were still nursing their babies on a part-time or full-time basis some six months later. It's a statistic that frustrates members of the American Academy of Pediatrics's Work Group on Breastfeeding—a group that would like to see breastfeeding become the norm for American women and their babies.

Although studies have shown that breastfeeding offers a number of health advantages to mothers and babies—advantages that bottle-feeding can't match—not all women will choose or be able to breastfeed. That's why we've chosen to include information on both breastfeeding and bottle-feeding in this chapter.

Getting breastfeeding off to the best possible start

As we mentioned in the previous chapter, newborns are particularly alert during the first hour after birth. If you're intending to breastfeed, this is the ideal time to try to establish a breastfeeding relationship.

The first time

The majority of healthy babies are born with a strong rooting reflex—a reflex that makes them open their mouth wide and move their mouth frantically in search of a nipple. You can stimulate your baby's reflex and encourage him to latch on by gently stroking his lower lip with the nipple. Your baby will then open his mouth widely, at which point you can move him toward your breast.

When your baby takes your nipple into his mouth, his jaws should close around the areola (the flat, pigmented area surrounding the nipple) rather than on the nipple itself. You can help him to latch on properly by grasping your breast with one thumb above the areola and the fingers and palms below it, and then gently compressing your breast. You can then direct your nipple into the baby's mouth. The nipple should be level or pointed slightly downward to avoid having it rub on the roof of your baby's mouth.

Let the baby nurse at the first breast for as long as he likes, and then put him on the other side until he stops nursing by himself.

You can tell that your baby is nursing properly (rather than just playing with the nipple) if you

- experience the let-down reflex (a tingling or tightening in your nipple that occurs as your milk is ejected);

- hear swallowing sounds (a sign that he is engaging in vigorous "nutritive sucking" rather than the more relaxed "non-nutritive sucking"—a source of emotional comfort to young babies);

- feel uterine cramping (something you will experience only during the first few days postpartum and might not experience much at all if this is your first baby);

- notice that your baby falls asleep after nursing and appears to be satisfied with the amount of food he received.

How breastfeeding works

Your baby's sucking movements trigger a series of complex biochemical responses in your body:

- The stimulation of the nerve fibers in your nipple signals your pituitary gland that your baby needs to be fed.

- In response to this stimulation, the pituitary gland releases prolactin (a hormone that stimulates the breasts to produce more milk) and oxytocin (a hormone that stimulates contractions of the tiny muscles surrounding the ducts in your breasts, ejecting the milk into the reservoir under the areola—the so-called let-down reflex). It generally takes about two to three minutes for the let-down reflex to kick in during your first few feedings. Within a week or two, however, the reflex will speed up considerably and your milk supply will increase dramatically.

Part of the beauty of breastfeeding is the fact that it works on the basis of supply and demand. Your body knows exactly how much milk to produce to meet your baby's needs. It also knows what type of milk your baby requires at his or her particular developmental stage.

Bright Idea
If colostrum or milk flows from one breast while your baby is sucking on the other, you can feel confident that your let-down reflex is working as it should. If you want to slow the flow of milk from your other breast, gently press on it with the palm of your hand.

The food your baby will receive during the first few feedings is colostrum—a yellowish substance that contains protective white blood cells capable of attacking harmful bacteria. It is high in protein and low in sugar and fat—an ideal first food for your baby. Within a couple of days, your milk will come in. When it comes in, your breasts may feel hot and extremely full of milk. If your breasts become overly full (that is, you experience engorgement), you can relieve some of the pressure by manually expressing a small amount of milk while you are in the shower. Sometimes the warm water from the shower will cause your milk to let down on its own. (Of course, if you are putting the baby to the breast frequently, engorgement won't be a problem.)

Just one quick word of caution: Don't express too much milk or you'll simply perpetuate the problem. Your body will think it needs to produce the same vast quantity of milk in the future in order to feed your baby.

Here are some other tips on managing engorgement:

- Wear a well-fitting nursing bra.

- Nurse your baby at least once every one to three hours, and use both breasts at each feeding. Encourage your baby to nurse for 10 to 20 minutes or longer at each breast.

- Gently massage the breast at which your baby is nursing in order to encourage the milk to start flowing and to relieve some of the tightness and discomfort you may be experiencing.

- If your areola is extremely firm, express a bit of milk from your nipple before you allow your baby to latch on. This will help prevent nipple soreness.

- If you are feeling particularly uncomfortable, take acetaminophen tablets or other pain-relief medications prescribed by your caregiver.

Aches and pains

You may experience some tenderness during the early days of nursing—especially during the first minute or two of nursing, when the baby first latches on and pulls the nipple into her mouth. If, however, you experience extreme soreness (if you are reluctant to put your baby to the breast because it hurts too much), you could be positioning your baby incorrectly.

If your nipples are tender, bruised, scabbed, or blistered at the tip, the tip of your nipple is probably rubbing against the roof of your baby's mouth while she is nursing.

If your nipple is tender or cracked at or near the base, it could be because your baby's gums are closing on the nipple rather than the areola—either because she isn't opening her mouth wide enough when she first latches on, because she is slipping off the areola onto the nipple (a common problem if the breast is engorged), or because she has developed thrush (a yeast infection in the mouth that will need to be treated with antibiotics).

If the undersides of your nipples are sore, this could be because your baby is nursing with his bottom lip tucked in. You can correct this problem by pulling the baby's bottom lip out several times during each feeding until he gets the hang of things.

If your nipples are red, slightly swollen, and feel burning hot, you could have nipple dermatitis—a reaction to a substance that has come into contact with your nipples (for example, vitamin E preparations, lanolin, or cocoa butter). The best thing to

Watch Out!
Babies who are given bottles or pacifiers before they've mastered the art of breast-feeding sometimes experience nipple confusion—a problem that can interfere with the establishment of breastfeeding. If you're committed to breastfeeding your baby, talk to your caregiver about what you can do to ensure that your baby is not inadvertently offered a bottle or a pacifier by one of his caregivers.

Unofficially...
Studies have shown that breastfeeding reduces your baby's chances of experiencing diarrhea, lower respiratory infections, ear infections, bacterial meningitis, botulism, and urinary tract infections. Some studies have also indicated that breastfeeding may help protect babies against SIDS, insulin-dependent diabetes mellitus, Crohn's disease, ulcerative colitis, lymphoma, allergic diseases, and other chronic digestive diseases.

put on sore or irritated breasts is breast milk. Just express a bit of breast milk at the end of a feeding and rub it on your nipples. Creams and lotions are unnecessary and merely contribute to other breast-feeding problems.

If your nipples are red, swollen, itchy, tender, or cracked and you find tiny curds stuck to them, you and your baby may have a thrush infection. (You can usually confirm this diagnosis by looking inside your baby's mouth. If you find white patches on her tongue, her cheeks, the insides of her lips, and her gums, she probably has a yeast infection. A few babies don't show any symptoms in the mouth but develop a painful diaper rash that resembles a mild burn.) Some newborn babies pick up yeast infections in the birth canal during delivery—something that frequently happens if the mother is diabetic. A thrush infection can also be triggered if the mother and baby are given antibiotics during or after the delivery. If you and your baby develop problems with thrush, you will need to be treated with an anti-fungal such as nystatin or gentian violet—a substance that will turn your baby's mouth, your breasts, and anything else it comes into contact with bright purple.

If your nipples burn, itch, flake, ooze, and crust, you could be experiencing an outbreak of eczema. You will need to seek the services of a dermatologist.

Here are some general tips on coping with sore nipples:

- Express a small amount of milk just before the baby latches on. This will help reduce some of the wear and tear on your nipples.

- Offer the least sore breast to your baby when she first starts to nurse. This is the side that will receive the most vigorous sucking because baby is hungriest.

Bright Idea
If you're having difficulty with afterpains (uterine contractions stimulated by the release of oxytocin while you nurse), take a painkiller before you put your baby to the breast.

■ Many lactation experts advise against using nipple shields as a means of coping with sore nipples, but if it's the only thing that's giving you any relief, you might consider using them as a temporary measure. Just be aware that they can sometimes make the soreness worse and may decrease your milk supply.

■ Massage your breasts before and during each nursing session to encourage the milk to flow.

■ Put your finger into the edge of your baby's mouth to break the suction before you remove her from the breast.

■ Allow your nipples to air-dry after each feeding.

■ Apply cold packs to your breasts for a short period after nursing. A well-positioned bag of frozen peas or corn can bring tremendous relief.

■ Avoid nipple creams. They will only irritate your nipples.

■ Change your nursing pads whenever they become wet. Avoid ones with plastic inserts because these increase your chances of developing a breast infection.

■ Look for a cotton bra and wear cotton T-shirts while you're nursing. Other fabrics don't allow for adequate air circulation.

■ Don't use soap on your nipples when you have your shower or bath.

About supplemental feedings

Most newborns don't require any fluids other than colostrum—the substance that is present in the breasts until your milk comes in about two days after the delivery. (The main exceptions are babies who have low blood sugar because their mother was diabetic, their birth weight was low, or they experienced unusual stress during labor and delivery.)

If you intend to breastfeed, it's important to avoid offering your baby a bottle during the early days of breastfeeding. Drinking from a bottle trains a baby to

- open her mouth less widely,

- wait to suck until she feels the firm bottle nipple in her mouth,

- encourage her to push her tongue forward—the opposite motion of what is required to nurse successfully.

What's more, a baby who has become accustomed to a bottle may not be willing to work at getting the milk out of a breast. Milk flows out of a bottle right away; it takes a minute or two to get the milk to start flowing out of a breast.

Everything you ever wanted to know about breastfeeding . . .

Breastfeeding is natural, but it doesn't always come naturally. Here are some answers to the most frequently asked questions about breastfeeding.

My newborn won't wake up long enough to nurse. Should I be concerned?

The bottom line is whether or not your baby is producing the number of wet or soiled diapers that is normal for a newborn baby. A minimum of five to six wet diapers, and one stool a day, is fine for babies up to the age of about six weeks.

If your baby isn't producing that many diapers, or isn't gaining weight as quickly as he should, you

> 66
> I wish I had educated myself more on breastfeeding. I was naive to think that it would come naturally. I wish I had attended breastfeeding classes before my baby was born.
> —Kim, 35, mother of one
> 99

might want to think about waking the baby up for more frequent feeds during the day. Try for a two- to three-hour interval between feedings during the daytime, when you're awake. Feed at least once during the night.

If you do decide to wake the baby up for more frequent feeds, don't just look at the clock: observe your baby's sleep stages. When he enters a period of light sleep (moving, eyelids flickering, and sucking), strip him down to his diaper. Do "baby sit-ups," if needed, until he is awake enough to nurse. If your baby slows down after nursing only a few minutes, gently stroking under the baby's chin or around his ears and head, or massaging your breast as he feeds, may keep him going stronger for longer.

How often should I feed my baby?

Most pediatricians recommend that breastfed babies follow a schedule of "demand feeding"—the mother feeds the baby when the baby is hungry. For breastfed babies, this typically translates into one feeding every two to three hours.

My nipples are really sore. I thought breastfeeding wasn't supposed to hurt.

Breastfeeding isn't supposed to hurt, but you might experience a bit of a tugging sensation. It should never be the kind of pain that would make you want to pull the baby off the breast immediately. If it hurts that much, there's a problem.

If your nipples are getting sore, take a look at how the baby is positioned at the breast. A lot of women will say, "It looks like he's latched on properly. He has a lot of the areola in his mouth."

However, mothers have this unique view from the top while they're nursing. You may find that the baby is simply positioned too high in the traditional

Unofficially...
Studies have shown that women who breastfeed return to their prepregnancy weights more quickly than women who bottle-feed.

cradle hold, with not enough areola on the side of his chin and jaw. Holding the baby on his side with his feet wrapped right around you makes a better angle so that you can get the nipple high against his palate, out of the way of the tongue action. His chin should be burrowing, both cheeks touching. If you have a hard time with this, move the baby down a bit so that he's "nose to nipple," and gently touch his lips to tease the mouth open into a wide gape as big as a yawn; then bring him in close quickly. This works in all positions: cradle (when you cradle your baby in one arm and hold him across your body), football (when you put his head in your hand and tuck his body under your arm like a football), and side-lying (when you lie on one side to nurse your baby). Initially, it's trial and error, but it gets easier with practice. A good latch helps prevent 90% of the most common breastfeeding problems.

My sister says she leaked milk constantly when she was nursing her baby. I haven't had much problem with leaking at all. Does this mean I don't have enough milk?

Everyone is different as far as leaking goes. The bottom line, again, is your baby's weight gain. If your baby is gaining weight, it doesn't matter if you leak or don't leak. For most women, leaking is simply a laundry problem. Some women who leak constantly and copiously, even in between feedings, may have a chronic oversupply. They can improve this situation by using one side rather than two at each feeding.

My baby often falls asleep while nursing on the first side. Should I make a point of offering my baby both breasts at each feeding?

Ten years ago, nursing mothers were advised to feed their babies for 10 minutes on the first side and as long as the baby wanted on the second side. Today, nursing mothers are being told to nurse their baby as long as the baby wants on the first side and then switch to the second breast if the baby is still hungry. When your baby first starts to nurse on a particular side, he receives foremilk (which is low in fat), followed by hindmilk (which is high in fat). If you switch breasts before your baby finishes the hindmilk, he is obtaining fewer calories and is likely to be less satisfied than if you gave him the chance to empty the first breast thoroughly and then move on to the second breast, if necessary.

Why does my baby spit up so much?

Spitting up is rarely cause for concern. If the baby spits up large quantities of milk, you might think about feeding on only one side because the baby may be sucking for comfort and getting a whole lot more milk than she really wants.

Another reason why some babies spit up more than others is that babies have different nursing styles. Some babies are so aggressive and excited at the breast that their breathe-suck-swallow rhythm isn't very smooth or relaxed. They take in more air, and they're apt to need more burping than other babies. These babies aren't always burped as soon as they need it because they are such aggressive nursers. When they do burp, up comes all this milk.

Small amounts of spitting up in an otherwise thriving, contented baby is not a problem. On the other hand, frequent vomiting of large amounts of milk should be brought to the attention of the baby's caregiver. For babies who cry a lot and suffer from gassiness or colic, eliminating certain foods in the mother's diet may be a help. The most frequent culprit in our culture is cow's milk. A lactation consultant or your baby's caregiver can help you to pinpoint any possible food sensitivities.

Moneysaver
According to the American Academy of Pediatrics, breastfeeding costs approximately $400 per year less than bottle-feeding, even when the extra calories required by the nursing mother are factored in.

Bright Idea
If you are intending to breastfeed your baby, be sure to check with your obstetrician or pediatrician about the safely of any prescription or nonprescription drugs you may be taking.

Are there certain foods I should avoid while I'm nursing?

If your baby develops colicky symptoms—that is, crying, fussing, nursing more frequently, and being extremely irritable—when you eat certain foods, you might want to avoid them. Perennial offenders include "gassy" foods such as cabbage, onions, garlic, broccoli, and turnips; cow's milk; and caffeine. If you eliminate the food that is causing the problem from your diet, you should see a marked improvement in your baby's temperament. If you don't see a change, the food you eliminated from your diet probably wasn't the problem.

I'm going back to work in a few months' time. Is it even worth my while to try to breastfeed my baby?

Nursing doesn't have to be all or nothing. Because of the tremendous health advantages to both you and your baby, any amount you can breastfeed is good. Four months is better than two months, two months is better than one month, one week is better than one day, and one day is better than nothing. Try to fit it into your lifestyle as best you can. You can find plenty of practical tips on breastfeeding and working in *The Unofficial Guide to Childcare,* by Ann Douglas.

When should I introduce a bottle?

If you want to introduce a bottle, you should be aware that some babies will develop a preference for the bottle over the breast. Try not to introduce it before six weeks of age if you are firmly committed to breastfeeding. On the other hand, try not to delay introducing the bottle past four months if you want your child to accept one. If your baby won't take a bottle, use a cup or spoon. Small cups work fine for small babies if you take it slowly. Then, nurse the baby when you get home.

What can I do to avoid getting a breast infection?

You're more likely to get a breast infection (mastitis) if you're run down. Your best defense against one is to take things slowly during the postpartum period and to be sure that you're getting enough rest.

If you do happen to develop mastitis—which is characterized by swelling, heat, and pain in one breast (often with a fever)—notify your doctor at once so that he can prescribe antibiotics. You should also continue to breastfeed because becoming engorged will only worsen the infection. The infection will not be transmitted to your baby through your breast milk, nor will the composition of your breast milk be affected.

Breastfeeding tips for special situations

Special situations call for special breastfeeding advice. Here are some tips on breastfeeding if you give birth to multiples, if you've previously had breast surgery, if you adopt a baby, or if your baby is premature.

Breastfeeding multiples

The biggest challenge to breastfeeding multiples is logistics. Whether you intend to nurse two babies at the same time or to alternate between nursings and bottle-feedings, you will need to come up with a game plan for feeding two or more babies.

If you decide to nurse both babies simultaneously, you will want to

■ find a comfortable spot to nurse (for example, a comfortable chair next to a table with a

Watch Out!
Avoid smoking and drinking alcohol while you are nursing. Cigarettes and alcohol contain substances that can interfere with your let-down, affect the content of your breast milk, and be harmful to your baby.

pitcher of water, the remote control for the TV, the cordless phone, and so on);

- choose a nursing position that is comfortable and that requires as few hands as possible (for example, the double football hold or the double cradle position;

- wake up the second baby when the first one wakes up to nurse and nurse both babies;

- jot down some notes about the feeding if you're worried that you'll forget important information later (for example, "Ben nursed well. Jessica kept dozing off and didn't appear to be particularly hungry.")

Here are some other tips for moms who are breastfeeding multiples:

- Drink plenty of fluids and eat plenty of nutritious foods. Breastfeeding demands approximately 500 calories per baby per day, so make sure that you're well fueled.

- Use a nursing pillow to position your babies so that you can keep one or both hands free.

- If you intend to express breast milk so that someone else can help out with feedings, rent a heavy-duty electric breast pump. Small electric and battery pumps simply aren't up to the task of pumping milk for two or more babies.

- Some mothers find it helpful to "assign" a particular breast to a particular baby rather than trying to remember which baby had which breast last.

- Remember that any amount of breast milk is better than nothing. If you're having difficulty keeping up with the breastfeeding demands of two or more babies, you may wish to consider supplementing with formula. On the other hand, if breastfeeding your babies exclusively is extremely important to you, rest assured that your breasts are almost certain to be up to the challenge.

Breastfeeding after breast surgery

Here are the facts on breastfeeding after breast surgery:

- A biopsy or removal of a lump seldom affects a woman's ability to breastfeed on the affected breast.

- A woman who has had a mastectomy can breast-feed on the remaining breast. In most cases, her remaining breast will still be able to produce more than enough milk for her baby.

- Women who have breast implants can usually breastfeed, as long as the milk ducts were not severed and there aren't any complications from the implants themselves.

- Women who have had breast reduction surgery may or may not be able to breastfeed, depending on the scope of the surgery. If, for example, the nipple was relocated, the milk ducts were probably severed and the milk supply may not be adequate. In this case, if the woman wanted to breastfeed her baby, she might have to nurse with the aid of a breastfeeding supplementation device (a tube-like device that is taped to the breast and that dispenses formula in a fashion that closely mimics regular breastfeeding).

Breastfeeding after adoption

You don't have to give birth to breastfeed a baby. An infant's suck is capable of stimulating milk production. That said, the majority of adoptive mothers will need to supplement their breast milk, at least initially, according to Kathleen Huggins, author of *The Nursing Mother's Companion.*

Although some people may advise you to try to initiate milk production before your baby is born by expressing or pumping milk from your breasts several times each day, the jury is still out on the effectiveness of this technique.

Your efforts to breastfeed an adopted baby are most likely to succeed if you start nursing your baby when she is still a newborn.

Breastfeeding a premature baby

If your baby is three to five weeks early, she will probably be able to breastfeed right away. If she is considerably more premature, you may need to express breast milk until the baby is healthy or mature enough to begin nursing on her own. As a rule of thumb, you should plan to express breast milk at least as often as your baby would normally nurse—eight or more times in a 24-hour period.

You will need to take particular care when sterilizing your breast-pump parts and bottles. All objects that come in contact with the milk or your breasts should be scrubbed thoroughly with hot, soapy water after each use and then sterilized in boiling water or a dishwasher twice daily.

Because expressing breast milk requires a lot of time and effort, you won't want to waste a single drop. Rather than overfilling a bottle, put a small amount of milk into two or more bottles. That way, there is less to waste if your baby isn't hungry after all. (Breast milk can't be kept once it has been thawed or warmed up.)

Choosing a breast pump

There are almost as many breast pumps on the market as there are automobiles, and—as is the case with cars—there's a model designed to suit every price range. If you will need to use your pump only occasionally, you can probably get away with purchasing a Chevrolet-type product. If, however, you are going to be using your pump on a daily basis and you want the best product on the market, you're best advised to invest in the Cadillac of breast pumps: a hospital-grade machine.

When you're shopping for a breast pump, you should keep your needs in mind:

- How often will you be pumping? Will you be pumping many times each day or just occasionally?

- Where will you be pumping? Will you have access to an electrical outlet? What about a sink for rinsing the various pump components?

- How much time will you have to devote to each pump session? If you're likely to be pressed for time, should you consider renting or purchasing a double-horned unit that will enable you to pump both breasts at once?

- Will you be taking the pump back and forth to work each day? If so, how portable is the unit?

- Does the pump have continuous or intermittent pressure? (Intermittent pressure is best because it more closely imitates the suck-release pattern used by nursing babies and because it is less likely to injure your breast.)

- How easy is the unit to clean?

Moneysaver
Some hospitals provide nursing mothers with a free horn, bottle, and tubing for use with a particular brand of electric breast pump. Be sure to find out if any such freebie is likely to come your way.

■ How expensive is it? If it's a less expensive machine, how well will it stand up to all the wear and tear?

As you might expect, there are advantages and disadvantages to each of the various types of pumps. Let's take a quick run-through of the basic types of models you can expect to find at your local drugstore or medical supply store:

Bicycle horn–style manual breast pumps

These contraptions look a lot like the bicycle horn you likely had as a kid. You squeeze the big bulb to get the milk flowing from your breasts. Not surprisingly, this type of breast pump is no longer recommended by lactation experts. Not only are they difficult to clean (and therefore quickly transformed into bacterial breeding grounds), but they don't work well and can actually cause trauma to the breast or nipple.

Syringe-style manual breast pumps

These pumps rely upon the suction produced by two cylinders that fit inside one another. They're portable, easy to use, easy to clean, and affordable. They're just not quite as efficient as some of the more powerful electrical models.

Convertible manual breast pumps

As you might gather from the name, these pumps offer the best of both worlds: the convenience of a manual pump combined with the added power of an electric. Many women consider them to be the next best thing to hospital-grade electric breast pumps.

Small battery-operated breast pumps

These pumps are convenient to use (that is, you can use them in your car or in a washroom stall at the mall!), but they don't have as much get up and go as their electrically powered counterparts. You'll also need to ensure that you tote around spare batteries—or risk looking like a lop-sided Chesty Morgan for the rest of your working day.

Small electric breast pumps
This type of pump generally works better than a comparable battery-operated unit, but it requires access to an electrical outlet and may burn out if you're using it a lot—a major consideration if you're pumping for twins.

Hospital-grade electric breast pumps
These types of pumps most closely resemble the sucking action of breastfed babies, cycling about 40 times per minute. Because they use a pumping action and level of suction similar to that of your own baby, you're likely to experience an efficient let-down and minimal breast soreness. Most units come with optional double-pump kits, a feature that can be a real timesaver for a busy working mom. The only problem with these units is that they're less portable than smaller pumps and can be very expensive to buy or rent.

If all this talk about pumps has left you feeling about as attractive and desirable as Bessie the Cow, take heart. If you're not comfortable with the idea of hooking an intimate part of your body up to a device that seems to have as much suction power as your vacuum cleaner, you can always fall back on the tried-and-true technique of hand-expressing. Although it takes a little practice to master this low-tech technique, it's convenient, portable, and incredibly cost efficient. You can learn the art of hand-expression from a lactation consultant or your local chapter of La Leche League, or you can follow

Bright Idea
Before you purchase a breast pump or sign a rental contract for an extended period of time, see if you can test-drive the unit first. There's no point in forking over a wallet full of cash only to discover that a particular model isn't going to do the job for you.

the step-by-step instructions provided by most books about breastfeeding. You can also find a wealth of information about breastfeeding at the La Leche League Web site: www.lalecheleague.org.

Pumping tips

66

The baby romped with me on the bed; we were delighted to come together, like lovers rushing back to the meeting-place, bringing presents.
—Writer Michele Landsberg reflecting on what it was like to nurse her toddler

99

One of the first things you're likely to learn about pumping is that it's not quite as easy as it looks. Although some women are able to fill eight-ounce bottles in a matter of minutes, they tend to be the exception rather than the rule. Most of us are happy when a pumping session results in the collection of two to three ounces of milk.

You might find it reassuring to learn that the amount of milk you are able to extract from your breast using a breast pump doesn't necessarily reflect the amount of milk your body is capable of producing. Some women simply have better results pumping than others. It's more a reflection of your relationship with the breast pump than any indication of your ability to produce ample quantities of milk for your baby. So don't sweat it if the other moms from your prenatal class seem to be capable of getting a much larger yield from their pumping sessions than you are able to get from yours. It could be that their breasts respond better to pumping. Or it could be that they're exaggerating their results a little. Either way, don't sweat it. Your body is fully capable of producing the quantity of milk your baby needs.

That said, there are some techniques you can use to maximize the amount of milk you're able to obtain by pumping.

Timing is everything

You will probably obtain the greatest quantity of milk if you pump first thing in the morning, when your breasts are particularly full. You're also likely to get more milk early in the week, when you're more rested, than toward the end of the week.

The numbers game

Increase the frequency of pumping sessions rather than the duration of each individual session. It's better to pump 4 times per day for 5 minutes a session than to settle in for a single 20-minute marathon.

The more the merrier

You can increase the amount of breast stimulation (and hence the amount of milk) by either double-pumping or nursing your baby on one side while you pump on the other. Pumping both of your breasts at the same time can help boost your milk supply by convincing your body that it needs to produce enough milk for two babies. Although the latter may sound like something that is best left to the more coordinated folks among us, it's actually not as difficult as it sounds. If your baby is a world-class wiggler and likes to let go of the breast a few times until your milk really gets flowing, you might find it easiest to get him latched on first and then put the pump to the other breast.

Different strokes for different folks

Some women find it helpful to spend a few minutes massaging their breasts before they try to pump. Basically, it's a matter of using the same techniques that you use when you conduct your monthly breast self-examination.

Here's how to get started:

- Sit in a comfortable position, ideally with your feet up.

- Place a warm towel across one breast (or both breasts, if you're double-pumping) for a minute or two, and then massage one or both breasts, using a circular motion. (For best results, start at the top and move around the sides and the bottom.)

- When you're finished massaging your breasts, lean over and shake them gently. This should encourage the milk to start flowing.

- Relax while you pump. This is an ideal time to catch up on some leisure reading, so be sure to keep the latest issue of your favorite magazine handy.

- If the flow of milk seems to be slowing down again, try massaging your breasts again.

A bit of inspiration

If you're pumping on one breast while you nurse your baby on the other, you've already got all the inspiration you need. But during those times when you're pumping while you're away from your baby, you may find it helpful to keep a snapshot of your baby (or of you nursing your baby) in front of you while you pump.

Switching sides

To maximize the amount of milk you obtain, switch breasts at least once per session (preferably twice). You'll be surprised how much more milk is actually left in a breast that initially appears to be empty.

Helping nature along

If you're still finding it difficult to get the milk flow-ing initially, ask your doctor for a prescription for an oxytocin nasal spray that you can use temporarily until you get into the whole pumping routine. Oxytocin is the hormone in your body that is responsible for causing your milk to let down. It's also responsible for the so-called nursing high that many nursing mothers experience. Bet you didn't realize that breastfeeding could be so addictive!

If pumping is becoming a chore and you're still not collecting enough milk to leave with your baby's childcare provider, you might want to consider supplementing with formula. Any amount of breast milk is beneficial to your baby (although, naturally, more is better). If you do decide to introduce formula to your baby's diet, don't try to force him to change his eating habits cold turkey. Mix breast milk with formula, gradually reducing the amount of breast milk over time as you ensure that your baby is able to tolerate the particular brand of formula you've selected. By proceeding slowly, you should be able to prevent your baby from becoming unduly constipated—an all-too-common problem when breastfed babies are suddenly switched to formula.

Storing breast milk

Breast milk can be stored at

- 0°F (–19°C) for six months or longer
- 32–39°F (0–4°C) for five to eight days
- 59°F (15°C) for up to 24 hours
- 66–72°F (19–22°C) for up to 10 hours
- 79°F (25°C) for 4 to 8 hours

Note: If you are freezing breast milk, be sure to date each container of milk so that you can make a point of using the oldest milk first.

Here are some additional pointers on storing breast milk:

- Breast milk should be refrigerated or frozen until use. Because freezing kills some of the antibodies in breast milk, it's best to refrigerate rather than freeze as much as possible.

■ Breast milk should be frozen in heavy plastic or glass containers or specially designed freezer bags. Disposable bottle liners simply aren't designed to tolerate the extreme change in temperature. If you freeze your breast milk in freezer bags, double-bag them or keep them in a larger container to protect them from punctures.

■ Freeze the milk in two- or three-ounce portions. If you fill an eight-ounce bottle with breast milk, you run the risk of having to throw it away if your baby drinks only a portion of it.

■ Refrigerate freshly pumped breast milk before adding it to frozen breast milk. This will prevent the warm milk from defrosting the top layer of frozen milk.

■ Breast milk often turns yellow when it has been frozen. This does not mean that the milk has spoiled.

■ Once breast milk has been thawed, it should not be refrozen. It can, however, be safely kept in the refrigerator for up to nine hours—perhaps even longer.

■ It's not unusual for breast milk to separate. If this occurs, simply shake your baby's bottle for a moment or two until the breast milk reconstitutes.

■ Breast milk should be thawed in running water. Don't heat it in the microwave or on the stove top. Not only do you run the risk of overheating the breast milk, but you also may destroy some valuable nutrients.

Bottle-feeding your baby

Although breast milk offers some advantages that formula can't provide, formula feeding is a perfectly acceptable alternative if you choose not to breastfeed your baby.

A generation ago, women fed their babies a mixture of evaporated milk, water, and sugar. Today, parents who decide to offer their babies bottles buy commercially prepared formulas that are designed to be easy to digest.

Your basic choices in formula are

- cow's milk–based formulas,

- soy-based formulas (for babies who cannot tolerate the lactose in cow's milk),

- specialized formulas designed to meet the needs of infants with particular disorders or diseases, as well as infants who are premature.

Most formulas are available in three different formats:

- premixed cans of ready-to-feed formula (the most convenient option but also the most expensive),

- concentrated cans of formula that need to be mixed with sterile water,

- powdered formula that needs to be mixed with sterile water.

Always check the expiration date on cans of formula and avoid purchasing any that are in dented or damaged cans.

There are three basic types of bottles on the market:

- plastic bottles with disposable liners (the most convenient option but also the most expensive),

Bright Idea
Premeasure the amount of powder you need to make a bottle, and carry it around in your baby's change bag in an empty bottle. If you find yourself away from home longer than anticipated and your baby gets hungry, you'll simply need to add water to mix up a bottle. You'll minimize any problems with lumping and clotting if you use slightly warm water.

Watch Out!
Nipples come in
different sizes.
The holes in
newborn nipples
are very small
(to slow the flow
of milk), whereas
the ones in tod-
dler nipples are
relatively large.
Ideally, when
you're feeding
your newborn,
formula should
drip out at the
rate of one drop
per second.

- plastic bottles that need to be cleaned with a bottle brush,

- glass bottles that need to be cleaned with a bottle brush.

To prepare bottles, you need to sterilize all of your equipment. The water you use to make formula should be brought to a rolling boil for at least one minute, cooled, and then mixed with the liquid or powdered formula. The bottles will then need to be stored in the refrigerator. They will keep for up to 24 hours.

When you go to feed your baby, you will probably want to warm the bottle up to room temperature by sitting it in a measuring cup filled with warm water. (*Note:* You don't need to purchase a commercial bottle warmer, and you should never heat a bottle in a microwave because doing so can result in hot pockets of milk that might burn your child.)

Newborn bottle-fed babies typically drink two to three ounces of formula per feeding and eat every three to four hours during the first few weeks of life. By the end of the first month, the baby should be taking about four ounces of formula and eating approximately once every four hours.

Do not reuse any formula that is left in your baby's bottle at the end of a feeding.

Now that you know what's involved in feeding your baby, let's talk about what else you need to know to survive the postpartum period—the subject of the next chapter.

Just the facts

- Nurse your baby as soon as possible after birth—ideally within one hour.

- Pay careful attention to positioning. Ninety percent of breastfeeding difficulties are caused by positioning problems.

- Plan to nurse your baby as often as she's willing—approximately 8 to 12 times in a 24-hour period.

- You can reduce your chances of developing a breast infection by ensuring that you're getting the rest you need.

- If you will be pumping milk on a regular basis—or for multiples—go for a heavy-duty hospital-grade breast pump. Small battery-operated and electric models aren't designed for large amounts of use.

- Breast milk should be refrigerated or frozen until it is needed. Freeze it in small quantities so that you won't have to waste a drop of this "liquid gold" if your baby isn't very hungry.

- A bottle-fed newborn eats almost as often as a breastfed newborn—every three to four hours.

GET THE SCOOP ON...
What babies are really like ▪ How to tell if your
baby is sick ▪ Caring for a premature baby or a
baby with special needs ▪ How you may be feeling physically ▪ Postnatal fitness ▪ How you
may be feeling emotionally ▪ Sex after baby

The Postpartum Survival Guide

N o matter how much time you've spent reading up on babies or how much time you've
spent around newborns, nothing can really
prepare you for the joys and challenges of the first
weeks of your baby's life. Some women recall the
early days postpartum as a wondrous time: a chance
to get to know their babies and to celebrate the act
of creation that brought them into being. Others
feel overwhelmed by the demands of new motherhood—the lack of sleep, the aches and pains of the
postpartum period, the need to be constantly at
their babies' beck and call, and the overwhelming
sense of responsibility that comes with parenthood.
Most women feel a mix of emotions—both euphoria
and exhaustion.

Katharine de Baun, the founder of Moms Online
(www.momsonline.com) remembers the postpartum period as a time of tremendous personal
growth: "In having to care 24 hours per day for a little baby, I was exhausted and overwhelmed, of
course, but I was also secretly relieved to be able to

633

stop being so obsessed with myself. When I became a mom I finally let go of the long-in-dying angst of my twenties; I felt like a true adult for the first time in my life. For me, motherhood was nothing less than a revolution in my identity, my priorities, my maturity."

Most women have a million questions about life after baby: what to expect from their babies, what to expect from their own bodies, and what to expect their lives to be like during the weeks and months ahead.

In this chapter, we address some of the most common concerns of new parents: newborn behavior, postpartum recovery, the "baby blues" and postpartum depression, postnatal fitness, and resuming sexual intimacy.

The truth about babies

If you've never been around a newborn baby before, you may be surprised by your baby's sleeping, eating, elimination, and crying patterns. Here's a sneak peek at what you can expect to experience during the first few weeks of your baby's life.

Sleeping

A long day of parenthood is finally drawing to a close. You abandon your plans to fold that last load of laundry, heading for bed instead. You no sooner fall into a deep sleep when you're awakened by the only member of your family who seems to be getting enough rest: your baby!

If you're feeling a bit frazzled and exhausted by your baby's erratic sleep patterns, you're not alone. According to Dr. Richard Ferber, author of *Solve Your Child's Sleep Problems,* newborn babies typically sleep about 16 or 17 hours per day, but rarely for more than a few hours at a time.

Fortunately for parents, babies' sleep patterns evolve over time. "During the first few weeks of life, a baby's patterns are erratic," said Dr. Deborah Lin-Dyken, a developmental pediatrician at the University of Iowa Hospitals and Clinics. "By age three to six months, however, most babies have switched to a circadian rhythm in which they sleep more at night than during the day."

It's at this point that most babies are ready to start sleeping through the night. According to pediatrician Dr. Alan Greene, babies are able to make this transition more easily if their parents have prepared the proper groundwork during their first weeks of life. Greene recommends that parents teach their babies the difference between night and day by exposing their babies to normal household noise during their waking hours and by engaging them in plenty of direct eye contact—something that babies find particularly stimulating.

"The most powerful wake-up activity is direct eye contact," Greene says. "When your baby locks eyes with you, it's almost like she's drinking a double latte. Her heart beat speeds up, her blood pressure rises a bit, and she becomes more awake."

Greene suggests that parents stroke their babies' feet during the daytime, because he says this stimulates the pineal gland, which helps in the regulation of the body's circadian rhythms. At night, the amount of stimulation should be kept to a minimum, and parents should rely upon a series of pre-bedtime rituals designed to cue the baby to the fact that the sandman awaits.

Whereas some babies start sleeping through the night largely on their own, others seem determined to stubbornly resist their parents' attempts to

Watch Out!
Don't lay your baby on her stomach when you tuck her into bed. The American Academy of Pediatrics recommends that babies be placed on their backs when they are sleeping—a position that has been proven to reduce the risk of sudden infant death syndrome.

Unofficially...
Although 16½ hours of sleep per day is the norm, some babies thrive on as few as 10 hours of sleep, whereas others need as many as 22 hours per day.

encourage them to abandon their nocturnal habits. Still, although it can be exhausting to have your sleep disrupted night after night, not everyone sees parenting a night-waking baby as a problem. Some parents—particularly ones with other children who demand their time and attention by day—may actually cherish a few stolen moments alone with their baby in the wee hours of the morning. Others—although not exactly overjoyed at the prospect of losing sleep—simply accept the fact that the baby is not yet ready to sleep through the night, and resolve to make the most of the situation while they wait for their baby's sleep patterns to mature.

Most sleep experts agree that any attempts to encourage a baby to sleep through the night should be left until the child is at least six months of age. "Prior to that time, a child's brain and nervous system are simply not sufficiently mature to enable him or her to sleep through the night," explained Dr. Charles Pohl, the director of the Pediatric Sleep Center at Thomas Jefferson University in Philadelphia, Pennsylvania.

The secret to making it through the newborn period without turning into a total zombie is to sleep when the baby sleeps—and to remind yourself that your life won't be like this forever. Studies have shown that 90% of babies will sleep six to eight hours at a stretch by the time they reach three months of age.

Eating

Whether your baby is breastfed or bottle-fed, she is going to spend a lot of time eating. Babies this age need to eat frequently in order to ensure that their small stomachs receive an adequate number of calories over the course of the day. Breastfed newborns typically nurse 12 times per day, and bottle-fed newborns usually eat at least eight times per day.

When you stop to consider the fact that the entire feeding cycle (feeding, burping, and diapering) can take as long as an hour, it quickly becomes apparent that a good part of your day is going to be spent feeding and caring for your baby. If you're breastfeeding, you may want to consider taking the baby into bed with you for a middle-of-the-night feeding. If you're bottle-feeding, you may want to trade off middle-of-the-night feedings with your partner: if you get the midnight feeding and your partner gets the 3:00 a.m. feeding, you each have a fighting chance of getting four or five consecutive hours of sleep.

Elimination

Ever wonder why the newborn packages of disposable diapers are sold in packages of 60? It's because newborns go through a phenomenal number of diapers during the first few weeks of life. During the first six weeks of life, most babies have at least one bowel movement a day—although some may have as many as 15. What's more, a typical newborn urinates 20 to 30 times each day, which means that you'll want to change your baby's diaper at regular intervals throughout the day. This doesn't mean you should panic if your baby only has six wet diapers each day, however. She may have urinated three or four times since you last changed her, but not enough to soak through her diaper.

The appearance of your baby's diapers will change tremendously during the first few weeks. Her first stools—made up of a greenish-black, sticky

Bright Idea
A baby who sleeps all day needs to nurse more frequently at night. Try to ensure that your baby nurses at least every three hours duing the daytime so that, over time, she will learn how to reserve her longest stretch of sleep for the time of day when you need it most—the middle of the night.

substance known as meconium—will be passed during the first few day or two of life. During the next few weeks, your baby's stools will become greenish-brown and semiliquid. Sometimes these so-called "transitional stools" are bright green and full of milk curds and mucus. When your baby gets to be about three weeks old, her stools will change again. Breastfed babies will develop orangey-yellow stools that are mustard-like in appearance and smell faintly of sour milk. Bottle-fed babies will develop solid, pale-brown bowel movements that have a stronger odor.

By the time she reaches six weeks of age, a breast-fed baby may be having as few as one bowel movement a week. This is because breast milk leaves very little solid waste to be eliminated from your baby's digestive system. Breastfed babies rarely experience problems with constipation. Any bowel movement that is looser than the consistency of peanut butter is perfectly normal for a breastfed baby.

Unofficially...
Most babies lose 5% to 10% of their birthweight during the first few days of life.

Bottle-fed babies are more likely to experience problems with constipation than breastfed babies. As a rule of thumb, bottle-fed babies should have at least one bowel movement per day. If your baby goes for more than a day without a bowel movement or appears to be straining, she may be constipated. Call your caregiver for advice.

Don't be alarmed if you notice a pinkish stain on your baby's diaper. This stain is usually a sign of highly concentrated urine, which has a pinkish color. As long as the baby is having at least four wet diapers per day, there's probably no need for concern, but if the pinkish staining persists or you notice any bright-red blood, get in touch with your baby's doctor.

Crying

The baby who sleeps all the time in the hospital and never utters so much as a whimper often has a surprise in store for his parents a week or two down the road. Long periods of crying typically set in during the second or third week of life, peaking in duration and frequency at about the six-week mark. Many babies have at least one daily crying session of 15 to 60 minutes that cannot easily be explained. More often than not, it hits in the evening when you want nothing more than to eat your dinner in peace or to curl up in bed with a book.

Your baby's cry is designed to elicit a powerful response in you so that you will respond to his needs right away. That's why most adults find it so distressing to listen to a baby's cry.

Although coping with a crying baby can be extremely difficult, some pediatricians, like Dr. Alan Greene, believe that there's a silver lining to these crying episodes. "Colic is a powerful rite of passage, a postnatal labor pain where new patterns of family life are born," he explains. "Even after the miracle of a new birth, many parents and families would revert back to their previous schedules and activities within a few weeks if the baby would only remain quiet and peaceful. Instead, the baby's exasperating fussy period forces families to leave their previous ruts and develop new dynamics, which include this new individual. Colic demands attention. As parents grope for solutions to their child's crying, they notice a new individual with new needs. They instinctively pay more attention, talk more to the child, and hold the child more—all because of the colic."

Although colic may be an effective anthropological tool for encouraging parents to spend time with their babies, it's easy to lose sight of its advantages when you've spent the past three hours walking a baby who is inconsolable. If your baby develops full-fledged colic (crying for a number of hours each day that typically lasts until the baby is three months of age), you may be desperate to find a way to soothe your baby.

Here are some techniques that have worked for other parents:

- rocking your baby (either in a rocking chair or in your arms as you sway from side to side);

- laying your baby tummy-down across your knees and gently rubbing her back (the pressure against her abdomen may help relieve her discomfort);

- gently stroking your baby's head or patting her back or chest;

- swaddling your baby snugly in a receiving blanket;

- singing or talking to your baby, or playing soft music;

- walking around with the baby in your arms, in a baby carrier (for example, a sling or Snugli), or in a stroller;

- taking your baby for a ride in the car;

- putting your baby in a baby swing (ideally a battery-operated model that doesn't need winding);

- exposing your baby to white noise (that is, low-level background noise like the sound that a vacuum cleaner or blow dryer makes);

Moneysaver
Rather than purchasing a commercially available baby-soother tape, make one of your own. Record "white noise" sounds that your baby finds particularly soothing: the dishwasher, the hair dryer, the vacuum cleaner, and so on.

- burping your baby to get rid of any trapped gas bubbles;
- bathing your baby in warm water.

If none of these techniques works, it could be because your baby is exhausted. Some babies engage in "discharge crying" when they are tired. They are inconsolable until you lay them in their cribs, at which point they fall into a deep sleep within a minute or two. (If you try this and your baby doesn't settle within five minutes or so, there's probably something else bothering him.)

Food sensitivities also contribute to fussiness in some babies. If you are nursing, try eliminating any foods that could be contributing to your baby's fussiness. Perennial offenders include milk products, caffeine, onions, and cabbage. If you are bottle-feeding, try switching from a milk-based formula to a soy-based formula to see if that helps with the problem. If food sensitivities are causing your baby's fussiness, you should see a marked improvement within a day or two of eliminating the problem foods.

If you feel that you're reaching your wits' end, have someone else care for your baby for an hour or two so that you can have a break. Even though you may feel guilty for leaving your baby in someone else's care and worry that no one else will be able to meet her needs as you can, it's important to recharge your parental batteries on a regular basis.

A crash course in baby care

Here's everything you need to know about caring for your newborn during the first few weeks of life.

Bathing

Until your baby's umbilical cord falls off (something that typically happens when she's about 10 days

Unofficially...
According to a recent story in the Associated Press, Ann Turner Cook, the original Gerber baby, is now a 72-year-old retired English teacher.

old), your baby should only have sponge baths. Here's how to give your baby a sponge bath:

1. Lay a towel on a flat surface in a warm area of your home.

2. Fill a bowl with warm water and place a bar of baby soap and a baby washcloth beside it.

3. Wrap your baby in a towel so that only the part of her body that you're washing at the time is exposed to the air.

4. Use a dampened washcloth (no soap) to wash her face.

5. Rinse the washcloth and then dip it in soap before washing the remainder of her body, finishing up with her diaper area.

Skin care

The best way to care for your baby's skin is to keep it clean and dry. Lotions, oils, and powders are rarely necessary. If your baby's skin becomes overly dry, it could be because you are bathing her too often. Cut back your baby's bath to once a week and see if that helps with the dryness.

Don't be alarmed if your baby develops "baby acne"—pimples that break out on the face during the fourth or fifth week of life. They are believed to be caused by the stimulation of oil glands in the skin by hormones passed across the placenta during pregnancy.

Other common skin conditions during the newborn period include cradle cap (scaly patches on the scalp, which usually disappear spontaneously within a couple of months) and diaper rashes (redness or small bumps on the lower abdomen, buttocks, genitals, and thigh folds, usually caused by prolonged exposure to urine or fecal material).

Both may require special treatments or medications if they become particularly severe. Contact your baby's caregiver if you're concerned.

Nail care

Newborn babies are often born with unbelievably long fingernails, and the nails continue to grow at a rapid pace. Keep your baby's fingernails as short and smoothly trimmed as possible so that he can't scratch himself. If you're reluctant to use nail scissors or clippers (even the baby-safe style), try biting your baby's nails while he's nursing or having his bottle.

How to tell if your baby is sick

One of the biggest worries of new parents is how to know when the baby is sick and requires medical attention. Here are some tips on dealing with fevers and other ailments your baby might develop.

Fevers

If you suspect that your baby has a fever, you should take her temperature so that you'll have a concrete reading to pass along to her doctor. The best way to take a young baby's temperature is by using a rectal thermometer.

You should call your baby's doctor immediately if

- your baby has a rectal temperature of 100.2°F (37.0°C) or higher and is less than two months old or 101°F (38.3°C) and is between two and six months old;

- your baby experiences a convulsion for the first time (her body stiffens, her eyes roll, and her limbs flail);

- your baby is crying as if she is in pain;

Bright Idea
To ensure that your baby stays warm without becoming over-heated, dress him in one more layer of clothing than what feels comfortable to you.

- your baby appears to be having difficulty breathing;

- your baby appears to have a stiff neck (for example, she resists when you try to pull her head forward toward her chest);

- your baby appears to be dehydrated or suffering from heat stroke.

Your baby's caregiver will probably advise you to

- keep the baby cool by removing excess layers of clothing,

- increase her fluid intake,

- give her a fever-reducing medication such as acetaminophen.

Other health problems

Fevers aren't the only types of health problems that warrant medical attention in a newborn. Here are some other medical conditions to watch for:

- **Abdominal distention:** If your baby's abdomen feels swollen and hard and he either has not had a bowel movement for a couple of days or is vomiting heavily, call your baby's caregiver. In the majority of cases, the problem is caused by gas or constipation, but it could potentially signal a more serious intestinal problem.

- **Severe vomiting:** Forceful vomiting (vomit that shoots out several inches from the mouth) can be an indication that your baby has an obstruction of the valve between the stomach and the small intestine. Contact your baby's caregiver.

- **Lethargy:** If your baby is rarely alert, doesn't wake up on his own for feedings, or seems disinterested in eating, contact his caregiver immediately. Your baby could be becoming dehydrated.

- **Respiratory distress:** If your baby experiences rapid breathing (more than 60 breaths in one minute), retractions (when the ribs stick out with each breath), flaring of the nose, grunting while breathing, or persistent blue skin color, your child could be experiencing respiratory distress. Contact his caregiver immediately.

- **An infected umbilical-cord stump:** If you notice pus at the base of the cord or red skin around the base of the cord, or if your baby cries when you touch the stump with your finger, your baby's umbilical-cord site may be becoming infected. Contact your baby's caregiver.

The facts about sudden infant death syndrome

One of the biggest fears of new parents is that their child will die as a result of sudden infant death syndrome (SIDS). Although SIDS is relatively rare—it happens to one to two out of every thousand apparently healthy babies between the ages of 4 and 16 weeks of life—certain babies are at greater risk of SIDS. These risks include

- low-birthweight male babies born in winter

- premature babies

- babies whose mothers smoke

- babies who sleep on their stomachs

Although scientists are still trying to unlock the mysteries of SIDS, it is widely believed that babies who die as a result of SIDS have immature arousal centers in their brains, something that predisposes them to stop breathing under certain circumstances.

A group of genetically inheritable metabolic disorders has also been identified as a rare (less than 5%) cause of SIDS. DNA testing can identify

Unofficially...
Babies are born with a number of important reflexes: the rooting reflex (rooting for the breast if her cheek or mouth is brushed), the Moro or startle reflex (throwing the arms and legs outward and crying loudly if startled), the palmar grasp reflex (grasping your finger when you stroke the palm of her hand), and the stepping reflex ("walking" when the feet are placed on a flat surface). Most of these reflexes disappear within the first six months of life.

carriers of these genes so that babies at risk can be identified and treatment procedures that can help prevent SIDS from occurring can be started after birth. This testing may be especially appropriate for those couples who have lost one baby to SIDS or have other history that places them at risk. A consultation with a genetics counselor is advised.

If you lose a baby to SIDS, you may experience powerful feelings of grief and depression. You will probably want to seek the services of a therapist and to join a support group for parents who have lost babies through similarly tragic circumstances.

Caring for a premature baby or a baby with special needs

Bright Idea
Rather than comparing your premature baby to a full-term baby born at the same time, compare your baby to other babies who were due at the same time that she was. During the early weeks, you might want to compare your baby to photos of fetuses still in utero who are at the same gestational age as your baby. (Lennart Nilsson's book *A Child Is Born* is an excellent source of such photos.)

If your baby is born prematurely or with birth-related or congenital problems, he may end up spending his first few weeks in the hospital—either in the neonatal intensive care unit or on the pediatric ward, depending on the extent of his health problems. You may find it extremely upsetting to leave the hospital without your baby, as Bridget, 36, did when her daughter, Jade, was born prematurely and with Dandy-Walker syndrome and other congenital anomalies. "You don't even feel like a mom because you don't have your baby," she recalls.

You may be worried about your baby, yet feel unsure about what questions to ask because everything about your baby's situation is utterly foreign to you. "It's like being in another country," Bridget explains. "You don't know the language or the customs."

Here are some tips on surviving your baby's hospitalization:

- Find out as much as you can about babies who are premature or who have special needs, either by talking to other parents or by having a family member do some research for you. (*Note:* Many hospitals have on-site pediatric reference libraries for the use of parents.) Ask someone in the unit—a parent or a nurse—to give you a crash course in ICU lingo so that you won't feel quite so intimidated.

▪ Bring a support person along when you're talking to the medical staff. "I didn't remember a lot of what the doctors were saying, so I made a point of having another relative there with me. It was good to have an extra set of ears to rely on," says Deirdre, 34, whose daughter experienced perinatal asphyxia and was left with multiple handicaps following the birth.

▪ Write down as much information about your baby's progress as you can. Note the baby's condition, medical treatments, medications, appearance, and alert periods, as well as your own thoughts and feelings about your baby. You may find it helpful to have this record of your baby's progress to refer to during the days ahead.

▪ Ask your baby's doctor if you can practice "kangaroo care." This involves laying your naked baby across your chest so that she can experience some skin-to-skin contact.

▪ Talk to a social worker or counselor about any concerns you may have about the care your baby is receiving. "I mentioned to the social worker that Rebecca was always sleeping when we were there," Deirdre explains. "She said she would ask the nursery staff about cutting down her medication or altering the time at which it was given so that she would be conscious during my visits. The next day I came in and found that they had taken Rebecca right off the medication that was causing her drowsiness."

- Ask if you can pump milk for the baby if she's unable to nurse. "Not only is it healthy for the baby; it makes you feel good to know that you are doing something that no one else can do for your baby," Deirdre explains.

- Don't become obsessed with all the monitors and high-tech equipment. "Let the nurses worry about them," Deirdre suggests.

- Personalize your baby's incubator by decorating it with balloons, stickers, and other items. If you want to buy a toy for your baby, however, make sure that it's made of plastic. Some hospitals won't allow stuffed animals around the incubators because they attract and hold bacteria.

- Don't beat yourself up if you aren't spending every waking moment at the hospital— particularly if your baby is hospitalized for an extended period of time. You won't be doing your baby any favors if you allow yourself to burn out.

- Ask if you can get special permission for someone other than you to spend time with your baby when you can't. "My aunt lives very close to the hospital where Rebecca was, so we made arrangements for her to visit with Rebecca as often as she wanted," says Deirdre. "It made me feel a lot better to know that she wasn't alone when we couldn't be there."

- Start preparing yourself for the day when your baby is discharged from the hospital. Participate as much as you can in your baby's day-to-day

Moneysaver
If your baby is being cared for out-of-town, ask if the hospital is able to help you to arrange any low-cost accommodations in the area.

care so that it won't be quite so scary when it's time to bring her home. Play with your baby when she is alert and awake, and sing to her during diaper changes. Start getting to know this precious little person who has just joined your family.

How you may be feeling physically

Your body went through a remarkable series of transformations while you were pregnant. Now your body is busy reversing those changes and returning to a nonpregnant state. Let's quickly run through some of the changes you can expect to experience during the postpartum period.

Weight loss

By the end of the postpartum period (six weeks after your baby's birth), you will probably be 17 to 20 pounds lighter than you were at the time you went into labor. This means that you will probably have at least a few extra pounds to lose—just as Mother Nature intended you to have. Just a quick reminder: Despite what the fashion moguls would have you believe, new mothers are supposed to have extra fat reserves so that they will have a fuel supply on hand for breastfeeding their babies. Clearly, the woman who slips into her prepregnancy jeans on her way home from the hospital is the exception rather than the rule. The majority of women look five to six months pregnant during the first week after the delivery.

Afterpains

The reason you still look six months pregnant is because your uterus is just beginning the process of returning to its prepregnant size (a process known as involution).

66

It took about three months before I could wear most of my prepregnancy clothing. Even though I lost all but five pounds by the time she was six weeks old, everything was somehow rearranged.
—Susan, 34, mother of one

99

During the first few weeks of the postpartum period, your uterus will alternately relax and contract. While this is happening, you may experience afterpains, which can range in intensity from virtually unnoticeable to downright painful. These afterpains tend to be more intense while you are nursing because the baby's sucking triggers the release of oxytocin, the hormone responsible for causing the uterus to contract.

Afterpains should not be confused with the symptoms of a serious infection or hemorrhage: extreme tenderness; severe, persistent cramping; or heavy bleeding. If you experience any of these symptoms, contact your caregiver immediately.

Lochia

The term *lochia* refers to the discharge that occurs as the uterus sheds its lining after birth. It typically lasts anywhere from 10 days to six weeks, starting out as a bright red, heavy flow, tapering down to a pinky-brown watery flow, and then becoming an almost colorless or yellowish discharge.

Many women find that their lochia turns bright red again if they engage in too much activity too soon. As Carl Jones cautions in *After the Baby is Born,* "A return of blood-tinged lochia after the discharge has faded usually means that you are overdoing things."

If you notice that your discharge suddenly becomes extremely heavy (that is, you soak more than one pad over the course of an hour) or it develops an extremely unpleasant odor, contact your caregiver immediately. You could be experiencing a postpartum hemorrhage or uterine infection.

Changes to the vagina

If you had a vaginal delivery, your vagina may feel stretched and tender during the weeks after the delivery, but it will soon return to its prepregnant state. Kegel exercises can help the process along and may prevent incontinence and gynecological problems.

Perineal pain

Your perineum is likely to be tender during the first few days after a vaginal birth—particularly if you had an episiotomy or a significant tear. This is because swelling in the perineal area can cause your stitches to pull, something that can be quite painful.

To reduce perineal pain, try one of the following techniques:

- Place ice in a washcloth or rubber glove and apply it to the swollen area (this technique is most effective during the first 12 to 24 hours after the delivery).

- Soak in a warm tub (either a bathtub or a sitz bath).

- Use a blow dryer to dry and warm your perineum.

Weakness in the pelvic floor muscles

The muscle that controls the openings of the vagina, urethra, and anus is stretched during both pregnancy and birth. If muscle tone isn't restored to the area, you may experience decreased vaginal tone; incontinence; or gynecological problems such as uterine, bladder, or rectal prolapse. (These problems are typically characterized by symptoms of pelvic pressure, an uncomfortable protrusion of tissues from the vaginal opening, painful or uncomfortable intercourse,

Watch Out!
If you decide to follow your mother's advice to use a heat lamp to promote healing of your stitches, make sure that you position the lamp at least a foot away from your perineal area and watch the clock closely to avoid giving yourself a burn in an already tender part of your body.

and the disruption of normal bladder and bowel function.) You can avoid many of these problems by doing your Kegel exercises religiously—even if you had a cesarean delivery.

Problems with urination

After months of running to the bathroom every couple of minutes, you may suddenly find yourself faced with the opposite problem: a decreased urge to urinate.

There are a number of reasons why you could experience this problem after the birth:

- Drugs and anesthesia used during the delivery may temporarily decrease the sensitivity of the bladder or your alertness to its signals.

- A low fluid intake both before and during labor, combined with an excessive loss of fluids through perspiration, vomiting, or bleeding, may mean that you simply don't need to urinate.

- Perineal pain may cause reflex spasms in the urethra (the tube that carries urine from the bladder), something that can make urination difficult.

- You may be afraid to urinate, fearing that the flow of urine over your perineum will be painful. (If this is the case, you might want to try urinating while you are sitting on the toilet saddle-style, when you are standing upright in the shower, or while you are pouring water across your perineum; or try drinking plenty of fluids so that your urine will be highly diluted and consequently less acidic.)

You can jump-start your waterworks by contracting and relaxing the pelvic area several times to stimulate the urethral response, running water, drinking lots of fluids, and placing hot or cold packs on your perineum—whichever one triggers your urge to urinate.

If you experience internal burning after urination or an intense, painful, and unusually frequent urge to urinate, you may have a urinary tract infection. Contact your caregiver to arrange for treatment.

Bowel movements

It's not unusual to go for two or three days without a bowel movement after you have given birth. This is because decreased muscle tone in the intestines, prelabor diarrhea, a lack of food during labor, perineal tenderness, and painful hemorrhoids may reduce your need or willingness to have a bowel movement.

If you become constipated during the postpartum period, simply increase your intake of fluids and fiber and remain active.

Breast changes

Even before you gave birth, your breasts were busy producing colostrum—your baby's first food. Sometime during the second or third day postpartum, your milk will come in. Your breasts can become very swollen and engorged during the 24 to 48 hours after that, regardless of whether or not you are nursing. You may also leak milk both during and in between nursings—a problem that is easily remedied by a hefty package of breast pads.

If you are breastfeeding, you can deal with engorgement by putting the baby to the breast more frequently or running warm water over your breasts and expressing just enough milk to relieve your discomfort.

> **"** My mom gave me this 'Mother's Journal' when I was pregnant. She wrote something in it for me, but her words just sounded corny before Ryan was born. But when I read it after he was born, her message made me cry. She had written, 'Welcome to the Club.' It brings tears to my eyes even now.
> —Tracy Moroney, mother of two, quoted in a recent article in the *Chicago Tribune* **"**

If you're bottle-feeding, you should keep your breasts tightly bound in a supportive bra (or two) and use ice packs, analgesics, or both to relieve the discomfort. Resist the temptation to express milk because you'll only prolong your misery: your body will increase milk production if it thinks that the milk is needed by your baby.

Sore nipples

If you are breastfeeding, you may experience some nipple tenderness during the first few days of nursing—particularly if your baby is a frequent or vigorous nurser.

The best way to treat sore nipples is to expose them to air and sunlight (or a heat lamp, if you're not into nude sunbathing). Walk around with the flaps of your nursing bra open, and stick to cotton—rather than synthetic—fabrics.

If nipple soreness doesn't disappear by the end of the first week, it's possible that a positioning problem is causing the discomfort. If in doubt, ask a lactation consultant, your local La Leche League leader, or an experienced breastfeeding mother to check your positioning.

Cesarean recovery

If you've had a cesarean birth, you may experience tenderness around your incision, gas buildup in your upper chest and shoulders, and fatigue. You've just been through major surgery. It's important to give yourself time to rest and recover.

The new you

Some of the changes your body experienced during pregnancy are permanent: your stretch marks won't fade away entirely, and your vagina may feel slacker than it did before. Other changes are temporary:

66

My husband and I love running together. After our baby was born, we bought a baby jogging stroller. It was a great way to make sure that we got to exercise together.
—Lynne, 32, mother of one

99

your flabby abdomen will eventually tighten up (with a little work on your part), and the day will come when you won't be dripping milk wherever you go. In the meantime, when you look at yourself in the mirror, remind yourself that you're not out of shape—you're in perfect shape for someone who has just had a baby.

Postnatal fitness

Some women are eager to start a postnatal fitness program right after the birth. Others prefer to use any baby-free moments to catch up on their sleep.

If you're one of the highly motivated few who manage to get their act together right after the delivery, be sure to take things slowly. Your body organs, system, and joints have undergone a tremendous amount of stress over the past nine months. Here are some tips on putting together an exercise program that's both safe and effective:

- Don't expect to be able to resume your prepregnancy fitness workout right away. Give yourself time to build up to your previous fitness level gradually. Stick to light workouts during the first two weeks postpartum. After that point, you can resume moderate physical activity, provided that you listen to your body if it tells you that you're working too hard.

- Rather than complicating things by trying to time your workout between feedings or arranging child care, find ways to include your baby in your workout. Push your baby in her stroller while you walk or run, take a baby aerobics class (where moms and babies are given opportunities to play together while the mother works out), or pop her in the Snugli while you ride on a stationary exercise bike.

Bright Idea
Hire a personal
trainer to design
a postnatal fit-
ness program you
can do in your
own home. If
you can afford
it, arrange to
have the trainer
come back
regularly to do
your workout
with you.

- Wear a sports bra or two nursing bras to provide your breasts with the support they need. If you are nursing, you may be more comfortable if you breastfeed your baby right before exercising.

- If you're having problems with incontinence, urinate before you start your workout and wear a panty liner to guard against leakage. Your problems with incontinence should disappear over time if you're diligent about doing your Kegel exercises.

- Make sure that your exercise program includes the following components: a warm-up, a cardio-vascular workout, strength training, flexibility training, and a cool-down. It should also include Kegels (to strengthen the muscles in your pelvic floor) and abdominal exercises such as curl-ups (to strengthen the muscles that support your stomach and your lower back).

- Keep your heart rate within the safe range for your age: 150 beats per minute if you're 20 to 25, 146 beats per minute if you're 25 to 30, 142 beats per minute if you're 30 to 35, 138 beats per minute if you're 35 to 40, 135 beats per minute if you're 40 to 45, and 131 beats per minute if you're over 45. (*Note:* These figures represent 75% of the maximum heart rate for nonpregnant women of the same ages.)

- Don't overdo it. Joint laxity (looseness) can be a problem for months after delivery. Perform all movements with caution and control, and avoid jumping; rapid changes of direction; jerky, bouncing, or jarring motions; and deep flexion or extension of joints. Also avoid knee-chest exercises, full sit-ups, and double leg lifts during the postpartum period.

■ Skip your workout if you're feeling particularly exhausted. Fatigue can lead to poor technique and possible injury.

■ Drink plenty of fluids before, during, and after your workout.

■ Stop exercising immediately and consult with a health-care professional if you experience any of the following symptoms: pain, faintness, dizziness, blurred vision, shortness of breath, heart palpitations, back pain, pubic pain, nausea, difficulty walking, or a sudden increase in vaginal bleeding.

■ To increase your strength and endurance, make a habit of exercising regularly—ideally two to three times per week.

■ Resist the temptation to diet—particularly if you're breastfeeding. You need an adequate intake of calories to cope with the demands of motherhood. Rather than drastically restricting your food intake, simply make healthier choices. (You might want to review the information on nutrition provided back in Chapter 8.)

How you may be feeling emotionally

As if the physical changes of new motherhood weren't enough to contend with, you may find yourself experiencing a lot of conflicting emotions during the postpartum period. One moment you may feel euphoric about being blessed with such a beautiful baby, and the next you may be crying because you can't even find 10 minutes to yourself to take a shower.

> 66
> I resumed my fitness program when my son was three months old. I simply used workout videos in my own living room while he was asleep.
> —Mary, 27, mother of one
> 99

Bright Idea
Save the squirt bottle that the hospital or birthing center gave you to clean your perineal site after the delivery. It's the ideal tool for rinsing shampoo out of your baby's hair.

You may also have other important issues to sort through: your feelings about the birth, your feelings about not being pregnant anymore, your feelings about your body, and your feelings about becoming a mother.

Your feelings about the birth

If your baby's birth followed your birth plan to the tee, you're probably euphoric about the way things went. If they didn't, you may be disappointed or angry about the way things went.

Leila, a 34-year-old mother of one, initially found it hard to accept the fact that she ended up with a cesarean section rather than the natural childbirth she had hoped for: "I hated myself for having a c-section. I was disappointed in my failure."

Women whose babies arrive prematurely often express similar feelings of disappointment. "I was sad when my first pregnancy ended because she was nearly seven weeks early," recalls Marilyn, a 43-year-old mother of three. "Physically and emotionally, I wasn't ready to let her go so early." Therese, a 31-year-old mother of one, experienced similar feelings: "I had the baby a month early and felt like I had been 'robbed' of a month of my pregnancy."

If you are not happy about some aspect of your birth, share your feelings with your partner, your caregiver, your doula, other support people who were at the birth, a trusted friend, or a therapist. It's important to resolve your feelings about such an important event in your life.

Your feelings about not being pregnant anymore

Some women feel a certain sadness after they give birth. Although they are delighted to have their babies, they miss being pregnant: "I missed feeling the baby move inside me," explains Therese.

Other women are delighted to have their pregnancies behind them: "I was so relieved not to be pregnant anymore," admits Anne, a 39-year-old mother of three. "I don't do pregnancy well."

Many women, like Mary, a 27-year-old mother of one, report a mix of emotions: "I felt both sad not to be pregnant anymore and glad to have my body back," she explains. "I missed the closeness and almost spiritual connectedness I felt while this baby was growing inside of me. I missed the warm looks I got from almost everyone, the attention, my own feeling of purpose and anticipation. But having my body back into shape and being able to wear the clothes I want, be sexy, be physically active, and even sip the occasional glass of wine is great."

Your feelings about your body

The first time you take a shower after having a baby, you may feel wonderfully slim. Gone is the huge stomach you've been carrying around for months, and you can even see your feet again.

Your feelings of svelteness are likely to last until you either try on a pair of prepregnancy pants or get a sideways glance at yourself in the mirror.

Some women find it hard to accept that they still look pregnant immediately after the delivery: "I felt very negative towards my body during the postpartum period," recalls Lisa, a 26-year-old mother of one. "It was very depressing to still have to wear those awful maternity pants when I wasn't pregnant anymore. I tried on a pair of my prepregnancy jeans a couple of days after I gave birth and almost burst into tears."

Other women—even those who have had a love-hate relationship with their bodies for much of their adult lives—finally make peace with their bodies.

Timesaver
Hang an empty plastic bag off the side of your baby's change table. As he outgrows outfits, toss them in the bag. When the bag is full, tie it closed and write the size and sex of baby clothes on the bag. That way, when it comes time to sell or reuse the garments, they'll all be organized according to size.

"I developed the most incredible respect, admiration, and sense of awe toward my body after the birth of my first child," says Marilyn, 43, who is currently expecting her third child. "Until I had a child, I knew nothing of my body's innate capabilities and how much it could do without my help. First it conceived and nurtured a fetus; then it birthed that child; then it fed that child in a way I could not have designed—first with colostrum and then with rich, nutritious milk in just the right amounts at the right times. I no longer looked at the outward flaws of my body; what I now felt was close to worship."

Jennifer, a 21-year-old first-time mother, experienced similar feelings: "I was in total amazement with my body after I had my daughter. I couldn't believe that my body had helped produce that beautiful baby. It was the most amazing thing."

Your feelings about becoming a mother

For first-time mothers, the biggest challenge of the postpartum period is adjusting to the fact that you are now someone's mother.

Mary, a 27-year-old first-time mother, remembers wishing that she was still pregnant: "In the first weeks after he was born, I felt overwhelmed by motherhood and longed for the days when he was safely tucked inside and all I had to do was dream and plan."

Jennifer, 25, who felt so empowered by the act of giving birth, resented the way her life changed after her baby's birth. "I felt like my life was over, like a life-term prison sentence had begun, and I hated my new role as mother and housewife."

Others are stunned to discover how quickly they begin to fall in love with their babies. "I remember being consumed with love for my first baby soon

> " The first days after my c-section, I felt this incredible, amazing love and respect and appreciation for my body and my gender. I was so proud of myself for having sustained that magnificent life in my body for nine months and given birth to her. I felt so beautiful and powerful—like I could climb Mount Everest.
> —Jennifer, 25, mother of one "

after she was born," recalls 43-year-old Marilyn. "I was in awe of and terrified of her power over me. I never felt so vulnerable in my love for another human being. What if something should happen to her? Would I survive?"

With this bond came a change in focus for Marilyn, a rethinking of priorities: "The moment I gave birth to her, an unexpected, involuntary transition took place. The universe no longer centered around me and what I wanted; instead, I stepped aside and placed her life and her well-being in the forefront."

Suzi, a 27-year-old mother of two, also views the moment she became a parent as a turning point in her life: "Becoming a parent has truly changed my life for the better. Everything I do has more meaning now. I work to provide for my children, I exercise so I can mentally handle being a mother and physically live longer and healthier to be here for my children. The house we bought, the neighborhood we live in, the cars we drive are all for our children. I want nothing more than to love my children and provide a nurturing environment for them to live in. I can't say one negative thing about parenting."

The baby blues versus postpartum depression

Given the massive physical and emotional challenges of the postpartum period, it's hardly surprising that some women report feeling depressed in the days following the delivery—the so-called baby blues.

"The day after giving birth—perhaps as a response to the incredible euphoria I'd experienced immediately after delivery and because of lack of sleep—I plunged into an abyss," confesses

I think the biggest thing about being a parent is how your perception of the world, yourself, and others changes. You are never able to watch a story involving a tragedy with a child without a lump in your throat, and you have sympathy for the lady in the supermarket with the child having a temper tantrum.
—Jodi, 30, mother of two

Unofficially...
According to a recent study in the *American Journal of Psychiatry,* 3% of fathers exhibit clear signs of depression after their babies are born. Men whose partners were suffering from postpartum depression were found to be at particular risk of experiencing depression themselves.

Marilyn, 43, who is currently pregnant with her third child. "I felt completely overwhelmed at the thought of taking care of a new baby—I felt completely inadequate and unprepared to do so. This feeling lasted for perhaps a week with both my babies."

If those feelings of inadequacy and depression last for longer than two weeks, leave you feeling completely exhausted or highly anxious, result in sleeping or eating disturbances, cause you to feel helpless or suicidal, or affect your ability to care for your newborn, you could be suffering from postpartum depression.

For some women, postpartum depression hits right after the birth: "I had major postpartum depression that started as soon as the baby was born," recalls Allison, 27, a mother of one. "I had to be put on antidepressants because I was so depressed that I wanted nothing to do with the baby. Thank God it finally subsided. But it lasted for about three months."

Others find that there's a delay before postpartum depression sets in: "I suffered from postpartum depression quite badly with all three pregnancies," recalls Karen, a 34-year-old mother of three. "It didn't kick in for a couple of months. I ended up getting help after my third child was born. I came to understand that I needed to drop some of my standards and accept that it was okay to use prepared foods sometimes, that I was entitled to sit with a latte for half an hour, and that, generally, I was doing a pretty good job."

"I didn't know I had postpartum depression until about eight months after the baby was born," says Anne, a 39-year-old mother of three. "I just realized I wasn't feeling spunky, happy, giggly, or sexy."

Some caregivers use the Edinburgh Postnatal Depression Scale (EPDS) as a tool for diagnosing postpartum depression. You can find a copy of this tool online at www.gp.org.au/cls/EDINB.html.

If you suspect that you are experiencing postpartum depression, it's important to seek help from your caregiver. You may also benefit from joining a postpartum-depression support group and sharing your experiences with other moms.

> 66
> Once I realized that I was dealing with postpartum depression, I was able to blame myself less.
> —Stephanie, 25, mother of one
> 99

Sex after baby

Although your caregiver will likely give you the go-ahead to resume sexual relations anywhere from two weeks until six weeks after your baby's birth, you may find that soreness in your perineal area, tenderness at the site of your cesarean incision, heavy lochia, or the mind-numbing fatigue that is so characteristic of the first few weeks postpartum serve to dampen your enthusiasm for sex at least for a while.

Here's what some of the members of our parent panel had to say about sex after baby:

"It took my husband and me a long time to resume our sex life. At first, we were just so completely exhausted. Sex was the last thing on our minds for about two months postpartum. Finally, at three months postpartum, things started calming down. The baby was sleeping more regularly, and we both were more rested.

"Often by the end of the day, I am 'touched out.' A nursing baby and a couple of other young children need a lot of physical contact. For my husband's sake, we began having sex again about two months after the baby was born. Once things got started, I enjoyed myself, but I had little desire to initiate things on my own."

"To be honest, my desire for sex was absolutely nil until the baby was about nine months old. Then it finally started to return."

"I lost my sex drive and still do not have it back fully after nine months. I love my husband dearly, but at night I just want to go to sleep and not worry about sex. We probably had sex about once a month from when our daughter was two months old until about eight months, and now it is getting better. It was really uncomfortable for about six months afterwards. We needed lots of lubrication because otherwise it was just painful."

"Honestly, for the first year after the baby was born, I couldn't have cared less if we ever had sex again. I just didn't feel sexy."

Even when the urge does resurface, some new parents find that their initial postbaby sexual experiences are anything but satisfying: "Our first attempt at intercourse was dreadful," recalls one first-time mother. "I had two significant tears, and even though they healed perfectly, I had a lot of pain when we tried intercourse. We tried lubricants, I tried relaxing, but nothing worked. We had several abandoned attempts over the course of a few weeks. My husband was very understanding, but I was very distressed and usually ended up crying. Finally, we decided to stop trying intercourse for a while, and expressed our intimacy in different ways. This helped immensely, both emotionally and physically. We were able to resume actual intercourse by six months postpartum, and it was completely pain-free for me then."

Not all couples find that having a baby puts a crimp in their style, however. Here's what one first-time mother had to say: "My husband and I started having sex again after two weeks. A little early, maybe, but we found creative ways to make it work. I've heard women say that they really had to plan for sex now that they have babies, but we found that the opposite was true: we perfected the quickie—anytime, anywhere, anyhow—because the baby slept so much."

Just because you'd rather sleep than cuddle up to your partner doesn't mean that your sex life is a thing of the past. Take it from this experienced mother: "First-time parents should realize that the frequency of sex will probably decrease significantly for the first few months. I know parents who didn't have sex for five months. However, things do get better."

> 66
> I didn't know the meaning of the word *tired* until after the baby was born. Utter exhaustion that words cannot describe.
> —Kim, 35, mother of one
> 99

Just the facts

- Newborn babies have erratic sleeping and eating habits and often have periods of unexplained crying. It's no wonder they need to be changed so often: a typical newborn urinates 20 to 30 times each day.

- The American Academy of Pediatrics recommends that babies sleep on their backs.

- A high fever (particularly one accompanied by a stiff neck), dehydration, abdominal swelling, severe vomiting, lethargy, respiratory distress, or an infection around the umbilical-cord stump all warrant a call to your baby's caregiver.

- Low-birthweight male babies born in winter, premature babies, babies whose mothers smoke, and babies who are put to sleep on their stomachs are at increased risk of falling victim to sudden infant death syndrome.

- If your baby is hospitalized for an extended period of time after the birth, it's important to take good care of yourself. Don't beat yourself up if you're not able to spend every waking moment at the hospital.

- You can expect to lose approximately 17 to 20 pounds of your pregnancy weight gain by the end of the postpartum period. You will probably still look five to six months pregnant during the first few days after you give birth because your uterus has not yet had a chance to return to its original size.

- Don't engage in any vigorous exercise for two weeks after a straightforward vaginal delivery—longer if you've had a cesarean or difficult birth. Stop exercising immediately if you experience pain, dizziness, a sudden increase in vaginal bleeding, or other worrisome symptoms.

- Don't be surprised if you experience a mix of emotions during the postpartum period. It's perfectly normal to feel this way.

- Although your caregiver will probably give you the go-ahead to resume sexual activity within two to six weeks after the delivery, it may take a little longer for your libido to kick in.

GET THE SCOOP ON...
Spacing your family ▪ The pros and cons
of various methods of contraception ▪
Preparing your older child for the birth
of a new baby

Your Next Pregnancy

E ven before you emerge from the postpartum fog, you should be giving serious thought to whether you want to have another baby. The reason is obvious: if you resume sexual relations before you have decided on a method of birth control, you're leaving an issue as important as the number and spacing of your children to fate.

In this chapter, we talk about a number of important issues related to family planning: the advantages and disadvantages of various methods of spacing a family, the pros and cons of various methods of contraception, and what you can do to prepare your older child for the birth of a new baby.

The space race

If you're planning to have more than one child, you'll need to consider the spacing of your family. Would you like to have your children in rapid succession—or would you prefer to have time to catch your breath before plunging into another pregnancy?

Having your children close together

There are clearly some advantages to having your children close together. You go through the diaper stage all at once, and your children have built-in playmates: one another.

"We had our first three children at nineteen-month intervals," says Marie, 34. "It was kind of wild when they were all little—we had a three year old, a nineteen month old, and a newborn at one point!—but now that they're a little older, it's great. They're never lonely because they always have one another to play with."

The downside to this scenario is obvious: parental exhaustion. If you have your children close together, you should expect to be tired for at least a year or two. Even if you're lucky enough to have both children on compatible sleeping schedules—and unfortunately it doesn't always work out that way—you will be dealing with the challenges of chasing after a toddler while you're trying to feed your newborn.

It's also important to factor in the sheer wear and tear on your body that can be exacted by two back-to-back pregnancies. Here's what Penelope Leach has to say about this whole issue: "If you have two babies eighteen months apart, you will be pregnant again when the first is only nine months old. You may ask your body to go straight from breast-feeding to intra-uterine feeding. You may be overwhelmed with nausea and/or sleepiness when your first child is at his most clingy and crawly, and when you are at your heaviest, he will still be young enough to need a lot of carrying."

Having your children further apart

For reasons like these, some families feel that it makes more sense to wait until their first child is a little older before having another baby. Susan, a 33-year-old mother of one, explains: "I'd like my first to be fairly independent and totally potty-trained before having another. I want each of my children to be 'the baby' for her fair share of time."

Some studies have shown that there are clear benefits to spacing your children a little further apart. As John Sussman and B. Blake Levitt note in *Before You Conceive:* "The spacing of pregnancies can be important, not just to help parents handle the increased workload of caring for children, but for the quality of life and development of the children themselves." Most studies of spacing issues indicate that children who are spaced two years apart or less from their siblings tend to have a lower IQ on average than children in families with greater gaps between births.

The downside to going this route, of course, is that your children may be too far apart in ages to enjoy playing together. A two year old and a ten year old are, for all intents and purposes, two "only children" who happen to share the same parents.

Sometimes, of course, the decision about the spacing of your children is taken out of your hands entirely. You may unexpectedly discover that you're pregnant again, or your best efforts to conceive your next child may be thwarted by an unanticipated episode of secondary infertility. (If you have difficulty conceiving, you may wish to review the material on fertility and infertility in Chapters 2 and 3.)

If you had difficulty conceiving the first time around, you may decide to start trying sooner than you normally would, just in case you experience fertility problems again: "Because of our battle with

Unofficially...
According to the U.S. Census Bureau, in 1997, there were 34,665,000 families with children under the age of 18. Of these, 41% had one child, 38% had two children, 15% had three children, 4% had four children, and 2% had five or more children.

Watch Out!
Studies have shown that closely spaced pregnancies are more likely to result in stillbirth, low birthweight, prematurity, and sudden infant death syndrome than more generously spaced pregnancies.

infertility and loss, we began trying immediately after the birth of our baby. We are still trying to conceive another child," notes Therese, a 31-year-old mother of one.

Contraceptive roundup

Although there are an ever-increasing number of contraceptive choices, the majority of U.S. adults continue to rely on three tried-and-true methods of controlling the size of their families: female sterilization (tubal ligation), the Pill, and the condom.

Table 20.1 gives a more detailed breakdown of who's using what, according to the National Center for Health Statistics Survey of Family Growth (1995).

As you've no doubt gathered by now, there's no such thing as an ideal method of birth control. They all have their downsides. Some are highly effective but may involve unacceptable risks or side effects. Others are relatively free of side effects or serious risks but have fairly high failure rates, especially for real-world users (for example, the real human beings who didn't use their condoms or diaphragm because they thought it was a "safe" time, or the woman with irregular cycles who practices the rhythm method). Bottom line? We know how to put a man on the moon, but we've yet to come up with a hassle-free and risk-free method of keeping the sperm from reaching the egg.

Let's take a quick run-through of the pros and cons of the various types of contraceptive products you're likely to find at your local pharmacy.

TABLE 20.1: CONTRACEPTIVE METHODS FOR WOMEN AGES 15–44 (NUMBERS ARE EXPRESSED AS PERCENT OF WOMEN IN EACH AGE GROUP)

	15–44	15–19	20–24	25–29	30–34	35–39	40–44
Female sterilization	17.8	0.1	2.5	11.8	21.4	29.8	35.6
Male sterilization	7.0	0	0.7	3.1	7.6	13.6	14.5
Pill	17.3	13.0	33.1	27.0	20.7	8.1	4.2
Implant (Norplant)	0.9	0.8	2.4	1.4	0.5	0.2	0.1
Injectable (Depo Provera)	1.9	2.9	3.9	2.9	1.3	0.8	0.2
Intrauterine device (IUD)	0.5	0	0.2	0.5	0.6	0.7	0.9
Diaphragm	1.2	0	0.4	0.6	1.7	2.2	1.9
Condom	13.1	10.9	16.7	16.8	13.4	12.3	8.8
Female condom	0	0	0.1	0	0	0	0

continues

Watch Out!
If having another baby right away would be a disaster for you and your partner, don't rely on breastfeeding as your sole method of birth control. Even though ovulation is generally suppressed in breastfeeding women who have had no periods since they gave birth, who are nursing on demand at least every four hours during the day and six hours at night, and who have babies under the age of six months, there is still a small risk of pregnancy.

	15–44	15–19	20–24	25–29	30–34	35–39	40–44
Periodic abstinence (rhythm)	1.5	0.4	0.6	1.2	2.3	2.1	1.8
Natural family planning	0.2	0	0.1	0.2	0.3	0.4	0.2
Withdrawal	2.0	1.2	2.1	2.6	2.1	2.3	1.4
Other methods*	1.0	0.3	0.9	1.2	1.3	0.9	1.8
Total percentage using contraception	64.2	29.8	63.4	69.3	72.7	72.9	71.5

*Other methods include morning-after pill, foam, cervical cap, Today™ sponge (currently not available in the U.S.), suppository jelly or cream (without diaphragm), and other methods not shown separately.

Condom

How it works: The male partner rolls the condom over his erect penis, leaving a small pocket at the end to collect sperm. The condom prevents sperm from reaching the cervix.

Effectiveness: 88% for average users

Pros:

- Condoms can be purchased right off the drugstore shelf. No prescription is required.

- They are relatively inexpensive ($.50 to $3.50 per use).

- They are a completely reversible method of birth control. You simply stop using them when you want to start trying to conceive.

- They can help protect against sexually transmitted diseases. (*Note:* Condoms made out of animal membranes do not protect against HIV.)

Cons:

- Condoms can interfere with the spontaneity of lovemaking. Just when things are getting interesting, one of you has to hop out of bed to try to find the box of condoms.

- Because condoms occasionally break or leak, most doctors recommend that they be used with contraceptive cream or jelly—something most users find to be unpleasant.

- If you use condoms while you are breastfeeding, you may also need to use a lubricant such as K-Y jelly. This is because the hormones associated with breastfeeding tend to dry up vaginal secretions, resulting in dryness that can cause soreness during intercourse.

- Some women are allergic to spermicides and latex, making condoms a poor choice.

Unofficially...
According to A. Christine Harris, author of *The Pregnancy Journal,* in certain tribes in New Guinea, couples are forbidden to resume sexual relations until after their baby has taken its first steps.

Female condom

How it works: A sheath is placed inside the vagina prior to intercourse.

Effectiveness: 75%–85% for average users

Pros:

- The female condom is available without a prescription.

- This birth-control method is fully reversible: simply stop using the product when you want to start trying to conceive.

- It can help protect against certain sexually transmitted diseases.

Cons:

- There is decreased vaginal sensation when the female condom is being used.

- The product protrudes outside the vagina, something that may bother you or your partner.

- It can be difficult to insert.

- Female condoms cost more than male condoms.

Diaphragm

How it works: A soft rubber dome is placed in the vagina in front of the cervix to stop the majority of sperm from making their way into the uterus. A spermicidal gel placed on the dome helps kill or immobilize those hardy sperm that do manage to make it that far.

Effectiveness: 82% for average users

Pros:

- The diaphragm is a relatively non-invasive method of birth control. You don't need to have surgery or take any hormones.

- It's relatively inexpensive: $20–$45 for the diaphragm plus $.50 or less per use for the gel.

- The diaphragm doesn't need to affect the spontaneity of lovemaking because it can be inserted in advance.

- The method is completely reversible. If you want to become pregnant, you simply stop using your diaphragm.

Cons:

- Diaphragms need to be prescribed and fitted by a health-care practitioner.

- They need to be refitted each time you give birth or lose or gain 10 pounds.

- Some women find them to be messy and awkward to use.

- Some women are allergic to spermicides and latex, making diaphragms a poor choice.

- Some studies have shown that women who use diaphragms are at increased risk of developing urinary tract infections due to the pressure they can exert against the bladder and urethra.

Cervical cap

How it works: A soft rubber dome is placed directly on the cervix to stop the majority of sperm from making their way into the uterus. A spermicidal gel placed on the dome helps kill or immobilize those hardy sperm that do manage to make it that far.

Effectiveness: 82% for average users

Pros:

- The cervical cap is a relatively non-invasive method of birth control. You don't need to have surgery or take any hormones.

Watch Out!
Don't think your diaphragm needs refitting only if you've had a vaginal delivery! If you had significant cervical dilation before having a cesarean section, your diaphragm may no longer fit properly. Don't take a chance. Have it refitted.

- It's relatively inexpensive: $20–$50 for the cervical cap plus about $.50 or less per use for the gel.

- The cervical cap doesn't need to affect the spontaneity of lovemaking because it can be inserted in advance.

- The method is completely reversible. If you want to become pregnant, you simply stop using your cervical cap.

Cons:

- Cervical caps need to be prescribed and fitted by a health-care practitioner.

- They are more difficult to insert properly than the diaphrams.

- They need to be refitted each time you give birth.

- Some women are allergic to spermicides and latex, making cervical caps a poor choice.

- The cervical cap has a higher failure rate in women who have given birth—even if they have been properly refitted. Some doctors suspect that this may have something to do with changes in the shape of the cervix after delivery.

- The cervical cap is not recommended for women who have a history of abnormal pap smears or toxic shock syndrome.

- The cervical cap can cause changes in the cells of the cervix, so you will need to have pap smears more frequently during the first one to two years of using this birth-control method.

Spermicides

How they work: Spermicides (creams, foams, vaginal suppositories, or vaginal film) are inserted into the vagina. These products then form a chemical barrier that either kills the sperm or prevents them from making their way past the cervix to the egg.

Effectiveness: 80% for average users

Pros:

- Spermicides are available without a prescription.

- They pose no known risks to human health (unless, of course, you are allergic to them).

- This method is fully reversible. If you wish to try to conceive, you simply stop using the spermicide.

- These products are relatively inexpensive (approximately $.50 or less per use).

Cons:

- Some women are allergic to spermicides; others experience minor vaginal irritations when exposed to these products.

- Spermicides can interfere with the spontaneity of lovemaking by necessitating a quick time-out in the heat of the moment. (Most of these products must be applied into the vagina within 30 minutes to an hour of ejaculation.)

- Spermicides aren't as effective as other methods of birth control (although their effectiveness can be increased if they are used along with condoms).

Oral contraceptives (also called "the pill")

How they work: Hormones (progesterone and estrogen in the regular pill or progesterone only in

Watch Out!
To reduce the risk of having an unwanted pregnancy, leave your diaphragm in place for 6 to 8 hours after intercourse. If you have intercourse again within that time, you will need to insert additional spermicide into your vagina via an applicator.

the mini-pill) are used to suppress the release of an egg, to change the conditions of the lining of the uterus, and to alter the quality of cervical mucus—the substance that helps transport the sperm to the egg.

Effectiveness: 97% for average users (higher when taken exactly as prescribed)

Pros:

- The Pill doesn't interfere with the spontaneity of lovemaking.

- It may help reduce the risk of ovarian and uterine cancer and pelvic inflammatory disease.

- It can be helpful in regulating the menstrual cycle and reducing the symptoms of PMS in certain women.

- The mini-pill (a progestin-only formulation) is often preferred for breastfeeding women and those who cannot or should not take estrogen (such as smokers in their mid-thirties or older, women with migraines, or those who get significant estrogen-related side effects).

Cons:

- Regular birth-control pills (pills that contain both estrogen and progestin) are not an ideal choice for women who are breastfeeding. They can decrease the mineral content of breast milk and reduce the milk supply.

- The Pill should not be used by women with a history of breast cancer, blood clots, liver disease, kidney disease, or unexplained uterine bleeding; who are smokers over the age of 35; or who are taking certain medications, certain antibiotics (such as rifampin), phenobarbital, phenytoin, and others that may decrease its effectiveness.

- It should be used cautiously by women with high blood pressure, diabetes, migraine headaches, depression, sickle-cell disease, or fibroids.

- Common side effects include nausea, breast tenderness, mid-cycle bleeding during the first few months, weight gain, an increase in appetite, mood swings, depression, headaches, and skin problems. Some rare side effects include phlebitis, liver disease, high blood pressure, gall-bladder disease, and migraine headaches.

- Taking the Pill can be expensive. A typical prescription will cost you approximately $25 to $45 each month (although generics, which appear to be equally effective, cost considerably less).

- You have to remember to take your pill each day—ideally at the same time of day. (*Note:* Although taking your pill at the same time of day is not necessary to ensure that the Pill is effective, doing so reduces the chances of unscheduled or "breakthrough" bleeding.)

Norplant implant

How it works: Six matchstick-sized tubes containing progesterone are surgically implanted into your upper arm under local anesthetic. They release progestin into your body on a continuous basis, disrupting ovulation, changing the quality of your cervical mucus, and making the uterine lining inhospitable to implantation by a fertilized egg.

Effectiveness: 99% for average users

Unofficially...
A recent study by researchers at Kaiser Permanente Medical Center in Oakland, California, challenges the controversial wisdom that women who take the contraceptive pill are at increased risk of heart attack. The study found that the only pill-users who face an increased risk of heart attack are those who are obese or who smoke.

Watch Out!
Some pregnancy books will tell you that bottle-feeding moms shouldn't start taking the Pill for at least 6 to 10 weeks after the births of their babies. Unfortunately, this is bad advice that reflects a lack of understanding of modern oral con-traceptives. Allowing this kind of gap can result in a very serious side effect: an unplanned pregnancy!

Pros:

- The Norplant implant is a hassle-free method of birth control. A Norplant implant can last for up to five years.

- It's reversible. Simply have the implant removed when you're ready to have your next child.

- It's believed to help protect against uterine cancer.

- It can be safely used while breastfeeding.

- It doesn't interfere with the spontaneity of love-making.

Cons:

- You'll have to come up with $450–$900 to have a Norplant inserted. (That works out to $90 to $180 per year over the five-year life of the implant.)

- It cannot be used by women who have liver disease, breast cancer, or unexplained uterine bleeding, or who have had previous problems with thrombophlebitis. It is not recommended for women with high blood pressure, gall-bladder disease, elevated cholesterol, irregular periods, headaches, or heart disease.

- Possible side effects of the Norplant implant include irregular bleeding, headaches, and nausea.

- A Norplant implant can be difficult to remove.

- Common side effects include irregular bleeding, prolonged periods, and light periods. A few women will also experience hair loss, acne, depression, or a decreased interest in sex.

- You may be able to see and feel your implant below the surface of your skin—something you may find disturbing.

Depo-Provera

How it works: Every three months, you receive an injection of progesterone. The progesterone prevents you from ovulating and causes changes to your cervical mucus, as well as the lining of your uterus.

Effectiveness: 99% for average users

Pros:

- Depo-Provera is extremely convenient. You simply schedule injections at three-month intervals.

- It helps protect against uterine cancer.

- It may reduce the severity of menstrual cramps.

- It is safe after childbirth and while breast-feeding.

- It is relatively inexpensive, costing $30–$65 for each three-month period.

- It does not interfere with the spontaneity of lovemaking.

Cons:

- Depo-Provera is not recommended for women with abnormal mammograms, high blood pressure, migraine headaches, asthma, epilepsy, diabetes, or other serious health complications.

- It cannot be used by women with thrombophlebitis, breast cancer, liver problems, or unexplained uterine bleeding.

- Possible side effects include irregular or absent periods, a decreased interest in sex, bloating, headaches, depression, and osteoporosis. Weight gain of five pounds during the first year and three to five pounds each year thereafter is not unusual.

- There can be a delay before your normal fertility resumes—anywhere from six months to two years after your last injection.

Bright Idea
Ask your caregiver to insert your Norplant implants, to give you an injection of Depo-Provera, or to provide you with a prescription for birth-control pills before you leave the hospital.

Emergency contraception (the "morning after" pill)

How it works: You take two combined estrogen/progestin birth-control pills within 72 hours of intercourse and two more 12 hours later, or you use a morning-after pill specifically designed for this use.

Effectiveness: 75%–95% for average users

Pros:

- Emergency contraception is a good backup measure if the condom breaks or your diaphragm or cervical cap becomes dislodged.

Cons:

- It can be prescribed only by a physician, and it is intended for use in emergency situations only (not as a routine method of birth control).

- If you had unprotected sex more than five days before the current episode of unprotected sex, you could be pregnant already and should take emergency contraceptive pills only after ruling out pregnancy with a sensitive blood pregnancy test.

- Common side effects include nausea, vomiting, bleeding, breast tenderness, and headaches. Serious side effects associated with longer term birth control use such as thrombophlebitis, heart attacks, strokes, liver problems, and high blood pressure do not seem to be a problem with emergency contraception.

(*Note:* If you are unable to use hormonal emergency contraceptives and you are at low risk of developing an IUD-related infection, your caregiver may recommend that you have an IUD inserted to attempt to prevent a pregnancy.)

Intrauterine device (IUD)

How it works: A T-shaped device is implanted in your uterus. It creates a uterine environment that is

> Emergency contraceptives are so safe. They could prevent, probably, if they were widely available, half of all unintended pregnancies in the United States and half of all abortions. All women should have an emergency contraceptive pill kit in their medicine chest, for themselves or a friend.
> —Dr. Bob Hatcher of Emory University Medical Center in Atlanta, quoted in a recent story at CNN.com

inhospitable to sperm by both interfering with the movement of sperm and preventing implantation. *Note:* There are two types of IUDs, a Copper-T IUD (ParaGard) and a progesterone-impregnated IUD (Progestasert).

Effectiveness: 99% for average users

Pros:

- An IUD is convenient. There's no need to think about birth control once it is in place (other than performing monthly checks of the IUD string to ensure that the IUD is still in place). A copper IUD can be left in place for 10 years, but a progesterone IUD needs to be changed annually.

- It can be used by breastfeeding women.

- It is easily reversed. You can start trying to become pregnant as soon as it is removed.

- It doesn't interfere with the spontaneity of lovemaking.

- You'll have to come up with $250 to $500 to have an IUD inserted. (That works out to $25 to $50 per year over the ten-year life of the ParaGard IUD.)

Cons:

- An IUD is not a good choice for a woman who is hoping to have children but has not yet started her family, because it is associated with an increased risk of infection, which might lead to fertility problems. Also, as noted below, there is a higher chance of expulsion.

- It should not be used by women with multiple sex partners or who have a history of pelvic inflammatory disease (PID) or ectopic

Timesaver
If you decide to go with an IUD, ask to have it inserted during your postpartum checkup.

pregnancy, because this compounds the risk of developing a serious pelvic infection.

- Possible side effects include cramping, backache, spotting, and heavy periods.

- You may experience some cramping and minor bleeding when the IUD is being inserted.

- IUDs are sometimes expelled during the first few months of use—something that can result in an unplanned pregnancy. (If you have had at least one child, you are less likely to expel the IUD from your uterus.)

- In about 2 out of every 1,000 cases, the IUD perforates the wall of the uterus during insertion.

- If you manage to become pregnant when an IUD is in place, you are at risk of experiencing a miscarriage, an ectopic pregnancy, or a premature birth.

Natural family planning

How it works: You monitor your basal body temperature and the quality of your cervical mucus to try to detect when you are most fertile, and then avoid intercourse during that time period.

Effectiveness: 75% for average users

Pros:

- Natural family planning is the least invasive method of birth control. Rather than relying on mechanical contraptions or hormonal methods to prevent the sperm from meeting the egg, you simply pay attention to your body's fertility signals and time intercourse accordingly.

Cons:

- You need to remember to take your basal body temperature each morning in order to learn more about your menstrual cycle and to monitor the quantity and quality of your cervical mucus over the course of your menstrual cycle.

- Couples who intend to use this method need to spend some time learning how to practice it correctly.

- You and your partner need to have the willpower to avoid making love during your most fertile period (or to rely on a secondary method of birth control).

- This method is not recommended for women with young babies because a woman's basal body temperature—one of the key sources of fertility information—isn't accurate unless she has had six hours of consecutive sleep—something most new mothers only dream of having.

- Women who are breastfeeding experience hormonal changes that affect cervical mucus, so they cannot rely upon the quality of their cervical mucus as a fertility sign.

- The fertile period is more difficult to predict in women with irregular cycles.

Tubal ligation

How it works: The fallopian tubes are cut and tied or otherwise surgically blocked to prevent the sperm and egg from meeting. The procedure is performed under either a local or a general anesthetic.

Effectiveness: 99%

Pros:

- Tubal ligation is a hassle-free permanent contraceptive solution for women who are certain that they don't want any more children.

Unofficially...
The Food and Drug Administration recently approved the Preven Emergency Contraceptive Kit—a kit that can prevent pregnancy when taken up to three days after a woman has unprotected intercourse. You can find out more about this product at www.PREVEN.com or by calling 1-888-PREVEN2

- A tubal ligation can be performed immediately after a vaginal or cesarean birth, or it can be performed via laparoscope two or more months after the delivery.

Cons:

- The procedure is not easily reversed, and if it is reversed, it is associated with a higher risk of ectopic pregnancy.

- Side effects after the procedure may include dizziness, nausea, slight abdominal pain or cramping, tiredness, shoulder pain, a gassy or bloated feeling, or general fatigue.

Vasectomy

How it works: The vas deferens—the tube that carries the sperm from the epididymis to the prostatic portion of the urethra—is cut and then tied off or cauterized.

Effectiveness: 99%

Pros:

- A vasectomy is far less invasive than a tubal ligation. It can be performed in a simple 20-minute procedure that can be performed in a urologist's office.

- A vasectomy doesn't interfere with either erection or ejaculation.

Cons:

- Occasionally, some bleeding or a minor infection may occur as a result of the procedure.

- Although the procedure is technically reversible, success rates vary and the expense is substantial. Therefore, it should not be used by anyone who is uncertain about whether he would like to have additional children.

Watch Out!
Vasectomies are not effective immediately. It can take 15 to 20 ejaculations—or more—for the male partner to clear out all remaining sperm from the male reproductive system. As a result, you and your partner will need to use another method of birth control until your partner gets the "all clear" signal following a semen analysis.

Coming soon to a drugstore near you

Here are a few of the most promising contraceptive methods for the future, according to *Parenting* magazine:

- the vaginal ring (a donut-shaped hormone-releasing ring that is inserted in the vagina for three weeks of each menstrual cycle),

- the transdermal patch, an adhesive patch that releases hormones through the skin,

- the male injection, a hormonal shot that would halt sperm production for up to three months.

Preparing your older child for the birth of a new baby

One of the biggest worries parents have when they are expecting their second or subsequent child is how the older children will react to the new baby. Although it's difficult to avoid any flare-ups of sibling rivalry—kids are only human, after all—you can do certain things to get your children's relationship off to the best possible start. Here are a few tips:

- Tap into your child's natural curiosity about babies. What child wouldn't be fascinated to learn that a newborn baby wets its diaper 20 to 30 times a day—or that it will triple its weight during the first year of life.

- Involve your older child in your pregnancy. Take him along to prenatal checkups so that he will have the opportunity to listen to the baby's heartbeat and to ask the doctor or midwife about the new baby.

- Resist the temptation to oversell the new sibling. Rather than focusing on how fun the baby will be in a year or two's time, let your child

Bright Idea
Want to give
your older child
a realistic idea of
what newborn
babies are really
like? *Baby
Science: How
Babies Really
Work,* by Ann
Douglas (one of
the co-authors of
this book), cov-
ers the basics of
infant develop-
ment in a child-
friendly way. You
can find out
more about the
book in
Appendix C.

know what the baby will be like when she first
arrives.

- Sign your child up for sibling preparation
classes. They are being offered by an increasing
number of hospitals, birthing centers, and
adoption agencies.

- Buy your child a small gift from the new baby—
perhaps a new book that the two of you
can enjoy together while the baby is eating or
sleeping.

- Take your child shopping with you when you're
picking out items for the new baby. Encourage
him to make as many purchasing decisions as
possible—what color of sleepers to buy, what
brand of diapers to pick out, and so on.

- Ask a friend or relative to do something special
with your older child shortly after the baby's
arrival. Some time alone with Grandma or
Grandpa may be all it takes to remind your
child that he's still as special as always.

- Encourage your child to participate in the
baby's care. Even a very young child can be
asked to pick out baby's outfit for the day or to
find a toy to entertain her. You might even
encourage your child to make a toy for the baby,
such as an eye-catching black-and-white mobile.

- When you pull out your camera, be sure to take
at least one shot of your older child. Otherwise,
he'll be quite disappointed when the film
comes back from the photo lab and there isn't a
single picture of him.

- Don't despair if sibling love doesn't blossom
overnight. It can take time for your older child

to develop feelings for the new baby, but that special sibling bond will begin to emerge over time.

No easy answers

There are no easy answers to the whole issue of family planning. There is no ideal method of spacing your children, no foolproof method of birth control, and certainly no guaranteed method of ensuring that your older child welcomes the new baby with open arms. Fortunately, the majority of couples manage to muddle through and make choices that—if not ideal—are at least ones they can live with.

Despite the fact that we now know more about the process of reproduction than at any other time in our history, we still have much to learn about the wondrous processes of pregnancy and birth. In fact, the reproductive landscape changes every day as research is conducted and discoveries are made. We hope you will use this book as a launching pad for your own ongoing research into these fascinating issues.

Just the facts

- If you have your children close together, you'll be perpetually exhausted for the first few years, but your children will have built-in playmates. If you have them further apart, you'll have a chance to catch your breath between pregnancies, but your children may be too far apart in age to be able to play well together.

- There's no perfect method of birth control. Some methods are difficult to reverse, others are expensive, and still others are either messy to use or have unacceptable side effects.

I was very open with David through my pregnancy—discussing the baby's development, my own changes, breast-feeding, and even conception. We looked through my prenatal books for pictures of fetuses in various stages of development and always identified the ones that were about the same 'age' as our baby.
—Elaine, 29, mother of two

- You can help prepare your older child for the baby's arrival by tapping into his natural curiosity about babies and by ensuring that there's a trusted relative or family friend on hand to shower your older child with special attention when the baby starts stealing the spotlight.

- If there's another baby in your future, make a point of staying up-to-date on the latest developments in reproductive health.

Glossary

Active labor The period of labor in which the cervix dilates from four to seven centimeters.

Afterbirth Another name for the placenta—your baby's physiological support system in utero.

Alpha-fetoprotein (AFP) testing A prenatal blood test performed between 15 and 18 weeks of pregnancy that is used to screen for both neural tube defects (high levels of AFP) and Down syndrome (low levels of AFP).

Amniocentesis A procedure that involves inserting a needle through the abdominal wall and removing a small amount of amniotic fluid from the sac surrounding the developing baby. The amniotic fluid is then used to test for fetal abnormalities or lung maturity.

Amniotic fluid The protective liquid, consisting mostly of water, that surrounds the baby inside the amniotic sac.

Amniotic sac (or amnion) The thin-walled sac within the uterus that contains the baby and the amniotic fluid.

Anencephaly   A birth defect resulting in a malformed brain and skull. Anencephaly leads to stillbirth or death soon after birth.

Apgar score   A measurement of a newborn's response to the stress of birth and life outside the womb. The test is performed one minute and five minutes after birth.

Areola   The flat, pigmented area encircling the nipple of the breast.

Biophysical profile   A prenatal test that assesses the well-being of the developing baby.

Bloody show   The mucus discharge—often tinged with blood—that indicates that the cervix is effacing or dilating.

Braxton Hicks contractions   Irregular contractions of the uterus that occur during pregnancy. They are felt most strongly during the late third trimester.

Breech presentation   When the fetus is positioned buttocks or feet down rather than head down.

Cephalopelvic disproportion   When the baby's head is too large for the mother's pelvis and birth canal.

Certified nurse-midwife (CNM)   A registered nurse who has received specialized training in caring for women during pregnancy, labor, and the postpartum period.

Cervical cap   A birth-control device, similar to a diaphragm, that is placed over the entrance to the cervix to block the passage of sperm.

Cervical dilation   The amount the cervix has opened up prior to or during labor. Cervical dilation is measured in centimeters (from 0 to 10). Ten centimeters is fully dilated and means that you're ready to push.

Cervical effacement   The thinning or drawing up of the cervix before and during labor.

Cervical incompetence   When a congenital defect or injury to the cervix causes it to open prematurely during pregnancy, causing miscarriage or a premature birth.

Cervix   The entrance to the uterus.

Cesarean section   The surgical procedure used to deliver a baby via an incision made in the mother's abdomen and uterus.

Chadwick's sign   A dark-blue or purple discoloration of the mucosa of the vagina and cervix during pregnancy.

Chlamydia   A common sexually transmitted disease that can render a woman infertile if left untreated. Antibiotics can be used to treat the disease.

Chloasma   Extensive brown patches of irregular shape and size on the face or other parts of the body that can occur during pregnancy.

Chorioamnionitis   An inflammation of the membranes surrounding the fetus.

Choriocarcinoma   A highly malignant cancer that can grow in the uterus during pregnancy or at the site of an ectopic pregnancy.

Chorion   The outer sac enclosing the fetus within the uterus.

Chorionic villus sampling (CVS)   A prenatal diagnostic test in which a few placental cells are extracted via a fine hollow needle or catheter inserted into the womb. DNA extracted from these cells is subsequently examined for genetic defects.

Chromosomal abnormalities   Problems that result from errors in the duplication of the chromosomes.

Chromosomes   Threadlike structures in the nucleus of a cell that transmit genetic information. The normal human chromosome number is 46, made up of 23 pairs.

Circumcision   Surgical removal of the foreskin of the penis.

CNM   See *certified nurse-midwife.*

Colostrum   The first secretion from the breasts following childbirth. Colostrum is high in protein and antibodies.

Conception   When the sperm meets the egg.

Conjoined twins   Identical twins who have not separated completely. More commonly known as Siamese twins.

Contraction   A painful, strong, rhythmic squeezing of the uterus that is experienced during labor.

Contraction stress test   A test that assesses the baby's well-being by monitoring its response to uterine contractions.

Cord prolapse   A rare obstetrical emergency that occurs when the umbilical cord drops out of the uterus into the vagina before the baby, leading to cord compression and oxygen deprivation.

Cordocentesis   See *Percutaneous umbilical cord sampling.*

Cytomegalovirus (CMV)   A group of viruses from the herpes virus family.

D & C (Dilation and Curettage)   A surgical procedure in which the cervix is dilated and the lining of the uterus is scraped.

DES (Diethylstilbestrol)   A synthetic form of estrogen given to women between the 1940s and 1970s to inhibit miscarriage. DES was later discovered to have serious effects on women and children, including cancer, infertility, and miscarriage.

Diastasis recti   Separation of abdominal muscles.

Dizygotic twins   See *fraternal twins.*

Doppler (doptone)   A handheld device that uses ultrasound technology to enable the caregiver to listen to the fetal heart rate.

Doula Someone who assists a woman and her family during labor and the postpartum period.

Due date The date on which a baby's birth is expected, calculated by adding 279 days to the first day of the woman's last menstrual period (LMP) or 265 days to the date of ovulation, if known.

Eclampsia A serious and rare condition that can affect pregnant or laboring women. It is usually preceded by preeclampsia. Symptoms of eclampsia include hypertension, edema, and protein in the urine. An emergency delivery may be required.

Ectopic pregnancy A pregnancy that occurs outside the uterus, usually in the fallopian tube.

Edema The accumulation of fluid in the body's tissues, resulting in swelling.

Electronic fetal monitor (EFM) An electronic instrument used to record the heartbeat of the fetus, as well as the contractions of the mother's uterus. Fetal monitors can be either external (placed on the abdomen) or internal (attached to the baby's scalp via the vagina).

Embryo A medical term for the baby during its first three months of development in the uterus.

Endometriosis The presence of uterine-lining tissue in or around other reproductive organs, particularly the ovaries and fallopian tubes.

Engagement When the baby's presenting part (usually the head) settles into the pelvic cavity.

Engorgement Congested or filled with fluid. This term refers to the fullness or swelling of the breasts that can occur between the second and seventh postpartum day, when a woman's breasts first start to produce milk.

Epidural Anesthetic injected in the epidural space at the base of the spinal cord.

Episiotomy A small incision made into the skin and perineal muscle at the time of delivery to enlarge the vaginal opening and facilitate the birth of the head.

Estimated Date of Confinement (EDC) The medical term for due date.

Estrogen A hormone that is produced in the ovaries and that works with progesterone to regulate the reproductive cycle.

External version A procedure in which the doctor turns the baby or babies in the uterus by applying manual pressure through the vagina and the outside of the mother's abdomen.

Face presentation A relatively uncommon labor presentation that occurs when the baby is head down but has its neck extended, as if it were looking down the birth canal.

Fallopian tube The tube that carries eggs from the ovaries to the uterus.

False labor When you experience regular or painful contractions that do not start to dilate or thin the cervix.

Fetal monitor See *electronic fetal monitor.*

Fetus The medical term used to describe the developing baby from the end of the third month of pregnancy until birth.

Forceps A tonglike instrument that may be placed around the baby's head to help guide it out of the birth canal during delivery.

Fraternal twins Twins who are the result of the union of two eggs and two sperm.

Fundal height The distance from the upper rounded part of a pregnant woman's uterus to her pubic bone.

Gestational diabetes Diabetes that occurs during pregnancy.

Glucose tolerance test   A blood test used to detect gestational diabetes. Blood is drawn at specified intervals following the ingestion of a sugary substance.

Group B strep   A bacteria found in the vaginas and rectums of some pregnant women. Women who test positive for group B strep may require antibiotics during labor to protect their babies from picking up a serious, potentially life-threatening infection.

Hemorrhoids   Swollen blood vessels around the anus or in the rectal canal that may bleed and cause pain, especially after childbirth.

Human chorionic gonadotropin (hCG)   The hormone produced in early pregnancy that causes a pregnancy test to be positive.

Hydramnios   See *polyhydramnios*.

Hyperemesis gravidarum   Severe nausea, dehydration, and vomiting during pregnancy.

Identical twins   When twins are the result of the fertilization and subsequent splitting of a single egg.

In vitro fertilization (IVF)   When eggs are inseminated in a petri dish and then implanted in the uterus.

Incomplete abortion   A miscarriage in which part, but not all, of the contents of the uterus are expelled.

Infertility   The inability to conceive or carry a child to term.

Intrauterine death   The death of an embryo or fetus within the uterus.

Intrauterine device (IUD)   A plastic or metal birth-control device inserted into the uterus to prevent fertilization.

Intrauterine growth restriction (IUGR)   When the baby's growth is less than what would normally be expected.

Jaundice See *newborn jaundice*.

Kegel muscles Muscles of the pelvic floor, including those of the urethra, vagina, and rectum.

Labor The process of childbirth, from dilation of the cervix to the delivery of the baby and the placenta.

Lightening A change in the shape of the pregnant uterus a few weeks before labor.

Linea nigra A dark line running from the navel to the pubic area that may develop during pregnancy.

Lochia The discharge of blood, mucus, and tissue from the uterus following childbirth.

Low birthweight Babies who weigh less than 5½ pounds at birth.

Mask of pregnancy See *chloasma*.

Mastitis A painful infection of the breast characterized by fever, soreness, and swelling.

Meconium The greenish substance that builds up in the bowels of a growing fetus and is normally discharged shortly after birth.

Miscarriage (spontaneous abortion) Expulsion of an embryo or fetus prior to 20 weeks' gestation.

Missed abortion When the embryo dies in utero but the body fails to expel the contents of the uterus. It is typically diagnosed by ultrasound.

Mittelschmerz Pain that coincides with the release of an egg from the ovary.

Molar pregnancy A pregnancy that results in the growth of abnormal placental cells rather than a fetus.

Monozygotic twins See *identical twins*.

Mucus plug The plug of thick and sticky mucus that blocks the cervical canal during pregnancy, protecting the baby from infection.

Neonatal death The death of a live-born infant between birth and 4 weeks of age.

Neonatal intensive care unit (NICU) An intensive care unit that specializes in the care of premature, low-weight babies and seriously ill infants.

Neural tube defects Abnormalities in the development of the spinal cord and brain in a fetus, including anencephaly, hydrocephalus, and spina bifida.

Newborn jaundice The yellowish tinge of a newborn's skin that is caused by too much bilirubin in the blood. It usually develops on the second or third day of life and lasts until the baby is 7 to 10 days old. Newborn jaundice can usually be corrected by special light treatment.

Nonstress test A non-invasive test in which fetal movements are monitored and recorded, along with changes in fetal heart rate.

Occiput anterior position When the baby's face is turned toward the back of the mother's pelvis in the birth canal.

Oligohydramnios A shortage of amniotic fluid.

Ovulation The point in the menstrual cycle in which a mature egg is released from the ovaries into the fallopian tubes.

Oxytocin The naturally occurring hormone that causes uterine contractions. A synthetic form of this hormone (Pitocin) is often used to induce or augment labor.

Pelvic floor muscles The group of muscles at the base of the pelvis that help support the bladder, uterus, urethra, vagina, and rectum.

Pelvic inflammatory disease (PID) An infection that can affect the uterus, fallopian tubes, ovaries, and other parts of the reproductive system.

Percutaneous umbilical cord sampling (PUBS) A diagnostic procedure that draws blood from the fetus's umbilical cord to test for abnormalities and genetic conditions.

Perineum   The muscle and tissue between the vagina and the rectum.

Phenylketonuria (PKU)   A genetic disorder in which a liver enzyme is defective, possibly leading to serious retardation. This disorder is detected through a blood test done at birth and may be controlled by a special diet.

Placenta   The organ that develops in the uterus during pregnancy, providing nutrients for the fetus and eliminating its waste products.

Placenta previa   A condition in which the placenta partially or completely blocks the cervical opening.

Placental abruption   The premature separation of the placenta from the uterus.

Placental infarction   The death of part of the placenta, which, if extensive enough, can cause stillbirth.

Polyhydramnios   An abnormal condition of pregnancy characterized by excess of amniotic fluid.

Postmature baby   A baby who is born after 42 completed weeks gestation. Note: The terms *post-term* or *postdates* are preferred.

Postpartum blues   Mild depression after delivery.

Postpartum depression (PPD)   Clinical depression that can occur following the delivery. Postpartum depression is characterized by sadness, impatience, restlessness, and—in particularly severe cases—an inability to care for the baby.

Postpartum hemorrhage   Loss of more than 15 ounces (450 ml) of blood at the time of delivery.

Preeclampsia/toxemia   A serious condition marked by sudden edema, high blood pressure, and protein in the urine.

Pregnancy-induced hypertension   A pregnancy-related condition in which a woman's blood pressure is temporarily elevated.

Premature baby   A baby who is born before 37 weeks of gestation.

Premature rupture of the membranes (PROM) When the membranes rupture before the onset of labor.

Progesterone   A female hormone that is produced in the ovaries and works with estrogen to regulate the reproductive cycle.

Prolactin   The hormone responsible for milk production that is released following the delivery of the placenta and the membranes.

Psychoprophylaxis   Intellectual, physical, and emotional preparation for childbirth. The term *psychoprophylaxis* is associated with the Bradley Method of husband-coached labor.

Quickening   When the pregnant woman first detects fetal movement (typically between the 16th and 20th weeks of pregnancy).

Round ligament pain   Pain caused by stretching ligaments on the sides of the uterus during pregnancy.

Rubella (German measles)   A mild, highly contagious viral disease that can cause serious birth defects in the developing baby.

Ruptured membranes   Loss of fluid from the amniotic sac. Also described as having your water break.

Sciatica   A common pregnancy-related condition. Pain in the leg, lower back, and buttock caused by pressure of the growing uterus on the sciatic nerve. Apply heat and rest to relieve the condition.

Show   See *bloody show.*

Siamese twins   See *conjoined twins.*

Spina bifida   A congenital birth defect that occurs when the tube housing the central nervous system fails to close completely.

Spinal anesthesia　A regional anesthetic that is injected into the spinal fluid.

Spontaneous abortion　See *miscarriage*.

Station　An estimate of the baby's progress in descending into the pelvis.

Stillbirth　A fetal death that occurs after the 20th week of pregnancy.

Stress test　A test that records the fetal heart rate in response to induced mild contractions of the uterus.

Stretch marks　Reddish streaks on the skin of the breasts, abdomen, legs, and buttocks that are caused by the stretching of the skin during pregnancy.

Teratogens　Agents such as drugs, chemicals, and infectious diseases that can cause birth defects in a developing baby.

Terbutaline　A medication used to stop contractions in preterm labor.

Threatened abortion　Bleeding during the first trimester of pregnancy that is not accompanied by either cramping or contractions.

Toxoplasmosis　A parasitic infection that can cause stillbirth or miscarriage in pregnant women and congenital defects in babies.

Transition　The third or final phase of the first stage of labor, when the cervix goes from 7 to 10 centimeters' dilation.

Transverse lie　When the fetus is lying horizontally across the uterus rather than in a vertical position.

Tubal ligation　A permanent sterilization procedure that involves tying off a woman's fallopian tubes to prevent conception.

Tubal pregnancy　A pregnancy that occurs in the fallopian tube.

Ultrasound　A technique that uses high-frequency sound waves to create a moving image, or sonogram, on a television screen.

Umbilical cord   The cord that connects the placenta to the developing baby, removing waste products and carbon dioxide from the baby and bringing oxygenated blood and nutrients from the mother through the placenta to the baby.

Vacuum extraction   A process in which a suction cup attached to a machine is placed on a baby's head to aid in delivery.

Vaginal birth after cesarean (VBAC)   A vaginal delivery after a woman had previously delivered a baby by cesarean section.

Varicose veins   Abnormally swollen veins, usually on the legs.

Vasectomy   A minor surgical procedure that involves cutting the vas deferens to block the passage of sperm.

VBAC   See *vaginal birth after cesarean.*

Vena cava   The major vein in the body that returns unoxygenated blood to the heart for transport to the lungs.

Vernix caseosa   A greasy white substance that coats and protects the baby's skin in utero.

Vertex   Head-down presentation.

Resource Directory

U.S. directory of organizations

Adoption

Adoptive Families of America
2309 Como Ave.
St. Paul, MN 55109
Phone: 615-645-9945
Fax: 651-645-0055

American Academy of Adoption Attorneys
Box 33053
Washington, DC 20033-0053
Phone: 202-862-2222
Fax: 202-293-2309
Web: http://adoptionattorneys.org
E-mail: trustee@adoptionattorneys.org

American Adoption Congress
Cherokee Station
P.O. Box 20137
New York, NY 10028-0051

Concerned United Birthparents (CUB)
2000 Walker Street
Des Moines, IA 50317
Phone: 515-262-2334

National Adoption Center
1500 Walnut Street, Suite 701
Philadelphia, PA 19102
Phone: 800-TO-ADOPT or 215-735-9988
Web: www.parentsoup.com/library/
organizations/bpfa013.html

National Adoption Information Clearinghouse
330 C Street SW
Washington, DC 20447
Phone: 888-251-0075 or 703-352-3488
Web: www.parentsoup.com/library/
organizations/bdfa012.html

North American Council on Adoptable Children
970 Raymond Avenue, Suite 106
St. Paul, MN 55114-1149
Phone: 612-644-3036

Birth centers
The National Association of Childbearing Centers
3123 Gottschall Road
RFD 1, Box 1
Perkiomenville, PA 18074-9546
Phone: 215-234-8068
Web: www.parentsoup.com/library/
organizations/bpdp006.html

Breastfeeding
Breastfeeding After Breast Cancer
P.O. Box 131
South Windham, ME 04082

FDA's Breast Implant Information Line
Phone: 800-532-4440

Global Maternal/Child Health Associations
P.O. Box 1400
Wilsonville, OR 97070
Phone: 503-682-3600
Fax: 503-682-3434
E-mail: waterbirth@aol.com

International Board of Lactation Consultant
Examiners
7309 Arlington Blvd., Suite 300
P.O. Box 2348
Falls Church, VA 22042
Phone: 703-560-7330
Fax: 703-560-7332
E-mail: IBLCE@erols.com

International Lactation Consultants Association
4101 Lake Boon Trail
Raleigh, NC 27607
Phone: 919-787-5181
Fax: 919-787-4916

La Leche League International
1400 North Meacham Road
Schaumberg, IL 60173-4840
Phone: 847-519-7330 or 708-455-7730 or
    800-LA LECHE
Web: www.lalecheleague.org

Natural Technologies Inc./White River
924 Callenegocio
San Clemente, CA 92673
Phone: 800-824-6351

Nursing Mothers Counsel
P.O. Box 50063
Palo Alto, CA 94303
Phone: 415-599-3669

Caregivers

American College of Obstetricians and
Gynecologists (ACOG)
Resource Center
409 12th Street SW
P.O. Box 96920
Washington, DC 20090-6920
Phone: 202-638-5577
Web: http://mgraves@acog.org

American Gynecological and Obstetrical Society
University of Utah
50 North Medical Drive, Suite 2B-200
Salt Lake City, UT 84132
Phone: 801-581-7647

Cesarean birth

International Cesarean Awareness Network, Inc.
1304 Kingsdale Ave.
Redondo Beach, CA 90278
Phone: 310-542-6400
Fax: 310-542-5368

Childbirth education

The Academy of Certified Childbirth Educators
2001 E. Prairie Circle, Suite I
Olathe, KS 66062
Phone: 800-444-8223

American Academy of Husband-Coached
Childbirth
Bradley Method
P.O. Box 5224

Sherman Oaks, CA 91413-5224
Phone: 800-4-A-Birth
Web: www.bradleybirth.com

American Society for Psychoprophylaxis in
Obstetrics
ASPO/Lamaze
1200 19th Street NW, Suite 300
Washington, DC 20036-2412
Phone: 800-368-4404 or 202-857-1128
Fax: 202-857-1102
Web: www.lamaze_childbirth.com
E-mail: lamaze@DC.sba.com

Association of Labor Assistants and Childbirth
Educators (ALACE)
P.O. Box 382724
Cambridge, MA 02238-2724
Phone: 617-441-2500

Association of Women's Health, Obstetric, and
Neonatal Nurses
700 14th Street NW, Suite 600
Washington, DC 20005-2006
Phone: 202-261-2400
Fax: 202-737-0575

Childbirth Without Pain Association
20134 Snowden
Detroit, MI 48235-1170
Phone: 313-341-3816

Coalition for Improving Maternity Services
c/o ASPO/Lamaze
1200 19th Street NW 5-300
Washington, DC 20036
Web: www.heathly.net/cims

Informed Homebirth/Informed Birth & Parenting
P.O. Box 3675
Ann Arbor, MI 48106
Phone: 313-662-6857
Web: www.parentsoup.com/library/
organizations/bpdp014.html

International Childbirth Education Association
& Bookcenter (ICEA)
P.O. Box 20048
Minneapolis, MN 55420
Phone: 612-854-8660 or 800-624-4934 (Book
   Center)
Fax: 612-854-8772

National Association of Childbirth Assistants
205 Copco Lane
San Jose, CA 95123
Phone: 408-225-9167

National Association of Postpartum Care
Services, Inc.
P.O. Box 1012
Edmonds, WA 98020
Phone: 206-672-8011

Waterbirth International
P.O. Box 5554
Santa Barbara, CA 93150

Childcare
National Association for the Education of Young
Children (NAEYC)
1509 16th Street, NW
Washington, DC 20036-1426
Phone: 800-424-2460 or 202-232-8777
Web: www.naeyc.org/naeyc/

National Association of Child Care Professionals
(NACCP)
304-A Roanoke Street
Christiansburg, VA 24073
Phone: 800-537-1118
E-mail: admin@naccp.org

National Association of Child Care Resource and
Referral Agencies (NACCRRA)
1319 F Street, Suite 810
Washington, DC 20004
Phone: 202-393-5501
Web: www.childcare-experts.org/ccx2.html

National Association of Family Child Care
(NAFCC)
206 6th Ave., Suite 900
Des Moines, IA 50309
Phone: 800-359-3817
Web: www.nafcc.org
E-mail: nafcc@nafcc.org

National Child Care Association (NCCA)
1016 Rosser Street
Conyers, GA 30012
Phone: 770-922-8198 or 800-543-7161
Web: www.nccanet.org/
E-mail: nccallw@mindspring.com

National Child Care Information Center (NCCIC)
243 Church Street NW
2nd Floor
Vienna, VA 22180
Phone: 800-616-2242

Contraception

Female Condom Information Line
875 N. Michigan Ave., Suite 3660
Chicago, IL 60611
Phone: 800-884-1601

Doulas

Doulas of North America
1100 23rd Avenue E
Seattle, WA 98112
Phone: 206-324-5440 or 206-325-1419
Fax: 206-325-0472
Web: www.dona.com

National Association of Postpartum Care Services
P.O. Box 1012
Edmonds, WA 98020
Phone: 718-631-2229

Endometriosis

Endometriosis Association
8585 North 76th Place
Milwaukee, WI 53223
Phone: 800-992-3636 (in United States) or
    800-426-2363 (in Canada)

St. Charles Medical Center
Endometriosis Treatment Program
2500 NE Neff Road
Bend, OR 97701-9977
Phone: 800-446-2177

Genetic counseling

Alliance of Genetic Support Groups
4301 Connecticut Avenue NW, Suite 404
Washington, DC 20008
Phone: 800-336-4363
Web: www.medhelp.org/

March of Dimes Birth Defects Foundation
1275 Mamaronek Avenue
White Plains, NY 10605
Phone: 914-428-7100 or 888-663-4637

National Society of Genetic Counselors
233 Canterbury Drive
Wallingford, PA   19086-6617
Phone: 610-872-7608
Fax: 610-872-1192
E-mail: nsgc@aol.com

Spina Bifida Association of America
4590 MacArthur Blvd. NW
Suite 250
Washington, DC 20009-4226
Phone: 800-621-3141
Fax: 202-944-3295
E-mail: spinabifida@aol.com

High-risk pregnancy
The Confinement Line
P.O. Box 1609
Springfield, VA 22151
Phone: 703-941-7183

DES Action USA
1615 Broadway, Suite 510
Oakland, CA 94612
Phone: 800-DES-9288
Web: www.desaction.org
E-mail: desact@well.com

For Teen Moms Only
P.O. Box 962
Frankfort, IL 60423-0962
Phone: 815-464-5465
Fax: 815-464-1855
Web: www.forteenmomsonly.com
E-mail: youngmoms@aol.com

Intensive Caring Unlimited (ICU)
P.O. Box 563
Newton Square, PA 19073
Phone: 610-876-7872

Sidelines Support Network
P.O. Box 1808
Laguna Beach, CA 92652
Phone: 949-497-2265
Web: www.sidelines. org

HMOs

The American Association of Health Plans
1129 20th Street, NW
Suite 600
Washington, DC 20036-3421
Phone: 202-778-3200
Fax: 202-331-7487
Web: www.aahp.org

Joint Commission on Accreditation of Healthcare
Organizations
One Renaissance Boulevard
Oakbrook Terrace, IL 60181
Phone: 630-792-5889
Fax: 630-792-5000
Web: www.jcaho.org

National Committee for Quality Assurance
2000 L Street, NW
Suite 500
Washington, DC 20036
Phone: 202-955-3500
Fax: 202-955-3599
Web: www.ncqa.org

Infant health

Allergy and Asthma Network
2751 Prosperity Avenue, Suite 150
Fairfax, VA 22031
Phone: 800-878-4403

American Academy of Pediatrics
141 Northwest Point Boulevard
Elk Grove Village, IL 60007-1098
Phone: 847-228-5005
Fax: 847-228-5097

Association for the Care of Children's Health
(ACCH)
7910 Woodmont Ave., Suite 300
Bethesda, MD 20814-3015
Phone: 301-654-6549 or 800-808-2224
Fax: 301-986-4553

Back to Sleep Campaign
National Institute of Child Health and Human
Development (NICHD)
31 Center Drive
MSC 2425
Bldg. 31, Room 2A32
Bethesda, MD 20892-2425
Phone: 301-496-5133 or 800-505-CRIB
Fax: 301-496-7101

National Association of Pediatric Nurse Associates
and Practitioners
1101 Kings Highway North, Suite 206
Cherry Hill, NJ 08034-1912
Phone: 609-667-1773
Fax: 609-667-7187
Web: www.napnap.org
E-mail: info@napnap.org

Infertility

American Society of Andrology
74 New Montgomery, Suite 230
San Francisco, CA 94105
Phone: 415-764-4823
Fax: 415-765-4915
E-mail: androlog@vic.edu

American Society for Reproductive Medicine
1209 Montgomery Highway
Birmingham, AL 35216
Phone: 205-978-5000
Fax: 205-978-5505

American Urological Association, Inc.
1120 North Charles Street
Baltimore, MD 21201-5559
Phone: 410-727-1100
Fax: 410-223-4374
Web: www.auanet.org

DES Action USA
1615 Broadway, #510
Oakland, CA 94612
Phone: 800-DES-9288 or 510-465-4011

Fertility Research Foundation
875 Park Avenue
New York, NY 10021
Phone: 212-744-5500

International Council on Infertility Information
Dissemination
P.O. Box 6836
Arlington, VA 22206
Phone: 520-544-9548 or 703-579-9178
Fax: 703-379-1593
Web: www.inciid.org
E-mail: INCIIDinfo@inciid.org

RESOLVE, Inc.
1310 Broadway
Somerville, MA 02144-1731
Business office: 617-623-1156
Help Line: 617-623-0744
Fax: 617-623-0252
Web: www.resolve.org
E-mail: resolveinc@aol.com

Society of Assisted Reproductive Technology
2140 11th Avenue S. #200
Birmingham, AL 35205-2800

Surrogates by Choice
P.O. Box 05257
Detroit, MI 48205
Phone: 313-839-4946

Maternal-infant health

American Foundation for Maternal and Child
Health
439 East 51st Street, 8th Floor
New York, NY 10022
Phone: 212-759-5510

Association of Maternal and Child Health Programs
1220 19th St. NW
Suite 801
Washington, DC 20036
Phone: 202-775-0436
Web: www.amchp1.org

Healthy Mothers, Healthy Babies Coalition
409 12th Street SW, Room 309
Washington, DC 20024-2188
Phone: 202-863-2458

Maternity Center Association
281 Park Avenue South
New York, NY 10010
Phone: 212-777-5000

National Center for Education of Maternal and
Child Health
2000 15th St. N
Suite 701
Arlington, VA 22201-2617
Phone: 703-524-7802
Fax: 703-524-9335
Web: www.ncemch.org
E-mail: infor@ncemch.org

National Maternal and Child Health Clearinghouse
2070 Chain Bridge Road, Suite 450
Vienna, VA 22182-2536
Phone: 703-356-1964
Fax: 703-821-2098
Web: www.circsol.com
E-mail: nmchc@circsol.com

The National Perinatal Information Center
One State Street, Suite 102
Providence, RI 02908
Phone: 401-274-0650
Fax: 401-455-0377
Web: www.npic.org
E-mail: npic@aol.com

Public Citizen's Health Research
1600 20th Street NW
Washington, DC 20009
Phone: 202-588-1000

Midwifery organizations

American College of Nurse-Midwives
818 Connecticut Avenue NW, Suite 900
Washington, DC 20006
Phone: 202-728-9860 or 888-MIDWIFE
Fax: 202-728-9897
Web: www.acnm.org
E-mail: info@acnm.org

Association for Childbirth at Home International
14140 Magnolia Blvd.
Sherman Oaks, CA 91423
Phone: 213-663-4996

Midwives Alliance of North America (MANA)
P.O. Box 175
Newton, KS 67114
Phone: 800-923-MANA (6262)
Web: www.mana.org
E-mail: manainfo@aol.com

Multiple births

Center for the Study of Multiple Births
333 E. Superior Street, #476 or #464
Chicago, IL 60611
Phone: 312-266-9093

International Twins Association
6898 Channel Road
Minneapolis, MN 55432
Phone: 612-571-3022

Louisville Twin Study
Child Development Unit
Health Sciences Center
School of Medicine
University of Louisville
P.O. Box 35260
Louisville, KY 40232

Minnesota Center for Twin and Adoption Research
University of Minnesota
Department of Psychology
75 East River Road
Minneapolis, MN 55455

MOST (Mothers of Supertwins)
(Triplets or more)
P.O. Box 951
Brentwood, NY 11717-0627
Phone: 516-434-MOST
Fax: 516-436-5653
Web: www.mostonline.org
E-mail: Maureen@mostonline.org

Multiple Births Foundation
Queen Charlotte's and Chelsea Hospital
Goldhawk Road
London, England W6 OXG
Phone: 081-748-4666, Ext. 5201

National Organization of Mothers of Twins
Clubs, Inc.
P.O. Box 23188
Albuquerque, NM 87192-1188
Phone: 505-275-0955 or 800-243-2276
Web: www.nomotc.org/
E-mail: NOMOTC@aol.com

Triplet Connection
P.O. Box 99571
Stockton, CA 95209
Phone: 209-474-0885 or 209-474-3073
Web: www.tripletconnection.org

Twin Services/Twinline
P.O. Box 10066
Berkeley, CA 94709

Phone 510-524-0863 or 415-524-0863
Web: www.parentsplace.com/readroom/twins

The Twins Foundation
P.O. Box 9487 or 6043
Providence, RI 02940-9487 or 02940-6043
Phone: 401-274-8946 or 401-751-4642

Twins Magazine
5350 South Roslyn, Suite 400
Englewood, CO 80111-2125
Phone: 800-328-3211
Fax: 303-290-9025
Web: www.twinsmagazine.com

Twin to Twin Transfusion Syndrome Foundation
411 Longbeach Parkway
Bay Village, OH 44140
Phone: 216-899-TTTS (8887)
Web: www.TTTS.org

Natural family planning organizations
Couple to Couple League
P.O. Box 111184
Cincinnati, OH 45211-1184
Phone: 513-471-2000
Web: www.parentsoup.com/library/
organizations/bpdp023.html

Diocesan Development Program for NFP
3211 4th Street NE
Washington, DC 20017-1194
Phone: 202-541-3240
Fax: 202-541-3054

Family of the Americas Foundation
P.O. Box 1170
Dunkirk, MD 20754-1170
Phone: 800-443-3395
Fax: 301-627-0847

National Coalition of Natural Family Planning
c/o Los Angeles Regional Family Planning Council
3600 Wilshire Boulevard, Suite 600
Los Angeles, CA 90010-2610
Phone: 213-386-5614
Fax: 213-368-4410

Parent support
National Association of Mothers' Centers
64 Division Avenue
Levittown, NY 11756
Phone: 800-645-3828
Fax: 516-520-1639

Postpartum Support, International
927 North Kellogg Avenue
Santa Barbara, CA 93111
Phone: 805-967-7636
Fax: 805-967-0608
Web: www.parentsoup.com/library/
organizations/bpdp011.html

Postnatal depression
Depression After Delivery
P.O. Box 1282
Morrisville, PA 19067
Phone: 800-944-4770

Pregnancy/infant loss
Abiding Hearts
P.O. Box 5245
Bozeman, MT 59717
Phone: 406-3888-8001
Fax: 406-587-7197
E-mail: hearts@imt.net

An Ache in Their Hearts
The University of Queensland
Department of Child Health
Clarence Court, Mater Children's Hospital
South Brisbane, QLD 4101 Australia
Phone 07-840-8154
Fax: 07-844-9069

AMEND (Aiding a Mother & Father Experiencing
Neonatal Death)
4324 Berrywick Terrace
St. Louis, MO 63128-1908
Phone: 314-487-7582
Web: http://amend.org

CLIMB
Center for Loss in Multiple Birth, Inc.
P.O. Box 1064
Palmer, AK 99645
Phone: 907-746-6123
Web: www.climb-support.org
E-mail: climb@pobox.alaska.net

The Compassionate Friends
National Office
P.O. Box 3696
Oak Brook, IL 60522-3696
Phone: 630-990-0010
Fax: 630-990-0246
Web: www.campassionatefriends.com
E-mail: tcf_national@prodigy.com

National Center for the Prevention of Sudden
Infant Death Syndrome
330 N. Charles Street
Baltimore, MD 21201
Phone: 301-547-0300 or
    800-638-SIDS

National SIDS Resource Center
2070 Chain Bridge Rd., Suite 450
Vienna, VA 22182
Phone: 703-821-8955
Fax: 703-821-2098

National Sudden Infant Death Syndrome
Foundation
2 Metro Plaza, Suite 205
8240 Professional Place
Landover, MD 20785
Phone: 301-459-3388

Pen Parents, Inc.
P.O. Box 8738
Reno, NV 89507-8738
Phone: 702-826-7332

Perinatal Loss
2116 NE 18th Avenue
Portland, OR 97212-2621
Phone: 503-284-7426
Fax: 503-282-8985

A Place to Remember
de Ruyter-Nelson Publications, Inc.
1885 University Avenue, Suite 110
St. Paul, MN 55104
Phone: 612-645-7045 or 800-631-0973
Fax: 612-645-4780
Web: www.aplacetoremember.com

SHARE (A Source of Help in Airing and Resolving
Experiences)
National Office
St. Joseph Health Center
300 First Capitol Drive

St. Charles, MO 63301-2893
Phone: 800-821-6819 or
    314-947-6164 (9am–5pm CT) or
    314-947-5000 or 618-234-2415
Fax: 314-947-7486
Web: www.nationalShareOffice.com

SIDS Alliance
1314 Bedford Avenue, Suite 210
Baltimore, MD 21208
Phone: 800-221-SIDS or 410-653-8226
Fax: 410-653-8709
Web: www.sidelines.org

Twinless Twins Support—ITA
11220 St. Joe Road
Fort Wayne, IN 46835
Phone: 219-627-5414

Premature infants
Parent of Premature and High Risk Infants
International, Inc.
c/o Sherri Nance, M.O.M
22940 W. Frisca Drive
Valencia, CA 913555
Phone: 805-254-2426

Premature, Inc.
Suite 100
10200 Old Katy Road
Houston, TX 77043

Premature and High Risk Infant Association
P.O. Box 37114
Peoria, IL 61614

Prenatal health
Registry of Pregnancies Exposed to
Chemotherapeutic Agents
Department of Human Genetics
University of Pittsburgh
Pittsburgh, PA 15261
Phone: 412-624-9951
E-mail: bgettig@helix.hgen.pitt.edu

Reproductive health
American Society for Colposcopy and Cervical
Pathology
20 West Washington St., Suite 1
Hagerstown, MD 21740
Phone: 800-787-7227
Fax: 301-733-5775

Safety
Danny Foundation
3158 Danville Boulevard
P.O. Box 680
Alamo, CA 94507
Phone: 800-83-DANNY
Web: dannycrib@earthlink.com
E-mail: www.dannyfoundation.org

Consumer Product Safety Commission
Washington, DC 20207
Phone: 800-638-2772 or
    800-628-8326 in Maryland and Alaska or
    800-492-8363 in Hawaii

Juvenile Products Manufacturers Assn.
236 Route 38 West, Suite 100
Moorestown, NJ 08057
Web: www.jpma.org

Sexually transmitted diseases (STDs)

American Social Health Association (ASHA)
P.O. Box 13827
Research Triangle Park, NC 27709-3827
Phone: 919-361-8400

Centers for Disease Control
Division of STD/HIV Prevention
1600 Clifton Rd., NE
Atlanta, GA 30333
Phone: 404-639-3311

National Herpes Hotline
P.O. Box 13827,
Research Triangle Park, NC 27709
Phone: 919-361-8488

Single parents

National Organization of Single Mothers
P.O. Box 68
Midland, NC 28107-0068
Phone: 704-888-KIDS

Parents Without Partners International, Inc.
401 North Michigan Ave.
Chicago, IL 60611-4267
Phone: 312-644-6610
Web: www.parentsoup.com/library/
organizations/bpdm012.html
E-mail: pup@sba.com

Single Mothers by Choice
P.O. Box 1642
Gracie Square Station
New York, NY 10028
Phone: 212-988-0993

The Whole Parent (support group for unwed parents during and after pregnancy)
5045 E. Thomas Street
Phoenix, AZ 85018
Phone: 602-952-1463
Fax: 602-952-8430

Special needs/birth defects

American Cleft Palate Foundation
1829 E. Franklin St., Suite 1022
Chapel Hill, NC 27514
Phone: 800-24-CLEFT
Fax: 919-933-9604

Association of Birth Defect Children (ABDC)
930 Woodcock Rd., Suite 225
Orlando, FL 32803
Phone: 800-313-2232 or 407-245-7035
Web: www.birthdefects.org
E-mail: abdc@birthdefects.org

Federation of Children with Special Needs
95 Berkley St. #104
Boston, MA 02116
Phone: 617-482-2915
Fax: 617-695-2939

Juvenile Diabetes Foundation
120 Wall Street, 19th Floor
New York, NY 10005
Phone: 800-223-1138
Fax: 212-785-9595

National Down Syndrome Congress
1605 Chantilly Dr., Suite 250
Atlanta, GA 30324
Phone: 800-232-NDSC
Web: http://members.carol.net/~ndsc
E-mail: NDSCcenter@aol.com

National Down Syndrome Society (NDSS)
666 Broadway
New York, NY 10012-2317
Phone: 800-221-4602
Web: www.pit.edu/~uclid/ndss.htm

National Information Center for Children and
Youth with Disabilities (NICHCY)
PO Box 1492
Washington, DC 20013-1492
Phone: 800-695-0285
Web: http://nichcy.org
E-mail: nichcy@aed.org

National Organization for Rare Disorders (NORD)
100 Rt. 37
P.O. Box 8923
New Fairfield, CT 06812-8923
Phone: 800-447-6673 (outside CT) or 203-746-6518
Fax: 203-746-6481
Web: www.rarediseases.org
E-mail: orphan@rarediseases.org

National Reye's Syndrome Foundation
P.O. Box 829
Bryan, OH 43506
Phone: 800-233-7393 or 800-231-7393 (Ohio only)
Web: www.bright.net/~reyessyn/

Parents Helping Parents
3041 Olcott St.
Santa Clara, CA 95054
Phone: 408-727-5775
Fax: 408-727-0182
Web: www.php.com

Surrogacy

Center for Surrogate Parenting
8383 Wilshire Blvd., Suite 750
Beverly Hills, CA 90211
Phone: 323-655-1974
Fax: 323-852-1310
Web: www.surroparenting.com
E-mail: centersp@aol.com

Organization of Parents Through Surrogacy
(OPTS)
P.O. Box 213
Wheeling, IL 60090
Phone: 847-394-4116
Fax: 847-394-4165

Working mothers

Center on Work and Family
Boston University
One University Road Room 215
Boston, MA 02215
Phone: 617-353-7225

Families and Work Institute
330 7th Avenue, 14th Floor
New York, NY 10001
Phone: 212-465-2044 or 212-465-8637
Web: www.familiesandworkinst.org

New Ways to Work
785 Market Street, Suite 950
San Francisco, CA 94103-2016
Phone: 415-995-9860
Fax: 415-995-9867
Web: www.nwww.org

NOW Legal Defense and Education Fund
99 Hudson St.
New York, NY 10013

Phone: 212-925-6635
Fax: 212-226-1006
Web: www.nowldef.org
E-mail: astrubel@nowldef.org

9 to 5, National Association of Working Women
1430 West Peachtree St., Suite 610
Atlanta, GA 30309
Phone: 216-566-9308 or 800-522-0925
E-mail: nat9th5@execpc.com

U.S. Equal Employment Opportunity Commission
1801 L Street NW
Washington, DC 20507
Phone: 800-669-4000 or 202-669-4900
Web: www.eeoc.gov

Women's Bureau
U.S. Department of Labor
200 Constitution Avenue NW, Room S-331
Washington, DC 20210
Phone: 800-827-5335

Work/Family Directions
930 Commonwealth Avenue West
Boston, MA 02215-1274
Phone: 617-278-4000
Fax: 617-566-2806

Canadian organizations

Adoption
Adoption Council of Canada
Box 8442
Stn. T
Ottawa, Ontario K1G 3H8
Phone: 613-235-1566
Web: www.adoption.ca
E-mail: jgrove@adoption.ca

Breastfeeding

INFACT Canada
(Infant Feeding Action Coalition)
10 Trinity Square
Toronto, Ontario M5G 1B1
Phone: 416-595-9819
Web: www.infactcanada.ca

LaLeche League Canada
18-C Industrial Drive
Box 29
Chesterville, Ontario K0C lH0
Phone: 613-448-1842
Breastfeeding Referral: 800-665-4324
Fax: 613-448-1845
E-mail: laleche@igs.net

Childcare

Childcare Advocacy Association of Canada
323 Chapel Street
Ottawa, Ontario K1N 7Z2
Phone: 613-594-3196
Fax: 613-594-9375

Contraception

The Bay Centre for Birth Control
790 Bay Street, 8th Floor
Toronto, Ontario M5G 1N9
Phone: 416-351-3700

Doulas

Labour Support Association and Registry (LSAR)
Maple Gove Village
P.O. Box 61058
Oakville, Ontario L6J 6X0
Phone: 905-842-3385
Fax: 905-844-0503
E-mail: Martensn@globalserve.net

Infant health

Canadian Foundation for the Study of Infant Deaths
586 Eglinton Avenue East, Suite 308
Toronto, Ontario M4P 1P2
Phone: 416-488-3260 (24 hours) or
    800-END-SIDS (outside Toronto)
Fax: 416-488-3864
Web: www.sidscanada.org/sids.html
E-mail: sidscanada@inforam.net

Canadian Institute of Child Health (CICH)
885 Meadowlands Drive East, Suite 512
Ottawa, Ontario K2C 3N2
Phone: 613-224-4144
Fax: 613-224-4145
Web: www.cich.ca
E-mail: cich@igs.net

Canadian Paediatric Society (CPS)
2204 Walkley Road, Suite 100
Ottawa, Ontario K1G 4G8
Phone: 613-526-9397
Fax: 613-526-3332
Web: www.cps.ca
E-mail: info@cps.ca

Parent to Parent Link
c/o The Easter Seal Society
1185 Eglinton Avenue East, Suite 706
Toronto, Ontario M3C 3C6
Phone: 416-421-8377 or
    800-668-6252 (outside Toronto)
Web: www.easterseals.org

Provincial I.O.D.E. Genetics Resource Centre
Children's Hospital of Western Ontario
800 Commissioners Road East
London, Ontario N6C 2V5
Phone: 519-685-8140
Fax: 519-685-8214
Web: www.lhsc.on.ca/programs/medgenet/
support.htm

Infertility
Infertility Awareness Association of Canada, Inc.
396 Cooper Street, Suite 201
Ottawa, Ontario K2P 2H7
Phone: 613-234-8585 or
    800-263-2929 (from Canada only)
Fax: 613-234-7718
Web: fox.nstn.ca/~iaac
E-mail: iaac@fox.nstn.ca

Midwives associations
College of Midwives of Ontario
2195 Yonge Street
4th Floor
Toronto, Ontario M4S 2B2
Phone: 416-327-0874
Fax: 416-327-8219
E-mail: admin@cmo.on.ca

Multiples
Parents of Multiple Births Association of Canada
(POMBA)
240 Graff Avenue
Box 22005
Stratford, Ontario N5A 7V6
Phone: 519-272-2203
Fax: 519-272-1926
Web: www.pomba.org
E-mail: office@pomba.org

Natural family planning organizations
Serena Canada
151 Holland Avenue
Ottawa, Ontario K1Y 0Y2
Phone: 613-728-6536
E-mail: serena@mlink.net

Other resources
The Consumer Health Information Service
Toronto Reference Library
789 Yonge Street
Toronto, Ontario M4W 2G8
Phone: 416-393-7056 or 800-667-1999
Fax: 416-393-7181
Web: www.mtrl.toronto.on.ca/centres/chis

Postpartum depression
Postpartum Adjustment Support Services—
Canada(PASS-CAN)
P.O. Box 7282, Station Main
Oakville, Ontario L6J 6L6
Phone: 905-844-9009
Fax: 905-844-5973
Web: www.passcan.com

Pregnancy/infant loss
Bereaved Families of Ontario
562 Eglinton Avenue East
Suite 401
Toronto, Ontario M4P 1P1
Phone: 800-BFO-6364 or 416-440-0290
Fax: 416-440-0304
Web: www.inforamp.net/~bfo
E-mail: bfo@inforamp.net

Perinatal Bereavement Services Ontario
6060 Highway 7
Markham, Ontario L3P 3A9
Phone: 905-472-1807
Fax: 905-472-4054

Reproductive health
The Canadian Pelvic Inflammatory Disease (PID)
Society
Box 33804, Station D
Vancouver, BC V6J 4L6
Phone: 604-684-5704

Vancouver Women's Health Collective
1675 West 8th Avenue, Suite 219
Vancouver, BC V6J 1V2
Phone: 604-736-5262
Fax: 604-736-2152
E-mail: vwhc@axionet.com

Women's College Hospital
Regional Women's Health Centre
790 Bay Street, 8th Floor
Toronto, Ontario M5G 1N8
Phone: 416-586-0211
Fax: 416-351-3727
Web: utl1.library.utoronto.ca/www/wch/index.htm

Safety
Infant and Toddler Safety Association (ITSA)
385 Fairway Road South, Suite 4A-230
Kitchener, Ontario N2C 2N9
Phone: 519-570-0181 (hotline)
Fax: 519-894-0739

Safe Start
B.C. Children's Hospital
4480 Oak Street
Vancouver, BC V6H 3V4

Phone: 604-875-3273
Fax: 604-875-2440
Web: www.childhosp.bc.ca/safestart

Transport Canada
Road Safety and Motor Vehicle Regulation
Place de Ville, Tower C
330 Sparks Street
Ottawa, Ontario K1A 0N5
Phone: 800-333-0371
E-mail: roadsafetywebmail@tc.gc.ca

Video
Ogle, Amy E. *Before Your Pregnancy: Prepare Your Body for a Health Pregnancy.* Order by calling 1-800-955-5115.

Web site directory
Hundreds of pregnancy-related Web sites are available online—more than you could possibly find time to visit in a mere nine months. To ensure that you are able to put your surfing time to the best possible use, we've hand-picked some of our favorites. Although we can't endorse the medical information available on these sites (mainly because their content is beyond our control), we can tell you that the sites we've picked are definitely worth a visit.

Please note: Because content on the World Wide Web is always changing, it's possible that some of these links may be outdated or the content on these sites may have changed by the time you decide to check them out. We'll post updates to our Web site (www.having-a-baby.com) from time to time, so be sure to let us know if you discover a dead or relocated link.

WEB SITE	HIGHLIGHTS
Adoption	
Adoption Council of Canada www.adoption.ca/	A good source of adoption-related information for Canadian parents.
National Adoption Information Clearinghouse www.calib.com/naic	As comprehensive as the name implies. You'll find online databases, publications, and links galore.
U.S. Department of Labor— Family and Medical Leave Act www.dol.gov/dol/esa/fmla.htm	Find out how the Family and Medical Leave Act applies to families who adopt.
Breastfeeding	
La Leche League www.lalecheleague.org	Packed with useful information on every conceivable aspect of breastfeeding.
U.S. Food and Drug Administration— "Breastfeeding: Best Bet for Babies" vm.cfsan.fda.gov/~dms/fdbrfeed.html	A detailed article outlining the benefits of breastfeeding and offering practical advice to women who are interested in breastfeeding their babies.
Childbirth Education and Labor Support	
Comparison of Well-Known Childbirth Organizations www.geocities.com/HotSprings/9947/cbetable1.html	A comparison of the various types of childbirth education philosophies. Includes links to the Web sites of the major childbirth education organizations.
Doulas of North America www.dona.com	Contains information on the benefits of using the services of a doula plus tips on finding and choosing a doula.

International Association of
Childbirth Educators
www.icea.org

Contains the contact information for
the International Association of
Childbirth Educators.

Lamaze International
www.lamaze-childbirth.com

Contains information on the Lamaze
philosophy of birth and information
about chapters across the country.

The Bradley Method of Natural
Childbirth
www.bradleybirth.com

Contains information on the Bradley
Method of natural childbirth. Allows
you to request a free directory of
childbirth educators who have been
trained in the Bradley Method.

Fertility/Infertility

American Society for
Reproductive Medicine's
"Selecting an IVF/GIFT Program"
www.asrm.org/current/press/select.html

Tips on choosing an IVF/GIFT program.

Atlanta Reproductive Health Center
www.ivf.com

Contains useful infertility information,
including the text to a book on
fertility. Not to be missed: The Advanced
Reproductive Technologies Photo
Gallery at www.ivf.com/multi.html.

Centers for Disease Control
and Prevention's Assisted
Reproductive Technology Success Rates
www.cdc.gov/nccdphp/drh/arts/index.htm

The first-ever report card for
fertility clinics. Contains detailed
ratings on fertility clinics across
the country, as well as some useful
information on comparing fertility
clinics.

continues

WEB SITE	HIGHLIGHTS
Fertile Thoughts www.fertilethoughts.net	Packed with useful information on infertility, including practical tips on dealing with your insurance company.
Fertility Infertility Treatment www.fertilitext.org	Comprehensive information on ovulation predictor kits, fertility drugs, and other aspects of fertility and infertility.
Infertility Resources www.ihr.com/infertility/ index.html	Contains articles on infertility, a directory of fertility clinics, and a list of online newsgroups and lists dedicated to the topic of infertility: www.ihr.com/infertility/newsgrp.html.
Infertility Update: On Fertile Ground homearts.com/depts/health/ 37upf1.htm	An article on high-tech fertility methods available to couples who are having difficulty conceiving.
Mediconsult's Infertility Education Material www.mediconsult.com/ infertility/shareware/	One of the most comprehensive sites of infertility information online.
RESOLVE, Inc. www.resolve.org	Information about RESOLVE, a national organization that provides support to couples struggling with infertility. The site is packed with useful articles on coping with infertility, as well as links to other related sites.

The International Council on Infertility Information Dissemination (INCIID) www.inciid.org	Contains fact sheets, articles, bulletin boards hosted by infertility experts, links to other sites, and much more. You'll definitely want to check this one out.

Health Information

AMA Health Insight—"Urinary Tract Infections" www.ama-assn.org/insight/ h_focus/wom_hlth/uti/uti.htm	Everything you could ever want to know about urinary tract infections.
American Medical Association's Contraceptive Information Center www.ama-assn.org/ special/ contra/contra.htm	Contains news stories and clinical information about various contraceptive methods.
American Dietetic Association www.eatright.org	Contains useful information on nutrition plus allows you to search for a dietitian in your area.
American College of Nurse-Midwives www.acnm.org	Detailed information about nurse-midwives, including a search engine that allows you to find a nurse-midwife in your area.
American Academy of Pediatrics www.aap.org	Although the site is primarily designed for pediatricians, there is some good content for families, including "Where We Stand," at

continues

WEB SITE	HIGHLIGHTS
	www.aap.org/advocacy/wwestand.htm (a concise summary of the American Academy of Pediatrics's stand on important pediatric-health-related issues).
Beatrice's Web Guide—"The Doctor Is In" www.bguide.com/webguide/health/plus/d0820Hmo.html	Online sources of information on choosing an HMO as selected by Ann Douglas, one of the authors of this book.
Centers for Disease Control and Prevention—"Group B Streptococcal Infections" www.cdc.gov/ncidod/diseases/bacter/strep_b.htm	Detailed and accurate information about what group B strep means to pregnant women and their babies.
Contraceptive Guide www.mjbovo.com/contracep.htm	A useful guide to contraceptive options written by Mary Jane Bovo, M.D.
Dieticians of Canada—"Make Nutrition Come Alive" www.dietitians.ca/eatwell/	Packed with useful information on all aspects of nutrition, including nutrition during pregnancy and the postpartum period.
Dr. Greene's House Calls www.drgreene.com	An amazing resource for families, this site—created by pediatrician Alan Greene—is packed with useful information on every conceivable aspect of pediatric care.
Health Answers www.healthanswers.com	Contains links to sites on fertility, infertility, contraception, pregnancy, and more.

Health Answers www.healthanswers.com	Answers health-related questions on various topics, including pregnancy.
Home Testing for Pregnancy kerouac.pharm.uky.edu/ hometest/pregnant/ptoc.html	Detailed information on various brands of home pregnancy tests.
Intelihealth www.intelihealth.com	A health information Web site developed by Johns Hopkins University. Contains useful information on all aspects of family health, including pregnancy and pediatric health.
Internet Health Resources www.ihr.com	Contains detailed information about infertility, homeopathic medicine, and other health-related topics.
Joint Commission on Accreditation of Healthcare Organizations www.jcaho.org	Tips on choosing a hospital.
March of Dimes www.modimes.org	Contains detailed information on various birth defects.
Mayo Health 0@sis www.mayohealth.org	Contains detailed information on all aspects of family health, including pregnancy. The due-date calculator located at www.mayohealth.org/mayo/common/htm/duedate/duedate.htm is particularly useful.

continues

WEB SITE	HIGHLIGHTS
MedicineNet www.medicinenet.com	Contains detailed information on diseases and drugs, a medical dictionary, and more.
Mediconsult.com www.mediconsult.com	Packed with journal excerpts, news stories, and more about fertility, infertility, pregnancy, and other health-related topics. Also contains a useful online medical glossary and links to other top-caliber health-related sites.
Motherisk motherisk.org	A good source of information on prenatal health for Canadian women, this Web site is operated by the Motherisk Clinic at Toronto's Hospital for Sick Children.
National Center for Health Statistics www.cdc.gov/nchswww/	The best place to search for health-related statistics.
National Association of Childbearing Centers—Birth Centers Online www.birthcenters.org	FAQs on birth centers, birth, and more.
New York Online Access to Health (Ask NOAH About Pregnancy) www.noah.cuny.edu/pregnancy	Useful information on family planning, prenatal care, and other health topics related to pregnancy.

New England Journal of Medicine www.nejm.org/public	Contains a searchable database of abstracts from this prestigious medical journal.
Obstetric Ultrasound home.hkstar.com/~joewoo/ joewoo2.html	Find out all about ultrasound technology and view real ultrasound photos of babies at various stages of development.
Parent Soup—"Understanding Prenatal Tests" www.parentsoup.com/ americanbaby/content/ prenataltest1.html	An article that explains prenatal tests in a straightforward manner.
The *New York Times* on the Web's Women's Health—Pregnancy www.nytimes.com/specials/ women/whome/pregnancy.html	Contains numerous articles and resources related to pregnancy, including excerpts from *The Merck Manual* (a medical reference book that contains detailed information on all aspects of reproductive health).
The Food Guide Pyramid www.nal.usda.gov:8001/py/ pmap.htm	Contains detailed information on The Food Guide Pyramid.
The Homebirth Choice www.efn.org/~djz/birth/ homebirth.html	An article from *Midwifery Today* magazine on the advantages of home birth.

continues

WEB SITE	HIGHLIGHTS
The Kitchen Counter homearts.com/helpers/calculators/caldocf1.htm	Provides nutritional information on common foods. Allows you to search by keyword or food category, and will keep a running tally of your entire day's menus.
Thrive Online www.thriveonline.com	An online version of the health magazine of the same name.
Traveling Pregnant www.travelhealth.com/preg.htm	Tips on traveling to exotic locales during pregnancy.
High Risk Pregnancy	
Hannah's Prayer www.hannah.org/risk.htm	A list of helpful resources related to high-risk pregnancy.
Sidelines www.sidelines.org	Provides information and e-mail support to women who are on bed rest during their pregnancies.
Multiples	
Famous Parents of Twins www.twinz.com/twins/parents.htm	A fun page that gives you the scoop on which famous people have been blessed with twins.
Parents of Twins/Multiples www.owc.net/~twins/freebie.htm	Packed with useful information for parents who are expecting more than one baby.
Parents of Multiples Birth Association www.pomba.org	Information and support for Canadian parents with twins and supertwins.

The Triplet Connection
www.tripletconnection.org

Information on The Triplet Connection, an organization for parents with three or more babies.

The Center for Study of Multiple Births
www.multiplebirth.com

Contains a detailed list of national and international organizations of interest to parents of multiples, as well as other useful material on twins and supertwins.

Twins World
www.twinsworld.com

Another fun site that celebrates what it means to be a twin.

Pregnancy and Parenting

Baby Bag Online
www.babybag.com

Contains articles and links on a range of parenting-related topics "from prenatal to preschool."

Baby Names
www.babynames.com

Looking for a baby name that really sizzles? Here are 18,000 baby names to inspire you.

Baby Science—"Encouraging Your Older Child to Welcome the New Baby"
www.babyscience.com/encourage.htm

Tips on preparing your older child for the birth of a new baby.

BabyCenter
www.babycenter.com

Packed with useful information on every conceivable aspect of pregnancy from preconception planning through

continues

WEB SITE	HIGHLIGHTS
	postpartum. There's everything from useful reference material to fun interactive tools such as a gizmo that allows you to time your baby's birth around major sporting events.
BabyZone www.babyzone.com	A fun pregnancy site that is packed with interactive tools such as gender detectors, as well as articles on celebrity baby names.
Beatrice's Web Guide—"Chats for Moms" www.bguide.com/webguide/parenting/plus/d0505Chat.html	Links to the best places to connect with other moms online.
Canadian Parents Online www.canadianparents.com	The leading Web site for Canadian families. Packed with articles, links, resources, bulletin boards, and more.
Childbirth.org www.childbirth.org	An extremely comprehensive pregnancy-related Web site that includes an interactive birth plan and numerous birth stories.
Crayola Family Play www.familyplay.com	Activities to keep your older child entertained while you're busy with the new baby.
CTW Family Workshop www.ctw.org/parents/0,1178,,00.html	Parenting information from the Children's Television Workshop, creators of Sesame Street.

Family.com
www.family.com

Contains the text of hundreds of parenting-related articles, bulletin boards where you can swap tips with other parents, and much more.

Fit Pregnancy
www.FitPregnancy.com

Contains excerpts from the glossy magazine of the same name. Not surprisingly, there's plenty of information on prenatal fitness on the site, including an eight-step prenatal workout.

How Your Baby Grows
homearts.com/depts/health/
fetal/fetal_calendar.html

A pregnancy calendar that includes detailed information about fetal development. Presented in partnership with the March of Dimes.

Interactive Pregnancy Calendar
www.pregnancycalendar.com

Plug in your due date and this interactive Web site will come up with a day-by-day customized pregnancy calendar for you.

Learn2.com
www.learn2.com

A fun site that provides "how to" instructions on a range of tasks, including burping a baby, coping with a crying child, childproofing your home, finding a nanny, changing a diaper, and—our personal favorite—improvising a diaper.

MomsOnLine
www.momsonline.com

A popular parenting Web site that contains some useful information about pregnancy and baby care.

continues

WEB SITE	HIGHLIGHTS
ParenthoodWeb www.parenthoodweb.com	Features articles on parenting, discussion boards, and more.
Parenting Q & A www.parenting-qa.com	A site packed with answers to the questions that are on every parent's mind. Contains a link to Parenting Q & A's sister site, The Cyber Mom Dot Com (www.thecybermom.com/), which is also worth a visit.
ParentSoup www.parentsoup.com	Another leading pregnancy site that contains lots of useful pregnancy-related articles, a smorgasbord of bulletin boards, and so on.
ParentsPlace www.parentsplace.com	Contains a whole library of material on parenting plus the most comprehensive site of parenting bulletin boards available online. There's a lot of midwife-friendly material on this site, including the popular "Ask the Midwife" column.
Parenttime www.pathfinder.com/	Contains excerpts from *Parenting* magazine, a baby name base, a special pregnancy section for expectant mothers, and more.
Pregnancy Today www.pregnancytoday.com	A site that is operated by two moms, one of whom was expecting twins as this book went to press. The site features chat forums, news stories, and an interactive pregnancy journal.

StorkSite www.storksite.com	One of the original pregnancy-related Web sites, StorkSite is one of the best places online to find answers to your pregnancy-related questions or chat with other expectant moms.
The Labor of Love www.thelaboroflove.com	Contains an online parenting magazine, message boards, a pregnancy and parenting search engine containing more than 1,500 entries, and more.
The Whole Nine Months homearts.com/depts/health/00ninec1.htm	A site packed with useful reading for parents and would-be parents.
The Baby Booklet members.aol.com/AllianceMD/booklet.html	A detailed guide to baby's first year by pediatrician Lewis Wasserman.
The Unofficial Guide to Having a Baby www.having-a-baby.com	The "Unofficial" Web site for this book. Check back periodically to get the scoop on updated links and more.
Pregnancy loss/Neonatal death	
Learn2.com—"Learn2 Avoid Junk Mail" www.learn2.com/05/0514/05142.html	Valuable tips on getting your name off baby-related mailing lists if you experience the loss of a baby.

continues

WEB SITE	HIGHLIGHTS
SIDS Network www.sids-network.org/	Contains information on sudden infant death syndrome (SIDS), as well as information on mailing lists and online resources for parents who have experienced miscarriage, stillbirth, neonatal death, or the death of an older child.
Subsequent Pregnancy After Loss www.inforamp.net/~bfo/spals	Contains subscription information for the online support group Subsequent Pregnancy After Loss (SPALS), as well as numerous other resources useful to women experiencing pregnancy after loss.
Wisconsin Stillbirth Service Program www.wisc.edu/wissp/when.htm	A compassionate and helpful site that provides coping tips for parents who experience stillbirth.
Safety	
Child Secure www.childsecure.com	Information on various aspects of child health plus product information on various child-safety items.
Child and Family Canada— "Garage Sales: Are the Savings Worth the Risks?" www.cfc-efc.ca/docs/00000620.htm	Provides practical guidelines on purchasing second-hand baby equipment at garage sales.
Juvenile Products Manufacturers Association www.jpma.org	Provides detailed information on what to look for—and what to avoid—when shopping for baby gear.

Kid Source ws1.kidsource.com/ kidsource/pages/recall.html	Links to the latest news on product safety recalls on juvenile products.
Pampers—"1996 Shopping Guide to Car Seats" www.pampers.com/wellbaby/ content/safety/2wbcarsa.htm	Contains slightly dated but still-useful car seat information from the American Academy of Pediatrics.
U.S. Consumer Product Safety Commission www.cpsc.gov	Contains detailed information on product recalls on a range of consumer goods, including juvenile products.

Special Circumstances

Beatrice's Web Guide—"Sites for Solo Parents" www.bguide.com/webguide/ parenting/plus/d0330Single.html	Contains links to the best sites for single parents.
A Guide to Lesbian Babymaking www.lesbian.org/lesbian-moms/ guide.html	Useful information on pregnancy and parenting for lesbians.
Midlife Mommies www.midlifemommies.com	A Web site dedicated to the joys and challenges of pregnancy and parenting at an older age.

Surrogacy

Court TV www.courttv.com/ legalhelp/family/surrogate.html	The legal status of surrogacy, according to the folks at Court TV.

continues

WEB SITE	HIGHLIGHTS
Motherhood in Question: Surrogates and Carriers www.msnbc.com/news/149876.asp	Part of an excellent series of articles about infertility by MSNBC. Includes a photo essay on surrogacy and links to discussion boards. Definitely worth a read.
Organization of Parents Through Surrogacy www.opts.com	Contains detailed information on surrogacy for both parents and surrogates. Includes updates on surrogacy-related legislation, summaries of media coverage of the surrogacy issue, bulletin boards for parents and surrogates, and more.
Sister, Can You Spare An Egg? www.usnews.com/usnews/issue/970623/23egg.htm	U.S. News Online takes a critical look at the whole surrogacy issue.
Surrogacy www.surrogacy.com	Contains detailed information on surrogacy: articles, links, FAQs, classified ads, a list of fertility- and surrogacy-related support groups, and more.
Surrogate Mothers Online www.SurromomsOnline.com/	Contains articles, bulletin boards, links, and more. Designed as a meeting place for surrogates and parents.

Working During Pregnancy

Beatrice's Web Guide—"From Here to Maternity" www.bguide.com/webguide/careers/plus/d0716Baby.html	Links to good sources of information on planning your maternity leave.
Department of Labor—Women's Bureau Clearinghouse www.dol.gov/dol/wb/public/programs/house.htm	Contact information and mission statement for the Department of Labor's Women's Bureau Clearinghouse.
The Unofficial Guide to Childcare www.childcare-guide.com	Packed with excerpts from *The Unofficial Guide to Childcare*, parenting articles, tips sheets, and more.
U.S. Equal Opportunity Commission www.eeoc.gov	A good source of information about pregnancy discrimination.
WomenCONNECT.com www.womenconnect.com/info/worklife/features/jan2398_wrkf.htm	Contains excerpts from *Working Woman* and *Working Mother* magazines.
Working Moms Refuge www.moms-refuge.com.index2.html	Contains articles about various aspects of being a working mother.

Further Reading

Barnes, Belinda and Suzanne Gail Bradley. *Planning for a Healthy Baby*. London: Vermilion, 1994.

Bert, Diana et al. *After Having a Baby*. New York: Dell Publishing, 1988.

Bert, Diana et al. *Having a Baby*. New York: Dell Publishing Co., Inc., 1984.

Bourne, Gordon. *Pregnancy*. London: Pan Books, Ltd., 1984.

Bryan, Elizabeth. *Twins, Triplets and More*. London: Penguin Books, 1992.

Campion, Mukti Jain. *The Baby Challenge: A Handbook on Pregnancy for Women with a Physical Disability*. London: Tavistock/Routledge, 1990.

Chalmers, Irena. *The Great American Baby Almanac*. New York: Viking Studio Books, 1989.

Chamberlain, David. *The Mind of Your Newborn Baby*. Berkeley: North Atlantic Books, 1998.

Cherry, Sheldon H. *Understanding Pregnancy and Childbirth*. New York: Bantam Books, 1984.

Clapp, James F. *Exercising Through Your Pregnancy.* Champaign, IL: Human Kinetics, 1998.

Colman, Libby Lee and Arthur D. Coleman. *Pregnancy: The Psychological Experience.* New York: The Noonday Press, 1991.

Cowan, Carolyn Pape and Philip A. Cowan. *When Partners Become Parents.* New York: Basic Books, 1992.

Curtis, Glade. *Your Pregnancy After 30.* Tucson: Fisher Books, 1996.

Curtis, Lindsay R., Mary Beard, and Yvonne Coroles. *Pregnant and Lovin' It.* New York: The Body Press/Perigee Books, 1992.

Dahl, Gail J. *Pregnancy and Childbirth Tips.* Vancouver: Innovative Publishing, 1998.

Davis, Deborah L. *Empty Cradle, Broken Heart.* Golden, Colorado: Fulcrum Publishing, 1996.

Doan, Helen McKinnon, *Every Pregnancy.* Toronto: Stoddart Publishing Co., Limited, 1990.

Donahue, Phil. *The Human Animal.* New York: Simon & Schuster Inc., 1985.

Douglas, Ann. *Baby Science: How Babies Really Work.* Toronto: Owl Books/Greey de Pencier Books, Inc., 1998.

Douglas, Ann. *The Unofficial Guide to Childcare.* New York: Macmillan/Alpha Books, 1998.

Edeiken, Louise and Johanna Antar. *Now That You're Pregnant.* New York: Macmillan Publishing Company, 1992

Eiger, Marvin S. and Sally Wendkos Olds. *The Complete Book of Breastfeeding.* New York: Bantam Books, 1987.

Eisenberg, Arlene, Heidi Murkoff, and Sandee Hathaway. *What to Expect the First Year.* New York: Workman Publishing Company, Inc., 1989.

Eisenberg, Arlene, Heidi Murkoff, and Sandee Hathaway. *What to Expect When You're Expecting.* New York: Workman Publishing Company Inc., 1996.

Fields, Denise and Alan. *Baby Bargains: Secrets to Saving 20% to 50% on Baby Furniture, Equipment, Clothes, Toys, Maternity Wear and Much, Much More.* Boulder: Windsor Peak Press, 1997.

Fisher, John J. *From Baby to Toddler.* New York: Perigee Books, 1987.

Gansberg, Judith M. and Arthur P Mostel. *The Second Nine Months.* New York: Tribeca Communications, Inc., 1984.

Ginsberg, Susan. *Family Wisdom: The 2,000 Most Important Things Ever Said About Parenting, Children, and Family Life.* New York: Columbia University Press, 1996.

Harris, A. Christine. *The Pregnancy Journal.* San Francisco: Chronicle Books, 1996.

Huggins, Kathleen. *The Nursing Mother's Companion.* Boston: The Harvard Common Press, 1990.

Iovine, Vicki. *The Girlfriends' Guide to Pregnancy.* New York: Pocket Books, 1995.

Jefferis, Benjamin Grant. *Safe Counsel.* Toronto: J.L. Nichols, 1894.

Jones, Carl. *After the Baby Is Born.* New York: Henry Holt and Company, Inc., 1990.

Jones, Carl. *Alternative Birth: The Complete Guide.* Los Angeles: Jeremy P. Tarcher, Inc., 1990.

Karlin, Elyse Zorn, Daisy Spier, and Mona Brody. *The Complete Baby Checklist*. New York: Avon Books, 1992.

Kitzinger, Sheila. *The Complete Book of Pregnancy and Childbirth*. New York: Albert A. Knopf, Inc. 1989.

Kitzinger, Sheila. *The Experience of Childbirth*. London: Penguin Books, 1987.

Klaus, Marshal H. and Phyllis H. *Your Amazing Newborn*. Reading, Mass: Perseus Books, 1998.

Kohner, Nancy and Alix Henley. *When a Baby Dies*. London: Pandora Press, 1991.

Korte, Diana and Roberta Scaer. *A Good Birth, a Safe Birth*. Boston: The Harvard Common Press, 1992.

La Leche League International. *The Womanly Art of Breastfeeding*. New York: Plume, 1991.

Landsberg, Michele. *Women and Children First*. Toronto: Penguin Books, 1983.

Lauersen, Niels H. and Colette Bouchez. *Getting Pregnant: What Couples Need to Know Right Now*. New York: Ballantine Books, 1992.

Leach, Penelope. *Babyhood*. London: Penguin Books, 1983.

Leach, Penelope. *Your Baby & Child*. New York: Alfred A. Knopf, 1996.

Lipper, Ari. *Baby Stuff: A No-Nonsense Shopping Guide for Every Parent's Lifestyle*. New York: Bantam Doubleday Dell Publishing Group, Inc., 1997.

Llewellyn-Jones, Derek. *Everywoman: a Gynaecological Guide for Life*. London: Faber and Faber Limited, 1986.

Louden, Jennifer. *The Pregnant Woman's Comfort Book*. New York: Harper Collins Publishers, 1995.

Maclean, Heather. *Women's Experience of Breast Feeding*. Toronto: University of Toronto Press, 1990.

Manginello, Frank P. and Theresa Foy DiGeronimo. *Your Premature Baby.* New York: John Wiley & Sons, Inc. 1998.

Marshall, Connie. *From Here to Maternity.* Rocklin, CA: Prima Publishing, 1991.

McKay, Sharon E. *The New Child Safety Handbook.* Toronto: Macmillan of Canada, 1988.

Mullens, Anne. *Missed Conceptions: Overcoming Infertility.* Scarborough: McGraw-Hill Ryerson Limited, 1990.

The New Baby and Child Care Encyclopaedia. Toronto: Family Communications, Inc., 1995.

Nilsson, Lennart and Lars Hamberger. *A Child Is Born.* New York: Dell Publishing, 1990.

Noble, Elizabeth. *Having Twins.* Boston: Houghton Mifflin Company, 1991.

Omichinski, Linda and Heather Wiebe Hildebrand. *Tailoring Your Tastes.* Winnipeg, Manitoba: TAMOS Boos, Inc., 1995. Order by calling 800-565-4847.

Paulson, Richard J. and Judith Sachs. *Rewinding Your Biological Clock.* New York, W.H. Freeman and Company, 1998.

Peoples, Debby and Harriette Rovner Ferguson. *What to Expect When You're Experiencing Infertility.* New York: W.W. Norton, 1998.

Peppers, Larry G., and Ronald J. Knapp. *How to Go On Living After the Death of a Baby.* Atlanta: Peachtree Publishers, Ltd., 1985.

Pullen, Heather and Jocelyn Smith. *Making Babies.* Mississauga: Random House of Canada Limited, 1990.

Queenan, John T. with Carrie Neher Queenan. *A New Life.* Toronto: Stoddart Publishing Co., Limited, 1986.

Refelman, Rachel. *Baby Gear for the First Year.* Toronto: Macmillan Canada, 1997.

Rich, Laurie A. *When Pregnancy Isn't Perfect.* New York: Dutton Books, 1991.

Rosenthal, M. Sara. *The Gynecological Sourcebook.* Los Angeles: Lowell House, 1994.

Rosenthal, M. Sara. *The Pregnancy Sourcebook.* Los Angeles: Lowell House, 1994.

Rothbart, Betty. *Multiple Blessings.* New York: Hearst Books, 1994.

Saunders, Peter. *Your Pregnancy Month-by-Month.* London: Hodder and Stoughton, 1996.

Sears, William, Martha Sears, and Linda Hughey Holt. *The Pregnancy Book.* Boston: Little, Brown and Company, 1997.

Serota, Cherie, and Jody Kozlow Gardner. *Pregnancy Chic: The Fashion Survival* Guide. New York: Villard, 1998.

Shelov, Steven P. and Robert E. Hannemann. *Caring for Your Baby and Young Child.* New York: Bantam Books, 1998.

Small, Meredith F. *Our Babies, Ourselves.* New York: Anchor Books, 1998.

Stoppard, Miriam. *Conception, Pregnancy and Birth.* Toronto: Macmillan Canada, 1993.

Stoppard, Miriam. *Dr. Miriam Stoppard's Pregnancy and Birth Book.* New York: Ballantine Books, 1987.

Sussman, John R. and B. Blake Levitt. *Before You Conceive: The Complete Pregnancy Guide.* New York: Bantam Books, 1989.

Vazquez, Liesl. *Babies Are Such a Nice Way to Start People.* White Plains, NY: Peter Pauper Press, Inc., 1997.

Weschler, Toni. *Taking Charge of Your Fertility.* New York: Harper Collins Publishers, Inc., 1995.

Zimmer, Judith. *Labor of Love: Mothers Share the Joy of Childbirth.* New York: John Wiley and Sons, Inc. 1997.

Important Documents

If you are alone and about to give birth

- Resist the urge to panic.

- Call your local emergency number and ask the person who takes the call to (1) dispatch an emergency response team and (2) notify your practitioner that you're about to deliver.

- Ask a neighbor to come over and stay with you until the emergency response team arrives.

- Pant if you feel the urge to push.

- Wash your hands and the vaginal area with detergent or soap and water.

- Spread a shower curtain, a plastic tablecloth, some clean towels, newspapers, or sheets on a bed, a sofa, or the floor, and lie down until someone arrives to help you.

- If your baby starts coming before help arrives, gently ease the baby out by pushing each time you feel the urge and catching the baby with your hands.

If you are with a mother who is about to give birth

- Resist the urge to panic, and try to comfort and reassure the mother.

- Call your local emergency number and ask the person who takes the call to (1) dispatch an emergency response team and (2) notify the mother's doctor or midwife that she is about to deliver.

- Encourage the mother to pant if she feels the urge to start pushing.

- Wash your hands and the mother's vaginal area with detergent or soap and water.

- Spread a shower curtain, a plastic tablecloth, some clean towels, newspapers, or sheets on a bed or table, and help the mother semi-sit in a reclining position at the edge with her buttocks hanging off and her knees apart. Support her head with one or two pillows.

- If she's in too much pain to climb onto the bed or table, place a stack of newspapers or folded towels under her buttocks so that she will be far enough off the floor for you to be able to deliver the baby's shoulders easily.

- If you are in an automobile, help the mother lie down on the seat with one foot on the floor and the other on the seat.

- If the woman needs to vomit, help her turn her head to the side in order to keep her mouth and airway clear.

- Keep a dishpan or basin handy to catch the amniotic fluid and blood.

- Once the baby's heard starts to appear, encourage the mother to pant or blow to slow the baby's exit from the birth canal. Then, apply gentle counterpressure to the baby's head to keep it from emerging too quickly.

- If you see a loop of umbilical cord around the baby's neck, gently pull on it and lift it over the baby's head. Abandon this effort if it won't come easily.

- If the baby's amniotic sac is intact, puncture the sac with a ball-point pen, being sure to hold the pen away from the baby's face, and carefully move the sac away from the baby's face. Clear the baby's mouth and nose immediately, by using a bulb syringe and gauze pad (if you have them) or by gently stroking the sides of the baby's nose in a downward direction and the neck and underside of the chin in an upward direction to help expel mucus and amniotic fluid.

- Take the baby's head in your hands and press it slightly downward, asking the mother to push at the same time. Then help ease the baby's shoulders out one at a time. Once the baby's shoulders have been delivered, the rest of the baby should slip out easily.

- Wrap the baby in a clean blanket or towel. Lay the baby across the mother's abdomen or place it at her breast if the cord is long enough.

- Don't try to pull the placenta out. If it is delivered before help arrives, wrap it in towels or a newspaper and elevate it above the level of the baby.

- Do not try to cut the cord.

- Keep both the mother and the baby comfortable until help arrives.

Birth plan

Fill out this birth plan and then make three copies.
Give one to your caregiver, put one in your labor
bag, and attach one to the preregistration form you
fill out at the hospital or birthing center.

Name:_____

Partner's name:_____

Home phone number:_____

Caregiver's name:_____

Due date:_____

I have prepared this birth plan to outline my wishes
for my baby's upcoming birth. I realize that medical
emergencies and other circumstances may necessitate deviations from this plan, but, as much as possible, I would like those who are present at my baby's
birth to respect the choices I have outlined in this
birth plan.

Birth location

I am planning to give birth in the following location:

___ hospital birthing unit

___ birthing center

___ home

People present

I intend to have the following people present at the
birth:

___ my partner (name): _____

___ my children (names and ages): _____
_____

___ other relatives (names and relationship): _____
_____

___ friend(s) (names and relationship): _____
_____

___ my doula (name): _____

___ other: _____

Laboring environment

While I am in labor, I would like (check as many as apply):

___ to have the lights dimmed.

___ to have noise and distractions kept to a minimum.

___ to be able to listen to music.

___ to be able to wear my own clothes.

___ to have my partner and/or other support person(s) with me at all times.

___ to leave my contacts in place throughout my labor, unless it becomes necessary for me to undergo anesthesia.

___ to be permitted to have photographs and/or videos taken of my labor and my baby's birth.

Labor choices

If my labor:

___ hasn't started when my water breaks, I'd like to wait at least 24 hours before an induction is attempted.

___ hasn't started and I am two weeks overdue, I would like to be induced.

___ hasn't started and I am two weeks overdue, I would prefer not to be induced.

___ hasn't progressed very far when I arrive at the hospital, I would like to be given the option of returning home to do more of my laboring there.

Students/residents

___ I am not willing to have students and residents present at my baby's birth.

___ I am willing to have students and residents present at my baby's birth, with the following limitations: _____

_____.

Laboring positions

While I am in labor, I would like:

___ to maintain my mobility as much as possible, and to be free to experiment with a number of different laboring positions.

___ to be able to labor in the bathtub or the shower.

___ to be permitted to consume clear fluids and ice chips during my labor.

Medical interventions

While I am in labor, I would like:

___ to have as few internal vaginal examinations as possible to minimize both pain and the risk of infection.

___ to avoid having an IV put in place unless there are specific medical reasons why I require one.

___ to avoid having an episiotomy unless absolutely necessary.

___ to have intermittent fetal monitoring rather than continuous monitoring (unless continuous monitoring becomes medically necessary).

Pain relief

I am planning to use the following pain-relief measures during my labor:

___ Relaxation

___ Breathing techniques/distraction

___ Positioning

___ Water therapy (shower and/or bathtub): ___ alone or ___ with my partner

___ Heat or cold therapy

___ Massage

___ Accupressure

___ Accupuncture

___ Hypnosis

___ Pain medications such as Stadol, Nubain, or Demerol

___ An epidural

___ Other (please specify): _____

Induction/augmentation of labor

If it becomes necessary to induce or augment my labor, I would prefer that the following technique(s) be used:

___ Natural methods of getting labor started (walking and sexual intercourse)

___ Nipple stimulation

___ Herbal induction (blue and black cohosh)

___ Castor oil

___ An enema

___ Prostaglandins gel

___ Synthetic oxytocin (Pitocin)

___ Stripping membranes

___ Amniotomy (rupturing the membranes)

Birthing equipment

I would like to have access to the following birthing equipment during labor:

___ birthing bed

___ birthing stool

___ birthing chair

___ squatting bar

___ birthing pool/tub

___ a mirror so that I can view my baby's birth

Pushing stage

I am intending to deliver my baby in the following position:

___ in a sitting position

___ on my side

___ squatting

___ on all fours

___ on my back

If I run into difficulties pushing and an assisted birth becomes necessary, I would prefer:

___ forceps

___ vacuum extraction

The birth

Once the baby has been delivered, I would like:

___ to have my baby placed on my chest as soon as possible.

___ to have my partner cut the umbilical cord.

___ to breastfeed my baby as soon as possible.

___ to avoid any unnecessary separation from my baby.

___ to have 24-hour rooming-in (sharing a room) with my baby.

Cesarean section

If I have a cesarean, I would like to have:

___ my partner present at the delivery.

___ my labor support person present at the labor.

___ a screen placed in front of my face to block my view of the delivery.

___ as much information as possible about what is happening on the other side of the screen.

___ as little information as possible about what is happening on the other side of the screen.

___ the delivery photographed or videotaped.

___ to touch my baby as soon as possible after the delivery.

___ to have my partner cut the cord.

___ to breastfeed as soon as possible.

Feeding

I am intending to:

___ breastfeed

___ bottle-feed

Circumcision

If my baby is a boy, I am intending to:

___ have him circumcised.

___ not have him circumcised.

Hospital stay

I am intending to leave the hospital within:

___ 6 hours of the delivery

___ 12 hours of the delivery

___ 24 hours of the delivery

___ 48 hours of the delivery

___ 3 to 5 days of the delivery

Sample letter of agreement with a doula

Agreement between

_____ (parents)

and

_____ (doula)

This letter of agreement spells out the obligations of both the parents and their doula in the period before, during, and after the birth.

The role of the doula

The doula is a trained professional who provides support to women during and after the births of their babies. She provides emotional support and physical comfort, and may assist the parents in communicating their wishes to the hospital or birthing-center staff or the midwife or other caregiver in attendance at a home birth. She cannot, however, perform clinical tasks such as checking blood pressure, the fetal heart rate, or cervical dilation; make decisions on the parents' behalf; or deal with the hospital staff on the parents' behalf.

The responsibilities of the doula
Before the birth:

- Meet with the parents at least once to discuss their plans for the birth and make herself available by phone to answer any questions or concerns about the upcoming birth.

- Discuss the use of pain relief during labor.

- Assist the parents in drafting a birth plan.

- Recommend any books, videos, or other resources that may be helpful to the parents.
- Give the parents an opportunity to meet her backup doula (name): _____.

During labor:

- Provide continuous labor support in the parents' chosen location for the birth (home, birthing center, or hospital).
- Help with relaxation, massage, positioning, and other techniques to provide comfort and encourage the labor to progress.
- Help the parents to carry out their plans for the birth as much as possible.
- Maintain a birth log that the parents may keep as a record of their baby's birth (as circumstances permit).
- Assist in photographing the labor, birth, and recovery (at the parents' request and as circumstances permit).

After the birth:

- Provide breastfeeding support and advice immediately following the delivery.
- Remain with the parents and the baby for a period of approximately _____ hour(s) after the birth.
- Provide postnatal support as follows (nature of role and duration of support):

  _____.

The responsibilities of the parents
Before the birth:

- Participate in childbirth education classes or otherwise educate themselves about labor and birth.

- Meet with the doula to discuss their plans for the birth and provide her with a deposit of 50% of the total cost of her services.

- Prepare a birth plan and/or fill out the doula's labor questionnaire.

During labor:

- Notify the doula as soon as possible once labor starts, allowing at least one hour for her to reach their home.

- Continue to communicate their wishes to the doula.

After the birth:

- Pay the balance of the doula's fee promptly.

- Pay an hourly fee of $_____ if visits beyond the scope of the original contract are provided.

Fees

A fee of $_____ will be paid in two installments: 50% at the end of the prenatal meeting and 50% after the birth. If the doula is not called to the birth because of reasons beyond the parents' control, she will keep the initial deposit, but no additional fee will be payable.

I/we have read this letter and agree to contract the doula's services as outlined above.

_____   _____
Parents   Doula

_____   _____
Parents   Doula

Dated this _____ day of _____, 19___, at _____.

Sample gestational surrogacy contract

This is a sample agreement for a gestational surrogacy arrangement. Because each surrogacy arrangement is unique, we do not recommend using this sample agreement as your actual surrogacy contract, but rather as a template or draft for discussion among the parties involved in the arrangement and their legal counsel.

THIS AGREEMENT is made this _____ day of _____, 19___, by and between _____ (hereinafter referred to as "Genetic Father and Genetic Mother," or collectively as "Genetic Parents") and _____ (hereinafter referred to as "Embryo Carrier").

The Parties are aware that surrogate parenting remains a new and unsettled area of law and that this Agreement may be held unenforceable in whole or in part as against public policy.

I. Purpose and Intent

The sole purpose and intent of this Agreement is to provide a means for _____ _____, Genetic Father, to fertilize in vitro an ovum from his wife _____ _____, Genetic Mother, for transfer and implantation into _____ _____, Embryo Carrier, who agrees to carry the ovum/embryo to term and relinquish custody of the child born pursuant to this Agreement to its Genetic Parents, _____.

II. Representations

_____ and _____ represent that they are a married couple, each over the age of eighteen years, who desire to enter into this Agreement. _____ and _____ further represent that to the best of their knowledge, they are respectively capable of producing semen and an ovum(s) of sufficient nature for in vitro fertilization and subsequent transfer into _____, Embryo Carrier, but make no representations as to _____'s ability or inability to conceive, carry to term, or give birth to a child.

_____ represents that she is a married woman, over the age of eighteen years, and that she desires to enter into this Agreement for the reasons stated above and not for herself to become the parent of any child conceived by _____ and _____ pursuant to this Agreement.

_____ further represents that to the best of her knowledge she is capable of carrying an implanted ovum/embryo to term.

III. Selection of Physicians and Counselor

A. Genetic Parents and Embryo Carrier will jointly select physician(s) to examine Embryo Carrier, order and review medical and blood tests for Genetic Parents, Embryo Carrier, and Carrier's Husband, and perform IVF procedures (the "Responsible Physician"). The parties will select a doctor in _____ to do the review and perform the IVF procedures.

B. The delivery doctor will be the Responsible Physician or Embryo Carrier's regular OB-GYN, whichever the parties jointly select.

C. At any time that Genetic Parents are advised it is appropriate, Genetic Parents and Embryo Carrier will jointly select an infertility specialist to become the Responsible Doctor.

D. Genetic Parents and Embryo Carrier will jointly select a psychologist for testing before the IVF procedures and counseling/mediating during pregnancy. The parties have selected _____ (the "Responsible Counselor") in _____, who is affiliated with _____.

IV. Physical Evaluations

A. Embryo Carrier will have a medical examination, blood and other tests, and psychological testing as determined by Genetic Parents and their advisors. _____ expressly waives the privilege of confidentiality and permits the release of any reports or information obtained as a result of said examination/testing to _____ and _____.

B. Embryo Carrier's Husband will have blood and sexually transmitted disease ("STD") tests as determined by the Responsible Physician. _____ expressly waives the privilege of confidentiality and permits the release of any reports or information obtained as a result of said examination/testing to _____ and _____.

C. Genetic Parents will have blood and STD tests as determined by the Responsible Physician. _____ expressly waives the privilege of confidentiality and permits the release of any reports or information obtained as a result of said examination/testing to _____ and _____.

V. Conditions

All parties' obligations under this Agreement (other than the obligation of Genetic Parents to reimburse

Embryo Carrier for expenses incurred) are conditioned on:

A. The approval of Genetic Parents and their advisors of results of Embryo Carrier's exams and tests.

B. The approval of Embryo Carrier and the Responsible Physician of results of Genetic Parents' STD tests.

VI. Medical Instructions

A. _____ agrees to adhere to all medical instructions given to her, including abstention from sexual intercourse as directed by the IVF Physician. _____ agrees to follow a transfer and prenatal medical examination schedule set by the attending Physician.

B. Embryo Carrier will not smoke, drink alcoholic beverages, use illegal drugs, non-prescription medication or prescription medication without approval of the Responsible Physician.

C. Embryo Carrier will undergo prenatal medical exams as directed by the Responsible Physician, will submit to other medical tests, and will take only drugs and vitamins recommended or prescribed by the Responsible Physician.

D. Embryo Carrier will do everything reasonably appropriate for her good health and the good health of the fetus during pregnancy.

E. Embryo Carrier will not engage in any hazardous or inappropriate activity during the pregnancy.

F. Embryo Carrier will not travel outside of _____ after second trimester of pregnancy, except in the event of extreme illness or death in the family (with doctor's approval).

VII. IVF Procedures

It is the parties' intention to do the following:

A. Try the number of cycles recommended by the Responsible Physician, but stop at any time that the physician recommends stopping.

B. Transfer a maximum of _____ embryos per cycle.

VIII. Early Termination of Agreement

Before Embryo Carrier becomes pregnant, the agreement may be terminated:

A. By Genetic Parents, if the Responsible Physician's opinion is that Embryo Carrier will not become pregnant within ____ cycles.

B. By Genetic Parents, if the Responsible Physician or counselor determines that Embryo Carrier is not a good candidate for carrying out this agreement.

C. By Genetic Parents or Embryo Carrier, if Embryo Carrier has not become pregnant after ____ cycles.

D. By Embryo Carrier, if the Responsible Physician determines that Genetic Parents are not good candidates for carrying out this agreement.

E. At the discretion of Genetic Parents or Embryo Carrier.

In the event of early termination, Genetic Parents will be responsible for Embryo Carrier's costs incurred up to date of termination.

IX. Termination of Pregnancy

The parties recognize that Embryo Carrier has the constitutional right to abort or not abort the pregnancy; however, the parties intend the following:

A. Genetic Parents and Embryo Carrier agree not to abort the pregnancy except to save the life of Embryo Carrier.

B. Genetic Parents and Embryo Carrier agree not to selectively reduce the number of fetuses in the case of a multiple pregnancy.

X. Birth

A. Location
Embryo Carrier will give birth at _____
in _____, _____.

B. Notice of Birth
Embryo Carrier will notify Genetic Parents as soon as she goes into labor so that Genetic Parents can join her at the hospital. Genetic Parents intend to be at the hospital and to be present during the delivery.

C. Responsibility for Child
Genetic Parents shall be responsible for any children born, whether healthy or not. Embryo Carrier waives the right to make medical decisions regarding the child after birth.

D. Child Born with Severe Birth Defects
If the child is born with birth defects so serious that life-sustaining equipment is required and physician recommends that the child not be placed on such equipment or not be resuscitated, Genetic Parents will make the decision. If Embryo Carrier disagrees, then she will be responsible for the child from that time, and Genetic Parents will have no further responsibility.

E. Name
Genetic Parents will name the child.

XI. Relinquishment/Adoption

Embryo Carrier will relinquish physical custody of the child to Genetic Parents upon birth. Embryo Carrier and Genetic Parents will cooperate in all proceedings for adoption of the child by Genetic Parents.

XII. Paternity Test

Embryo Carrier, Embryo Carrier's Husband, and Genetic Parents agree that the child will have paternity tests, if Genetic Parents request.

XIII. After Birth Contact

A. Embryo Carrier can see the child while in the hospital, but the child will be in the care of Genetic Parents from birth forward.

B. After Genetic Parents take the child from the hospital, Embryo Carrier and Embryo Carrier's Husband agree not to try to view or contact the child. Genetic Parents intend to keep Embryo Carrier informed by sending a picture and a letter about the child's progress at least on an annual basis, if Embryo Carrier wishes. Embryo Carrier agrees that she will be reasonably available if child has questions about his/her birth mother.

XIV. Counseling

A. Counseling Sessions

It is the parties' intention that Embryo Carrier will attend at least ____ counseling sessions per month with the Responsible Counselor in _____ during the pregnancy. It is also the parties' intention that Embryo Carrier will attend more counseling sessions if:

(i) Embryo Carrier wants to attend the sessions;

(ii) Genetic Parents want Embryo Carrier to attend the sessions; or

(iii) Embryo Carrier's attendance is strongly recommended by the Responsible Counselor.

Embryo Carrier will use her reasonable efforts to attend the meetings, but will not be penalized for not attending if she does not feel well.

B. Disagreements

The parties intend that if they have disagreements among them that they are unable to resolve quickly or if there are issues that they want to bring up before a third party, that they will discuss the disagreements or issues in a conference call or meeting under the direction of the Responsible Counselor. The parties acknowledge that the Responsible Counselor is very experienced in surrogacy matters and agree to be guided by her recommendations.

XV. Fees, Reimbursement, Insurance, and Other Expenses

A. Embryo Carrier's Fee

1. Genetic Parents agree to pay Embryo Carrier as compensation for services provided the sum of $_____. The compensation shall be paid in 10 equal monthly installments, the first being paid after the pregnancy is confirmed.

2. In the case of a multiple pregnancy, Genetic Parents agree to pay Embryo Carrier a bonus fee of $2,000 per additional child. Bonus fee will be added to the original fee of $_____ and disbursed in equal monthly installments.

3. Escrow Account—Genetic Parents will open an escrow account and will place all fees in the account before IVF procedures begin. Genetic Parents' attorney will be authorized to disburse funds from the account per the payment schedule set out above (Section XV, Part A, Paragraph 1 and 2).

4. Embryo Carrier will receive the total fees set out above (Section XV, Part A, Paragraph 1 and 2), provided she carries the child(ren) at least 32 weeks.

5. In the event that a cesarean is ordered in either a single or multiple birth, Embryo Carrier will be paid an additional $500.

6. Genetic Parents will place $_____ in the aforementioned escrow account (v) to pay for any medical expenses not covered by insurance.

7. For a completed cycle that does not result in a pregnancy, Embryo Carrier will be paid a sum of $500.

B. Termination of Pregnancy

1. If Embryo Carrier miscarries (through no fault of her own) or is advised by the Responsible Physician that an abortion is necessary to save her own life, then the payment plan outlined in Section XV, Part A, will cease and all payments to date will belong to Embryo Carrier. Any outstanding uninsured or unreimbursed medical expenses will be the responsibility of the Genetic Parents.

2. If Embryo Carrier aborts the pregnancy when not directed to do so by the Responsible Physician and Genetic Parents, Genetic Parents will have no responsibility for surrogacy fee or expenses other than Embryo Carrier's expenses incurred to that date.

C. Insurance

1. Genetic Parents will be responsible for term life insurance for Embryo Carrier.

2. The policy will be bought before the first IVF cycle and will remain in effect until 2 months after delivery or end of pregnancy. It will cost approximately $_____ premium for $250,000 face amount of insurance. The beneficiaries will be Embryo Carrier's Husband and Embryo Carrier's Children.

D. Counseling

1. Genetic Parents responsible for costs of psychological screening for Embryo Carrier.

2. Genetic Parents responsible for costs of counseling for Embryo Carrier at a monthly rate of $_____.

3. Genetic Parents responsible for up to 5 counseling sessions for Embryo Carrier with the Responsible Counselor after the birth, if needed.

E. Medical Payments

1. Genetic Parents responsible for the reasonable costs of medical screening for Embryo Carrier, Embryo Carrier's Husband, Genetic Mother and Genetic Father.

2. Genetic Parents responsible for all medical costs related to conception, pregnancy, and birth not covered by medical insurance.

3. Embryo Carrier's medical insurance policy will be the primary insurance coverage for medical costs related to pregnancy and birth.

4. If a medical specialist for high-risk pregnancy is recommended by the Responsible Physician and not covered by insurance, Genetic Parents will be responsible for all related costs.

F. Attorney's Fees

Genetic Parents responsible for Embryo Carrier's attorney's fees to review contract, as well as those related to the adoption procedure.

G. Other Payments

1. Reimbursement for child care expenses related to Embryo Carrier's travels to doctor visits.

($_____/hr or _____/day for overnight care)

2. Reimbursement for gas and travel expenses at $.27 per mile for car, airline tickets, and hotel in connection with doctor or counseling visits.

3. Household helper: Genetic Parents will provide $100 per week (paid monthly in advance) in the case of multiple pregnancy or high-risk pregnancy in which the Responsible Physician requires Embryo Carrier to be on bedrest or drastically reduce her activity.

4. Maternity clothes: $500.00

5. Stillborn

Genetic Parents will be responsible for any funeral or cremation expenses.

6. Genetic Parents are not responsible for any charges or costs unless provided for in this Agreement.

XVI. Other Issues

A. Publicity/Confidentiality

1. Embryo Carrier will not disclose information about Genetic Parents or about this arrangement to the media unless Genetic Parents approve the disclosure.

2. Genetic Parents will not disclose information about Embryo Carrier or about this arrangement to the media unless Embryo Carrier approves the disclosure.

B. Death of Genetic Mother or Genetic Father Precedes Birth of Child(ren)

1. If Genetic Father should die before child is born, the child shall be placed with Genetic Mother as the mother, and all terms of this Agreement continue.

2. If Genetic Mother should die before child is born, the child shall be placed with Genetic Father as the father, and all terms of this Agreement continue.

3. If both Genetic Mother and Genetic Father should die before child is born, they have chosen _____ to be child's guardian and take custody at birth.

4. In the event of the death of both Genetic Mother and Genetic Father, _____ will be responsible for all expenses related to the surrogacy.

XVII. Arbitration

Any and all disputes relating to this Agreement or breach thereof shall be settled by arbitration in _____, _____, in accordance with then-current rules of the American Arbitration Association, and judgment upon the award entered by the arbitrators may be entered in any Court having jurisdiction hereto. Should one party either dismiss or abandon the claim or counterclaim before hearing thereon, the other Party shall be deemed the "Prevailing Party" pursuant to this Agreement. Should both parties receive judgment or award on their respective claims, the party in whose favor the larger judgment or award is rendered shall be deemed the "Prevailing Party" pursuant to this Agreement.

XVIII. SIGNATURES

Successors & Assigns:
This agreement shall insure to the benefit of and be binding on the parties, their heirs, personal representatives, successors, and assigns. IN WITNESS WHEREOF, the parties have executed this agreement on the date first written above.

Dated this _____ day of _____, 19___ at _____, _____

_____, Embryo Carrier

By:

_____, Genetic Father

By:

_____, Genetic Mother

Reprinted with permission. This is a sample agreement for a gestational surrogacy arrangement.
Because each surrogacy arrangement is unique, we
do not recommend using this sample agreement as
your actual surrogacy contract, but rather as a template or draft for discussion among the parties
involved in the arrangement and their legal counsel.

Important Statistics

These baby growth charts will give you a rough indication of how quickly your baby will grow during his or her first year of life. Remember, every baby is different, so don't panic if your baby is growing more quickly or more slowly that the "average".

Appendix E

National Center for Health Statistics
Girls' Weight by Age Percentiles
Ages Birth-36 Months

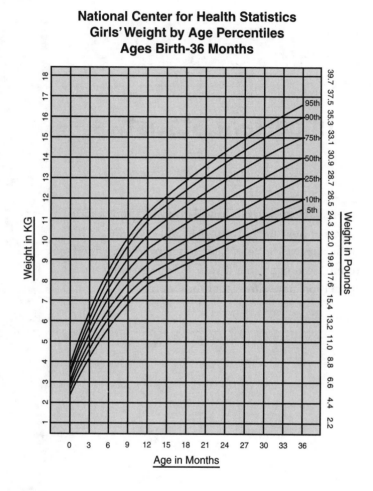

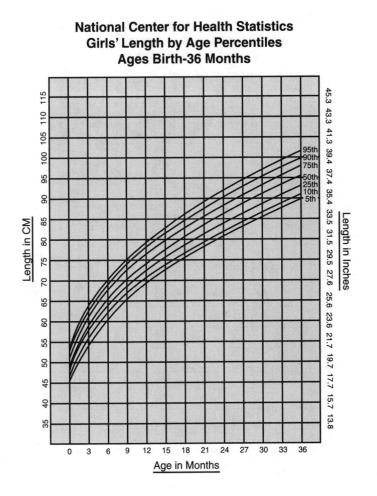

**National Center for Health Statistics
Girls' Length by Age Percentiles
Ages Birth-36 Months**

National Center for Health Statistics
Boys' Weight by Age Percentiles
Ages Birth-36 Months

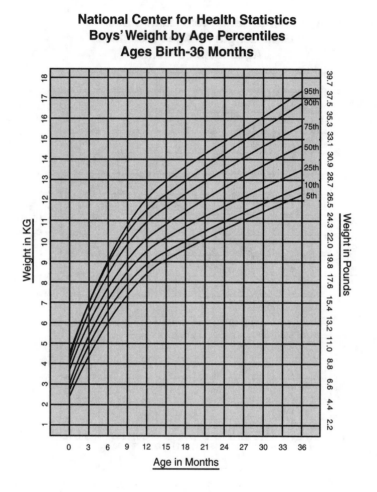

National Center for Health Statistics
Boys' Length by Age Percentiles
Ages Birth-36 Months

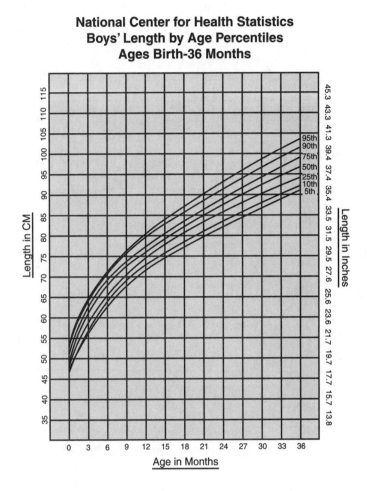

The *Unofficial Guide*™ Reader Questionnaire

If you would like to express your opinion about having a baby or this guide, please complete this questionnaire and mail it to:

The *Unofficial Guide*™ Reader Questionnaire
Macmillan Lifestyle Group
1633 Broadway, floor 7
New York, NY 10019-6785

Gender: ___ M ___ F

Age: ___ Under 30 ___ 31–40 ___ 41–50 ___ Over 50

Education: ___ High school ___ College ___ Graduate/Professional

What is your occupation?

_____

How did you hear about this guide?
___ Friend or relative
___ Newspaper, magazine, or Internet
___ Radio or TV
___ Recommended at bookstore
___ Recommended by librarian
___ Picked it up on my own
___ Familiar with the *Unofficial Guide*™ travel series

Did you go to the bookstore specifically for a book on having a baby? Yes ___ No ___

Have you used any other *Unofficial Guides*™?
Yes ___ No ___

If Yes, which ones?

_____
_____
_____

What other book(s) on having a baby have you purchased?

_____

_____

_____

Was this book:
___ more helpful than other(s)
___ less helpful than other(s)

Do you think this book was worth its price?
Yes ___   No ___

Did this book cover all topics related to having a baby adequately?   Yes ___   No ___

Please explain your answer:

_____

_____

_____

Were there any specific sections in this book that were of particular help to you?   Yes ___   No ___

Please explain your answer:

_____

_____

_____

On a scale of 1 to 10, with 10 being the best rating, how would you rate this guide? ___

What other titles would you like to see published in the _Unofficial Guide_™ series?

_____

_____

Are _Unofficial Guides_™ readily available in your area?   Yes ___   No ___

Other comments:

_____

_____

_____

_____

Get the inside scoop...with the
Unofficial Guides™!

The Unofficial Guide to Acing the Interview
   ISBN: 0-02-862924-8 Price: $15.95

The Unofficial Guide to Alternative Medicine
   ISBN: 0-02-862526-9 Price: $15.95

The Unofficial Guide to Buying or Leasing a Car
   ISBN: 0-02-862524-2 Price: $15.95

The Unofficial Guide to Buying a Home
   ISBN: 0-02-862461-0 Price: $15.95

The Unofficial Guide to Childcare
   ISBN: 0-02-862457-2 Price: $15.95

The Unofficial Guide to Cosmetic Surgery
   ISBN: 0-02-862522-6 Price: $15.95

The Unofficial Guide to Dieting Safely
   ISBN: 0-02-862521-8 Price: $15.95

The Unofficial Guide to Divorce
   ISBN: 0-02-862455-6 Price: $15.95

The Unofficial Guide to Earning What You Deserve
   ISBN: 0-02-862716-4 Price: $15.95

The Unofficial Guide to Hiring and Firing People
   ISBN: 0-02-862523-4 Price: $15.95

The Unofficial Guide to Hiring Contractors
   ISBN: 0-02-862460-2 Price: $15.95

The Unofficial Guide to Investing
   ISBN: 0-02-862458-0 Price: $15.95

The Unofficial Guide to Planning Your Wedding
   ISBN: 0-02-862459-9 Price: $15.95

All books in the *Unofficial Guide™* series are available at your local bookseller, or by calling 1-800-428-5331.

About the Authors

Ann Douglas and Dr. John R. Sussman can tell you everything you need to know about having a baby. Ann is an experienced journalist and author who specializes in writing about pregnancy and parenting, and she is the mother of four children ages one to ten.

Ann writes for a variety of print and online publications, including *The Chicago Tribune, Crayola Family Play,* and *StorkSite.* She is also the author of six books for parents and children, including *The Unofficial Guide to Childcare* (Macmillan, 1998), *Baby Science: How Babies Really Work* (Owl Books, 1998), and *The Family Tree Detective Book* (Owl Books, 1999).

Ann also has a great deal of personal knowledge of the issues described in this book, having experienced the joy of giving birth to four living children as well as the heartbreak of infertility and losing a child through stillbirth. Few writers can match her passion for or knowledge of fertility, pregnancy, childbirth, breastfeeding, and the newborn period.

Ann can be contacted via e-mail at pageone@kawartha.com.

Dr. John R. Sussman is the Chief of the Medical Staff at New Milford Hospital, New Milford, CT. Previously he was Chief of Obstetrics and Gynecology at New Milford Hospital. He is Assistant Clinical Professor in the Department of Obstetrics and Gynecology at the University of Connecticut School of Medicine. Dr. Sussman is the co-author (with B. Blake Levitt) of *Before You Conceive: The Complete Prepregnancy Guide* (Bantam, 1989).

During his career, Dr. Sussman has delivered more than 2,000 babies. He is the father of two children, one of whom he delivered.